T0331081

"There is a vast academic literature on global value chains in developing countries and an equally vast literature on corporate social responsibility. However, there is painfully little research that links together the two academic fields. The book edited by Lund-Thompson, Hansen, and Lindgreen makes a welcome contribution to this neglected but important area of academic research."
— *Peter Nolan, Chonghua Professor of Chinese Development (Emeritus),*
University of Cambridge, Director, China Centre, Jesus College, Cambridge, UK.

"These experienced and informed editors have brought together a rich but diverse set of chapters that look at many dimensions of business and development. The chapters reflect how the topic of development in the Global South has itself become more complex. The dimensions explore the well established such as global value chains, but extend to less well understood topics such social entrepreneuring. What is common and holds the collection together is the concern about the relationships between business and global development. For those of us who believe that we cannot understand development as simply an economic phenomenon, the chapters relate well to understanding business as socially and culturally embedded. The book brings together a range of current, up to date and relevant views, knowledge and expertise about what's happening and how we can begin to better understand what's going on in the South. If nothing else, the diversity of the chapters demonstrates the importance of understanding how business shapes development."
— *Alistair R. Anderson, Distinguished Professor of Entrepreneurship,*
Lancaster University Management School, UK

"The book provides a much needed contribution to fill a forgotten gap in the business management field. Even though businesses heavily impact development processes, and vice-versa, there are very few scholars in business management community who serious study the links between business and development studies. The book brings refreshing contributions and analyses of the different connections between business and development from a worldwide group of scholars."
— *Professor Jose A. Puppim de Oliveira, Fundação Getulio Vargas (FGV) &*
São Paulo School of Management (EAESP), Brazil

"In a world with increasing challenges and a rising humanitarian funding gap, there is a strong need for exploring new models, beyond classic corporate social responsibility, where companies and humanitarian/development actors create shared value and impact. Here, this important book and the broad research it captures will inspire us and move the debate forward."
— *Christian Friis Bach, Secretary General of the Danish Refugee Council (Dansk Røde*
Kors), former Minister of Development Cooperation, Denmark, and former Under-Secretary
General and Executive Secretary of United Nations Economic Commission for Europe

"At the Danish investment fund IFU, we are operating in the interface between business and development on a daily basis, assisting businesses with their investments in developing countries while at the same time contributing to economic and social development. The book *Business and Development Studies: Issues and Perspectives* edited by Thomsen, Hansen, and Lindgreen is a highly timely exploration of the potential of private enterprise in development and it will no doubt be read with great interest by development and business practitioners working in this field".

— *Torben Huss, CEO, IFU, Investment Fund for Developing Countries, Denmark*

"The 2015 UN Sustainable Development Goals have assigned the private sector a pivotal role towards solving some of the most pressing global development problems. In the anthology *Business and Development Studies: Issues and Perspectives* (edited by Peter Lund-Thomson, Michael W. Hansen, and Adam Lindgreen), a diverse group of eminent scholars and emerging academics sets out to scrutinise whether businesses can indeed contribute to inclusive and sustainable development efforts or remain part of the deeply entrenched problems of inequality, poverty and injustice in the Global South. The 19 chapters make important and novel contributions from both empirical and theoretical angles. They provide in-depth and critical analyses of the potential and trade-offs of business operations towards achieving various economic, social and ecological goals in the Global South. The editors have also developed innovative ideas for future theoretical and methodological pathways in business and development studies. This collection is a must-read for researchers, students, development practitioners and policy makers who work at the interface of global business and international development and are interested in the historical trajectories and contemporary challenges of involving the private sector in global development agendas."

— *Andreas Neef, Professor in Development Studies,*
University of Auckland, New Zealand

"The demise of both statist development strategies and extreme forms of market fundamentalism has created the space for a more nuanced view of the potential contribution and associated limitations of the private sector as an agent of development. This book is a pioneering attempt to bring together the different strands of research that address the role of business in development. It goes beyond a narrow focus on Corporate Social Responsibility and a preoccupation with the 'business case' that tends to characterize the international business literature. The contributors bring a wealth of theoretical and empirical insights from their engagement with development issues often based on extensive fieldwork in the Global South. It will be essential reading for students and others interested in the opportunities and problems that business involvement in development present."

— *Professor Rhys Jenkins, Director MA in Globalization, Business and Sustainable Development, School of International Development, University of East Anglia, UK*

"This important collection provides a rich body of conceptual and empirical chapters that cover a breadth of issues on business and development studies. It underlines need to understand better the interactions between state, business and society in the development process, and to consider this both as a critical research agenda and a discipline in its own right."

— *Khalid Nadvi, Professor of International Development, Global Development Institute, School of Environment, Education and Development, University of Manchester, UK*

Business and Development Studies

Business and Development Studies: Issues and Perspectives provides a comprehensive collection of cutting-edge theoretical and empirical contributions to the emerging field of business and development studies.

Compared to more traditional business-school accounts of business in developing countries which focus on the challenges and opportunities of doing business in developing countries, this anthology explores whether, how, and under what conditions business contributes to the achievement of economic, social, and environmental goals in developing countries. The book consolidates the current status of academic work on business and development, identifies state of the art in relation to this academic field, and establishes a future research agenda for 'business and development studies' as an emerging academic discipline within the social sciences.

The book will be of interest to researchers and students, including economists, geographers, sociologists, political scientists, corporate social responsibility specialists, and development scholars who are seeking an in-depth overview of current debates about the role of business as a development agent in the Global South. The book is also of relevance to practitioners that are engaged in work with the private sector seeking to enhance the positive effects and minimize the negative economic, social, and environmental consequences of business activity in the Global South.

Peter Lund-Thomsen is Professor of Corporate Social Responsibility and Sustainability in the Global South at the Copenhagen Business School, Denmark. He is Associate Editor of *Competition and Change* and has been Associate Editor of *Business Ethics: A European Review*.

Michael Wendelboe Hansen is Associate Professor at the Copenhagen Business School in Denmark. He has done extensive empirical research on Danish multinational companies and emerging markets, on outward foreign direct investment from developing countries (in particular from India), and on private-sector development.

Adam Lindgreen is Professor of Marketing at Copenhagen Business School where he heads the Department of Marketing. He also is Extraordinary Professor with the University of Pretoria's Gordon Institute of Business Science.

RIOT! Routledge Studies in Innovation, Organizations and Technology

For more information about the series, please visit www.routledge.com/Routledge-Studies-in-Innovation-Organizations-and-Technology/book-series/RIOT

Business and Development Studies

Issues and Perspectives

Edited by Peter Lund-Thomsen,
Michael Wendelboe Hansen and
Adam Lindgreen

Routledge
Taylor & Francis Group

LONDON AND NEW YORK

First published 2020
by Routledge
2 Park Square, Milton Park, Abingdon, Oxon OX14 4RN

and by Routledge
605 Third Avenue, New York, NY 10017

First issued in paperback 2021

Routledge is an imprint of the Taylor & Francis Group, an informa business

© 2020 selection and editorial matter, Peter Lund-Thomsen, Michael Wendelboe Hansen and Adam Lindgreen; individual chapters, the contributors

The right of Peter Lund-Thomsen, Michael Wendelboe Hansen and Adam Lindgreen to be identified as the authors of the editorial material, and of the authors for their individual chapters, has been asserted in accordance with sections 77 and 78 of the Copyright, Designs and Patents Act 1988.

All rights reserved. No part of this book may be reprinted or reproduced or utilised in any form or by any electronic, mechanical, or other means, now known or hereafter invented, including photocopying and recording, or in any information storage or retrieval system, without permission in writing from the publishers.

Trademark notice: Product or corporate names may be trademarks or registered trademarks, and are used only for identification and explanation without intent to infringe.

Publisher's Note
The publisher has gone to great lengths to ensure the quality of this reprint but points out that some imperfections in the original copies may be apparent.

British Library Cataloguing-in-Publication Data
A catalogue record for this book is available from the British Library

Library of Congress Cataloging-in-Publication Data
Names: Lund-Thomsen, Peter, editor. | Wendelboe Hansen, Michael, editor. | Lindgreen, Adam, editor.
Title: Business and development studies : issues and perspectives / edited by Peter Lund-Thomsen, Michael Wendelboe Hansen and Adam Lindgreen.
Description: Abingdon, Oxon ; New York, NY : Routledge, 2020. | Series: Routledge studies in innovation, organisations and technology | Includes bibliographical references and index.
Identifiers: LCCN 2019033665 (print) | LCCN 2019033666 (ebook) | ISBN 9781138059870 (hardback) | ISBN 9781315163338 (ebook)
Subjects: LCSH: International business enterprises—Developing countries. | Economic development—Developing countries.
Classification: LCC HD2932 .B87 2020 (print) | LCC HD2932 (ebook) | DDC 338.9009172/4—dc23
LC record available at https://lccn.loc.gov/2019033665
LC ebook record available at https://lccn.loc.gov/2019033666

ISBN 13: 978-1-03-208775-7 (pbk)
ISBN 13: 978-1-138-05987-0 (hbk)

Typeset in Bembo
by Apex CoVantage, LLC

To all the students, researchers, and practitioners in the field of business and development studies. May this book become a useful reference for your work in this area. – Peter

To the hundreds of students that over the past 15 years have studied business and development studies at Copenhagen Business School. – Michael

For Joëlle, the best mom that my two lovely daughters, Vic and Zazou, ever could have. – Adam

Contents

Figures

Tables

About the editors

Peter Lund-Thomsen

Peter Lund-Thomsen is Professor of Corporate Social Responsibility and Sustainability in the Global South at the Copenhagen Business School, Denmark. His research focuses on the linkages among global value chains, industrial upgrading, and corporate social and environmental responsibility (CSER) in developing countries. He theorizes and empirically investigates how the CSER policies of internationally branded companies are implemented in global supply chains and how they affect supplier competitiveness, work conditions, and the environment in the South.

To date he has published 30 articles in internationally peer-reviewed journals. He is Associate Editor of *Competition and Change* and has been Associate Editor of *Business Ethics: A European Review*. He co-edited special issues on micro, small, and medium-sized enterprises and CSER in developing economies; global value chains, local economic organization, and CSER in the BRICS countries (Brazil, Russia, India, China, and South Africa); and the relationship between industrial clusters and CSER in the Global South in journals such as *Business & Society*, *Journal of Business Ethics*, and *Competition and Change*.

Michael Wendelboe Hansen

Michael Wendelboe Hansen is an associate professor at the Copenhagen Business School in Denmark. His main research interest is related to firm strategy, organization, and management in emerging markets and developing countries. A key theme is how conventional business theories and research methodologies need to be modified to analyze firms in emerging markets and developing countries. Theoretically, he works with various international business perspectives, including transaction cost economics, resource and capability perspectives, and spillover and linkage theories. He has done extensive empirical research on Danish multinational companies and emerging markets related to outward foreign direct investment from developing countries (in particular, India) and private-sector development.

Adam Lindgreen

After studies in chemistry (Copenhagen University), engineering (Engineering Academy of Denmark), and physics (Copenhagen University), Professor Adam Lindgreen completed an MSc in food science and technology at the Technical University of Denmark. He also finished an MBA at the University of Leicester. He received his PhD in marketing from Cranfield University. His first appointments were with the Catholique University of Louvain (2000–2001) and Eindhoven University of Technology (2002–2007). Subsequently, he served as Professor of Marketing at Hull University's Business School (2007–2010); University of Birmingham's Business School (2010), where he also was the research director in the Department of Marketing; and University of Cardiff's Business School (2011–2016). Under his leadership, the Department of Marketing and Strategy at Cardiff Business School ranked first among all marketing departments in Australia, Canada, New Zealand, the United Kingdom, and the United States, based upon the hg indices of senior faculty. Since 2016, he has been Professor of Marketing at Copenhagen Business School, where he also heads the Department of Marketing. Since 2018, he also is Extraordinary Professor with the University of Pretoria's Gordon Institute of Business Science and a Visiting Professor with Northumbria University's Newcastle Business School.

Adam has been a visiting professor with various institutions, including Georgia State University, Groupe HEC, and Melbourne University. The recipient of the "Outstanding Article 2005" award from *Industrial Marketing Management* and the runner-up for the same award in 2016, he serves on the board of several scientific journals; he is Co-Editor-in-Chief of *Industrial Marketing Management*. His research interests include business and industrial marketing management, corporate social responsibility, and sustainability. He has been awarded the Dean's Award for Excellence in Executive Teaching.

Adam also is a member of the International Scientific Advisory Panel of the New Zealand Food Safety Science and Research Centre (a partnership among government, industry organizations, and research institutions), as well as of the Chartered Association of Business Schools' Academic Journal Guide (AJG) Scientific Committee in the field of marketing.

Beyond these academic contributions to marketing, Adam has discovered and excavated settlements from the Stone Age in Denmark, including the only major kitchen midden – Sparregård – in the southeast of Denmark; because of its importance, the kitchen midden was later excavated by the National Museum and then protected as a historical monument for future generations. He is also an avid genealogist, having traced his family back to 1390 and published widely in scientific journals related to methodological issues in genealogy, accounts of population development, and particular family lineages.

Contributors

Sameer Azizi is Assistant Professor of Business Studies at the Department of Social Sciences and Business, Roskilde University, Denmark. He received his PhD from Copenhagen Business School in 2017. His research interests include CSR by multinational corporations in developing countries seen from the theoretical perspectives of areas of limited statehood and critical management studies.

Joanne Bauer is a co-founder of Rights CoLab and Adjunct Professor of International Affairs at Columbia University, where she teaches the seminar, "Corporations and Human Rights," as well as a year-long "Business and Human Rights Clinic." She is the editor of *Forging Environmentalism: Justice, Livelihood and Contested Environments* (2006) and co-editor of *The East Asian Challenge for Human Rights* (1999). An expert in business and human rights, Dr. Bauer's current work focuses on realigning business and society.

Michael Brookes is Professor of Work and Employment at the University of Hertfordshire. He has extensive and long-standing experience supporting a variety of community-based organizations in South Africa. His main research interests are employment relations, comparative and international human resource management, and employability and community wealth building.

Frederik Claeyé is an associate professor at Lille Catholic University. He is the holder of the chair of enterprise and social impact business. He obtained his PhD from Middlesex University Business School. His research interests include social entrepreneurship in Africa and entrepreneurship at the base of the pyramid.

Anabella Davila is Professor of Management at EGADE Business School, Tecnologico de Monterrey, Mexico. Dr. Davila received her PhD from Pennsylvania State University. She holds the Research Chair on Strategy and Management of Organizations in Emerging Economies and has co-edited several research books and chapters on Latin American human resource management. Her research interests include labor culture, human resource management, human development, and sustainability. Her work examines the social logic that governs Latin American organizations. She is a member of the Mexican Researchers System (Tier II).

Michael Flint is an independent evaluation consultant. He has an MA in social and political sciences from Cambridge University and an MSc in agricultural economics from Reading University. His research interests include corporate social responsibility, international supply chains, and the living wage.

Gary Gereffi is Professor of Sociology and Founding Director of the Global Value Chains Center at Duke University (https://gvcc.duke.edu/). He received his BA from the University of Notre Dame and his PhD from Yale University. Dr. Gereffi has published numerous books and articles on globalization, industrial upgrading, and social and economic development, and he is one of the originators of the global value chains framework. Current projects include (1) investigating the impact of U.S. protectionism on jobs and regional trade agreements; (2) evaluating how the digital economy and Industry 4.0 are likely to affect international business strategies and industrial upgrading; and (3) shifting regional interdependencies in East Asia and North America, with a focus on China, South Korea and Mexico vis-à-vis the United States.

Silvia Grandi is adjunct professor in geography of the territory and geopolitics, finance, and international development at the University of Bologna, where she received her PhD. She is also a permanent director of the Italian Ministry of Economic Development and member of various policy advisory committees. She has authored three books in Italian on the geography of development (2010, 2013, 2018) and other international publications. Her current research interests include development policies, geography of finance, and geography of sustainable energy.

Franque Grimard is an associate professor in the Department of Economics at McGill University. Dr. Grimard received his PhD from Princeton University. His research specialties are development and health economics, in which domain he applies statistical analysis to applied policy issues such as poverty and social protection, health, gender empowerment, public finance management, corporate social responsibility and extractive industries, and sustainable development.

Ahmad Hassan is a PhD fellow in the Department of Management, Aarhus University, Denmark. He earned a master's of social sciences in economics and business administration from Roskilde University, Denmark. His research interests include sustainability standards, particularly multistakeholder initiatives; corporate social responsibility in global production networks; and gender-related issues in developing countries.

Mohamad Hossary is a graduate student at the American University of Beirut, specializing in Business Analytics. He has contributed to several textbooks and case studies, as well as research papers, that deal with strategy, management, and education. He also worked on multiple book chapters that cover CSR and the sustainable development goals (SDGs).

Dima Jamali is a professor in the Olayan School of Business, American University of Beirut, and currently the National Representative for Global Compact Network Lebanon (GCNL), a network of businesses committed to advancing sustainability and SDGs in Lebanon. She has a PhD in social policy and administration from the University of Kent at Canterbury. Her research and teaching revolve primarily around corporate social responsibility and social entrepreneurship. She is the author and editor of four books and more than 80 high-level international publications, focusing on different aspects of sustainability, sustainable development, and CSR in developing countries in general and in the Middle East specifically.

Johanna Järvelä is a PhD candidate at Cass Business School. She holds a master's degree in development studies from University of Helsinki and is a Fellow at the ETHOS Centre for Responsible Enterprise at Cass, as well as the Centre for Corporate Responsibility (CCR) in Helsinki. Her research focuses on the roles of state, politics, and regulation in corporate responsibility production and critical development studies.

Søren Jeppesen is Associate Professor of Business, Development and Entrepreneurship at the Centre for Business and Development Studies, Department of Management, Society and Communication at Copenhagen Business School, Denmark. He has published in a variety of journals. His research interests include small- and medium-sized enterprises and CSR in developing countries, developing country firms, linkages, and upgrading.

Ans Kolk is a full professor at the University of Amsterdam Business School, The Netherlands. Her areas of expertise are in corporate social responsibility, sustainable development, and sustainability, especially in relation to international business. She has published numerous articles in international reputable journals, as well as book chapters and books. Dr. Kolk won the Elsevier-wide Atlas award for social impact for her single-authored article, "The Social Responsibility of International Business," and received the prestigious Aspen Institute Faculty Pioneer European Award (Lifetime Achievement Award), which recognizes exceptional faculty who are leaders in integrating environmental and social issues into their research and teaching both on- and off-campus. Her article (co-authored with Niccolò Pisani, Arno Kourula, and Renske Meijer) "How Global Is International CSR?" was selected as the best paper published in the field in 2017 by the International Association for Business and Society. Dr. Kolk is senior editor of *Journal of World Business*, consulting editor of *Journal of International Business Policy*, and an editorial board member on many other mainstream and specialized journals. For more information and an overview of publications, see www.anskolk.eu

Arno Kourula is Associate Professor of Strategy at the University of Amsterdam Business School, the Netherlands, and Docent at Aalto University, Finland. His primary research and teaching interests are cross-sector social interaction and corporate sustainability. Dr. Kourula's articles have appeared (or are forthcoming) in many journals. He has received several awards for research, teaching, and reviewing. He is the co-editor for special issues of *Journal of Business Ethics*, an associate editor at *Business & Society*, and on the editorial boards of *Journal of World Business* and *Journal of International Business Policy*.

Philip Mader is a co-editor of the *Routledge International Handbook of Financialization* (2019). He completed his PhD at the Max Planck Institute for the Study of Societies in Cologne on *The Political Economy of Microfinance*, for which he won two awards. He is a research fellow at the Institute of Development Studies and convenes the MA in Globalisation, Business and Development.

Valerie Nelson is Professor of Sustainable Development. She has a BA in anthropology from Cambridge University and an MSc in rural resources and environmental policy. Her research interests focus on sustainable agriculture, forestry, and rural development. She leads the Sustainable Trade and Responsible Business Programme at the Natural Resources Institute, University of Greenwich.

Niccolò Pisani is Associate Professor of International Management at the University of Amsterdam in the Netherlands. He holds a PhD in management from IESE Business School. His research focuses on the international management domain, and the topics of his scholarly enquiry range from global business strategy to international corporate social responsibility. His research has appeared in a variety of journals. His work has also been published in leading European newspapers and featured in popular online news platforms.

Sandra Ramos is currently undertaking a PhD in management sciences at Lille Catholic University, France. She has been teaching organizational behavior, intercultural management, social business, and social economics at the same institution. Her research interests are focused on the performance, growth, and impact of social enterprises. She holds a master's degree in social economics from Minho University, Portugal.

Jacobo Ramirez is Assistant Professor of Latin American Business Development in the Department of Management, Society and Communication (MSC), Copenhagen Business School (CBS). Dr. Ramirez's research interests focus on human resource management, leadership, and organizational change in complex institutional environments (e.g., security risks, social unrest, displacement, fragile states).

Gerrit Rooks is assistant professor of sociology at the School of Innovation Sciences at Eindhoven University of Technology. Dr. Rooks received his

PhD from Utrecht University. His research interests include networking of entrepreneurs and gender differences in network perceptions. He recently published *Social capital of entrepreneurs in a developing country: the effect of gender on access to and request for resources*, Social Networks (with G. Solano).

Erinch Sahan is Chief Executive of the World Fair Trade Organization, a global community and verifier of 400 social enterprises that fully practice Fair Trade. Previously, he spent seven years at Oxfam, where he founded its Future of Business Initiative and led campaigning teams. Prior to joining Oxfam, Dr. Sahan worked in business, including at Procter & Gamble, and later in government as a development advisor to Australian trade negotiators. He holds both law and business degrees, and an honorary Doctorate from Oxford Brookes University. Dr. Sahan has lectured at various universities on sustainable business.

Georges Samara is an assistant professor at the American University of Beirut. He is the winner of the extraordinary doctorate award in Spain and several international best research paper awards. His main research areas are family business management and ethical and socially responsible business behavior. His research has addressed both topics independently and simultaneously. Dr. Samara serves as associate editor for *Business Ethics: A European Review* and as a reviewer for *Journal of Business Research*, *International Entrepreneurship and Management Journal*, *Management Decisions*, the Academy of Management Annual Conference, and the Academy of International Business.

Giacomo Solano is a policy and statistical analyst for the Migration Policy Group, a Brussels-based think tank. He holds a PhD in sociology from the University of Amsterdam and University of Milan-Bicocca (joint degree). He previously worked as a postdoc researcher at Eindhoven University of Technology on a project on entrepreneurship in Uganda, on which this chapter is based. His research interests include migration studies (e.g., migrant entrepreneurship and integration policies) and entrepreneurship in developing countries. On this topic, he recently published *Social capital of entrepreneurs in a developing country: the effect of gender on access to and request for resources*, Social Networks (with G. Rooks).

Nikodemus Solitander is a director of the Centre for Corporate Responsibility (CCR) and a researcher at Hanken School of Economics in Helsinki. He holds a PhD in economic geography, and his research focuses on the intersections of business and politics, critical studies of corporate responsibility, and responsible management education.

Jodie Thorpe is leader of the Business, Markets, and the State research cluster and a research fellow at the Institute of Development Studies in the UK. She is an expert on inclusive business, private-sector development, and cross-sector partnerships. Over the course of her career, she has advised a wide range of companies in developed and emerging markets. She holds an MSc in comparative politics and wrote her thesis on the politics of institutional reform.

Peter Wad is Associate Professor Emeritus at Copenhagen Business School. He graduated as Mag. Art. (MSc research) from Copenhagen University in 1979 and was employed at Copenhagen Business School as a research associate professor in 1995 and associate professor from 2002. He has contributed to various journals and anthologies pertaining to development strategy, business linkages, employment and industrial relations, and innovation policy. He reported to the United Nations Industrial Development Organization (UNIDO) and International Labour Organization (ILO) on issues regarding automotive industries in the Global South during the financial crisis of 2008–2009.

Michelle Westermann-Behaylo is Assistant Professor of International Management at the University of Amsterdam Business School. She holds a PhD in strategic management from George Washington University and a JD from Vanderbilt University. Her research generally focuses on how organizations manage stakeholders and use nonmarket strategies for both strategic and social performance. She also writes about the role of business in promoting peace, human dignity, and human rights. Her research has received financial support from, among others, the Netherlands Organization for Scientific Research, the Aspen Institute, the Institute for Economics and Peace, and the One Earth Future Foundation.

Mahinda Wijesiri is a postdoctoral research fellow at University of Québec – TELUQ. He earned his PhD in interdisciplinary studies (management and economics) at University of Bergamo, Italy. His research lies at the intersection of three domains – social entrepreneurship, new social business forms, and social responsibility of nonprofit organizations – to explore managerial and organizational issues at the intersection of business and society. His research has received financial support from, among others, the Fonds de recherche du Québec – Nature et technologies (FRQNT) and the International Development Research Centre Canada (IDRC).

Part I

Introduction

1 Business and development studies

Issues and perspectives

*Peter Lund-Thomsen, Michael Wendelboe Hansen,
and Adam Lindgreen*

Introduction

With the liberalization of world trade, privatization of state enterprises, and deregulation of national economies, the role of business in the Global South has become increasingly important (Utting, 2005). The rise of the BRICS (Brazil, Russia, India, China, and South Africa) and firms originating from these countries also challenges the traditional hegemony of Western multinational companies as market leaders and trendsetters in international business (Knorringa and Nadvi, 2016; Lund-Thomsen and Wad, 2014; Matthews, 2006; Ramamurti, 2012). A recently adopted development agenda – Sustainable Development Goals (SDGs) – depicts a key role for the private sector, responsible for delivering capital, innovations, goods, and services to help resolve development issues, as well as engaging in partnerships with other development agents (GRI/UN Global Compact/WBCSD, 2015).

In academic terms, literature on the role of business in the Global South spans a range of interrelated topics, such as global value chain/global production network analysis (Gereffi et al., 2005; Yeung and Coe, 2015); multinational companies and spillovers on local industries (Blomstrom and Kokko, 1998; Narula and Pineli, 2016); linkages and foreign direct investment (Altenburg, 2000; Giroud and Scott-Kennel, 2009); base-of-the-pyramid strategies (Hart, 2005; Prahalad, 2005); the role of industrial clusters in promoting local economic development (Giuliani, 2016; Schmitz, 1999); (social) entrepreneurship (Gough et al., 2014) and microfinance (Yunus, 2007); corporate social responsibility (Jamali, 2010; Jeppesen and Lund-Thomsen, 2010); business and climate change (Newell, 2012); and business and poverty reduction (Blowfield and Dolan, 2014; Kolk and Tulder, 2006; Nunnenkamp, 2004). These literature streams, whether directly or indirectly, all examine how business affects development. Yet even as all these studies address the impact of business on development, we note a lack of consolidation and integration of these streams and the knowledge they have produced. Such a gap may miss opportunities for cross-fertilization and synergy (Hansen and Schaumburg-Müller, 2010).

This book aims to consolidate the current status of academic research on business and development and identify the state of the art within this emerging academic discipline. It offers a comprehensive collection of cutting-edge theoretical and empirical contributions to the field. Compared with more traditional, academic accounts of business in the Global South that focus on the related challenges and opportunities, this anthology instead prioritizes questions of whether, how, and in what conditions business can contribute to advance the achievement of economic, social, and environmental goals in the Global South.

Business and development studies as an emerging academic discipline

To start this discussion, we posit that business and development studies represent an emerging academic discipline in its own right, so we explore its characteristics. Specifically, business and development studies constitute (1) an academic research discipline, (2) a profession, and (3) an applied social science subject.

According to Turner (2000, 47), an academic discipline refers to "collectivities that include a large proportion of persons holding degrees with the same differentiating specialization name." Academic disciplines can be described according to their level of institutionalization, or the extent to which they are manifest in (1) degree-granting units, typically within universities; (2) persons holding these degrees; and (3) degree holders being employed in positions relevant to their creed. According to Turner (2000, 52), being a member of an academic discipline thus entails what he describes as "communicative competence," such that "what disciplinary training serves to do is to create a community or audience of persons who can understand what is said." But to the best of our knowledge, few research groups, centers, or departments grant degrees in business and development studies, a limited number of students hold degrees in this subject area, and even fewer are currently employed in positions that refer specifically to business and development studies. Notable exceptions include the University of Sussex Center for Business and Development (established in 2014), which also provides a master's program in Globalization, Business and Development, and the Copenhagen Business School Center for Business and Development Studies (established in 2005), which hosts a master's program in Business and Development Studies.

Nevertheless, it is possible to identify common themes in published studies that arguably constitute a foundation for business and development studies as an academic discipline. In particular, an important aspect of business and development studies is that the various accounts primarily take a problem-driven approach to understanding private-sector development in the Global South. In this view, private-sector companies have the potential to contribute to solving pressing economic, social, and environmental challenges in the Global South. However, they also may be part of the cause of these challenges, such as due to their exploitation of workers or pollution of the environment. Theorizing also is important for business and development studies. For example, it is possible to theorize about the role of private-sector companies in the industrialization strategies of the Global South or the interplay of public and private sectors in such strategies. Or we might theorize about the ways in which "local" developing firms are tied into global production networks or how developing country firms internationalize their operations globally from their home base.

This academic discipline also has a clear policy orientation. In terms of its analytical focus, substantial attention has been devoted to governance efforts to make private-sector firms more efficient, profitable, and able to serve broad stakeholder and societal concerns. In this context, understanding the scarcity of economic and environmental resources and the politics of distribution, both within and between countries in the Global South, is a key insight for understanding the role of the private sector in enhancing or undermining economic, social, and environmental aspects of development. Business operations cannot be studied in isolation from the politics of distribution in the Global South. Whether in local or export-oriented industries, the division of profit between labor and management is a constant subject of contention. In resource extraction industries such as mining or timber, another vital issue relates to the distribution of the profits and broader benefits/costs of operations in these industries. If profits accrue through the extraction of minerals, they may be reaped by corporate actors with a global reach beyond the communities in which they operate. But the mining operations also impose environmental costs that tend to hinder the health and living conditions of residents in the immediate vicinity of these mines. The potential compatibility and trade-offs among the financial, social, and environmental impacts of business operations in the Global South are at the heart of business and development studies.

Furthermore, research in business and development studies is characterized by extended fieldwork in the Global South to understand the ground-level reality as perceived by local stakeholders. Obtaining an in-depth understanding of the local contexts in which multinational and local firms operate and are embedded within the Global South is a core concern in business and development studies, reflecting the goal of determining how the broader institutional environment in the Global South affects firm operations.

A common assumption in business and development studies is that the formal structures of the institutional environment feature greater volatility, uncertainty, and unpredictability than what might exist in developed country contexts. However, business and development studies also seek to theorize about and empirically investigate how firms – multinational or local – influence the institutional contexts within which they operate. This influence might entail not only their attempts at determining the formal aspects of the institutional environment (e.g., national laws governing subsidies, inflows of foreign direct investment) but also more informal elements of the institutional environment, such as the rules and norms that guide firm operations. For example, multinational companies sourcing from the Global South sometimes insist that no child labor should be involved in the production of goods and services for export markets.

Business and development studies may take a historical perspective on the role of business in the economic, social, and environmental development of countries in the Global South. Even after many years of independence, private sectors continue to be influenced by the historical legacies of colonialism in some developing country contexts. For example, colonial trading companies (e.g., British East India Company) severely exploited both natural resources and inhabitants of the Global South. Such historical legacies also translate into present-day realities, including inequality in wealth and resource access. In turn, business and development studies are concerned with understanding the evolutionary nature of firm activities in the Global South, including the possibility that "former" developing countries such as China advance their enterprises to such a level that they become dominant actors in foreign direct investment and world trade in particular industries.

Because business and development studies are normative in approach, writings in this academic discipline tend to feature policy recommendations about what businesses, states, nongovernmental organizations, trade unions, and other stakeholders should do to promote the development and regulation of the private sector. An increasing ambition of many countries in the Global South is that the private sector should act as an engine of growth and employment. Business and development studies research seeks such an understanding of how the private sector may contribute to universal development goals, such as the SDGs of the United Nations, or whether it actually undermines these goals in practice.

A continuing challenge for business and development studies is that traditional understanding of what constitutes "developed" and "developing" countries is becoming more fluid; the World Bank gave up this distinction in 2016 (World Bank, 2016). In turn, it is important to acknowledge the heterogeneity of countries in the Global South; some countries offer relatively well-established environments for specific businesses, such as the information technology industry in Bangalore, India, even as other industrial areas in the same country continue using very basic forms of technology and function in highly poverty-stricken areas. Similar concerns apply to China, with a distinction between relatively affluent coastal regions and the rural hinterland in some inner provinces. Moreover, across countries, we find vast heterogeneity, such as between highly industrialized South Africa and less industrialized countries in Central Africa. Understanding the diversity of institutional contexts within which private-sector development takes place in the Global South is a vital concern of business and development studies.

We thus summarize some key characteristics of business and development studies research in Table 1.1.

Table 1.1 Characteristics of business and development studies research

Business as a Source of Progress or Harm in the Global South
Politics of Scarcity
Local Institutional Environments
Policy-Oriented
Extended Fieldwork in Challenging Settings
Historical Perspective
Normative Approach

Four literature streams in business and development studies

Building on this broad conceptualization of business and development studies and the increasingly blurred geographical imagery of "South" and "North," we propose that four streams of literature reflect the core facets of business and development studies research: business, governance, and development; transnational flows, business, and development; international business, corporate social responsibility (CSR), and development; and local firms, organizations, and development. We delineate each of these four research streams next.

Business, governance, and development

This literature stream explicitly deals with the institutional context and the actors that shape the possibilities for businesses to influence human well-being, positively or negatively, at various geographical scales, from international to national to regional to local levels of analysis.

Wad's contribution to this book accordingly sets out the historical context for understanding state–business relations in the period following the Second World War. According to Wad, states might be categorized as business challenging or business supporting, according to how they embody both public–private institutional capacity. Vulnerable ruling elites enabled "catching-up" efforts during the Cold War (1948–1991). However, it is less clear what it takes for states in the Global South to catch up in terms of economic development in the post–Cold War era that has been characterized by the rise of global value chains and network governance. According to Wad, the "Made in China 2025" industrial plan moves the state–market debate to a new realm in which the old North–South tensions in trade relations may be replaced by new trade wars, escalating the risk of a new Cold War between the United States and China.

Thorpe and Mader also seek to outline a broader research agenda for state business relations and development. Their targeted agenda would encourage investigations of how state–business relations might contribute to general outcomes in the sustainable development era. They review several key themes: the developmental state, patterns of embedded autonomy, aspiring 21st-century developmental states, the deals framework, and formal versus informal institutions. They thus argue that most studies of formal state–business relations zoom in on how such relations might affect economic development, but they ignore other development aspects. By outlining a more complete research agenda, Thorpe and Mader attempt to shift the focus, beyond economic growth considerations, to foreground how processes (agency, patterns of exchange, idea, ideologies) and structures (power and resources, formal and informal institutions) shape development outcomes in the Global South.

In his chapter, Hansen argues that despite the relevance of multinational companies (MNCs) to development, they typically are not covered by the international business (IB) literature – which was not always the case. Rather, the IB literature grew out of a broader concern for societal and developmental agendas, reflecting grand questions about why MNCs exist, how and why their international activities expand into more regions and sectors, and how MNC activity affects the welfare and development of societies. Yet starting in the early 2000s, the IB literature seemingly lost sight of these broader questions and began to become immersed solely in theoretically determined questions. With this shift, the IB literature lost much of its relevance for practical policy. Hansen accordingly calls for the IB literature to return to its roots and its grand questions to advance current development discourses.

For Järvelä and Solitander, the state actor is key to facilitating businesses' contributions in the Global South. Addressing a traditional topic, development aid, they analyze the functions of development finance institutions in the context of wider financialization processes. These authors argue that increased reliance on the logics of finance must be understood in a broader historical context, namely, the post–Washington Consensus. Development finance institutions act to accelerate financialization processes in ways that "responsibilize" market mechanisms through discourses related to CSR and public–private partnerships. They identify four particular modes of financialization: through organization, through inward financing, through outward investment, and through valuation.

Transnational flows, business, and development

This second research stream deals with global economic organization and financial flows across country borders. The resulting analyses also cross scales, including international, national, regional, and local levels. Some studies attest to how multinational companies invest in the Global South, with influences on economic, social, and environmental aspects of development within and across countries in the area. Others deal with how global economic organization takes place through interfirm networks, which are typically orchestrated by multinational corporations, with implications for both local economic development and social and environmental upgrades in diverse localities in the Global South.

The post–Cold War period in particular has seen an increase in interfirm networks and global value chains (GVCs), highlighting the continued importance of multinational companies in business and development studies. Whereas the chapters contained in the business, governance, and development research stream centered on how businesses interact with states within given national boundaries, studies of GVCs explicitly highlight the importance of business activities that traverse national boundaries through the transnational organization of interfirm networks. Gereffi discusses some recent governance trends related to such networks, including organizational consolidation within GVCs and geographic concentration associated with the growing significance of emerging economies as central actors in political and economic spheres. This chapter also points to the diverse roles of emerging economies in GVCs. Extending beyond serving as major exporters of intermediate and final manufactured goods and primary products, emerging economies now represent meaningful end-consumer markets, and trade among countries in the Global South has substantially increased in the aftermath of the modern global economic recession.

The rise of GVCs as a dominant form of international trade implies that local producers in the Global South confront new social and environmental demands from so-called lead firms. Concerned about protecting their brands and reputations in their home markets, international retailers have adopted ethical guidelines for suppliers, such as mandating the absence of child labor, minimum wages and overtime pay, workers' rights to organize in trade unions and bargain collectively, and so forth. In their chapter, Lund-Thomsen and Lindgreen outline two approaches to addressing such concerns in GVCs: compliance and cooperation. After detailing the drivers, features, conceptual underpinnings, and limitations of these paradigms, they argue that a cooperation paradigm cannot alter power relationships in GVCs or ensure sustained improvements to workers' conditions. Such insights also suggest avenues for research related to purchasing practices and labor standard noncompliance, CSR capacity building among local suppliers, and improved local CSR monitoring in the developing world.

Whereas Lund-Thomsen and Lindgreen adopt a fairly narrow perspective on vertical relations (buyer–supplier linkages), Nelson and Flint take a broader view on responsible business initiatives in GVCs that seek to change corporate behavior. Their overall theory of responsible business initiatives highlights the diverse mechanisms they apply, including enabling, pressure, and ideational strategies, to achieve positive outcomes for workers, communities, and environments. Nelson and Flint also explore interventions supported by civil society, companies, or donors in terms of their potential complementarity (or substitutivity) with voluntary, private governance approaches. This chapter concludes with a summary of the systemic constraints on responsible business initiatives and a call for research that focuses on the root causes of poor corporate performance.

The final chapter of this section cites a specific responsible business initiative, using the same terminology that Nelson and Flint outline in their chapter. That is, Hassan explores the opportunities and challenges of multistakeholder initiatives for improving the working conditions of female employees in GVCs. Their labor must be perceived according to multiple contexts, spanning both the productive economy (paid work) and the reproductive economy (unpaid household activities, usually carried out by women). Using the multistakeholder Better Cotton Initiative as an example, Hassan argues that such initiatives can improve the income and health of female workers through training and capacity-building activities, but they cannot change the embedded roles of women in performing household activities or their overall role in society.

International business, corporate social responsibility, and development

Another research stream deals particularly with the function of international business in the Global South in terms of discharging economic, social, and environmental responsibilities. Although the previous stream of research, on transnational flows, also acknowledges the role of international business, the third research stream focuses on their embeddedness within particular socio-economic and sociocultural contexts in the Global South. The related research accordingly explores how the local embeddedness of multinational companies in the Global South contributes positively or negatively to the human welfare of local stakeholders, including corporate employees, local workers, and local communities.

For example, Jeppesen and Azizi argue that there is no simple way to under-stand the relationship between CSR and development, because so much depends on the theoretical or disciplinary perspective adopted. They detail three main perspectives, as well as their very different takes on whether CSR in the Global South positively enhances or negatively hinders economic, social, and environ-mental development aspects in the Global South: the business perspective, the development perspective, and the critical political economy perspective. This classification is clearly useful for identifying some underlying assumptions and methodological considerations inherent to CSR and development research, but other methods also exist to assess whether CSR has positive or negative devel-opment implications. Using a summary of key themes and debates in CSR and international business research in recent decades, Kolk et al. thus introduce several frameworks that might predict which businesses are likely to contribute positively to the achievement of SDGs. They close this chapter by reflecting on the SDGs within broader business and development debates, as well as offering suggestions for research that specifies how businesses contribute to SDGs.

Along with general analytical perspectives and frameworks for understand-ing the effects of CSR, studies of CSR and development continuously call for a better understanding of the embeddedness of international firms in different national contexts and the potential implications of this embeddedness for local development outcomes (Jeppesen and Lund-Thomsen, 2010). In turn, Jamali et al. seek to integrate the CSR strategies of MNCs with the SDGs and path-ways to sustainable development. For most MNCs, their CSR efforts vary with the market characteristics and with the size of their subsidiaries. In this sense, governmental intervention may be necessary to expand the scope and impact of their CSR activities. Their chapter thus resonates with the importance that both Wad and Thorpe and Mader assign to the governance context in the first chapters. The governance context and contextual embeddedness also are important themes in Davila's discussion of the social practices of multinational companies in Latin America. Her proposed analytical framework identifies pat-terns regarding how MNCs understand and implement CSR in Latin America. In terms of embeddedness, the analysis indicates that MNCs are quite distant from Latin American communities.

This lack of responsiveness in the CSR efforts of some MNCs also highlights the potential that CSR initiatives serve to hide more fundamental, potentially negative implications of the MNCs' activities in the Global South. The impact of businesses on human rights remains a hotly debated topic. Bauer and Sahan cite the lack of protection of human rights, noting that though recent legal, policy, and normative developments suggest new efforts, it remains that businesses, civil society organizations, and governments in the Global South fail to address human rights violations that implicate multinational enterprises. Thus, Bauer and Sahan acknowledge the benefits of alternative models of business operations that take a more balanced approach to stakeholder power and distribution, but they still call for ways to ensure that business and human rights interventions address power asymmetries between powerful corporations and the people they affect. In a similar vein, Ramirez highlights the potentially negative human rights effects of energy investments involving government and private, often multinational investors, on local economic regions. Using internal colonialism and environmental justice theories, Ramirez outlines indigenous people's opposition to wind energy investments at the Isthmus of Tehuantepec, Oaxaca, Mexico. His findings indicate that indigenous people's social unrest stems from their perceptions of uneven regional development and environmental injustice.

Local firms, organizations, and development

The fourth research stream relates to the role of local firms, organizations, and development, with a focus on how local businesses and nonprofit organizations (using business practices and techniques) contribute to or undermine human welfare in local economic regions and communities in the Global South. Most of the related analyses consider how local firms and organizations, whether at the micro or regional level, act to enhance or undermine human welfare.

An important theme relates to the business strategies of micro, small, and medium-sized enterprises (MSMEs), which typically account for 80 to 90 percent of all employment, often in informal economy settings. Individual enterprises can be especially important. As Solano and Roots argue, such businesses make important contributions to innovation in the Global South and thus to economic growth. An increasing number of studies addresses small business innovation, yet no established consensus exists regarding which factors influence small business innovation in the Global South. Solano and Roots present the results of a large-scale survey in Uganda, which demonstrate that entrepreneurs in rural areas, with long-established businesses, who are better educated and more proactive, and who have more self-confidence, are most likely to innovate.

However, it is not only individual MSMEs that make important contributions to economic, social, and environmental development in the Global South. They also can act collectively, with positive and negative effects on localized forms of development. As Grandi argues, MSME clusters – operating in proximity to one another in related industries and within a confined geographical area – can benefit from their co-location both passively and actively. Passively, they gain access to a trained workforce, support institutions, local input suppliers, specialized consultants, and a constant flow of co-located knowledge.

Actively, they might cooperate with other stakeholders to promote economic, social, and environmental upgrades within the cluster. Grandi proposes transporting cluster models from one context to another, as in a project in which the Indian government and World Bank sought to conserve and revitalize the leather and textile craft clusters in Rajasthan by using Italian industrial cluster models. The transmission is easier said than done, though; despite the potential similarities between Italy's industrial cluster models and India's leather and textile clusters, no one single model exists for organizing industrial districts or rural craft clusters. Models cannot be moved from one context to another without significant adaptations to the process.

It also is important to recognize the organizations operating at micro or regional levels in the Global South that use business techniques or models derived from business settings, even though they do not operate on a for-profit basis. For example, Wijesiri and Grimard cite microfinance institutions as organizations that allegedly can promote women's socioeconomic empowerment and reduce gender inequality. In reality, though, the evidence is mixed. Using a survey of female entrepreneurs in rural Nepal, the authors demonstrate that women's participation in microfinance programs has a significant, positive effect on their financial empowerment, but this impact is less pronounced when it comes to women's social development outcomes. Similarly, Claeyé et al. investigate how a South African social enterprise seeks to make a dent in the rampant unemployment problem of South Africa. Analyzing a unique single case study, the authors show how a social enterprise, well embedded in its institutional context, can make a difference.

Pathways for business and development studies

Although this volume contains 19 chapters, none of them fully unpack the notions of business and development or how they are conceptually interlinked. Accordingly, a promising avenue for further research would be to analyze the roles that business should play, according to well-developed theoretical traditions, such as modernization theory, dependency theory, or post-development approaches. Similarly, a more critical investigation should consider whether businesses have a role to play in promoting human development. Several policy documents have initiated such discussions, often trying to make a kind of business case for corporate involvement in promoting various conceptions of development. However, from an academic perspective, we need more in-depth scrutiny of the policies and claims of advocates that link business and development in various ways. Further research in the business and development studies domain thus should work to link the terms conceptually.

We also suggest a second area for research in business and development studies. We organize this book according to four literature streams (business, governance, and development; transnational flows, business, and development; international business, CSR, and development; and local firms, organizations, and development), but in this introductory chapter, we have not really explored key methodologies for supporting business and development studies. We thus see plenty of scope for a more in-depth investigation of the types of research methods used by scholars in this academic discipline. Do business and development studies scholars use qualitative or quantitative methods in particular institutional contexts? What ethical and normative challenges and dilemmas arise during research in difficult or remote contexts? How do business and development scholars "give back" to the organizations, communities, workers, and other stakeholders that they study? How do business and development scholars communicate the results of their research, and does this effort have any broader policy impacts? If so, how can these impacts be measured or assessed? These questions represent exciting research topics that can usefully be explored in the future.

References

Altenburg, T. (2000). Linkages and spillovers between transnational corporations and small and medium-sized enterprises in developing countries: Opportunities and best policies. In UNCTAD (Ed.), *TNC-SME linkages for development: Issues – experiences – best practices*, United Nations, New York and Geneva.

Blomstrom, M., Kokko, A. (1998). Multinational corporations and spillovers, *Journal of Economic Surveys*, 12(3), 247–277.

Blowfield, M., Dolan, C. (2014). Business as a development agent: Evidence of possibility and improbability, *Third World Quarterly*, 35(1), 22–42.

Gereffi, G., Humphrey, J., Sturgeon, T. (2005). The governance of global value chains, *Review of International Political Economy*, 12(1), 78–104.

Giroud, Axele, Scott-Kennel, J. (2009). MNE linkages in international business: A framework for analysis, *International Business Review*, 18(6), 555–566.

Giuliani, E. (2016). Human rights and corporate social responsibility in developing countries' industrial clusters, *Journal of Business Ethics*, 133(3), 39–54.

Gough, K., Langevang, L., Namatovu, R. (2014). Researching entrepreneurship in low-income settlements: The strengths and challenges of participatory methods, *Environment and Urbanization*, 26(1), 297–311.

GRI/UN Global Compact/WBCSD. (2015). *The SDG compass – the guide for business action on the SDGs*, United Nations, New York.

Hansen, M.W., Schaumburg-Müller, H. (2010). Firms in developing countries: A theoretical probe into the borderland of business studies and development studies, *European Journal of Development Research*, 22(2), 197–216.

Hart, S. (2005). *Capitalism at the crossroads – the unlimited business opportunities in solving the world's most difficult problems*, Prentice Hall, Upper Saddle River, NJ.

Jamali, D. (2010). The CSR of MNC subsidiaries in developing countries: Global, local, substantive or diluted? *Journal of Business Ethics*, 93(2), 181–200.

Jeppesen, S., Lund-Thomsen, P. (2010) Special issue on "new perspectives on business, development and society", *Journal of Business Ethics*, 93(2), 139–142.

Knorringa, P., Nadvi, K. (2016). Rising power clusters and the challenges of local and global standards, *Journal of Business Ethics*, 133(1), 55–72.

Kolk, A., Van Tulder, R. (2006). Poverty alleviation as business strategy? Evaluating commitments of frontrunner multinational corporations, *World Development*, 34(5), 789–801.

Lund-Thomsen, P., Wad, P. (2014). Global value chains, local economic organization and corporate social responsibility in the BRICS countries, *Competition and Change*, 18(4), 281–290.

Matthews, J. (2006). Dragon multinationals: New players in 21st century globalization, *Asia Pacific Journal of Management*, 23(1), 5–27.

Narula, R., Pineli, A. (2016). *Multinational enterprises and economic development in host countries: What we know and what we don't know.* Discussion Paper No: JHD-2016–01, John H. Dunning Center for International Business, University of Reading, UK.

Newell, P. (2012). *Globalization and the environment – capitalism, ecology, and power*, Polity Press, Cambridge.

Nunnenkamp, P. (2004). To what extent can foreign direct investment help achieve international development goals? *The World Economy*, 27(5), 657–677.

Prahalad, C.K. (2005). The fortune at the bottom of the pyramid: Eradicating poverty through profits. *Vikalpa*, 30(2), 149–152.

Ramamurti, R. (2012). What is really different about emerging market multinationals? *Global Strategy Journal*, 2(1), 41–47.

Schmitz, H. (1999). Global competition and local cooperation: Success and failure in the Sinos Valley, Brazil, *World Development*, 27(9), 1627–1650.

Turner, S. (2000). What are disciplines? And how is interdisciplinarity different? In P. Weingart, N. Stehr (Eds.), *Practising interdisciplinarity*, University of Toronto Press, Toronto, pp. 46–65.

Utting, P. (2005). Corporate responsibility and the movement of business, *Development in Practice*, 3–4, 375–388.

Yeung, H., Coe, N.M. (2015). Toward a dynamic theory of global production networks, *Economic Geography*, 91(1), 29–58.

Yunus, M. (2007). *Creating a world without poverty – social business and the future of capitalism*, Public Affairs, The Nobel Foundation, Stockholm.

World Bank. (2016). *World development indicators*, IBRD, World Bank, Washington, DC.

Part II

Business, governance, and development

2 Governance, business and development

Peter Wad

Introduction

The worldwide *systemic conflict* during the Cold War (1948–1991) entailed a contradistinction between the market-economic system in the West and the plan-economic system of the East. With the collapse of the Soviet Bloc and USSR as a superpower, the understanding of the state-market mechanism for economic development changed. With the emergence of a globally integrated market economy, many more powerful actors were around playing the game, and national governments were no longer able to govern unilaterally within their borders, nor outside their territory of sovereignty (Levy-Faur 2012). Governments no longer governed, but engaged in governance by way of interactively steering and coordinating political affairs with other states and nonstate actors (Jessop 1998; Peters 2012). In practice, political "sovereignty" was translated into the state's "relative autonomy" within and across its territory.

Although "corporate governance" had been an established term in business studies for a long time, the notion of "governance" became part of the international development agenda in 1992, when the World Bank (WB) launched the "good governance" agenda as an extension of its structural adjustment program (World Bank 1992). The concept of governance was defined as "the manner in which power is exercised in the management of a country's economic and social resources for development" (WB 1992, p. 1), and good governance was understood as "sound development management" (WB 1992, p. 1) and as "an essential complement to sound economic policies" (WB 1992, p. 1). More specifically, good governance entailed rule by law (legal framework for governance), accountability, transparency, and effective and efficient public-sector management. The new discourse presumed a market economy and was an attempt by the WB to reintroduce a smaller and more effective version of the state as a development agent of its Washington Consensus of neoliberalism.

Around the same time development research disclosed that developmental states in East Asia displayed sustained rapid economic growth, industrialization, educational development, and poverty reduction (Chu 2003; Lall 2004; Wade 2018). The economic and social success of developmental states were based on states "getting prices wrong" (Amsden 1989) and "governing the market"

(Wade 1990). Linda Weiss (1995) depicted the particular governance form as "governed interdependence" entailing strategic industrial policymaking with close coordination and consultation between interdependent public authorities and private investors, producers, and redistributors. Thus, *private business* was a key component, actor, or partner of development, while state power was normally in the hands of authoritarian governments (military or civilian) that did not involve independent popular organizations or civil society in the art of governing the country.

During the Cold War era developing countries became increasingly differentiated in terms of economic growth and industrial development to the point where the common "Third World" classification lost its meaning (Harris 1986; Harris et al. 2009). But in spite of the contradictions between different types of capitalist market economies and socialist plan economies, all parties during the Cold War era subscribed by and large to a common understanding of economic development as "modernization" entailing economic growth, industrialization, and mass consumption as the key yardsticks of national economic advancement. With the turn to postmodernity the conception of economic organization was translated into customized mass production and consumption ("flexible specialization"), and with the transition to postindustrial information and knowledge societies, industrial societies are no longer the most economically advanced societies in the world. However, the mainstream conceptualization of *economic development* is still at least theoretically understood as strongly attached to processes of industrialization (Haraguchi et al. 2017). The mainstream conception of standard economic development does still entail the structural transformation of agrarian economies into industrial economies (Reinert 2007). Jumping the industrial phase into a high-income service economy is the exception and reserved for minor countries with special links to larger countries (e.g., logistics, tourism, tax heavens).

A further complication for understanding, explaining, and improving the governance of economic development is the processes of globalization that accelerated with the post–Cold War regime of the World Trade Organization (WTO) of 1995. Much research was undertaken on private governance of interfirm relations at the local level (industrial clusters) or at the global level (global commodity chains, value chains, or production networks) during the 1990s (Humphrey and Schmitz 2000). The study of global value chains (GVCs) and global production networks intensified during the 2000s and 2010s and included research on the linkages between local and global forms of business governance and their impacts on industrial upgrading (Bair 2009; Coe and Yeung 2015; Fold and Larsen 2008; Gereffi 2018; Gibbon and Ponte 2005; Schmitz 2004). Public governance had internationalized with supra-national regional trade agreements like the North American Free Trade Agreement (NAFTA), the European Union's (EU) internal market, and the Association of Southeast Asian Nations' (ASEAN) ASEAN Free Trade Area (AFTA), and with global multistakeholder initiatives like the United Nations' (UN) Millennium Development Goals (MDGs), UN Sustainable Development Goals (SDGs) and the UN Global Compact (UNGC) (Humphrey et al. 2014). Thus, public–private governance emerged into international standard setting and multiactor networks for international monitoring and compliance (Ponte et al. 2011). With public-sector reforms, including decentralization and the "third wave" of democratization, public–private partnerships (PPPs) and local policy networks added to the governance complexity and dynamic at multiple levels (Brogaard and Petersen 2018; Faguet 2014; Huntington 1993; Therkildsen 2008).

During the early 21st century we have seen a declining research interest for the national level and political center (national or central government) in the study of governance, business, and development. But the concept of "political governance" of economic development assumes today the existence of state formations that do not rule over state-controlled plan economies, but interact at multiple levels of market economies with domestic nonstate economic actors (private business, labor, local communities) and foreign actors (other states, multinational corporations [MNCs], international financial institutions [IFIs], international nongovernmental organizations [INGOs]). In this context, we understand "political governance" as more than a mode of governing (WB 1992) and rather as a state-related process of policymaking, institutional mediation and implementation, and power politics about the (re)allocation of scare resources for private and public consumption and investment (Lauridsen 2012; Leftwich 2006).

The purpose of the chapter is to provide an overview of the political economy of development (PED) perspective regarding the study of the interplay between the state and the domestic private sectors and identify pertinent research issues for the future. However, we delimit our review and discussion to the question: How has the political economy literature about industrialization dealt with the political governance of the domestic business sector in developing countries and what are the major gaps? The literature considered includes both research on the Third World of the Cold War era with decolonization and new postcolonial states and research on the Global South of the post–Cold War era with rapid globalization and emerging market economies like China, India, Brazil, and South Africa. Moreover, we review cross-over research from three established streams or schools: the economic nationalist approach (mercantilism, neo-mercantilism), the market approach (liberalism, neo-liberalism), and the critical approach (Marxism, post-Marxism) (O'Brien and Williams 2007, Ch. 1). And we add a fourth stream of literature (the new political economy perspective), including a cross-disciplinary, historical-institutionalist approach to investigate supra-national regional political economies (Rasiah and Schmidt 2010) and a global network approach to the governance of politics, business, and society at multiple levels (Mayer et al. 2017; Yeung 2009, 2014).

The chapter is delimited in various ways. It is focused on political governance of domestic business, that is, local/indigenous or foreign subsidiaries/affiliates businesses operating in the developing country. International business like northern transnational corporations (TNCs) or global production networks (GPNs) are not an object per se. Finally, empirical evidence is not used for theory testing but for conceptual and theoretical illustration, clarification, or argumentation.

The chapter is structured in the following way. After the introduction the second section presents and discusses the cross-disciplinary field of PED that frames our object of inquiry: political governance, business, and industrialization. Thereby, the analytical framework and approach of the chapter are outlined. The third, fourth, and fifth sections review and discuss how domestic business is treated in the literature on industrial development policy, developmental state institutions, and the politics of industrialization, respectively. In the sixth section we reflect on the gaps in the literature and related research issues for the future. We conclude the chapter in section seven.

The political economy of development perspective

Political economy and development studies

Political economy (PE) as a field is defined by Robert Gilpin as "the interaction of the market and powerful actors" (Gilpin 2001, p. 45). This definition assumes, first, that economies are market economies and not plan economies or other kinds of nonmarket economies. In the post–Cold War era this became increasingly the reality, with the formation of the global market economy, whereby Gilpin's delineation of the PE perspective becomes even more relevant for the analysis of the Global South. However, with the emergence of the GVC perspective on the organization of firms in market economies, the very conceptualization of the market as the defining criterion is questioned. Now, the global market is composed of various forms of business organizations like GVCs or GPNs that are governed by other mechanisms than the market and the hierarchy (Gereffi et al. 2005; Henderson et al. 2003; Humphrey and Schmitz 2000). Various kinds of interfirm networks evolved, and competition changed from between thousands of corporate buyers and sellers to between corporate networks with oligopolistic or monopolistic power and driven by complex forms of coordination (Gibbon 2008; Gibbon and Ponte 2005).

Second, Gilpin's conceptualization allows for inclusion of powerful companies like MNCs and business groups, but small and medium-sized firms (SMEs) seem to be subsumed under the market concept. Only if they align into a powerful business association or informal business networks might they count as powerful collective actors (Doner and Schneider 2000). But the question regards also the gray borderline between commercial state-owned enterprises (SOEs), government-linked-companies (GLCs), and private corporations and what it takes to qualify as a market economy.

In the WTO today no agreed-upon definition of a market economy prevails, but for antidumping matters, a level playing field of corporate competition is a must in order to achieve *market economy status* (MES). MES requires the establishment of a national economy with market-based pricing of costs of inputs and remunerations of outputs, transparent and independently audited accounting records, clear and enforced bankruptcy and property laws, financial and productive efficiency related to market dynamics and not to a former position in a nonmarket economy, and exchange rate conversions reflected in the market price (Barone 2015, p. 20, note 31). But it is up to the individual member countries to decide whether a country like China complies with these criteria, and the MES can even be granted to individual companies.

Third, the PE approach of Gilpin (2001, p. 3) prioritizes the "national system of political economy" in the workings of the international and global political economy but where MNCs and international organizations are important players, too. Acknowledging that (supra-national) regionalization of economies has evolved and deepened, Gilpin denies that this phenomenon undercuts state power: "Regionalization is not an alternative to the nation-state, as some believe, but rather embodies the efforts of individual states to collectively promote their vital national interests and ambitions" (Gilpin 2001, p. 11).

Conceived in the Gilpin way the PE perspective fits well with the definition of 'development studies' by John Martinussen (1997), because development research is focused on *macro-level, societal economic transformation* of relatively poor societies. In addition, societal change is normatively valued in terms of the economic and social benefits that are captured by the population over time in terms of, for example, reduced poverty. Development studies are therefore constituted as *social science* or rather as a *cross-disciplinary field* of social sciences (economics, political science, sociology, anthropology) and social components of other (natural or life) sciences (e.g., cultural and economic geography).

Choosing a PED perspective, we concur with Martinussen that its main object is the society and thereby that the focus of research is on the national, macro, or societal level, but we take the interface between politics and the economy (including its micro-foundation of companies) at local, national, and global levels to be determining for the structure and dynamics of the societies of the Global South in the 21st century. Therefore, we prioritize the cross-disciplinary approach of political science, economics, and business studies as constituting the social science base of economic development studies. Yet the relevance and appropriateness of such a conceptualization is challenged by the globalization of national economies and political systems, the global centralization of corporate power (MNCs) relative to the decentralized forms of political governance, and the emergence of the (subnational) local/regional space as the focal territory of global-local economic (Coe and Yeung 2015).

Governance, business, and development

Governance has become a key concern in the PED literature (Balland et al. 2010; Bresser-Pereira 2008; Lauridsen 2012; Leftwich 2005a; Whitfield et al. 2015), but also in new economic sociology (Evans 2005; Wad 2001; Whitley 2001) and political anthropology (Hansen and Stepputat 2001; Sharma and Gupta 2006; Stacey and Lund 2016). The core stream of relevant literature is located in the subfield of state–business relations (SBR) studies that date back to the 1990s (Doner 1991b, 1992; MacIntyre 1994; Maxfield and Schneider 1997).

In the SBR literature the concept of "business" is understood as a wide-ranging concept that "can mean anything from a particular legal entity to the sum of all economic activity outside the household" (Haggard et al. 1997, p. 36). Thus, the concept connotes business as capital (national economy level), industry (sector level), firm (organizational level), network (informal interfirm linkages), and association (formal cross-firm collaboration). The governance of business entails business policy, institutions, and politics that regard the micro-organization of commercial activities and the rules and regulations that market players have to follow: corporate governance, competition policy, standards of products, production, sales and innovation, internal and external employment and work conditions, code of conduct, financial transactions, tax management and liabilities, free trade and antitrust institutions, etc.

The SBR approach has seen a revival in recent years (Ayele et al. 2016; Lemma and te Velde 2018). SBR has been given research priority by new institutional economists or historical institutionalists (Cimoli et al. 2009), and even by development economists (Page and Tarp 2017). However, with Terence Gomez's (2002a, pp. 2–6) conception of 'political business,' an anthropological-sociological approach (Gomez 2010; Gomez and De Micheaux 2017) has been added to the SBR stream of research. In Malaysia, political business manifested itself in various ways, for example, as "partisan business" (companies controlled by political parties in order to accumulate financial resources that can be mobilized in support for partisan politics, e.g., during elections) (Gomez 1994, 2002b). But more common was networks of political patrons and business clients (Gomez and Jomo 1997). Many of these business clients defaulted during the East Asian financial crisis and so did some of their political patrons, too, enabling or forcing the Malaysian state to "re-nationalize" and re-finance firms that were "too big to fail" in a Malaysian context. A new segment of government-linked investment companies (GLICs) and government-linked companies (GLCs) evolved, and they came to dominate the domestic economy of Malaysia during recent decades (Gomez 2017).

Analytical approach of the chapter

In the PED literature there has been an undercurrent of structuralism in the analytical approach to grasp political interventions in developing countries, thus taking political-economic structures to determine, or at least condition, the outcome of industrial policy (Doner et al. 2005; Khan 2010; Stallings 1978; Whitfield et al. 2015). The classic "structure–agency" methodology has been elaborated into a meta-perspective of "structure–institution–agent" in the recent literature on international development assistance, labeled the "Drivers of Change" approach by the British Department for International Development (Dahl-Østergaard et al. 2005; DFID 2004; Leftwich 2006). Adding political analysis to the PED perspective, Leftwich (2005a) lifted the analytical

framework to the present state, where power structures frame political settlements and coalitions that form mechanisms of state and state–business institutions with relevant actors (agents) that again act in terms of policymaking
and implementation (agency) and affect social change and eventually economic
transformation.

The Drivers of Change approach can be understood as relational and
dynamic more than structural and deterministic, because it articulates a double lane of feedback processes from structure to agents (and agency) via institutions and from agents (or agency) to structure via institutions. Thus, the
"Drivers of Change" can be elaborated to comprise the interplay between
political-economic power structures, state–business institutions and agents, and
the agency of industrial policy. A similar analytics is used by Lauridsen (2012),
contrasting the WB's orthodox "good governance" approach with a heterodox
"developmental governance" approach. Our review of the PED literature on
industrial development will follow the evolution of this thinking, starting with
industrial policy, then move on to state–business institutions and actors, and
finally discuss research on industrial politics.

From industrial policy to business policy –
and back again?

Changing the conceptualization of industrial policy

The classic concept of industrial development policy had a rather narrow focus
on industrial diversification, with an immanent assumption of industrial deepening (through production of intermediary goods) and industrial upgrading
(through production of capital goods). Diversification was imperative because
postcolonial states seldom had manufacturing industries and imported most
industrial goods while relying on commodity export of raw materials to earn
foreign currency for import. Diversification was addressed by the application
of trade-related industrial policies aiming for import-substitution industrialization (ISI) or export-oriented industrialization (EOI) graded along three levels:
labor-intensive consumer goods (level 1), capital-intensive intermediary goods
(level 2), and technology-intensive capital goods (level 3) (Haggard 1990).
"Infant industry" policies were often added in order to help establish local
firms in protected industries, sometimes with the intention to create "national
champions," as in the Malaysian national automotive policy (Wad and Chandran 2011).

An alternative strategy of "product champions" was used in Thailand, where
the goal was to establish a huge domestic automobile market and economies of
scale for the one-ton pickup truck (Thoburn and Natsuda 2017). With beneficiary lower taxation on sales of minivans and subsidization of domestic assem-
bling and component production, foreign auto makers choose Thailand as the
hub of Southeast Asian automobile manufacturing. When the Thai market col-
lapsed after the East Asian financial crisis in 1997, the auto MNCs switched

idle capacity to export production and expanded this segment tremendously (Doner and Wad 2014).

ISI policies were highly popular among Third World governments in the 1950s and 1960s, although the strategy of agricultural demand-led industrialization (ADLI) seemed to be the best option in terms of linkage and employment generation, but due to protectionist agricultural policies in the North, this policy was not feasible in most cases, as expanding agricultural output would have to be exported.

ISI policies comprised trade-related investment measures (TRIMs) that should protect domestic firms by regulations that included tariffs, quotas, local content requirements, demand for local capital participation in joint ventures with foreign capital, export commitments to generate foreign currency, financial regulations, including repatriation of profits, etc. (Dicken 2015, p. 190). EOI policies included support for industrial relocation (tax exemption for foreign direct investment [FDI], etc.) and agglomeration through infrastructure investment in free trade zones (FTZ) or export-processing zones (EPZ), tariff-free warehouses, export promotion, etc. FTZs and EPZ policies for attracting FDI and MNCs multiplied during the 1970s and beyond, and especially in Southeast Asia and the Caribbean.

A more offensive approach to external economic expansion emerged in middle-income countries with rising capital accumulation. Here, governments could ease regulation of private and public capital flows and enabled the expansion of "emerging MNCs" (EMNCs) to the point where outward FDI (OFDI) and EMNCs have become key components of a new industrial development strategy (Gammeltoft and Kokko 2013; Paul and Benito 2018; Rasiah et al. 2010).

Enterprise-related conceptualization of industrial policy emerged with the studies on industrial organization at the firm level (Humphrey 1995), the interfirm level of industrial clustering (Schmitz 1995; Schmitz and Nadvi 1999), and the international level of GVCs (Humphrey and Schmitz 2000; Schmitz 2004) and global production networks (Henderson et al. 2003). Industrial policymaking became much more related to the facilitation and development of business capabilities in the pursuit of corporate competitiveness, linkage formation, and collective efficiency at the local or regional level and industrial productivity enhancement through product, process, function, or chain upgrading, including new ways of exploiting local natural resources (Hansen et al. 2015; Morris et al. 2012). Industrial clustering can be supported through infrastructure investment in industrial districts and vendor and linkage programs, and industrial upgrading was assisted through research and development (R&D) services, innovation and entrepreneurial programs, venture capital funding, public procurement, etc. (Chandran et al. 2012; Lundvall et al. 2009; Lema and Lema 2012; Lema et al. 2015).

Although the old industrial policies were framed in either a trade perspective (ISI, EOI) or in a domestic perspective (corporate expansion, diversification, and clustering), their overall objective was to counter the disarticulation of the postcolonial economy and contribute to the generation of an independent and *nationally integrated economy*, often articulated in a national development strategy and implemented through development planning (Wad and Jeppesen 2006). In this perspective Laurids Lauridsen's conceptualization of "strategic industrial policy" (SIP) is taken to be key to defining the core features of national economic development.

SIP is understood as policies aiming "to foster new industrial capacity, diversify production, create inter-sectoral and inter-industry linkages, promote learning, improve productivity and shift economic activity towards higher technology and higher value-added activities" (Lauridsen 2010, p. 8). Thus, Lauridsen lines up with Cimoli et al. (2009) who advocated similar thoughts about economic development, seeing it to be immanently tied to the formation of industrial capabilities in the developing country. The SIP concept of *industrialization* differentiates between industrial *diversification* (from one to multiple industries), *industrial deepening* (adding intermediary products and components, linking and clustering producers and suppliers), and *industrial upgrading* (increasing productivity by reducing costs and enhancing the sales value of products and services) (Lauridsen 2010).

National industrial policy: from domestic integration to global integration?

Facing a global trend of geographic fragmentation of industries through offshoring and outsourcing and functional integration of production functions in GVCs and GPNs, the agenda for national industrial policymaking is set to move from facilitating the development of industrial clusters and linking them together in a dynamic domestic economy toward linking firms and clusters with competitive and expanding GVCs/GPNs. Political sovereignty is not enough anymore, although the size of the domestic market matters (e.g., China and India). International business and political networks gain importance in the hunt for manufacturing and servicing tender options and contracts.

The literature on this issue is not that vast, and it contains a highly relevant paradox, as noticed by Laurids Lauridsen (2018, p. 330):

> On the one hand, it is stated that well-designed and well-implemented industrial policy is essential for developing more dynamic, robust and rewarding production structures in a globalized world. On the other hand, it is argued that non-integrated and dispersed supply and value chains have foreclosed the traditional role of industrial policy in economic development.

Lauridsen concludes that "even in a highly globalizing economy, effective industrial and productive development policies are needed for economic and social transformation" (Lauridsen op. cit.). Considering three strands of this new industrial policy (NIP) thinking, Lauridsen dismisses the policies advocated by the WTO and Organisation for Economic Co-operation and Development (OECD) because these organizations substitute or translate the old "building development" approach with a new "joining development," thus downplaying the capacity building and integration of the domestic economy (Lauridsen op. cit.).

At least two types of analyses open up the new terrain of industrial policy thinking: GVC-oriented industrial policy studies and the GPN-related "strategic coupling" analysis. In the GVC-oriented literature, researchers reflect on the immediately perceived similarity between the old ISI policy and the new GVC-oriented policy, aiming for the establishment of local production, innovation capacity, and more advanced market demands (Gereffi and Sturgeon 2013). Yet the most important difference regards the role that developing countries can play in the global supply chain of lead firms.

First, GVC-oriented policy must target first-tier global suppliers, not global lead firms (producers and buyers) because global sourcing is a must, and global suppliers will therefore be huge industrial investors in the Global South. Second, industrial policy must focus on specialization of domestic firms in niches of higher-value-adding activities where local suppliers can serve multiple global customers as long as industrial capacity and capability building comply with the increasing demand. Third, localization of global first-tier suppliers will be critical for local industrial upgrading because they can function as hub-and-spoke catalyzers for local clustering of domestic firms and even functional upgrading over time.

In the GPN approach, strategic coupling became the core new conceptualization of development strategy. This thinking came in two versions: GPN 1.0 and GPN 2.0. The first version (Henderson et al. 2003) aimed to explore the analytical aspects of the concept, while the second version aimed to provide an explanatory framework for strategic coupling (Coe and Yeung 2015, p. 21). Strategic coupling targets the subnational regional level as the territory and space of economic development because firms are located in specific geographical places with their regional assets and embedded in particular regional institutions. Strategic coupling between regionally situated firms and GPNs is formed by consultations, negotiations, and cooperation between the regional institutions (state agencies, business associations, and labor organizations); GPN lead firms; and networks of subsidiaries, suppliers, service providers, and customers. The dynamics of the strategic coupling affect regional assets and translate into regional economic development (value capture, industrial and social upgrading, sustainable growth) (Coe and Yeung 2015, p. 19). Coe and Yeung (2015, p. 184) outline three basic modes of strategic coupling;

- *Indigenous coupling* that is based on emerging "national champions" (big business) and lead firms in new production networks supported by SIP and mediated by highly skilled migrant labor (expatriate management, engineers). This is a coupling from the inside to the outside, preserving autonomy and control.
- *Functional coupling* that is based on the emergence of strategic partners and localization of global MNC activities supported by politically driven skills,

infrastructure, and technology upgrading and mediated by transnational flows of business information and technology. This is strategic coupling from both sides, inside-out and outside-in.

- *Structural coupling* that is based on runaway or weakly linked transplants and subcontractors located in externally open and efficient infrastructure (EPZs, FTZs) with tax subsidies, minimum labor legislation, etc. This is strategic coupling from outside-in.

Appointing MNCs as the key strategic players of GPNs the GPN researchers converge partly with the GVC literature emphasizing *lead firms* as governing the GVCs (Gereffi et al. 2005). Yet the whole problematic of corporate GVC governance is highly debated. We notice, first, that multifirm alliances may be the actual drivers, not single lead firms (Fold 2002). Second, governance may vary across the GVC depending on the tier level of the GVC and the target of governance: the binary interfirm relation (coordination) or the larger chain from supply to distribution (producer versus buyer driven, or governance by corporate standards) (Gibbon 2008; Gibbon and Ponte 2005). And third, lead firms may not necessarily be leaders but might align with or follow first-tier suppliers that control the core technology of the product or production process (Wad 2008; Wong 2018). Gereffi and Sturgeon (2013) thus emphasize that the proliferation and complexity of global supply chains offer developing countries new opportunities for accessing and moving up the industrial ladder, where the focus should shift from lead firms to lead suppliers or supply niches (bottlenecks, etc.).

Reflecting on the situation of least developed countries (LDCs) Flintø and Ponte (2017) conclude that "adaptive states" must explore GVC opportunities and avoid nonfeasible GVC options. Here, 'nimble' industrial policies can overcome supply-side obstacles and facilitate the virtuous cycle of global integration. Thereby, Flintø and Ponte join the critical stance of researchers towards 'lead firm' thinking as the only option for business and economic development in an era of GVCs and networks. There are virtuous and vicious ways of coupling, recoupling, and decoupling between local and global nodes of GVC/GPNs, including commodity extraction (Morris et al. 2012; Hansen et al. 2015). But "strategic coupling" presumes expanding imports of commodities, components, and parts in a timely manner (just-in-time if necessary), not reduced imports a la the ISI strategy. Strategic import expansion requires again advanced logistics and an advanced external and internal infrastructure for transportation and communication.

From passive to active industrial policy?

Taking domestic firms as the target group of industrial policy, governments have two options according to Ben Schneider (2015): hands-off and hands-on. Both these options are framed and substantiated by policymaking: a hands-off policy changes a state-driven or regulated domain of the economy into a

market-driven domain of the economy through business-friendly privatization of state-owned enterprises or agencies, deregulation of "unfriendly" business legislation and execution, and liberalization with competition-enhancing
decisions and implementations. Schneider (2015) calls this "passive" industrial
policy. "Active" industrial policy includes selective subsidies, quotas, local content requirements, equity participation, venture capital, loans and credit, export
and import support, etc. But the policy support is to be combined with more
or less explicit objectives and performance targets to be accomplished by firms
being privileged with grants, cheap loans, contracts, and licenses.

The most controversial and contested claim by some active industrial policy
advocates is that governments can "pick winners" by identifying and creating
successful domestic companies that are able to compete in international markets. Such firms have been labelled 'national champions,' and they were taken
to mark industrial achievements by developing country governments. Neo-
classical economists reject this possibility, arguing that only the market can do
so (e.g. World Bank 1993). Yet Dani Rodrik (2007), a neo-classical economist
with an institutional orientation, qualifies the dictum:

> Yes, the government cannot pick winners, but effective industrial policy
> is predicated less on the ability to pick winners than on the ability to cut
> losses short once mistakes have been made. In fact, making mistakes ("pick-
> ing wrong industries") is part and parcel of good industrial policy when
> cost discovery is at issue.
>
> (Rodrik 2007, p. 150)

This was exactly what they did in South Korea. Low-performing companies were not closed down but merged with or forced into acquisition
by competing and well-performing firms (Wad 2002). From Rodrik's Latin
American experiences, he contends that "it is difficult to come up with real
winners in the developing world that are not a product of industrial policies
of some sort" (Rodrik 2007, p. 151). But as mentioned before, it failed in
Malaysia (Natsuda et al. 2013; Wad and Chandran 2011), and the research jury
is out concerning China.

Aiming to simplify the literature on industrial policy in developing countries
during and after the Cold War, Hubert Schmitz (2007) classified the policies
along their firm-related challenging and supporting features. The Washington
Consensus was deemed to be challenging without support, the ISI protectionist
package was seen as supportive without challenge, and a policy package of both
challenging and supporting measures was coined "active industrial policy." The
Washington Consensus policy was applied primarily in Latin America and sub-
Saharan Africa, while active industrial policies were pursued by the East Asian
developmental states.

Depending on the context, active industrial policy was not a one-size-fits-
all policy, as the Washington Consensus policy has been nicknamed. According to Hubert Schmitz (2007), the sector- or industry-specific strategy should

be designed according to the technological and marketing gaps that domestic firms face relative to their international competitors and partners:

- If domestic firms faced both steep technological and marketing gaps, governments should rely on inward foreign direct investment (IFDI) by MNCs. IFDI- and MNC-friendly location policies should be put in place, like FTZ/EPZ infrastructure construction projects.
- If domestic firms had marketing leverage but not up-to-date technological capabilities, joint ventures with foreign MNCs and international licensing would be appropriate for building technological capacity.
- If domestic firms faced a marketing gap but possessed adequate techno-logical capabilities, the indigenous firms could link up with lead MNCs as suppliers in their GVCs and production networks, and the government should support this with linkage and vendor programs.
- Only if domestic firms had adequate technological and marketing capabili-ties to compete locally and internationally could the government pursue an export supporting policy, including export-promotion credit, advertis-ing, brand marketing, OFDI risk sharing, innovation and development, etc.

Export support could typically become an option after a period of "first stage" labor-intensive and low-technology ISI, as seen in, for example, textile and garment industries, where local firms might have been learning the tricks on their own or as joint venture partners. Yet if no firm capabilities were avail-able domestically in a particular product or service market segment, it would be rather difficult to build technological and marketing capacity from scratch without relying on MNCs as international buyers or JV technology partners. The exception might be if indigenous managerial capability is available in large domestic business groups (like the chaebols in South Korea) because manage-rial resources can be deployed in new businesses if supported and challenged by a proper industrial policy program providing capital, technology, and out-lets for new entrepreneurial projects and activities. The South Korean shipyard industry was established that way and reached a high level of international competitiveness.

Thus, scarcity of entrepreneurial, managerial, and organizing talent and experience might be the critical bottleneck for private business development. As such, the Korean chaebols formed a container of managerial talent that could carry corporate diversification with state guidance and support, while the scarcity of automotive industrial-managerial capability was narrowed down to nearly a single person in Malaysia. Due to the selective ethnic Malay affirmative policy and the strategic goal to form a Bumiputera Commercial and Industrial Community (BCIC) ethnic Chinese auto industrialists and entrepreneurs were excluded from taking leading roles in the Proton-national automotive project of the 1980s, whereas Japanese automaker took the lead in a state-MNC joint venture (Jomo 1994). Being acquired by a Malay industrialist with automotive experience in the mid-1990s, the Proton project (now DRB-HICOM) ended up in dire straits when the owner died in a helicopter crash just before the East Asian crisis hit Malaysia in 1997 (Wad 2001). Proton was rescued by the state and ended up as a government-linked company before being privatized again in 2012 (Wad and Chandran 2011) and essentially acquired by Chinese automaker Geely in 2017 (Zhang et al. 2017).

Political space for industrial policy in a global market economy

What is left of policy space for active or strategic industrial policy in the WTO era is highly contested in the literature (Haggard 2018). The space is left especially for corporate and product taxation, product and process standards, public procurement, finance, innovation, vocational education, and infrastructure (Natsuda et al. 2013; Natsuda and Thoburn 2014). The space varies with membership conditions accessing the WTO and on the country's locational advantages, that is, market attractiveness; raw material availability; cheap or skilled labor; industrial clustering; and industrial assets for acquisition, mergers or partnering (Lauridsen 2018; Rasiah 2005; Rodrik 2007; Wade 2003, 2010, 2018). Intellectual property right (IPR) institutions are often fragile, and even if formalized IPRs are open to informal political influence and violation. IPR regimes are highly contested issues in international trade and investment debates, including the China–US trade debacle (Morrison 2018).

The recent literature on industrial policy in a PED perspective converges more or less on what is the new focus of strategic interest: competitiveness, productivity, innovation, learning, and upgrading (Coe and Yeung 2015; Lauridsen 2010; Lundvall et al. 2009; Rasiah 2017; Rodrik 2007; Schmitz 2007). What is partly overlooked is the challenging function of market competition that Hubert Schmitz emphasized in his active industrial policy thinking. Formal markets for manufactured goods are often monopolistic or oligopolistic in developing countries dominated by foreign MNCs or domestic business groups. Competition policy was originally thought of as a complementary part of active industrial policy. The dilemma of industrial policy is that the creating of "national champions" through subsidies and market control turn these firms into oligopolies or monopolies. Japan, the original "developmental state," mastered by and large the phasing out of state support and increasing competition between the selected firms in order to make them commercially viable at the home and later in international markets (Johnson 1982).

Focusing on nonmarket corporate governance, competition between GVCs and production networks within the same product market might appear as a research gap. Competition-based *market* upgrading or downgrading has also been rather overlooked in GVC theory (Gibbon and Ponte 2005; Wad 2006). Competition policy as part of an active industrial policy needs to be brought out of the shadow of neoliberalism and Washington Consensus, and it may require the conceptualization and theorizing of a new state formation: the competition state (Cerny 1997). The political governance of Malaysia's economic development was probably highly influenced and disciplined by its open economy (Hill

2012), but the competition policy was only enacted very late in Malaysia, in fact at a time (2010) when deindustrialization had started (Lee 2012).

So, international policy space matters, but so, too, does policy commitment and institutional capability to prepare for and leapfrog into global competitive markets and catch up in GPNs on a ladder of rising institutional complexity and steep learning curves. The theme of institutional capacity and effectiveness is addressed in particular by the SBR literature, as highlighted in the next section.

State–business institutions

With the "institutional turn" in development research in the late 1980s, the literature focused on the critical question of how to design institutions that could mobilize investment capital and govern the interplay between state and firms in a productive and developmental way (Evans 2005). Studies focused increasingly on the variety of state formations (Evans 1995, 1997; Kohli 2004), with particular focus on 'developmental states' as the abode of developmental effectiveness (Leftwich 1995); on state–business consultative mechanisms (Evans 1995; Schneider 2015) as a prerequisite for developmental success; and on big business or business associations (Doner and Schneider 2000) as key players in the policymaking, implementation, and monitoring. In the other end of the scale Evans (1995) portrayed "predatory state" formations as kleptocratic regimes based on neo-patrimonial or patron–client networks with rampant corruption and fraud prevailing at all levels. In between, "intermediary states" were defined as states with "pockets of efficiency" yet without effective centrally planning and coordinating.

State–business relations: Embedded autonomy and beyond

Peter Evans's (1995) concept of embedded autonomy came to dominate the thinking of the relationship between developmental states and domestic businesses, although it had its critics (Moore 1998). Evans acknowledged the contradictory composition of "autonomy" and "embeddedness" but argued that this dialectic was possible if the state had a strong cohesive, rule-based, meritocratic bureaucracy that carried out policymaking for the common good, sidestepping particularistic claims from interest groups, while consulting relevant businesses and other actors during policy formulation and implementation, thereby exchanging information and enabling coordination, monitoring, and adjusting.

The alternatives to embedded autonomy were alternatives of failure: "Autonomy without embeddedness" implied policy failure due to misinformation and lack of feedback (e.g., plan economy), and "embeddedness without autonomy" implied development failure because state agencies were captured by special interests and broader development goals would not be accomplished. Thus, the developmental state was narrowly defined and constituted by an autonomous state bureaucracy and ongoing state–business consultation. But states differed in terms of embedded autonomy, from centralized and comprehensive state efficiency to "pockets of efficiency" at sector, industry, or local/regional levels, which characterized intermediate state formations. The institutional configuration among rapidly growing and industrializing East Asian countries varied a lot, which also gave way to selective institutional imitation, recomposition, and innovation outside East Asia (Evans 1998). The business component was not explicated, but this is not to say that business people like street vendors cannot be institutional entrepreneurs even in an informal economy like Zambia's (Larsen 2012).

Yet the business component was a rather black spot in the research literature on embedded autonomy. Or the assumption was probably that business is "big business" (Coe and Yeung 2015; Gereffi 1990b) in the form of private business groups (e.g., Korean chaebols), SOEs (e.g., in Taiwan), or foreign MNCs (e.g., in Singapore). According to Schneider (2012) a combination of domestic big businesses and foreign MNCs are often found in so-called "hierarchical market economies" in Latin America and Southeast Asia. In Malaysia, ethnic Chinese business groups and MNCs became supplemented with GLCs governed by GLICs, and the CLICs/GLCs became the primary drivers in tandem with the foreign MNCs of the highly internationalized Malaysian economy (Gomez 2017; Hill 2012). But in spite of being excluded from state financial and other supports, Chinese-family SMEs did surprisingly well in economies like Malaysia and Taiwan.

Now, successful developmental states "dug their own grave," so to speak. If the starting point is "big state–small business," the relationship evolves into a "big state–big business," with the implementation of the strategic industrial policy. Big business may then internationalize to access new markets, resources, and corporate assets, on the one hand, and, in line with the neo-liberal consensus, lobby for "de-development" of the big developmental state, on the other hand, and if realized the "small state" outcome may again pressure the political elite to seek new allies and broaden the alliance (Evans 1997). As seen in South Korea, this process of state devolution began in the early 1980s, and after democratization from 1987, deregulation accelerated in the 1990s (Chang et al. 1998). Yet the state returned strongly during the financial crisis in 1998, and tripartism with corporatist state–labor–business negotiations was initiated, aiming to restructure the chaebols (dominant conglomerates) and to make the labor market more flexible (Wad 2002). The attempt was only partly successful – no "Korea Incorporated" regime matured as it had in Japan in the 1960s. Malaysia tried to imitate the key institutions of both Japan and South Korea in the 1980s with its "Look East" policy, but the MNCs did not want to include labor (at the micro-level as in Japan), and the ruling coalition marginalized indigenous (ethnic Chinese) managerial capabilities (contrary to South Korea that was not ethnically divided) (Jomo 2007). The "Malaysia Incorporated" policy failed (Jomo 2014), and Malaysia faced premature deindustrialization (Rasiah 2011) and a "middle-income trap" (Yusuf and Nabeshima 2009). Doner and Schneider argue more generally that middle-income traps emerge due to mismatches between institutional capacity to pursue policies for industrial upgrading, and that institutional inefficiency is conditioned by political obstacles to institutional upgrading (Doner and Schneider 2016).

In the "low-income trap" of "predatory state" formations, or at least weak, fragile, or failed state formations, states were often weak relative to society (Migdal 1988) and with structures of embeddedness without autonomy. Corruption has often been identified as a key explanatory factor behind the misery. Yet "rents" may serve many purposes, and political rents may be part of a vicious cycle of neo-patrimonial and antidevelopmental governance, but they can also serve the purpose of creating and sustaining a progressive political coalition (developmental political settlement) that can pursue and drive structural transformations of the relatively unproductive economy (Altenburg 2011; Khan 2000a, 2000b, 2010; Khan and Jomo 2000). The virtuous circle seems to be articulated in the two larger East Asian newly industrializing and now industrialized countries (South Korea and Taiwan), while the city-state of Singapore, with an open economy and a state–labor ruling alliance, looks like an authoritarian developmental state with a relatively "clean" political system (Pereira 2008).

Reconsidering state-business institutions and networks

Schneider (2015) reflects critically on the contribution of the Maxfield and Schneider anthology of 1997. Schneider acknowledges that it was too general and less substantial regarding state–business forms of collaboration and explanations for the variety of SBRs in terms of collaboration and/or collusion. He admits this ideal combination of best practices is seldom realized – with the South Korean export councils of 1960–1970 and (partly) the Korean technology councils of the 1980s and 2000s as an exception. Schneider emphasized also that state–business councils should include information exchange, authoritative allocation of resources, measures to check rent seeking, and active industrial policymaking. According to Khan and Blankenburg (2009), the point is that the match or mismatch between industrial policy and institutional capacity is key to the success or failure of state interventions in market economies of Latin America and Asia. Or as Lauridsen (2012) expressed it, "best fit" is preferable to "best practice." Merilee Grindle (2007) articulated the problem as "good enough governance."

Lemma and te Velde (2017) focus on the institutions of effective SBRs and critically appraise the research literature for Africa and East Asia. Acknowledging the rather limited empirical evidence that is available on the matter, they conclude

> that effective SBRs can matter a lot. The case studies based on careful, qualitative analysis suggest that SBRs can be effective (Mauritius) but also ineffective (Malawi). The quantitative evidence further suggests that high scores of SBRs measures are related to higher economic growth and

firm-level productivity. However, we need consider in more detail possible ways how to assess the effectiveness of SBRs in practice.

(Lemma and te Velde 2017, p. 76)

This caution about the applicability of the SBR terminology is corroborated by Charles et al.'s (2017) study of SBR in three East African countries, Zambia, Kenya and Tanzania, because they could not decisively conclude whether the SBRs were collaborative or collusive, at least as perceived by management.

Reviewing the SBR literature for Latin America, Schneider (2015) argued that the construction of approximations to the ideal type of SBRs is facilitated by political systems of coherent and centralized bureaucracies and peak business associations for labor-intensive accumulation in the era before economic globalization. However, relatively decentralized and technological inclusive systems for high-tech innovation and development seem more appropriate in an era of democratization and globalization.

Thus, Schneider is very much in line with Rodrik's (2007) conclusions, but Rodrik drives his argumentation about institutional quality further. He contends that the wider political regime of authoritarianism or democracy makes a difference in the long term, claiming that democratic institutions condition stable long-term growth and higher short-term stability, absorb economic shocks better, and achieve more just distributional outcomes and less inequality (Rodrik 2007, p. 169).

However, the relationship between capitalist development and democratization is highly contested in the PED literature. Research delivers evidence for at least two alternative propositions besides Rodrik's that there is a long-term trend of correlation between the development of capitalist economies and liberal democratic regimes. Adrian Leftwich (2005b) argued that there are institutional incompatibilities between economic development and political democratization, while Atul Kohli (2003) claimed, after studying industrial and developing countries across the Global South, that there is a contingent historical-contextual relationship between economic development and liberal democracy. The wider state–society relationship is highly relevant for the more specific politics of industrialization and its outcome.

The politics of state–business relations

Understanding governance as political processes of SBRs makes power a central part of the larger explanation of forms and dynamics of governance (Hyden 2006). SBRs are carried by elites that muster public and private authority and resources that are activated in their interaction, be it cooperative or conflictual, subdued or co-opted, and conditioned by goal alignments and inequality of power among actors. Recent studies contend that *the vulnerability of political and business elites* seems to have a decisive effect on the policies and practices of these elite to build and develop SBRs, although researchers may disagree on the way such vulnerability affects industrial policymaking and institutional development.

This dynamic has been analyzed empirically for East Asia during the Cold War, and sub-Saharan Africa and Latin America during the post–Cold War era.

The survival of political elites in East Asia

Rick Doner et al. (2005) wondered why developmental states only emerged in few developing countries, when these developmental institutions seemed to secure rapid economic growth and industrialization. In search for the political genesis of developmental states, they took on the question: Under which conditions are ruling elites driven to deliver growth-enhancing public goods and services and hence to build developmental institutions? Deliberately choosing a structural-deterministic approach, they explained the rise of developmental states in South Korea, Taiwan, and Singa-pore by the "systemic vulnerability" of their ruling elites.

Doner et al. (2005) defined a "developmental state" narrowly as a state that possesses a coherent bureaucracy and public–private consultative mechanisms, thus following Evans (1995). The theoretical argument is that holders of state power are "systemically vulnerable" when they face external security threats and internal social pressure to build broader coalitions and distribute benefits (side payments), while facing scarce natural resource endowments that cannot easily and quickly be translated into financial means. These ruling elites are squeezed financially and politically because the external threats (being in the frontline of the Cold War) and internal threats (suppressed and poorly paid hard-working laborers, farmers and self-employed businesspeople) require huge financial, economic, and technological resources to withstand or overcome. Due to the countries' lack of resource abundance, the structural vulnerability can only be countered by rapid economic growth, and such growth requires state capacity and collective willingness to mobilize and invest capital and labor strategically in rapid industrialization.

Paradoxically, with the *Systemic Vulnerability Theory* (SVT), Doner, Richie, and Slater (2005) argue that resource scarcity can be a fortunate situation for economic development if political leaders know how to handle it. This proposition contrasts the "resource curse" theory, where resource availability is hypothesized to lead to low growth, collusive exploitation of valuable resources by foreign and local elites, and overall development failure (John 2005, 2011; Ross 1999). Considering the resource curse enigma, Michael Ross (1999) diagnosed the PED thinking as a particularly weak political theory to explain the inability of governments to handle the "standard" problems of commodity export, that is, declining relative commodity prices and price volatility. However, today sovereign wealth funds may be effective financial policy tools to handle wealth preservation, developmental initiatives, or financial protectionism, thus proactively avoiding the resource curse situation (Jen 2007; Xu 2010). But they are not "water-tight" institutions and can be corrupted, as seen with the 1MDB fund that was exploited during the 2010s by Malaysia's former prime minister, Najib Razak (2009–2017).

Empirically, Doner et al. (2005) compared and contrasted the three "tiger economies" with four ASEAN countries (Malaysia, Thailand, Indonesia, and the Philippines). This comparison revealed that none of the ASEAN-4 countries had "developmental states," although Malaysia came close with moderate bureaucratic capacity and some consultation mechanisms (intermediary state formation with pockets of efficiency). These countries also displayed natural resource abundance that positioned ruling elites in less precarious situations. Moreover, they did not face external threats or internal pressure to the same degree as the tiger economies, it is argued. Thus, the ASEAN-4 fit the negative explanatory configuration implied by the theory that if ruling elites face no systemic vulnerability, no developmental state will be built and sustained.

The survival of political and business elites in sub-Saharan Africa

Contrary to East Asia, sub-Saharan Africa never industrialized (Hyden 1983) and even faced deindustrialization of its small industrial sector before the millennium (Lall 2004). Thus, Whitfield et al. (2015) searched for a theory of the (in)effectiveness of industrial policy in sub-Saharan Africa aiming to explain the successes as well as failures at a sector or industry level. They dismissed, on the one hand, the developmental state approach as a too state-centric model for understanding rapid economic growth and development, and the state–business model, on the other hand, because it emphasized in a too narrow way collaborative SBRs, excluding the broader state–society context of politics.

Instead they adopted the "political survival of ruling elites" approach like Doner, Richard, and Slater (2005), but they chose to take a broader "state-in-society" perspective, selecting Mushtaq Khan's (2010) Political Settlements theory as the starting point for theorizing the varied performance of African industrial policy and capitalist development (Whitfield et al. 2015, pp. 11–14).

The Whitfield group (2015) agrees with Khan's thinking regarding the importance of political contexts for industrial policymaking and the importance of the power positions and technical-industrial capabilities of capitalists and entrepreneurs. But they underlined that Africa differs significantly from other developing countries (e.g., Latin America, Asia) with regard to the weak position of indigenous capitalist classes (Whitfield et al. 2015, p. 25).

The research group also revised Khan's theory by adding a triangle stipulating three conditions for a successful industrial policy in the context of sub-Saharan African politics: (1) mutual interests between ruling elites and capitalist firms/farms, (2) pockets of efficiency between ruling elites and state bureaucrats, and (3) learning for productivity between capitalists and state bureaucrats (Whitfield et al. 2015, pp. 17–22). This triangle of state–business institutions corresponds to Chalmers Johnson's (1982) conception of the Japanese developmental state, although it explicates and emphasizes aspects of learning processes.

To explain what generates these conditions for successful industrial policymaking Whitfield et al. (2015) construed the Elaborated Political Settlement Theory (EPST). The theory is composed of two layers: the power structure of society with its particular political settlement and the configuration of industrial policy triangles. The concept of "political settlement" is operationalized into two sets of four variables: the ruling elite's external vulnerability and internal contestation and the political influence and technological capabilities of domestic capitalists. The particular form of the political settlement explains the particular conditional factors for industrial policymaking.

Following Mushtaq Khan, they model four types of political settlements, including "Competitive clientelism" (Ghana), "Vulnerable authoritarianism" (Mozambique), "Weak dominant party" (Tanzania), and "Strong dominant party" (Uganda, yet turning towards competitive clientelism). The strong dominant party type of political settlement is an adjustment of Khan's "potential developmental coalition,: displaying low vulnerability and contestation of the ruling elite (actualized in South Africa and Mauritius) because the group's sampling of country cases for research did not include a case of potential developmental coalition but only an approximation (Uganda) where some kind of contestation existed among ruling elites (Whitfield et al. 2015, pp. 105–107).

The Whitfield group's overall conclusion is that contemporary African political settlements are in general not conducive for effective industrial policy, with ruling elites being vulnerable and contested and with domestic capitalists having low technological capabilities (Whitfield et al. 2015, p. 294). The most feasible effective alliances are between ruling elites and foreign capitalists with higher technological capabilities and where higher mutual interests can be established by consultation, lobbying, or ideological consensus. Such alliances can generate sectoral economic growth, but not secure or sustain sector-wise deepening and upgrading, nor nationally integrated development.

Ruling elite vulnerability and survival: a paradox?

The two studies of Doner et al. (2005) and Whitfield et al. (2015) respectively disagree conceptually and theoretically on the explanatory power of vulnerability for effective industrial policymaking: positive in the SVT and negative in the EPST. More specifically, in the EPST vulnerability (outside pressure on the ruling coalition) does affect the establishment of pockets of efficiency but it does not condition alignments of "mutual interests" (between ruling coalition and domestic capitalists) or "learning for productivity" (among domestic capitalists) (Whitfield et al. 2015, p. 104). Moreover, the EPST looks more into the internal aspects (contestation) of the ruling elite alliance, something that is left unelaborated in the SVT. Finally, the SVT is focused on political elites, while the EPST enlarges the focus to political, bureaucratic, and business elites and bundles them in the notion of "political settlement" at the national level and "effective industrial policy" at the sector level. In retrospect, a vulnerability analysis of the business component of both theories might also be relevant and theoretically inspiring (Fuentes and Pipkin 2016).

Governing business for strategic industrial development: research issues and implications

Taking stock of the PED literature regarding the advances and drawbacks of conceptualizing and theorizing the problematic of political governance of business for industrial development, we now consider a few pertinent topical, conceptual, theoretical, and methodological issues that need research attention, clarification, elaboration, and validation in the future. By and large, we abstain from drawing any political-practical development implications, for the SBR based on this account because the problem area is reviewed and discussed in a broad and explorative way and not analyzed in a time- and context-specific situation that embeds political and business actors and influences their related agency (policymaking and strategizing).

The contemporary relevance of understanding political governance and industrial policy

In 2015 China launched the "Made in China 2025" industrial policy that aims to bring China into the frontier of technological development in ten high- and smart-tech industries where American, European, Japanese, or other OECD-based firms have been or are expected to be leading (ISDP 2018; Malkin 2018). "Made in China 2025" is a package of industrial strategies that includes massive state-linked financial assistance to Chinese firms to build or acquire advanced corporate assets through domestic R&D and innovation, sourcing of high-tech at international markets, and FDI or corporate acquisitions.

Traditionally MNCs from the Global North have been most competitive, exploiting competitive advantages in leveled global markets, but EMNCs from larger developing countries have been getting ahead with home-government support. China has pursued an explicit policy of "Going Out" or "Going Global" since 1999, and with massive state support for outward FDI, the acquisition of sensitive corporate assets and infrastructures in the West triggered the issue of dual use (for civil and military purposes) of components, parts, and final products. This concern for national security has been raised and used to block Chinese FDI, import, and corporate acquisitions among Western countries.

China may in fact seem to prove the effectiveness of strategic industrial policy in an age of economic globalization where multilateral trade is governed by the WTO regime of most-favored nation, and national treatment prohibiting discrimination between foreign and domestic firms in member countries. But industrial policy is selective and discriminatory in order to further national industrial development in market economies and has been used by countries throughout industrial history (Chang 2002). Moreover, China classified itself as a socialist market economy in 1993, and it was again classified as such when accessing the WTO in 2001. But the WTO regime of multilateral trade denies national discrimination between foreign and domestic firms in member countries, with exceptions for the transition period of entry, qualified developing country needs, national security, and environmental concerns. China was expected to obtain the MES in 2016, and many countries in Southeast Asia have granted China the MES, but not the United States, the EU and Japan!

The non-MES of China among advanced northern countries entails that member countries can easily launch antidumping investigations about the pricing of China's export of products and services, complying with the WTO rules. With the giant Chinese socialist market economy (Sigley 2006), the United States and other advanced market economies face a situation where SOEs and government-linked corporations, together with an expanding private sector – 57.6 million firms and 300 million employees (Warner 2018) – challenge the very foundation of globalized market economies and the WTO quest for fair competition and international trade between firms and countries in genuine market economies (O'Connor 2018).

The assumption has been that China would move toward a full market economy where companies could compete on a level playing field. But in the late 2010s, we cannot say whether China moves toward a mature market economy or consolidates as a socialist (one-party state) market economy. China's development planning has changed and become much more complex and flexible since the abandonment of central planning in 1993. Heilmann and Melton (2013) concluded that it defies easy classification:

> The hallmark of Chinese development planning lies in the dynamics of recombined governance based on loosely institutionalized, malleable, and adaptive policy processes. These governance mechanisms go beyond standard explanatory models of the command economy, the East Asian developmental state, or the regulatory state.
>
> (Heilmann and Melton 2013, p. 617)

Thus, the international competition among countries and firms has peaked in the clash between China and the United States in 2018 about strategic industrial policy, where an escalating trade war is translated into a question of national security and threatens to start a new Cold War. The state–market debate about industrial policy recurs.

Theoretical loopholes and opportunities

Recent advances in the PED followed the stream of "the survival of ruling elites" (Doner et al. 2005; Whitfield et al. 2015). But this does not come without critical responses. Benjamin Selwyn (2016) delegitimizes key development theories for being 'elitist', that is, taking the viewpoint of capital (or a capitalist state) while pledging concerns for the poor. According to Selwyn, elitist development theory includes the Washington Consensus, post–Washington Consensus, statist political economy, modernization Marxism, and various pro-poor growth theories.

The survival of the ruling elite approach suffers from this downgrading or neglecting of labor as a driver of industrial development – if organized labor is not an explicit part of the ruling coalition, and it seldom is. Selwyn (2016) suggests that an alternative "labor-centered" development theory must be founded in the collective actions of the laboring classes, understood as people who make a living by supplying wage work to capital on labor markets, inclusive of unemployed people.

In developing countries since the Cold War, politics cross class coalition formation and normally excludes organized labor and represses labor mobilization, organization, and political participation (Deyo 1987, 1989, 2012). If we look for organized labor (labor parties, trade unions) in the so-called "power bloc" (linked to the governing institutions as governments), Singapore and Chile are examples of countries that managed to catch up and achieve a high-income status but at the cost of political subordination in an authoritarian regime in Singapore (Rodan and Jayasuriya 2009) and a bloody political disaster in Chile (Stallings 1978) with a military dictatorship (1993–1990) before returning to a constrained democracy yet with sustained center-left governments for two decades.

Less successful economically, but more democratic, is Costa Rica (Sandbrook et al. 2007) or Mauritius, which is taken to be a showcase of effective SBRa (Lemma and te Velde 2017). Labor may more often be part of the ruling alliance in the role of economic beneficiaries (target group of social policies of populist government) or ideological supporters (voters for governing labor-oriented populist parties) (Stallings 1978), but not in Mauritius (Ulriksen 2012).

The historical inclusion or exclusion of organized labor in Latin America also had important implications for the emerging political regimes (Collier and Collier 1991). With the emergence of democratic institutions of governance, organized labor through labor parties or components of political alliances will be able to push for social reforms and welfare benefits (Sandbrook et al. 2007). This may even be the case when organized labor is not part of the governing coalition but acts as an active oppositional force with other social movements, e.g., South Korea since the start of democratization in 1987 or as trade unions with labor market, industry-wide, and/or workplace agency of collective bargaining and action (Wad 2017). But the dire strait of the state–labor–employer tripartism in the Global South is demonstrated again and again by the ILO (ILO/OECD 2018).

Beyond focusing on the omission of organized labor as a core political-economic actor, the "elite" focus should be deepened by elaborating and integrating research on formally or informally organized business (business associations and networks) (Bräutigam et al. 2002; Charles et al. 2017; Chibber 2004; Doner and Schneider 2000; Larsen 2012; Lucas 1997; Schneider 2004; Sinha 2005; Taylor 2012). Formally and strongly organized business has been a relatively rare sight in the Global South, but to make advances toward more sustainable economic development, it is important that firms join hands both as industrialists and as employers to facilitate corporatist and democratic governance of economic development at local, national, and global levels.

In contrast to the significance of network governance in GVC/GPN research is the literature on domestic policy networks, which is rather thin and conceptually meager. It turned out as a catchword with a high potential to grasp more complex and multilevel governance in the early 21st century (Witte et al. 2003). It became part of the institutional theory of business strategizing linking government and business (B2G relations) (Peng 2003; Peng and Zhou

2005) and most famously so regarding Chinese "guanxi" informal personal relations (Yeung 2004). A recent debate about the evolution of the socialist market economy between development planning, market forces, and policy experimentation in China also reflects the importance of policy networking in a fluent period of transition or relapse (Heilman and Melton 2013; Naughton 2013). Finally, a policy network has also been used in studies to describe public–private governance of local industrial clusters (Humphrey and Schmitz 2000), and the concept of the "triple helix" was construed to articulate local innovation clusters of universities, firms, and local governments (Etzkowitz and Leydesdorff 2000).

However, development-oriented policy network analysis has not yet made much progress conceptually and theoretically relative to such research in the Global North, where new public governance, democratic networking, and meta-governing have been on the research agenda (Sørensen and Thorfing 2009, 2017). These approaches to policy network analysis might be inspiring for a re-examination of the concepts and theories of systemic vulnerability and political settlement that have advanced our knowledge about the state–business nexus at the national and sector level of economic development.

Methodological deficiencies and new tools of investigation

The dominant approach in the PED has been nicknamed "methodological nationalism," emphasizing the nation, state, or country as its object of analysis (Gore 1996). Ontologically, nation-states are the basic real entities of social life and the abode of national structures that are taken to explain varieties of country performance (methodological holism). In contrast, methodological individualism takes the micro-actor (human beings) as the micro-foundation and explanatory unit for social and societal outcomes, as explicated by Amarty Sen (1999). Building a micro-foundation for theories of macro-economic development is a challenge in itself that includes overcoming the classic social science impasse of structure–agency analysis (Little 1998).

Applying methodological nationalism on a Third World or Global South of limited N-country cases invites *comparative macro analysis* in the field of PED, although neo-institutionalist governance studies have made extensive use of quantitative variable-based studies (Balland et al. 2010). The "classic" accounts of the comparative approach applied historical-comparative perspectives on the transitions to capitalism and the consequential political regime changes (e.g., Barrington Moore 1966; Skocpol 1979; Collier and Collier 1991), but they also complemented their structural-comparative analysis with process tracing of temporal sequences of events and processes in comparable cases. Comparative country analysis was extensively applied by political economic researchers aiming for understanding divergent trajectories of economic development between developing countries and regions (Gereffi 1990a; Haggard 1990) and more specifically among the Murdoch school focusing on the dynamics of capitalism and political changes in Southeast Asia (Rodan et al. 1997, 2006).

Analytically, Doner, Ritchard, and Slater (2005) used a classic comparative methodology framed by a critical rationalist research philosophy of induction and deduction in a contextual sequence of discovery and justification of the SVT. In fact, they used a research strategy of abduction, abstracting the hypotheses with the method of similarity (South Korea and Taiwan) and testing the hypotheses by using the method of similarity and difference for the developmental state of Singapore and the nondevelopmental states of the ASEAN-4 (Thailand, Malaysia, Indonesia, the Philippines). But they did not stop here. They added the *method of process tracing* of the political events and decisions that evolved into the full-fledged formation of developmental states in South Korea, Taiwan, and Singapore and that blocked or derailed the process in the ASEAN-4. Thus, they based their analysis on the *logic of qualitative comparative correlation* and deepened their analysis with the *logic of colligation* validating the claims for causality by way of disclosing the processes and events that transmitted the causes into consequences.

The sophisticated analysis by Doner, Ritchie, and Slater (2005) did not save them from criticism. Richard Stubbs (2009) dismissed their argumentation and conclusion because he found the empirical evidence unreliable and the analytics without a geo-political perspective on the relational dynamics of the region. Stubbs's multilevel and dynamic analytical perspective is highly relevant due to the regional influence of the United States and the linkages between successive wars (Korea and Vietnam) for the reactivation of national economies (e.g., Japan's and South Korea's), respectively. It is in line with Rasiah and Schmidt's (2010) outline of a new political economy with a Southeast Asia perspective moving beyond methodological nationalism, an endeavor that has also been pursued by a new generation of the Murdock school (Hameiri and Jones 2014).

However, Stubbs's critique of the empirical evidence is flawed. US military and development assistance in the 1950s was huge to the point of creating an externally induced resource curse of rampant political corruption (Wad 2002). But US aid declined over the 1960s to a point where Doner et al. (2005) are right in claiming that South Korea, Taiwan, and Singapore faced resource scarcity (Casse 1985; Gray 2013; USAID undated). Thus, external resource flows declined simultaneously with the evolution of developmental state institutions and interventions. Yet Stubbs's point, that external resource support matters, is pertinent and complements Doner et al.'s qualification of the national security threats toward ruling elites as external and internal!

The comparative research strategy was also explored by Whitfield et al. (2015) increasing the analytical complexity by investigating the phenomenon of the politics of industrial policy in four sub-Saharan countries at the national and the sector levels. Yet it was not carried to the ultimate end, leaving out a comparative country matrix. This could have validated the findings of the study, but it could also have called for a *retroductive research strategy* (Ragin 1994) that entails an ongoing abductive, deductive, inductive, and retroductive (repeated) process of new reflections over fits and misfits between evidence and hypotheses from the investigation.

The logic of colligation and the method of process tracing have been useful analytical tools in historical and political science research (Georg and Bennett 2004; Bennett and Checkel 2014; Mahoney 2012; Mahoney et al. 2009; Roberts 1996). They have also been increasingly applied in development research and policy cum project evaluations and particular in impact evaluation (Barnett and Munslow 2014). Thus, considering the under-researched area of business impact at multiple levels, process tracing methodology is a highly relevant and appropriate tool to be consulted and eventually applied. Exemplary studies in a political business perspective are done by Gomez (2009) on the evolution of Malaysian companies and by Gomez and De Micheaux (2017) on the theoretical aspects of understanding corporate history in a non-Western political-economic context.

Empirically, qualitative comparative research has dominated PED, partly justified by the focus on the societal and macro-level of development, nicknamed "methodological nationalism." With a shift to multilevel analysis and the inclusion of firms as key actors individually or collectively (business associations or networks), case studies with process tracing of (successful) corporate histories are still highly relevant. But quantitative measures based on surveys of hundreds and thousands of companies can be used for quantitative statistical analysis (e.g., correlation and regression analysis) (Lemma and te Velde 2017). Time series data of firm features might provide opportunities for causal statistical case studies that could take business studies much further and elaborate the dimension of political business in the PED literature. However, such data will often have to be generated as primary data because the statistical sources are unreliable or outright missing in large parts of the Global South.

Conclusions

Within the larger research field of governance, business, and development the chapter has explored the questions: How has the PE literature about industrialization dealt with the political governance of the domestic business sector in developing countries, and what are the major gaps?

We discussed political governance as a matter of industrial policy, state–business institutions, and the politics of industrialization. Considering the literature, we dare say that some kind of academic settlement has been concluded, at least in the heterodox camp of researchers within the PED perspective. Industrial policy has always been and is still used by states for reasons of national security, trade, and economic development. Using strategic industrial policy during the Cold War, the East Asian development states (South Korea, Taiwan, Singapore) were able to build competitive advantages of domestic businesses in selectively protected national economies mediated by strong state–business institutions of consultation, coordination, and collaboration; high levels of savings and subsidized investments; and exploitation of preferential access to foreign market opportunities in the Global North.

With the post–Cold War era and the WTO regime of international trade starting in 1995, developing country members have had their industrial policy space reduced after a transition period. China joined the WTO in 2001 after having pursued a market-oriented strategic industrial policy (socialist market economy) since 1993, and China has been catching up very fast since then, surpassing Germany as the largest export nation and the second largest economy in the world after the United States. With "Made in China 2025" the Chinese one-party state decided in 2015 to take China to the frontline of technological innovation and manufacturing. But with the Trump administration, the United States initiated trade sanctions against several countries but picked China as the primary scapegoat for the US trade deficit. The emerging trade war is underpinned by another emerging new Cold War on national security between the United States and China.

Thereby, the state–market dispute is revitalized. Smaller developing countries have been and might be allowed to continue (some) active industrial policies by liberal market democracies if they are set on transforming to proper market economies, but not a one-party-ruled giant of a socialist market economy attacking the high-tech positions of Northern TNCs. The "fallacy of composition" recurs in international relations.

The urgency and durability of state intervention in developing (market) economies often emerged when political and business elites were in dire straits under conditions of systemic vulnerability, but the literature diverges on the conceptualization and qualitative impact of systemic vulnerability. We contend that a more comprehensive conceptualization and dynamic multilevel comparative cum relational analysis can clarify the matter. It is a highly complex problematic that will have to draw on research from the Global South and Global North and require independently governed research collaboration within and across borders and disciplines

What is particularly missing in the PED perspective by the late 2010s is not so much valid political-economic theorizing about macro-level problems (macroeconomic policy, institutions and politics), nor sector-level industrial issues (active and strategic industrial policy, institutional design, and sector politics). Bridging the local-global linkages of value chains and production networks has also been on the research agenda for the last two decades. What is partly missing is the integration of the global-local framework with the national framework of economic (and social) development. GVCs and GPNs might contribute to local/regional development through various kinds of strategic coupling and industrial upgrading, depending on the modalities of governance applied. But how various types and trajectories of corporate governance interact with various kinds of political governance is still rather unclear and unsettled theoretically.

Thus, the "political business" of national development is to be considered a subfield of the PED perspective that should be given research priority by way of studying policy networks of public and private actors and their scaling up and down of collaborative and/or conflictual initiatives across local/regional, national, and regional/global levels of the political economies of the Global South. Without exploring and understanding the feedback loops from the micro-level to the meso- and macro-level, we will not be able to advance our theorizing of political governance of national economic development in more open economies with complex, fluent, and flexible policy networking of multiple actors.

References

Altenburg, T. (2011), "Can Industrial Policy Work Under Neopatrimonoial Rule?" UNU-WIDER. *Working Paper* No. 2011/41. Helsinki: UNU-WIDER.

Amsden, Alice (1989), *Asia's Next Giant: South Korea and Late Industrialization*. Oxford: Oxford University Press.

Ayele, Seife, Philip Mader, and Jodie Thorpe (2016), "State-Business Relations Beyond Growth: Bringing in Development," *Evidence Report* No. 215 with Jing Gu, Mar M. Morales and Philip Reed. Brighton, Sussex: Institute of Development Studies (IDS).

Bair, Jennifer (ed.). (2009), *Frontiers of Commodity Chain Research*. Stanford: Stanford University Press.

Balland, Jean-Marie, Karl O. Moene, and James A. Robinsson (2010), "Governance and Development," in *Handbook of Development Economics*, Dani Rodrik and Mark Rosenzwig, eds. Amsterdam: Elsevier, 4597–4656.

Barone, Barbara (2015), *One Year to Go: The Debate Over China's Market Economy Status (MES) Heats Up*. Bruxelles: European Parliament.

Barnett, Chris, and Tamlyn Munslow (2014), "Process Tracing: The Potential and Pitfalls for Impact Evaluation in International Development," Evidence Report 102. Brighton: IDS.

Bennett, Andrew, and Jeffrey T. Checkel (eds.). (2014), *Process Tracing: From Metaphor to Analytical Tool*. Cambridge: Cambridge University Press.

Bräutigam, Deborah, Lise Rakner, and Scott Taylor (2002), "Business Associations and Growth Coalitions in Sub-Saharan Africa," *Journal of Modern African Studies*, 40 (4), 519–547.

Bresser-Pereira, Luiz C. (2008), "Globalization, Nation-State and Catching Up," *Brazilian Journal of Political Economy*, 28 (4), 557–576.

Brogaard, Lena, and Ole H. Petersen (2018), "Public-Private Partnerships (PPPs) in Development Policy: Exploring the Concept and Practice," *Development Policy Review*, 36, 729–747.

Casse, Thorkil (1985), "The Non-Conventional Approach to Stability: The Case of South Korea. An Analysis of Macro-Economic Policy, 1979–84," CDR Research Report No. 5. Copenhagen: Centre for Development Research.

Cerny, Philip G. (1997), "Paradoxes of the Competition State: The Dynamics of Political Globalization," *Government and Opposition*, 32 (2), 251–274.

Chandran, V.G.R., Rajah Rasiah, and Peter Wad (2012), "Malaysia's Manufacturing Innovation Experience," in *Innovation and Industrialization in Asia*, Rajah Rasiah, Yeo Lin, and Yuri Sadoi, eds. London: Routledge, 128–150.

Chang, Ha-Joo (2002), *Kicking Away the Ladder: Development Strategy in Historical Perspective*. London: Anthem Press.

Chang, Ha-Joo, Hong Jae-Park, and Chul Gyue Yoo (1998), "Interpreting the Korean Crisis: Financial Liberalisation, Industrial Policy and Corporate Governance," *Cambridge Journal of Economics*, 22, 735–746.

Charles, Goodluck, Søren Jeppesen, Paul Jamau, and Peter Kragelund (2017), "Firm-Level Perspectives on State-Business Relations in Africa: The Food-Processing Sector in Kenya, Tanzania and Zambia," *Forum for Development Studies*, 44 (1), 109–131.

Chibber, V. (2004), "Reviving the Developmental State? The Myth of the National Bourgeoo-isie," *eScholarship*, University of California, http://escholarship.org/uc/item/2bq2753n

Chu, Yun-Han (2003), "East Asia: Development Challenges in the Twenty-First Century," in *States, Markets, and Just Growth: Development in the Twenty-First Century*, Atul Kohli, Chung-in Moon and Georg Sørensen, eds. New York: United Nations University Press, 127–163.

Cimoli, Mario, Giovanni Dosi, and Joseph E. Stiglitz, (eds.). (2009), *Industrial Policy and Development. The Political Economy of Capabilities Accumulation*. Oxford: Oxford University Press.

Coe, Neil M., and Henry W-C. Yeung (2015), *Global Production Networks: Theorizing Economic Development in an Interconnected World*. Oxford: Oxford University Press.

Collier, Ruth B., and David Collier (1991), *Shaping the Political Arena: Critical Junctures, the Labor Movement, and Regime Dynamics in Latin America*. Notre Dame, IN: University of Notre Dame Press, 2002 Edition.

Dahl-Ostergaard, Tom, David Moore, Vanessa Ramirez, Mark D. Wenner, and Ane Bonde (2005), "Community-Driven Rural Development: What Have We Learned?" Inter-American Development Bank Sustainable Development Department Technical Paper Series. Washington, DC (accessed March) www.iadb.org/sds/doc/RUR-COWIE.pdf.

Department for International Development (DFID) (2004), "Drivers of Change," Official document. London: DFID.

Deyo, Frederic C. (ed.). (1987), *The Political Economy of the New Asian Industrialism*. Ithaca: Cornell University Press.

Deyo, Frederic C. (1989), *Beneath the Miracle*. Berkeley: University of California Press.

Deyo Frederic C. (2012), *Reforming Asian Labor Systems. Economic Tensions and Worker Dissent*. Ithaca: Cornell University Press.

Dicken, Peter (2015), *Global Shift. Mapping the Changing Contours of the World Economy*. London: Sage, 7th Edition.

Doner, Richard F. (1991), "Approaches to the Politics of Economic Growth in Southeast Asia," *The Journal of Asian Studies*, 50 (4), 818–849.

Doner, Richard F. (1992), "Limits to State Strength: Toward an Institutionalist View of Economic Development," *World Politics*, 44 (3), 398–431.

Doner, Richard F., and Ben R. Schneider (2000), "Business Associations and Economic Development: Why Some Associations Contribute More Than Others," *Business and Politics*, 2 (3), 261–288.

Doner, Richard F., and Ben R. Schneider (2016), "More Politics than Economics," *World Politics*, 68 (4), 608–644.

Doner, Richard F., Brian K. Richie, and David Slater (2005), "Systemic Vulnerability and the Origins of Developmental States: Northeast and Southeast Asia in Comparative Perspective," *International Organization*, 59 (2), 327–361.

Doner, Richard F., and Peter Wad (2014), "Financial Crises and Automotive Industry Development in Southeast Asia," *Journal of Contemporary Asia*, 44 (4), 664–687.

Etzkowitz, Henry, and Leydesdorff, Loet (2000), "The Dynamics of Innovation: From National Systems and 'Mode 2' to a Triple Helix of University – Industry – Government Relations," *Research Policy*, 29, 109–123.

Evans, Peter (1995), *Embedded Autonomy: States and Industrial Transformation*. Princeton: Princeton University Press.

Evans, Peter (1997), "State Structures, Government-Business Relations, and Economic Transformation," in *Business and the State in Developing Countries*, Sylvia Maxfield and Ben R. Schneider, eds. London: Cornell University Press, 63–87.

Evans, Peter (1998), "Transferable Lessons? Re-Examining the Institutional Prerequisites of East Asian Economic Policies," *The Journal of Development Studies*, 34 (6), 66–86.

Evans, Peter (2005), "The Challenges of the 'Institutional Turn': New Interdisciplinary Opportunities in Development Theory," in *The Economic Sociology of Capitalism*, Victor Nee and Richard Swedberg, eds. Princeton: Princeton University Press, 90–116.

Faguet, Jean-Paul (2014), "Decentralisation and Governance," *World Development*, 53, 2–13.

Flintø, Daniel, and Stefano Ponte (2017), "Least-Developed Countries in a World of Global Value Chains: Are WTO Trade Negotiations Helping?" *World Development*, 94, 366–374.

Fold, Niels (2002), "Lead Firms and Competition in 'Bi-Polar' Commodity Chains: Grinders and Branders in the Global Cocoa. Chocolate Industry," *Journal of Agrarian Change*, 2 (2), 228–247.

Fold, Niels, and Larsen, Marianne N. (eds.). (2008), *Globalization and Restructuring of African Commodity Flows*. Uppsala: The Nordic Africa Institute.

Fuentes, Alberto, and Seth Pipkin, (2016), "Self-Discovery in the Dark: The Demand Side of Industrial Policy in Latin America," *Review of International Political Economy*, 23 (1), 153–183.

Gammeltoft, Peter, and Ari Kokko (2013), "Introduction: Outward Foreign Direct Investment from Emerging Economies and National Development Strategies: Three Regimes," *International Journal of Technological Learning, Innovation and Development*, 6 (1–2), 1–20.

Georg, Alexander L., and Andrew Bennett (2004), *Case Studies and Theory Development in the Social Sciences*. Cambridge: MIT Press.

Gereffi, Gary. (1990a), "Paths of Industrialization: An Overview," in *Manufacturing Miracles. Paths of Industrialization in Latin America and East Asia*, Gary Gereffi and Donald L. Wyman, eds. Princeton: Princeton University Press, 3–31.

Gereffi, Gary (1990b), "Big Business and the State," in *Manufacturing Miracles. Paths of Industrialization in Latin America and East Asia*, Gary Gereffi and Donald L. Wyman, eds. Princeton: Princeton University Press, 90–109.

Gereffi, Gary (2018), *Global Value Chains and Development: Redefining the Contours of 21st Century Capitalism*. Cambridge: Cambridge University Press.

Gereffi, Gary, John Humphrey, and Timothy Sturgeon (2005), "The Governance of Global Value Chains," *Review of International Political Economy*, 12 (1), 78–104.

Gereffi, Gary, and Timothy Sturgeon (2013), "Global Value Chain-Oriented Industrial Policy: The Role of Emerging Economies," in *Global Value Chains in a Changing World*, Deborah K. Elms and Patrick Low, eds. Geneva: WTO, Fung Global Institute and Temasek Foundation Centre for Trade & Negotiations, 329–360.

Gibbon, Peter (2008), "Segmentation, Governance and Upgrading in Global Clothing Chains – a Mauritian Case Study," in *Globalization and restructuring of African commodity flows*, Niels Fold and Marianne N. Larsen, eds. Uppsala: The Nordic Africa Institute, 184–209.

Gibbon, Peter, and Stefano Ponte (2005), *Trading Down: Africa, Value Chains, and the Global Economy*. Philadelphia: Temple University Press.

Gilpin, Robert (2001), *Global Political Economy: Understanding the International Economic Order*. Princeton: Princeton University Press.

Gomez, Edmund T. (1994), *Political Business: Corporate Involvement of Malaysian Political Parties*. Cairns: James Cook University Press.

Gomez, Edmund T. (2002a), "Introduction: Political Business in East Asia," in *Political Business in East Asia*, Edmund T. Gomez, ed. London: Routledge, 1–33.

Gomez, Edmund T. (2002b), "Political Business in Malaysia: Party Factionalism, Corporate Development and Economic Crisis," in *Political Business in East Asia*, Edmund T. Gomez, ed. London: Routledge, 82–114.

Gomez, Edmund T. (2009), "The Rise and Fall of Capital: Corporate Malaysia in Historical Perspective," *Journal of Contemporary Asia*, 39 (3): 345–381.

Gomez, Edmund T. (2010), "The Politics and Policies of Corporate Development: Race, Rents and Redistribution in Malaysia," in *Malaysia's Development Challenges: Graduating from the Middle*, Hal Hill, Tham Siew Yean and Ragayah Maji Mat Zin, eds. London: Routledge, 63–82.

Gomez, Edmund T. (2017), Minister of Finance incorporated. *Ownership and Control of Corporate Malaysia*. Petaling Jaya: Strategic Information and Research Development Centre.

Gomez, Edmund T., and Elsa Lafaya De Micheaux (2017), "Diversity of Southeast Asian Capitalisms: Evolving State-Business Relations in Malaysia," *Journal of Contemporary Asia*, 47 (5), 792–814.

Gomez, Edmund T., and Kwame Sundaran Jomo (1997), *Malaysia's Political Economy: Politics, Patronage and Profits*. Cambridge: Cambridge University Press.

Gore, Charles (1996), "Methodological Nationalism and the Misunderstanding of East Asian Industrialisation," *The European Journal of Development Research*, 8 (1), 77–122.

Gray, Kevin (2013), "Aid and Development in Taiwan, South Korea, and South Vietnam," WIDER. *Working Paper* 2013/085. Helsinki: UNU-WIDER.

Grindle, Merilee S. (2007), "Good Enough Governance Revisited?" *Development Policy Review*, 25 (5), 553–557.

Haggard, Stephan (1990), *Pathways from the Periphery: The Politics of Growth in the Newly Industrializing Countries*. Ithaca: Cornell University Press.

Haggard, Stephan (2018), *Developmental States*. Cambridge: Cambridge University Press.

Haggard, Stephan, Sylvia Maxfield, and Ben Ross Schneider (1997), "Theories of Business and Business-State Relations," in *Business and the State in Developing Countries*, Sylvia Maxfield and Ben R. Schneider, eds. London: Cornell University Press, 36–60.

Hameiri, Shahar, and Lee Jones (2014), "Murdoch International: The 'Murdoch School' in International Relations," Conference Paper. Hong Kong: City University of Hong Kong.

Hansen, Michael W., Lars Buur, Anne M. Kjær, and Ole Therkildsen (2015), "The Economics and Politics of Local Content in African Extractives: Lessons from Tanzania, Uganda and Mozambique," *Forum for Development Studies*, 26, 1–28.

Hansen, Thomas B., and Finn Stepputat (eds.). (2001), *States of Imagination: Ethnographic Explorations of the Postcolonial State*. Durham: Duke University Press.

Haraguchi, Nobuya, Charles F.C. Cheng, and Eveline Smeets, (2017), "The Importance of Manufacturing in Economic Development: Has This Changed?" *World Development* 94, 293–315.

Harris, Dan, Mick Moore, and Hubert Schmitz (2009), "Country Classifications for a Changing World," *IDS Working Paper 326*. Brighton: IDS.

Harris, Nigel (1986), *The End of the Third World: Newly Industrializing Countries and the Decline of an Ideology*. London: I. B. Tauris.

Heilmann, Sebastian, and Oliver Melton (2013), "The Reinvention of Development Planning in China, 1993–2012," *Modern China*, 39 (6), 580–628.

Henderson, Jeffrey, Peter Dicken, Martin Hess, Neil Coe M., and Henry W-C. Yeung (2003), "Global Production Networks and the Analysis of Economic Development," *Review of International Political Economy*, 9 (3), 436–464.

Hill, Hal (2012), "Malaysian Economic Development: Looking Backward and Forward," in *Malaysia's Development Challenges: Graduating from the Middle*, Hal Hill, Tham Siew Yean, and Ragayah Maji Mat Zin, eds. London: Routledge, 1–42.

Humphrey, John (1995), "Introduction (Industrial Organization and Manufacturing Competitiveness in Developing Countries," *World Development*, 23 (1), 1–7.

Humphrey, John, and Hubert Schmitz (2000), "Governance and Upgrading: Linking Industrial Cluster and Global Value Chain Research," IDS Working Paper, No 120. Brighton: Institute of Development Studies.

Humphrey, John, Steven Spratt, Jodie Thorpe, and Spencer Henson (2014), "Understanding and Enhancing the Role of Business in International Development: A Conceptual Framework and Agenda for Research," *IDS Working Paper* 440. Brighton: IDS.

Huntington, Samuel (1993), *The Third Wave: Democratization in the Late Twentieth Century*. Norman: University of Oklahoma Press.

Hyden, Göran (1983), *No Shortcut to Development: African Development Management*. London: Heineman.

Hyden, Göran (2006), "Beyond Governance: Bringing Power into Policy Analysis," *Forum for Development Studies*, 33 (2), 215–236.

ILO/OECD (2018), "Building Trust in a Changing World of Work," The Global Deal for Decent Work and Inclusive Growth Flagship Report 2018. Geneva: ILO.

Institute for Security and Development Policy (ISDP) (2018), "Made in China 2025," *Backgrounder*, June.

Jen, Stephen (2007), "Sovereign Wealth Funds: What They Are and What's Happening," *World Economics*, 8 (4), 1–7.

Jessop, Bob (1998), "The Rise of Governance and the Risks of Failure: The Case of Economic Development," *International Social Science Journal*, 155, 29–45.

John, Jonatan Di (2005), "Oil Abundance and Violent Political Conflict: A Critical Assessment," *Journal of Development Studies*, 45 (6), 961–986.

John, Jonatan Di (2011), "Is There Really a Resource Curse? A Critical Survey of Theory and Evidence," *Global Governance*, 17, 167–184.

Johnson, Chalmers (1982), *MITI and the Japanese Miracle: The Growth of Industrial Policy, 1925–1975*. Stanford: Stanford University Press.

Jomo, K.S. (1994), "The Proton Saga: Malaysian Car, Mitubishi Gain," in *Japan and Malaysian Development: In the Shadow of the Rising Sun*, Jomo K.S., eds. London: Routledge, 263–290.

Jomo, K.S. (2007), "Industrialization and Industrial Policy in Malaysia," in *Malaysian Industrial Policy*, Jomo K.S, eds. Singapore: NUS Press, 1–34.

Jomo K.S. (2014), "Malaysia Incorporated: Corporatism a la Mahathir," *Institutions and Economies*, 6 (1), 73–94.

Khan, Mushtaq H. (2000a), "Rents, Efficiency and Growth," in *Rents, Rent-Seeking and Economic Development: Theory and Evidence in Asia*, Mushtaq H. Khan and Jomo K.S., eds. Cambridge: Cambridge University Press, 21–69.

Khan, Mushtaq H. (2000b), "Rent-Seeking as Process," in *Rents, Rent-Seeking and Economic Development: Theory and Evidence in Asia*, Mushtaq H. Khan and Jomo K.S., eds. Cambridge: Cambridge University Press, 70–144.

Khan, Mushtaq H. (2010), "Political Settlements and the Governance of Growth-Enhancing Institutions," *Paper*.

Khan, Mushtaq H., and Stephanie Blankenburg (2009), "The Political Economy of Industrial Policy in Asia and Latin America," in *Industrial Policy and Development: The Political Economy of Capabilities Accumulation*, Mario Cimoli, Giovanni Dosi, and Joseph E. Stiglitz, eds. Oxford: Oxford University Press, 336–377.

Khan, Mushtaq H., and K.S. Jomo (2000), "Introduction," in *Rents, Rent-Seeking and Economic Development: Theory and Evidence in Asia*, Mushtaq H. Khan and Jomo K.S., eds. Cambridge: Cambridge University Press, 1–20.

Kohli, Atul (2003), "Democracy and Development: Trends and Prospects," in *States, Markets, and Just Growth: Development in the Twenty-First Century*, Atul Kohli, Chung-in Moon and Georg Sørensen, eds. New York: United Nations University Press, 39–63.

Kohli, Atul (2004), *State-Directed Development: Political Power and Industrialization in the Global Periphery*. Cambridge: Cambridge University Press.

Lall, Sanjaya (2004), "Reinventing Industrial Strategy: The Role of Government Policy in Building Industrial Competitiveness," *G-24 Discussion Paper Series* No. 28. New York: UNCTAD.

Larsen, Marcus M. (2012), "Institutional Entrepreneurship in the Informal Economy: The Case of the Zambia National Marketeers Association," in *Entrepreneurship in the Informal Economy: Models, Approaches and Prospects for Economic Development*, Mai T. T. Thai and Ekatarina Turkina, eds. New York: Routledge, 114–126.

Lauridsen, Laurids S. (2010), "Strategic Industrial Policy and Latecomer Development: The What, the Why and the How," *Forum for Development Studies*, 37 (1), 7–32.

Lauridsen, Laurids S. (2012), "From Good Governance to Developmental Governance – How Policies, Institutions and Politics Matter," *Forum for Development Studies*, 39 (3), 337–366.

Lauridsen, Laurids S. (2018), "New Economic Globalization, New Industrial Policy and Late Development in the 21st Century: A Critical Analytical Review," *Development Policy Review*, 36, 329–346.

Lee, Cassey (2012), "Microeconomic Reform in Malaysia," in *Malaysia's Development Challenges: Graduating from the middle*, Hal Hill, Tham Siew Yean, and Ragayah Maji Mat Zin, eds. London: Routledge, 155–173.

Leftwich, Adrian (1995), "Bringing Politics Back, in: Towards a Model of the Developmental State," *The Journal of Development Studies*, 31 (3), 400–427.

Leftwich, Adrian (2005a), "Politics in Command: Development Studies and the Rediscovery of Social Science," *New Political Economy*, 10 (4), 573–607.

Leftwich, Adrian (2005b), "Democracy and Development: Is There Institutional Incompatibility?" *Democratization*, 12 (5), 686–703.

Leftwich, Adrian (2006), "Drivers of Change: Refining the Analytical Framework. Part I and Part II," *Mimeo*. DFID.

Lema, Rasmus, and Adrian Lema (2012), "Technology Transfer? The Rise of China and India in Green Technology Sectors," *Innovation and Development*, 2 (1), 23–44.

Lema, Rasmus, Ruy Quadros, and Hubert Schmitz (2015), "Reorganising Global Value Chains and Building Innovation Capabilities in Brazil and India," *Research Policy*, 44, 1376–1386.

Lemma, Alberto, and Dirk W. te Velde (2017), "State-Business Relations as Drivers of Economic Performance," in *The Practice of Industrial Policy: Government-Business Coordination in Africa and East Asia*, John Page and Finn Tarp, eds. Oxford: Oxford University Press, 63–79.

Levy-Faur, David (2012), "From 'Big Government' to 'Big Governance'?" in *Oxford Handbook of Governance*, David Levi-Faur, ed. Oxford: Oxford University Press, 3–18.

Little, Daniel (1998), *Microfoundations, Method, and Causation: On the Philosophy of the Social Sciences*. New Brunswick: Transaction Publishers.

Lucas, John (1997), "The Politics of Business Associations in the Developing World," *The Journal of Developing Areas*, 32 (1), 71–96.

Lundvall, Bengt-Åke, K. J., Christina Chaminade, and Jan Vang (2009), *Handbook of Innovation Systems and Developing Countries. Building Domestic Capabilities in a Global Setting*. Cheltenham, UK: Edward Elgar.

MacIntyre, Andrew (1994), "Preface," in *Business and Government in Industrialising Asia*, Andrew MacIntyre, ed. Ithaca: Cornell University Press, ix–x.

Mahoney, James (2012), "The Logic of Process Tracing Tests in the Social Sciences," *Sociological Methods & Research*, 41 (4), 570–597.

Mahoney, James, Erin Kimball, and Kendra L. Koivu (2009), "The Logic of Historical Explanation in the Social Sciences," *Comparative Political Studies*, 42 (1), 114–146.

Malkin, Anton (2018), "Made in China 2025 as a Challenge to Global Trade Governance. Analysis and Recommendations," *CIGI Papers* No. 183, August 2018.

Martinussen, John D. (1997), *Society, State and Market: A Guide to Competing Theories of Development*. London: Zed Books.

Maxfield, Sylvia, and Ben R. Schneider (eds.). (1997), *Business and the State in Developing Countries*. London: Cornell University Press.

Mayer, Frederick W., Nicola Philips, and Anne C. Posthuma (2017), "Introduction: The Political Economy of Governance in a 'Global Value Chain World'," *New Political Economy*, 22 (2), 129–133.

Migdal, Joel S. (1988), *Strong Societies and Weak States: State-Society Relations and State Capabilities in the Third World*. Princeton: Princeton University Press.

Moore, Barrington (1966), *Social Origins of Dictatorship and Democracy*. Boston: Beacon.

Moore, Mick (1998), "Review," *Economic Development and Cultural Change*, 46 (2), 427–432.

Morris, Mike, Raphael Kaplinsky, and David Kaplan (2012), "One Thing Lead to Another – Commodities, Linkages and Industrial Development," *Resource Policy*, 37, 408–416.

Morrison, Wayne M. (2018), *The Made in China 2025 Initiative: Economic Implications for the USA*. Washington: Congressional Research Service, Updated August 29.

Natsuda, Kaoru, and John Thoburn (2014), "How Much Policy Space Still Exists Under the WTO? A Comparative Study of the Automotive Industry in Thailand and Malaysia," *Review of International Political Economy*, 21 (6), 1346–1377.

Natsuda, Kaoru, Noriyuki Segawa, and John Thoburn (2013), "Liberalization, Industrial Nationalism, and the Malaysian Automotive Industry," *Global Economic Review*, 42 (2), 113–134.

Naughton, Barry (2013), "The Return of Planning in China: Comment on Heilmann-Melton and Hu Angang," *Modern China*, 39 (6), 640–652.

O'Brien, Robert, and Marc Williams (2007), *Global Political Economy: Evolution and Dynamics*. New York: Palgrave Macmillan.

O'Connor, Sean (2018), *SOE Megamergers Signal New Direction in China's Economic Policy: The US-China Economic and Security Review Commission*. Staff Research Report. Washington: US-China Commission.

Page, John, and Finn Tarp (eds.). (2017), *The Practice of Industrial Policy. Government-Business Coordination in Africa and East Asia*. Oxford: Oxford University Press.

Paul, Justin, and Gabriel R.G. Benito (2018), "A Review of Research on Outward Foreign Direct Investment from Emerging Countries, Including China: What Do We Know, How Do We Know and Where Should We Be Heading?" *Asia Pacific Business Review*, 24 (1), 90–115.

Peng, Mike W. (2003), "Institutional Transitions and Strategic Choices," *Academy of Management Review*, 28, 275–296.

Peng, Mike W., and Jessie Q. Zhou (2005), "How Network Strategies and Institutional Transitions Evolve in Asia," *Asia Pacific Journal of Management*, 22, 321–336.

Pereira, Alexius A. (2008), "Whither the Developmental State? Explaining Singapore's Continued Developmentalism," *Third World Quarterly*, 29 (6), 1189–1203.

Peters, Guy (2012), "Governance as Political Theory," in *Oxford Handbook of Governance*, David Levi-Faur, ed. Oxford: Oxford University Press, 19–32.

Ponte, Stefano, Peter Gibbon, and Jacob Vestergaard (eds.). (2011), *Governing Through Standards: Origins, Drivers and Limitations*. London: Palgrave Macmillan.

Ragin, Charles (1994), *Constructing Social Research: The Unity and Diversity of Method*. Thousand Oaks: Pine Forge Press.

Rasiah, Rajah (2005), "Trade-Related Investment Liberalization Under the WTO: The Malaysian Experience," *Global Economic Review*, 34 (4), 453–471.

Rasiah, Rajah (2011), "Is Malaysia Facing Negative Deindustrialization?" *Pacific Affairs*, 84 (4), 715–736.

Rasiah, Rajah (2017), "The Industrial Policy Experience of the Electronics Industry in Malaysia," in *The Practice of Industrial Policy: Government-Business Coordination in Africa and East Asia*, John Page and Finn Tarp, eds. Oxford: Oxford University Press, 123–144.

Rasiah, Rajah, Peter Gammeltoft, and Yang Jiang (2010), "Home Government Policies for Outward FDI from Emerging Economies: Lessons from Asia," *International Journal of Emerging Markets*, 5 (3–4), 333–357.

Rasiah, Rajah, and Johannes D. Schmidt (2010), "Introduction," in *The New Political Economy of South East Asia*, Rajah Rasiah and Johannes D. Schmidt, eds. Cheltenham, UK: Edward Elgar, 1–43.

Reinert, Erik (2007), *How Rich Countries Got Rich . . . and Why Poor Countries Stay Poor*. London: Constable and Robinson.

Roberts, Clayton (1996), *The Logic of Historical Explanation*. University Park: Pennsylvania State University Press.

Rodan, Garry, and Kanishka Jayasuriya. (2009), "Capitalist development, Regime Transitions and New Forms of Authoritarianism in Asia," *The Pacific Review*, 22 (1), 23–47.

Rodan, Gary, Kevin Hewison, and Ricvhard Robison (eds.) (1997), *The Political Economy of South-East Asia: An Introduction*. Melbourne: Oxford University Press.

Rodan, Gary, Kevin Hewison, and Richard Robison (eds.) (2006), *The Political Economy of Southeast-Asia: Markets, Power and Contestation*. Melbourne: Oxford University Press.

Rodrik, Dani (2007), *One Economics – Many Recipes: Globalization, Institutions and Economic Growth*. Princeton: Princeton University Press.

Roos, Michael L. (1999), "The Political Economy of the Resource Curse," *World Politics*, 51 (2), 297–322.

Sandbrook, R., March Edelman, Patrick Heller, and Judith Teichman (2007), *Social Democracy in the Global Periphery: Origins, Challenges, Prospects*. Cambridge: Cambridge University Press.

Schmitz, Hubert (1995), "Collective Efficiency: Growth Path for Small Scale Industry," *The Journal of Development Studies*, 31 (4), 529–566.

Schmitz, Hubert (ed.) (2004), *Local Enterprises in the Global Economy. Issues of Governance and Upgrading*. Cheltenham, UK: Edward Elgar.

Schmitz, Hubert (2007), "Reducing Complexity in the Industrial Policy Debate," *Development Policy Review*, 25 (4), 417–428.

Schmitz, Hubert, and Khalid Nadvi (1999), "Clustering and Industrialization: Introduction," *World Development*, 27 (9), 1503–1517.

Schneider, Ben R. (2004), *Business, Politics, and the State in Twentieth-Century Latin America*. Cambridge: Cambridge University Press.

Schneider, Ben R. (2012), "Contrasting Capitalisms: Latin America in Comparative Perspective," in *The Oxford Handbook of Latin American Political Economy*, Javier Santiso and Jeff Dayton-Johnson, eds. Oxford: Oxford University Press, 381–402.

Schneider, Ben R. (2015), *Designing Industrial Policy in Latin America: Business-State Relations and the New Developmentalism*. New York: Palgrave Macmillan.

Selwyn, Benjamin (2016), "Theory and Practice of Labour-Centred Development," *Third World Quarterly*, 37 (6), 1035–1052.

Sen, Amartya (1999), *Development as Freedom*. New York: Alfred A. Knopf.

Sharma, Aradhana, and Akhil Gupta (eds.). (2006), *The Anthropology of the State: A Reader*. Oxford: Blackwell.

Sigley, Gary (2006), "Chinese Governmentalities: Government, Governance and the Socialist Market Economy," *Economy and Society*, 35 (4), 487–508.

Sinha, Aseema (2005), "Understanding the Rise and Transformation of Business Collective Action in India," *Business and Politics*, 7 (2), 1–35.

Skocpol, Theda (1979), *States and Social Revolutions*. Cambridge: Cambridge University Press.

Sørensen, Eva, and Jacob Torfing (2009), "Making Governance Networks Effective and Democratic Through Metagovernance," *Public Administration*, 87 (2), 234–258.

Sørensen, Eva, and Jacob Torfing (2017), "Metagoverning Collaborative Innovation in Governance Networks," *American Review of Public Administration*, 47 (7), 826–839.

Stacey, Paul, and Christian Lund (2016), "In a State of Slum: Governance in an Informal Urban Settlement in Ghana," *Journal of Modern African Studies*, 54 (4), 591–615.

Stallings, Barbara (1978), *Class Conflict and Economic Development in Chile, 1958–1973*. Stanford: Stanford University Press.

Stubbs, Richard (2009), "What Ever Happened to the East Asian Developmental State? The Unfolding Debate," *The Pacific Review*, 22 (1), 1–13.

Taylor, Scott D. (2012), "Influence Without Organizations: State-Business Relations and Their Impact on Business Environments in Contemporary Africa," *Business and Politics*, 14 (1), 1–35.

Therkildsen, Ole (2008), "Public Sector Reforms and the Development of Productive Capacities in LDCs," *Background Paper No. 1*. Geneva: UNCTAD.

Thoburn, John, and Kaoru Natsuda (2017), "Comparative Policies for Automotive Development in Southeast Asia," in *Cars, Automobility and Development in Asia: Wheels of Change*, Arve Hansen and Kenneth B. Nielsen, eds. London: Routledge, 17–36.

Ulriksen, Marianne S. (2012), "Welfare Policy Expansion in Botswana and Mauritius: Explaining the Causes of Different Welfare Regime Paths," *Comparative Political Studies*, 45 (12), 1483–1509.

USAID. (Undated). *South Korea: From Aid Recipient to Aid Donor*. Washington: USAID (accessed 15 April 2015), www.usaid.gov/location/asia

Wad, Peter (2001), "Business Systems and Sector Dynamics: The Case of the Malaysian Auto Industry," in *Understanding Business Systems in Developing Countries*, Gurli Jakobsen and Jens E. Torp, eds. New Delhi: Sage, 87–127.

Wad, Peter (2002), "The Political Business of Development in South Korea," in *Political Business in East Asia*, Edmund T. Gomez, ed. London: Routledge, 182–215.

Wad, Peter (2006), "The Automotive Supplier Industry Between Localizing and Globalizing Forces in Malaysia, India and South Africa," in *Transnational Corporations and Local Firms in Developing Countries – Linkages and Upgrading*, Michael W. Hansen and Henrik Schaumburg-Müller, eds. Køge: Copenhagen Business School Press, 233–261.

Wad, Peter (2008), "The Development of Automotive Parts Suppliers in Korea and Malaysia: A Global Value Chain Perspective," *Asia Pacific Business Review*, 14 (1), 47–64.

Wad, Peter (2017), "The Asian Automotive Industry and Labour Organizing," in *Cars, Automobility and Development in Asia. Wheels of Change*, Arve Hansen and Kenneth B. Nielsen, eds. London: Routledge, 37–61.

Wad, Peter, and V.G.R. Chandran (2011), "Automotive Industry in Malaysia: An Assessment of Its Development," *International Journal of Automotive Technology and Management*, 11 (2), 152–171.

Wad, Peter, and Søren Jeppesen (2006), "Development Strategy, Industrial Policy and Cross Border Inter-Firm Linkages," in *Transnational Corporations and Local Firms in Developing Countries – Linkages and Upgrading*, Michael W. Hansen and Henrik Schaumburg-Müller, eds. Køge: Copenhagen Business School Press, 311–338.

Wade, Robert H. (1990), *Governing the Market: Economic Theory and the Role of Government in East Asian Industrialization*. Princeton: Princeton University Press.

Wade, Robert H. (2003), "What Strategies Are Viable for Developing Countries Today? The World Trade Organization and the Shrinking of 'Development Space'," *Review of International Political Economy*, 10 (4), 621–644.

Wade, Robert H. (2010), "After the Crisis: Industrial Policy and the Developmental State in Low-Income Countries," *Global Policy*, 1 (2), 150–161.

Wade, Robert (2018), "The Developmental State: Dead or Alive?" *Development and Change*, 49 (2), 518–546.

Warner, Malcom (2018), "Book Review: Entrepreneurship in China: The Emergence of the Private Sector," *Asia Pacific Business Review*, published online April 18, https://doi.org/10.1080/13602381.2018.1463627

Weiss, Linda (1995), "Governed Interdependence: Rethinking the State-Business Relationship in East Asia," *The Pacific Review*, 8 (4), 589–616.

Whitfield, Lindsay, Ole Therkildsen, Lars Buur, and Anne Mette Kjær (2015), *The Politics of African Industrial Policy. A Comparative Perspective*. New York: Cambridge University Press.

Whitley, Richard (2001), "Developing Capitalisms: The Comparative Analysis of Emerging Business Systems in the South," in *Understanding Business Systems in Developing Countries*, Gurli Jakobsen and Jens E. Torp, eds. New Delhi: Sage, 25–41.

Witte, Jan Martin, Thorsten Brenner, and Wolfgang H. Reinicke, (2003), "Innovating Global Governance Through Global Public Policy Networks: Lessons Learned and Challenges Ahead," *Brookings Review*, 1.

Wong, Wilson K.O. (2018), *Automotive Global Value Chain: The Rise of Mega Suppliers*. London: Routledge.

World Bank (1992), *Governance and Development*. Washington, DC: World Bank.

World Bank (1993), *The East Asian Miracle: Economic Growth and Public Policy*. Washington, DC: Oxford University Press for the World Bank.

Xu, Yi-chong. (2010), "The Political Economy of Sovereign Wealth Funds," in *The Political Economy of Sovereign Wealth Funds*, Xu Yi-chong and Gawdat Bahgat, eds. Basingstoke: Palgrave Macmillan.

Yeung, Henry W-C. (2004), "Strategic Governance and Economic Diplomacy in China: The Political Economy of Government-Linked Companies from Singapore," *East Asia*, 21 (1), 40–64.

Yeung, Henry W-C. (2009), "The Rise of East Asia: An Emerging Challenge to the Study of International Political Economy," in *Routledge Handbook of International Political Economy*, Mark Blyth, ed. London: Routledge, 201–215.

Yeung, Henry W-C. (2014), "Governing the Market in a Globalizing Era: Developmental States, Global Production Networks and Inter-Firm Dynamics in East Asia," *Review of International Political Economy*, 21 (1), 70–101.

Yusuf, Shahid, and Kaoru Nabeshima (2009), *Tiger Economies Under Threat: A Comparative Analysis of Malaysia's Industrial Prospects and Policy Options*. Washington, DC: The World Bank.

Zhang, Miao, Rajah Rasiah, and John L. K. Yes (2017), "Navigating a Highly Protected Market: China's Chery Automobile in Malaysia," *Journal of Contemporary Asia*, 47 (5), 774–791.

3 State–business relations and development[1]

Toward a more complete research agenda

Jodie Thorpe and Philip Mader

Introduction

In developing countries as much as in developed countries, what businesses do, how they do it, and how their actions in turn affect society depend profoundly on their interactions with states. These relations between sovereign states, businesses, and societal aspirations for development are the subject of this chapter, in which we assess the state of existing research and present an analytical framework based on the concept of negotiation. This allows us to plot an enhanced research agenda focused on how structures and processes of negotiation shape progress on development outcomes, and thus to contribute to the study of political economy as part of business and development studies, an emergent interdisciplinary research field in the social sciences.

To frame the issue of state–business relations, it is worth noting that in September 2015, when world leaders adopted the 17 Sustainable Development Goals (SDGs) with the aim of ending all forms of poverty, fighting inequalities, and promoting environmental sustainability, they charged governments with taking ownership of these goals and establishing national frameworks for their achievement. At the same time, the SDG signatories called upon a wide range of businesses – from micro-enterprises to cooperatives to multinationals – "to apply their creativity and innovation" to address these sustainable development challenges.[2] This emphasis on the role of business as a development actor resonates with much contemporary thinking and practice (Humphrey et al. 2014). Yet here, as elsewhere, significant gaps are evident in terms of how to theorize and analyze the relationship of business with the state, particularly in relation to goals that go beyond a narrow focus on economic growth. A more complete research agenda for state–business relations in development must illuminate what structures and processes help attain the broader developmental aspirations enshrined in the SDGs.

This chapter begins by defining core concepts: state, business, power, and development. It then reviews key literatures that have illuminated the effects of state–business relations on development but have mainly focused on economic growth and industrialization, as well as the variables which influence the nature and outcomes of these interactions. Finally, it proposes a broadened research agenda for an empirical evaluation of state–business relations that would focus on structures and processes of negotiation between different actors and how these shape development outcomes beyond growth.

Key concepts

State–business relations can be understood as interactions of political and economic authorities over time through which they seek to influence and constrain each other. Through this "mutual adjustment amongst authorities" (Lindblom 1977, p. 175), public affairs (decisions that affect society) are determined. These state–business relations typically are characterized by structured, iterative processes, which are shaped by both institutional arrangements and the relative power and interests of state and business actors (Ayele et al. 2016). Our emphasis is on how states and businesses interact over longer periods of time, not in one-off, discreet, or arbitrary events, but rather through ongoing, often complex, and iterative engagements which we conceptualize as "negotiations" (which we elaborate in the final main section of this chapter).

Many of these concepts that matter for the analysis of state–business relations and development effectiveness are plagued by widely differing assumptions, and in some cases are highly contested. This section clarifies our understanding of key concepts central to the study of state–business relations as part of business and development studies.

"State" and "business"

There are multiple and contending views of what the state is and how it exercises influence, just as there are divergent views of what business is (Haggard, Maxfield, and Schneider 1997). Rather than being a single, unified actor, the state is better understood as a collection of agencies collectively endowed with the legal mandate to represent a population within a defined geography. The boundary may be local, subnational, or national.

Although embedded in society, the state is largely autonomous in its own right – indeed it must be, to conduct the day-to-day affairs of society – and its agency shapes social, political, and economic processes (Evans, Rueschemeyer and Skocpol 1985). The state includes multiple ministries, agencies, civil servants, and politicians – "state managers" – each with potentially distinctive interests and capacities (Jessop 2001). However, more generally, the state is the political organization that persists beyond any particular individual or administration. It has the "*monopoly* of the *legitimate* use of physical force"' to enforce order (Weber 1978, p. 54), although under capitalism the power of the state is far from absolute, and its interests are indeterminate and interdepend with others' interests (Jessop 2001). The basis of the state's legitimacy and authority may be rational (legal), traditional, or charismatic (Weber 1978); and this legitimacy and authority will influence the ways in which states engage with businesses.

If the "state" has political authority, then "business" has authority over the day-to-day allocation of many economic resources. Business makes choices about technology, the structure of work, and the allocation of resources, which cannot easily be mandated, even in authoritarian states (Lindblom 1977). Like the state, business is embedded in social networks and institutions, including the policies of the state (Granovetter 1985). Haggard et al. (1997) conceptualize business based on the factors that shape its power and preferences, proposing to understand business as capital, as sectors, as firms, as associations, and as a network (Table 3.1). Each conceptualization highlights different types of power that "business" may exert: the structural power of capital, of the business sector as a whole, and of large firms; the instrumental power of business associations pursuing specific business interests; and the power of networks of individual business-people. This analysis reminds us that businesses are heterogeneous, ranging from large global companies to individual entrepreneurs, across agriculture, industry, and services, and varying in its capacity to negotiate with the state.

Table 3.1 Theories of business

Conceptualization	Features of business in this conceptualization
Business as "capital"	• Business (as capital) exerts structural power. • Businesses share collective interests. • Capital "votes twice": by lobbying and by deciding on investment. • The state is constrained by business' control of investment resources; this can be positive where it constrains a predatory state.
Business as "sector"	• Business (as the business sector) exerts structural power. • Characteristics of sectors (factor intensity, degree of industrial concentration) shape business preferences. • Sector composition and representation in the political system affect state–business relations. • Contending interests of different sectors constrain the state.
Business as "firm"	• Businesses (large firms) exert structural power. • Firm size (concentration) and diversity (conglomeration) affect both preferences and leverage of business. • Multisector conglomerates have diverse interests and may support changing policy priorities. • How firms acquire capital (family, foreign, shareholder ownership) may also shape their interests.
Business as "association"	• Instrumental power of business (actively exerting influence). • Business associations matter: if a small number of businesses with large economic weight organize, their power is great. • Associations serve to aggregate and intermediate business interests. • Associations can be rent-seeking, but 'encompassing multisectoral associations' can limit the pursuit of particularistic interests.
Business as "network"	• Power of individuals in business. • Influence of managers and owners through personal connections, shared worldviews, and overlapping roles. • Repeated interaction leads to trust and cooperation with state elites, but no guarantee of "good" policy. • Networks between business and government can also lead to clientelism.

Source: Adapted from Ayele et al. (2016, p. 22); based on Haggard et al. (1997)

Power

Given that states and businesses seek, possess, and exert influence over one another, we must ask: What exactly is "power"? Although this short section cannot do justice to the vast theoretical debates in the social sciences, it outlines key concepts for understanding state–business relations in the development context.

Fuchs and Lederer (2007) provide a useful framework for assessing business power, based on instrumental, structural, and discursive elements. *Instrumental* power is relational and causal, exerting power directly over other actors, for instance, through business lobbying. *Structural* power is determined by the economic structures of capitalism and implies that business has influence even before lobbying or active influencing begins. As a result of structural power, for example, a government may refrain from adopting, or even considering, new environmental or tax policies, fearing businesses will divest. *Discursive* power is the power of ideas and norms, which shape the framing of problems and potential solutions. Narratives, storylines, images, and symbols are used to build legitimacy; for instance, discourses of "corporate citizenship" create new routes of action for businesses and states.

Another distinction in the forms of power (Gaventa 2006) contrasts "power over" and "power with." "Power over" is understood as a controlling force, constraining the choices of others; this type of power is often countered by checks and balances. However, some theorists also understand power as a constructive force. "Power with" involves aggregating resources to render them useful and potent for the collective good (Moore 2005).

Relevant to ideas about power, finally, is the notion of the "spaces" in which it is felt. Policy spaces are arenas where power and influence are exercised as different actors and interests interact. Spaces may be "closed," where decisions are taken among elites behind closed doors, with limited involvement of non-elites, and often little transparency and accountability. "Invited" spaces allow more open participation, but are still created (and thus often access-controlled) by more powerful authorities which invite others to participate, often in a consultative rather than executive way. "Claimed" spaces, finally, are ones which less powerful actors create for themselves, often in opposition to closed or invited spaces (Gaventa 2006).

Development and development effectiveness

The literature on state–business relations in development has traditionally, explicitly or implicitly, been interested primarily in investment, growth, and industrialization. However, although investment and growth have often been linked to development, they are not the whole story, and economic and social development have often not followed in step with economic growth.

Amartya Sen, for example, proposes a pluralistic definition of development as the expansion of "capabilities," although rejected calls for him to detail specifically which capabilities are required. Development refers to enhancing people's opportunities to act: "having the freedom to choose one kind of life rather than another" (Sen 2004, p. 12). The United Nations Development Programme's Human Development Index (HDI) is based on the measurement of a few core "capabilities" related to health, education, and income. Another approach, taken by the Institute of Development Studies (IDS), has been to outline a set of contemporary global challenges to be addressed in order to overcome poverty and injustice (IDS 2015). These are to reduce inequalities, accelerate sustainability, and build more inclusive and secure societies. These, too, are relatively abstract and multidimensional, although more normative, in defining desired end goals and directions of travel.

Our understanding of development effectiveness aligns with such broader visions of development, not least to reflect and support the process of global goal definition and targeting led by the United Nations. The most recent iteration, the SDGs (see Table 3.2), set out 17 multidimensional goals (composed

Table 3.2 The 17 sustainable development goals

Goal	Short description
1: No Poverty	End poverty in all its forms everywhere
2: Zero Hunger	End hunger, achieve food security and improved nutrition, and promote sustainable agriculture
3: Good Health and Well-being	Ensure healthy lives and promote well-being for all at all ages
4: Quality Education	Ensure inclusive and equitable quality education and promote lifelong learning opportunities for all
5: Gender Equality	Achieve gender equality and empower all women and girls
6: Clean Water and Sanitation	Ensure availability and sustainable management of water and sanitation for all
7: Affordable and Clean Energy	Ensure access to affordable, reliable, sustainable, and modern energy for all
8: Decent Work and Economic Growth	Promote sustained, inclusive, and sustainable economic growth; full and productive employment; and decent work for all
9: Industry, Innovation, and Infrastructure	Build resilient infrastructure, promote inclusive and sustainable industrialization, and foster innovation
10: Reduced Inequality	Reduce inequality within and among countries
11: Sustainable Cities and Communities	Make cities and human settlements inclusive, safe, resilient, and sustainable
12: Responsible Consumption and Production	Ensure sustainable consumption and production patterns
13: Climate Action	Take urgent action to combat climate change and its impacts
14: Life Below Water	Conserve and sustainably use the oceans, seas, and marine resources for sustainable development
15: Life on Land	Protect, restore, and promote sustainable use of terrestrial ecosystems; sustainably manage forests; combat desertification; and halt and reverse land degradation and halt biodiversity loss
16: Peace and Justice Strong Institutions	Promote peaceful and inclusive societies for sustainable development; provide access to justice for all; and build effective, accountable, and inclusive institutions at all levels
17: Partnerships to Achieve the Goal	Strengthen the means of implementation and revitalize the global partnership for sustainable development

Source: Own work, based on *https://sustainabledevelopment.un.org/sdgs*

of 169 targets). SDG 2 on "Zero Hunger," for instance, commits the world to "end hunger, achieve food security and improved nutrition and promote sustainable agriculture," while pointing to enhanced agricultural productivity, farmers' access to land and other inputs, market access, building sustainable production systems, and maintaining genetic seed diversity as ways to achieve zero hunger. Only one of the goals (Goal 8) makes any direct reference to economic growth, and few others directly imply economic growth (Goals 1, 9, and 10). Although many of the goals may be positively related to economic growth, others may also be unconnected to growth, or in some cases, growth could even be inimical to their pursuit (for instance, Goals 13–15). As with the Millennium Development Goals previously, the last goal is a process goal focused on implementation. Cutting across all of the SDGs is the pledge that "no one will be left behind."[3]

The multidimensional and global nature of the SDGs means that achieving these goals is a complex problem shared by states and businesses, or at least affected by their actions and interactions, which consequently requires negotiation of strategies and priorities. Development effectiveness will therefore depend on patterns of behavior which emerge through the relationships between actors and evolve over time.

State–business relations in development: the focus on growth

In this next section, we review how scholarship has previously conceived of how state–business relations shape developmental outcomes. This draws upon a literature that spans (heterodox) economics, political science, international political economy, sociology, business studies, and development studies. The appropriate roles of state and market, and how (if at all) states should intervene in markets and the affairs of business, are central development debates, harking back to classical political economy. Given that an improved research agenda for state–business relations in development will build on such past findings and debates, we start our review with a brief introduction to the developmental state as the concept which most strongly has foregrounded state–business relations in development. We then review key literatures that have applied and adapted the concept to analyze the effects of state–business relations on growth.

States, markets, and the "developmental state"

One of the fundamental development debates is about the appropriate division of labor between states and markets in driving economic development. However, this classical debate, which counter-posed state-led and market-led approaches, was turned on its head by the real-world examples of countries such as Japan, South Korea, and Taiwan and their failure to conform to the expectations of either statists or (neo-)liberal economists.

The experience of these countries underpins the thesis of the developmental state and its role in successful economic development (Woo-Cummings 1999). The central proposition is that in late-industrializing states, free markets are insufficient to create development, and the state plays a central role in driving industrialization (Johnson 1982). State managers, working within a powerful and talented bureaucracy, are uniquely able to take a longer-term view in planning the economy. These managers act independently of the short-term interests of different sectors of society (e.g., business or labor), strategically formulating industrial policy and supporting new industries through subsidies and protections that temporarily insulate them from market competition as they strive towards international competitiveness.

The East Asian developmental states challenge the accepted wisdom that state support which insulates private actors from competition necessarily leads to rent-seeking, undermining incentives for businesses to invest productively and to innovate in pursuit of profitable returns (Krueger 1974). Rent-seeking companies derive profits from their relationship with the government, expending otherwise productive resources in pursuit of these rents, and reducing the efficiency and aggregate income in the economy (Ellis 2010; Olson 1982). However in developmental states, rents are created in ways that support rather than undermine productive investment by offering temporary protection from competition while businesses build their capabilities. Linda Weiss (1995) described four manifestations of such state–business interaction in the East Asian experience: "disciplined support," where support for business comes attached to performance conditions; "public risk absorption," where the state lowers the risk of establishing new or emerging industries; "private-sector initiative in public policies," business shaping the state or colluding with it; and finally, "public-private innovation alliances" around acquiring, developing, upgrading, and diffusing technology (*ibid.*: 607–11). The early work on the developmental state theory was later complemented by efforts to isolate the factors which support "effective" state–business relations in countries beyond East Asia, particularly in sub-Saharan Africa and South Asia (discussed later).

Embedded autonomy

Peter Evans (1995), in his influential work on embedded autonomy, attempted to pinpoint structural characteristics of the developmental state. He identifies two key factors that together were crucial to the East Asian model: (1) bureaucrats being embedded in a web of ties with business and broader society, providing channels for continual interaction and negotiation, and (2) a bureaucracy that is simultaneously sufficiently autonomous to protect the state from capture by private interests. The emphasis is on a dense network of ties and mutual trust leading to rapid and effective policy implementation. Through this embedded autonomy, the state supports groups, notably business groups and capitalists who share its developmental vision, to overcome collective action problems.

Elements posited as having been vital to the emergence of a developmental state in several Asian countries (and later also in countries such as Botswana, Mauritius, Chile, and Costa Rica) include the state's ability and determination to work with the private sector in an often symbiotic relationship between (at least some) state agencies and key industries; a shared vision and elite consensus on the importance of building a national state and economy, which may be spurred on by disruptions in the traditional order; legitimacy derived from leadership oriented towards development; and state power to co-ordinate the private sector with the aim of achieving growth (Ansu et al. 2016; Castells 1992; Leftwich 2000; Routley 2012).

Another branch of scholarship has been predominately concerned not with the emergence of collaboration, but with the inherent risk that the embeddedness of the state with industrial capital will lead to collusion rather than supporting development. This work proposes a more specific set of factors that encourage what have been termed "developmental coalitions," rather than collusive "distributional coalitions" (Olson 1982; Sen 2015). These include the participation of multisectoral firms or business associations (rather than firms with narrow, specific interests, such as extractive industries); economies where leading productive sectors have low barriers to entry, are labor-intensive, and are vulnerable to market fluctuations; the autonomy of state managers from politically motivated pressures to distribute resources; and state–business networks based on formal structures that are open, transparent, and competitive (Brautigam, Rakner and Taylor 2002; Haggard, Maxfield and Schneider 1997; Schneider and Maxfield 1997). The countervailing organization of other social groups, such as labor or environmental groups, and their having access to policy processes and resources may also inhibit collusion and rent-seeking (Schneider and Maxfield 1997).

21st-century developmental state

Yet the conditions for economic development today are different from those facing the early developmental states. Globalization has led to a fragmentation of production alongside deeper political-economic interconnections across economies. Even more significant, perhaps, is the decline in industries that were so integral to the story of East Asian development. In the 21st century, developing countries are exhausting industrialization opportunities sooner and at lower levels of income than early industrializers (Rodrik 2016), and manufacturing employs a declining percentage of the population. The service sector has become more important, although it is bifurcated between highly rewarded business and financial services and poorly rewarded personal service sectors. In his updated work on the "21st-century developmental state," Evans (2008, p. 6) finds that this decline of industry poses new challenges:

> viewing shifts in the historical character of economic growth through the lens of modern development theory suggests that state capacity will

have an even greater role to play in societal success in the coming century than it did in the last century. But, it also suggests that the specific kind of "embeddedness" or "state-society synergy" that was crucial to 20th century success – dense networks of ties connecting the state to industrial elites – will have to be replaced by much broader, much more "bottom up" set of state society ties to secure developmental success in the current century.

The 21st-century developmental state must manage economies that generate intangible assets (ideas, skills, and networks) rather than physical assets like machinery, and hence must be capability-enhancing (Evans 2010, p. 38), because growth is no longer the driver of human development, but rather human development is what drives growth. In some cases, dense business–state networks will pose an impediment to 21st-century developmental states, because social returns from state action to enhance human capabilities are greater than private returns, leaving public and private interests misaligned[4] (Evans 2008).

Growth acceleration vs. growth maintenance

While still primarily concerned with growth, a group of researchers has moved the analytical lens from relationships that can kickstart growth (growth acceleration) to the institutions and relations that can maintain it. To describe how these models work in practice, Pritchett and Werker (2012) and ESID (2014) use the term "deals." Deals are negotiated and agreed actions, which may, however, only be selectively enforced. Moving from growth acceleration to growth maintenance requires a move from one type of deal to another (rather than from deals to "rules," as promoted through "good governance" agendas). Whereas growth *acceleration* is supported by a movement from disordered to ordered deals through the type of repeated personalized interactions familiar from the developmental state, ESID (2014) argue that growth *maintenance* requires a shift from closed to open deals (Table 3.3). Open deals are ones that are widely available to all investors, bringing diversity, competition, and innovation.

Studies using the deals framework have found that the main challenges to long-term growth maintenance are institutional rigidity and path dependency, which hinder a movement from one type of deal to another. In Ghana, for example, the deals space that emerged from the country's political settlement supported growth, but not structural transformation. Changing this deals space in a way that promotes sustained growth has proven difficult (Osei et al. 2015). In Rwanda, Behuria and Goodfellow (2016) find the deals space failed to progress from closed and disordered to open and ordered deals; growth maintenance has been achieved, but through carefully protected closed deals in strategic nodes of certain sectors. Continued disorder in other sectors may threaten long-term growth. In India, economic growth was found to be episodic and prone to

Table 3.3 The "deals" space

		Closed deals	*Open deals*
Kickstarting growth	Disordered deals	Only those with political connections can make deals, and even they cannot be certain that officials will deliver.	Anyone can make a deal, but no one is certain that officials will deliver.
	Ordered deals	Only those with political connections can make deals, but they can be confident that officials will deliver.	Anyone can make a deal, and they can be certain that officials will deliver.
		Maintaining growth. ⟶	

Source: ESID 2014

collapse, because institutions failed to evolve, and some even deteriorated (Sen, Kar and Sahu 2014).

Institutions and "effective" state–business relations

In the last decade, one strand of research on the developmental state has empiri-cally explored state–business relations in developing countries beyond East Asia. Using primarily quantitative methods, it has focused on the institutions that support close state–business ties and their role in reducing policy uncertainty, supporting information exchange, establishing trust and credibility between public and private actors, raising investments, boosting productivity at the industry and firm levels, and ultimately bringing about economic growth and structural transformation (Calì, Mitra and Purohit 2011; Calì and Sen 2011; Te Velde and Alberto 2015; Qureshi and Te Velde 2013).

This body of work explores the formal institutional structure of state–business relations in relation to their effectiveness. Elements of the formal institutional structure are the level of private-sector organization *vis-à-vis* the public sector (e.g., through an umbrella business organization); public-sector organization to offer credible commitments to the private sector (e.g., an investment promo-tion agency); regular interactions (such as formal public–private dialogue) with information sharing, consultation, coordination, and reciprocity; and mecha-nisms to avoid harmful collusion (such as competition policy).

Testing these characteristics in 19 sub-Saharan African countries (Sen and Te Velde 2009) and across 15 states of India (Cali, Mitra and Purohit 2011; Cali and Sen 2011), researchers find that state–business relations significantly explain differences in economic growth.[5] Studies from Ghana, Mauritius, South Africa, and Zambia also find that formal consultative forums matter by enabling businesses to transparently influence government budget decisions (Te Velde and Leftwich 2010). Approaching these issues from the firm per-spective, Qureshi and Te Velde (2013) find that firm membership in a business association enhances productivity by 25 to 35 percent (*ibid*, p. 925) and that organized state–business relations improve a country's investment climate and labor productivity.

Informal institutions

However, other studies draw different and more nuanced conclusions. For example, using survey data from 171 local firms in Kenya, Tanzania, and Zambia, Charles et al. (2017) found that a significant number of firms did not participate in business associations or joined more than one, splitting and weakening their voices in engaging with governments. They highlight instead the ongoing importance of *informal* relations between states and businesses and emphasize the need to explore the linkages and dynamics between formal and informal channels further. Coming from a different angle, Schneider (2015), in his study of Brazil, highlights the central role that state-owned enterprises played in industrial transformation and technological improvement in sectors such as steel, automobiles, mining, ethanol, and aircraft manufacturing. These state-owned enterprises effectively internalized state–business reciprocity, bypassing the need for formal mediating institutions and resulting in investments in human capital development and the generation of jobs that made use of skilled workers.

In fact, much of what really lies behind "good" state–business relations may not be formal, observable, or straightforwardly measurable. Researchers from the Centre for the Future State[6] investigated these issues through case study analysis in Brazil, China, Egypt, Indonesia, and Vietnam. Abdel-Latif and Schmitz (2010), for example, found that informal relationships – social networks based on shared social roots and professional backgrounds – facilitated effective public–private interactions in raising investment and economic growth in Egypt, provided that interactions took place in settings that minimized opportunities for corruption and patronage and maximized inclusiveness, accompanied by strong monitoring agencies, including a free media. Moore and Schmitz (2008) reach similar conclusions from their study of China in the 1970s and 1980s, when "relationship-based" informal mechanisms were used to provide assurances to investors. On the other hand, barriers to effective state–business relations identified by researchers using the deals framework described earlier include the lack of a stable political settlement between business and political elites and a large part of the business elite situated in high rent and noncompetitive sectors, as well as significant fragility, conflict, and corruption.

Although these studies are generally sensitive to the risks of collusion and crony-capitalism, they emphasize the importance of understanding how state–business relations work *in practice* (rather than emphasizing interactions that are formally enshrined in policy), including through channels that may not necessarily be visible. They suggest that regulatory reforms that place too much stress on formal arm's-length relationships between business and the state in weak governance environments may even undermine more effective informal interactions. Thus, in assessing state–business relations, the emphasis must be on the *function* and *practice* of state–business relations rather than on particular institutional *forms* (ESID 2014; Sen 2015); formal structure is often even "myth and ceremony," as governments and business groups emulate others in creating particular formal institutional arrangements that have little bearing on practice (Meyer and Rowan 1977).

Toward a more complete research agenda

Although the literature discussed earlier clarifies that good relations between state and business matter for economic growth and industrial development, it raises many new questions, including: What is the role and sequencing of formal versus informal state–business relations? What kind of processes lead to outcomes that benefit not just states and businesses or state and business elites but also generate wider benefits to society? And if we agree that function matters more than the form of state–business relations, what exactly are these functions and how might we recognize them analytically?

Moreover, if we return to our initial concern with state–business relations and the developmental aspirations enshrined in the SDGs, the review of the literature provides relatively few clues of how state–business relations could support their attainment. Issues of citizen well-being, social advancement, civil and political rights, and environmental sustainability have not been central to the developmental state analysis, which is concerned with gross economic performance first. The story of developmental states and "effective" state–business relations is primarily a story of GDP growth and specific processes leading to it, such as investment in technological improvement, human capital development, firm productivity, industrial transformation, and export expansion (Bräutigam, Rakner and Taylor 2002; Schneider and Maxfield 1997; Evans 2008). Other goals have sometimes been described as intentions or outcomes of developmental states, such as generating jobs and increasing incomes, and more broadly contributing towards poverty reduction, taxation, improved transparency, and accountability (Sen 2015). East Asian developmental states did improve the material well-being of citizens, and their governments derived legitimacy from doing so (Routley 2012). However, these achievements often came as by-products or delayed benefits from growth, and other empirical evidence points to some developmental states achieving economic growth yet failing to deliver broader social advancement. Brazil in the 1980s and 1990s, for example, achieved industrial transformation in some key sectors but failed to promote overall social welfare and regional equality (Schneider 2015). Botswana's economic growth ran far in advance of its achievements in terms of the HDI (Meyns and Musumba 2010: 42–56). The early developmental states of East Asia are also associated with authoritarian regimes or illiberal democracies, meaning that growth was achieved at the expense of civil and political rights and the prioritization of business interests over those of the citizenry. Their environmental record, at least during their strongest "developmental" phase, was very poor. All this has evident implications for their relevance as models for other developing countries.

Key questions that arise therefore include: What types of businesses and state–business relationships support progress toward the broader developmental objectives set out in the SDGs? What kind of "deals" or negotiations may be able to achieve broader developmental objectives, even without growth? Is there potential for alignment between "effective" state–business relations for growth with ones that are effective for other developmental outcomes? And even, perhaps, what kind of state–business relations would help manage potential contradictions between developmental goals, such as growth versus environment-related goals? A more complete research agenda on state–business relations is needed, focusing on broader development outcomes beyond growth. We propose to begin with the idea of negotiation as a key form of interaction.

A framework of negotiation

As we noted at the outset, "state–business relations" are interactions of political and economic authorities over time, through which they influence and constrain each other, a process which Lindblom (1977, p. 175) described as "mutual adjustment amongst authorities." The literatures employing the concepts of embedded autonomy, "effective" relations that facilitate coordination and "deals" as deliberated and agreed-upon rules or compromises, all point to the importance of forms of engagement that allow states and businesses to articulate and reconcile competing, but not necessarily incompatible, interests through negotiation. In order to clarify our concept of negotiation (and set out what it is not), in Figure 3.1 we identify a number of different types of possible interactions in the policy space, which differ depending upon how

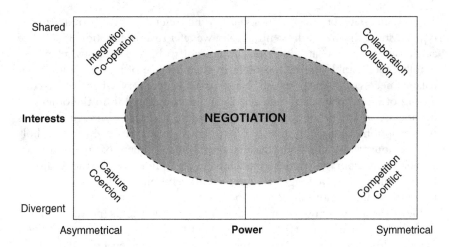

Figure 3.1 The realm of negotiation

Source: Ayele et al. (2016)

equally matched business and state actors are (symmetrical or asymmetrical interaction, horizontal axis) and how shared or divergent their interests are (vertical axis).

In the extreme corners of this stylized policy space, we find co-optation, capture, collaboration, and competition. In the top–right corner, state and business actors who have relatively equal power and share interests are most likely to engage in very close cooperation and partnerships for practical solution-seeking (collaboration); less desirably, they may also cooperate at the expense of wider societal interests (collusion) (Sen 2015). Both are manifestations of exerting "power with." Collusion between state and business is likely to arise when elites calculate their interests to be best served by rent-seeking or exchange of favors (e.g., state protection, subsidies, bribes) in order to redistribute wealth to themselves (Olson 1982; Sen 2015). In the opposite corner, where power is highly asymmetrical, unequal state and business agents interact (Manor 1991). Very powerful businesses may capture[7] the state, shaping policies and regulations to their own benefit, or predatory states may capture and subjugate businesses. These outcomes are both manifestations of "power over." In the bottom–right corner, actors with quite equal power but divergent interests are liable to be in competition or conflict. In such a "state versus markets" scenario, irreconcilable goals lock them into entrenched struggles for supremacy; likely both are weakened as a result. At the top left, finally, under conditions of unequal power but compatible interests, integration and co-optation are likely; the weaker actor is incorporated into (or led by) the other. In such scenarios, the state may effectively lead business and integrate it into its agendas, as with "state capitalism" or state-owned enterprises. Vice versa, a dominant business elite might effectively co-opt and integrate a pliant and weak state or subvert particular agencies of the state, as many argue has been the case with financial regulation in recent decades (Storm 2018).

But many state–business relations also do not resemble these extreme archetypes. Instead, they lie in the central realm we refer to as negotiation. Here, state and business interests are different enough not to be coterminous, albeit not wholly incompatible either, and there is some balance of power, without this balance necessarily being "equal." Negotiation is necessary when, under conditions of interdependency, each actor requires something from the other and cannot use power or authority alone to achieve its goals. Although instances of corruption, capture, or conflict often garner greater attention from scholars and journalists, and policymakers and business leaders often rhetorically emphasize collaboration and "partnership," many (if not most) of the meaningful and policy-effective long-term interactions between state and business work through the interactions of negotiation.

Negotiation also draws attention to not only the structures (power, interests) that produce a particular type of engagement but also the process of engagement itself. Actors' orientations – their interests – are often fluid and can be shaped and reshaped by the interaction and exchange of ideas. As ideas are exchanged over time, new interpretations are found and common interests may be established, leading to new "deals" and emergent institutions. Negotiated state–business relations allow common understandings of interests, problems, and potential solutions to be found, and sometimes even "win–win" outcomes to be pursued through discovering the other's preferences, building trust, and identifying mutually acceptable solutions (Lewicki et al. 2010, pp. 125–143). There are, of course, well-known perils along the way: the good faith of one actor may be taken advantage of, negotiators may lose accountability to their constituency (as with "cognitive capture" of regulators), or negotiation may be increasingly pursued for its own sake (Lewicki et al. 2010, p. 37).

These forms of (inter-)action reflect understandings of agency developed in social theory by the pragmatist tradition (e.g., Mead 2015) and in sociology and political science by proponents of institutional theory, particularly "actor-centred institutionalism" (Mayntz and Scharpf 1995). Moreover, they follow themes developed in some of the literature reviewed earlier. Evans (1995, p. 12), for instance, argued that developmental states lead through "the continual negotiation and renegotiation of goals and policies." Haggard, Maxfield and Schneider (1997, p. 83) argued against painting state–business relations in terms of an autonomous state and a relatively passive private sector, instead portraying them as negotiations through which governments seek political support, investment, and information, and businesses seek predictable and stable environments and relevant incentives.

Key themes in a broadened research agenda

Processes of negotiation. The recognition of informal institutions, and the idea that formal institutions emerge gradually, points to the importance of process-oriented analyses of negotiation and the concepts of "networked negotiation" and "policy-directed concession-exchange" (Ayele et al. 2016). Institutions that may appear as structural factors at a later point of development grew gradually in strength and accreted over time (Djelic and Quack 2003). In line with the deals framework earlier, which evaluates state–business relations as shifting political arrangements for reaching compromises on policy, a focus on processes that lead to more formalized rules or that renegotiate established rules means tracing the concrete interactions and steps through which arrangements are found, solidified, and rearranged. Three insights can guide this research.

First, insights can be generated through focusing on understanding how formal and informal networks shape ongoing policy dialogue through *networked negotiations*. This follows from Haggard, Maxfield and Schneider's (1997) category of "business and government as a network" and suggests studying how, through repeat interactions, interlinked representatives of business coordinate with state actors. For instance, they may share information and technical expertise or engage in collective learning and consensus building about policy preferences and work towards more collaborative arrangements, which can become institutionalized over time. This process would, in the framework in Figure 3.1, be the use of negotiation to move gradually towards the top-right corner and stronger collaboration (or, if the networks are closed and unaccountable, collusion).

The importance of networked policy dialogue and agenda-setting suggests paying closer attention particularly to "who knows whom" and where and how they interact. But the notion of networked interaction should also not distract from issues of relative power. In some cases, information flow and collaboration could also be part of competition for dominance in patterns of "networked hierarchy" (integration and co-optation in the top-left corner of Figure 3.1), where success in business is a key to rewards in the political realm, and vice versa (Lin and Milhaupt 2013).

Second, studies of process should explicitly focus on how resources are exchanged in negotiation. The notion of *policy-directed concession exchange* takes the prerogative of states at initiating negotiation as given, particularly in the case of countries with a stronger "developmental" agenda, but highlights how often a quid pro quo exchange with business is necessary for states to effectively pursue their policy priorities. Although activist states may possess the initiative, they nonetheless need to ensure the cooperation of business in order to gain the resources with which to pursue their agenda. They often do so through negotiations that emphasize the exchange of concessions and resources in stages (cf. Alfredson and Cungu 2008). For instance, in an effort to create jobs, governments may offer businesses preferential access to resources like land in exchange for businesses' efforts to improve product quality and export competitiveness. Either side may offer more at a later stage, once the benefits of the arrangement are clear. Over time, the negotiating actors may realize that the size of the "pie" being negotiated is not fixed and rigid modalities are no longer necessary, leading to greater trust and larger win-win outcomes, and perhaps the type of "embedded autonomous" scenario emphasized by the developmental states literature.

Third, whereas structural analyses are likely to focus on power, institutions, and interests, a process analysis can focus on how *ideas and ideologies* shape negotiation over time. Reflecting how discursive power shapes the framing of problems and potential solutions, process-oriented research can illuminate how the negotiation process draws upon the beliefs and convictions of the negotiating agents. For instance, shared ideologies about what constitutes modernity and progress, such as pursuing inclusion or emulating successful developmental states, can profoundly shape state–business relations. Of particular interest are the ways in which narratives, storylines, images, and symbols bestow legitimacy to actors and to the outcomes of negotiation and how new ideas and shared understandings of problems and solutions can evolve through the negotiation process itself.[8] Although ideas and ideologies alone cannot explain or create functional state–business relations, we would suggest they have very powerful effects in being able to move relations along the vertical axis in the matrix in Figure 3.1 and thus are a key variable.

Structures of negotiation. Negotiation processes do not start from a blank slate, however. Research is also needed on (1) the structural factors that initially condition negotiation and the emergence of formal and informal institutions that make functional networks, concession-exchange, and shared beliefs possible, or hinder them; and (2) the structures that subsequently make negotiation effective or ineffective, in terms of the pursuit of particular development outcomes. The lens of negotiation suggests focusing on the structural interdependence between business and state actors as a catalyst for seeking solutions and identifying how power and resources that may be exchanged (financial resources, productive factors, information, skills, expertise, support, etc.) are initially distributed.

One obvious area to consider are the *institutions* of the nation-state and of business organization. Structural institutional conditions that were highlighted earlier as conducive to noncollusive, relatively open state–business relations include the existence of formal mechanisms to ensure transparency, well-organized negotiating groups (e.g., associations), strong constituencies that hold their negotiators accountable, and the presence of a "Weberian" bureaucracy insulated from particular interests. Yet defining noncollusive relations based on these factors also sets an unrealistically high bar that many developing countries may not meet. To quote Rodrik (2013, p. 31), such prescriptions would essentially suggest, "if you want to become rich, you need to look like rich countries"; or more broadly that, to develop, a country would need to already have the institutional structures of a developed country. Rodrik instead advocates exploring heterodox "second-best" (or nonoptimal) strategies, which may be found through negotiation processes that build from nonoptimal institutional starting points.

Given how much formal-legal institutions often diverge from what actually happens, a challenge for structural analyses is to better evaluate and understand how institutions work in practice, including *informal institutions*. Informal networks can be powerful, if often invisible, structural constraints or enablers of negotiation. Earlier studies of state–business relations acknowledged the importance of informal institutions (Abdel-Latif and Schmitz 2010; Moore and Schmitz 2008), which include not only extra-formal networks but also actors' shared cultural-cognitive and normative frames. Despite acknowledging the relevance of these informal institutions, methodological challenges mean that quantitative studies have tended to focus only on formal and visible institutions. Moreover, often, informal institutions have been explained away as a mere stepping-stone on the way to more formal structures. Particularly in places with weaker formal institutions, we would suggest instead that case-study designs that illuminate how informal institutions work in and across contexts, and how they emerge and persist, and why, may expose possible pathways and roadblocks to "second-best" strategies. But informal institutions are not just starting points for formalization. Of particular interest is the interplay between formal and informal institutions, which may have different short-term and long-term effects (Unsworth 2010), and the importance of informal relationships of trust, loyalty, and friendship, which can emerge over time through formal interactions, further strengthening formal institutions.

Broadening the actor cast. It may appear obvious that successful outcomes of state–business relations require engaging the right actors for given policy objectives. But the implications for practice and research are far-reaching and not always initially clear. Who must be included, and who can realistically be included? For example, negotiations of a government ministry with a small number of large companies within a concentrated sector can be far less costly and complex compared to attempting to engage a very diffuse set of micro- and small-scale enterprises. Yet under particular circumstances, such as address-ing issues related to the informal sector, finding ways of working with these actors – who lack formal organization or representation – may be essential to effectively addressing the challenge at hand.

Although much of the existing literature emphasizes business associations as key contributors to effective state–business relations, the question for policy-makers is whether the formally organized sector is always the best (or the only necessary) negotiating partner. Moreover, formal associations can also be rent-seeking, and doubts have arisen as to whether their role is overstated. Under certain conditions, actors outside of the state or business realm, such as labor unions, nongovernmental organizations (NGOs), interest groups or civil soci-ety organizations, can also hold the key to negotiating progress on particular development outcomes, possibly as interlocutors or important constituencies. This does not necessarily mean always speaking of "state–business–society rela-tions," but the challenge for researchers is to understand where, when, and how actor groups beyond organized formal state and business representations facili-tate state–business relations that can effectively pursue development outcomes.

A second issue to consider is the role of international actors and multilevel governance networks (Smith 2004). Existing research on state–business rela-tions has mostly taken a national-level approach for granted, at the expense of reflecting how many policy fields and communities are increasingly transna-tionally constituted (Djelic and Quack 2010), as well as the extent to which foreign actors (such as international donor agencies or investor groups) shape domestic policies, particularly in low-income countries. In some countries, for instance, large parts of government spending are financed by international donor funds, making these donors participants in state–business relations. On the private-sector side, in some countries such as Ethiopia or the Philippines, large diasporas and remittance-sender communities play a crucial role in driv-ing domestic investments. Understanding state–business relations thus means evaluating the role of international actors such as donors, diasporas, interna-tional advisors, and NGOs more clearly and moving beyond "methodological nationalism" (Gore 1996).

Methodological pluralism. It is evident from the preceding agenda that the research needed will have to be multidisciplinary and involve mixed methods. It would ideally include quantitative surveys on state–business relations and different SDG targets, or on state–business relations and inclusion or exclu-sion of other actors from policy processes, learning from earlier variable-based research on effective state–business relations. This work would be able to draw on data being collected as part of the SDG global indicator framework, along-side other datasets (e.g., governance, economic). From this, new hypotheses can be distilled and relevant or interesting cases for in-depth investigation can be identified: high-achieving countries in which the processes behind particular achievements can be traced or countries that underperform or overperform on the SDG targets compared to their peers at a particular level of development or in a particular governance context. Intracountry comparisons between sectors are another promising route, because they hold many other contextual factors constant.

Detailed qualitative case studies would involve a mapping and analysis of actors and their interactions, employing, for example, network mapping and political economy analysis to offer insights into factors that contributed to more or less effective relationships and stronger or weaker development out-comes. In this work it will be important to deepen an understanding of the nature of the private sector and of state–business relations in the country and sector(s) in question. What is the nature of the domestic private sector, situat-ing actors (firms, associations) within the economic and political structure of the sector? Who knows whom within business and the state, and what is the nature of the spaces through which policies, discourses, decisions, and relation-ships are shaped? This analysis requires understanding not only the structure and processes of state–business interactions but also the inclusion or exclusion of other societal actors (labor, civil society), as well accounting for the interna-tional dimension.

As far as possible, this analysis should include informal as well as formal rela-tions. Although good information may be hard to obtain from existing data, ignoring the existence and importance of informal interactions or automati-cally condemning all informal relationships as collusion risks ignoring much of what may lie behind the outcomes observed. The approach poses methodologi-cal challenges which may be overcome by drawing on methods less familiar to the study of state–business relations, such as ethnographic approaches or dis-course analysis, to understand the motivations or social networks of key actors.

Conclusions

We began this chapter by arguing that the sustainable development era requires a broadened research agenda on state–business relations. After clarifying dif-ferent meanings of state and business, the notion of power, and discussing the broadening of the development agenda and the SDGs, we reviewed different strands of existing scholarship on state–business relations in development. Here we saw the emergence of the idea of the "developmental state" and patterns of "embedded autonomy" and more recent empirical literatures on what may con-stitute "effective" state–business relations and growth-oriented political "deals," as well as the importance of formal and informal institutions. This scholarship has focused almost exclusively on the economic dimensions of development and the state and business as protagonists, paying comparatively little attention to other dimensions and other actors. In outlining a more complete research agenda, we highlighted the role of networks, resource exchange, and ideas and ideologies in negotiation; the importance of research into informal as well as formal institutional structures; and the roles of other actors, including international ones. We finally sketched how a methodologically pluralistic agenda could practically explore how state–business relations shape development.

Research on state–business relations as part of business and development studies needs to go beyond a focus on growth alone and encompass the state–business–society politics of positive social and economic transformations (cf. Scoones, Leach and Newell 2015). The literature on effective state–business relations, as we saw clearly, points to the importance of particular types of engagement for economic growth and structural change and proposes – although it does not necessarily reach a consensus on – key ingredients of "effective" collaboration. The question of how state–business relations could contribute to, or conversely may undermine, other aspects of development remains unresolved.

The most evident starting point here are the SDGs, as the present policy embodiment of a more holistic development agenda (see Table 3.2). It is clear that the achievement of the SDGs will depend in part on the ways in which states and businesses engage with one another. Enshrined in SDG 17 is the call for a "global partnership" involving public–private and multistakeholder partnerships in pursuit of the goals. The question is: What structures and processes contribute to state–business relations that promote such a partnership? How are these structures and processes different in different contexts? Which actors must be involved for success?

Our proposition for research on state–business relations is therefore simple but compelling: to take seriously the SDGs with a research agenda that empirically and conceptually foregrounds the interactions of states and businesses over specific parts of the SDGs. This research should also focus more sharply on illuminating how and why state–business relations that aim for growth may fail to produce economic and social development in the broader sense, or even at times hinder it. Research on state–business relations can illuminate more clearly the trade-offs, contradictions, and complexities involved in pursuing different development goals and how these are negotiated. To clarify this with two examples: research focused on SDG 2 (hunger and nutrition) would explore how structures and processes of negotiation have led to different levels of attainment in terms of ending hunger, achieving food security, and improving nutrition in different political and economic conditions. Research focused on SDG 8 (inclusive and sustainable growth) would explore how negotiations lead to inclusivity or job quality in particular (e.g., labor-intensive) sectors. An analysis of state–business relations with respect to these goals would thus illuminate how, by whom, and under what conditions more or less effective strategies for the pursuit of these goals can be negotiated – not as by-products of economic growth, but rather as goals that are analytically separate from growth, and may even be at odds with it. The same, we envision, would apply to an analysis of the other 14 substantive SDGs.

The challenge of developing adequate frameworks for understanding evolving (and often informal) state–business relations in complex development processes remains large. If the body of work on effective state–business relations in support of economic growth has not produced clear consensus on what is needed to make these relationships effective, the challenge in the case of SDGs is multiplied. Although detailed case work will not provide policy blueprints that can be replicated, it will stimulate new ways of thinking that are relevant to other contexts. Given the renewed calls for states and businesses to work together to achieve the global goals, this deserves a central place on the business and development studies research agenda.

Notes

1 Acknowledgement: This chapter draws upon research conducted as part of a project on 'State-business relations beyond growth' by Seife Ayele, Phil Mader, Jodie Thorpe, Jing Gu, Mar Maestre Morales, and Philip Reed, funded by UK aid from the UK government. The views expressed do not necessarily reflect the UK government's official policies. We also thank Martin Gardner for his assistance. Any errors or omissions in the final work are entirely the authors' own.
2 www.un.org/sustainabledevelopment/development-agenda/
3 United Nations, Transforming our world: the 2030 Agenda for Sustainable Development https://sustainabledevelopment.un.org/post2015/transformingourworld (last accessed 15 July 2017)
4 Evans gives the example of early childhood education as a case where markets would lead to underinvestment because they channel investment to areas where total returns are lower but private returns appear higher, particularly in the short term.
5 Calì and Sen (2011, p. 1543) add that this explanatory power is greater than any other conventional growth determinant (such as geography or access to the sea).
6 www2.ids.ac.uk/futurestate/ (accessed 15 September 2016)
7 Unlike corruption, which involves entities (often companies) paying bribes to officials to influence how existing laws are *implemented* with respect to the bribe payer, capture results from structural power influencing how laws are *formed* (Hellman and Kaufmann 2001).
8 This premise stands in contrast to a rational choice approach that would assume fixed and known preferences.

References

Abdel-Latif, A. and Schmitz, H. (2010), "State-Business Relations and Investment in Egypt," in *Effective State-Business Relations, Industrial Policy and Economic Growth*, Dirk Willem te Velde, Massimiliano Cali and Karen Ellis, eds. London: Overseas Development Institute, 23–24.

Alfredson, Tanya and Cungu, Azeta (2008), *Negotiation Theory and Practice: A Review of the Literature*, Rome: Food and Agricultural Organization of the United Nations.

Ansu, Yaw, David Booth, Tim Kelsall and Dirk Willem te Velde (2016), *Public and Private Sector Collaboration for Economic Transformation*. Paper presented at the 2016 African Transformation Forum, Kigali.

Ayele, Seife, Philip Mader, Jodie Thorpe, Jing Gu, Mar Maestre Morales and Philip Reed (2016), "State – Business Relations Beyond Growth: Bringing in Development," *IDS Evidence Report* (Vol. 215). Brighton: Institute of Development Studies.

Behuria, Pritish and Tom Goodfellow (2016), "The Political Settlement and 'Deals Environment' in Rwanda: Unpacking Two Decades of Economic Growth", *ESID Working Paper* (Number 57). Manchester: University of Manchester: Effective States and Inclusive Development Research Centre.

Bräutigam, Deborah, Lise Rakner and Scott Taylor (2002), "Business Associations and Growth Coalitions in Sub-Saharan Africa," *Journal of Modern African Studies*, 40(4), 519–547.

Calì, Massimiliano, Siddhartha Mitra and Purnima Purohit (2011), "Measuring State-Business Relations Within Developing Countries: An Application to India States," *Journal of International Development*, 23, 394–419.

Calì, Massimiliano and Kunal Sen (2011), "Do Effective State Business Relations Matter for Economic Growth? Evidence from Indian States," *World Development*, 39(9), 542–1557.

Castells, M. (1992), "Four Asian Tigers with a Dragon Head: A Comparative Analysis of the State, Economy and Society in the Asian Pacific Rim," in *State and Development in the Asian Pacific Rim*, Richard P. Appelbaum and Jeffrey William Henderson, eds. London: Sage Publications, 33–70.

Charles, Goodluck, Søren Jeppesen, Paul Kamau and Peter Kragelund (2017), "Firm-Level Perspectives on State-Business Relations in Africa: The Food-Processing Sector in Kenya, Tanzania and Zambia," *Forum for Development Studies*, 44(1), 109–131.

Djelic, Marie-Laure and Sigrid Quack (2003), "Theoretical Building Blocks for a Research Agenda Linking Globalization and Institutions," in *Globalization and Institutions*, Marie-Laure Djelic and Sigrid Quack, eds. Cheltenham: Edward Elgar Publishing, 15–34.

Djelic, Marie-Laure and Sigrid Quack, eds. (2010), *Transnational Communities: Shaping Global Economic Governance*. Cambridge: Cambridge University Press.

Ellis, K. (2010), "How State-Business Relations Trumps Market Forces in Determining Commercial Success," in *Effective State-Business Relations, Industrial Policy and Economic Growth*, Dirk Willem te Velde, ed. London: Overseas Development Institute.

ESID (2014), *Researching the Political Economy Determinants of Economic Growth: A New Conceptual and Methodological Approach*. Manchester: University of Manchester: Effective States and Inclusive Development Research Centre.

Evans, Peter B. (1995), *Embedded Autonomy: States and Industrial Transformation*. Princeton, NJ: Princeton University Press.

Evans, Peter B. (2008), "In Search of the 21st Century Developmental State," *The Centre for Global Political Economy Working Paper* (Number 4). Brighton: The Centre for Global Political Economy.

Evans, Peter B. (2010), "Constructing the 21st Century Developmental State: Potentialities and Pitfalls," in *Constructing a Democratic Developmental State in South Africa: Potentials and Challenges*, O. Adigheji, ed. Cape Town: HSRC Press, 37–58.

Evans, Peter B., Dietrich Rueschemeyer and Theda Skocpol, eds. (1985), *Bringing the State Back In*. Cambridge: Cambridge University Press.

Fuchs, Doris and Markus M.L. Lederer (2007), "The Power of Business," *Business and Politics*, 9(3), 1–17.

Gaventa, John (2006), "Finding the Spaces for Change: A Power Analysis," *IDS Bulletin*, 37(6), 23–33.

Gore, Charles (1996), "Methodological Nationalism and the Misunderstanding of East Asian Industrialisation," *The European Journal of Development Research*, 8(1), 77–122.

Granovetter, Mark (1985), "Economic Action and Social Structure: The Problem of Embeddedness," *American Journal of Sociology*, 91(3), 481–510.

Haggard, Stephan, Sylvia Maxfield and Ben Ross Schneider (1997), "Theories of Business and Business-State Relations," in *Business and the State in Developing Countries*, Sylvia Maxfield and Ben Ross Schneider, eds. Ithaca: Cornell University Press, 36–60.

Hellman, Joel and Daniel Kaufmann (2001), "Confronting the Challenge of State Capture in Transition Economies," *Finance & Development*, 38(3), 31.

Humphrey, John, Stephen Spratt, Jodie Thorpe and Spencer Henson (2014), "Understanding and Enhancing the Role of Business in International Development: A Conceptual Framework and Agenda for Research," *IDS Working Paper* (Vol. 440). Brighton: Institute of Development Studies.

IDS (2015), *Engaged Excellence for Global Development: Strategy 2015–20*. Brighton: Institute of Development Studies.

Jessop, Bob (2001), "Bringing the State Back in (Yet Again): Reviews, Revisions, Rejections, and Redirections," *International Review of Sociology*, 11(2), 149–173.

Johnson, Chalmers (1982), *MITI and the Japanese Miracle: The Growth of Industrial Policy, 1925–1975*. Stanford: Stanford University Press.

Krueger, Anne O. (1974), "The Political Economy of the Rent-Seeking Society," *The American Economic Review*, 64(3), 291–303.

Leftwich, Adrian (2000), *States of Development: On the Primacy of Politics in Development*. Cambridge: Polity Press.

Lewicki, R., D. Saunders and B. Barry (2010), *Negotiation: Readings, Exercises and Cases*. New York: McGraw-Hill.

Lin, Li-Wen and Curtis J. Milhaupt (2013), "We Are the (National) Champions: Understanding the Mechanisms of State Capitalism in China," *Stanford Law Review*, 65, 697–759.

Lindblom, Charles E. (1977), *Politics and Markets: The World's Political Economic Systems*. New York: Basic Books.

Manor, James (1991), *Rethinking Third-World Politics*. New York: Routledge.

Mayntz, Renate and Fritz W. Scharpf (1995), "Der Ansatz des akteurzentrierten Institutionalismus," in *Gesellschaftliche Selbstregelung und Politische Steuerung*, R. Mayntz and F. Scharpf, eds. Frankfurt: Campus.

Mead, George Herbert (2015), *Mind, Self and Society*. Chicago: The University of Chicago Press.

Meyer, John W. and Brian Rowan (1977), "Institutionalized Organizations: Formal Structure as Myth and Ceremony," *American Journal of Sociology*, 83(2), 340–363.

Meyns, Peter and Charity Musumba (2010), "The Developmental State in Africa Problems and Prospects," *INEF-Report 101/2010*, University of Duisburg-Essen Institute for Development and Peace.

Moore, Mick (2005), "Methods of Analysing Power: Consultant's Report on Published Studies, Principally on Burkina Faso and Ethiopia," *Methods of Analysing Power – A Workshop Report*. Stockholm: SIDA.

Moore, Mick and Hubert Schmitz (2008), *Idealism, Realism and the Investment Climate in Developing Countries*. Brighton: Institute of Development Studies.

Olson, Mancur (1982), *The Rise and Decline of Nations: Economic Growth, Stagflation, and Social Rigidities*. New Haven and London: Yale University Press.

Osei, Robert Darko, Charles Ackah, George Domfe and Michael Danquah (2015), "Political Settlements, the Deals Environment and Economic Growth: The Case of Ghana," *ESID Working Paper No. 53*. Manchester: University of Manchester: Effective States and Inclusive Development Research Centre.

Pritchett, Lant and Eric Werker (2012), "Developing the Guts of GUT (Grand Unified Theory): Elite Commitment and Inclusive Growth," *ESID Working Paper No. 16*. Manchester: University of Manchester: Effective States and Inclusive Development Research Centre.

Qureshi, Mahvash Saeed and Dirk Willem Te Velde (2013), "State-Business Relations, Investment Climate Reform and Firm Productivity in Sub-Saharan Africa," *Journal of International Development* 25(7), 912–935.

Rodrik, Dani (2013), "The Past, Present, and Future of Economic Growth," *Global Citizen Foundation Working Paper* (Number 1). New Delhi: Global Citizen Foundation.

Rodrik, Dani (2016), "Premature Deindustrialization," *Journal of Economic Growth*, 21(1), 1–33.

Routley, Laura (2012), "Developmental States: A Review of the Literature," *ESID Working Paper* (Vol. 3). Manchester: University of Manchester: Effective States and Inclusive Development Research Centre.

Schneider, Ben Ross (2015), "The Developmental State in Brazil: Comparative and Historical Perspectives," *Brazilian Journal of Political Economy*, 35(1), 114–132.

Schneider, Ben Ross and Sylvia Maxfield (1997), "Business, the State, and Economic Performance in Developing Countries," in *Business and the State in Developing Countries*, Sylvia Maxfield and Ben Ross Schneider, eds. Ithaca: Cornell University Press.

Scoones, Ian, Melissa Leach and Peter Newell, eds. (2015), *The Politics of Green Transformations*. London: Routledge.

Sen, Amartya (2004), "Development as Capability Expansion," in *Readings in Human Development: Concepts, Measures and Policies for a Development Paradigm*, A.K.S. Kumar and S. Fukuda-Parr, eds. New Delhi and New York: Oxford University Press, 3–16.

Sen, Kunal (2015), *State-Business Relations: Topic Guide*. Birmingham: GSDRC.

Sen, Kunal, Sabyasachi Kar and Jagadish Sahu (2014), "The Political Economy of Economic Growth in India 1993–2013," *ESID Working Paper* (Number 44). Manchester: University of Manchester: Effective States and Inclusive Development Research Centre.

Sen, Kunal and Dirk Willem Te Velde (2009), "State Business Relations and Economic Growth in Sub-Saharan Africa," *Journal of Development Studies*, 45(8), 1267–1283.

Smith, Michael (2004), "Toward a Theory of EU Foreign Policy-Making: Multi-Level Governance, Domestic Politics, and National Adaptation to Europe's Common Foreign and Security Policy," *Journal of European Public Policy*, 11(4), 740–758.

Storm, Servaas (2018), "Financialization and Economic Development: A Debate on the Social Efficiency of Modern Finance," *Development and Change*, 49(2), 302–329.

Te Velde, Dirk Willem and Lemma Alberto (2015), "State-Business Relations as Drivers of Economic Performance," *WIDER Working Paper 2015/098*. Helsinki: KOICA/ UNU-Wider.

Te Velde, Dirk William and Adrian Leftwich (2010), *State-Business Relations and Economic Growth in Sub-Saharan Africa: A Review of Case Studies in Ghana, Mauritius, South Africa and Zambia*. Manchester: Research Programme Consortium on Improving Institutions for Pro-Poor Growth (IPPG).

Unsworth, Sue (2010), *An Upside-down View of Governance*. Brighton: Institute of Development Studies.

Weber, Max (1978), *Economy and Society: An Outline of Interpretive Sociology* (Vol. 1). Berkeley, CA: University of California Press.

Weiss, Linda (1995), "Governed Interdependence: Rethinking the Government-Business Relationship in East Asia," *The Pacific Review*, 8(4), 589–616.

Woo-Cumings, Meredith, ed. (1999), *The Developmental State*. New York: Cornell University Press.

4 International business and economic development

Michael Wendelboe Hansen

Introduction

Multinational corporation (MNC) activity potentially has enormous implications for development (Bhagwati, 2012; Cypher and Dietz, 2004). MNCs invest massively across borders to integrate economic activity. MNCs possess advanced technology and knowledge that are key to industrial and economic development. They provide market access and organize exports. They engage in country arbitrage and force countries into races to attract investments. They sell goods and services that are essential to human development. Their organizational and managerial practices may have immense implications for industry structure and competition in host countries. They exert influence on policy and politics and play key roles in shaping global technical, management, social, and environmental standards. All these consequences derive from the multinational nature of MNCs: the fact that they organize value-adding activities across borders. In recent decades, the context of international business activity has changed profoundly, making MNCs' development role even more critical: (1) MNCs are increasingly present in developing countries; (2) MNCs are increasingly coming from developing countries; (3) Countries around the world increasingly look to MNCs for solutions to the grand challenges related to sustainable and economic development; and (4) MNCs increasingly seek to transform their intended or unintended impacts on host countries into sustainable competitive advantage.

Hence, it would seem obvious and unavoidable that the study of MNCs *par excellence*, international business (IB), would relate intensely to the role of MNCs in development. However, this is not the case. Instead, whereas early IB research was strongly engaged in the developmental and societal role of IB, the IB research agenda has since then gradually moved toward more narrow questions related to MNC strategy, organization, and management and has effectively made itself superfluous to practical development policy. This chapter will describe how IB lost sight of the development dimension and discuss how the study of MNCs' development role can be reintroduced into IB so that IB can contribute to addressing the grand development questions of our time.

The IB literature and developing countries

The early IB literature

The IB field took shape during the 1960s and 1970s and was essentially a spin-off from economics, especially the subfields of international trade economics and industrial organization (IO): international trade economics had long studied international flows of goods and capital but lacked a clear concept of the role of firms (i.e., MNCs) in shaping international capital and trade flows. As a consequence, international trade economics had difficulties explaining the then emerging phenomenon of foreign direct investment (FDI) (i.e., cross-border capital flows aimed at gaining management control of foreign activities). Inspired by IO (Bain, 1956), the Canadian economist Stephen Hymer (1960/76) and American economist Raymond Vernon (1966, 1973), proposed that FDI and MNC activity should be understood in terms of large firms' need to extend dominant (oligopolistic) market positions in home markets to foreign markets. Later, scholars such as British Peter Buckley and Mike Casson (1976) and Belgian Francois Hennart (1982) questioned that extension of market power was the key driver of international business activity, instead arguing that firms undertook FDI to overcome transactional market failures related to licensing and exports.

A key characteristic of the early MNC literature was that it was highly engaged in questions related to the societal implications of MNC activity. IO-inspired scholars adopted relatively critical views of MNCs' development role, as large MNCs essentially extended oligopolistic positions from rich core countries to the poor periphery (Vernon, 1973; Kindleberger, 1973). This literature intensively discussed the positive and negative welfare consequences of oligopolistic industries organized by MNCs spreading into developing countries (Caves, 1996. See Hansen and Hoenen (2016) for a review of that literature). After having finalized his seminal PhD thesis (Hymer (1960/75), Stephen Hymer even moved toward Marxian economics–inspired ideas about modern capitalism and the uneven nature of development (Dunning & Pitelis, 2008). Also development economists engaged in critical analysis of MNCs' role in development, see, for example, Lall & Streeten, 1977; Lall, 1978, 1980, 2000).

The Coase (1937)–inspired transaction cost stream within the emerging IB field was much more sympathetic to large MNCs, as their global reach, according to this view, mostly could be attributed to attempts to circumvent market failures in cross-border transactions. In IB jargon, rather than creating market failures (so-called "structural market failures"), as argued by the IO tradition, MNCs circumvented transactional market failures (so-called "natural market failures") (Hennart, 1991). In developing countries, market failures were assumed to be particularly widespread, and the inflow of FDI would consequently help these countries organize activities that, without the presence of MNCs, would have been very difficult to organize (Rugman, 1981). Later, Penrose (1958)–inspired resource and capability based perspectives of MNCs argued that MNCs were effectively bridging advanced economies and developing countries and providing a channel through which modern technology, products, and organizational practices could travel across geographical spaces (Forsgren, 2002). As argued by John Dunning – the main figure of the early IB literature – MNCs were "trail blazers of modernity" (Narula & Dunning, 2000).

In his seminal stock-taking analysis of MNCs' global expansion and their impact on economic development, Caves (1996) discussed the positive and negative aspects of MNCs' activities in developing countries. He concluded that the negative aspects related to oligopolistic practices of MNCs were limited and overwhelmed by the positive effects deriving from organization of markets and technology transfer.

The IB literature maturing

By the 1990s, IB was focused on "big" questions, such as why FDI took place, why MNCs existed, and how MNCs interacted with the deepening of internationalization called globalization (Buckley et al., 2017). Huge advances in the understanding of MNCs were made: MNCs existed because markets for intermediaries in foreign countries were nonexistent or inefficient (Buckley & Casson, 1976) and/or because firms possessing a lead position in home markets wanted to extend this position to foreign markets (Hymer, 1976). The deeper internationalization compared to previous internationalization incidents was described via the increasingly globally figured MNC value chain and the coordination of internationally dispersed activities (Porter, 1986). The literature converged around a number of core theories – in particular, transaction cost economics, resource based/capability perspectives, and market power perspectives – all of which were attempted to be integrated by John Dunning's so-called OLI (ownership, location and internalization) framework (1977, 2006). During the 1980s and 1990s, IB evolved into a discipline, with its own associations, journals, core theories, methodologies, etc., and the discipline witnessed a growing specialization and higher levels of rigor in terms of model development and testing. In short, by the early 2000s, IB was a fully fledged and highly dynamic discipline involving many thousand researchers around the world, addressing tangible questions related to IB activity.

In 2002, one of IB's founding fathers, Peter Buckley, expressed fear that the IB agenda, after more than 30 years of rapid expansion and success, had "run out of steam" (Buckley, 2002). The IB agenda had now – successfully – addressed the grand questions, and new grand questions were not in sight. In particular, Buckley lamented that the literature had abandoned its empirical drivenness based on phenomena of the world economy for a predisposition for questions that derived from theoretical puzzles. Buckley argued that IB, in its pursuit of ever-increasing theoretical and methodological refinement, had lost sight of the societal role of the MNC. At the same time, another key IB scholar, Ravi Ramamurti, argued that during the last 15 to 20 years, the study of the societal and developmental implications of MNC activity had been marginalized to more or less isolated research groups at the fringes of IB (Ramamurti, 2004). Claus Meyer, one of the leading young IB scholars of that time argued that "International business (IB) scholars pay too much attention to the interests and challenges facing MNEs and not enough to how MNEs help or hurt developing countries" (Meyer, 2004). Similarly, Mats Forsgren (2002, 2017) called for a reinvigoration of the societal impact stream in IB and argued that especially MNC organizational theory may help inform the discussion of MNCs' development impacts.

Now 15 years later, were Buckley, Ramamurti, Meyer, and Forsgren right that the IB literature lost track of its roots and failed to develop big new research agendas? In particular, were they right that the IB literature lost sight of the developmental role of MNCs and instead became preoccupied with MNC strategy, organization, and management? To these questions we will turn in the following sections.

A survey of the development orientation of the IB literature

In order to understand how the IB literature has dealt with development issues, two things were done: First, a quantitative analysis of development key words – so-called "markers of development orientation" – was conducted in three leading IB journals in order to conclude how important these key words are and how their use has evolved over time. Second, a qualitative analysis of development orientation of the IB literature was conducted based on a review of the main contributions to the development-oriented IB literature.

Markers of development orientation in the IB literature

Methodology

The three leading IB journals examined were the *Journal of International Business Studies* (JIBS), *Journal of World Business* (JWB), and *International Business Review* (IBR). Other main IB journals not analyzed are *Global Strategy Journal* (GSJ), *Management and Organization Review* (MOR), and *Management International Review* (MIR). The development orientation of the three journals was analyzed through a search for markers of development orientation in texts. The development orientation markers were:

- *Developing countries*: This term broadly denotes countries that, according to the United Nations (UN), are developing countries. This consists of approximately 150 countries that define themselves as "developing."
- *Emerging markets*: This term is akin to the term developing countries but is sometimes used to denote developing countries with relatively high gross domestic product (GDP) growth rates and relatively well-functioning market institutions.

- *Spillovers and developing countries*: One of the most valid development markers may be "spillovers," that is, unintended (positive) side effects of business activity on host countries. Inflow of FDI may lead to productivity, growth, and employment spillovers on the host economy (e.g., through linkages to local industry or through competition and demonstration effects).
- *Linkages and developing countries*: The term linkage is used to denote the channels through which MNCs interact with local industries and firms. The presence of linkages will typically indicate an impact on local firms and industries (e.g., in the form of upgrading and expanded business activity).
- *Sustainable development*: The term sustainable development won prominence with the 1992 United Nations Conference on Environment and Development (UNCED) conference in Rio and refers to development processes that do not erode their own ecological foundation. Recently, with the adoption of the UN Sustainable Development Goals, the term sustainable development has experienced a renaissance in development discourse.
- *Corporate social responsibility*: Corporate social responsibility (CSR) denotes activities – profitable or not – undertaken by companies to meet some kind of societal expectation. As developing countries often lack the institutions and regulations to prevent externalities from business activity, it is sometimes expected that MNCs voluntarily prevent such externalities from occurring through CSR practices.
- *Bottom of the pyramid (BOP)*: Some MNCs adopt strategies aimed at catering to the poorest segments of developing countries – the so-called bottom of the pyramid (BOP) – based on an assumption that collectively, the BOP can provide a profitable market if sufficient scale can be achieved.

Overall development orientation in the three journals

Overall, around one-third of the articles in all three journals refer to "developing countries" and around one-fourth to the more recent marker "emerging markets." However, many of these references are to MNCs' marketing or outsourcing in developing countries and do not engage the question of the development role and impact of MNCs. The markers "linkages and developing countries" and "spillovers and developing countries" refer more directly to the MNC development role. Around 20 percent of all articles in the three journals refer to linkages and around 10 percent to spillovers. Around 5 percent refer to CSR, and fewer to sustainable development, although JWB focused significantly more on this marker (Figure 4.1).

The historical evolution in the development orientation of the three journals

The probably best impression of the evolution in IB research can be obtained through JIBS, as this journal has existed since 1970 and it is the highest ranking of the IB journals proper. Our survey shows that JIBS is not a journal

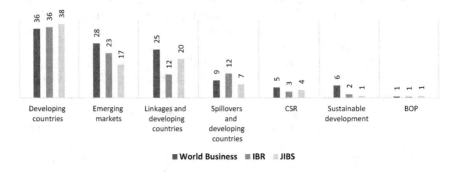

Figure 4.1 Percentage of articles in journals that refer to development marker, all years

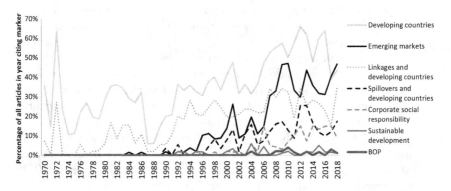

Figure 4.2 Markers of development orientation in *Journal of International Business Studies*

exclusively for MNCs in the developed economies: almost 40 percent of the articles in JIBS mention developing countries. "Developing countries," except for a brief decline in citations during the late 1980s, was always relatively high on the JIBS agenda; by the 2010s approximately half the papers cite "developing countries." The waning interest in "developing countries" in JIBS in the late 1980s is most likely explained by the strong concentration of MNC activity in developed countries, due to the debt crises of much of the developing world in the late 1980s. From the survey it is also clear that the up-and-coming word for locations outside developed countries is "emerging markets," which since the late 1980s has moved to prominence in JIBS articles and by 2018 has become more frequently cited than "developing countries" (Figure 4.2).

However, the high interest in "developing countries" and/or "emerging markets" in JIBS does not necessarily reflect an interest in MNCs' role in development. If we look at the markers specifically related to MNC developmental role and impact, it becomes evident that development, thus understood, figures much less prominently in JIBS: around 20 percent of the abstracts in a given year refer to "linkages and developing countries" and less than half this number mentions "spillovers and developing countries." The interest in these types of issues seems to grow from the early 1990s until the onset of the financial crises, where this interest seems to stagnate or even decline. "CSR" is a recent marker of development role of MNCs, and we can see that since the mid-2000s there has been a continuous increase in interest for "CSR," moving to a level around 10 percent in recent years.

An analysis of IBR (which only goes back to 1994) suggests a low interest in all development markers until around 2004, after which we see a slow increase in references to development markers. However, this increase is mainly detectable in relation to the markers "developing countries" and "emerging markets." "Spillovers" is mentioned in around 10 percent of the articles, "linkages" more rarely. As was the case with JIBS, references to "spillovers" and "linkages" alike seem to be stagnating after the financial crises, although at a relatively high level of around 20 percent. "Sustainable development" and especially "CSR" has gained in importance since the mid-2000s, however at a very low level (Figure 4.3).

Finally, the analysis of JWB reveals a slightly different story, possibly because this journal explicitly has chosen to prioritize MNCs' development role. For instance, the journal was exceptional in the sense that at a very early stage it engaged in sustainability issues in response to the 1992 Rio conference (Kolk & Tulder, 2010). Consequently, we can see that "sustainable development" references are comparatively common in this journal compared to JIBS and IBR. Also "linkages and developing countries" appears relatively important in this journal throughout its existence. Other development markers are more or less at the same level as for the two previously analyzed journals, and we also see a movement to a higher level of interest in the development aspects of

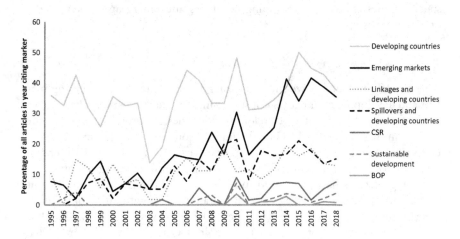

Figure 4.3 Markers of development orientation in *International Business Review*

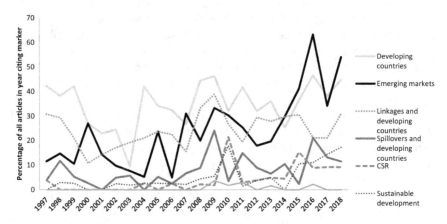

Figure 4.4 Markers of development orientation in *Journal of World Business*

MNCs from around 2003 to around the financial crises and then stagnation (Figure 4.4).

A content analysis of the development orientation of the IB literature

Looking in more detail at the content of IB journals, it becomes evident that although around one-third of the papers mention "developing countries" and "emerging markets," they overwhelmingly adopt a business perspective on these regions; only a small proportion deals explicitly with development impact and role as indicated through the markers "spillovers," "linkages," "sustainable development," BOP, and CSR. We will in the following briefly analyze what specific issues related to developing countries and emerging markets the IB literature takes up.

Business perspectives on MNCs in development

That the IB literature, as we showed earlier, has moved toward emerging markets and developing countries is not surprising. By the 2010s, more than 50 percent of global FDI went to developing countries. As growing opportunities emerge in these regions, MNC marketing and sourcing strategies in developing countries/emerging markets have generated large interest in the IB literature. In particular, various aspects of MNC marketing in developing countries and emerging markets have generated much interest in the IB literature. The literature on marketing analyzes how MNCs are dealing with emerging market/developing country conditions (Kearney, 2015; Ghemawat, 2001) and seeking to exploit the market potentials there (Arnold & Quelch, 1998; Dawar & Chattopadhay, 2002; Douglas & Craig, 2011). The expanding literature on marketing in developing countries is partly a reflection of the fact that more business activity is gravitating toward developing countries and emerging markets, but also that business environments are improving so that it becomes increasingly relevant to develop marketing strategies that relate to the specific market conditions of such countries, for example, the low levels of market segmentation, underdeveloped marketing infrastructures, and high growth rates. A specific branch of marketing literature analyzes MNC marketing strategies that cater to the poor, the so-called BOP strategies (Prahalad & Hammond, 2002; London & Hart, 2004; Simanis, 2011). According to this literature, MNCs need to modify their business models to cater to the poorest segments. In our survey, a small but growing percentage of papers refer to marketing in developing countries/emerging markets.

Mirroring the marketing stream of IB, a stream of literature focuses on upstream internationalization by MNCs into emerging markets and developing countries. The simultaneous global configuration and disintegration of MNC value chains (Porter, 1986) have evidently led to a focus in IB research on how MNCs can optimize through exploiting low-cost or asset-rich locations of developing countries and emerging markets (Doh, 2005). For instance, the offshoring and outsourcing literature has focused on placement of value chain functions in developing countries and emerging markets (see Quinn & Hilmer, 1994; Mudambi & Venzin, 2010) and analyzed how MNCs locate increasingly advanced functions in these countries (Jensen & Pedersen, 2012).

Much of the literature on MNCs in developing countries finds inspiration in the institutional strategy perspective (Peng, 2002; Peng et al., 2009; Kostova & Zaheer, 1999; Meyer, 2005; Hoskisson et al., 2000; Kostova et al., 2009; Wright et al., 2005, Xu & Meyer, 2013), which essentially holds that strategy research on MNCs operating in countries with weak institutions, changing institutions, and/or dominant informal institutions needs to take into account such institutional specificities of such locations (Khanna & Palepu, 2010). This array of theories discussing how and why institutions matter for firms (Gelbuda et al., 2008) has had a profound influence on the MNC literature and is in many ways the pivot for current developing country and emerging market strategy research.

Another empirical development pushing the IB agenda toward developing countries and emerging markets is the growing FDI coming out of developing countries. By the mid-2000s, developing countries themselves became major outward investors, so that now more than 40 percent of all outward FDI comes from these countries. This development gave impetus to a surge in research on emerging market multinationals (EMNCs). The themes of this research were essentially whether EMNCs are different from Western MNCs, that is, whether they have particular ownership-specific (O) advantages, such as strong abilities to collaborate and acquire skills through networks, and/or location-specific (L) advantages, such as privileged government access and low-cost bases (Ramamurti, 2012; Matthews, 2006; Narula, 2006; Hennart, 2012; Buckley, 2009).

Development role of MNCs

While the survey of development markets in the IB literature demonstrated that IB has substantially engaged in research on business activity in and from developing countries and emerging markets, it was also demonstrated that most of the papers focused on MNCs' strategy, organization, and management in those locations and only rarely focused specifically on MNC roles and impacts. Nevertheless, a substantial proportion of 10 to 20 percent of the research published in the main IB journals somehow refers to MNC development roles and impacts.

From economics, IB has "imported" a stream of research that analyzes positive externalities from MNC activity, so-called spillovers (see e.g. Blomstrøm & Kokko, 2000; Markusen & Venables, 1999). This spillover literature examines how MNCs, as an unintended consequence of their investments, create positive spillovers on host countries, for example, in the form of productivity increases or improved market access (Blomstrøm & Kokko, 2000). Spillovers can partly happen indirectly through demonstration and competition, and partly directly through collaboration between the MNC and local firms (i.e., linkages) (Narula & Pinely, 2016). One of the points of the spillover literature is that the larger the technological and organizational gap between MNCs and local industry, the less likely spillovers will be (Nunnenkamp, 2004). Whether spillovers happen will furthermore depend on the absorptive capacity of local industries (i.e., their ability to learn from collaboration with MNCs) (Narula & Marin, 2003). Most of the spillover studies are examining interactions between FDI aggregates and proxies for development effects (e.g., productivity) through econometric analysis (see Meyer and Sinani (2009) for a review of this literature). Rarely, if ever, do these studies analyze spillovers at the firm level, and it is generally unclear to what extent and in what way the spillovers can be attributed to MNCs qua being MNCs (Rugraff & Hansen, 2011). In other words, although the notion of spillovers has led to publication in IB journals, this stream of research tends to neglect the firm-level perspective.

Inspired by Porter's value chain thinking (Porter, 1986), economic geography has developed a strong research agenda focusing on the configuration of economic activities between developed and developing countries, the so-called "global value chain literature." This economic geography value chain literature has significantly affected and inspired IB research (see e.g. Buckley & Ghauri, 2004; Buckley et al., 2009; Strange & Humphrey, 2018). Global production is essentially configured through close-knit interfirm relationships – value chains – led by typically Western-based buyer and producer lead firms (i.e., large MNCs). The configuration of value chains is largely determined by the market power of the involved firms, in combination with the transaction costs of interfirm exchange. The configuration of value chains essentially determines the abilities of developing country firms to become integrated into the value chains, as well their ability to upgrade their products, processes, and value-adding activities within the value chains (Gereffi, 1999; Humphrey & Schmitz, 2004). This literature will tend to be relatively pessimistic with regard to developing country firms' ability to benefit from value chain integration (Humphrey & Schmitz, 2004).

Another and somewhat related literature is the literature on MNC linkages (Lall, 1980; Altenburg, 2000; Giroud & Scott-Kennel, 2009; Hansen et al., 2009). Already back in the 1950s, development economists argued that a key impediment to economic development was related to the lack of rich industrial infrastructures and networks in developing countries, making it difficult for firms to create a sharp division of labor and engage in specialization (Hirschman, 1958). Due to a lack of linkage opportunities, MNCs – especially in extractives – would often form enclaves in developing countries, with few impacts on local industry. The recent linkage literature, however, points out that in many instances MNCs will foster linkages upstream and downstream in their value chain in order to gain local inputs, reduce costs of imports, and improve relations to local communities (Morris et al., 2012). Contrary to the spillover literature mentioned before, the linkage literature has actually tried to connect MNC characteristics with development impacts, arguing that impacts on local linkage partners are partly conditioned by MNCs' organization and strategies (Scott-Kennel & Endervick, 2005; Hansen et al., 2009), in addition to capacities of local firms and industries and host country characteristics (Altenburg, 2000; Giroud & Scott-Kennel, 2009; Hansen & Schaumburg-Müller, 2006).

From the CSR literature – which is partly informed by organizational stakeholder theory (Freeman, 2010) – emanates a growing interest in CSR within IB. The idea here is that MNCs in developing countries often operate in a "moral free space" (Donaldson, 1996; Pisani et al., 2017) due to regulatory and institutional voids. In some locations, MNCs will benefit from internalizing these regulatory voids through CSR. In line with this, several IB scholars have argued that CSR necessarily should be part of the study of MNCs (Buckley & Ghauri, 2004; Dunning, 2006; Kolk & Thulder, 2010). Heeding this argument, numerous IB scholars have engaged the CSR agenda. The IB literature on CSR is strongly inspired by the strategic view of CSR, according to which CSR is seen as an investment in risk reduction, in reduction of liabilities, in capturing new markets, and in obtaining a social license to operate (Buckley et al., 2017). Hence, it is the business case for CSR rather than the moral case for CSR that interests the IB literature. A related research stream focuses on MNC partnerships and alliances for development, arguing that MNCs can and should engage with development issues by fostering mutually beneficial partnerships with nongovernmental organizations (NGOs) aimed at solving development problems (Oetzel & Doh, 2009). A main problem of the CSR literature on MNCs is that it, with a few exceptions (see e.g. Jamali, 2010), rarely relates to the CSR practices of MNCs that derive specifically from their multinational nature.

Assessment

Looking at the interest of leading IB journals in development issues prior to the mid-2000s, we can understand why IB scholars such as Ramamurti, Forsgren,

Meyer, and Buckley argued that IB's interest in developing countries and development issues was weak. However, our survey suggested that since the early 2000s there has been a growing interest in emerging markets and developing countries, especially up to and around 2010. Hence, it does not seem that the IB literature "ran out of steam" after 2002 when Buckley wrote his seminal article, at least not as far as the engagement in developing country–related research is concerned. Instead, new agendas or big questions entered IB and provided new dynamics, all agendas more or less directly related to developing countries: organizing, managing, and strategizing to exploit growing market potentials in developing countries; the emergence of multinationals coming from developing countries and emerging markets; the growing disintegration of MNC value chains and sourcing of activities in low-cost locations; and the growing interest in how MNCs respond to calls for social responsibility and sustainability.

However, the survey also indicated that the bulk of IB research on developing countries and emerging markets is related to MNC strategy, organization, and management, and less frequently touches upon the role and impact of MNCs in development processes. At best, 10 to 15 percent of abstracts deal with spillover issues and issues related to CSR and only little more deal with linkages and development. Moreover, much of IB's so-called development research is the offspring from other disciplines and is not really drawing on the core theories of IB. Hence, the IB spillover research has essentially imported theories and methodologies from development and trade economics, the value chain research from economic geography, and the CSR research from organizational stakeholder theory. Rarely does the research on the MNC developmental role draw on what can be seen as IB's main contribution: its ability to understand MNCs and their impacts qua being MNCs.

The modest IB focus on MNCs' development role is partly understandable, as IB has had an important mission in explaining and understanding the MNC and, indeed, has succeeded hugely in that mission. But as argued, IB may have an important contribution to development debates due to its unique understanding of cross-border firm activity and how this cross-border nature affects host countries (Ramamurty, 2004). IB can help overcome the often embryonic conceptualization of cross-border firm strategy and organization that is inherent to development research coming from adjacent disciplines such as political economy, development and trade economics, economic geography and the organizational CSR literature (Hansen & Schaumburg-Müller, 2010). As a consequence of its lacking engagement with development issues, IB has suffered from a lack of impact on related disciplines – here in particular development economics – as well as on practical development policy. This lack of engagement with practical development policy is a natural consequence of disciplinary specialization and pursuit of methodological rigor (Buckley et al., 2017). But we would argue that IB has gone too far in removing itself from practical development policy; as argued by Buckley et al. (2017), "IB can play a more constructive and vital role by tackling expansive topics at the business – societal interface." In the remaining parts of this chapter we will seek to identify which research agendas related to MNCs' development role could inspire future IB research.

IB development research issues for the future

> We call upon IB scholars to address grand challenges, with the purpose of advancing IB theory, contributing to important debates with scholars in allied social sciences, as well as actually helping to resolve these difficult challenges our generation is currently facing.
>
> (Buckley et al., 2017)

Although IB has evolved into an immensely successful discipline over the last 30 years, it has failed to fully engage with issues related to MNCs' developmental and societal role as it matured. There are two problems with this: The first is that where – arguably – development economics, economic geography, and political science all have been highly successful in informing and shaping development policy and practice, this is not the case with IB. Consequently, policymakers and practitioners must look to IB for inspiration and answers in vain. The second problem is that spillovers from IB to adjacent disciplines dealing with development-related issues rarely happen. Hence, disciplines that have engaged intensely with development issues (e.g., development economics, economic geography, and political science) rarely refer to the IB literature.

What would a revitalization of IB's engagement in research on MNCs' development role look like? We argue that a revitalized development agenda in IB would focus on three issues: (1) Directing focus to MNCs' development role qua being MNCs; (2) Re-discovering the empirical problem orientation of earlier IB literature; and (3) Opening more up for qualitative and inductive methodologies.

Directing focus toward MNCs' development role qua being MNCs

Buckley et al. (2017, 1052) argues that "IB scholarship may move away from its historical, narrow focus on the differences between MNEs and domestic firms, and instead leverage existing and new knowledge to contribute to efforts by social and behavioral scientists to make sense of critical global phenomena." We disagree with this argument. In our view, any revitalization of the IB agenda should draw on what we consider the comparative advantage of IB: that it understands MNCs qua being MNCs. IB is unique in its explicit focus on firms that organize value-adding activities across geographical borders and thereby produce some impacts that are different from those generated by other types of business enterprise. However, as we argued earlier, much of IB's world on the development role of MNCs fails to attribute that role specifically to the cross-border nature of MNCs. An emerging IB research agenda on the development role of MNCs would explicitly focus on how and in what ways the cross-border strategy, organization, and management practices of MNCs have implications for the impacts they have on developing countries (Pearce, 2006).

Toward greater empirical problem orientation

The second element in a revitalization of IB research on MNCs' development role would be to return to the strong empirical problem-orientation of the early IB literature. In line with Doh et al. (2016), we argue that IB scholars should to a higher degree initiate research with inspiration in a phenomenon or problem, and subsequently choose methods and theories that are most appropriate for analyzing that phenomenon or problem, instead of driving research agendas by ever more specific theoretical puzzles.

What are those empirical problems, then, that could and should inspire future IB research on MNCs' development role?

The SDG agenda: A definite driver of future problem-oriented IB research could be the UN-led Sustainable Development Goals (SDG) agenda. This agenda is likely to inform and shape the development intervention for the next 15 years. The SDG agenda formulates 17 goals for key development challenges, such as poverty, energy, water, inequality and injustice, and climate change, and outlines specific activities for how these goals can be achieved. Contrary to the Millennium Development Goals 2000–2015 (MDGs) agenda, which preceded the SDGs, the SDG agenda has assigned a key role to business, including international business. The question in relation to IB research hence is how MNCs, in exploiting their core advantages, can contribute to the finance and implementation of the 17 SDGs. Currently, IB is only to a limited extent involved in such research; according to Kolk and Thulder (2010, 120) "the impact of MNEs on sustainable development is. . largely unclear and needs further investigation."

Market and industry structure: Strangely, whereas much of the IB literature on emerging markets and developing countries is drawing on the institutional perspective, it rarely focuses on the specific market structures of developing countries (other than to the extent that these can be attributed to institutional voids). Hence, the lack of competition, the widespread structural market failures, and the asymmetric power relations between MNCs and local firms, etc., that characterize MNC activity in developing countries are rarely explicated in IB research. One exception is Buckley et al. (2009), who introduced the notion of the global factory to direct attention toward the role of powerful MNCs in organizing global production systems and their ability to curb developing country local producers' growth and upgrading. Similarly, Hansen and Hoenen (2016) call for a re-discovery of Hymer's original insights regarding the role played by oligopolistic industry structures in shaping MNC activities and impacts in developing countries.

Endogenizing institutions in strategy analysis: Although, as mentioned, a dynamic and sizable literature has emerged that focuses on MNCs and institutions in developing countries and emerging markets, this literature typically looks at the influence of institutions on MNC strategy and not the reverse relationship. Hence, an overlooked research agenda in relation to MNCs' development role relates to how MNCs influence the shape of institutions. It has long been acknowledged that MNCs may "fix" market failures by internalizing imperfect markets in their operation (Hennart, 1991), but the same is probably true for institutions, that is, that MNCs may "fix" some of the widespread institutional voids that characterize developing countries by building or influencing institutions (Hoskisson et al., 2000; Rugman & Verbeke, 2000). A more sinister interpretation of MNCs' interaction with institutions would be that MNCs capture institutions and/or use them to close markets. For instance, the migration and dissemination of standards from North to South, a process to a large extent orchestrated by MNCs, is effectively paving the way for MNCs at the expense of local firms not able to meet such standards (Gereffi et al., 2005).

MNCs' internalization of the development agenda: The spillover literature rests on the implicit assumption that development outcomes are produced as a collateral effect of market transactions. However, in modern business, the distinction between spillovers and core business activities is increasingly obliterated. For instance, upgrading taking place in linkages with suppliers and subcontractors can hardly be labeled spillovers, as they often are part of the market transaction and factored into contracts (Narula & Pineli, 2016). Moreover, we see how MNCs increasingly are seeking to appropriate the value of development spillovers by measuring and reporting on these spillovers, hence potentially improving their competitive position. Documented positive development contribution may constitute a "social license to operate" in some industries and countries. It may give MNCs marketing advantages in relation to customers increasingly scrutinizing producers for their development role. Likewise, the strategic use of CSR adopted by growing numbers of MNCs may play a key role in the survival, growth, and competitive position of MNCs (Kolk & Thulder, 2010; Porter & Kramer, 2006). The obliteration of the sharp distinction between CSR, spillovers, and core business in developing countries raises a whole lot of exciting research agendas for IB

MNCs and industrial policy: IB needs to engage much more actively with development policy and industrial policy agendas. MNCs are increasingly mobilized for development purposes, and governments are looking to MNCs for solutions to development challenges, for example, accessing technology, upgrading standards, providing market access, developing infrastructures, or providing finance. However, too often, government intervention in FDI rests on a poor understanding of how MNCs operate (Rodrik, 2004; Hansen, 2017). As a consequence, FDI interventions become ineffective, or even detrimental, to what they set out to achieve. An example is the so-called "local content requirements" that increasingly are used by developing countries to ground MNCs in the local economy. Such measures are seen not just in mining and extractives but increasingly also in manufacturing industries. More often than not, these requirements are based on a poor understanding of how MNCs operate (i.e., their global procurement strategies, their quality and safety standards, etc.). As a consequence, such measures either fail or they become ineffective (Hansen, 2013, 2017). Another example of an area where IB can contribute to debates on industrial policy is that many developing countries and emerging markets have liberalized their FDI legislation to attract FDI without introducing the related legislation that protects host industries against external shocks from FDI. This has frequently caused crowding out of local investment, entrepreneurial talent, and jobs (Chang, 2002, 2004; Altenburg & von Drachenfels, 2006). A better informed industrial policy based on a firm understanding of MNCs' competitive impacts would help avoid such side effects of liberalization.

Toward more quantitative and inductive research

In his plea for IB to engage the grand issues of our time, Buckley et al. argue that "tackling such issues, however, will require a widening in scope of what has come to be accepted as the appropriate expanse of the IB domain, and a loosening of the constraints that have been self-imposed regarding theory, method, and research approaches" (Buckley et al., 2017). We agree with this statement. As a logical consequence of the greater problem orientation advocated earlier, IB must open up for more flexible and eclectic research approaches that are better geared to capture the dynamics of the empirical field. Arguably, the routinization and formalization of current IB research around model development, stringent hypotheses testing, and advanced econometric analysis have marginalized more qualitative research aimed at identifying real-life problems and dynamics, and developing theories and understandings related to current development challenges.

Conclusions

> Only if IB scholars take grand challenges seriously, accept that these phenomena are distinct, develop innovative research designs, and concede to the sometimes-equivocal nature of their findings, will they develop novel and interesting theoretical insights that are also relevant to society at large. Therefore, building on the heritage of John Dunning and Stephen Hymer, among many others, we believe that IB scholars require a widening, rather than a narrowing, of their theoretical and epistemological horizons. IB must become, once again, an aspirational discipline.
>
> (Buckley et al. 2017, 1061)

In this chapter, we have explored how the IB literature deals with the key issue of MNCs' development role and impact. Although this issue certainly was at the core of early IB research, it seems that it has been partly marginalized in more recent IB research. It is not that IB is not interested in MNC activity outside the developed countries. It is more that this interest has not embraced the development roles and impacts of MNCs. Instead, IB has focused mainly on MNC strategy, organization, and management in emerging markets and developing countries, as well as on the emerging phenomenon of MNCs coming from such regions. The limited IB research on MNC development role that exists (e.g., research on spillovers, linkages, sustainability, and CSR) is to a large extent imports from adjacent disciplines such as development economics, economic geography, political science, and organization studies, and rarely focuses on the role and impact of MNCs qua being MNCs (i.e., qua being companies that organize value-adding activities across borders).

Hence, in light of the pertinent issues related to development and the need for policy and business practice to be informed by IB research, we suggested a research agenda on MNC development role and impact that (1) takes its point of departure in the comparative advantage of IB vis-a-vis other related disciplines, namely that it focuses specifically on cross-border business activity; (2) returns to the strong empirical problem orientation that characterized early IB research; and (3) loosens some of the methodological orthodoxies that have put IB on a path toward increasing theory-driven, and, would many practitioners argue, esoteric research agendas.

References

Altenburg, T. (2000). Linkages and spillovers between transnational corporations and small and medium-sized enterprises in developing countries: Opportunities and best policies. In: UNCTAD (Ed.), *TNC-SME Linkages for Development: Issues – Experiences – Best Practices*. New York and Geneva: United Nations.

Altenburg, T. and C. von Drachenfels (2006). The "new minimalist approach" to private-sector development: A critical assessment. *Development Policy Review* 24 (4): 387–411.

Arnold, D.J. and J.A. Quelch (1998). New strategies in emerging markets. *Sloan Management Review* 40 (1): 7–20.

Bain, J. (1956). *Barriers to New Competition*. Cambridge: Harvard University Press.

Bhagwati, Jagdish N. (2012). Multinational corporations and development: Friends or foes. Institutional Theory in International Business and Management. *Advances in International Management* 25: 5–14.

Blomström, M. and A. Kokko (2000). Multinational corporations and spillovers. In M. Blomström, A. Kokko and M. Zejan (Eds.), *Foreign Direct Investment: Firm and Host Country Strategies*. London: Palgrave Macmillan.

Buckley, Peter J. (2002). Is the international business research agenda running out of steam? *Journal of International Business Studies* 33: 365–373.

Buckley, Peter J. and M. Casson (1976). *The Future of the Multinational Enterprise*. London: Palgrave Macmillan.

Buckley, Peter J., Jonathan P. Doh and Mirko H. Benischke (2017). Towards a renaissance in international business research? Big questions, grand challenges, and the future of IB scholarship. *Journal of International Business Studies* 48(9): 1045–1064.

Buckley, Peter J. and Pervez N. Ghauri (2004). Globalisation, economic geography and the strategy of multinational enterprises. *Journal of International Business Studies* 35(2): 81–98.

Buckley, Peter J. et al. (2009). The impact of the global factory on economic development. *Journal of World Business*: 131–143.

Caves, R. (1996). *Multinational Firms and Economic Analysis*. Cambridge: Cambridge University Press.

Chang, H.J. (2004). Regulation of foreign investment in historical perspective. *The European Journal of Development Research*, 16(3): 688–710 = 22.

Chang, H.J. (2002). Breaking the mould: An institutionalist political economy alternative to the neo-liberal theory of the market and the state. *Cambridge Journal of Economics* 26: 539–559.

Coase, R.H. (1937). The nature of the firm. *Economica* (4).

Cypher, J. and S. Dietz (2004). Transnational corporations and economic development. In *The Process of Economic Development*. London: Routledge.

Dawar, N. and A. Chattopadhay (2002). Rethinking marketing programs for emerging markets. *Long Range Planning* 35: 457–474.

Doh, Jonathan P. (2005). Offshore outsourcing: Implications for international business and strategic management theory and practice. *Journal of Management Studies* 42(3): 695–704.

Doh, Jonathan P., Fred Luthans and John Slocum (2016). The world of global business 1965–2015: Perspectives on the 50th anniversary issue of the *Journal of World Business*: Introduction to the special issue: 1–5.

Donaldson, T. (1996). Values in tension: Ethics away from home. *Harvard Business Review*, 74(5), 48–62.

Douglas, S. and C. Samuel Craig (2011). Convergence and divergence: Developing a semi global marketing strategy. *Journal of International Marketing*, March, 19(1): 82–101.

Dunning, John H. (2006). The eclectic paradigm as an envelope for economic and business theories of MNE activity. *International Business Review* 9(2): 163–190.

Dunning, John H. (1977). Trade, location of economic activity and the MNE: A search for an eclectic approach. In *The International Allocation of Economic Activity*. London: Palgrave Macmillan, 395–418.

Dunning, John H. and Christos N. Pitelis (2008). Stephen Hymer's contribution to international business scholarship: An assessment and extension. *Journal of International Business Studies* 39(1): 167–176.

Forsgren, Mats (2002). Are multinational firms good or bad? In V. Havila, M. Forsgren, H. Håkanson (Eds.), *Critical Perspectives on Internationalization*. Oxford, UK: Elsevier Science Ltd, 29–58.

Forsgren, Mats (2017). *Theories of the Multinational Firm: A Multidimensional Creature in the Global Economy*. Cheltenham: Edward Elgar Publishing.

Freeman, R. Edward (2010). *Strategic Management: A Stakeholder Approach*. Cambridge: Cambridge University Press.

Gelbuda, Modestas, Klaus E. Meyer and Andrew Delios (2008). International business and institutional development in Central and Eastern Europe. *Journal of International Management* 14(1): 1–11.

Gereffi, Gary (1999). International trade and industrial upgrading in the apparel commodity chain. *Journal of International Economics* 48(1): 37–70.

Gereffi, Gary, J. Humphrey and T. Sturgeon (2005). The governance of global value chains. *Review of International Political Economy*, 12 (1): 78–104.

Ghemawat, Pankaj (2001). Distance still matters. *Harvard Business Review* 79(8): 137–147.

Gibbon, Peter and Stefano Ponte (2005). *Trading Down: Africa, Value Chains, and the Global Economy*. Philadelphia: Temple University Press.

Giroud, Axele and Joanna Scott-Kennel (2009). MNE linkages in international business: A framework for analysis. *International Business Review* 18(6): 555–566.

Hansen, M.W. (2013). *From enclave to linkage economies*. DIIS Working paper.

Hansen, M.W. (2017). *Local content and MNC strategy*. Paper presented to EIBA, 2017 in Milan.

Hansen, M.W. and Anne Kristin Hoenen (2016). Global oligopolistic competition and foreign direct investment: Revisiting and extending the literature. *Critical Perspectives on International Business* 12(4): 369–387.

Hansen, M.W. and H. Schaumburg-Müller (Eds.) (2006). *Transnational Corporations and Local Firms in Developing Countries – Linkages and Upgrading*. Copenhagen: Copenhagen Business School Press.

Hansen, M.W. and H. Schaumburg-Müller (2010). Firms in developing countries: A theoretical probe into the borderland of business studies and development studies. *The European Journal of Development Research* 22.2 (2010): 197–216.

Hansen, M.W., Torben Pedersen and Bent Petersen (2009). MNC strategies and linkage effects in developing countries. *Journal of World Business*: 121–131.

Hennart, Jean Francois (1982). *A Theory of Multinational Enterprise*. Ann Arbor: University of Michigan Press.

Hennart, Jean François (1991). The transaction cost theory of the multinational enterprise. In C. Pitelis and C. Sudgen (Eds.), *The Nature of the Transnational Firm*. London: Routledge.

Hennart, Jean François (2012). Emerging market multinationals and the theory of the multinational enterprise. *Global Strategy Journal* 2(3): 168–187.

Hirschman, A. (1958). *The Strategy of Economic Development*. New Haven: Yale University Press.

Hoskisson, R., L. Eden, C.M. Lau and M. Wright (2000). Strategy in emerging economies. *Academy of Management Journal* 43:249–267.

Humphrey, John and Hubert Schmitz (2004). Chain governance and upgrading: Taking stock. *Local Enterprises in the Global Economy*. Cheltenham: Edward Elgar Publications.

Hymer, S. (1960). *The International Operations of National Firms: A Study of Direct Foreign Investment*. Cambridge, MA and London: MIT Press (published in 1976).

Hymer, S. (1976). *The International Operations of National Firms: A Study of Direct Foreign Investment*. Cambridge: MIT Press.

Jamali, Dima (2010). The CSR of MNC subsidiaries in developing countries: Global, local, substantive or diluted? *Journal of Business Ethics* 93(2): 181–200.

Jensen, Peter D. Ørberg and Torben Pedersen (2012). Offshoring and international competitiveness: Antecedents of offshoring advanced tasks. *Journal of the Academy of Marketing Science* 40(2): 313–328.

Kearney, AT.T. (2015). *Foreign Direct Investment Confidence Index®, Miscellaneous Years*. www.atkearney.dk/research-studies/foreign-direct-investment-confidence-index/2015.

Khanna, T. and K.G. Palepu (2010). Multinationals in emerging markets, Ch 4. In T. Khanna and K.G. Palepu (2010). *Winning in Emerging Markets – A Road Map For Strategy and Execution*. Boston, MA: Harvard Business School Press, 83–123.

Kindleberger, Charles Poor (1973). *The Formation of Financial Centers: A Study in Comparative Economic History*, Boston: MIT.

Kolk, Ans and Rob Van Tulder (2010). International business, corporate social responsibility and sustainable development. *International Business Review* 19(2): 119–125.

Kostova, Tatiana, Kendall Roth and M. Tina Dacin (2009). Theorizing on MNCs: A promise for institutional theory. *Academy of Management Review* 34(1): 171–173.

Kostova, Tatiana and Srilata Zaheer (1999). Organizational legitimacy under conditions of complexity: The case of the multinational enterprise. *Academy of Management Review* 24(1): 64–81.

Lall, S. (1978). Transnationals, domestic enterprises, and industrial structure in host LDCs: A survey. *Oxford Economic Papers* 30(2): 217–248.

Lall, S. (1980). Vertical inter-firm linkages in LDCs: An empirical study. *Oxford Bulletin of Economics and Statistics* 42(3): 203–226.

Lall, S. (2000). *FDI and Development: Policy and Research Issues in the Emerging Context*. Queen Elizabeth House Working Paper Series – QEHWPS43, University of Oxford.

Lall, S. and P. Streeten (1977). *Foreign Investment, Transnationals and Developing Countries*. London: Macmillan.

London, T. and S.L. Hart (2004). Reinventing strategies for emerging markets: Beyond the transnational model. *Journal of International Business Studies* 35: 350–370.

Markusen, J. and A. Venables (1999). Foreign direct investment as a catalyst for industrial development. *European Economic Review* 43: 335–356.

Mathews, J. (2006). Dragon multinationals: New players in 21st century globalization. *Asia Pacific Journal of Management* 23: 5–27.

Meyer, K. (2004). Perspectives on multinational enterprises in emerging economies. *Journal of International Business Studies* 35(4): 259–276.

Meyer, K. (2005). Foreign direct investment in emerging economies. *Policy Discussion Paper:* 1–33.

Meyer, K. and E. Sinani (2009). When and where does foreign direct investment generate positive spillovers? A meta-analysis. *Journal of International Business Studies* 40: 1075–1094.

Morris, Mike, Raphael Kaplinsky and David Kaplan (2012). "One thing leads to another" – Commodities, linkages and industrial development. *Resources Policy* 37(4): 408–416.

Mudambi, Ram and Markus Venzin (2010). The strategic nexus of offshoring and outsourcing decisions. *Journal of Management Studies* 47(8): 1510–1533.

Narula, R. (2006). Globalization, new ecologies, new zoologies, and the purported death of the eclectic paradigm. *Asia Pacific Journal of Management* 23(2): 143–151.

Narula, R. and J. Dunning (2000). Industrial development, globalization and multinational enterprises: New realities for developing countries. *Oxford Development Studies* 28(2): 141–167.

Narula, R. and A. Marin (2003). Foreign Direct Investment Spillovers, Absorptive Capacities and Human Capital Development: Evidence from Argentina. Geneva: International Labour Office Working Paper no. 96.

Narula, R. and André Pineli (2016). *Multinational enterprises and economic development in host countries: What we know and what we don't know. No. 020.* United Nations University-Maastricht Economic and Social Research Institute on Innovation and Technology (MERIT).

Nunnenkamp, P. (2004). To what extent can foreign direct investment help achieve international development goals. *The World Economy* 27(5): 657–677.

Oetzel, J. and J. Doh (2009). MNEs and development: A review and re-conceptualization. *Journal of World Business* 44: 108–120.

Pearce, R. (2006). Globalisation and development: An international business strategy approach. *Transnational Corporations* 15(1): 39–74.

Peng, M. (2002). Towards an institution-based view of business strategy. *Asia Pacific Journal of Management* 19: 251–267.

Peng, Mike W., et al. (2009). The institution-based view as a third leg for a strategy tripod. *The Academy of Management Perspectives* 23(3): 63–81.

Penrose, E.T. (1958). *The Theory of the Growth of the Firm.* New York: Wiley.

Pisani, Niccolò, et al. (2017). How global is international CSR research? Insights and recommendations from a systematic review. *Journal of World Business* 52(5): 591–614.

Porter, M.E. (1986). Competition in global industries: A conceptual framework. In M.E. Porter (Ed.), *Competition in Global Industries.* Cambridge, MA: Harvard Business School.

Porter, M.E. and M.R. Kramer (2006). Strategy & society: The link between competitive advantage and corporate social responsibility. *Harvard Business Review* 84(12): 78–92.

Prahalad, C.K. and A. Hammond (2002). Serving the world's poor, profitably. *Harvard Business Review* 80(9): 48–58.

Quinn, J. and F. Hilmer (1994). Strategic outsourcing. *Sloan Management Review* 35(4) (Summer): 43–55.

Ramamurti, R. (2004). Developing countries and MNEs: Extending and enriching the agenda. *Journal of Business Studies* 35: 277–283.

Ramamurti, R. (2012). What is really different about emerging market multinationals? *Global Strategy Journal* 2(1): 41–47.

Rodrik, D. (2004). *Industrial Policy for the Twenty-First Century*. Cambridge, MA: Harvard University. www.ksg.harvard.edu.

Rugman, A.M. (1981). *Inside the Multinationals: The Economics of Internal Markets*. London: Croom Helm.

Rugman, A.M. and A.Verbeke (2000). Multinational enterprises and public policy. In C. Millar et al. (Eds.), *International Business: Emerging Issues and Emerging Markets*. London: Macmillan, 21–43 = 22.

Rugraff, Eric and Michael Wendelboe Hansen, eds. (2011). *Multinational Corporations and Local Firms in Emerging Economies*. Amsterdam: Amsterdam University Press.

Scott-Kennel, J. and P. Enderwick (2005). FDI and inter-firm linkages: Exploring the black box of the IDP. *Transnational Corporations* 14(1): 105–130.

Simanis, Erik (2011). Needs, needs, everywhere, but not a BoP market to tap. *Next Generation Business Strategies for the Base of the Pyramid*: 103–126.

Strange, Roger and John Humphrey (2018). What lies between market and hierarchy? Insights from internalization theory and global value chain theory. *Journal of International Business Studies*: 1–13.

Vernon, R. (1966). International investment and international trade in the product cycle. *Quarterly Journal of Economics* (May): 80, 190–207.

Vernon, R. (1973). *Sovereignty at Bay*. Harmondsworth: Penguin.

Wright, M., I. Filatotchev, R. Hoskisson and M. Peng (2005). Strategy research in emerging economies: Challenging the conventional wisdom. *Journal of Management Studies* 42(1): 1–34.

Xu, Dean and Klaus E. Meyer (2005). Linking theory and context: "Strategy research in emerging economies" after Wright et al. (2005). *Journal of Management Studies* 50(7).

5 The financialization and responsibilization of development aid

Johanna Järvelä and Nikodemus Solitander

Development: a changing play field for finance

The last 20 years have seen some major changes and shifts in how the intersections of development and business are constructed, understood, and operationalized. New actors and alliances have emerged, establishing new interventions and mechanisms in North–South relations (Richey and Ponte 2014). Arguably, one of the most prevalent changes has occurred within the realm of development finance. The emphasis on the importance of the private sector as a source of finance and as an enabler of development has become a dominant idea in the international development agenda for North–South relations (van Waeyenberge, Fine and Bayliss 2011). By the time of the Monterrey development finance negotiations in 2002, private-sector development had emerged as a prevalent doctrine, coupled with the idea that a larger part of development funding needed to come from financial markets and through the development of financial instruments (van Waeyenberge 2015). This private-sector turn in development is just one example of a larger financialization of society, indicating an "increasing role of financial motives, financial markets, financial actors and financial institutions in the operation of domestic and international economies" (Epstein 2005, p. 3) and a "pattern of accumulation in which profit making occurs increasingly through financial channels rather than through trade and commodity production" (Krippner 2005, p. 14). Although grounded in a larger context of neoliberalism, here construed in relation to "state promotion of private capital in general and of finance in particular" (van Waeyenberge, Fine and Bayliss 2011, p. 8), the financialization of development aid can be seen as inherently linked to the post–Washington Consensus (PWC), a "more state and poverty friendly" form of development aid than the neoliberalism of the Washington Consensus (ibid, p. 9).

The PWC was clearly visible in the outcomes of the Busan development aid financing conference in 2011. As Mawdsley, Savage and Kim (2014) note, in many respects the Busan conference saw the end of the so-called Paris regime, which had focused on poverty reduction and aid effectiveness and had guided all development aid since the Paris Declaration on Aid Effectiveness in 2005. Busan marked the start of a new development regime, one that brought in new actors and further strengthened the role of the private sector by putting economic growth in the center of development cooperation. It also extended the idea of development financing outside of official development aid (ODA). The emphasis in this new regime lay on the necessity of private capital in general, but finance in particular (van Waeyenberge, Fine and Bayliss 2011). This meant that new forms of finance, such as export credits and state-sponsored financial instruments (e.g., development finance funds and private equity funds), were claimed to be crucial for development (Bracking 2012). Moreover, this happened alongside the reconfiguration of responsibilities of actors in the public–private partnerships, such as private equity firms, development finance institutions (DFIs), and various (quasi-)state actors.

At the same time, there was a need for the PWC approach to respond to the critique of the dysfunctions caused by the withdrawal of state intervention and the unfolding "market failures" of business dealing with poverty (van Waeyenberge, Fine and Bayliss 2011), such as exacerbating income inequalities, exploiting the conditions of the poor, and the destruction of nature (Craig and Porter 2006; Blowfield and Dolan 2014). One way of reframing the market as responsible was the rollout of public–private partnerships to deal with the failures of an unbridled market approach (Bäckstrand and Kylsäter 2014; Liese and Beisheim 2011; McGoey 2014), while at the same time deploying the state in such partnerships to sustain the promotion of finance capital (van Waeyenberge, Fine and Bayliss 2011, p. 9). In this context, it is important to note how state actors have increasingly relied on business discourses to create meaning to "responsible markets" and "responsible private corporations." As a way to construct the societal benefits and the benign development effects and to legitimize the financialization and privatization of aid to larger groups of stakeholders, there has been an increased use of corporate social responsibility (CSR) discourse. CSR discourse is of central interest because it establishes corporations as legitimate actors ethically capable (and accountable) of taking over some of the traditional responsibilities of governments. It is through CSR that firms increasingly make sense of, measure, and vocalize their developmental impact, CSR is there to ensure the (discursive) production of the social good (Heal 2005). CSR discourse is also useful in the development context because of how it portrays success as something nonconflictual and dissent as a perversion (Banerjee 2007; Blowfield 2005; Fougère and Solitander 2009). Such nonconflictual win-win narratives tend to be especially important in the intersections of public–private partnerships and CSR. These win-win narratives, however, can stand at odds with the impacts of financialization in development aid, where, for example, conflicts related to human rights, land rights, or indigenous rights are fueled and triggered by large-scale investments by international finance institutions (Zoomers 2010). Celebrated business logic ventures into development, such as microfinance, also have a dark side, with a risk of accumulation by dispossession and debt peonage, facilitating surplus extraction through credit relations, instead of contributing to meaningful development (Bond 2013; Mader 2015). Further adverse effects on development are found in the strong links between financialization and the use of tax havens/offshore centers, which further drain resources from developing countries (Bracking 2012; Garcia-Arias 2015).

In this chapter, we analyze the increasing financialization of development aid. We particularly look at the role of state-owned DFIs as (1) drivers for financialization (2) in responsibilizing the market, particularly through the discourses of CSR and public–private partnerships. We position the increased role of DFIs in larger historical-political economy shifts and its implications for sustainable local development in the South. In line with the book's problem–driven approach to understanding private-sector development in the Global South, we problematize the effects of increased financialization, investments, and mechanisms that are inserted between the state and their investment impacts in local communities in developing regions. As an illustration, throughout the chapter we analyze the shifting roles of European DFIs, with a particular focus on the Finnish state-owned DFI, Finnfund.

The Finnish case serves as a good illustration of the shifting landscapes, as Nordic countries have been historically important actors in development cooperation, with a political focus on human rights and democracy. The so-called Nordic aid model has emphasized poverty alleviation and welfare, as well as health, education,n and women's rights. As a part of the model, the allocation of funds has been grant driven and focused on the least developed countries. This model, which was active from the 1970s until the late 1990s in Denmark, Finland, Norway, and Sweden, gained a reputation for generosity and the ideals of solidarity, altruism, and humanitarianism (Oden 2015; Elgström and Delputte 2016). However, since the beginning of this millennium, the Nordic model has faded, and differences between the Nordic countries' approaches have started to emerge (ibid). The private turn in Nordic development policies has accentuated private-sector-led growth, market solutions for development, and fund allocation for business and investment – resulting in less emphasis on governments as drivers of development (Elgström and Delputte 2016). Simultaneously, the role of state-owned DFIs as the most important vehicle for the new development aid model has increased.

The chapter is structured as follows: In the first section, we briefly trace the changing role of the private sector in development aid and finance. We show how financialization of development aid is the latest phase of the PWC and the implications of it. In the second section, we focus on the role of DFIs in the financialization of development. DFIs are state-owned finance institutions that are posited as a means to correct the market failures and fairness issues in the Global South born out of the Washington Consensus, while at the same time contributing to the acceleration of the financialization of development. In the third section, we look at the CSR-related governance and accountability mechanisms that steer the activities of DFIs. Finally, we conclude the chapter by offering some reflections on the uneasy relationship of the private sector and development and discuss possible future avenues for research.

A brief history of the financialization of development aid

The idea that the private sector spearheaded by multinational firms could and should be harnessed to work for the poor is not new. Starting from the neoliberal reforms of the 1980s in the form of the structural adjustment programs (SAPs), the role of a private sector, global financial flows, and attractive national policies have been strengthened in development discourse and praxis. The reforms of the 1980s came under increasing critique as inequality in the global economy appeared to have increased during the era of neoliberal restructuring, and economic growth per se was insufficient to deal with the problem of endemic poverty (Öniş and Senses 2005). Although the Poverty Reduction Strategy Papers (PRSPs) of 1990s continued the "making markets work for the poor" idea, they emphasized at the same time country ownership and civil society participation as two of the key principles in development cooperation and set the scene for PWC (Ruckert 2006). These Poverty Reduction Strategies were International Monetary Fund (IMF)– and World Bank–led programs that targeted the developing country governments and policies to open up their domestic markets to attract foreign direct investment (Booth 2003; Mawdsley, Savage and Kim 2014; Tarp 2000). These programs were complemented with the "Aid for Trade" programs, bilateral trade agreements with a development component, bilateral aid programs with a trade component, and multilevel programs to facilitate development country governments to enhance private-sector development in their countries (Langan 2011). However, all of these were agreements between governments. Although these initial PWC efforts can be seen as neither representing a fundamental break from the Washington Consensus nor an attempt to reproduce exactly the neoliberal policy regime of the 1980s, they laid the foundation for the following phase in the business-focused development discourse (Ruckert 2006; Van Waeyenberge, Fine and Bayliss 2011).

The next phase in development policy discourse was brought by the new millennia, as the focus shifted from macroeconomic policies and bilateral and multilateral action to the actions of global corporations and particularly the financial flows of private capital. This ideological shift meant changing the role of government from the driver to the backseat in development assistance (Blowfield 2005; Langan 2011). This shift was partly legitimized through the notion of "weak" and "absent" states and "governance gaps," where the need for private-sector and corporate activity was deemed necessary (Banks et al. 2016; Blowfield and Frynas 2005). At the same time, it signaled a departure from the Washington Consensus by inserting a more poverty-focused business discourse (van Waeyenberge, Fine and Bayliss 2011). This phase of the PWC also presented a non-agonistic view of the state, that is, the state together with business (through private–public partnerships) promotes market solutions (through state intervention if necessary) to deal with market failures and fairness issues in developing regions (ibid.). The idea of "making markets work for the poor" transformed itself into responsible and sustainable business. But the private turn of development since the early 2000s has not only meant bringing in corporations to the toolbox for development, but more importantly, it has signified an increasing emphasis of different private-sector-driven financial instruments in development aid, and as such, the financialization of the whole system (Mawdsley 2018), and arguably of poverty itself (Mader 2015).

The explanatory factors behind this shift were diminished ODA levels and other sources of public funding and the overall growth of the financial sector. As noted in the Reality of Aid (2012) report, the renewed interest in private-sector development happened concomitantly with falling rates of ODA and even further discrepancies between the promises made and the level of actual ODA flows. Mobilizing private-sector flows burdens less the national budgets of donor countries and can be used to enhance the national trade endeavors. Furthermore, what is calculated in the private sector development allocations varies between the donor countries, but there is a growing trend in the role of DFIs in them. The donor rationale and its legitimation present the private sector as the main driver for economic growth, which in turn is seen as a key factor for development (ibid.).

To illustrate through the Finnish case, when a new center-right government entered office in 2015, it introduced a new development policy that put a strong emphasis on the role of the private sector in policy and financial mechanisms. The government allocated 100 million euros for the Finnish Development Finance Institute, Finnfund, while at the same time cutting 300 million euros from the traditional development cooperation channels. The shift in the role of Finnfund in the development policy landscape was accentuated by the fact that it had requested 60 million less (Finnwatch 2015). Government officials legitimized the shift by explicitly referring to the Addis Ababa Agenda, which had "emphasized the role of the private sector," and the UN Post-2015 Development Agenda, which "sets explicit targets for the private sector" (Torvinen in Development Policy Committee 2015). In the historical context, the policy shift towards DFIs also marked a return to instrumentalism, where domestic interests explicitly override the developing country interests as the motivation of the policy (Ylönen 2016). Finnfund's aim is to finance companies in which a Finnish interest is involved – as well promoting inclusive economic and social development in developing regions. The expectation is that through increased financialization of development and by financing Finnish business endeavors and interests in the Global South, it will fulfill local development objectives in sustainable, nonconflictual ways. This illustrates the political discourse that has been referred to as postpolitical (Mouffe 2005), with an emphasis on win–win politics, promoting solutions and ideas that are supposedly beneficial for everyone in society (Garsten and Jacobsson 2013). In the following section, we will analyze in more depth the intersections of the financialization of development assistance, the growth of DFIs, and the responsibilizing discourse that is supposed to govern the market failures caused by financialization and the private turn of development.

Public–private partnerships and the rise of development finance institutions

As stated in the previous section, PWC recognizes the failure of structural adjustment programs to address issues connected to sustainable development, such as pollution or deforestation (often framed as "market failures") or increasing income inequalities (framed as "fairness issues") and emphasizes the role of the state to correct these issues. However, there is an assumption that these corrections by the state will be made through market mechanisms and in partnerships with private capital (van Waeyenberge, Fine and Bayliss 2011). Since the early 2000s, the United Nations (UN) has actively been pushing the partnership ideology, and the launch of the Global Compact in the year 2000 marked an important turning point in the development discourse. While recognizing market failures and unfairness, instead of seeing development as correcting the structural inequalities of power and wealth, the Global Compact "posits development as a collective challenge to be met by the combined efforts of diverse stakeholders, whose potentially conflicting interests are elided via the language of participatory pluralism" (Bair 2007, p. 488). Both the partnership discourse and the responsibilizing role of the state can be seen in the way the role of state-owned DFIs, which will be introduced in-depth in the following section, is construed, here illustrated through an interview with the chair of the Organisation for Economic Co-operation and Development's (OECD) Development Assistance Committee:

> The [state-owned] DFIs can go into markets where private investors are not already going on their own and they can maintain high standards in terms of environment and working conditions. Too many in the public sector talk about the private sector rather than with the private sector. DFIs may act as an important link between the private sector and policy-makers. They are in a better position to have a genuine dialogue with private investors – including banks, insurance companies, pension funds – about the barriers facing their investment in poor countries.
>
> (Solheim in EDFI 2016, p. 7)

This illustrates how (1) DFIs are embedded in a partnership discourse where it is portrayed as a necessity that governments partner with the private sector to solve the "systemic barriers to sustainable development" (EDFI 2016, p1), and in the legitimization of DFIs, both the UN SDGs and the Addis Ababa Agenda of 2015 are frequently referred to through their explicit emphasis on private capital and public–private partnerships. (2) DFIs are portrayed as inserting responsibility in the market through their state ownership "they can go to markets where private actors will not; they can maintain high environmental and social conditions where private actors cannot" (EDFI 2016, p. 7). As Bracking et al. (2010) note, DFIs often claim that they are a "civilizing influence" in funds, promoting better CSR standards and praxis. (3) DFIs are presented as

hybrid financial market actors who understand the ideology of private investments better than other public entities.

Development finance institutions and the financialization of poverty

Although the history of development banks goes back to the 1950s and postwar
reconstruction (c.f. Bruck 1998), we focus on the growth of DFIs since the
PWC. DFIs are defined by the European Development Finance Institutions
(EDFI, the association of bilateral European DFIs) as "government-backed
institutions that invest in private sector projects in low- and middle-income
countries in order to promote job creation and sustainable economic growth"
(EDFI 2016, p.VI).

It is possible to distinguish between multilateral DFIs such as the International Finance Corporation (IFC) and the Multilateral Investment Guarantee
Agency, regional DFIs such as the African Development Bank Group (AfDB)
and the Inter-American Development Bank (IADB), and what is the focus in
this chapter, bilateral DFIs. The growth of DFIs during the last 20 years has
been rapid. Currently, bilateral DFIs make up 35 percent of DFIs donor-backed
capital flows to private-sector investment in developing countries, and the total
portfolio of investments for European DFIs has tripled in ten years to €36.3 billion at the end of 2015 (EDFI 2016). Table 5.1 outlines some of the main DFIs
and their characteristics.

Table 5.1 Major DFIs

DFI	Country	ownership	Total portfolio (M€), **2015**	% financial sector of total investment portfolio	ODA, (M$), 2015
BIO	Belgium	100% state	622	40	377
CDC	UK	100% state	5998	16	3815
COFIDES	Spain	53% state	865	2	77
DEG	Germany	83% state	7191	32	1602
FINNFUND	Finland	93.4% state	602	12	235
FMO	Netherlands	51 % state	9256	37	465
IFU	Denmark		572	9	384
NORFUND	Norway	100% state	1573	29	728
OeEB	Austria	100% export credit agency	973	62	41
PROPARCO	France	64% AFD (state)	5623	46	1090
SIFEM	Switzerland	100% state	555	15	618
SIMEST	Italy		2097		280
SOFID	Portugal	59.99% state	11		52
SWEDFUND	Sweden	100% state	376	40	847
OPIC	USA		21500	55	9121

Some DFIs are full government finance institutions, whereas others are cor-porate legal entities with a banking license (of the 15 European DFIs, 5 have a banking license), and most of the DFIs are governed by specific laws (Bruck 1998). DFIs usually operate by providing high-risk loans, equity, and guarantees to private rather than public actors in developing regions. The aspect of sustain-able development and/or poverty reduction is often explicitly referred to in the statutes of the DFIs and in some cases contributes to the eradication of poverty and social development, which can be stipulated in law.[1] The European govern-ments, however, generally also expect their bilateral DFIs to promote national economic interests and to mobilize the activities of domestic businesses.

The DFIs are themselves deeply entrenched in the global growth of financialization – we identified five main modes of financialization in relation to DFIs:

1 Financialization through organization. As organizations' DFIs are part of what Stockhammer (2010) labels the shadow banking system, the "motor for finan-cialization . . . [the] substantial and growing part of the financial sector [that] does not take the form of (traditional) banking (or insurance)" is composed of "institutions such as investment funds, money market funds, hedge funds, private equity funds and special purpose vehicles." Although the European DFIs are dominantly state-owned, 8 of the 5 European DFIs have private entities as significant minority shareholders (EDFI 2016). For the most part, these shareholders are banking institutions in the DFI's home country.

2 Financialization through inward financing. In terms of inward financing, it is increasingly common that the European DFIs leverage their shareholders' equity to finance their own investments through "loans from institutional investors, their shareholders and other liabilities" (EDFI 2016, p. 11). Of the European DFIs, five operate with a banking license, and these typically have leverage on their balance sheets from institutional investors. The EDFI states that "DFIs are structured and operate to promote financial participa-tion from private sectors counterparts" (ibid, p. 23), where "private sec-tor" should be read as "finance sector." In the Finnish case, when in 2015 Finnfund was granted 130 million euros, the total funding was divided into direct replenishment from the government and a loan by the government. The government claimed the capitalization of Finnfund (which is a not-for-profit entity) as a "financial investment" and thus it would not count as a cost in the national accounts (Government Budget Draft 2016, p. 11, transl.) – with this also claiming that the cuts in development assistance (nonfinan-cial discourse) were not connected to the increase of funding for the DFI (finance discourse). As the director of Finnfund put it, "the capitalization of Finnfund is not away from other [development assistance], but rather the choice is between the capitalization of Finnfund and another finance invest-ment" (Kangasniemi in Development Policy Committee 2015, p. 2, transl.)

3 Financialization through outward investment. When considering the inter-section of business and development, the DFIs steer large parts of their

outward investments towards the finance sector in developing countries (see Table 5.1), thus further accelerating financialization. When looking at the European DFIs, the largest sector by investments is financial services, at 30 percent of total investments (followed by the energy sector at 18 percent and manufacturing at 12 percent) (EFDI 2016, p. 18). The investments target investment funds, microfinance institutions, and other financial intermediaries. The DFIs often have as an explicit target to expand the finance sector in particular. Finnfund states that the finance sector has "significant multiplier effects" (Finnfund Investment Report 2016, p. 14) in developing countries, and by targeting the finance sector, it promotes "operational transparency, [and] improve[s] the management of environmental and social risks" (ibid.). The EDFI states that the finance sector is to be targeted because DFIs' investment portfolio should be focused on sectors that "generate the highest development impact" (EDFI 2016, p. 18). It further states that:

> DFIs have played an important role in building the private equity industry in emerging markets. . . . This has contributed to the expansion of the private equity industry in these markets over the past 10–15 years and, over time, to significant fundraising from private investors . . . investments in private equity funds grew from US$3.5 billion in 2003 to US$44 billion in 2015 with 70% in Asia and 9% in Sub-Saharan Africa . . . In 2015, the European DFIs invested €1.3 billion in approximately 30 investment funds and the total investment fund portfolio reached €8.3 billion in approximately 400 different funds at the end of 2015, up from €4.5 billion in 2008 . . . [IFC] created a group dedicated to investment in funds in 2000 with the goal of investing in 8–10 funds annually. The activity level was later raised based on the good performance of these investments. The portfolio reached US$5 billion in 270 funds by 2015.
>
> (ibid, p. 23)

It is noteworthy that when looking at how social impact and the development targets are met and measured, the financial sector is often increasingly at the center stage, for example, the US DFI Overseas Private Investment Corporation (OPIC) states that through its current investment portfolio it will create 75,980 jobs in nonfinancial sectors and will create 391,406 jobs in the financial sector, adding that the percentage of managerial jobs created will be double that of non–financial-sector jobs (OPIC 2017, p. 2). Similarly, Finnfund reports that half of the jobs it has directly contributed to are either in development finance institutions or in investment funds (Finnfund in Finnwatch 2017, p. 14). As Table 5.1 shows, there is a difference between the DFIs in terms of how large the investment flows towards the finance sector are (ranging from under 10 percent for COFIDES and IFU to over 50 percent for OPIC), but the trend is that its role is increasing across the board. The increased role of the finance sector as a recipient of investments strengthens the analysis that DFIs explicitly are driving a model of center–periphery financialization (Garcia-Arias 2015), meaning that (Western) donor countries increase the influence of the finance sector in the developing economies, and as the sector grows, it increases the role of financial innovation through both products (securitizations, derivatives, etc.) and instruments (microfinance, hedge funds, etc.). For example, a number of European DFIs have identified "significant gaps in access to finance for [firm in LDCs] because they are neither served by microfinance nor by foreign direct investment" (EDFI 2016, p. 22), and as a response they have set up special investment funds such as the DFID Impact Fund, managed by the CDC Group (the UK's DFI) and the MASSIF, AEF, and IDF funds managed by FMO (the DFI of the Netherlands).

4   Financialization through secrecy jurisdictions. DFI investment flows are often arranged through tax havens, as they are inherently intertwined in the same logics and thus reproduce the same harmful structures as the private investors (Bracking et al. 2010). The recent Paradise and Panama papers showed that several European DFIs, such as Finland's Finnfund and Denmark's IFU (Investment Fund for Developing Countries), have invested in equity funds registered in tax havens such as the Cayman Islands and Mauritius. The director of Finnfund underlined the normalcy of such practice within finance services with the following: "The unfortunate fact is that you cannot pay your taxes in poor countries due to absent tax governance. Because of this you are forced to operate through e.g. Mauritius" (Kangasniemi in Development Policy Committee 2015, transl.). "From the perspective of a fund investor, the Cayman Islands is a stable country with predictable arrangements" (Kangasniemi in Yle 2017). It would be exceptional to casually legitimize such arrangements as a state-funded and state-owned development agency, but because the DFI sees itself as a market actor within the finance sector, this is seen as normalized praxis.

5   Financialization through valuation. The DFIs and the funds they invest in operationalize development at a distance, and the way they construct a meaning of impact is highly influenced by financialization. This point will be further elaborated in the next section, but as financialization of development is increasingly operationalized through various private funds where

> "investors pool their funds, and then Fund Managers invest in other companies, who may then invest in yet others, or set up a corporate entity with the special purpose of actually building, mining or drilling. Distal investment is efficacious for money-holders since, by their nature, energy, mining and infrastructure tend to generate contestation with local communities and environmental activists."
>
> (Bracking 2012, p. 275)

Financialization creates various challenges (especially for the state owners) in how to make sense of social and environmental impacts at a distance and how to legitimize its own actions and inactions. Herein, financialization plays a central role, as a number of calculative technologies are utilized for valorizing social and environmental impacts; as Bracking (2012, p. 276) notes, through these technologies "development" is generally defined "as an aggregate of social, economic, financial, governance and environmental components." Finnfund, like many DFIs, uses a tool referred to as a "development effect assessment tool" (DEAT), which quantifies three aspects: corporate sustainability principles, economic development impact, and the role of Finnfund. We will analyze the DEAT tool further in the next section.

These five identified modes of financialization support the analysis by van Waeyenberge, Fine and Bayliss (2011, pp. 1–2) that the PWC cannot be understood outside of financialization and that the PWC is about "making markets work . . . but the markets working, or advancing, most over the period of the PWC have been those of finance." The most recent phase of the private turn of development has turned poverty into a problem of finance (Mader 2015). What is missing, however, is a deeper debate on the responsibilities and accountabilities of both the DFIs, as financialization also increases the likelihood of economic, banking, financial, and currency crises (Garcia-Arias 2015); the negative effects of the hegemonic ideal within finance of encouraging the use of tax havens and increasing capital flight; and the potential risks for income and wealth distribution by favoring capital over labor (Arestis and Caner 2010; Garcia-Arias 2015).

State legitimation and the governance of DFIs through CSR

The Western donors of development aid have increasingly turned to CSR as a discourse to legitimize the shift towards the privatization of development. In this section we will show how on a discursive level states and state actors make sense of the responsibilization of private capital/actors of societal tasks (poverty/development) and how private capital and, by extension, financialization is framed as something desirable and good for development. On a practical level, we will show how DFIs use and reproduce certain logic and tools associated with CSR, such as reliance on standards and voluntary codes of conduct.

CSR as a win-win rhetoric for development. The OECD Development Assistance Committee's (DAC) Busan Conference marked a significant shift in the development aid rhetoric when firms were framed as "equal partners" and the focus shifted from poverty reduction to economic growth (Banks et al. 2016). As outlined in the previous section, instead of talking about ODA flows, this PWC discourse emphasizes the broader understanding of development finance, which includes export credits, state-sponsored financial instruments (DFIs), and other forms of private capital flows (Mawdsley, Savage and Kim 2014). This private-sector partnership discourse, which draws on CSR with its postpolitical rhetoric of partnerships, consensus, and win-win solutions for development, has moved into mainstream political thought in both donor countries and development agencies. In the Finnish case, the government's development policy rests on four pillars of which one aims specifically to generating economic growth by job creation in developing countries, specifying that:

> Finland possesses know-how as a promoter of resource-wise and account-able business and economic activity . . . From 2016 to 2019, Finland will contribute over EUR 500 million to mobilise investments for sustainable development in developing countries. This contribution will be in the form of capital investments and loans . . . Development policy investments aim to achieve development impacts in the partner countries. At the same time, however, the funds must yield revenue and the invested capital must be returnable, that is, it is expected to eventually reflow back to Finland.
>
> (formin.finland.fi)

This shows a reproduction of a core idea within contemporary CSR discourse: that it is possible to make development a sustainable business model, where the poor win (through impact) and, in this case, the Finnish economy wins (through revenue flows back to Finland). As the report of the International Business Forum organized by the World Bank and the UN Global Compact in 2005 states: "[CSR is] intended to curb some of the more extreme behav-ior found in free markets . . . [it is] intended to complement government action or inaction – recognizing that a lack of public policy frameworks cre-ates uncertainty and governance voids that undermine business confidence" (IBF 2005, p. 13). The UN, through the launch of the Global Compact in 2000, played an important role in reframing poverty as a "business opportu-nity." When channeling funds to the DFIs, state actors frequently cite the UN millennium goals and the SDGs for increasingly focusing its development efforts on the strengthening of responsible private flows of capital to bolster responsible business in developing countries, here illustrated through the Danish DFI, IFU:

> Development aid cannot stand alone. In order to create sustainable societies in the developing world, private capital and investments are vital. This is also the conclusion in the new Sustainable Development Goals (SDGs) set forward by the UN to end poverty, fight inequality and injustice, and tackle climate change by 2030 . . . When IFU invests in sustainable development in developing countries through public-private partnerships (Goal 17), we are supporting the achievement of a range of the SDGs.
>
> (www.ifu.dk/)

Many DFIs have in their founding charters and steering documents explicit reference to sustainable development and CSR discourse, for example: "Central to our ethos is a firm commitment to responsible investment . . . stipulate[ing] environmental, social and governance standards that are often above those required by local law" (CDC Mission statement) and "Finnfund's strength as a tool for development is its ability to achieve sustainable development through finance" (Finnfund, owner's steering document) and "The objectives of the company's operations are . . . to contribute to the creation of conditions for improved standards of living for people who live in poverty and oppression" (Swedfund, Mission statement).

The CSR agenda and partnership model are based on voluntary agreements between "mutual beneficiaries" or stakeholders; however, as noted, the power imbalance and corporate-led initiatives also might lead to more business than development; that is, how one frames the problem implies also nature of the action: If the problem is seen to be the lack of clean water, the solution might be building a well, or if the problem is the lack of money, a microcredit scheme might be the solution. In "inclusive capitalism" models the problem of poverty is often seen as a market problem; hence, the solution will be to correct it by making the poor part of the global market system (Blowfield and Dolan 2014). Additionally, the problems that business and the market deem significant and the solutions proffered often accord more with the needs of capital than the needs of the poor (ibid, p. 30). As Banks et al. (2016) note, for corporate actors to contribute meaningfully to local development, they need to take the community perspective and give decision-making power to local people. However, there is a tendency in the current development policy discourse to measure impact through the state- and national economy–level "developments" and emphasize job creation and economic growth as the foremost objectives and tools for development. The problem of delinking from local-level impact is further aggravated in the financialized development model, where development is operationalized at a distance (Bracking 2012), and where an increased number of actors, investments, and mechanisms are inserted between the donor/investor state and their investment impacts in local communities in developing regions.

The question of impact and distance is of essence, as there have been a number of reported cases of growing violence,[2] land grabs,[3] tax avoidance,[4] and human rights violations congruently with the official narrative of job creation[5] tied to DFI investments. A significant part of DFI investments go to large-scale energy and agriculture projects (Reality of Aid Report 2012), and these are often celebrated as exemplary projects (Finnfund Annual report 2016). But as much of the political ecology literature on land grabs shows, this dynamic of large-scale and land-intensive investments in developing countries is prone to cause local destruction in the form of dislocation, loss of livelihoods, and poverty (White et al. 2012). A large body of literature has been critical of the suggested partnership discourse of development as mainstreaming Western values, seeing the "others" as in need of development but unable to notice or address the power relations and imbalances between the parties (Cooke and Kothari 2001; Mohan and Stokke 2000; Enns, Bersaglio and Kepe 2014). But what is perhaps most noteworthy with DFIs is not so much the idea that private actors and the market can solve poverty issues, but rather the idea that the state should "blend" its development assistance *through* private actors and financial flows.

CSR as DFI practice. The previous section outlined CSR as discourse, how it legitimizes the blending and channeling of public funds with private financial

capital in a partnership discourse. In this section we will look at CSR as a practice. If a rationale of the blending is achieved through state involvement to curb
certain "extreme and unsustainable behavior found in the free market," and
if the DFIs can go into markets where private investors are not going, while
"maintain[ing] high standards in terms of environment and working conditions" (EFDI 2016, p. 7), then how is this supposed to be achieved? By looking
at the governance of the European DFIs, it becomes clear that it is the same
voluntary CSR mechanisms that govern the free market actors that govern the
state-owned DFIs; thus, the standards are the same as those private investors
utilize to legitimize their social responsibilities: the Global Compact, Principles
for Responsible Investment (PRI), and some DFI-specific voluntary principles and guidelines such as the EDFI Principles for Responsible Financing,
the International Finance Corporation (IFC) Performance Standards, and the
World Bank Group's Environmental, Health, and Safety Guidelines, which are
most commonly referred to as providing the private governance frameworks
responsibility. These are, in the words of Shamir (2008, p. 7), "the markets of
authority" where "laws, rules and regulations, are partially replaced by a variety
of guidelines, principles, codes of conduct and standards do not necessarily
enjoy the coercive backing of the state, and they are not an ordering activity."
These CSR principles and guidelines are also voluntary and not mandated by
the laws that otherwise govern the DFIs. They serve to instrumentalize morality with respect to the goals of the organizations while disregarding the moral
substance of the goals themselves (Herlin and Solitander 2017). There is a cir-
cularity in reasoning, as the CSR guidelines become proxies for sustainable
action. When Honduran activist Berta Cáceres was assassinated for her opposition of the construction of a hydroelectric dam in a river considered sacred
by the Lenca community (Watts 2016), Finnfund and FMO (the Dutch DFI)
repeatedly made sense of the situation only by asking if they had interpreted the
Global Compact and IFC standards correctly. This shows how in CSR actions/
inactions are rendered neither "good" nor "bad," only "correct" or "incorrect"'
(Herlin and Solitander 2017). Additionally, CSR guidelines/principles are not
able to secure the rights or well-being of the marginalized and poor because of
the structural limitations, that is, imposition of particular economic and social
norms, and the inability to recognize noncapital forms of relationships and their
significance (Banerjee 2018; Dolan 2008). This is well illustrated in the discussion of the value of the hydroelectric dam in Honduras, which is construed
dominantly through its supposed economic benefits (Finnfund 2016b).

This brings us to the measurement aspects. The DFIs use various calculative technologies to measure the development impact when making investment decisions. As Bracking (2012) notes, valorizing social and environmental
impacts tend to become more common as the DFIs get involved. It is part of
financialization, as it converts the social and the environment into calculated
items in the private equity funds' risk and profit assessment (ibid). These calcu-
lations are central to the trade-off logic that often comes into play when the
win–win logic that exists at the outset is questioned. In the case of Honduras

and the negative effects on the indigenous Lenca community, the tension was immediately made sense of by Finnfund in terms of an instrumentalist logic wherein the indigenous claims to holy lands were offset with other communities' access to electricity measured in GWh. But studies such as that of Bracking (2012) also find severe problems with how the DFIs use a weighting system in their impact assessment which favors financial criteria, "combined with an aggregation system which allows poor environmental effect scores to be offset by the more points available in the financial section" (ibid.p. 279) and giving "points in an arbitrary manner." The assessments are often made as desktop research or outsourced to consultants with little knowledge of the particular issues in the affected regions. As Blowfield and Frynas (2005) point out, quite often the analyses on business as problem solvers lack the historical understanding of why and how the problem was created, that is, underlying logics that might have an effect on how and what is seen as an appropriate solution.

The DEAT used by Finnfund is presented in Table 5.2. Each category is mostly rated using a 4-point scale from no effect, neutral/limited effect, positive effect, and significant positive effect, and given a weighted score. Noteworthy is that on top of measuring the impact of projects in terms of corporate sustainability and economic impact, Finnfund also evaluates and weights its own role and the significance of its presumed effects – opening up questions about what Bracking (2012) calls the thin, partial, and pseudo-mathematical methods of assessing impact.

Table 5.2 DEAT impact assessment categories

Corporate Sustainability Principles	*Economic Development Impact*	*Role of DFI*
Climate change mitigation	Financial sustainability of the project	Additionality of client risk
Environmental and social effects	Effect on direct job creation/direct employment	Additionality from country risk
Promotion of good corporate governance	Effect on indirect job creation/indirect employment	Catalytic role of DFI
Commitment to gender equality in employment	Payment to government	Nonfinancial role of DFI
ODA status of project country	Effect on the balance of payment	
Promotion of economic activity and employment creation in fragile states	Effect on customers/end users	
Effect on low-income and vulnerable groups	Effect on local producers/suppliers	
Effect on society through CSR activities	Effect on local competition and marker development	

Another serious difficulty with CSR is the lack of accountability of the both the DFIs themselves and the CSR standards and tools they follow. From the cases of the European DFIs, the state owners appear largely passive over issues regarding social and environmental responsibilities, outsourcing the governance to the earlier-mentioned markets of authorities. The DFIs see themselves as financial actors answering to the market – they follow the same norms as other financial-sector actors, including aggressive tax planning, the use of offshore arrangements, and a tight veil of secrecy. In the case of Finnfund, the DFI has repeatedly declined to publish its social impacts assessments by appealing to "bank secrecy norms" towards its clients.

As noted by Richey and Ponte (2014, p. 13), many of the new actors in development (referring to companies but also celebrities and private foundations) "are active as development tools – but [are] not responsible for development." Blowfield and Frynas (2005) make critical notions on the ideational use of CSR and the stakeholder dialogue model, as, for the most part, it does not account for power inequalities or the challenges, especially in the developing country context, that the stakeholder engagement model might include because of differences in language, culture, values, or education. The power to decide who is included in these stakeholder engagement models has no legal basis but is dependent on the business case (ibid). Thus, corporations can also use their power to delegitimize stakeholders opposing their projects (Banerjee 2018). Banerjee (ibid) points out also how the tension between normative and instrumental views of CSR remain yet to be resolved, meaning that while the normative prescriptions for CSR build on the win-win idea, the accounts on instrumental deployment of CSR describe win-lose situations, where profit is made at the expense of marginal stakeholders. Furthermore, as Banks and Hulme (2014) note, there has been a great challenge even for nongovernmental organizations (NGOs) to be accountable to the poor or marginalized groups, raising the question of how DFIs who see themselves as financial service corporations answering to the market will be able to tackle this problem in a more satisfactory manner.

Conclusions

In this chapter we have showed how the recent increased intertwining of private financial flows with the funding of development aid is positioned in a historical continuum of the PWC and the realpolitik choice in cutting ODA flows. However, this development is not unproblematic. We have highlighted here the critique on the compatibility of the market logic of the PWC and the development objectives of ending poverty, hunger and child mortality, or enhancing women's rights. We have also elaborated on the role the CSR discourse has played in establishing private capital and markets as responsible, and as a way to "offset" the negative effects of capitalism in the development context. Perhaps the most significant change of the latest development turn is the reformulation of the role of the state, this time as the enabler (through private–public partnerships) of the social consciousness of the market and financial flows. But through financialization, the state plays another pivotal role, that of an underwriter of private risks – because despite the win–win logic of CSR, development finance discourse is fast to point to the impossibility of the private sector being able to invest in developing regions using normal financial risk logic. This is perhaps most visible in the latest buzzword within development finance, that of "blended finance" – the strategic use of public development capital through DFIs for the mobilization of additional external private finance often framed as a necessity to achieve the SDGs. Blended finance explicitly reconfigures the risks, as the role of government is to be "risk cushions" (Business and Sustainable Development Commission 2018, p. 7) for private investors but also incentivizes DFIs to hedge risks inherent in least developed countries (LDCs), by "shift[ing] DFI portfolios . . . toward more stable middle-income countries" (ibid, p. 7). The pivotal role the state seems to play in the PWC suggests something new, but as Fine (2013, p. 58) reminds us,

> neoliberalism is not about the withdrawal of state (economic) intervention; it has always been associated with a strong not a weak state . . . On the contrary, the distinguishing role of the (advanced) neoliberal state has primarily been to promote the interests and internationalization of capital in general and of finance in particular, an important example being the extent that state finance itself has been financialized.
>
> (Fine 2013, p. 58)

But equally, in the spirit of public–private partnerships, the financialization of development is about private actors and private financial flows and about adopting certain logics of finance. PWC underlines the necessity of private capital in general, but finance in particular, for sustainable development. The increased role of DFIs reframe poverty as being mostly a problem of finance (Mader 2015). We have identified five central modes through which DFIs and, by extension, states parttake and act as key accelerators of the financialization of development, namely (1) financialization through organization, (2) financialization through inward financing, (3) financialization through outward investment, (4) financialization through secrecy jurisdictions, and (5) financialization through valuation.

DFIs explicitly drive a model of center– periphery financialization (Garcia-Arias 2015), where financialization emerging in developed economies is exported and imposed on the LDCs, exponentially increasing the influence of the finance sector in the developing economies. From a development perspective, financialization is problematic, as it increases the likelihood of economic, banking, financial, and currency crises (Garcia-Arias 2015; Lapavitsas 2013); encourages the use of tax havens and increasing capital flight; increases risks for income and wealth distribution by favoring capital over labor (Arestis and Caner 2010; Garcia-Arias 2015); and can lead to accumulation by dispossession and debt peonage, facilitating surplus extraction through credit relations (Bond 2013; Mader 2015).

Through the increased use of financial intermediaries, the funding decisions are distanced from the beneficiaries of the aid and the local development it should enhance. The power is of the former, although the latter should be empowered. Through the financialization of development, there has also been an increased use of private equity funds (PEFs) by the DFIs, which exacerbates the issue of distance between donor states and recipient locales. Using a CSR and impact investment logic, DFIs often claim that they are a civilizing influence in funds, promoting better standards than would prevail in the absence of their involvement. But if and when tensions and problems arise, the DFIs are fast to point out how they cannot have control or insight into the investment of the PEFs. For PEFs, reputational damage is rarely an issue due to the complex and anonymous nature of the financial investment circuit, and thus the effects of CSR are seldom visible.

Although it is clear that the DFIs operate with different investment logics and, to an extent, favor different kinds of investment targets, it is clear that many direct investments target large-scale industrial projects. But reported adverse effects of these projects, for example, in the form of land grabs (Borras and Franco 2013), raise the question of the need for baseline knowledge and use of development frameworks to measure and monitor unintended as well as intended consequences of these projects. Also, as we have noted, the use of DFIs as a development tool has led to the use of somewhat problematic measurement for development such as the overall growth of the economy (gross domestic product [GDP]) and amount of jobs created, which do not capture the quality of the development or quality of the jobs, including if a living wage is paid or not. This question links to the discussion on trade-offs between different development objectives. Often, the negative impacts are legitimated with positive impacts, but there is a moral question of how much inequality and harm can be caused, especially with public funding in the name of development.

We have discussed how the growing financialization and role of the private sector in development aid is more problematic than the official discourse of partnership and CSR make it seem. Therefore, this apparent contradiction should be acknowledged and suitable policies, guidelines, and tools developed to minimize the risks. The tools DFIs have been using thus far are not adequate. The ability of DFIs to incorporate social and environmental issues is at the moment questionable and should be addressed before further advancement of the private sector in development. As owners, the states have the ability to make the DFIs more accountable for social, environmental, and taxation issues. If voluntary CSR tools are to govern the DFIs, then accountability mechanisms for failure to comply with these need to be formulated and put in place.

For the research in the intersection of business and development, the role and operations of the DFIs provide a great opportunity. A lot of high-quality critical research has focused on the World Bank, but much less research has been done on multilateral and especially bilateral DFIs. As hybrid actors operating with a deeply financialized and market-based logic, while being state-owned entities, they provide interesting objects of study from a wide variety of perspectives. This chapter has hopefully shown that business and development research can be combined to research the role of financialization in the development but also in the creation of uneven (financialized) development.

Notes

1 For example, in Finland, the so-called Finnfund Act stipulates that Finnfund shall promote "the economic and social development of countries which the Development Assistance Committee (DAC) of the Organization for Economic Cooperation and Development (OECD) has classified as developing countries."
2 www.gaipe.net/wp-content/uploads/2017/10/Exec-Summ-Dam-Violencia-EN-FINAL.pdf
3 www.grain.org/fr/bulletin_board/entries/5798-are-european-taxpayers-funding-land-grabs-and-forest-destruction
4 https://yle.fi/uutiset/osasto/news/paradise_papers_finnish_development_finance_agency_holds_8_mil_in_tax_haven_fund/9919282
5 https://www.ciel.org/glass-half-full-the-state-of-accountability-in-development-finance/

References

Arestis, Philip, and Asena Caner (2010). "Capital account liberalization and poverty: How close is the link?" *Cambridge Journal of Economics*, 34(2), pp. 295–323.
Bäckstrand, Karin, and Mikael Kylsäter (2014). "Old wine in new bottles? The legitimation and delegitimation of UN public – private partnerships for sustainable development from the Johannesburg summit to the Rio+ 20 summit", *Globalizations*, 11(3), 331–347.
Bair, Jennifer (2007). "From the Politics of Development to the Challenges of Globalization", *Globalizations*, 4(4), 486–499.
Banerjee, Subhabrata Bobby (2007). *Corporate Social Responsibility: The Good, the Bad and the Ugly*. Cheltenham: Edward Elgar Publishing.
Banerjee, Subhabrata Bobby (2018). "Transnational power and translocal governance: The politics of corporate responsibility", *Human Relations*, 71(6), 796–821.
Banks, Glenn, Regina Scheyvens, Sharon McLennan, and Anthony Bebbington (2016). "Conceptualising corporate community development", *Third World Quarterly*, 37(2), 245–263.
Banks, Nicola, and David Hulme (2014). "New development alternatives or business as usual with a new face? The transformative potential of new actors and alliances in development", *Third World Quarterly*, 35(1), 181–195.
Blowfield, Michael (2005). "Corporate social responsibility: Reinventing the meaning of development?" *International Affairs*, 81(3), 515–524.
Blowfield, Michael, and Catherine S. Dolan. (2014). "Business as a development agent: Evidence of possibility and improbability", *Third World Quarterly*, 35(1), 22–42.
Blowfield, Michael, and Jedrzej George Frynas. (2005). "Editorial – setting new agendas: Critical perspectives on corporate social responsibility in the developing world", *International Affairs*, 81(3), 499–513.
Bond, Patrick (2013). "Debt, uneven development and capitalist crisis in South Africa: From Moody's macroeconomic monitoring to Marikana microfinance mashonisas", *Third World Quarterly*, 34(4), 569–592.
Booth, David (2003). "Introduction and overview: Are PRSPs making a difference? The African experience", *Development Policy Review*, 21(2): 131–159.

Borras, Saturnino M. Jr, and Jennifer C Franco (2013). "Global Land Grabbing and Political Reactions 'From Below'", *Third World Quarterly*, 34(9), 1723–1747.

Bracking, Sarah (2012). "How do Investors value environmental harm/care? Private equity funds, development finance Institutions and the partial financialization of nature-based industries", *Development and Change*, 43(1), 271–293.

Bracking, Sarah, David Hulme, David Lawson, Kunal Sen and Danture Wickramasinghe (2010). *The Future of Norwegian Development Finance*. Norwegian official document no: 0902364–55. Oslo: Government of Norway, available at www.osisa.org/sites/default/files/schools/bracking_on_development_finance.pdf

Bruck, Nicholas (1998). "Role of development banks in the twenty-first century", *Journal of Emerging Markets*, 3, 39–68.

Business and Sustainable Development Commission (2018). *Better Finance, Better World*. Consultation Paper of the Blended Finance Taskforce, available at http://s3.amazonaws.com/aws-bsdc/BFT_BetterFinance_final_01192018.pdf

Craig, David Alan, and Doug Porter (2006). *Development Beyond Neoliberalism? Governance, Poverty Reduction and Political Economy*. London: Routledge.

Cooke, Bill, and Uma Kothari (2001). *Participation: The New Tyranny?* London: Zed.

Development Policy Committee (2015). *Minutes of Plenary Session of the Finnish Development Policy Committee*, September 10, available at http://docplayer.fi/45015894-Kehityspoliittisen-toimikunnan-taysistunto-to.html

Dolan, Catherine S. (2008). "Arbitrating risk through moral values: The case of Kenyan Fairtrade", in Geert De Neve, Luetchford Peter, Jeffrey Pratt, Donald C. Wood (eds.), *Hidden Hands in the Market: Ethnographies of Fair Trade, Ethical Consumption, and Corporate Social Responsibility* (Research in Economic Anthropology, Volume 28), Bingley: Emerald.

EDFI (2016) *EDFI Flagship Report 2016: Investing to Create Jobs, Boost Growth and Fight Poverty*, Association of European Development Finance Institutions, available at: www.edfi.eu/wp/wp-content/uploads/2017/10/EDFI-Flagship-Report-2016.pdf

Enns, Charis, Brock Bersaglio, and Thembela Kepe (2014). "Indigenous voices and the making of the post-2015 development agenda: The recurring tyranny of participation", *Third World Quarterly*, 35(3), 358–375.

Elgström, Ole, and Sarah Delputte (2016). "An end to Nordic exceptionalism? Europeanisation and Nordic development policies", *European Politics and Society*, 17(1), 28–41.

Epstein, Gerald A. (ed.) (2005). *Financialization and the World Economy*. London: Edward Elgar.

Fine, Ben (2013). "Financialization from a Marxist perspective", *International Journal of Political Economy*, 42(4), 47–66.

Finnfund (2016a). *Annual Report*, available at https://annualreport.finnfund.fi/2016/en

Finnfund (2016b). *FAQ on the Agua Zarca Run-of-the-River Hydroelectric Generation Project*, available at www.finnfund.fi/ajankohtaista/uutiset16/en_GB/faq_agua_zarca/

Finnfund (2016c). *Investment Report 2016*, available at https://annualreport.finnfund.fi/2016/filebank/1010-Financial_Statements_2016.pdf

Finnwatch (2015). *Järjestöiltä leikataan 49 miljoonaa, Finnfundille ohjataan 100 miljoonaa*, 13.8.2015, available at www.finnwatch.org/fi/uutiset/326-jaerjestoeiltae-leikataan-49-miljoonaa,-finnfundille-ohjataan-100-miljoonaa

Finnwatch (2017). *Salkut Auki: Finnfundin rahastosijoitusten kohdeyritykset*, April, available at: www.finnwatch.org/images/pdf/Salkut_auki_Finnfund.pdf

Fougère, Martin, and Nikodemus Solitander (2009). "Against corporate responsibility: Critical reflections on thinking, practice, content and consequences", *Corporate Social Responsibility and Environmental Management*, 16(4), 217–227.

Garcia-Arias, Jorge (2015). "International financialization and the systemic approach to international financing for development", *Global Policy*, 6(1), 24–33.

Garsten, Christina, and Kerstin Jacobsson (2013). "Post-political regulation: Soft power and post-political visions in global governance", *Critical Sociology,* 39(3), 421–437.

Government Budget Draft (2016). *Talousarvioesitys 2016,* Ministry of Finance, Finland, available at http://budjetti.vm.fi/indox/download.jsp;jsessionid=2C6F1B7EE7664D1FD955 42C94DFF1D77?lang=fiandfile=/2016/tae/valtiovarainministerionKanta/Yksityiskoh-taisetPerustelut/24/24.pdf

Heal, Geoffrey (2005). "Corporate social responsibility: An economic and financial framework", *The Geneva Papers on Risk and Insurance-Issues and Practice,* 30(3), 387–409.

Herlin, Heidi, and Nikodemus Solitander (2017). "Corporate social responsibility as relief from responsibility: NPO legitimizations for corporate partnerships in contested terrains", *Critical Perspectives on International Business,* 13(1), 2–22.

IBF (2005). *Fighting Poverty: A Business Opportunity,* report of the 10th International Business Forum on the topic Business and the Millennium Development Goals: An Active Role for Globally Responsible Companies, available at http://siteresources.worldbank.org/CGCSRLP/Resources/report_IBF05-screen.pdf

Krippner, Greta R. (2005) "The financialization of the American economy", *Socio-Economic Review,* 3(2), 173–208.

Langan, Mark (2011). "Private sector development as poverty and strategic discourse: PSD in the political economy of EU-Africa trade relations", *Journal of Modern African Studies,* 49(1), 83–113.

Lapavitsas, Costas (2013). *Profiting Without Producing: How Finance Exploits Us All.* London: Verso Books.

Liese, Andrea, and Marianne Beisheim (2011). "Transnational public-private partnerships and the provision of collective goods in developing countries", in T. Risse (ed.), *Governance Without a State? Policies and Politics in Areas of Limited Statehood* (pp. 115–143). New York: Columbia University Press.

Mader, Philip (2015). "The financialization of poverty", in *The Political Economy of Microfinance* (pp. 78–120). London: Palgrave Macmillan.

Mawdsley, Emma (2018), "Development geography II: Financialization." *Progress in Human Geography,* 42(2): 264–274.

Mawdsley, Emma, Laura Savage, and Sung-Mi Kim (2014) "A 'post-aid world'? Paradigm shift in foreign aid and development cooperation at the 2011 Busan high level forum", *The Geographical Journal,* 180(1), 27–38.

McGoey, Linsey (2014) "The philanthropic state: Market – state hybrids in the philanthrocapitalist turn", *Third World Quarterly,* 35(1), 109–125.

Mohan, Giles, and Kristian Stokke (2000). "Participatory development and empowerment: The dangers of localism", *Third World Quarterly,* 21(2), 247–268.

Mouffe, Chantal (2005) *On the political, thinking in action.* London: Routledge.

Oden, Bertil (2015). "The Africa policies of Nordic countries and the Erosion of the Nordic aid model -a comparative study", Nordiska Afrikainstitutet, Discussion Paper 55.

Öniş, Ziya, and Fikret Senses (2005). "Rethinking the emerging post-Washington consensus", *Development and Change,* 36(2), 263–290.

OPIC (2017). *Annual Report on Development Impact Fiscal Year 2016,* Overseas Private Investment Corporation, available at www.opic.gov/sites/default/files/files/FY16_Annual_Development_Report_Final.pdf

Reality of Aid Report (2012). *Aid and Private Sector: Catalysing Poverty Reduction and Development?* Available at www.realityofaid.org/wp-content/uploads/2013/02/ROA_Report_2012-Aid_and_the_Private_Sector1-final.pdf

Richey, Lisa Ann, and Stefano Ponte (2014). "New actors and alliances in development", *Third World Quarterly*, 35(1), 1–21.

Ruckert, Arne (2006) "Towards an inclusive-neoliberal regime of development: From the Washington to the Post-Washington consensus", *Labour, Capital and Society / Travail, capital et société*, 34–67.

Shamir, Ronen (2008). "The age of responsibilization: On market-embedded morality", *Economy and Society*, 37(1), 1–19.

Stockhammer, Engelbert (2010). *Financialization and the Global Economy*, Political Economy Research Institute Working Paper, 242.

Tarp, Finn (ed.) (2000). *Foreign Aid and Development: Lessons Learnt and Directions for the Future*. London: Routledge.

van Waeyenberge, Elisa (2015). *The Private Turn in Development Finance*. FESSUD: Working Paper Series, 140.

van Waeyenberge, Elisa, Ben Fine, and Kate Bayliss (2011). "The World Bank, neo-liberalism and development research", in K. Bayliss, E. van Waeyenberge, and B. Fine (eds.), *The Political Economy of Development: The World Bank, Neoliberalism and Development Research* (pp. 3–25). London: Pluto.

Watts, Jonathan (2016). "Berta Cáceres, Honduran human rights and environment activist, murdered", *The Guardian*, March 4, available at www.theguardian.com/world/2016/mar/03/honduras-berta-caceres-murder-enivronment-activist-human-rights

White, Ben, Saturnino M. Borras Jr, Ruth Hall, Ian Scoones, and Wendy Wolford (2012). "The new enclosures: Critical perspectives on corporate land deals", *The Journal of Peasant Studies*, 39(3–4), 619–647.

YLE (2017). *Paradise Papers: Finnish Development Finance Agency Holds 8 Mil in Tax Haven Fund*, 6.11.2017, available at https://yle.fi/uutiset/osasto/news/paradise_papers_finnish_development_finance_agency_holds_8_mil_in_tax_haven_fund/9919282

Ylönen, Matti (2016). "Yksityinen käänne: kehitysrahoituksen uusi instrumentalismi", *Politiikka* 58(1), 69–79.

Zoomers, Annelies (2010). "Globalisation and the foreignisation of space: Seven processes driving the current global land grab", *The Journal of Peasant Studies*, 37(2), 429–447.

Part III

Global value chains, business, and development

6 Global value chains, development, and emerging economies[1]

Gary Gereffi

Global value chains and international competition

Globalization has given rise to a new era of international competition that is best understood by looking at the global organization of industries and the ways in which countries rise and fall within these industries (Gereffi 2011). Using core concepts like "governance" and "upgrading," global value chains (GVCs) highlight the ways in which new patterns of international trade, production, and employment shape prospects for development and competitiveness. GVC analysis documents the international expansion and geographic fragmentation of contemporary production networks and focuses primarily on the issues of industry (re)organization, coordination, governance, and power in the chain (Gereffi and Lee 2012). Its concern is to understand the causes and consequences of the organizational reconfiguration taking place in global industries.[2] The GVC approach also explores the broader institutional context of these linkages, including trade policy, regulation, and standards.

In the past two decades, profound changes in the structure of the global economy have reshaped global production and trade and have altered the organization of industries and national economies (Gereffi 2014). As supply chains became global in scope, more intermediate goods were traded across borders, and more imported parts and components were integrated into exports (Feenstra 1998; Krugman 1995). In 2009, world exports of intermediate goods exceeded the combined export values of final and capital goods for the first time, representing 51 percent of nonfuel merchandise exports (WTO and IDE-JETRO 2011, p. 81). Because of the unique ability of the GVC framework to show how international supply chains link economic activities at global, regional, national, and local levels within particular industries, international organizations such as the United Nations Conference on Trade and Development (UNCTAD), the Organisation for Economic Co-operation and Development (OECD), the World Bank, and the World Economic Forum, are utilizing the GVC approach to structure new donor initiatives and data collection programs on global trade and development (Cattaneo et al. 2010; OECD 2013; UNCTAD 2013; World Economic Forum 2013).

Emerging economies are playing significant and diverse roles in GVCs (Gereffi and Sturgeon 2013). During the 2000s, they became major exporters of intermediate and final manufactured goods (China, South Korea, and Mexico) and primary products (Brazil, Russia, and South Africa). However, market growth in emerging economies has also led to shifting end markets in GVCs, as more trade has occurred between developing economies (often referred to as South–South trade in the literature), especially since the 2008–2009 economic recession (Staritz et al. 2011, pp. 1–12). China has been the focal point of both trends: it is the world's leading exporter of manufactured goods and the world's largest importer of many raw materials, thereby contributing to the primary product export boom.

The rise of GVCs

In the 1970s and 1980s, US retailers and global brands joined manufacturers in the search for offshore suppliers of most categories of consumer goods. This led to a fundamental shift from what had been "producer-driven" commodity chains, which include capital- and technology-intensive industries like automobiles and electronics, to "buyer-driven" chains, which include a broad range of consumer products, like apparel, footwear, toys, and sporting goods (Gereffi 1994a). The geography of these chains expanded from regional production-sharing arrangements to full-fledged global supply chains, with a growing emphasis on East Asia (Gereffi 1996). In the 1960s and 1970s, large, vertically integrated transnational corporations dominated the landscape in most international industries (Vernon 1971), and the prevailing development strategy was import-substituting industrialization (ISI). Well established in Latin America, Eastern Europe, and parts of Asia since the 1950s, ISI was a state-led effort to build domestic industries by requiring foreign manufacturers to replace imports with locally made products, beginning with the assembly of final goods and working back to key components, in return for guaranteed market access (Gereffi 1994b). These domestic industrial policies were intended to nurture a set of full-blown national industries in key sectors that could significantly reduce, if not fully eliminate, imports from the industrialized nations (Baldwin 2011).

The death knell for ISI, especially in Latin America, came from the oil shock of the late 1970s and the severe debt crisis that followed it (Urquidi 1991). The ISI approach was creating large and persistent trade deficits because the manufacturing sectors in ISI countries were simply importing intermediate goods rather than reducing imports altogether, and escalating debt service payments led to a net outflow of foreign capital that crippled economic growth in the 1980s.

Under pressure from the International Monetary Fund (IMF) and the World Bank, many developing countries made the transition from ISI to export-oriented industrialization (EOI) during the 1980s (Gereffi and Wyman 1990; Haggard 1990). This new outward-oriented development model focused on exports to the global market by local firms, and it removed the state requirement that foreign firms had to produce for protected domestic markets, which mainly benefitted larger developing economies. There was an equally profound reorientation in the strategies of transnational corporations (Grunwald and Flamm 1985). The rapid expansion of industrial capabilities and export propensities in a diverse array of newly industrializing economies in Asia and Latin America encouraged transnational companies to accelerate their own efforts to outsource relatively standardized activities to lower-cost production locations worldwide. Precisely this change in the strategies of transnational companies enabled the transition from ISI to EOI in developing economies, and it corresponds with the shift from producer-driven to buyer-driven commodity chains at the level of global industries (Gereffi 1994a, pp. 97–100).

The rise of GVCs occurred in a period of falling trade barriers, the emergence of the World Trade Organization (WTO), and the policy prescriptions associated with the "Washington Consensus," that is, that governments had only to provide a strong set of "horizontal" policies (such as education, infrastructure, and macroeconomic stability) and be open to trade in order to succeed (Gore 2000). Of course, many observers noted that the dynamic emerging economies did much more than establish a set of economy-wide enabling institutions for growth. They frequently also targeted key domestic industries for support, under either ISI or EOI policies that tended to alternate over time in both Latin American and East Asian nations (Gereffi and Wyman 1990; Haggard 1990).

Today, industrial policy is on the upswing (Crespi et al. 2014; OECD Development Centre 2013; Salazar-Xirinachs et al. 2014). WTO accession often comes with allowances for selective industrial policies (e.g., trade promotion, local content rules, taxes, tariffs, and more indirect programs that drive local production) to remain in force for specified periods. Bilateral trade agreements can supersede such allowances under WTO rules, and a handful of relatively large and advanced emerging economies (such as those in the G20) that have more clout in the institutions of global governance are using them to create policy space to design and implement activist industrial policies.

The organization of global industries into GVCs in which production and trade networks are spread across many countries and regions has reinvigorated industrial policy debates (Baldwin 2011). There is not likely to be a return to the ISI and EOI policies of old, however. Domestic industries in both industrialized and developing countries no longer stand alone, competing mainly through arm's-length trade. Instead, they have become deeply intertwined through complex, overlapping business networks created through recurrent waves of foreign direct investment and global sourcing. Companies, localities, and entire countries have come to occupy specialized niches within GVCs. Because of this, today's industrial policies have a different character and generate different outcomes than before. Intentionally or not, governments currently engage in GVC-oriented industrialization when targeting key sectors for growth (Gereffi and Sturgeon 2013).

New governance structures reinforce the organizational consolidation occurring within GVCs and the geographic concentration associated with the growing prominence of emerging economies as key economic and political actors (Gereffi 2014, pp. 15–17). After 1989, the breakup of the Soviet Union, the opening of China to international investment and trade, and the liberalization of India brought a number of very large economies onto the global stage, known initially as BRICs (Brazil, Russia, India, and China).[3] This resulted in what Richard Freeman called "the great doubling" of the global labor pool from about 1.5 billion workers to 3 billion workers (Freeman 2008). The rise of the BRICs spurred the globalization process, as GVCs began to focus their investment and sourcing operations in big and dynamic emerging economies that offered abundant raw materials, large pools of low-wage workers, highly capable manufacturers, and rapidly growing domestic markets.

Faced with slow growth at home, large transnational lead firms in GVCs rushed to set up operations in BRIC countries, especially China, in an effort to carve out brand recognition and market share in rapidly expanding consumer markets and to cut costs on goods produced for export back to home markets (Naughton 1997; Ross 2006). In producer-driven chains, the lead firms that to a large degree defined the structure of these industries were largely global manufacturers like General Motors, Ford, IBM, and HP. In buyer-driven chains, the lead firms were a mix of retailers (like Walmart, JCPenney, and Carrefour), global marketers (such as Nike, Liz Claiborne, and Polo Ralph Lauren), and supermarkets and food multinationals (like Tesco, Sainsbury's, Kraft Foods, and Nestlé) (Gereffi 1994a). The lead firms in buyer-driven chains were particularly influential in the globalization process because they accelerated the process of "global sourcing" based on orders from developed countries, which relied almost entirely on production carried out in developing economies (Dicken 2011; Gereffi 1999).

As retailers and branded manufacturers in wealthy countries became more experienced with global sourcing, developing countries enhanced their infrastructure, and suppliers in those countries upgraded their capabilities in response to larger orders for more complex goods.[4] In the 1990s, many US- and Europe-based manufacturers quickly became huge global players, with facilities in scores of locations around the world (e.g., Siemens, Valeo, Flextronics) (Sturgeon 2002; Sturgeon and Lester 2004). A handful of elite East Asian suppliers (e.g., Pou Chen, Quanta, Foxconn) and trading companies (e.g., Li & Fung[5]) also took on more tasks for multinational affiliates and global buyers (Appelbaum 2008). These firms expanded production throughout Asia and, more recently, in Africa, Eastern Europe, and Latin America (Hernández et al. 2014; Morris et al. 2011; Pickles and Smith 2011; Smith et al. 2014).

Lead firms themselves are getting bigger and increasing their global market shares through mergers, acquisitions, and the decline of many rivals (Gereffi 2014, p. 16). This has been coupled with a growing recognition of the strategic vulnerabilities of global supply chains, linked to the risk of single-source relationships and the danger of lead firms losing access to critical inputs and raw material supplies (Lynn 2005). This is particularly apparent in the agri-foods sector, in which consumer goods firms such as Cadbury, Coca-Cola, and Unilever are expanding their direct involvement in the procurement and sustainability of the raw material sides of their value chains, such as those involving cocoa, coffee, and sugar (Barrientos and Asenso-Okyere 2008; Oxfam, 2011). This is also evident in the automobile and electronics industries, in which concern about the availability of raw materials such as lithium and coltan (Nathan and Sarkar 2011), respectively, are spurring greater engagement between GVC lead firms and host country suppliers and governments (Sturgeon and Kawakami 2011; Sturgeon and Van Biesebroeck 2011). These examples suggest that a number of GVCs, especially in natural resource–based industries, are giving greater attention to strategic collaboration as a counterweight to the long-term trend toward specialization and fragmentation of supply chains.

Governance and upgrading in GVCs

The GVC framework focuses on globally expanding supply chains and how value is created and captured therein (Gereffi and Lee 2012). By analyzing the full range of activities that firms and workers perform to bring a specific product from its conception to its end use and beyond, the GVC approach provides a holistic view of global industries from two contrasting vantage points: top-down and bottom-up (Gereffi and Fernandez-Stark 2011). The key concept for the top-down view is the "governance" of GVCs, which focuses mainly on lead firms and the organization of global industries, and the main concept for the bottom-up perspective is "upgrading," which focuses on the strategies used by countries, regions, and other economic stakeholders to maintain or improve their positions in the global economy (Gereffi 2011, pp. 39–40).

The concept of governance is the centerpiece of GVC analysis. It examines the ways in which corporate power can actively shape the distribution of profits and risk in an industry and the actors who exercise such power through their activities. Power in GVCs is exerted by lead firms. In the governance typology outlined in Figure 6.1, the market and hierarchy poles of the GVC governance continuum are driven by price and ownership within vertically integrated firms, respectively. The remaining three categories are stable forms of network governance (modular, relational, and captive), in which different kinds of GVC lead firms control to a large degree the ways in which global supply chains operate and the main winners and losers within these chains (Gereffi et al. 2005).

Although governance issues have attracted a good deal of attention among GVC scholars, the research on economic upgrading has been at least as important because many of the people who use the GVC framework have a very strong development focus (Gereffi 2018). "Economic upgrading" is defined as the process by which economic actors – firms and workers – move from low-value to relatively high-value activities in GVCs (Gereffi 2005, p. 171). The challenge of economic upgrading in GVCs is to identify the conditions under which developing and developed countries and firms can "climb the value chain" from basic assembly activities using low-cost and unskilled labor to more

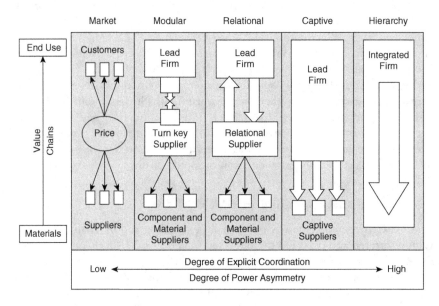

Figure 6.1 Five types of global value chain governance

advanced forms of "full package" supply and integrated manufacturing (Humphrey and Schmitz 2002).

Connecting GVCs to economic development

GVCs matter for economic development in several ways because the ability of countries to prosper depends on their participation in the global economy, which is largely a story about their role in GVCs (Gereffi and Lee 2012). Connecting countries to GVCs involves both investment and trade, which rely heavily on efficient global supply chains in order to contribute to growth.[6] A key factor in such efficiency is infrastructure development, which enables global trade though the construction and improvement of the physical facilities that link national economies: ports and canals, airports, roads, and a wide range of information and communication technologies (Dicken 2011, pp. 400–406; WTO and IDE-JETRO 2011, pp. 28, 30). Improving trade flows at the border can be enhanced by infrastructure investments inside the border (i.e., in roads and facilities that connect rural regions and small firms to larger domestic markets), and also by investments beyond the border, especially in infrastructure facilities that connect a country to its nearby neighbors in regional supply chains (Mayer and Milberg 2013). These regional markets are often underappreciated because of the importance given to developed country markets in the 1990s and early 2000s, but in the current era, regional value chains are becoming a new focus for investment planning by development banks and international organizations (Gereffi and Lee 2012, pp. 28–29).

GVC studies are pervasive in academic publications that examine a wide range of global industries.[7] The framework has also been adopted by many of the most important international organizations concerned with economic development, such as the WTO, UNCTAD, the OECD, the World Bank, and the World Economic Forum (Gereffi 2019).[8] The international institutions that have provided the underpinning for the Washington Consensus (such as the World Bank, the IMF, and the WTO) and major bilateral donors (such as the US Agency for International Development [USAID] and the UK's Department for International Development [DFID]) have embraced new models of development thinking, with an emphasis on sectoral analysis that links macro issues such as international trade and investment more closely with the micro development issues of employment, gender dynamics, and sustainable livelihoods (M4P 2008; Milberg and Winkler 2013; Staritz and Reis 2013). In addition, new alliances have emerged among diverse UN and other international agencies (such as the World Bank and the International Labour Organization [ILO]) to promote joint research agendas that explore the links between economic and social upgrading, explicitly using the GVC framework (Barrientos et al. 2011; Cattaneo et al. 2010; Rossi et al. 2014).

This is an area in which GVC analysis and supply chain management research can be mutually beneficial. Sophisticated value chain data disaggregated by business functions can complement existing country-level trade statistics and industry-level input–output data, providing a clear picture of who is gaining and losing in GVCs (Sturgeon and Gereffi 2009). When combined with data on employment, they will greatly advance our understanding of both economic and social development opportunities in the global economy.

Today virtually all major bilateral and multilateral donor agencies use value chain analysis as an instrument of private-sector development (Gereffi 2014). According to Altenburg (2007), there are two principal reasons for the increasing popularity of the GVC approach within the international donor community since the end of the 1990s: first, the accumulating evidence of a link between economic growth driven by the private sector and poverty reduction; and second, the fact that global integration of trade and production through GVCs transmits the pressures of global competition to domestic markets in developing economies, leaving less space for local firms to design, produce, and market on their own. Given the pervasiveness of GVCs, the question for many is not *if*, but *how*, to integrate into value chains in a balanced way that addresses both competitiveness and equity issues and that allows for the incorporation of a growing proportion of the workforce while increasing productivity and output.

There is no simple way to connect GVC analysis to private-sector development, given that the firms in a value chain range from transnational corporations to microenterprises, and the institutional context and geographic scope of value chains vary enormously. Generally, however, donor interventions have four objectives: strengthening the weakest link to address potential bottlenecks; improving flows of knowledge and resources to make all firms in the chain more productive; working on specific links between firms to improve efficiency; and creating new or alternative links in the chain to promote diversified outcomes (Humphrey and Navas-Alemán 2010).

Much of this research and theoretical work has focused on how lead firms in specific GVCs have driven this process in various ways. Decisions about outsourcing and offshoring are, after all, strategic decisions made by managers. But such decisions are not made in a vacuum. The policies and programs of countries and multilateral institutions set the context for corporate decision making, and there has been an evolution in the form and effects of industrial policy along with the evolution of the business networks that comprise GVCs.

Today the organization of the global economy is entering a new phase – what some have referred to as a "major inflection point" (Fung 2011) – that could have dramatic implications for firms and workers in emerging and industrialized countries. As world trade rebounds from the 2008–2009 economic crisis, emerging economies have become a major engine of growth.

Developing economies in GVCs: upgrading experiences in diverse sectors

Many examples could be provided to illustrate how developing countries are participating in GVCs. For purposes of this chapter, we will focus on three aspects of GVCs particularly relevant to economic upgrading and inclusive development goals: (1) building export capabilities – the cases of coffee, apparel, and automobiles; (2) leveraging services to build knowledge capabilities and move to high-value niches in GVCs – the cases of a traceability system for the cattle industry in Uruguay and environmental services in Costa Rica; and (3) the role of public–private partnerships to narrow the human capital gap in India and Latin America and to develop the aerospace industry in Mexico.

Promoting growth and upgrading in export-oriented GVCs

The coffee value chain in Central America and East Africa. The world coffee market is large, with retail sales of US$70 billion and demand growing steadily at about 2.5 percent annually.[9] The biggest global producers are Brazil and Vietnam, followed by Colombia and Indonesia. The United States is the largest consumer market, spending an estimated $30 billion in 2009. Within the coffee GVC, there are important quality distinctions that translate into significant price variations for coffee producers, as well as distinct market segments for large branded manufacturers in the coffee sector. The two main varieties of coffee are arabica (higher quality) and robusta (lower quality). These correspond to segmentation at the retail end of the GVC: there is a commercial-grade segment (e.g., Folgers), which sells large volumes at relatively low prices, and a specialty or high/quality gourmet segment (e.g., Starbucks, Illy coffee), which sells in niche markets and commands premium prices. Within the United States, the specialty coffee market has grown rapidly, with a number of boutique and super-high-grade coffees, and this offers great potential for growth by developing country coffee producers (Ponte 2002).

Central America is recognized as one of the world's leading specialty coffee producers. In most countries of the region, over half of their production is classified as premium coffee (i.e., above commercial grade). Guatemala and Honduras are perhaps the best established Central America coffee suppliers in global markets, with Nicaragua and Panama rapidly gaining market share in the specialty coffee segment. In 2010, Guatemala's coffee exports were valued at $718 million, involving more than 171,000 producers; Nicaragua exported $351 million of coffee produced by nearly 90,000 growers (World Bank 2012, p. 19). Whereas specialty coffee accounted for just 20 percent of Guatemala's coffee exports in 1980s, it now accounts for over 80 percent.

Most specialty coffee in Central America comes from small producers, and the challenge is how to provide them with a sustainable niche in the specialty coffee GVC. The potential economic, social, and environmental upgrading gains of specialty coffee are not in question. Smallholders growing for the specialty market can sell their coffee at premiums significantly higher than certified coffee and receive a larger share of the retail price. For example, compared to the 2014 minimum price established for fair trade, organic certified coffee, $1.90 per pound, the average price specialty coffee growers received during the first nine months of 2014 was $2.72, and as high as $3.60 (Farmers to 40 2014). Consumers tend to prefer single-origin coffee with an emphasis on new and unique varietals[10] and source authenticity (like premium wine), and there is a high value attached to socially and environmentally sustainably grown coffee as well.

There are various difficulties, however, in capturing these price premiums within Central America. The specialty coffee value chain is typically dominated by a few large exporters, along with roasters who are located near the final consumers in North America, Europe, and increasingly East Asia. Infrastructure investments are required to build the wet processing plants to assure the quality of premium coffee. For smallholders, it is usually not economical to have washing stations on the farm, and thus they are built at the cooperative level or by private firms.[11] Given infrastructure needs and the relatively high cost of inputs (e.g., fertilizer), inadequate short-term financing for Central American smallholders is a major obstacle in the specialty coffee segment. In addition, given the importance of quality control, branding, and coordination across the chain, the creation of strong national or regional coffee associations could provide a major boost to export producers in Central America.

The coffee value chain is considered an important sector for economic upgrading of smallholder farmers in other regions of the world, including South America, Asia, and sub-Saharan Africa (Daviron and Ponte 2005; Talbot 2004). Within East Africa, coffee represents a significant share of agricultural exports in Ethiopia, Kenya, Uganda, Rwanda, Tanzania, and Burundi. Despite nearly ideal growing conditions for the arabica coffee needed to produce specialty coffee, production in the Rwandan coffee sector declined sharply in the 2000s. Struggling to regain its economic growth after the 1994 Rwandan genocide, many of Rwanda's smallholders had abandoned coffee production, leaving about 400,000 still committed to the sector in 2002 (Abdulsamad et al. 2015, p. 31).

In 2000, USAID initiated several projects to help smallholder coffee growers in Rwanda improve the quality of their coffee to meet specialty status, which substantially increased shareholder revenues. To ensure the sustainability of these gains, USAID implemented a development alliance made up of US and Rwandan universities, enterprises, and nongovernmental organizations (NGOs), which over a 10-year period proved highly successful.[12] The positive outcomes for smallholders required the establishment of cooperatives and coffee washing stations to create a local processing infrastructure that permitted smallholders to partner with specialty roasters in the coffee value chain.[13] This established some balance of power between smallholders and large international coffee buyers and allowed specialty roasters to introduce the prestigious Cup of Excellence coffee competition to Rwanda in 2008, the first such competition ever held in Africa (Abdulsamad et al. 2015, p, 36). As in Central America, Rwandan smallholders growing coffee for the specialty market sold their coffee at higher price premiums than certified coffee and for a larger share of the retail price, without having to pursue a costly certification process (Abdulsamad et al. 2015, p. 39–40).

Nicaragua, Lesotho, and Swaziland in the apparel manufacturing global value chain.

The Nicaraguan apparel industry's exports nearly doubled from US$716 million in 2005 to $1.36 billion in 2011 (Bair and Gereffi 2014, p. 256). Nicaragua mainly participates in the low-value "cut-make-trim" stage of the apparel value chain (see Figure 6.2). Leveraging the country's competitive wage advantage, the industry employed more than 51,300 people in 2010[14] (Portocarrero

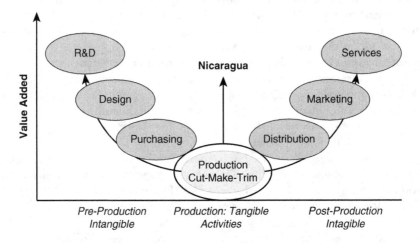

Figure 6.2 Curve of value-added stages in the apparel global value chain: Nicaragua

Lacayo and Victoria 2010). In 2009, 89 percent of Nicaraguan apparel exports were destined for the United States. The country is still considered a small regional supplier, but since 2004 it has steadily gained US market share in certain segments such as woven pants and cotton shirts as a result of its preferential trade status within the Dominican Republic–Central American Free Trade Agreement (Bair and Gereffi 2014). Apparel manufacturers in Nicaragua focus on trousers, mainly denim jeans and twill pants, as well as t-shirts.

The industry consists of a large proportion of foreign-owned firms, with very few locally owned companies. Among the foreign firms, Korean and US ownership dominates, with the remainder coming from El Salvador, Honduras, Mexico, and Taiwan. A significant proportion of these firms are part of larger global or regional networks; particularly in Central America, this structure allows global firms to provide full-package services for their clients by leveraging the interactions of multiple country operations. Knit-based firms sell to buyers such as Walmart, Target, and Ralph Lauren. Woven apparel firms are more regionally focused, with operations in neighboring countries such as Guatemala, Honduras, and Mexico, and leading buyers include Levi Strauss, Cintas, and Kohl's.

Between 2005 and 2010, the volume of Nicaragua's apparel exports grew by 8.6 percent, but despite this increase, Nicaragua has had limited success in moving up the apparel value chain and mainly competes through low-cost apparel assembly. The country's apparel exporters have not achieved significant product upgrading; the value of exports only increased by 4.5 percent (ProNicaragua 2010). Rather, this period was characterized by an increase in the production of t-shirts and knitwear, which are low-value-added product segments. Prior to the economic crisis, the country had seen increases in the value of its exports in woven trousers, but due to the economic slowdown in the United States, 2009 exports fell back to their 2006 levels.

Nicaragua remains vulnerable in terms of economic upgrading because its apparel exports are dependent on US trade policy (specifically, the Tariff Preference Level, or TPL, exception offered to Nicaragua that allowed it to import textiles from East Asia). However, the country has shown advances in social upgrading, due in large part to the efforts of the tripartite National Free Trade Zones Commission to join the interests of workers, the private sector, and government. It also has become part of the Better Work program by the ILO (Bair and Gereffi 2014).

The trade-policy dependency of Nicaragua and other Central America Free Trade Agreement (CAFTA) countries on the US market is paralleled by the similar dynamics found in sub-Saharan Africa's apparel-exporting economies that are covered by the African Growth and Recovery Act (AGOA), such as Lesotho and Swaziland (Morris et al. 2011). As with Nicaragua, apparel exports by Lesotho and Swaziland are concentrated on the US market, which absorbs over 98 percent of clothing exports from both countries. However, the phase-out of the Multi-Fibre Arrangement (MFA) in 2004, which ended the apparel quota system, and the 2008–2009 global economic crisis prompted a sharp drop in clothing exports by both countries to the United States. Many of the Taiwanese firms that concentrated on supplying the US market left in the wake of the crisis.

However, sub-Saharan Africa had a different dynamic that buffered Lesotho and Swaziland from the global economic recession. A new type of investor – South African clothing manufacturers – moved into Lesotho and Swaziland not as a production base to take advantage of AGOA preferences for access to the US market, but rather because of their lower labor costs in comparison to South Africa as a new export market. The South African Customs Union provides duty-free access for apparel produced in member countries (which include Lesotho and Swaziland), which allows South African retailers to maintain low prices and a growing market share (Morris et al. 2011, p. 98). Furthermore, South African–owned firms are far more likely than their Taiwanese counterparts to utilize local production, supervisory, and management skills in their apparel operations in Lesotho and Swaziland, thus promoting additional upgrading prospects in these countries. Sustaining these advantages, however, would require more active government policies to incentivize added skill development within local clothing manufacturers in both countries (Morris et al. 2011, pp. 115–117)

Automobiles in Mexico and Brazil.

The automobile industry typifies the sharp contrast in patterns of GVC participation found within Latin America's manufacturing sector.[15] Beginning in the 1980s and accelerated by Mexico's entry into the North American Free Trade Agreement (NAFTA) in 1994, Mexico shifted from an ISI strategy to an export-oriented model in its automotive sector, which relied on low-cost Mexican workers and extensive foreign direct investment (FDI) from the United States, Europe, and Japan interested in establishing a strong network of car makers and auto parts suppliers that could turn Mexico into a world-class export hub, focused on sales to the US market. On the basis of its strategic proximity to the United States and its trade agreements with over 40 countries, Mexico has become one of the top automotive export countries in the world. Although this has created significant job opportunities, the relatively low level of wages has not kept pace with Mexico's growing productivity, and the industry still has relatively weak linkages with local suppliers.

The model of GVC participation in Brazil's automotive sector is quite different. The Brazilian strategy is to emphasize sales to its large internal market and regional connections with its MERCOSUR partners (mainly Argentina, but also Paraguay, Uruguay, and Venezuela), using high tariffs on automotive products imported from outside of MERCOSUR to increase the technological capabilities of Brazilian affiliates of foreign car makers. In addition, Brazil has introduced various incentives for exports, higher levels of local content, and investment in new plants in the country.

Both Brazil and Mexico attract significant amounts of FDI into the automotive sector.[16] However, the role played by transnational corporations (TNCs) is different. In Brazil the exports are lower, but local suppliers are more fully integrated into the operations of the TNCs, with higher levels of local innovation and research and development (R&D) capabilities. In Mexico, the range of activities in the automotive value chain is more diverse because it supplies the needs of Japanese, German, and American auto makers in both Mexico and the US market. The automotive GVC has created more jobs in Mexico, but higher skill levels and technological capabilities in Brazil. The current development policies in each country related to autos are intended to fill in the gaps left by their current strategies.

Leveraging local knowledge to add value in resource-based GVCs

Creating knowledge: a traceability system for the cattle industry in Uruguay.

With over 12 million head of cattle in Uruguay, cows outnumber people by four to one and beef is Uruguay's leading export. In 2010, Uruguay exported U$1.1 billion in bovine products (UNComtrade 2012). The global beef industry, however, is extremely vulnerable to health and food safety problems. Uruguay has not been immune to these difficulties. A 2000 outbreak of foot-and-mouth disease led to a multiyear ban on exports to the United States and the European Union, as well as numerous other countries, including Chile, Israel, and South Korea. In order to mitigate the impact of these challenges on key export revenues, Uruguay embarked on the development of a sophisticated bovine traceability system, which would allow the country to quickly and efficiently track the source of and contain potential problems, and maintain consumer and regulatory confidence of their products in the developed world.

The livestock traceability system was developed through a collaborative multistakeholder initiative bringing together producers, local governments, transport personnel, the private sector, information technology companies, and the central government (the Ministry of Agriculture, in particular). Today, this is the only system in the world with real-time monitoring of 100 percent of the national cattle herd. A chip implanted in each cow's ear at birth allows the system to keep centralized and accurate information regarding the animal from birth through to sales and distribution points. Approximately 2.5 million new animals are registered on an annual basis (Crescionini 2012; SONDA 2012).

Uruguay has a great opportunity to capitalize on its knowledge and experiences, exporting these services to other countries that face similar issues. Indeed, Colombia has already begun to roll out this information system for its cattle herd. This means that Uruguay can participate in different segments of the cattle value chain. In addition to continued beef exports, Uruguay now has the potential to export advanced services not only for the beef industry but the broader livestock sector as well. In the face of rising concerns in meeting increasingly strict global food safety standards, this is a tremendous competitive advantage for the country.

Environmental services offshoring: an opportunity for Costa Rica.

Costa Rica is recognized worldwide for its unique approach to environmental protection and is a leader in the field among both developing and developed countries alike. As a result of conservation incentives put in place in the 1980s, today tropical forest covers more than half of the country. Illegal farming is down to just 15 percent, and farmers are paid to manage and protect their natural surroundings (Conservation International 2012). To date, however, this know-how has been used principally to support domestic priorities. Experts work for national NGOs and foundations, and the country has not yet seized the opportunity to commercialize the significant expertise it has built over many years. With the rising prominence of climate change on the global development agenda, there is significant demand for services in these areas.

Due to its critical mass of qualified human capital to sustain this niche (Chassot 2012; Rodriguez 2012), Costa Rica is in an excellent position to export high-demand environmental services, such as natural resources management, environmental impact studies, threatened and endangered species assessments, protected areas evaluations, and environmental education and training, among many others. More than 18 other countries, including China, have consulted Costa Rica to learn about its conservation policies (Conservation International 2012). As with many developing countries, however, limited knowledge of potential markets and undeveloped entrepreneurship skills undermine the potential for translating these consulting opportunities into profitable service exports (Chassot 2012). The promotion of this industry will require the internationalization of local firms, on one hand, and the attraction of foreign environmental firms, on the other, to use Costa Rica as a platform to export environmental services. Linking these two types of firms will be critical for the development of this niche activity.

Skills for upgrading

Public–private partnerships to narrow the human capital gap in India and Latin America.

National "finishing schools" represent a promising tool to narrow the gap between the human capital needs of GVCs and the skills supplied by national education systems. The finishing school model has been tested in India and the Philippines, and recently applied in Latin America with the support of the Inter-American Development Bank (IDB). These schools help recent graduates and workers develop high-demand skills, making them more employable. In turn, by increasing workforce employability, finishing schools can help a country improve its position in the value chain.

Finishing schools build upon the fundamental skills acquired in academic institutions, filling in specific gaps in knowledge and soft skills. These gaps are determined by the skill sets needed by a particular industry, as compared with the workforce's current skills. In India, the most effective finishing schools were those that collaborated with companies to identify the desired skill sets and match trainings to these gaps (Tholons 2012). In the global services industry, these skills often include technical (IT) skills, English abilities, and soft skills such as relational skills, confidence, and presentation skills. Programs at finishing schools that train workers for careers in IT services can run from five weeks to up to one year in duration (Tholons 2012, p. 14). Often, these schools target youths who have recently graduated from high school or university, but they can also play a role in retraining adult workers (IDB 2012).

Public–private partnerships are central to creating effective financing and governance mechanisms to support finishing school programs in developing countries. Although in India, finishing schools may be run by either the government or a private institution, in Latin America there is increasing recognition that collaborative policies and institutions provide the most effective support to finishing school initiatives.[17] The public–private model offers two key advantages: (1) such partnerships create opportunities for co-financing, reducing the cost burden borne by any one sector; and (2) the content of the programs is determined by the employers themselves, ensuring that the skills developed match industry needs (IDB 2012). Thus, the finishing school model recognizes the role of all stakeholders, "the State, the academe, and industry – in shaping the capabilities of the labor pool towards in delivering information technology and business process outsourcing services" (Tholons 2012, p. 14).

The aerospace industry in Querétaro, Mexico.[18]

The aerospace industry in Querétaro has grown rapidly. Bombardier – one of the leading companies in the sector, based in Canada – arrived in the area in 2006, marking the entry of Querétaro into the aerospace GVC. The French group Safran and Spanish airframe manufacturer Aernnova quickly followed suit, establishing operations in 2007. Under the leadership of the Secretariat for Sustainable Development, Querétaro's aerospace cluster has since become one of the four leading locations in Mexico. By 2012, there were over 30 foreign firms operating in the state, with projected employment of over 6,000, about 20 percent of the country's aerospace workforce. Mexico's exports in the sector had reached US$4.5 billion by 2011, up from US$1.3 billion in 2004.

Growth was supported by a clear commitment to the development of the industry by the state government, including the creation of the National Aeronautics University of Querétaro (UNAQ) in 2007, which housed several technical programs developed in public–private initiatives and created the first aerospace engineering program in the country. State investments in UNAQ amounted to US$21 million by 2009. In addition to training teaching staff in both Canada and Spain, UNAQ drew teachers from aerospace firms working in the region. By 2012, there were 488 technical and professional students at UNAQ. UNAQ's contributions to human capital development in the state added to an already strong engineering training base. In 2009, engineering graduates accounted for 41 percent of undergraduate degrees, and 65 percent of master's degree programs available in the state were in engineering fields (Casalet et al. 2011).

Additionally, in 2007 an aircraft maintenance program was established in Querétaro by the National Mexican Technical Training Institute, which graduates 90 technicians annually. This has supported the ongoing development of the state's maintenance and repair operations capacity and helped capture large investments, including the 2012 Delta-Aeromexico deal to establish a US$50 million maintenance, repair, and overhaul (MRO) facility in Querétaro with seven production lines to serve both airlines.

The heterogeneity of emerging economies and their export profiles

Focusing on a set of seven contemporary emerging economies – China, India, Brazil, Mexico, Russia, South Korea, and South Africa – will give a broader sense of the role of GVCs and development policies in the developing world. They are all centrally involved in distinct types of GVCs in agriculture, extractive industries (mining, oil, and gas), manufacturing, and services (Gereffi and Sturgeon 2013). Together, these seven emerging economies account for 45 percent of the world's population, 25 percent of global exports, and 24 percent of gross domestic product (GDP) in 2013, and their GDP growth rates are substantially higher than the world average (3.2 percent versus 2.2 percent) (see Table 6.1). The economic and social characteristics of these countries are quite diverse, however. The specific roles of these countries in the global economy vary according to their openness to trade and foreign investment; their endowments of natural, human, and technological resources; their geopolitical relationships to the world's most powerful countries; and the characteristics of their immediate neighbors.

As GVCs have expanded in scope and complexity, emerging economies have clearly benefitted, surging ahead of the advanced industrial countries in terms of export performance. Between 1995 and 2007, the global export market shares of the United States and Japan fell by 3.8 percent and 3.7 percent, respectively, whereas China more than doubled its market share from 4 percent in 1995 to 10.1 percent in 2007, making it the world's export leader (ahead of Germany, the United States, and Japan). South Korea, Mexico, Turkey, South Africa, and the former transition countries in central Europe also increased their export market shares during this period. Even more surprising, emerging economies made their most significant gains in high- and medium-technology industries, which previously were the stronghold of OECD countries. This phenomenon was mainly driven by processing exports from China, whose share of high-technology exports soared by 13.5 percent in the period 1995–2007, moving it ahead of the United States as the world's largest exporter of electronics (Beltramello et al. 2012, pp. 9–10).

Although collectively these seven nations have considerable economic clout, China is the global pacesetter of the group. Although China and India are the most populous countries in the world, with 1.36 and 1.25 billion inhabitants, respectively, China is the undisputed export leader, with $2.2 trillion in exports in 2013. China's export total is greater than that of Russia, South Korea, India, Brazil, Mexico, and South Africa *combined* ($2.14 trillion), and its GDP has grown by over 9 percent per year for over 30 years. It is now the second-largest

Table 6.1 Seven selected emerging economies in comparative perspective, 2013

Country	Population (Millions)[1]	Exports ($Billions)[2]	GDP ($Billions)[1]	GDP/ capita (USD)[1]	GDP/ capita (PPP)[1]	GDP growth YoY (%)[1]	Percent of GDP[3]		
							Agriculture	Industry	Services
China	1,357	$2,209	$9,240	$6,807	$11,906	7.7	10	44	46
South Korea	50	$560	$1,305	$25,977	$33,140	3.0	3	39	58
Russia	143	$527	$2,096	$14,611	$24,114	1.3	4	38	58
Mexico	122	$380	$1,261	$10,307	$16,463	1.1	4	36	60
India	1,252	$337	$1,877	$1,498	$5,412	5.0	17	26	57
Brazil	200	$242	$2,246	$11,208	$15,038	2.5	6	26	68
South Africa	53	$95	$351	$6,618	$12,507	1.9	3	29	68
Total or Avg.	3,177	$4,350	$18,376	$11,004	$16,940	3.2	7	34	59
World Total	7,125	$17,635	$75,593	$10,610	$14,397	2.2			
% of World Total	45%	25%	24%	104%	118%	146%			

Sources: World Bank: http://data.worldbank.org; United Nations Comtrade, International Trade Center.

Notes:

(1) World Bank, World Development Indicators: http://data.worldbank.org

(2) UN Comtrade, International Trade Center: http://comtrade.un.org/

(3) CIA World Factbook, Country Profiles: www.cia.gov/library/publications/the-world-factbook/

Table 6.2 Export profiles of emerging economies, 2000–2013

	Share of exports by sector in 2013*					Total Export Value ($ Billions)	Change in total export value, 2000–2013	Percentage point change in share of exports by sector, 2000–2013				
	Primary Products	Resource Based	Low-Tech	Medium-Tech	High-Tech			Primary Products	Resource Based	Low-Tech	Medium-Tech	High-Tech
China	3%	8%	32%	23%	34%	2,209	786%	–4	0	–10	4	11
South Korea	2%	17%	9%	43%	28%	560	226%	0	6	–8	10	–8
Russia	55%	29%	2%	8%	2%	527	412%	6	10	–3	–3	–2
Mexico	16%	8%	9%	42%	22%	380	129%	3	3	–6	4	–6
India	14%	38%	20%	18%	8%	337	702%	0	9	–19	7	3
Brazil	33%	33%	5%	21%	4%	242	340%	13	6	–7	–4	–8
South Africa	25%	31%	6%	27%	3%	95	265%	8	1	–3	1	–1

Legend: $x \leq -6$ | $-5 \leq x \leq 0$ | $0 \leq x \leq 9$ | $x \geq 10$

*Exports totals do not include uncategorized exports, and therefore they may not equal 100%.

Sources: United Nations Comtrade, SITC Rev. 2.

economy in the world (after only the United States) and has overtaken Germany as the world's largest exporter (Beltramello et al. 2012, p. 9). Notwithstanding its rapid economic growth, however, its GDP per capita in US dollars was the third lowest among these emerging economies in 2013 ($6,807), well ahead of India ($1,498) and a little larger than South Africa ($6,618), but only 60 percent that of Brazil ($11,208), less than half the per capita income of Russia ($14,611), and just over one-quarter that of South Korea ($25,977). On average, the GDP per capita of these seven emerging economies was about 18 percent above the world average in 2013, using purchasing power parity (PPP) indicators.

The export profiles of these emerging economies indicate the roles that they play in GVCs. Using a classification scheme that categorizes traded goods according to primary products plus four types of manufactured exports (resource-based, low-tech, medium-tech, and high-tech) (Lall 2000), Table 6.2 highlights some of the differences between the export profiles of these countries in 2013. Three of the emerging economies are heavily oriented toward primary product or resource-based exports: Russia (84 percent), Brazil (66 percent), and South Africa (56 percent). Over half of India's exports are resource oriented, and another 20 percent are low-tech (primarily apparel products) manufactured goods.[19] China, South Korea, and Mexico, by contrast, are heavily involved in manufacturing GVCs. About 90 percent of China's exports are manufactured goods, while a preponderance of the exports of South Korea (71 percent) and Mexico (64 percent) are medium-tech (automotive, machinery) and high-tech (mainly electronics) exports.

China's export success has been a particular challenge for Latin America's two largest economies, Brazil and Mexico. In 2010, China was Brazil's largest trading partner, accounting for about 15 percent of Brazil's exports and imports. Between 2000 and 2010, Brazil's exports to China increased almost 30-fold, and since 2002, imports have grown 16-fold. Although the Lula administration in Brazil was keen to develop a strong economic partnership with China, concern has arisen due to both the composition of Brazil's exports to China (the "primarization" of Brazilian exports) and their concentration in a relatively small number of products and exporting firms. About 70 percent of Brazil's global exports in 2011 were primary products or resource-based manufactures. Furthermore, these two categories accounted for just over 60 percent of Brazilian exports to countries other than China in 2009, compared to almost 90 percent to China (Sturgeon et al. 2013, pp. 29–30). Brazil's exports to China are concentrated in a very limited number of products, with iron ore and soybeans alone accounting for over two-thirds of the total in 2009.[20]

What is particularly notable about Brazil's trading relationship with China is that it is skewed to the export of products (both primary commodities and manufactured goods) with a very low level of processing, whereas imports tend to be technology intensive components and machinery. The soybean value chain is a good example of the former. About 95 percent of Brazil's soybean exports to China in 2009 were unprocessed beans. In contrast, there were virtually no exports of soybean meal, flour, or oil to China. In order to pursue its strategy of promoting the Chinese soybean processing industry, China imposed a tariff of 9 percent on soybean oil imports, whereas the tariff on unprocessed soybean imports was only 3 percent. More processed imported soybean products also paid a higher value-added tax rate in China than unprocessed beans. This same protectionist policy of tariff and nontariff barriers imposed by the Chinese government to protect its domestic producers was applied to a range of other primary and processed intermediate products from Brazil, including leather, iron and steel, and pulp and paper (Jenkins 2012, pp. 28–29).

On the import side, Brazil has also been influenced by China's structure of international trade. In 1996, low-technology products accounted for 40 percent of Brazil's imports from China, whereas high-technology products accounted for 25 percent. By 2009, the pattern was nearly reversed: high-technology products were 41 percent of the total, and low-technology products were 21 percent. If we look at this trend in terms of the end use of imports, consumer goods imports from China to Brazil fell from 44 percent to 16 percent between 1996 and 2009, whereas the imports of capital goods and their parts doubled (Jenkins 2012, pp. 29–31). Thus, Brazil has been subordinated to occupy the lowest rungs of the value-added ladder in its trade with China in recent decades, which poses long-term structural imbalances for Brazil if the situation does not change.

From a GVC perspective, which focuses on the location of value added in global production systems, high-technology imports from Mainland China are most often driven by the products and strategies of firms based in OECD countries, along with their business partners (e.g., trading companies, contract manufacturers, and component producers) based elsewhere in the world, especially Taiwan, Hong Kong, and Singapore. Thus, the historic reliance of Brazil on the "Global North" for technology-intensive products has in essence remained, even as China's importance as a trading partner has risen. In other words, China has become a major conduit for technology from the Global North.

Notwithstanding the unprecedented momentum of China's rise in the global economy, these competitiveness problems for Brazil can be ameliorated, or even reversed. Mexico, which is Latin America's second-largest economy, appears to be in the midst of a remarkable turnaround, based on a little publicized manufacturing revolution that is allowing the country to become a credible competitor to China, after losing US market share to China for more than a decade (Gereffi 2009). Mexico currently exports more manufactured products than the rest of Latin America combined, and it has begun to diversify its export profile, with exports to the United States falling from 90 percent of total exports a decade ago to less than 80 percent today.

The main elements of Mexico's success include a very high degree of trade openness: it has free trade agreements with 44 countries, which is more than twice as many as China and four times more than Brazil. Rising wages and fuel prices have made it increasingly expensive to export from China to the US market. Mexico's wages, which used to be nearly four times higher than China's a decade ago, are just 29 percent higher today. Also, although Mexico still has an abundance of cheap labor (more than half of its population of 112 million is under 29), its workers are also becoming more skilled, with growing proportions of graduates in engineering, architecture, and other professions (Thomson 2012). Furthermore, Mexico's geographic proximity to the United States allows shorter supply chains, lower transport costs for bulky items, and quicker delivery times in the context of increasingly popular "fast fashion," "just in time," and other "rapid response" business models. However, this turnaround is not based on the success of domestic firms. As with China, Mexico is a platform for multinational enterprises seeking to locate labor-intensive aspects of GVCs (including both manual and knowledge work) in a country that is both low cost and close to the huge US market.

The role of industrial policies in GVCs

Industrial policies that take the new realities of GVCs into account include traditional measures to regulate links to the global economy, especially the regulation of trade, FDI, and the exchange rates used in ISI and EOI policies that sought to elevate the position of "national champions" (Salazar-Xirinachs et al. 2014). Today, GVC-oriented industrial policy focuses to a greater extent than in the past on the intersection of global and local actors, and it takes the interests, power, and reach of lead firms and global suppliers into account, accepts international (and increasingly regional) business networks as the appropriate field of play, and responds to pressures from international NGOs (Crespi et al. 2014; OECD Development Center 2013).

There are three distinguishable types of industrial policies: "horizontal" policies that affect the entire national economy, "selective" (or "vertical") industrial policies targeted at particular industries or sectors, and GVC-oriented industrial policies that leverage international supply chain linkages or dynamics to improve a country's role in global or regional value chains (Gereffi and Sturgeon 2013, pp. 342–343). "Horizontal" policies focus on the basic building blocks of competitive national economies, such as education, health, infrastructure, and R&D expenditures. Although these areas all provide attractive opportunities for private investors, the public sector typically plays a role in providing widespread access to these factors as public goods. Domestic industrial policies tend to be "selective" or "vertical" because they are associated with prioritizing particular industries or activities at the national level. GVC-oriented industrial policies go beyond the domestic economic focus of ISI-style policy regimes, which try to re-create entire supply chains within a national territory. Given the expansion of international production networks associated with GVCs, this new type of industrial policy explicitly utilizes extraterritorial linkages that affect a country's positioning in global or regional value chains.

Several major features highlight the distinctive nature of GVC-oriented industrial policies (Gereffi and Sturgeon 2013, pp. 353–354). One is the role of global suppliers. GVC-oriented industrial policies require an increasingly sophisticated understanding of the global-scale patterns of industrial organization that have come to the fore in GVCs since at least the 1990s. Lead firms are relying on global suppliers and intermediaries for an array of processes, specialized inputs, and services, and demanding that their most important suppliers have a global presence. Hence suppliers, not lead firms, are making many of the new investments that developing countries are seeking to capture. In many cases, suppliers generate the bulk of exports as well. The capability to serve multiple customers also takes on heightened importance.[21] Thus, it is no accident that Brazil sought investments from Foxconn, rather than Apple, in its desire for iPhones and iPads to be produced in the country for domestic consumption and export elsewhere in Latin America.

A second feature of industrial policies in the GVC era is global sourcing and value chain specialization. Policies that promote linkages to GVCs have very different aims than traditional industrial policies that intend to build full-blown, vertically integrated domestic industries (Baldwin 2011). Policies can target specialized niches in GVCs. These can be higher-value niches suited to existing capabilities, or they can be generic capabilities pooled across foreign investors. Either of these can serve both domestic and export markets. This sort of value chain specialization assumes an ongoing dependence on imported inputs and services. Global sourcing means that the entire value chain may never be captured, but it also assures ongoing involvement in leading-edge technologies, standards, and industry best practices.

Third, firms in emerging economies like China and Brazil are seeking to move to the head of GVCs, at least regionally if not globally. Encouraging global suppliers to establish facilities within a country has long-term advantages. Local lead firms can rely on global suppliers in their midst and on broader GVCs for a wide range of inputs and services, from design, to production, to logistics, to marketing and distribution. This can lower risk and barriers to entry for local firms, provide access to capabilities and scale that far outstrip what is available domestically, and ensure that products and services are up to date.

The use of industrial policies by emerging economy policymakers should not come as a big surprise. Both developed and developing countries have deployed these policies in the past, often with considerable sophistication, as in the case of East Asian economies such as Japan, South Korea, Singapore, Taiwan, and now China. Looking towards the future, the traditional rule-making and finance-oriented international organizations of the Washington Consensus era, such as the WTO, the IMF, and the World Bank, face the challenge of constructing a new global economic order that aligns with the shifting roles of both the emerging and developed economies. A stable foundation for sustainable development will require both bold vision and a flexible pragmatism to guide a new generation of inclusive growth policies and institutional arrangements within the global economy.

Conclusions

Economic globalization is a by-product of international production and trade networks organized by transnational firms, and it is embedded in various kinds of regulation, including rules of the game established by international institutions, national government policies, and various forms of private govern-ance that nonstate actors use to manage activities in GVCs (Mayer and Gereffi 2010). Public governance will likely

> be called upon to play a stronger role in supplementing and reinforc-ing corporate codes of conduct, product certifications, process standards, and other voluntary, non-governmental types of private governance that have proliferated in the last two decades, and multi-stakeholder initiatives involving both public and private actors will arise to deal with collective action problems.
>
> (Gereffi 2014, p. 29)

The challenge is to link economic and social upgrading of both material work conditions and the quantity and quality of jobs created in contemporary GVCs (Barrientos et al. 2011). For developing countries, the trade, investment, and knowledge flows that underpin GVCs provide mechanisms for rapid learn-ing, innovation, and industrial upgrading (Staritz et al. 2011). GVCs can provide local firms with better access to information, open up new markets, and cre-ate opportunities for fast technological learning and skill acquisition. Because transactions and investments associated with GVCs typically come with quality control systems and prevailing global business standards that exceed those in developing countries, enterprises and individuals in developing countries can acquire new competencies and skills by participating in GVCs.

Still, GVCs are not a panacea for development. Very rapid or "compressed" GVC-driven development can create a host of new economic and social policy challenges in areas such as health care and education (Whittaker et al. 2010). GVCs can create barriers to learning and drive uneven development over time, even as they trigger rapid industrial upgrading, because of the geographic and organizational disjunctures that often exist between innovation and production. There is considerable evidence that greater profits accrue to lead firms in the value chain that control branding and product conception (e.g., Apple) and to the "platform leaders" that provide core technologies and advanced compo-nents (e.g., Intel). At the same time, contract manufacturers and business process outsourcing service providers (e.g., call centers) tend to earn slim profits and may never develop the autonomy or capabilities needed to develop and market their own branded products. Typically, firms that provide routine assembly tasks and other simple services within GVCs earn less, pay their workers less, and are more vulnerable to business cycles, not least because they are required to sup-port large-scale employment and fixed capital (Lüthje 2002).

As developing economies have become key players in GVCs, a new set of issues has emerged regarding how countries can maximize their upgrading opportunities in the global economy. Central to this challenge is how coun-tries can move up the value chain by engaging local firms, assimilating new knowledge, and improving employment conditions, with appropriate policies and institutions to facilitate economic, social, and environmental upgrading.

The various examples of GVC participation reviewed in this chapter highlight a variety of options that countries would be wise to consider in trying to improve their international competitiveness. Several targeted recommendations outlined below highlight what developing countries can do to improve their positions in GVCs.

Infrastructure. Large-scale infrastructure development projects involving roads, shipping terminals, and airports are a major focus of development banks and national governments in their efforts to modernize economies and improve their access to global markets. Increasingly, China and other emerging economies are stepping in to fill what they perceive as a significant infrastructure gap for developing economies.[22] However, our GVC case studies reveal that more specific forms of infrastructure can be highly beneficial to upgrading local economies. As the coffee cases in Central America and East Africa illustrated, sector-specific infrastructure like coffee washing stations that permit wet milling are essential for smallholder farmers to attain the quality needed for specialty coffee exports. For many of the higher-value services, world-class information technology infrastructure is essential, which increases connectivity for small and large users alike.

Trade policy. A prominent feature of the global economy in the last several decades has been the rapid growth of regional trade agreements (e.g., NAFTA, CAFTA-DR, and MERCOSUR in Latin America; AGOA in sub-Saharan Africa; and ASEAN [Association of Southeast Asian Nations] in Asia), and the proliferation of bilateral trade agreements as well (e.g., Mexico has over 40 such agreements and Chile more than 20). Although these policies have greatly facilitated the access of developing economies to world-class imports and key export markets, regional agreements can also have a restrictive impact in terms of their country-of-origin requirements. In Nicaragua's apparel industry, for example, the country was able to negotiate a 10-year TPL agreement with the United States to give them access to non-US fabrics (mainly from Asia) for their apparel exports. However, the expiration of the TPLs in 2014 has created considerable uncertainty among foreign investors and could lead to an outflow of FDI that could cripple the country's apparel exports (Frederick et al. 2014).

Developing countries should be wary of building up their competitive advantage in GVCs on the basis of short-term trade policy advantages. Many of the preferential trade agreements have market access aspects that are of limited duration. Countries should view these as "windows of opportunity" that permit the development of capabilities that could lead to more sustainable niches in specific GVCs. Often, this involves the creation of backward or forward linkages, like textiles in apparel and cold-storage facilities in the fresh fruit value chain. Global buyers in GVCs prefer "one-stop shopping." If these capabilities cannot be built at a national level in terms of scale or cost constraints, then another option would be to develop the capabilities that could permit functional upgrading in the GVC with nearby countries in the region.

Industrial policy. There has been a long history of industrial policy in developing economies, built around the ISI strategy of the 1950s to 1970s, especially in Latin America and East Asia (Gereffi and Wyman 1990). From the 1980s through the early 2000s, state-led industrial policy fell out of favor, and the "Washington Consensus" championed by the World Bank and the IMF advocated EOI based on the East Asian model. Due to a variety of factors, including the global economic recession of 2008–2009 and the rise of large emerging economies such as China, India, and Brazil, the Washington Consensus is now in disarray and industrial policy is back (Gereffi 2014). However, as a result of economic globalization and the predominance of GVCs, a return to traditional ISI industrial policy based on protected domestic markets, local content requirements, mandatory joint ventures, and other measures from the ISI toolkit is unlikely to be effective.

Industrial policy in the GVC era needs to recognize that many of the multinational corporations that act as lead firms in GVCs are streamlining their supply chains from hundreds or even thousands of suppliers spread across dozens of countries in every continent of the world,[23] to a much smaller number (perhaps just 20 to 30) of larger, more capable and strategically located manufacturers. In addition, there is considerable geographic concentration, in which a few countries are controlling larger shares of global output in each industry (Gereffi 2014). These shifts imply a much greater concentration of industrial production within the Global South, higher levels of South–South trade, and the rise of emerging economy TNCs that play a far more significant role in GVCs.

In this context, several key features of GVC-oriented industrial policy are likely to become more significant in developing economies (Gereffi and Sturgeon 2013): (1) GVC-oriented industrial policies may want to target global suppliers or contract manufacturers that make significant investments in developing economies, rather than the branded lead firms in GVCs;[24] (2) value-chain specialization heightens the importance of joining rather than building GVCs (Baldwin 2012; Cattaneo et al. 2013), and the policies that promote linkages to GVCs are very different from those intended to build vertically integrated domestic industries; (3) industrial policies should seek to identify GVC lead firms and global contractors that have an interest in partnering with and developing the capabilities of local firms; and (4) in a GVC-oriented world, the industrial policies among emerging economies are increasingly likely to be in conflict, with China often finding itself in the middle of these controversies.

Workforce development. A skilled workforce is an essential ingredient of GVC upgrading, especially for high-value services, which case studies show can add value to virtually every kind of industry: extractive, agricultural, manufacturing, professional services, and even tourism. In the context of GVCs, however, the skills required for upgrading must be oriented to highly dynamic global demand, as defined by key private-sector actors. Therefore, workforce development programs should involve a combination of basic education and more specialized training, with private companies supplementing the role played by public agencies (Gereffi et al. 2011; Wadhwa et al. 2008).

Standards and certifications. Global production must meet very high international standards for quality and safety, especially for industries related to food, health, and with a potentially big environmental impact (like oil and mining). A dizzying array of industry standards and product certifications are linked to GVCs. Although there are often significant price premiums for producers of qualifying products, acquiring appropriate certifications can be costly and complex, especially for small firms. Financing to support certifications is likely to facilitate entry by small and medium enterprises (SMEs) into GVCs, but the gains from certification are not guaranteed unless the global demand and prices for these products continue to be high.[25] Therefore, complying with standards and certifications is best seen as a necessary but not sufficient condition for economic upgrading, which is most likely to affect SMEs.

Public–private partnerships. Given the key role played by the private sector in GVCs, international donors and development agencies have shown a great deal of interest in supporting public–private partnerships in developing countries (Bella et al. 2013; UNGC 2011; USAID 2014). Because private capital and trade flows in the global economy dwarf official donor assistance, these global flows in GVCs have heightened concerns over how to make sure that positive development trajectories are related not only to economic but also social and environmental objectives. Thus, multilateral and bilateral donors have engaged the private sector to take on a variety of pro-poor development roles. Although public–private partnerships can positively affect growth at the industry level through increased investment, output, exports, and employment, the economic gains do not automatically translate to smallholders, SMEs, and local households due to the power asymmetries that are embedded in many GVC relationships (Mayer and Milberg 2013). Therefore, the wide variety of "Aid for Trade" schemes and other forms of public–private partnerships should seek to assure that SMEs and other targeted beneficiaries of inclusive development projects acquire the productive capabilities needed to respond to dynamic markets through appropriate financing of required infrastructure, affordable certification, technical assistance, improved information flows, and mechanisms to enhance bargaining power to protect worker rights and community development objectives.

There is no magic bullet to improve international competitiveness in GVCs, given the great diversity of experiences and interests within developing regions of the world. However, by acknowledging and addressing the new realities of the global economy, emerging economies and less-developed countries alike can improve their ability to define manageable goals and capture a greater share of the gains in GVCs.

Notes

1 Acknowledgements: This chapter first appeared as a UNIDO/UNU-MERIT background paper for UNIDO's *Industrial Development Report 2016*: IDR 2016 WP 10.
2 The seminal publication is *Commodity Chains and Global Capitalism*, which applied the global commodity chains concept for the first time to a broad range of contemporary industries (Gereffi and Korzeniewicz 1994). In the early 2000s, the global commodity chains research agenda helped to spawn the closely related global value chain and global

production network approaches (for comprehensive literature reviews, see Bair 2005, 2009 (ch. 1), Gereffi 1994b, 2005. 2018, and Lee 2010.

3 Jim O'Neill (2011), the Goldman Sachs executive who coined the term BRICs in the early 1990s, now argues that there are a much larger number of "growth economies" (BRICs plus 11) that fall into this category, including South Korea, Mexico, Turkey, and Indonesia, among others.

4 See Hamilton and Gereffi (2009, pp. 153–159), who describe how US, European, and Japanese buyers worked with suppliers in South Korea and Taiwan to create the necessary conditions for expanding and diversifying exports of a broad array of consumer goods in both economies.

5 Li & Fung, the largest trading company in the world, has about 30,000 suppliers globally and operates in 40 countries (Fung 2011).

6 According to a recent study, reducing supply chain barriers to trade could increase gross domestic product up to six times more than could removing tariffs (World Economic Forum 2013, p. 13).

7 As of July 27, 2018, nearly 1,100 GVC publications and more than 780 researchers are listed on the Global Value Chains website (https://www.globalvaluechains.org/publications), which is maintained at Duke University.

8 Illustrative publications include Cattaneo et al. 2010, 2013; OECD 2013; UNCTAD 2013; World Bank-IDE-JETRO 2011; World Economic Forum 2013. Many more publications and interviews with members of international organizations that have utilized the GVC framework are available at the website for the Duke Global Summit (see https://dukegvcsummit.org/). This conference, which was held at Duke University on October 29–Nov. 1, 2014, brought together 30 organizations and more than three dozen academic and practitioner participants who were actively involved in GVC programs and research related to international development agencies in order to explore topics related to development, economic and social upgrading in GVCs; advances in GVC metrics related to value creation and value capture; and the future of global governance.

9 The material for this section is drawn primarily from the World Bank (2012, pp. 19–32).

10 Guatemala alone produces seven distinct varietals of specialty coffee due to its diverse geography.

11 In Guatemala, estimates for larger producers show the following distribution of costs across the coffee value chain: 15 percent for producers with wet mills (who buy from small farmers that do not possess wet mills, which reduces their share of the value chain), 13 percent for traders, and 72 percent for the roasters (World Bank 2012, p. 25).

12 For a detailed analysis of the varied public–private partnerships in Rwanda's coffee sector, see Abdulsamad et al. (2015).

13 Between 2000 and 2010, the number of coffee washing stations in Rwanda increased from 2 to 187, and the fully washed coffee value chain grew from exporting 32 tons of coffee in 2002 and 5,800 tons in 2010 (Oehmke et al. 2011). An audit conducted in 2010 estimated that these partnership projects delivered 82 percent higher incomes for beneficiaries, as well as a 17 percent lower incidence of poverty by 2010 (Abdulsamad et al. 2015, p. 37).

14 The industry reached a peak in employment in 2007, with 88,700 employees. However, pressures from the economic crisis forced layoffs and closures during 2008 and 2009.

15 This section draws on the discussion of these two industries in UNCTAD (2014, pp. 67–69).

16 In Brazil, FDI to the automobile industry (assembly and auto parts) soared from an annual average of $116 million in 2007–2010 to $1.6 billion in 2011–2012 (UNCTAD 2013, p. 61). Between 2007 and 2012, the automotive industry in Mexico had an influx of $3.6 billion in announced FDI (PwC Mexico 2013, p. i).

17 The IDB replicated the public–private partnership models developed in India to its first pilot projects in Uruguay and Colombia.

18 The description of this case is drawn from Fernandez-Stark et al. (2014).

19 Lall's categories only cover goods, however, and India is also the world leader in exports of offshore services, with 45 percent of the global total. See Fernandez-Stark et al. (2011), which defines and analyzes recent trends in the offshore services industry using a GVC approach.

20 This is reflected in Brazil's top 10 exports in 2011, where the top seven items are primary products or processed intermediates (see Sturgeon et al. 2013, Table 3).

21 Multiple customers provide global suppliers with sufficient business to justify capital-intensive investments that may have high minimum-scale requirements, such as electronic displays and automated production lines.

22 China has taken the lead in launching a new Asian Infrastructure Investment Bank, which appears to be winning the support of US allies not just in Asia (such as Australia, New Zealand, South Korea, Singapore, and Thailand) but in Europe as well (Britain, France, Germany, and Italy have all expressed interest in joining the bank as founding shareholders). China is also a central player in the new "BRICS" Development Bank (with Brazil, Russia, India, and South Africa), and a proposed Silk Road development fund to boost connectivity with its neighbors in Central Asia (*The Economist* 2015).

23 In 2011, for example, Nike's products were made in 930 factories in 50 countries, employing more than 1 million workers. However, Nike itself had just 38,000 direct employees, most of whom work in the United States. All of the other workers in Nike's global supply chain were employed by subcontractors based in developing economies (Locke 2013, p. 48). Over 80 percent of Walmart's more than 60,000 suppliers are located in China alone (Gereffi and Christian, 2009, p. 579).

24 Foxconn Technology Group, the largest electronics contract manufacturer in the world, has its home office in Taiwan, but its production and exports for leading brand-name multinationals like Apple are concentrated in mainland China, where it employs more than 1 million workers, making it by far the largest private employer in the country. Li & Fung, the largest trading company in the world, is headquartered in Hong Kong but does most of its sourcing from China, and it has extensive operations in the Americas (Fung 2011).

25 As we saw in the coffee case, the price for specialty coffee could be double that for certified organic or Fair Trade coffee.

References

Abdulsamad, Ajmal, Shawn Stokes, and Gary Gereffi (2015), "Public-private partnerships in global value chains: Can they actually benefit the poor?" Report prepared for USAID, Leveraging Economic Opportunity (LEO) Report #8, (February), https://gvcc.duke.edu/wp-content/uploads/2015-02_PublicPrivatePartnerships_in_GVCs_Can_they_actually_benefit_the_poor_LEO_report508.pdf.

Altenburg, Tilman (2007), "Donor approaches to supporting pro-poor value chains," Report prepared for the Donor Committee for Enterprise Development, Working Group on Linkages and Value Chains, www.enterprise-development.org/page/download?id=38

Appelbaum, Richard P. (2008), "Giant transnational contractors in East Asia: Emergent trends in global supply chains," *Competition & Change*, 12 (1), 69–87.

Bair, Jennifer (2005), "Global capitalism and commodity chains: Looking back, going forward," *Competition & Change*, 9 (2), 153–180.

Bair, Jennifer (ed.). (2009), *Frontiers of Commodity Chain Research*. Stanford, CA: Stanford University Press.

Bair, Jennifer, and Gary Gereffi (2014), "Towards better work in Central America: Nicaragua and the CAFTA context," in *Towards Better Work: Understanding Labour in Apparel Global Value Chains*, Arianna Rossi, Amy Luinstra and John Pickles, eds. Basingstoke, UK: Palgrave Macmillan and the International Labour Office, 251–275.

Baldwin, Richard (2011), *Trade and Industrialisation After Globalisation's 2nd Unbundling: How Building and Joining a Supply Chain Are Different and Why It Matters*. Cambridge, MA: National Bureau of Economic Research, Working Paper 17716 (December), www.nber.org/papers/w17716.

Baldwin, Richard (2012), "Global supply chains: why they emerged, why they matter, and where they are going?" CEPR Discussion Paper No. 9103, August.

Barrientos, Stephanie, and Kwadwo Asenso-Okyere (2008), "Mapping sustainable production in Ghanaian cocoa: Report to Cadbury," Institute of Development Studies (University of Sussex, UK) and the University of Ghana, www.bwpi.manchester.ac.uk/medialibrary/research/ResearchProgrammes/businessfordevelopment/mappping_sustainable_production_in_ghanaian_cocoa.pdf.

Barrientos, Stephanie, Gary Gereffi, and Arianna Rossi (2011), "Economic and social upgrading in global production networks: A new paradigm for a changing world," *International Labour Review*, 150 (3–4), 319–340.

Bella, Jose Di, Alicia Grant, Shannon Kindornay, and Stephanie Tissot (2013), *Mapping Private Sector Engagement in Development Cooperation*. Ottawa, Canada: The North-South Institute, www.nsi-ins.ca/wp-content/uploads/2013/09/Mapping-PS-Engagment-in-Development-Cooperation-Final.pdf.

Beltramello, Andrea, Koen De Backer, and Laurent Moussiegt (2012), "The export performance of countries within global value chains," *OECD Science, Technology and Industry Working Papers*, 2012/02. OECD Publishing, www.ecb.europa.eu/home/pdf/research/compnet/Beltramello_DeBacker_Moussiegt_2012.pdf.

Casalet, Mónica, Edgar Buenrostro, Federico Stezano, Rubén Oliver, and Lucía Abelenda (2011), *Evolución y complejidad en el desarrollo de encadenamientos productivos en México: Los desafíos de la construcción del cluster aeroespacial en Querétaro*. Santiago: CEPAL.

Cattaneo, Olivier, Gary Gereffi, Sebastien Miroudot, and Daria Taglioni (2013), "Joining, upgrading and becoming competitive in global value chains: A strategic framework," The World Bank, Policy Research Working Paper 6406, April, http://documents.worldbank.org/curated/en/254001468336685890/pdf/wps6406.pdf.

Cattaneo, Olivier, Gary Gereffi, and Cornelia Staritz (eds.). (2010), *Global Value Chains in a Postcrisis World: A Development Perspective*. Washington, DC: The World Bank.

Chassot, Olivier (2012), "Servicios medioambientales," Personal communication with K. Fernandez-Stark, November 2.

Conservation International (2012), "Costa Rica," www.conservation.org/where/north_america/costarica/Pages/costarica.aspx.

Crescionini, Eduardo (2012), *Sistema de trazabilidad bovina en Uruguaya*. Monteverde: Ministerio de Ganadería, Agricultura y Pesca, www.imaginar.org/taller/agrotic/eduardo_crescioni_ministerio_agricultura_uruguay.pdf.

Crespi, Gustavo, Eduardo Fernández-Arias, and Ernesto Stein (eds.). (2014), *Rethinking Productive Development: Sound Policies and Institutions for Economic Transformation*. Washington, DC: Inter-American Development Bank.

Daviron, Benoit, and Stefano Ponte (2005), *The Coffee Paradox: Global Markets, Commodity Trade and the Elusive Promise of Development*. London: Zed Books.

Dicken, Peter (2011), *Global Shift: Mapping the Changing Contours of the World Economy*, 6th ed. New York: Guilford.

The Economist (2015), "The infrastructure gap: The Asian infrastructure investment bank," (accessed March 21, 2018).

Farmers to 40 (2014), "Analyzing fair trade proof data," (accessed January 14, 2015), www.farmersto40.com/blog/.

Feenstra, Robert C. (1998), "Integration of trade and disintegration of production in the global economy," *Journal of Economic Perspectives*, 12 (4), 31–50.

Fernandez-Stark, Karina, Penny Bamber, and Gary Gereffi (2011), "The offshore services value chain: Upgrading trajectories in developing countries," *International Journal of Technological Learning, Innovation and Development*, 4 (1–3), 206–234.

Fernandez-Stark, Karina, Penny Bamber, and Gary Gereffi (2014), "Global value chains in Latin America: A development perspective for upgrading," in *Global Value Chains and World Trade: Prospects and Challenges for Latin America*, René Antonio Hernández, Jorge Mario Martínez-Piva, and Nanno Mulder, eds. Santiago: UN Economic Commision for Latin America and the Caribbean and German Cooperation (GIZ), 79–106.

Frederick, Stacey, Jennifer Bair, and Gary Gereffi (2014), "Nicaragua and the apparel value chain in the Americas: Implications for regional trade and employment," *Duke CGGC*, March 18, www.cggc.duke.edu/pdfs/2014-03-25a_DukeCGGC_Nicaragua_apparel_report.pdf.

Freeman, Richard (2008), "The new global labor market," *Focus*, 26 (1), 1–6, www.irp.wisc.edu/publications/focus/pdfs/foc261.pdf.

Fung, Victor K. (2011), "Global supply chains – past developments, emerging trends," Speech to the Executive Committee of the Federation of Indian Chambers of Commerce and Industry, October 11, www.fungglobalinstitute.org/en/global-supply-chains-%E2%80%93-past-developments-emerging-trends.

Gereffi, Gary. (1994a), "The organization of buyer-driven global commodity chains: How US retailers shape overseas production networks," in *Commodity Chains and Global Capitalism*, Gary Gereffi and Miguel Korzeniewicz, eds. Westport, CT: Praeger Publishers, 95–112.

Gereffi, Gary (1994b), "The international economy and economic development," in *The Handbook of Economic Sociology*, Neil J. Smelser and Richard Swedberg, eds. Princeton, NJ: Princeton University Press, 206–233.

Gereffi, Gary (1996), "Commodity chains and regional divisions of labor in East Asia," *Journal of Asian Business*, 12 (1), 75–112.

Gereffi, Gary (1999), "International trade and industrial upgrading in the apparel commodity chain," *Journal of International Economics*, 48 (1), 37–70.

Gereffi, Gary (2005), "The global economy: Organization, governance, and development," in *The Handbook of Economic Sociology*, Neil J. Smelser and Richard Swedberg, eds., 2nd ed. Princeton, NJ: Princeton University Press, 160–182.

Gereffi, Gary (2009), "Development models and industrial upgrading in China and Mexico," *European Sociological Review*, 25 (1), 37–51.

Gereffi, Gary (2011), "Global value chains and international competition," *Antitrust Bulletin*, 56 (1), 37–56.

Gereffi, Gary (2014), "Global value chains in a post-Washington consensus world," *Review of International Political Economy*, 21 (1), 9–37.

Gereffi, Gary (2018), *Global Value Chains and Development: Redefining the Contours of 21st Century Capitalism*. Cambridge, UK: Cambridge University Press.

Gereffi, Gary (2019), "Global value chains and international development policy: Bringing firms, networks and policy-engaged scholarship back in," *Journal of International Business Policy*, 2, 3: 195-210.

Gereffi, Gary, and Michelle Christian (2009), "The impacts of Wal-Mart: The rise and consequences of the world's dominant retailer," *Annual Review of Sociology*, 35, 573–591.

Gereffi, Gary, and Karina Fernandez-Stark (2011), "Global value chain analysis: A primer," Center on Globalization, Governance & Competitiveness, Duke University, Durham, NC, https://gvcc.duke.edu/wp-content/uploads/2011-05-31_GVC_analysis_a_primer.pdf.

Gereffi, Gary, Karina Fernandez-Stark, and Phil Psilos (2011), *Skills for Upgrading: Workforce Development and Global Value Chains in Developing Countries.* Durham, NC: Duke Center on Globalization, Governance & Competitiveness and the Research Triangle Institute, www.cggc.duke.edu/gvc/workforce-development/.

Gereffi, Gary, John Humphrey, and Timothy Sturgeon (2005), "The governance of global value chains," *Review of International Political Economy*, 12 (1), 78–104.

Gereffi, Gary, and Miguel Korzeniewicz (eds.). (1994), *Commodity Chains and Global Capitalism.* Westport, CT: Praeger.

Gereffi, Gary, and Joonkoo Lee (2012), "Why the world suddenly cares about global supply chains," *Journal of Supply Chain Management*, 48 (3), 24–32.

Gereffi, Gary, and Timothy Sturgeon (2013), "Global value chains and industrial policy: The role of emerging economies," in *Global Value Chains in a Changing World*, Deborah K. Elms and Patrick Low, eds. Geneva: World Trade Organization, Fung Global Institute and Termasek Foundation Centre for Trade and Negotiations, 329–360.

Gereffi, Gary, and Donald L. Wyman (eds.). (1990), *Manufacturing Miracles: Paths of Industrialization in Latin America and East Asia.* Princeton, NJ: Princeton University Press.

Gore, Charles (2000), "The rise and fall of the Washington consensus as a paradigm for developing countries," *World Development*, 28 (5), 789–804.

Grunwald, Joseph, and Kenneth Flamm (1985), *The Global Factory: Foreign Assembly in International Trade.* Washington, DC: The Brookings Institution.

Haggard, Stephan (1990), *Pathways from the Periphery: The Politics of Growth in the Newly Industrializing Countries.* Ithaca: Cornell University Press.

Hamilton, Gary G., and Gary Gereffi (2009), "Global commodity chains, market makers, and the rise of demand-responsive economies," in *Frontiers of Commodity Chain Research*, Jennifer Bair, ed. Stanford, CA: Stanford University Press, 136–161.

Hernández, René A., Jorge Mario Martínez-Piva, and Nanno Mulder (eds.). (2014), *Global Value Chains and World Trade: Prospects and Challenges for Latin America.* Santiago, Chile: United Nations Economic Commission for Latin America and the Caribbean and German Cooperation (GIZ).

Humphrey, John, and Lizbeth Navas-Alemán (2010), *Value Chains, Donor Interventions and Poverty Reduction: A Review of Donor Practice.* Brighton, UK: Institute of Development Studies at the University of Sussex, IDS Research Report 63.

Humphrey, John, and Hubert Schmitz (2002), "How does insertion in global value chains affect upgrading in industrial clusters?" *Regional Studies*, 36 (9), 1017–1027.

IDB (Inter-American Development Bank) (2012), "What is the inter-America development bank doing about BPO labor in Latin America?" www.nearshoreamericas.com/interamerica-development-bank-bpo-labor-latin-america/.

Jenkins, Rhys (2012), "China and Brazil: Economic impacts of a growing relationship," *Journal of Current Chinese Affairs*, 1, 21–47.

Krugman, Paul (1995), "Growing world trade," *Brookings Papers on Economic Activity*, 1, 327–377.

Lall, Sanjaya (2000), "The technological structure and performance of developing country manufactured exports, 1985–98," *Oxford Development Studies*, 28 (3), 337–369.

Lee, Joonkoo (2010), "Global commodity chains and global value chains," in *The International Studies Encyclopedia*, Robert A. Denemark, ed. Oxford, UK: Wiley-Blackwell, 2987–3006.

Locke, Richard M. (2013), *The Promise and Limits of Private Power: Promoting Labor Standards in a Global Economy.* New York and Cambridge: Cambridge University Press.

Lüthje, Boy (2002), "Electronics contract manufacturing: Global production and the international division of labor in the age of the Internet," *Industry and Innovation*, 9 (3), 227–247.

Lynn, Barry C. (2005), *End of the Line: The Rise and Coming Fall of the Global Corporation*. New York: Doubleday.

M4P (Making Markets Work Better for the Poor) (2008), *Making Value Chains Work Better for the Poor: A Toolbook for Practitioners of Value Chain Analysis*. London: UK Department of International Development.

Mayer, Frederick, and Gary Gereffi (2010), "Regulation and economic globalization: Prospects and limits of private governance," *Business and Politics*, 12 (3), Article 11, www.bepress.com/bap/vol12/iss3/art11/.

Mayer, Frederick, and William Milberg (2013), "Aid for trade in a world of global value chains: Chain power, the distribution of rents, and implications for the form of aid. Capturing the gains," Working Paper 34, www.capturingthegains.org/publications/workingpapers/wp_201334.htm.

Milberg, William, and Deborah Winkler (2013), *Outsourcing Economics: Global Value Chains in Capitalist Development*. New York and Cambridge: Cambridge University Press.

Morris, Mike, Cornelia Staritz, and Justin Barnes (2011), "Value chain dynamics, local embeddedness, and upgrading in the clothing sectors of Lesotho and Swaziland," *International Journal of Technological Learning, Innovation and Development*, 4 (1–3), 96–119.

Nathan, Dev, and Sandip Sarkar (2011), "Blood on your mobile phone? Capturing the gains for artisanal miners, poor workers and women," Capturing the Gains Briefing Note, No. 2, February, www.capturingthegains.org/pdf/ctg_briefing_note_2.pdf.

Naughton, Barry (ed.). (1997), *The China Circle: Economics and Technology in the PRC, Taiwan, and Hong Kong*. Washington, DC: The Brookings Institution.

OECD (2013), *Interconnected Economies: Benefitting from Global Value Chains*. Paris: Organisation for Economic Cooperation and Development, www.oecd-ilibrary.org/science-and-technology/interconnected-economies_9789264189560-en.

OECD Development Centre (2013), *Perspectives on Global Development 2013: Industrial Policies in a Changing World*. Paris: OECD, www.oecd.org/development/pgd/pgd2013.htm.

Oehmke, James F., Alexandre Lyambabaje, Etienne Bihogo, Charles B. Moss, Jean Claude Kayisinga, and Dave D. Weatherspoon (2011), "The impact of USAID investment on sustainable poverty reduction among Rwandan smallholder coffee producers: A synthesis of findings," www.jfoehmke.com/uploads/9/4/1/8/9418218/rwanda_synthesis_document_final_draft_oct_2011.pdf.

O'Neill, Jim (2011), *The Growth Map: Economic Opportunity in the BRICs and Beyond*. New York: Penguin.

Oxfam (2011), "Exploring the links between international business and poverty reduction: The Coca-Cola/SABMiller value chain impacts in Zambia and El Salvador," *Oxfam Policy and Practice: Private Sector*, www.oxfamamerica.org/static/oa3/files/coca-cola-sab-miller-poverty-footprint-dec-2011.pdf.

Pickles, John, and Adrian Smith (2011), "Delocalization and persistence in the European clothing industry: The reconfiguration of trade and production networks," *Regional Studies*, 45, 167–185.

Ponte, Stefano (2002), "The 'latte revolution'? Regulation, markets and consumption in the global coffee chain," *World Development*, 30 (7), 1099–1122.

Portocarrero Lacayo, and Ana Victoria (2010), *El sector textil y confección y el desarrollo sostenible en Nicaragua*, January. Geneva: International Centre for Trade and Sustainable Development.

ProNicaragua (2010), "Investment opportunities: Textiles and apparel," www.pronicaragua.org/index.php?option=com_content&view=article&id=35&Itemid=98&lang=en.

PwC Mexico (2013), "Doing business in Mexico: Automotive industry," (accessed May, 2018), www.pwc.com/mx/doing-business-automotive.

Rodriguez, Carlos Manuel (2012), "Servicios medioambientales." Personal communication with K. Fernandez-Stark, August 22.

Ross, Andrew (2006), *Fast Boat to China: Corporate Flight and the Consequences of Free Trade*. New York: Pantheon Books.

Rossi, Arianna, Amy Luinstra, and John Pickles (eds.). (2014), *Towards Better Work: Understanding Labour in Apparel Global Value Chains*. New York: Palgrave Macmillan and International Labour Office.

Salazar-Xirinachs, José M., Irmgard Nübler, and Richard Kozul-Wright (2014), *Transforming Economies: Making Industrial Policy Work for Growth, Jobs and Development*. Geneva: International Labour Office and United Nations Conference for Trade and Development.

Smith, Adrian, John Pickles, Milan Buček, Rudolf Pástor, and Bob Begg (2014), "The political economy of global production networks: Regional industrial change and differential upgrading in the East European clothing industry," *Journal of Economic Geography*, 14 (6), 1023–1051.

SONDA (2012), "Un sistema de trazabilidad para el ganado bovino de Uruguay que asegura calidad sanitaria," (accessed December, 2012), www.sonda.com/caso/10/.

Staritz, Cornelia, Gary Gereffi, and Olivier Cattaneo (eds.). (2011), *International Journal of Technological Learning, Innovation and Development*, 4 (1–3). Special issue on "Shifting end markets and upgrading prospects in global value chains."

Staritz, Cornelia, and José Guilherme Reis (eds.). (2013), *Global Value Chains, Economic Upgrading, and Gender: Case Studies of the Horticulture, Tourism and Call Center Industries*. Washington, DC: The World Bank, www.capturingthegains.org/pdf/GVC_Gender_Report_web.pdf.

Sturgeon, Timothy J. (2002), "Modular production networks: A new American model of industrial organization," *Industrial and Corporate Change*, 11 (3), 451–496.

Sturgeon, Timothy J., and Gary Gereffi (2009), "Measuring success in the global economy: International trade, industrial upgrading, and business function outsourcing in global value chains," *Transnational Corporations*, 18 (2), 1–36.

Sturgeon, Timothy J., Gary Gereffi, Andrew Guinn, and Ezequiel Zylberberg, (2013), "O Brasil nas cadeias globais de valor: implicações para a política industrial e de comércio," *Revista Brasileira de Comércio Exterior*, 115, 26–41.

Sturgeon, Timothy J., and Momoko Kawakami (2011), "Global value chains in the electronics industry: Characteristics, crisis, and upgrading opportunities for firms from developing countries," *International Journal of Technological Learning, Innovation and Development*, 4 (1–3), 120–147.

Sturgeon, Timothy J., and Richard K. Lester (2004), "The new global supply base: New challenges for local suppliers in East Asia," in *Global Production Networking and Technological Change in East Asia*, Shahid Yusuf, M. Anjum Altaf, and Kaoru Nabeshima, eds. Washington, DC: The World Bank and Oxford University Press, 35–87.

Sturgeon, Timothy J., and Johannes Van Biesebroeck (2011), "Global value chains in the automotive industry: An enhanced role for developing countries?" *International Journal of Technological Learning, Innovation and Development*, 4 (1–3), 181–205.

Talbot, John M. (2004), *Grounds for Agreement: The Political Economy of the Coffee Commodity Chain*. Lanham, MD: Rowman & Littlefield.

Tholons (2012), *Outsourcing & National Development in Latin America*. New York: Tholons. www.google.com/url?sa=t&rct=j&q=&esrc=s&source=web&cd=1&cad=rja&ve d=0CD0QFjAA&url=http%3A%2F%2Fwww.tholons.com%2Fnl_pdf%2FTholons_ Whitepaper_Tholons_Outsourcing_and_National_Development_Whitepaper_February_ 2012.pdf&ei=eAi5UK3pIJSw8ATChoHYCQ&usg=AFQjCNGzetmK9aZXhHlKjKX Ok7ROE9Y_Gw&sig2=n4Rj-utYcgJ5bCnpMUo8Fw.

Thomson, Adam (2012), "Mexico: China's unlikely challenger," *Financial Times*, September 19, www.ft.com/content/9f789abe-023a-11e2-b41f-00144feabdc0

UN Comtrade (2012), "United Nations commodity trade statistics database," https://comtrade.un.org/

UNCTAD (2013), *World Investment Report, 2013 – Global Value Chains: Investment and Trade for Development.* Geneva: United Nations Conference for Trade and Development.

UNCTAD (2014), *World Investment Report, 2014 – Investing in the SDGs: An Action Plan.* Geneva: United Nations Conference for Trade and Development.

UNGC (2011), "Partners in development: How donors can better engage the private sector for development in LDCs," United Nations Global Compact, United Nations Development Program, and BertelsmannStiftung, www.unglobalcompact.org/docs/issues_doc/development/Partners_in_Development.pdf.

Urquidi, Victor L. (1991), "The prospects for economic transformation in Latin America: Opportunities and resistances," *LASA Forum*, 22 (3), 1–9.

USAID (2014), *Global Development Alliances.* Washington, DC: United States Agency for International Development, www.usaid.gov/gda.

Vernon, Raymond (1971), *Sovereignty at Bay: The Multinational Spread of U.S. Enterprises.* New York: Basic Books.

Wadhwa, Vivek, Una Kim de Vitton, and Gary Gereffi (2008), "How the disciple became the guru: Workforce development in India's R&D labs," Report prepared for the Ewing Marion Kauffman Foundation, July 23, http://papers.ssrn.com/sol3/papers.cfm?abstract_id=1170049.

Whitttaker, D. Hugh, Tianbiao Zhu, Timothy Sturgeon, Mon Han Tsai, and Toshie Okita (2010), "Compressed development," *Studies in Comparative International Development*, 45, 439–467.

World Bank (2012), "Unlocking Central America's export potential – 2. Unlocking potential at the sector level: Value chain analyses," http://documents.worldbank.org/curated/en/2012/10/17211219/unlocking-central-americas-export-potential-vol-2-4-unlocking-potential-sector-level-value-chain-analyses.

World Economic Forum (in collaboration with Bain & Company and the World Bank) (2013), "Enabling trade: Valuing growth opportunities," http://www3.weforum.org/docs/WEF_SCT_EnablingTrade_Report_2013.pdf.

WTO and IDE-JETRO (2011), "Trade patterns and global value chains in East Asia: From trade in goods to trade in tasks," *World Trade Organization and Institute of Developing Economies*, Geneva and Tokyo, www.ide.go.jp/English/Press/pdf/20110606_news.pdf.

7 Corporate social responsibility in global value chains[1]

Where are we now, and where are we going?

Peter Lund-Thomsen and Adam Lindgreen

Introduction

On September 11, 2012, more than 300 workers died in a fire in the Ali garment factory in the commercial hub of Karachi, Pakistan. Workers were burned alive, succumbed to smoke inhalation, or died after trying to jump from the top floors of the factory building to escape the fire. Many of the windows and exit doors had been blocked by factory managers, preventing workers from escaping the blaze (Walsh and Greenhouse, 2012). Shortly before the fire broke out, the factory complex also had been certified with a SA8000 label – a seal of legitimacy for factories that comply with international labor standards (AFL-CIO, 2013). In November 2012, another 112 workers died in a factory fire in Dhaka, the capital of Bangladesh, when they found themselves trapped on the upper floors of a factory and the fire spread from the bottom to the top floors. This factory supplied Walmart and Sears, both of which (along with other international retailers) claimed they had not been aware that their products were being produced in the Dhaka factory, despite the extensive social and environmental auditing programs they had in place for their suppliers (Yardley, 2012).

Such recent events, including the massive collapse of Bangladesh's Rana Plaza factory in May 2013 that killed more than 1,100 workers, have sparked renewed concerns about the lack of national labor regulations and the inadequacy of existing private social auditing schemes that seek to ensure a basic level of safety and decent work conditions for laborers in export-oriented industries located in developing countries (Locke, 2013). In this chapter, we seek to advance the debate over private social auditing schemes in global value chains. We trace the development of social auditing back to the early 1990s, when international retailers and supermarkets came under public scrutiny for their sourcing practices, after revelations that workers in developing countries were laboring under highly exploitative conditions. Private social auditing – also known as the compliance model – emerged in response to these criticisms. However, during the 2000s and early 2010s, impact assessments of corporate codes of conduct have shown that social auditing schemes (or corporate codes of conduct) at best have brought about limited improvements in workers' conditions, especially in developing country export industries. A broad-based coalition of leading international retailers, private consultants, academics, and nongovernmental organizations (NGOs) thus has started advocating a new cooperative policy paradigm for instituting corporate social responsibility (CSR) in global value chains.

For the purposes of this chapter we use Blowfield and Frynas' (2005, p. 503) definition of CSR,

> an umbrella term for a variety of theories and practices all of which recognize the following: (a) that companies have a responsibility for their impact on society and the natural environment, sometimes beyond legal compliance and the liability of individuals; (b) that companies have a responsibility for the behaviour of others with whom they do business (e.g. within supply chains); and (c) that business needs to manage its relationship with wider society, whether for reasons of commercial viability or to add value to society.

This chapter is not the first to review criticisms of compliance-based models (e.g., AFL-CIO, 2013; De Neve, 2009; Locke et al., 2007, 2009; Locke and Romis, 2007; Lund-Thomsen, 2008; Ruwanpura and Wrigley, 2011) but it makes a unique contribution to critically assess the potential of and limits to an alternative model, namely, the cooperation paradigm for working with CSR in global value chains. We argue that the measures proposed by this paradigm are unlikely to alter power relationships in global value chains fundamentally. Despite the good intentions of its advocates, it cannot deliver sustained improvements in working conditions across developing country export industries, according to our analysis. Drawing on a critical review of the cooperation paradigm, we conclude by suggesting other avenues for research on CSR in global value chains.

Compliance-based paradigm

Drivers

Since the fall of the Berlin Wall in 1989, capitalism has dominated economic activity across the globe (Khara and Lund-Thomsen, 2012). In the 1980s and 1990s, privatization of state-owned enterprises, deregulation of national economies, and liberalization of international trade combined to create an environment in which it was highly attractive for multinational companies to conduct business in developing countries (Utting, 2005). The arrival of new communication technologies such as the Internet and the facsimile, reduced costs for international air travel, and better transportation infrastructure also made it possible for international retailers and supermarkets to source products from countries in Asia, Africa, and Latin America (Haufler, 2001). These countries promised abundant labor supplies, necessary skills and manufacturing capabilities, and much lower wages, such that international buyers reduced their cost structures through extensive outsourcing (Tokatli et al., 2008).

However, the rise of global value chains, through which Western retailers and supermarkets controlled vast networks of suppliers dispersed throughout the world, also raised substantial concerns about the social and environmental conditions in which the goods and services were being manufactured (Seidman, 2007). Campaigns initiated by NGOs, trade unions, student organizations, and the media highlighted the use of child and slave labor, as well as the existence of sweatshops that produced items destined for Western markets (Klein, 2000). Initially, the campaigns largely focused on reforming international policy actors, such as the World Trade Organization (Locke, 2013). As it became increasingly clear that efforts to introduce universal minimum labor and environmental standards would not succeed due to resistance by developing country governments (AFL-CIO, 2013), labor rights and environmental activists turned their attention to campaigning against Western retailers and supermarkets (Bair and Palpaceur, 2012). These campaigns prompted what we call the "compliance-based model" for working with CSR in global value chains (Locke et al., 2009).

Main features

The compliance-based model assumes that NGOs, trade unions, and the media could bring sufficient pressure on international supermarkets and retailers, whether with naming and shaming campaigns in the public media or by mobilizing consumer boycotts of corporations that failed to ensure safe, hygienic work conditions in their supplier factories in developing countries (Locke et al., 2009). Such pressure then should force international companies to develop corporate codes of conduct or ethical guidelines, stipulating the social and environmental conditions in which their products and services were to be produced in developing countries. Compliance with these guidelines could be checked through social and environmental audits undertaken by first-, second-, or third-party monitors to confirm compliance with international buyers' codes of conduct (O'Rourke, 2003, 2006). In theory, factories that displayed a high level of compliance with a buyer's code of conduct would be rewarded with longer-term trading relationships and more orders. Factories that did not attempt to comply with codes of conduct instead would have their orders reduced or even be completely excluded from global supply chains (AFL-CIO, 2013). Our emphasis on "in theory" is deliberate. In practice, we find limited evidence that international buyers systematically cut ties with factories in response to their low social or environmental compliance levels. Nor is there evidence to suggest that suppliers that display high levels of social and environmental compliance receive rewards in the form of more orders (Ruwanpura and Wrigley, 2011).

This description of the compliance-based model is idealized; in reality, various formulations and implementations have emerged across different geographical contexts. As Hughes et al. (2007) observe, some companies and multistakeholder initiatives have focused less strictly on auditing than others. For example, the UK-based Ethical Trading Initiative (ETI) and some of its NGO and company members adopt more aspirational, developmentally oriented approaches, with a focus on long-term improvements in labor conditions in global value chains. Multistakeholder initiatives and corporations in the United States instead tend to adopt a more short-term, compliance-oriented approach. Nevertheless, in both the United States and Europe, widespread agreement admits that the compliance-based model has brought about limited improvements in work conditions in developing country export industries (AFL-CIO, 2013; Locke, 2013; Locke et al., 2007, 2009; Lund-Thomsen et al., 2012; Ruwanpura, 2012).

Throughout the 2000s and into the early 2010s, impact assessment studies showed that codes of conduct improved tangible work conditions, such as the payment of minimum wages, occupational health and safety, and the reduction of overtime work (Barrientos and Smith, 2007; Egels-Zandén, forthcoming; ETI, 2006). Although not directly framed as an impact assessment study, a recent article by Raj-Reickert (2013) indicates that it may not be clear whether measures used in the implementation of corporate codes of conduct (such as indicators, benchmarks, and audits) have any effect on the health and safety of workers.

But codes of conduct had little effect on less tangible issues, such as freedom of association and the right to collective bargaining (Barrientos and Smith, 2007; McIntyre, 2008; Oxfam, 2013). In some cases, it was unclear whether improvements in work conditions resulted from code implementations or other factors, such as a predisposition among supplier managers to treat the workforce well, or broader environmental factors, such as changes in national legislation (Nelson et al., 2007). Such studies also noted inherent problems with this compliance model. First, discrepancies often arose between the commercial practices of international buyers (e.g., demand for lower prices, seasonal products, completion of orders within a short time span) and their insistence on compliance with their codes of conduct (Barrientos, 2013). To meet price points, suppliers could not pay their workers the minimum wage; to address seasonal demand, they could not provide stable employment year round; and they often were compelled to make workers engage in overtime work to meet last-minute orders (or changes) (Oxfam, 2004; Ruwanpura and Wrigley, 2011; Tokatli et al., 2008). The incoherence between international buyers' purchasing practices and their codes of conduct even became institutionalized in their separate purchasing and CSR departments (Harney, 2008). These distinct departments would visit supplier factories at different times and make contradictory demands, such that the purchasing department might require price cuts a week before the CSR compliance staff insisted on higher wages for workers in supplier factories (Khara and Lund-Thomsen, 2012; Ruwanpura and Wrigley, 2011).

Second, this lack of consistency across buyers' purchasing and social auditing practices pushed some local suppliers to engage in auditing fraud – a practice that became particularly widespread in China (Egels-Zandén, forthcoming; Oxfam, 2013). These suppliers trained workers to provide "correct" answers to auditors and used tailored computer programs to falsify worker records. Thus, they met the commercial requirements of international buyers while maintaining the appearance of compliance with corporate codes of conduct (Harney,

2008). When third-party monitors discovered such auditing fraud, they often lacked sufficient incentives to "rock the boat" by demanding significant changes in work conditions from either buyers or suppliers. These monitors usually were commercial auditing firms, so their continued business depended on maintaining good relations with either buyers or suppliers – that is, the clients that paid for the audits to take place. Thus, doubts arose regarding whether the rarely publicized third-party audits could really generate credible evidence about work conditions inside supplier factories (O'Rourke, 2003, 2006). Even more recently, dangerous factory conditions that have caused the deaths of hundreds or thousands of garment workers raised serious concerns about the validity of social auditing, considering that the Karachi-based factory and some of the buildings in Rana Plaza had been certified as compliant with international standards shortly before the deadly incidents (AFL-CIO, 2013; Clean Clothes Campaign/SOMO, 2013).

Conceptual underpinnings

Many assumptions inherent to the compliance paradigm are reminiscent of those in the global value chain framework. For example, Gereffi (1994) proposes that "lead firms," such as European and North American supermarkets and retailers, drive global value chains. Their role is to "govern" the global value chain by determining what kinds of products/services to produce, in which quantity, when, where, and at what price, using dispersed networks of suppliers across the developing world. According to this perspective, suppliers are generally "powerless," with few or limited options for influencing the governance of the chain by the lead firms. Gereffi et al. (2005) add nuance to this view by proposing a theory to explain the nature of value chain relationships among international buyers and their first-tier suppliers in the developing world. These relationships can range from arm's-length, market-based relationships (buyers have full control over suppliers) to hierarchies (buyers own suppliers). In between, modular or relational value chains might be characterized by more equal power relationships between buyers and suppliers.

The compliance-based paradigm similarly assumed that lead firms had the power to dictate and control how products were produced by supplier factories in the developing world. This assumption further indicated that international supermarkets and retailers could control both working and environmental conditions in export-oriented industries. Although this compliance-based paradigm avoided the assumption that all lead firms owned their suppliers (hierarchy), power relationships in the chain were regarded as highly unequal, with first-tier suppliers held "captive" to the social and environmental requirements of buyers.

Gereffi's (1994) original conceptualization of global value chain analysis mentions the role of institutional contexts as part of the global value chain framework. However, this element remained generally underdeveloped until relatively recently, when authors began elaborating on the institutional part of the framework (Nielson and Pritchard, 2009, 2010). In this view, the functioning of global value chains can be understood only in relation to vertical and horizontal dimensions. The vertical dimension refers to the question of who determines the kinds of products that are to be purchased, when, and at what price in global value chains (Gibbon and Ponte, 2005). The horizontal dimension instead entails local socioeconomic contexts of work and employment affected by global value chains. These local institutional contexts include both formal rules of the game, such as economic, social, and environmental laws, and the enforcement agencies charged with implementing such laws (De Neve, forthcoming).

Institutions also refer to the informal rules of the game, or norms and values that various actors hold in relation to what constitutes global value governance (Nielson and Pritchard, 2010). For example, there may be sharply contrasting ideas about "local" and "global" perceptions of whether child labor should be allowed. International NGOs, trade unions, supermarkets, and retailers often insist on prohibitions of child labor; domestic producers may take the view that child labor constitutes a form of job training for children that will enable them to earn a livelihood, particularly if formal schooling options are either nonexistent or of very poor quality (Lund-Thomsen, 2008). As Neilson and Pritchard (2009) argue, the interaction of global value chains and local institutional contexts thus creates struggles over which norms and values should guide export-oriented production in developing countries.

The compliance-based paradigm focused primarily on vertical relations (i.e., trading relationship between international buyers and their suppliers). It has not paid much explicit attention to how horizontal relations (i.e., local socioeconomic and sociocultural contexts of employment in which global value chains are embedded) affect social and environmental compliance levels in developing country export industries. Drawing on Hess (2004), we assert that the compliance-based paradigm tends to ignore the societal embeddedness of global value chain participants (i.e., actors' origins and the influences on their actions without or outside of their societies of origin), as well as their territorial embeddedness (i.e., the extent to which individual actors are anchored in places that facilitate or constrain their actions). Instead, the main focus has been on how the value chain could improve social and environmental conditions in developing country export industries. Implicitly at least, the compliance-based approach seems to have been developed as a response to territorial embeddedness. For example, NGOs and trade unions started campaigning against international lead firms after they realized that many developing country governments were failing to safeguard workers' rights and control environmental pollution levels (Locke, 2013). Thus, they turned to multinational companies to control the social and environmental side effects of outsourcing production to suppliers in developing countries (AFL-CIO, 2013). At the same time, there was perhaps an implicit recognition of the need to ensure the societal embeddedness of corporate codes of conduct. Multinational companies designed codes of conduct to ensure that local suppliers abided by their national laws, such as those dictating how old a person had to be before she or he could be legally employed in a company. These codes of conduct deferred to national laws, even if they also stipulated tougher requirements than those ensconced in national laws (Kolk and Van Tulder, 2004).

Cooperation paradigm

Drivers

In light of these limitations of the compliance-based paradigm, a broad-based coalition of actors began pushing for the adoption of what we call a more cooperative policy paradigm to working with CSR in global value chains (Lund-Thomsen et al., 2012). First, academic researchers have actively cooperated with large multinational companies to research the limitations of the compliance-based paradigm and document alternative ways that international brands might cooperate with suppliers to achieve sustained improvements in work conditions (Locke, 2013; Locke et al., 2007, 2009; Locke and Romis, 2007).

Second, multistakeholder initiatives, such as the UK ETI, Dutch Sustainable Trade Initiative, Danish Ethical Trade Initiative, and Norwegian Sustainable Trade Initiative cooperate across members to find "development-oriented" approaches for improving ethical trade (DIEH, 2013). To some extent, their work has been informed by results from prior impact studies of codes of conduct (e.g., ETI, 2006). These initiatives continue "learning by doing," developing and trying new approaches through projects and working groups, with the aim of establishing best practices for ethical trade. The constant search for new and improved methods of improving CSR in global value chains thus is compatible with the organizational mandates of these initiatives. Various NGOs similarly have participated in broad-based coalitions of actors, pushing for a more cooperative approach to working with CSR in global value chains (IDH, 2009). Oxfam-UK asserts that business can serve an important function for poverty reduction in developing countries (Clay, 2005), so it supports the development of various reports and briefings that document the impact of businesses on society but also how companies – and multinationals in particular – contribute to improving these impacts (Oxfam, 2013). In 2010, Oxfam-UK published a briefing, "Better Jobs in Better Supply Chains," to document how improved labor standards in developing country factories might help boost sales and improve staff recruitment and retention.

Third, private-sector consultants have pioneered a new, cooperation-based approach to CSR in global value chains. For example, the London-based consultancy IMPACTT describes itself as a "leading consultancy company in the area of ethical trade, human rights, labor rights, and international development" (IMPACTT, 2013). In its 2011 report, it detailed how international brands and supermarkets have tried to persuade and instruct suppliers to comply with national labor laws and international labor standards but also why their efforts have made little difference for the conditions of workers at the bottom of global value chains. This report contains several case studies that highlight ways for international brands, suppliers, and workers to identify the "sweet spot" at which their interests intersect. Thus, international brands and suppliers could compete in "an increasingly uncertain world by harnessing the power of the workforces to produce better products more efficiently" (IMPACTT, 2011). In short, various actors – including international buyers, academics with an interest in CSR in global value chains, consultancy companies, and NGOs – have pushed for the adoption of a new paradigm to working with CSR in global value chains.

Main features

In a somewhat stylized fashion, we can identify the main characteristics of the new cooperative paradigm to working with CSR in global value chains. First, international buyers need to review their purchasing practices and provide better prices to their suppliers so that the latter can afford to pay workers higher wages. These buyers also might introduce better production planning to provide business to suppliers throughout the year and avoid last-minute orders (Barrientos, 2013). Maintaining long-term trading relationships with suppliers, instead of shopping around for the cheapest deal, thus becomes crucial for securing better work conditions at the bottom of global value chains (Oxfam, 2010). In addition, coordination between purchasing and CSR departments could enhance the consistency of the demands that these buyers place on suppliers (IDH, 2009).

Second, instead of expecting suppliers to shoulder all of the costs of compliance with codes of conduct, buyers might invest in capacity development for both local supplier managers and workers employed in the factories (Oxfam, 2010). Local factory managers should receive training in human resources management, product quality, and production processes. Instead of seeing workers as a costly input factor, local factory managers need to be trained to understand them as an important company resource (Nike, 2010). Improving worker–management relations also could help reduce the high turnover rates at supplier factories (IMPACTT, 2011). By involving workers more actively in decision-making processes while promoting teamwork and fault finding on factory floors, such tactics could increase productivity (Locke et al., 2009). Moreover, some recommendations include offering workers training in their basic rights and responsibilities in the workplace. Then traditional code implementation and auditing could provide top-down pressures on manufacturers to improve conditions, while workers aware of their rights apply a simultaneous bottom-up pressure to receive safe working conditions (Lund-Thomsen and Coe, 2013). However, a prerequisite for these initiatives was closer cooperation and frequent interactions between the sourcing and CSR personnel of international brands and local factory management. Without such interactions, it would not be possible to secure the simultaneous objectives of enhancing factory competitiveness and work conditions (Locke and Romis, 2007).

Third, considering the poor track record of mainstream social auditing methods, a new range of policy measures has aimed to transform standard setting and auditing in global value chains. With participatory social auditing, auditors would need to be knowledgeable of the local contexts and able to communicate in the native languages of workers (Auret and Barrientos, 2004). These auditors then could move beyond a tick-box approach and short fly in–fly out visits, which rarely revealed fundamental violations. Instead, they would have opportunities to be creative, such as leaving their own contact information with workers, who then could call after the visit if they wanted to convey something outside the usual working hours (Harney, 2008). Some companies started experimenting with off-site visits to interview workers in their homes, where they might feel less pressured to provide particular answers to an auditor's questions. Moreover, cooperation between corporations and local resources, such as NGOs and trade unions, would enable closer, more independent, year-round monitoring of work conditions (Oxfam, 2010). Working with such local resources provided a means to discover unauthorized outsourcing of production to local subcontractors, which otherwise would be difficult to discover through normal snapshot audits.

Conceptual underpinnings

In conceptual terms, the shift to the cooperation-based paradigm marks a change in the nature of value chain governance between international buyers and first-tier suppliers. With its emphasis on long-term, trust-based relationships and close collaboration between international buyers and suppliers, this paradigm mirrors relational value chains, which are characterized by high degrees of mutual dependency in the design, production, and marketing of products/services between buyers and suppliers. Similarly, the cooperation paradigm envisages close collaboration by buyers and first-tier suppliers related to issues such as the introduction of new production techniques or the reorganization of work processes on the factory floor.

The original global value chain approach considered how local suppliers could improve their position in global value chains, with the aim of extracting greater financial benefits from their participation in the global economy (Schmitz, 1999, 2006). The global value chain approach assumed local suppliers could learn from their interactions with global buyers, such as how to improve their products (product upgrading) and production processes (process upgrading). In addition, by learning production skills during interactions with global buyers in one industry, suppliers might transfer these skills and become more competitive in other industries (intersectoral upgrading) (Humphrey and Schmitz, 2002; Schmitz and Nadvi, 1999).

Yet for suppliers to move up the value chain, they also would have to adopt higher-level functions, such as designing and branding their own products (functional upgrading). A consensus emerged that lead firms likely would bar suppliers' functional upgrading, because this step would encroach on their own core competence and turn the suppliers into competitors or new lead firms (Schmitz, 2006). The compliance-based paradigm basically ignored the potential benefits that developing country suppliers might obtain from engaging in social and environmental upgrades to their factories. Instead, they became the "culprits" who failed to address social and environmental concerns, whereas more powerful, international buyers would develop codes of conduct and enforce them rigorously.

In contrast, the cooperation-based paradigm places more emphasis on creating opportunities for product and process upgrading. It emphasizes the business case for social compliance, such that building suppliers' human resources management and production organization capabilities enhance worker productivity and ensure consistent manufacturing of high-quality products (IMPACTT, 2011). Such cooperation also implies a commitment to social upgrading, including increasing the quality and conditions of work by training workers on their legal rights and the relevant codes of conduct (Lund-Thomsen and Coe, 2013). This stylized account of the cooperation paradigm does not place much emphasis on local institutional contexts, particularly the territorial embeddedness of global value chains, but some early signs suggest that this issue is gaining in importance. For example, the ETI (2012) recently announced that its future work would focus on a limited number of value chains (food and farming, hard goods and household, and apparel/textiles), instead of concentrating on thematic issues such as child labor or homework per se (though work continues on these issues). Therefore, the ETI can concentrate on mapping workers' rights violations in specific value chains that entail distinct societal contexts (e.g., southern India). According to this initiative (ETI, 2012, p. 3), "Addressing workers' issues in the context in which they occur will enable us to develop models for wider change that are rooted in reality."

This new approach seems to fit well with insights gained in research highlighting the importance of a good understanding of how CSR becomes embedded in national institutional contexts, in both developed and developing countries (Jamali and Neville, 2011; Matten and Moon, 2008). Institutional perspectives on CSR focus on explaining how and why CSR differs across national or institutional contexts (Brammer et al., 2012; Gond et al., 2011), as well as the potential role of CSR as a global homogenizing force. In this sense, Western conceptions of CSR might spread across the globe as various organizations (and private companies in particular) seek to achieve legitimacy with external stakeholders and respond to mimetic, coercive, and normative pressures (Jamali and Neville, 2011). This search for legitimacy informs the new cooperation-based paradigm, with its focus on international buyers cooperating with local resources, such as NGOs and trade unions that theoretically can provide independent, year-round monitoring of work and environmental conditions at local supplier factory sites. These local resources should provide insights into local work conditions at the bottom of global value chains. From this perspective, the cooperation-based paradigm encompasses a global production networks approach (Henderson et al., 2002). In the global production networks approach, the starting point is the network metaphor, which appears better able to capture global economic organizations than a chain metaphor (Coe et al., 2008).

In practice, lead firms cannot govern their value chains completely. Instead, the governance of global production networks is "spread out," and diverse actors, such as international organizations, national governments, NGOs, trade unions, business associations, workers, and communities, help determine which products to produce, when, where, in what quantities, and at what price (Henderson et al., 2002). The emphasis in the global production networks approach includes all relevant actors in the production network, not just the direct relationship between international buyers and first-tier suppliers, to understand how such networks are governed (Coe et al., 2004). This line of thinking is reflected in the cooperation-based paradigm, in which the effective monitoring of work and environmental conditions at supplier factories cannot be limited to lead firms and suppliers. A wider set of actors is necessary to govern the value chain effectively, including local, place-based NGOs and trade unions with the necessary expertise to assist lead firms in monitoring work conditions in export-oriented industries in developing countries.

The new cooperation paradigm: a critical assessment

Can this new paradigm for CSR in global value chains deliver sustained improvements in workers' conditions, as its many advocates hope and believe? We briefly examine some of the main tensions that exist for the new paradigm.

First, just how widespread is the new cooperation-based paradigm for working with CSR in global value chains? In other words, is this new paradigm being taken up by international retailers and supermarkets, or is it mostly an ideal, preached rather than practiced in global value chains? Despite the dearth of research into the actual practices of the new cooperation paradigm, there are several reasons to question just how widespread it is at the moment. Locke and colleagues (2009) document the cooperation between Nike and some of its suppliers in Central America and Asia, which brought about improvements in workers' conditions. Barrientos (2013) and Lund-Thomsen and Coe (2013) also detail how international brands, NGOs, and trade unions have sought to collaborate on issues such as improving purchasing practices and year-round capacity building. However, Barrientos (2013) also notes that international buyers resist the adoption of responsible practices, and Lund-Thomsen and Coe (2013) describe how the global financial crisis and stakeholder politics partly undermined Nike's attempts to link better supplier incentives, factory management training, and awareness-raising activities among the workers employed at a Pakistani supplier. These important examples suggest how the new cooperation paradigm may work in practice, but we find little evidence to suggest that international brands have fundamentally revised their purchasing practices, engaged in long-term capacity building with suppliers, or cooperated with local NGOs and trade unions to train workers and undertake constant factory monitoring. Both Barrientos (2013) and Lund-Thomsen and Coe (2013) instead offer examples of how the measures advocated by the cooperation paradigm might fail. Moreover, Locke et al.'s (2009) examples do not necessarily reflect the general approach Nike takes to working with its suppliers. The rhetoric surrounding cooperation sounds valid, but it is difficult to imagine how vast corporations such as Nike can realistically engage in close cooperation with more than 800 first-tier suppliers. Collaboration might be feasible with a few selected suppliers engaged in pilot projects; it appears nearly impossible to replicate such close cooperation across hundreds of suppliers, considering just the logistical challenges. Instead, traditional forms of compliance monitoring likely will continue to offer the dominant approach to working with CSR in global value chains, supplemented with occasional pilot projects that seek to develop functional alternatives.

Second, the cooperation-based paradigm emphasizes long-term relationships and investments in capacity building, but few "Southern" voices have taken part in defining this new paradigm. Rather, it appears advocated mainly by international brands, Northern-based consultants, academics, and NGOs. The voices of developing country suppliers, workers, and communities have remained largely silent. This is hardly a new critique of CSR approaches that originate in Europe and North America (Blowfield and Frynas, 2005; Prieto-Carron et al., 2006), but the absence of Southern voices in advocating this change to working with CSR in global value chains can reinforce existing inequalities in global value chain governance. The new cooperation paradigm thus appears to do little to change the basic status quo, in which only certain actors (i.e., international retailers) dictate the terms of their trade with local suppliers. From this perspective, the cooperation paradigm can do little to alter suppliers' perceptions that CSR in global value chains is a form of economic and cultural imperialism (Khan and Lund-Thomsen, 2011). In economic terms, some actors demand that workers be hired as permanent, full-time employees and paid compensation after layoffs, but if they cannot guarantee sufficient work throughout the year – or at least not in the same quantity – it becomes financially impossible for local suppliers to keep a permanent workforce employed at factories (Lund-Thomsen, 2008). These same corporations often insist that local suppliers pay the costs associated with upgrading factories; that is, they demand improvements but are not willing to share the costs of achieving them (Ruwanpura and Wrigley, 2011). In cultural terms, the norms and values underlying CSR rhetoric often represent impositions on developing country suppliers that operate in diverse contexts (Nadvi, 2008) distinct from those that determine the norms of Western Europe or North America. For example, whereas child labor is a social evil in Western views of the world, it offers a means of informal education and family support in some areas of South Asia (A. Khan, 2007). This "education" not only helps support the family but also enables children to learn a profession that will sustain them later in life. In contexts characterized by desperate poverty and unavailable schooling, child labor may be part of broader livelihood strategies, used to stay alive (F.R. Khan, 2007; Ruwanpura and Roncolata, 2006).

Another question pertains to whether the cooperation-based approach even is feasible in the context of wider capitalist competition. For example, international consumers seemingly dictate the price and quality requirements for particular goods and services (Gibbon and Ponte, 2005). International corporations respond to these consumer demands by designing products with matching price and quality ranges. Then they place orders reflecting the quantity, quality, and price ranges demanded by consumers across vast networks of suppliers in developing countries that engage in fierce competition to attract and sustain this business (Gereffi, 1994). In response to supply chain pressures, local suppliers structure networks of contractors, contractors, and workers to obtain the required inputs at the lowest possible price. In this competitive context, there is very little scope for cooperation beyond the limits set by international consumer markets that demand simultaneously constant price decreases, shorter lead times, and maintenance of product quality (Khara and Lund-Thomsen, 2012; Tokatli et al., 2008). Even were improved cooperation between buyers and suppliers to arise, nothing in the new paradigm ensures a revised sharing of the benefits across the value chain participants. As Kaplinsky (2000) illustrates, securing effective returns on value chain participation depends on the kinds of rents that value chain participants can obtain. Economic rents may be attained through differential productivity (among enterprises or workers) and the erection of barriers to entry (Kaplinsky, 2005). To the extent that international buyers still command the most rents in the value chain, through their control of the design, branding, market, and distribution of consumer products and services, shifting to a cooperation paradigm is unlikely to increase supplier incomes substantially enough to sustain improvements in work conditions and living standards. That is, the cooperation paradigm does not fundamentally challenge the inequality inherent in global value chains. Drawing on Lund-Thomsen (2008), if a local worker is paid 60 cents for stitching a football in Pakistan, the management of the local supplier might be paid 5 dollars for selling that ball to an international brand, before it is sold in an outlet store in Europe or North America at a price of US$100. In other words, international retailers continue to capture most of the value from global value chain participation; suppliers and workers in developing countries obtain marginal shares of the overall value generated. Nor does the new paradigm do anything to alter the basic system of "sweating" (Miller, 2012). Garment manufacturing had already taken on a pyramid shape in the early 20th century in the United States and Germany: At the top sat so-called "jobbers" that had developed their own designs (and sometimes manufacturing capabilities). They increasingly used production mediators ("sweaters") that could "extract[] the most labour . . . at the lowest possible price from manufacturing units with the most vulnerable workers that could be found" (Miller, 2012, p. 1). In reference to Blackburn (2007), Miller argues that this system works in contexts marked by an oversupply of labor and no union organization, varying or seasonal demand, and a lack of proper management. The discourse in the cooperation paradigm aims to address root causes of poor working conditions at the bottom of global value chains, but it does little, if anything, to change the pyramid-shaped, unequal, exploitative (global) production system. Perhaps the strongest critique of the cooperation paradigm is that it fails to grant workers sufficient agency in governing the global value chains. An emerging body of literature notes local workers in export-oriented industries who prefer not to work in CSR-compliant factories (De Neve, 2009; Lund-Thomsen, 2013). The main point is to show the diversity of lived experiences among workers engaged in export-oriented manufacturing, particularly in South Asia. Workers are not a uniform input factor; they are living, sentient beings with great diversity in their sex, age, family, economic, cultural, and caste backgrounds. Such diversity influences their preferences to opt into or out of different work practices and places. Carswell and De Neve (2013) demonstrate that young, unmarried, female migrant workers appear content working in formalized, export-oriented factories in Tiruppur, Tamil Nadu, India, because this type of work helps them maximize their earnings and savings, which will help them later in their lives. Once these workers marry, they often are expected to adopt primary child-rearing and domestic household responsibilities, such that full-time factory-based work in the city may no longer be feasible for them. Instead, home-based work likely offers a more appealing option, enabling them to earn some income, even if relatively meager, while balancing their domestic duties with income-generating means (see also Lund-Thomsen, 2013).

Conclusions

With this chapter, we have argued that leading retailers, consultants, NGOs, and academics recognize the limitations of traditional compliance-based models of working with CSR in global value chains. With this model, international NGOs, trade unions, student organizations, and the media pressured multinational companies to adopt voluntary social and environmental guidelines for the performance of their supplier factories in developing countries. In theory (but rarely in practice), this approach would reward CSR-compliant factories and punish those that did not comply. In practice, the compliance model induced relatively modest improvements in work conditions for laborers in export-oriented industries in developing countries. Therefore, a coalition of academics, consultants, leading retailers, and NGOs has advocated a new, cooperation-based paradigm to rectify the shortcomings of the compliance-based paradigm. In the new paradigm, international buyers revise their purchasing practices, help build the capacity of local factory management and workers, and cooperate with local resources (e.g., NGOs, trade unions) to improve factory monitoring and thus labor standard compliance.

By critically assessing the potential and limitations of this new paradigm, we argue that it is unlikely to alter the power relations of international buyers, suppliers, and workers in global value chains. In particular, the new paradigm seems unable to secure significantly higher incomes or improved conditions for workers, considering the constraints imposed by worldwide competition among suppliers. International markets instead appear likely to remain volatile, ever-changing, and demanding, such that suppliers realistically cannot undertake significant upgrades in the conditions of employment for workers without the threat that corporations will relocate their production to other capable, cheaper (and less compliant) suppliers elsewhere in the developing world. Furthermore, the verdict is still out regarding whether this cooperative paradigm will receive wider recognition and uptake among international brands. Several themes could guide important investigations into the effects of this new paradigm, including (1) the link between buyer purchasing practices and labor standard (non) compliance in developing country factories, (2) efforts to develop the capacity of local supplier management in the area of human resources management, and (3) cooperation between international buyers and local resources.

Purchasing practices and labor standard noncompliance

Multiple NGO reports and academic articles have pointed to the potentially adverse consequences of corporate purchasing practices on labor standard compliance in developing country factories (Barrientos and Smith, 2007; Oxfam, 2004; Traidcraft, 2006), yet the topic lacks sufficient insights from CSR research in global value chains (cf. Barrientos, 2013). Further investigations of the new CSR paradigm should fill this gap by linking the hitherto unconnected literature streams related to supply chain/operations management and labor standards/codes of conduct in global value chains. In the former, the focus has been mainly on how to optimize processes for sourcing products from domestic or overseas suppliers and pay the lowest possible price for the best possible product, delivered in the shortest possible time frame. Labor research in global value chains instead has addressed how workers (1) benefit from participation in global value chains, (2) are affected by corporations' ethical guidelines and economic upgrading or downgrading processes by local supplier firms, and (3) actively exert their agency to influence their work conditions (Barrientos et al., 2011; Nadvi, 2004; Riisgaard, 2009; Riisgaard and Hammer, 2011). Investigations of the effects of the new cooperative paradigm on CSR in global value chains thus could help build a bridge between operations and supply chain management studies and research into labor standards in global value chains by theorizing and empirically investigating how corporate purchasing practices affect labor standard compliance levels, whether positively or negatively, in developing country export industries.

Another research focus could detail the performance systems in which purchasing managers operate to determine how different policies reward and/or punish decision making that integrates economic, social, and environmental criteria in purchasing practices. Such investigations would require more in-depth analyses or interviews with purchasing managers and personnel regarding pricing, lead times, product quality, the use of particular production technologies, and management systems. An important theme in this direction might consider how purchasing managers deal with the multiple sustainability dilemmas they face when executing purchasing/sourcing/CSR activities. Researchers would need to ask when and why "classical" purchasing practices seem compatible or conflict with social and environmental sustainability criteria. Research attention also might address resolutions to the sustainability dilemma, including the strategies that purchasing managers already employ when they face multiple requirements. For example, what decision-making processes do managers adopt when they must choose between responding to price pressures by buyers or devoting resources to improving their social/environmental performance? On the other side, how do buyers decide whether to shop around for the cheapest possible bargain or to engage in long-term cooperation with their suppliers?

CSR capacity building among local suppliers

Research into the effects of the new cooperative paradigm on CSR should investigate whether pilot projects that have attempted to improve human resources management capacity at local supplier factories have been successful. The new cooperation paradigm predicts that improved human resources management leads to greater labor standard compliance (IMPACTT, 2011). Theoretically, this assumption is reminiscent of Grimshaw and Rubery's (2005) mutual gains approach, according to which the formal employment relationship provides guarantees to workers (e.g., formal contracts, limits to overtime work, health insurance) in return for workers' cooperation, such that both parties gain. That is, employers gain access to a skilled and committed workforce, turnover declines, and productivity increases, while workers enjoy stable work, income, and productive employment. Empirically, the question is whether such an approach is feasible or realistic in competitive international environments marked by declining piece rates, shorter lead times, increasing quality demands, and demands for buyers and suppliers to maintain flexibility to respond quickly to changing market needs (Tokatli et al., 2008).

We thus call for studies that empirically investigate whether attempts at building suppliers' capacity, such as in human resources management, really improve relations between management and workers, despite the broader competitive pressures that global value chain participation entails. Research attention also should consider how power relationships in the value chain affect possibilities for sustaining upgrades. For example, there may be differences in the ways large retailers and small or medium-sized importers engage in capacity building. For large retailers with hundreds or thousands of suppliers, long-term capacity building measures may be infeasible beyond a few select suppliers, chosen specifically for this benefit. Smaller importers with fewer suppliers instead may be better positioned to engage in long-term cooperation, such that a mutual gains approach could be more applicable. If small and medium-sized importers depend on single suppliers in relational chains, their incentives to invest in long-term CSR upgrading efforts at local factories in the developing world likely are greater.

Improved CSR monitoring by local resources

The third part of a research agenda related to the new cooperation paradigm should consider the use of local resources that act as the eyes and ears of international retailers and supermarkets on the ground, offering year-round monitoring of work conditions in supplier factories (Oxfam, 2010). Similar to the issue with capacity building, this theme has important implications for power relations. According to the cooperation paradigm, local resources might extend the power of international retailers and supermarkets to control social and environmental conditions in supplier factories – but at a price. For example, local NGOs risk becoming financially dependent on international corporations, creating questions about their ability to assess work conditions independently (Baur and Schmitz, 2012). Such cooperation with international firms also creates the risk that the more radical advocacy agendas of NGOs might get toned down in favor of maintaining cooperative relationships (Newell, 2001).

Similarly, local trade unions would confront challenges were they to engage in year-round monitoring of work conditions in local export industries. Traditionally, unions have cited freedom of association and the right to collective bargaining as the most important labor rights and the best means to facilitate improved working conditions in factory-based work settings. Without the right to organize collectively and negotiate for improved work conditions, real changes in compliance with labor standards may be unlikely (AFL-CIO, 2013). From this point of view, serving as a local resource that monitors work conditions at local supplier factories for international corporations might dilute the very *raison d'etre* of trade unions. Instead of taking a seat at the table and engaging in collective bargaining, unions might suddenly find themselves part of the private regulatory efforts of Western companies, whose standards have been determined unilaterally. Further investigations of the new cooperation paradigm for CSR in global value chains thus should attend carefully to both the possibilities and the challenges that such forms of cooperation present, not only for international firms but also for the freedom and independence of local NGOs and trade unions.

Note

1 Acknowledgement: This manuscript has appeared in *Journal of Business Ethics*: 2014, Vol. 123, No. 1, pp. 11–22. Rights to reprint the paper as part of this collection has been obtained from Springer.

References

AFL-CIO (2013). *Responsibility outsourced: social audits, workplace certification and twenty years of failure to protect workers' rights.* AFL-CIO, Washington, DC.

Auret, D. and Barrientos, S. (2004). *Participatory social auditing – a practical guide to developing a gender sensitive approach.* IDS Working Paper no. 237, Institute of Development Studies, University of Sussex, Brighton.

Bair, J. and Palpaceur, F. (2012). From varieties of capitalism to varieties of activism. *Social Problems*, 59(4), 522–543.

Barrientos, S. (2013). Corporate purchasing practices in global production networks – a socially contested terrain. *Geoforum*, 44(1), 44–51.

Barrientos, S., Gereffi, G. and Rossi, A. (2011). Economic and social upgrading in global production networks: a new paradigm for a changing world. *International Labour Review*, 150(3–4), 319–40.

Barrientos, S. and Smith, S. (2007). Do workers benefit from ethical trade? Assessing codes of labour practice in global production systems. *Third World Quarterly*, 28(4), 713–729.

Baur, D. and Schmitz, H.P. (2012). Corporations and NGOs: When accountability leads to cooptation. *Journal of Business Ethics*, 106(1), 9–21.

Blackburn, S. (2007). *A fair day's wage for a fair day's labour – sweated labour and the origin of minimum wage legislation in Britain*. Ashgate, Alderton.

Blowfield, B. and Frynas, J.G. (2005). Editorial. Setting new agendas: critical perspectives on corporate social responsibility in the developing world. *International Affairs*, 81(1), 499–513.

Brammer, S., Jackson, G. and Matten, D. (2012). Corporate social responsibility and institutional theory: new perspectives on private governance. *Socio-Economic Review*, 10(1), 3–28.

Carswell, G. and De Neve, G. (2013). Labouring for global markets: conceptualising labour agency in global production networks. *Geoforum*, 44(1), 62–70.

Clay, J. (2005). *Exploring the links between international business and poverty reduction*. Oxfam, Unilever, Oxford.

Clean Clothes Campaign/SOMO (2013). *Fatal fashion – analysis of recent factory fires in Pakistan and Bangladesh: a call to protect and respect garment workers' lives*. Clean Clothes Campaign/SOMO, Amsterdam.

Coe, N.M., Dicken, P. and Hess, M. (2008). Introduction: global production networks: debates and challenges. *Journal of Economic Geography*, 8(3), 267–269.

Coe, N.M., Hess, Yeung, H.W.C., Dicken, P. and Henderson, J. (2004). Globalizing regional development: a global production networks perspective. *Transactions of the Institute of British Geographers*, 29(4), 468–484.

De Neve, G. (2009). Power, inequality and corporate social responsibility: the politics of compliance in the south Indian garment industry. *Economic and Political Weekly*, 44(22), 63–71.

De Neve, G. (forthcoming). Fordism, flexible specialization and CSR: how Indian garment workers critique neoliberal labor regimes. *Ethnography*.

DIEH (2013). *Annual report 2012 ("Årsrapport 2012")*. Danish Ethical Trading Initiative, Copenhagen.

Egels-Zandén, N. (forthcoming). Revisiting supplier compliance with MNC codes of conduct: recoupling policy & practice at Chinese toy suppliers. *Journal of Business Ethics*.

Ethical Trading Initiative (ETI) (2006). *ETI code of labor practice – Do workers really benefit?* Institute of Development Studies, University of Sussex, Brighton.

Ethical Trading Initiative (ETI) (2012). *Ethical trade initiative – annual review 2011*. ETI, London.

Gereffi, G. (1994). The organization of buyer-driven global commodity chains: how US retailers shape overseas production networks. In: Gereffi, G. and Korzeniewicz, M. (Eds.), *Commodity chains and global capitalism*. Praeger, Westport, CT, 95–122.

Gereffi, G., Humphrey, J. and Sturgeon, T. (2005). The governance of global value chains. *Review of International Political Economy*, 12(1), 78–104.

Gibbon, P. and Ponte, S. (2005). *Trading down: Africa, value chains and the global economy*. Temple University Press, Philadelphia, PA.

Gond, J.P., Kang, N. and Moon, J. (2011). The government of self-regulation: on the comparative dynamics of corporate social responsibility. *Economy and Society*, 40(4), 640–671.

Grimshaw, D. and Rubery, J. (2005). Inter-capital relations and the network organisation: redefining the work and employment nexus. *Cambridge Journal of Economics*, 29(6), 1027–1051.

Harney, A. (2008). *The China price – the true cost of competitive advantage*. Penguin Press, London.

Haufler, V. (2001). *A public role for the private sector – industry self-regulation in the global economy*. Carnegie Endowment for International Peace, Washington, DC.

Henderson, J., Dicken, P., Hess, M., Coe, N.M. and Yeung, H.W-C. (2002). Global production networks and the analysis of economic development. *Review of International Political Economy*, 9(3), 436–464.

Hess, M. (2004). Spatial relationships? Towards a reconceptualization of embeddedness. *Progress in Human Geography*, 28(2), 165–186.

Hughes, A., Buttle, M. and Wrigley, N. (2007). Organisational geographies of corporate responsibility: a UK-US comparison of retailers' ethical trading initiatives. *Journal of Economic Geography*, 7(4), 491–513.

Humphrey, J. and Schmitz, H. (2002). How does insertion in global value chains affect upgrading in industrial clusters? *Regional Studies*, 36(9), 1017–1027.

IDH (2009). *Beyond auditing – tapping the full potential of labor standards promotion*. Dutch Sustainable Trade Initiative (IDH), Amsterdam.

IMPACTT (2011). *Finding the sweet spot: smarter ethical trade that delivers more for all*. IMPACTT, London.

IMPACTT (2013). *About us*, www.impacttlimited.com/about-us (accessed 28 April 2013).

Jamali, D. and Neville, B. (2011). Convergence vs. divergence in CSR in developing countries: an embedded multi-layered institutional lens. *Journal of Business Ethics*, 102(4), 599–621.

Kaplinsky, R. (2000). Globalisation and unequalisation: what can be learned from global value chain analysis? *Journal of Development Studies*, 37(2), 117–146.

Kaplinsky, R. (2005). *Globalization, poverty, and inequality – between a rock and a hard place*. Polity Press, Cambridge.

Khan, A. (2007). *Power, policy and the discourse on child labour in the football manufacturing industry of Sialkot*. Oxford University Press, Karachi, Pakistan.

Khan, F.R. (2007). Representational approaches matter. *Journal of Business Ethics*, 73(1), 77–89.

Khan, F.R. and Lund-Thomsen, P. (2011). CSR as imperialism: towards a phenomenological approach to CSR in the developing world. *Journal of Change Management*, 11(1), 73–90.

Khara, N. and Lund-Thomsen, P. (2012). Value chain restructuring, work organization, and labor outcomes in Football manufacturing in India. *Competition and Change*, 16(4), 261–280.

Klein, N. (2000). *No logo: taking aim at the brand bullies*. Taylor & Francis, New York.

Kolk, A. and Tulder, R.V. (2004). Ethics in international business: multinational approaches to child labor. *Journal of World Business*, 39(1), 49–60.

Locke, R.M. 2013. Lead essay: can global brands create just supply chains? *Boston Review*, May–June.

Locke, R.M., Amanguel, M. and Mangla, A. (2009). Virtue out of necessity: compliance, commitment, and the improvement of labor standards. *Politics & Society*, 37(3), 319–351.

Locke, R.M., Qin, F. and Brause, A. (2007). Does monitoring improve labor standards? Lessons from Nike. *Industrial and Labor Relations Review*, 61(1), 3–31.

Locke, R.M. and Romis, M. (2007). Improving work conditions in global supply chains. *MIT Sloan Management Review*, 48(2), 54–62.

Lund-Thomsen, P. (2008). The global sourcing and codes of conduct debate: five myths and five recommendations. *Development and Change*, 39(6), 1005–1018.

Lund-Thomsen, P. (2013). Labour agency in the football manufacturing industry of Sialkot, Pakistan. *Geoforum*, 44(1), 61–71.

Lund-Thomsen, P. and Coe, N. (2013). *CSR and labor agency: the case of Nike in Pakistan*. Working Paper, 3/2013, Center for Corporate Social Responsibility, Copenhagen Business School, Copenhagen.

Lund-Thomsen, P., Nadvi, K., Chan, A., Kahra, N. and Xue, H. (2012). Labour in global value chains: work conditions in football manufacturing in China, India and Pakistan. *Development and Change*, 43(6), 1211–1237.

Matten, D. and Moon, J. (2008). Implicit and explicit CSR: a conceptual framework for a comparative understanding of corporate social responsibility. *Academy of Management Review*, 33(2), 404–424.

McIntyre, R. (2008). *Are worker rights, human rights?* University of Michigan Press, Ann Arbor, MI.

Miller, D. (2012). *Last nightshift in Savar: the story of the Spectrum sweater factory collapse.* McNidder and Grace, Alnwick.

Nadvi, K. (2004). Globalisation and poverty: how can global value chain research inform the policy debate? *IDS Bulletin*, 35(1), 20–30.

Nadvi, K. (2008). Global standards, global governance and the organisation of global value chains. *Journal of Economic Geography*, 8(3), 323–343.

Neilson, J. and Pritchard, B. (2009). *Value chain struggles: institutions and governance in the plantations of South India.* Wiley-Blackwell, Gloucester.

Neilson, J. and Pritchard, B. (2010). Fairness and ethicality in their place – the regional dynamics of fair trade and ethical sourcing agendas in the plantation districts of South India. *Environment and Planning A*, 42(8), 1833–1851.

Nelson, V., Martin, A. and Ewert, J. (2007). The impacts of codes of practice on worker livelihoods. *Journal of Corporate Citizenship*, 28, 61–78.

Newell, P. (2001). Managing multinationals: the governance of investment for the environment. *Journal of International Development*, 13(7), 907–919.

Nike (2010). Corporate social responsibility report – FY 07, 08, 09. Nike, Beaverton, OR.

O'Rourke, D. (2003). Outsourcing regulation: analyzing non-governmental systems of labor standards and monitoring. *Policy Studies Journal*, 31(1), 1–29.

O'Rourke, D. (2006). Multi-stakeholder regulation: privatizing or socializing global labor standards. *World Development*, 34(5), 899–918.

Oxfam (2004). *Trading away our rights: women working in global supply chains.* Oxfam International, Oxford.

Oxfam (2010). Better jobs in better supply chains. *Briefings for Business no. 5.* Oxfam, Oxford.

Oxfam (2013). *Labour rights in Unilever's supply chain: from compliance towards good practice.* Oxfam International, Oxford.

Prieto-Carron, M., Lund-Thomsen, P., Chan, A., Muro, A. and Bhushan, C. (2006). Critical perspectives on CSR and development: what we know, what we don't and what we need to know. *International Affairs*, 82(5), 977–987.

Raj-Reichert, R. (2013). Safeguarding labour in distant factories: health and safety governance in an electronics production network. *Geoforum*, 44(1), 23–31.

Riisgaard, L. (2009). Global value chains, labor organization and private social standards: lessons from East African cut flower industries. *World Development*, 37(2), 326–340.

Riisgaard, L. and Hammer, N. (2011). Prospects for labour in global value chains: labor standards in the cut flower and banana industries. *British Journal of Industrial Relations*, 49(1), 168–190.

Ruwanpura, K. (2012). *Ethical codes: reality and rhetoric – a study of Sri Lanka's apparel sector.* University of Southampton, Southampton, GB.

Ruwanpura, K. and Roncolata, L. (2006). Child rights: an enabling or disabling right? The nexus between child labor and poverty in Bangladesh. *Journal of Developing Societies*, 22(4), 359–378.

Ruwanpura, K. and Wrigley, N. (2011). The costs of compliance? Views of Sri Lankan apparel manufacturers in times of global economic crisis. *Journal of Economic Geography*, 11(6), 1–19.

Schmitz, H. (1999). Global competition and local cooperation: success and failure in the Sinos Valley, Brazil. *World Development*, 27(9), 1627–50.

Schmitz, H. (2006). Learning and earning in global garment chains. *European Journal of Development Research*, 18(4), 546–571.

Schmitz, H. Nadvi, K. (1999). Clustering and industrialization: special issue. *World Development*, 27(9), 1503–14.

Seidman, G. (2007). *Beyond the boycott – labor rights, human rights, and transnational activism.* Russel Sage Foundation, New York.

Tokatli, N., Wrigley, N. and Kizilgün, O. (2008). Shifting global supply networks and fast fashion: made in Turkey for Marks & Spencer. *Global Networks*, 8(3), 261–280.

Traidcraft (2006). *Buying matters – consultation – sourcing fairly from developing countries.* Traidcraft, London.

Utting, P. (2005). Corporate responsibility and the movement of business. *Development in Practice*, 15(3–4), 375–388.

Walsh, D. and Greenhouse, S. (2012). Certified safe, a factory in Karachi still quickly burned. *The New York Times*, December 7.

Yardley, J. (2012). Horrific fire revealed a gap in safety for global brands. *The New York Times*, December 6.

8 Critical reflections on responsible business initiatives and systemic constraints for achieving a safe and just operating space for humanity[1]

Valerie Nelson and Michael Flint

Prospects for responsible business and alarm bells

There is a sustainability gap between current business performance and the changes needed to achieve sustainability (GRI, UNGC, WBCSD, 2015, p. 19).[2] From a sustainable development perspective, as defined in "Our Common Future" (Brundtland, 1987), development must not only satisfy current human needs but the needs of all future generations. Later work grounds this broad-ranging definition of sustainable development in scientific definitions of planetary environmental (Steffen et al., 2009) and social thresholds (Raworth, 2017), within which human activity should be confined to provide a '*safe and just operating space for humanity*' (Raworth, 2017). In this chapter we analyze prospects for changes in business behavior, such that business impact enables the achievement of this goal of sustainable development within safe and just boundaries, rather than undermining it.

The United Nations Sustainable Development Goals (SDGs) provide a new set of global aspirations, and many large companies are rapidly aligning their activities to these (KPMG, 2017). However, global business impact is intimately intertwined with the current global ecological crisis, and the globalizing economy is linked to social inequality and wealth concentration.[3] Questions arise as to whether global business and the global economy in their current forms can enable the delivery of the SDGs. In this chapter, we consider whether current efforts to achieve responsibility in business are effective in light of the urgent need to achieve sustainable and equitable development.

Donors are increasingly supporting private-sector-led development. Many leading businesses and some business management literature already recognize the need for rapid action. Winston (2014) suggests corporate strategies conduct a "big pivot" to respond to sustainability challenges. There are inescapable challenges in a "resource-constrained" economy for core business models (Blowfield, 2013). However, what is not clear is the extent of actual change in corporate practice.

Definitions of responsible business and corporate responsibility are the subject of extensive academic debate, but all share the belief that companies have a responsibility for the public good (Blowfield and Murray, 2014). Approaches range from incremental modifications in business behavior via risk management, to approaches in which businesses are actively diligent, transparent, and accountable with sustainability impacts to radical changes in ownership and business models. However, the delineation of which are the morally significant actors worthy of attention and the issues judged "material" to companies or wider stakeholders still largely depends upon on perspective and position. Anchoring "responsibility" in business, we suggest, should be linked to clear science-based environmental targets and internationally recognized human rights

Initiatives seeking to influence corporate responsibility proliferate. Responsible business initiatives (RBIs) are external to companies and mostly nongovernmental in nature. Earlier RBIs provided product sustainability standards and promoted corporate sustainability reporting. More recent initiatives employ a wider set of approaches to influence companies, but there has been limited articulation of their theories of change (see the third section). We review the available evidence on RBI effectiveness and impact in the fourth section, drawing upon (1) a comprehensive review of the academic and gray literature and (2) long-standing interactions with RBIs through a series of donor-funded evaluations, impact studies, and academic research on private standards governance. We conclude with a preliminary exploration of complementary and alternative approaches.

Responsible business initiatives: an overarching theory of change

To conceptualize RBIs and how they seek to effect change, we develop a generic theory of change, which sets out the anticipated causal steps and assumptions (Figure 8.1).

When effectively implemented, the theory of change anticipates that the responsible business capacity of companies and other stakeholders is enhanced. Stronger capacity (knowledge, skills and attitudes, opportunity such as change in business case, motivation) is anticipated to lead to a change in company practices (e.g., standards for workplace employees) and in corporate procurement in supply chains. A spectrum of behavior change is feasible, from public aspirations and commitments, through policy development or modifications, to more concrete changes in management systems and practices. The length of the causal chain is longer in long and complex global supply chains. Corporate behavior change in supply chains comprises changes in purchasing and recruitment practices. The latter are a pivotal step in the theory of change: without these changes, it is unlikely that supplier behavior will also change. Note that in some industries, suppliers are increasingly powerful and the negotiating power of buyers is less strong. There are often multiple sets of suppliers in supply chains in developing countries (tier 1, tier 2, etc.), and for responsible business to be

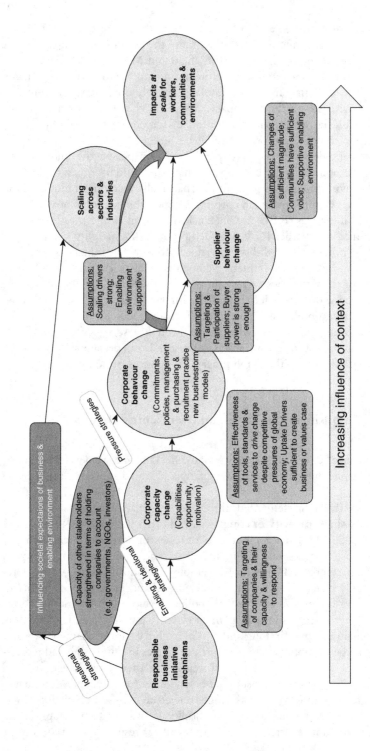

Figure 8.1 A generic theory of change for responsible business initiatives

achieved requires changes at each stage in terms of improved supplier capacity and incentives, as well as behaviors.

It is important to note that changes are unlikely to be as linear in practice: companies can move forward on an issue and then backtrack again; progress on some issues might be accompanied by backwards steps on others; leaps forward may be undertaken with new leadership or as technological and market factors create different opportunities and pressures.

Ultimately, responsible business in operations and among suppliers is antici- pated as leading to positive benefits and impacts for workers, communities, and environments. Moving beyond individual companies entails scaling processes in which practices are not confined to market leading companies, but other com- panies crowd in, new start-ups disrupt business models, and/or governments step in to create a level playing field, institutionalizing and promoting higher standards of responsible business through policies and regulatory changes.

Multiple assumptions underpin this theory of change: diverse preconditions need to be in place for the *theory* of change to hold true in *practice* at every step of the way. In the next section, we unpack the evolving strategies employed by RBIs, before analyzing evidence of their comparative and overall effectiveness.

Conceptualizing responsible business initiative strategies

To date, there has been limited conceptualization of *how* RBIs work. One report on "Inclusive Capitalism" (Said Business School, Oxford University, 2016) names key influencing strategies,[4] which we draw upon and adapt, cat- egorizing them into three types of strategies and extending the analysis to how they are anticipated to cause change, namely, (1) enabling strategies, (2) pressure strategies, and (3) ideational strategies.

First, enabling strategies support companies to improve their understanding, attitudes, and skills on responsibility issues, and possibly responses, and to create new opportunities and motivation for action. RBIs provide tools and services, such as setting and operationalizing standards for products and businesses to strengthen corporate capacity. Many corporate sustainability reporting princi- ples, guidelines, and standards are now mature initiatives and share the aim of increasing corporate disclosure and transparency, with other actors expected to use this disclosed information to hold companies to account. Capacity strengthening for business and sectors includes bespoke training (e.g., human rights training). Many RBIs also engage corporate leaders in safe spaces and seek to shift mind-sets and co-generate ideas, using peer comparisons to stimu- late stronger corporate leadership.

Second, pressure strategies are tools used as a way of stepping up pressure on companies on sustainability issues. Examples include the rating of companies in public benchmarks on specific areas of performance, such as the Access to Medicines Index. The publication of these ratings is anticipated as increasing pressure on those that do not perform well to do more and potentially reward- ing those that score highly to sustain or improve their practices. Mobilizing investor pressure is an increasingly common approach: RBIs seek to inform investors and pressure them to raise issues with investees. This is a form of financial pressure which is anticipated to lead to changes in the business case for corporate action.

Third, ideational strategies are used by RBIs aiming to shift societal expectations about what is "good" enterprise by changing cultural norms and advocating for governance innovations such that "good" enterprise is more feasible. Some RBIs rely upon their convening power to do this: for example, the United Nations (UN) Global Compact seeks to inform global discourse by engaging companies, governments, and civil society. Others seek to intervene more directly. For example, B Lab has created the concept of benefit corporations in which corporate forms require and enable companies to balance societal as well as shareholder interests. Legal roadmaps are identified, social movements and civic networks are established, and impact tools are provided so that companies can self-assess their sustainability impact. Some RBIs advocate changes in governmental policies and normative frameworks for a more level playing field in the enabling environment.

Assessing the evidence of responsible business initiative effectiveness and impact

RBIs vary in the responsible business issues they focus on. Some tackle individual issues; others are comprehensive in approach. Many of the issues tackled are highly relevant to poverty reduction agendas. Most RBIs work with companies and sectors involving large numbers of poor people. However, RBIs do not necessarily prioritize poverty reduction or specifically target workers in global supply chains or the poor communities affected by businesses. In terms of corporate targeting and reach, many RBIs operate from headquarters in end markets anticipating a trickle-down effect along complex supply chains to workers, communities, and environments in developing countries (i.e., the impact pathway is long with many inherent assumptions).

Uptake of RBI services/products beyond market leaders is less strong. There are signs of more extensive uptake of reporting, but the quality is highly variable and there remain some companies and sectors where reporting is not yet normalized (KPMG, 2017[5]). There are positive membership trends for many RBIs (e.g., Global Reporting Initiative [GRI], ISEAL, B Lab, Ethical Trading Initiative [ETI], UN Global Compact [UNGC]), indicating that some global businesses perceive value in adoption. However, adoption could also be used to protect reputations, rather than signaling actual intent to change practices. Research finds that more polluting companies are the most likely to engage in corporate reporting. From a global business perspective, only a small minority of companies are willing to participate. Although membership may be growing, this can be from a very small base: one of the largest RBIs – United Nations Global Compact – only covers 2 percent of listed companies and global gross domestic product (GDP). Further, uptake is not an indicator of the extent of change within companies. Topple et al., 2017, find a falling away of implementation beyond company headquarters.

RBIs generally target multinational companies, yet small and medium-sized enterprises (SMEs) are the bulk of global business, constituting 80 to 90 percent of employment in developing countries, generating a large part of the employment in the lower tiers of global supply chains, but often characterized by the worst working conditions.[6] Several RBIs are seeking to tailor their standards and guidance for SMEs, but this is rarely a prime focus, and compliance costs can be prohibitive. Sector coverage among global industries has also been highly uneven.

Beyond these issues for RBIs in terms of adoption and coverage, we now turn to the question of how effective RBIs are, considering the different types of strategies – enabling, pressure, and ideational.

Enabling strategies

Corporate reporting, standards, and tools

Voluntary, nonfinancial reporting is a comparatively mature mechanism. Diverse guidelines, standards, and tools exist to enable companies to measure and report on their sustainability performance. Some standards and guidelines (e.g., UNGC principles or ETI base code) are offered as voluntary, learning approaches, whereas others are intended for monitoring, accreditation, and enforcement (e.g., Global Reporting Initiative standards). Other examples include the Integrated Reporting approach.[7] Performance benchmarks also exist. Public benchmarks comparing corporate performance are discussed under pressure strategies.

There has been rapid growth in voluntary and mandatory corporate reporting (Bartels et al., 2016; KPMG, 2017), spurred by public pressure and aided by new rules from stock exchanges and legislation.[8] Voluntary reporting by large companies is increasingly common practice, with GRI being the most widely adopted standard. New topics emerge and fall under the spotlight: for example, a current focus is on human rights, modern slavery, and child labor issues and single-use plastics. Reporting on environmental performance has a longer history, as it is easier to measure.

Despite this expansion, there are still large companies, and many SMEs, that are not reporting (KPMG, 2017) and view nonfinancial reporting as an unnecessary cost item. Implementation beyond headquarters to country-based operations, subsidiaries, and along supply chains is uneven, especially beyond tier-one suppliers. Emerging evidence suggests that although some management practices associated with international standards, principles, and conventions are adopted within headquarters, they do not filter down to subsidiary companies, and although more companies are paying attention to the social and environmental practices of their supply chain, only 16 percent have a comprehensive sustainability policy in place for it (Topple et al., 2017).

There is more reporting and there may be instances of improved report-ing quality; however, evidence that mainstream corporate reporting is signifi-cantly improving in *quality* is lacking. An academic literature review suggests that reporting quality remains poor, with a lack of standardization, complete-ness, accuracy, and comparability. Academic research is lacking, and what exists includes little evidence of a positive causal relationship between reporting and corporate behavior change, and still less on resulting changes for workers, com-munities, and the environment.[9] There are cases in the literature where report-ing and practices are more aligned in terms of positive responsible behavior but causal links are not evident. A great deal of the potential evidence on corpo-rate practice change is never made public for reasons of commercial sensitiv-ity, so positive change can be hidden. But it is very hard for external actors to judge progress. The poor quality of reporting undermines the ability of external stakeholders to assess performance.

Trends identified by independent ratings of corporate performance suggest very limited progress. For example, the Corporate and Human Rights Bench-mark database finds the following: "Some clear leaders, but improvements can still be made," "the results skewer significantly to the lower bands," "lowest performing companies must improve urgently," and "commitments must be followed through," "engagement with those potentially affected is lacking," and "there is a gap between responding publicly to serious allegations and taking appropriate action" (CHRB, 2017, pp. 2–3). Many of what the International Trade Union Confederation (ITUC) rate as the "world's worst countries for workers" are also seen by business as the world's best places to source from.[10] This type of wider evidence, which reviews sectors and not just market leaders, indicates a serious lack of significant change.

Social indicators have been underserved, but efforts exist to strengthen social impact metrics. On poverty impact reporting, a recent GRI report (2017) finds that more companies are reporting on poverty impacts, but through a lens of philanthropy and community engagement, excluding consideration of inclusive growth issues. The report does not provide evidence that corporate reporting is driving change on corporate poverty impacts.

It is assumed that external users, such as investors and nongovernmental organizations (NGOs), will use disclosed information from corporate reports to hold companies to account, but this assumes adequate capacity and resources. Yet many NGOs have miniscule resources compared with corporate budgets and the resources available to high-net-worth individuals, and this limits their relative capacity to influence public narratives. The operating space for civic actors is under pressure in many countries, with downward trends reported by the monitoring organization, CIVICUS.[11] Human rights and environmental activists continue to be subject to violence and repression.

Thus, we suggest that more evidence is needed that corporate reporting is effectively driving change, not just that there is more reporting of existing performance. The risk is that ineffective approaches not only mask inaction, but they occupy space in public narratives, preventing more politically engaged citizen campaigns. Braam et al. (2016) argue that some corporate responsibility strategies (including corporate reporting) are merely "legitimization strategies," allowing business as usual to continue and, at worst, deflecting stakeholder pressure.

Recently, newer RBIs are offering approaches to corporate reporting focused more outcomes, The B Lab impact standard includes some business management practices at the more meaningful end of the spectrum. However, they still tend to rely upon corporate self-assessment, and the stringency of indicators and standards remains an issue. FutureFit (2018)[12] is something of an exception, providing a public benchmark linking corporate performance to sustainability goals and science-based targets. However, mainstream adoption will be highly challenging.

Does more reporting equate with a change in behavior? The more established RBIs promoting corporate reporting have been slow to demonstrate this. The UK's ETI has a unique tripartite approach (companies, NGOs, and trade unions) and has always employed a collaborative, learning-by-doing approach. Although the ETI may have changed corporate practices, it is not possible for external actors to know if this is the case: it is not possible to assess corporate members' progress, because their reports to the ETI are not yet published.[13] Plans are now in place for a transparent reporting framework, but its rigor and the willingness of members to participate remain to be seen. The last impact assessment for the organization was produced in 2006 (IDS, 2006).

Supply chain transparency, accountability, and traceability tools

The extent to which technological innovation can empower workers in global supply chains or marginalize them further is uncertain. Some companies are moving ahead with technology-enabled systems for enhanced transparency in supply chains, including uptake of product coding/serialization, Blockchain, distributed ledgers and digital finance, and real-time monitoring tools for unified in-house data analysis and industry collaborations (Niforos et al., 2017).[14] Blockchain can deliver value chain transparency with respect to transactions, but there are ethical risks. Companies can benefit when such innovations enable them to deliver on sustainability claims, but potentially carry risks for less powerful actors. For example, buyers may decide to source only from small-holder agriculture producers in areas that they find are less risky using information from new technology-enabled traceability systems, rather than investing in improvements for producers currently supplying them.

Technological innovations hold potential to amplify worker voice, supported by NGOs and researchers, but the latter can find access challenging, and there are ethical risks of recriminations for participating workers. Companies use such tools to hear workers' views in their supply chains: for example, LaborLink and LaborVoices collect anonymous feedback using mobile phones from frontline supplier employees about working conditions to inform global brands. Worker representation should be founded on freedom of association, and it is the role of unions to represent worker's interests. However, given capacity deficits among many unions and restrictions upon them in many countries, such complementary measures afforded by new technologies could be used by civil society, including trade unions, to amplify worker voice and increase pressure on companies. As with other RBIs, worker voice initiatives need to demonstrate effectiveness and impact – including on more challenging issues and for vulnerable groups.

Business and industry capacity strengthening

Many RBIs seek to enhance individual corporate capacity on responsible business issues by providing standardized advice, bespoke advisory services, training packages, or more proactive, structured learning processes. Beyond RBIs, a huge consultancy industry provides similar services. International NGOs also engage in different ways, campaigning for change, but also acting as a critical friend in some cases. Targeted work by RBIs may strengthen corporate capacity in terms of understanding responsible business issues and strategies. Many RBIs provide important guidance for companies on a growing range of issues (e.g., Shift-Mazars, 2015, and ETI-developed detailed guidance and training on human rights due diligence), but evidence is required that capacity strengthening leads to behavior change.

Learning-by-doing approaches actively engage stakeholders in structured, social learning processes (e.g., the ETI with its tripartite structure jointly engages NGOs, trade unions, and corporate members). Other RBIs provide bespoke training for individual companies (e.g., Shift trains small groups of companies on human rights issues). More passive approaches include the provision of global reporting standards (e.g., by GRI) or open platforms for knowledge/guidance (e.g., as UNGC seeks to do for all companies globally). Several RBIs (e.g., B Lab, GRI, and UNGC) have begun to establish a greater presence within emerging markets and developing countries, with support for local fora, hubs, and networks, to build capacity in specific geographies. Although closer stakeholder engagement is desirable, the ETI has facilitated pilots on its base code and country programs for many years with mixed evidence of success (Nelson et al., 2007). Comparative analysis of differing corporate capacity-strengthening approaches would be instructive.

Moving beyond individual corporate engagement, there is a distinct shift in development cooperation aiming to support industry-wide initiatives for more systemic approaches, involving multiple stakeholders in processes of dialogue and coordination to achieve governance innovations and changes in incentives. Multistakeholder initiatives are viewed as a critical path to wider scaling in sector transformation (Molenaar et al., 2015), with agricultural sector initiatives leading the way. The IDH Sustainable Trade Programme claims impacts on the Malawi Tea sector, although evaluation evidence is limited.[15] Initiatives are now springing up in other sectors, for example, a "Race to the Top" initiative in Vietnamese apparel and footwear,[16] including a national public–private platform (IDH, 2018, p. 53). However, despite this new enthusiasm, the politics and equity of multistakeholder processes are sometimes overlooked (Nelson and Tallontire, 2014).

The Bangladesh Accord on Fire and Building Safety was established after an industrial accident and in the absence of an effective national regulatory body on workplace safety, reportedly achieving improved safety conditions through factory inspections and worker training over five years, although poor practices continue, and a Transition Accord is still needed.[17] Progress on enabling rights is much less evident. Initial findings from a Bangalore, India, apparel sector study, based on secondary evidence, finds uneven progress on sector business responsibility, with a predominance of isolated pilots.[18] For some practitioners, the Bangladesh Accord demonstrated a new way of working, linking buyers and suppliers in common action: the Action Collaboration Transformation (ACT) initiative aims to tackle the structural barriers to living wages, now on a global scale in apparel,[19] engaging brands and retailers in the garment and textile industries with a global trade union federation, IndustriALL, building a framework for action to establish enabling rights in global supply chains. Such initiatives are relatively new, and the issue is adoption: the Accord agreement occurred because of the scale of the tragedy of the Rana Plaza building collapse. Change by most mainstream companies sourcing from Bangladesh would entail the adoption of a completely new business model, which may account for the limited progress on more systemic issues. Pilot responsible business innovations were useful in Vietnam apparel, but macro-pressures, domestic politics, an upcoming trade deal, and labor organization shaped government responses and opened the door for them, not the reverse (Evans, 2018).

Product and supply chain sustainability standards

Product and supply chain sustainability standards are voluntary approaches offering services to companies. They have defined and operationalized sustainability in many sectors, but there are limits to their effectiveness as a sole agent of change. Sustainability standards have been more widely evaluated than other RBIs, although evidence findings are mixed, especially in the peer-reviewed literature (De Fries et al., 2017; Oya et al., 2017). This is unsurprising given the number of factors shaping rural livelihoods (Nelson and Martin, 2013). A four-year study found positive net benefits but highly context-specific outcomes and a clear indication that sustainability standards are insufficient mechanisms for poverty eradication and tackling environmental issues at landscape scales, so complementary and alternative measures may be needed for rural transformations (Nelson and Martin, 2013; Nelson and Phillips, 2018). The weak reach of standards beyond a top tier of rural smallholders, the exclusionary costs of compliance for less organized/capitalized producers, and unaddressed systemic sustainability issues are all factors in this regard (Nelson and Martin, 2013[20]). Coordination is needed among diverse landscape stakeholders (Molenaar et al., 2015), but community empowerment in development planning and fair value chain relations are also critical for equitable outcomes (Nelson and Phillips, 2018).

Many agri–food multinational companies are under pressure to increase the responsibility of their land investments and sourcing practices. Some companies are investing in "own-brand" supply chain initiatives for reputational benefit and greater flexibility (Nelson and Phillips, 2018). Landscape and jurisdictional approaches catalyze market forces to facilitate multistakeholder processes, governance, and incentives innovations, but more research is needed on conditions for success and on power issues (Nelson and Phillips, 2018).

Sustainability standards are evolving as a result of scrutinizing impacts. Changes include adopting more outcome-focused standards, promoting demand for sustainable products in emerging economies, using digital technologies to increase transparency and monitor environmental outcomes, and collaborative work on living incomes and wages. Some standards organizations are moving away from certification, to focus on capacity strengthening support, facilitation of dialogue, and learning platforms; for example, Bonsucro is consulting on becoming a "change platform" to achieve wider reach and to focus on capacity strengthening for mills and smallholders, providing company performance validation and facilitation of national-sector improvement.[21] These trust-based, collaborative models have cost and flexibility advantages, but carry risks of reduced accountability and standard stringency.

Pressure strategies

Engaging investors

Many RBIs are increasingly targeting investors to encourage them to lean on their investees and, potentially in the longer term, changing their own investment decisions. Examples include the Carbon Disclosure Project (CDP), socially responsible investment in emerging markets,[22] and investor activism/shareholder advocacy.

One RBI approach is to provide investors with a means of assessing the sustainability performance of companies in their portfolio through performance ratings systems. Another is to engage investors on a specific topic – providing information and pressuring investors to use their influence in discussions with their investees. Engaging investors has a huge potential given the financial muscle of investors, but the length and indirectness of the impact pathway are potential concerns, as is the ability of such mechanisms to change investor priorities. Evaluation evidence is limited, partly due to the confidential nature of investor decision making.

B Lab has developed a rating tool approach for use by investors and seeks linkages with investors and business associations, encouraging them to engage companies in impact management. B Corporations are required to report on environmental, social, and governance (ESG) considerations every two years to determine the path for corporate structure and the state of incorporation and to sign an official public commitment. Companies that are GIIRS-rated[23] go through ESG reporting annually. The B Analytics tool can be used to assess a portfolio of companies on their ESG performance. It is early yet, so evaluation evidence is not available, and confidentiality issues may make this challenging.

The ShareAction Workforce Disclosure Initiative leverages institutional investors to pressure investees. A survey of companies (supported by investors) generates detailed, comparable evidence on corporate performance on workforce and supply chain working conditions and informs and engages investors to push them to raise workplace conditions with investees. Corporate survey fatigue and data quality are both issues, and it is not yet clear what action companies will take.[24] Investor engagement effects are likely to be visible only in the longer term, with improvements in global measures on decent work.

One program encouraged investors to engage investees on labor standards in agricultural supply chains, covering 34 global food and beverage companies, and 23 reportedly showed improvements in reporting and on some practices, especially governance and certified sourcing, but the report lacks details, especially on causality and the scope of improvements (Principles for Responsible Investment Programme, 2016).

The investment landscape is neither homogenous or static: passive investment is expanding[25] (i.e., investment strategies with limited ongoing buying and selling, with a focus on long-term appreciation and limited maintenance), and the implications for responsibility in business are unclear.[26] Socially responsible investment approaches (e.g., divestment from harmful companies, impact investment) have gained attention[27]) and present major opportunities for achieving improved business outcomes, but mainstreaming within investment is necessary, as is evaluation. Many factors play a role (e.g., regulatory changes, government actions, and the work of advocacy groups), and different types of SRI have different kinds of impacts (IFC, 2013).[28]

There are systemic constraints on responsible business. Globalization processes have enabled many companies to seek cheaper labor, usually achieved through lower standards. Investor willingness to act is uncertain: Some "ethical" funds essentially only exclude weapons and tobacco investments. Production of an adequate modern slavery assessment statement is widely seen as an adequate improvement and may be an investor requirement, but corporate behavior may not have changed.

The key driver in corporate decision making is the strength of the shareholder business case for treating workers better. Shareholders prioritize profits, dividends, and share prices. A weak business case involves paying lip service to workers' rights, due diligence and audits, and reducing the risk of major reputational damage. Arguably, there is a far stronger shareholder case that companies prioritize production in the cheapest sourcing locations, where factories can meet basic capability requirements, regardless of workers' rights. Whereas some companies may modify their policies and practices in response to investor pressure, it is not clear that investors will demand sufficiently robust implementation of sufficiently strict standards over and above the standards already applied by many of the companies surveyed to make a significant difference to working conditions in supply chains or on other sustainability issues.

Public benchmarks

Some RBIs publish ratings of corporate performance to raise pressure on companies to act more responsibly. Publication may lead to impacts, but the effects may also be felt beforehand when companies are informed of their inclusion. Evaluation of public benchmark impact is limited. One exception is an evaluation of the Access to Medicines Index (2016), although this only includes a small number of corporate cases and does not measure change in corporate behavior.

A 2013 "Behind the Brands" campaign by the NGO, Oxfam, was based on a scorecard of the ten largest food and beverage companies on seven themes, such as transparency, farmers, etc. The assessment analyzes publicly available information (e.g., annual reports, sustainability reports, supplier codes), but does not assess actual practices.[29] A 2016 progress report finds companies have made more commitments, but more implementation is required.[30] A key challenge is getting access to data on actual practices.

A key aspect of irresponsible business is purchasing practices (Starmanns, 2017), yet few RBIs publish ratings on business practices affecting suppliers' capacity to act responsibly. A new initiative, the Better Buying Practices Index (BBPI) is addressing this, capturing confidential data from suppliers who rate the performance of their buyers. Data are collected, scored, and made available to buyers and suppliers, with ratings updated every six months. Eventually the data will be made public along with buyer comments. Guidance and feedback are provided to individual buyers. The first BBPI benchmark report (Dickson, 2018) ranked 65 brands/retailers, finding 60 percent of the suppliers ranked do *not* have incentives to comply with buyer codes of conduct, yet such incentives are essential for changing supplier practices. Relationship length between buyers and suppliers does not affect the quality of buyer purchasing practices, but direct relationships between buyers and suppliers do lead to better ratings for buyers, compared with buyer–supplier relations mediated by third parties (Dickson, 2018). The focus on key buying practices is an advantage, compared with more limited assessments focused upon public commitments and management practices in less critical areas. Whether the public nature of the rating can build pressure for change and whether companies adopt improvement strategies (i.e., more "predictable business, adequate lead times, fair financial deals, and incentives for compliant factories") is yet to be known. Individual corporate performance ratings are not yet published. Combined with stakeholder engagement, the tool may be effective, but evidence of effectiveness is needed. A similar rating of buy-in from other sectors, such as agri-food sourcing, is desirable.

Ideational strategies

Creating new legal forms and enterprise models

Corporate sustainability is influenced by enterprise forms, internal governance, and ownership (Oxfam and Donor Committee for Enterprise Development,

2016), but clear patterns are hard to find. Corporate leaders have differing values with varied effects for enterprise responsibility. Patterns of public offerings are also changing in different markets with potential ramifications. Conflicting evidence is presented for employee-owned enterprises (Oxfam and Donor Committee for Enterprise Development, 2016). Standard company forms prioritize profit maximization and shareholder returns, although some jurisdictions allow for enlightened shareholder value maximization, with expanded definitions of shareholder values (Oxfam and Donor Committee for Enterprise Development, 2016). Beyond this traditional form, there are social enterprises which prioritize social benefits (e.g., community interest companies in the UK) which can enjoy tax benefits in some countries. Cooperatives are locally controlled by members, rather than outside investors. Industrial foundations are foundations that own companies (Mayer, 2016).

In addition, two key innovative forms include (1) Benefit Corporations[31] – hybrid structures that shield directors from liability so it is easier to prioritize social mission over short-term shareholder interest (Oxfam-DCED, 2016) and (2) in jurisdictions where a Benefit Corporation is not yet possible, companies can achieve BCorp certification, with directors required to consider the interests of all stakeholders. B Lab works on enabling fiduciary law and advocating for public policy reform to change the rules on corporate accountability. Its emphasis on a wider pursuit of social and environmental impact alongside financial returns could potentially transform individual companies. A collective of B companies could have a potential role as market disruptors, potentially influencing traditional private-sector actors more widely (Sistema B blog[32]). Combined with impact investment, the Benefit Corporation model is a potentially transformative approach to social entrepreneurship (Servigon Caballero, 2017; Mayer, 2016).[33] Global minimum standards are still necessary (e.g. on human rights, living wages), plus other statutory corporate forms could be developed, e.g. industrial foundation models (Mayer, 2016). However, it cannot be assumed, in the short term at least, that responsibility is always or necessarily financially profitable for traditional companies. The business case for B Lab adoption by existing companies may change over time, as the case against 'business-as-usual' becomes clearer, but mainstreaming is likely to be challenging. Current participants tend to have a sustainability ethos. Multi-national and public company participation is needed, but few examples currently exist (e.g. Danone).

Changing leaders' mindsets via ideational and peer pressure strategies

Many RBIs use their convening power to bring together business leaders and reward positive change by showcasing good practice, holding high profile events and seeking to exert peer pressure. Such approaches potentially normalize discussions on sustainability and/or help to change norms about business responsibility, promoting a 'good purpose'. However, it is not clear how far such approaches are effective in changing norms and driving change in mainstream practices or merely mask wider inaction. Many established RBIs, such as Global Reporting Initiative and the UN Global Compact, hold international conferences and thematic events, and convene different stakeholder groups. The UK's Ethical Trading Initiative runs regular meetings for specific sector-stakeholders, drawing on representation from its tripartite members (i.e. unions, NGOs, corporates) to support learning. Convening CEOs is a key plank of the UNGC theory of change, but there is no robust, independent organisational evaluation demonstrating change in corporate practice has resulted beyond the making of public commitments from such activities and others.[34]

Beyond responsible business initiatives

Beyond responsible business initiatives, there are other interventions which share common aims. Examples include policy advocacy by NGOs seeking to influence the rules of the game. The literature on the regulation of business is vast and cannot be covered here – suffice it to say that with processes of globalization there has been a shift in power away from national governments and communities to global companies and private governance initiatives. There is renewed interest in regulation, as the limits of voluntary initiatives has become clearer. The Brazilian moratorium on soy, for example, has been successful in preventing further soy-induced expansion into Amazonian forests by large commercial concerns, but such regulations require sustained national-level political will, and there may be leakage issues across borders where government rules are not aligned. Hybrid governance innovations in forest-landscape initiatives at multiple scales include landscape compacts for companies encouraging commitments on sourcing. Yet their effectiveness in achieving diverse public goods, including zero deforestation, are not yet clear, and there are potential equity issues.

Consumer campaigns can raise awareness and build consumer pressure. There are successful examples of civil society actors holding businesses to account, especially multiscale alliances, but they are disadvantaged compared to growing corporate and elite power and the connections between companies and governments in developing countries. Next we discuss three approaches which companies, academics, donors, and governments have variously supported in recent years to explore their potential role in advancing responsibility in business.

Shared value approaches

Porter and Kramer (2011) suggest business contributes to sustainable development by creating benefits both for firms and society in "shared value" approaches, that is, the overall size of the pie in terms of value increases, rather than there being a fairer distribution of an existing pie (fair share of value). Several "hard-nosed" companies have initiated shared value investments according to Porter and Kramer (2011), for example, Nestlé invested in smallholder coffee producers trapped in low productivity, poor quality, and environmental degradation cycles, giving advice on farming practices, support to access inputs, and payment of a premium for better beans, leading to higher yields and quality, better incomes, lower negative environmental impacts, and a stronger coffee supply for the company. However, critics suggest that such "win-win" projects may still leave an "'ocean of unsolved environmental and social conflicts'" untouched, and although it may support integration of activities into one social strategy, it does not support a responsible, corporation-wide strategy and thus does not redefine the purpose of the corporation as claimed (Crane et al., 2014, p. 139). Further, legal and ethical standards compliance is assumed, as is adequate mitigation of any harms caused. The concept fails to capture the messy, trade-offs that occur in the real world (Crane et al., ibid). One issue is the potential for increased smallholder producer dependency on specific corporate buyers.

Labor clauses in trade agreements

In foreign trade agreements, labor clauses[35] are increasingly being included in primary trade agreement or as side agreements.[36] Existing research compares institutional designs, particularly the extent to which sanctions for noncompliance are included ("conditional" provisions), versus "promotional" provisions only (e.g., dialogue and technical cooperation) and analyzes why labor clauses are included in trade agreements, but lacks evidence on their effectiveness *viz* working conditions and labor market outcomes.[37] Siroën and Andrade (2016) compared the effects of labor clauses in trade agreements on the ratification of ILO conventions and worker rights practices, finding that labor provisions have not played a significant role in the improvement of labor practices, their effect has been limited to the ratification of ILO conventions, and trade agreements do not demand strong enforcement mechanisms. Calls are growing for enhanced enforceability in labor clauses in trade agreements, plus giving equal weight to labor and sustainable development provisions versus commercial, technical, and tariff issues, plus improved promotional provisions, capacity building activities, and stronger monitoring of core labor standards application.[38]

A study of the Vietnamese Garment industry (Evans, 2018) explores stakeholder perceptions of what led to recent improvements in labor relations (wages, social dialogue, and freedom of association). Strikes occurred among workers. Manufacturers wanted to prevent strikes and retain lucrative contracts with reputation-sensitive buyers. At the same time, a trade deal, the Trans-Pacific Partnership, emerged on the political horizon, potentially offering improved market access and economic growth, but pre-ratification conditionalities were proposed, relating to compliance with international labor standards, including independent unions. Recognizing the growing support for the trade deal due to regional geopolitics and economics, the likelihood of the inclusion of labor reform requirements in the trade deal and the importance of tackling strikes to sustain regime credibility, the Vietnamese government sought to engage in exploratory workshops and pilots (Evans, 2018). Donor-funded programs played a role in enabling experimentation on labor reforms, but they did not cause the reforms to happen (Evans, 2018). When windows of opportunity arise, RBIs may enable improvement strategies, but are unlikely to be able to create such conditions on their own.

Development cooperation programs

Donors are increasingly investing in inclusive growth initiatives to reach bottom-of-the-pyramid markets and looking to support private-sector-led development. Here we focus upon the latter. In sectors involving factory settings, such as apparel, product certification adoption is very limited. Donor engagement previously supported corporate code systems, but these are widely regarded as being ineffective. More recently donors have sought to fund core business strategy approaches (e.g., sustainability and sourcing strategy should be addressed together) and incubation/blended finance approaches to support such approaches. The Trade and Global Value Chains Initiative (TGVCI), supported by the UK Department for International Development, tested whether corporate investment in the workforce (social upgrading) could lead to business benefits (economic upgrading) for more sustainable, resilient global supply chains in partnership with companies. Evaluation of a diverse range of initiatives in collaboration with private companies indicates promising pilots (e.g., women worker health interventions, intensive coaching on life and technical skills, social dialogue approaches, and human resource/productivity training for middle managers), but also found that more challenging, structural issues were not tackled (e.g., living wages, housing, or environmental impacts) and were in design stages, and there was no effort to build sector-wide stakeholder engagement (Nelson et al., 2017).

The ILO Better Work Programme monitors and provides advice to garment factories to support compliance with national and international labor standards, plus capacity-strengthening activities (training of workers, union leaders, and factory managers). An impact evaluation finds positive improvements on certain issues (e.g., child labor and compensation), but less improvement on overtime, with most firms not complying (Drusilla et al., 2016). Vietnamese stakeholders reported that the program enabled experimentation, but much wider geopolitical factors determined what was possible in practice and buyer pressure was more influential (Evans, 2018). Although pilots can help to change cultural norms about what can be done and how, macro-scale pressures shape regime openness to reforms, and the strength of labor, transnational polities, and governance issues is influential (Evans, 2018).

Finally, donors are still learning how to work with companies, and from a development question the issue is how far this modifies their own practice. The Donor Committee for Enterprise Development advises that donors should treat companies as "equal actors" and create demand-led, longer term (less transactional) relationships, flexible funding models, and improved staff–private sector experience (DCED, 2017). Changes in donor language and ways of operating to accommodate private-sector priorities carries risks as well as potential rewards, but the latter are inadequately recognized. Donors should frame their decisions as an investor in aid interventions addressing priority development as framed by local communities and civil society, rather than changing their language and norms as if they were a business themselves.

Discussion

Despite a clear increase in the attention businesses are giving to sustainability issues (UNGC DNV, 2015), evidence on the effectiveness and impact of RBIs is limited. The lack of data is unsurprising, given the challenges of accessing private-sector data and the limited incentives for corporate transparency. In some areas, such as product standards, there is more evidence, but results are mixed. In other areas, there are more data, but no clear answers (e.g., on the business case). On other RBI approaches such as public benchmarks, new corporate forms, and corporate and sector capacity strengthening, there is very little available evidence. Overall, the evidence base for knowing what works in responsible business is thin, despite the public resources invested and given the scale of business sustainability impacts. The evidence available suggests that some of the assumptions in the later stages of the generic RBI theory of change may not hold true, particularly the causal steps from commitments to policies and from policies to actual changes in behavior (e.g., purchasing and sourcing practices). This has implications both for RBIs and for supporting donors.

The assumption that there is a business case for companies to improve their behavior, as well as a moral imperative, is key to many RBIs, as well as to voluntary approaches more generally. If responsibility is in the self-interest of business, the necessity for government regulation is reduced, and the case for investing in RBIs as a vehicle for win-win gains for both business and society is enhanced. However, although it may be right that "a commitment to ethical principles should outweigh financial justification" (World Economic Forum, 2015, p. 4), if the financial justification is hard to make, or even runs contrary to ethics, this suggests that there is a limit to what *voluntary* RBIs can achieve. That there is a general business case (and increasing regulatory pressure) which would support some improvements in business behavior for some companies does not mean that there is as yet a universal business case for improving all business behavior for all companies.

The reality is that the business case for responsible business is variable and uncertain. It should not be assumed that responsibility makes business sense for companies that need to meet shareholder demands or that are privately owned by an owner that does not have a strong values motivation, at least in the short term. The International Finance Corporation (IFC) states that "companies that do good by the environment, their labour force, and communities do well financially."[39] However, the literature on the overall business case for responsibility is more mixed. Some studies show a positive correlation between corporate social responsibility (CSR) and financial profitability (Carroll and Shabana, 2011; Orlitzky et al., 2003; Beurden and Gossling, 2008; Thorpe and Prakash

Mani, 2003; Wang et al., 2015). Some do not (See Mulyadi and Anwar, 2012); Aras et al., 2010); Nelling and Webb, 2009). One study found higher investment returns for "sin stocks" (Hong and Kacperczyk, 2009). A later paper did not (Blitz and Fabozzi (2017). Overall, the relationship is complex and heterogeneous, and the direction of causation remains unanswered. A recent meta-review of the benefits of sustainability standards found that benefits are difficult to quantify and highly context dependent (AidEnvironment, 2017).

Progress towards responsibility in business has been heavily concentrated in a small minority of reputation-sensitive companies and sectors and in a very small minority of companies. UNGC, the world's largest corporate sustainability initiative with over 9,500 business members, covers just 2 percent of global GDP, 2 percent of listed companies, and 4 percent of people working in the private sector.[40] Many international supply chains are very long, complex, and opaque. Just understanding these, let alone acting to improve conditions, has proved to be a huge undertaking for highly committed companies. If companies do not know what is going on – or do not want to – achieving impact is virtually impossible. There tends to be a sharp fall-off from commitments to action, particularly action in distant subsidiaries, supply chains, or beyond tier 1 suppliers. A much higher percentage of companies have policies on human rights than carry out impact assessments, monitor or evaluate performance, or disclose information on policies and practices.[41] Such improvements as have been achieved in supply chains focus on easier issues such as health and safety, rather than on freedom of association and excessive working hours.[42] Corporate codes of practice in two African agricultural export industries mainly benefitted permanent workers on material indicators, with limited effect on temporary workers and on empowerment indicators (Nelson et al., 2007). An evaluation of the ETI base code found a similar picture (IDS, 2006). Dima Jamali, Lund-Thomsen, and Khara (2017) found that developing country suppliers often emphasize their action on high-profile issues such as child labour, but this can mask decoupling on less visible issues leaving the fundamental challenges for workers unaddressed. Problems relating to working conditions, such as purchasing practices and living wages, correctly identified in ethical trade circles more than a decade ago are still being discussed.

The systemic context within which international firms operate needs to be considered. Much of the persistence of poor working conditions and labor rights, and negative community and environmental impacts are the result of the "causal drivers of global production networks in terms of the competitive dynamics (optimizing cost-capability ratios, market imperatives, and financial discipline) and risk environments" (Yeung and Coe, 2014). Poor working conditions and insecure labor rights are a product of these systemic business and economic models that link large retailers and global brands in highly unequal and price-sensitive relationships with a mass of, generally small, competing suppliers in countries with weak governance and poor labor rights. "Upstream" business practices have major "downstream" effects on suppliers and their workers (Locke, 2013, p. 175). "When supplier firm margins are squeezed by the asymmetry of market structure in global value chains, these firms in turn are under enormous pressure to keep wages and labour standards low" (Milberg and Winkler, 2013). This model, combined with the poor governance in supplier countries, contributes to the weak or limited business case for responsibility, which in turn explains the limited coverage and uptake of RBIs and limited progress on so many indicators of supply chain sustainability, especially on enabling rights.

The rise of polycentric trade and Asian consumption growth (Horner and Nadvi, 2017) is another challenge, because of more limited awareness of ethical and environmental issues in emerging markets. Technological innovations are supporting disruptive business models with unclear sustainability implications. Civic action (e.g., citizen online petitions, NGO campaigns and trade union strikes, etc.), as well as civic inaction (e.g., consumer ignorance and indifference to human rights abuses in international supply chains), also forms part of the contextual picture. Regulation sets the enabling environment for business and trade, but governance gaps allow the continuation of poor business practices. The elite power of the super wealthy should be problematized, not only because of the lack of accountability of such individuals in terms of the sustainability impact of their generally high levels of consumption but also because of their growing political influence, combined with interests in weakening regulatory frameworks (see Standing, 2016, on the "thinning of democracy"). There is a closure of global civic space, which also means that the space for campaigning and resistance by citizen campaigners such as human rights activists is decreasing.

Figure 8.2 captures not only the generic theory of change for responsible business as envisaged by responsible business actors but also visualizes the diverse dynamics at play in the global economy, with (changing) pressures for and against more responsible business: RBIs seek to influence corporate behavior, but there are many assumptions involved (e.g., weak business cases), and external pressures and societal expectations of business also shape outcomes. The diagram includes both changes within existing types of business, but also notes the potential for more radical change in business models and "forms of enterprise." The diagram also notes the importance of evaluating performance with respect to science-based goals and internationally recognized human rights and social policies.

In the midst of a rather depressing analysis, lessons and possible ideas for positive drivers of change are discussed next:

- Increase a focus on the key aspects of corporate behavior, rather than on public commitments and policies, and consider issues such as purchasing and sourcing practices, as these drive change among suppliers. Supplier ratings on purchasing and sourcing practices might assist in this regard.
- Attention and support should focus on sector- and industry-wide transformation approaches, moving beyond the existing corporate-centric focus on market leaders.

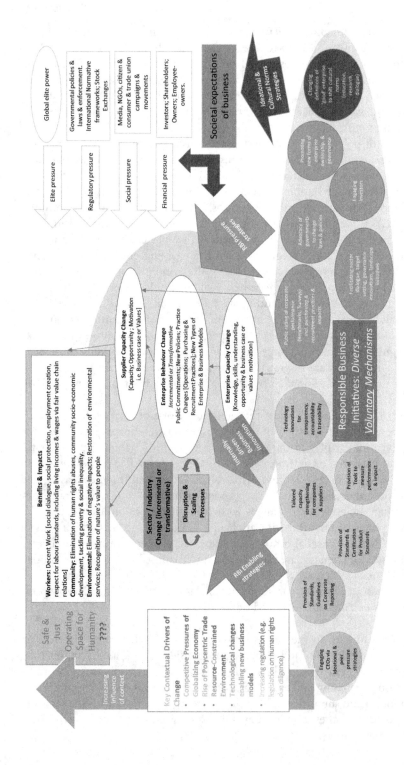

Figure 8.2 Contextualizing the responsible business initiative theory of change (drivers, enterprise change, thresholds)

- Sector- and industry-wide approaches should address systemic issues, such as enabling rights (i.e., in addition to those that work on easier issues such as building safety) and landscape governance and finance in agriculture and forestry.
- Multi-stakeholder initiatives represent a means of facilitating stakeholder coordination, dialogue, and action, but more investment is needed in foundational processes, as well such as public participation in economic development planning and consideration of different enterprise forms and economic models, land tenure security, and community and civil society capacity strengthening. This is necessary to achieve more equitable outcomes. Representation and the voice of marginal groups should be central and given specific attention.
- Research and independent evaluation are needed on responsibility in business and economic development, given the propensity of corporate actors to overstate their performance and the vested interests among RBIs for positive evaluation evidence.
- Sector and industry studies are a priority to establish levels of responsibility performance and impact *across* sectors and industries, measured against appropriate science-based and social policy targets. More support for decent work, community empowerment, and environmental data in different countries is a priority.
- The perspective of workers and local communities is missing from most responsible business literature and discourse, in part due to ethical and logistical challenges, but also because of oversight. More effort is needed to support worker and community agency in all dimensions to participate in economic development.
- More critical reflection should be injected into development and responsible business debates. A focus on what really drives change, whether positive change is occurring (based on robust evidence), and what the effective mechanisms are is greatly overdue and should inform future strategies by civil society, donors, and enterprises. More attention should be paid to new enterprise forms, financial systems, and progressive economic development.
- Consideration of the magnitude of change required to have any hope of developing an economy that supports human development, while not exceeding planetary boundaries (Raworth, 2017), is necessary. New forms of enterprise ownership, governance, and forms may enable greater responsibility and should be identified and promoted, including potential means of accessing finance that enables more equitable outcomes.

Conclusions

"Being on a journey" is a well-used responsible business cliché. What is far from clear is what the *end* of the journey is envisaged to be, *when* we will reach it, and *whose* interests are served? Indeed, it is hard to know whether companies, sectors, and industries are progressing on this journey and on what time frame, or whether we are even headed in the right direction. The broad evidence on global sustainability challenges suggests that the direction and speed of travel are seriously problematic. On certain issues, such as climate change, the evidence is clear that we are heading in the wrong direction, with major consequences for societal integrity. On many environmental measures we are exceeding scientifically advised thresholds for a safe planet for humanity. Global inequality and elite power are increasing, which also suggests that on social measures, the opportunities for a "just" operating space for humanity are diminishing, not increasing. There may be individual areas of improvement, but on many of the major indicators we are in very serious trouble.

Although initially formulated to reduce the negative impacts of corporate actions, the evidence reviewed suggests that responsible business and the associated products and services offered by RBIs to deliver it are increasingly being used by companies to boost corporate reputation/political power and to deflect regulation. Even though the current business and society discourse suggests that companies are integrating sustainability into their core business models, there is limited evidence that for incumbent companies and industries that this is the case. Although corporate leaders and champions can have a values motivation and there are instances of corporate leadership and improvement, the business case for responsible business practice is generally weak, compared with that for irresponsible business.

There is often a major mismatch between the rhetoric of responsible business actors and what the evidence suggests. Looking at the bigger picture, coverage by RBIs is highly partial in terms of business practice and effects, both within and across sectors. The evidence on RBI effectiveness is either weak or nonexistent (depending on the mechanism in question) apart from sustainability standards. Even for the latter the evidence is mixed. More research is needed to evaluate the effectiveness of more recent RBI approaches. RBIs need to demonstrate that they can be effective and that this is an urgent task for their own credibility, learning, and improvement. However, critical reflection is also needed to establish which, if any, RBIs can have an influence and under what conditions (for example, they may be used when a window of opportunity opens in the wider context). Some newer approaches are starting to focus more clearly on the root causes of irresponsible business and trying to design more systemic approaches, such as promoting different kinds of enterprise governance, ownership, and legal status. Other examples are global alliances promoting worker enabling rights, sector-wide transformation programming, ratings by suppliers of buyer purchasing and sourcing practices, and trade negotiations which include labor clauses including enforcement requirements, etc. Donor cooperation programs on responsible business may support experimentation by progressive actors, but it is not clear that RBIs can drive change in corporate behavior. Systemic change requires combined sets of pressure and incentives of significant magnitude – not only incremental change in corporate behavior but also more far-reaching changes in business models, finance, and economic development approaches. It is unlikely that we can achieve a safe and just operating space for humanity with "business as usual," and that means that RBIs need to articulate and test their theories of change, and wider actors need to reflect upon and design complementary and alternative strategies. Scaled-up civic action is critical to pressure for stronger regulation and supportive policies and to change norms on "good" enterprise and economies.

Whatever benefits/impacts may be achieved by RBIs and other interventions, evaluation should consider the thresholds for a safe and just operating space for humanity. If the combined achievements by RBIs are not likely to meet these thresholds, this suggests, at a minimum, that improvements are needed, but most likely radical changes in direction by all those concerned with our common future, including among responsible business actors.

Notes

1 Acknowledgement: The UK Department for International Development funded evaluation and learning of the Responsible, Accountable and Transparent Enterprise Programme, findings from which inform this chapter. However, the views are entirely those of the authors.
2 Rather than comparing with historical data, current trends, or projected future performance and benchmarking against the performance and goals of industry peers, companies should consider how best to meet external societal needs and adopt science-based targets.
3 www.unrisd.org/80256B3C005BD6AB/(httpEvents)/845A4834BECE32D3C12582F D004389A9?OpenDocument
4 The University Said Business School (2016, p6) framework of "inclusive capitalism" organizations, that is, organizations with "*missions to incite businesses to act in a more inclusive, just, fair, sustainable, conscious, pro-social, or responsible manner,*" includes influencing strategies, namely, networking/convening leaders, research/thought leadership, movement building/community organizing, policy/advocacy, new standards/organizational forms, business education, public engagement, and advisory services.
5 Corporate sustainability reporting is now "*standard practice for large and mid-cap companies around the world, with around three quarters of the 4,900 companies studied issuing CR reports and two thirds of reports analysed in this survey applying the GRI G4 Guidelines or Standards*" (KPMG, 'The Road Ahead', 2017). However, although reporting rates among the G250 have been stable over the past four surveys (at 90 to 95 percent), for the N100 companies there have been higher levels of growth in reporting, largely due to new regulation (KPMG, 2017, p. 9). This means that one-quarter of the N100 companies are not currently reporting on their sustainability. At the sector level, the KPMG survey finds that 60 percent of companies across all industry sectors are reporting on corporate responsibility, which means that 40 percent are still not reporting.
6 Decent work in global supply chains, ILO (2017, p. 7).
7 "Integrated Reporting is a broad-based framework for business and investment decisions that are long term, inclusive and with purpose" https://integratedreporting.org/
8 Such as the EU Non-Financial Reporting Directive requiring large public-interest EU companies with more than 500 employees to report.
9 Two key research questions include (1) To what extent is corporate reporting effective in changing corporate behavior and (2) What is the evidence that this leads to positive social and environmental benefits? Four databases were reviewed using 18 search terms, and following a screening process, 66 articles were selected as being of direct relevance. The studies reviewed exhibit variable methodological rigor and, although comprehensive, our study was not a systematic review: Abdullah et al, 2015; Ackers and Eccles, 2015; Adams Frost, 2008; Anas et al, 2015; Anstatt and Volkert, 2016; Aragon-Correa et al,

2016; Barkemeyer et al, 2015; Barkemeyer and Stringer, 2015; Belal et al, 2015; Biswas and O'Grady, 2016; Blanco et al, 2016; Boiral & Heras-Saizarbitoria, 2017; Braam et al, 2016; Bonsón, and Bednárová, 2015; Brown et al, 2016; Calderon et al, 2016; Caritte et al, 2015; Delmas and Blaas, 2010; Dennis et al, 2015; Doda et al, 2016; Emel et al, 2012; Farag et al, 2015; Fatima et al, 2015; Gallego-Alvarez, 2008; Islam and Jain, 2013; de Jongh and Möllmann, 2014; Hamman et al, 2009; Lauwo, et al, 2016; McPhail and Adams, 2016; Momin and Parker, 2013; Morali and Searcy, 2013; Morhardt, 2009. Pérez-López, et al, (2015); Salazar, et al, 2012; Sardinha et al, 2011; Sethi and Schepers, 2014; Sorensen, 2012; Toppinen and Korhonen-Kurki, 2013; Tsang et al, 2009.

10 ITUC Global Rights Report 2017.
11 The CIVICUS Monitor analyzes the extent to which the three civil society rights are being respected and upheld and the degree to which states are protecting civil society: https://monitor.civicus.org/globalfindings0417/
12 http://futurefitbusiness.org/
13 Unlike the Fair Wear Foundation, which publishes annual Brand Performance Checks.
14 https://hbr.org/2010/10/the-transparent-supply-chain
15 "IDH-supported sector initiatives lead to (better) worker – management dialogue, which can lead to collective bargaining agreements (CBAs). For instance, within the tea sector, the Malawi Tea 2020 coalition has already seen real progress – helping build the capabilities of both management and workers' organizations to engage in effective collective bargaining, resulting in the first CBA in the Malawian tea industry in August 2016. The CBA is a key milestone toward a living wage in the sector, as it immediately led to an increase in nominal wage of 18–24%" (www.idhsustainabletrade.com/uploaded/2017/06/IDH-How-we-are-making-a-difference1-web.pdf, p. 53).
16 A pre-competitive, locally owned, multistakeholder initiative in the Vietnamese apparel and footwear sector promoting and enabling locally embedded sustainable manufacturing practices. Provides capacity building for increasing worker-management dialogue, productivity training to workers, supervisors, and management in factories in Vietnam and discusses labor policies with the Vietnamese government and international organizations (www.idhsustainabletrade.com/uploaded/2017/06/IDH-How-we-are-making-a-difference1-web.pdf, p. 53).
17 https://fashionunited.uk/news/business/the-need-for-the-bangladesh-accord-persists-5-years-after-rana-plaza/2018041829172
18 An ongoing sector study has reviewed 77 studies on the Tamil Nadu industry and assessed the evidence against a conceptual framework based on the Higgs Facility Tools, which are used in the apparel industry and developed by the Sustainable Apparel Coalition (SAC) (https://apparelcoalition.org/the-sac/). These tools measure the social and environmental performance of individual factories, but we have adopted sector-level assessments.
19 https://actonlivingwages.com/
20 Nelson, V., & Martin, A., 2013. Assessing the poverty impact of sustainability standards. NRI report commissioned by DFID. Chatham, UK. www.nri.org/images/documents/project_websites/AssessingPovertyImpacts/AssessingThePovertyImpactOfSustainability Standards.pdf
21 www.bonsucro.com/wp-content/uploads/2017/10/Microsoft-Word-Public-Theory-of-Change-Draft_HQ.docx.pdf
22 https://www.ifc.org/wps/wcm/connect/topics_ext_content/ifc_external_corporate_site/sustainability-at-ifc/publications/publications_report_towardssri__wci__131957 7575212
23 GIIRS Ratings are the gold standard for funds that manage their portfolio's impact with the same rigor as their financial performance. http://b-analytics.net/giirs-funds
24 For example, on the living wage, the WDI only asks whether companies "engage with critical suppliers" (yes/no) and asks for "details on the engagement process and the progress that has been made."
25 www.n3d.eu/_medias/n3d/files/PBC_1057026.pdf

26 www.ftadviser.com/opinion/2017/07/24/passive-managers-are-increasingly-interested-in-esg/?page=1
27 www.economist.com/news/finance-and-economics/21731640-millennials-are-coming-money-and-want-invest-it-responsibly-sustainable. Nov. 5th, 2017.
28 www.ifc.org/wps/wcm/connect/39514780488555c0b7ecf76a6515bb18/IFC_Breif_responsibilty_online.pdf?MOD=AJPERES&CACHEID=39514780488555c0b7ecf76a6515bb18
29 www.behindthebrands.org/images/media/Download-files/BtB%20Methodology%20document_final_Sept%202014.pdf
30 https://d1tn3vj7xz9fdh.cloudfront.net/s3fs-public/file_attachments/bp-journey-to-sustainable-food-btb-190416-en.pdf
31 http://benefitcorp.net/faq
32 http://blog.academiab.org/2017/06/04/sistema-b-pioneers-affecting-systemic-change-in-latin-america/
33 There remain "almost no empirical insights on the implementation of the ten principles in corporations . . . the impact of the Compact on existing business practices . . . for instance, whether and how participating firms have changed existing routines (e.g. on supplier relations)."
34 That is, binding commitments on labor issues as defined by the core ILO labor standards and upholding of domestic labor laws, with potential additional references to occupational safety and health, working hours, and wages.
35 Eighty percent of new trade agreements that have entered into force since 2013 contain a clause relating to respect for labor standards, and 136 countries worldwide are signatory to at least one trade agreement with labor standards provisions (ILO, 2016) "Assessment of Labour Provisions in Trade and Investment Arrangements." Available at: https://www.ilo.org/global/publications/books/WCMS_498944/lang--en/index.htm
36 See Ergon News: http://ergonassociates.net/labour-clauses-trade-agreements-operate-can-improved/
37 See Ergon News: http://ergonassociates.net/labour-clauses-trade-agreements-operate-can-improved/
38 www.ifc.org/wps/wcm/connect/topics_ext_content/ifc_external_corporate_site/sustainability-at-ifc/business-case
39 UNGC Accenture, 2013; UNGC/DNV (2015), p. 60).
40 2017 UNGC Progress Report. UNGC (2017, p. 47).
41 R. M. Locke (2013, p. 174).

References

Abdullah, M., et al., 2015. Risk management disclosure P. Othmar M. Lehner, ed. *Journal of Applied Accounting Research*, 16(3), pp. 400–432. Available at: www.emeraldinsight.com/doi/10.1108/JAAR-10-2014-0106 [Accessed January 9, 2017].

Ackers, B., & Eccles, N.S., 2015. Mandatory corporate social responsibility assurance practices. *Accounting, Auditing & Accountability Journal*, 28(4), pp. 515–550. Available at: www.emeraldinsight.com/doi/10.1108/AAAJ-12-2013-1554 [Accessed January 9, 2017].

Adams, C.A., & Frost, G.R., 2008. Integrating sustainability reporting into management practices. *Accounting Forum*, 32(4), pp. 288–302.

Aidenvironment, 2017. The business benefits of using standards – A meta-review. Report for ISEAL.

Anas, A., Rashid, H.M.A., & Annuar, H.A., 2015. The effect of award on CSR disclosures in annual reports of Malaysian PLCs. *Social Responsibility Journal*, 11(4).

Anstatt, K., & Volkert, J., 2016. Corporate social responsibility: Impacts on sustainable human development: Recent findings and consequences. *Ekonomski Vjesnik*, 29(1), pp. 193–210.

Available at: http://apps.webofknowledge.com/full_record.do?product=WOS&search_mode=GeneralSearch&qid=48&SID=Z1rpPM1x1LefHTO1ean&page=3&doc=73 [Accessed January 9, 2017].

Aragon-Correa, J.A., Marcus, A., & Hurtado-Torres, N., 2016. The natural environmental strategies of international firms: Old controversies and new evidence on performance and disclosure. *Academy of Management Perspectives*, 30(1), pp. 24–39. Available at: http://amp.aom.org/cgi/doi/10.5465/amp.2014.0043 [Accessed January 9, 2017].

Aras, G., Aybars, A., & Kutlu, O., 2010. Managing corporate performance: Investigating the relationship between corporate social responsibility and financial performance in emerging markets. *International Journal of Productivity and Performance Management*, 59, 229–254.

Barkemeyer, R., Preuss, L., & Lee, L., 2015b. On the effectiveness of private transnational governance regimes – Evaluating corporate sustainability reporting according to the global reporting initiative. *Journal of World Business*, 50(2), pp. 312–325.

Bartels, W., Fogelberg, T., Hoballah, A., & Van der Lugt, C., 2016. Carrots and sticks: Global trends in sustainability reporting regulation and policy. KPMG, GRI, UNEP, Centre for Corporate Governance in Africa. Available at: https://assets.kpmg.com/content/dam/kpmg/pdf/2016/05/carrots-and-sticks-may-2016.pdf [Accessed March 24, 2017].

Barkemeyer, R., Stringer, L.C., et al., 2015. Corporate reporting on solutions to wicked problems: Sustainable land management in the mining sector. *Environmental Science & Policy*, 48, pp. 196–209.

Belal, A.R., Cooper, S.M., & Khan, N.A., 2015. Corporate environmental responsibility and accountability: What chance in vulnerable Bangladesh? *Critical Perspectives on Accounting*, p. 33.

Beurden, P. van, & Gossling, T., 2008. The worth of values – A literature reivew on the relation between corporate social and financial performance. *Journal of Business Ethics*, October, 82, p. 407.

Biswas, S., & O'Grady, W., 2016. Using external environmental reporting to embed sustainability into organisational practices. *Accounting Research Journal*, 29(2), pp. 218–235. Available at: www.emeraldinsight.com/doi/10.1108/ARJ-04-2015-0063 [Accessed January 9, 2017].

Blanco, C., Caro, F. & Corbett, C.J., 2016. The state of supply chain carbon footprinting: Analysis of CDP disclosures by US firms. *Journal of Cleaner Production*, 135, pp. 1189–1197. Available at: http://linkinghub.elsevier.com/retrieve/pii/S0959652616308095 [Accessed January 9, 2017].

Blitz, D., & Fabozzi, F., 2017. Sin stocks revisited: Resolving the sin stock anomaly. *Journal of Portfolio Management*, 44(1).

Blowfield, M., 2013. *Business and Society*. Oxford University Press, Oxford, ISBN 978-0-19-964298-4.

Blowfield, M., & Murray, A., 2014. *Corporate Responsibility*. Third Edition. Oxford University Press, Oxford.

Boiral, O., & Heras-Saizarbitoria, I., 2017. Managing biodiversity through stakeholder involvement: Why, who, and for what initiatives? *Journal of Business Ethics*. 140(3), pp. 403–421.

Bonsón, E., & Bednárová, M., 2015. CSR reporting practices of Eurozone companies, *Revista de Contabilidad*, 18(2), pp. 182–193, ISSN 1138-4891, https://doi.org/10.1016/j.rcsar.2014.06.002.

Braam, G.J.M., et al., 2016. Determinants of corporate environmental reporting: The importance of environmental performance and assurance. *Journal of Cleaner Production*, 129. Available at: http://linkinghub.elsevier.com/retrieve/pii/S0959652616301068 [Accessed January 9, 2017].

Brown, Drusilla, et al., 2016. *The Impact of Better Work* (Tufts University). file:///C:/Users/reall_000/Downloads/Tufts-University-Final-IA.pdf

Brundtland, G.H., 1987. *Our Common Future.* UN World Commission on Environment and Development.

Calderon, A., Harris, J.D., & Kirsch, P.A., 2016. Health interventions used by major resource companies operating in Colombia. *Resources Policy*, 47, pp. 187–197. Available at: http://linkinghub.elsevier.com/retrieve/pii/S0301420715000197 [Accessed January 9, 2017].

Caritte, V., Acha, S., & Shah, N., 2015. Enhancing corporate environmental performance through reporting and roadmaps. *Business Strategy and the Environment*, 24(5), pp. 289–308. Available at: http://doi.wiley.com/10.1002/bse.1818 [Accessed January 9, 2017].

Carroll, A.B., & Shabana, K.M., 2011. The business case for corporate social responsibility: A new review of concepts, research and practice. *International Journal of Management Reviews*, 12(1).

CHRB, 2017. Corporate Human Rights Benchmark: Key Findings 2017, www.corporatebenchmark.org/sites/default/files/styles/thumbnail/public/2017-03/Key%20Findings%20Report/CHRB%20Key%20Findings%20report%20-%20May%202017.pdf

Crane, A., Palazzo, G., Spence, L.J., & Matten, D., 2014. Contesting the value of 'creating shared value'. *California Management Review*, 56(2), Winter, University of California, Berkeley.

Delmas, M., & Blass, V.D., 2010. Measuring corporate environmental performance: The trade-offs of sustainability ratings. *Business Strategy and the Environment*, 19(4).

Delmas, M., & Blass, V.D., 2010. Measuring corporate environmental performance: The trade-offs of sustainability ratings. *Business Strategy & the Environment*, 19(4), pp. 245–260. Available at: http://web.b.ebscohost.com/ehost/detail/detail?vid=154&sid=cab002ee-11b2-4e91-96d1-c794a04685d8@sessionmgr106&hid=102&bdata=JnNpdGU9ZWhvc3Qtb Gl2ZQ==#AN=49388808&db=8gh [Accessed January 9, 2017].

DeFries, R.S., Fanzo, J., Mondal, P., Remans, R., & Wood, S.A., 2017. Is voluntary certification of tropical agricultural commodities achieving sustainability goals for small-scale producers? *Environmental Research Letters*, 12(3). doi: 10.1088/1748-9326/aa625e

de Jongh, D., & Möllmann, C.M., 2014. Market barriers for voluntary climate change mitigation in the South African private sector. *South African Journal of Economic and Management Sciences*, 17(5).

Dennis, P., Connole, H., & Kraut, M., 2015. The efficacy of voluntary disclosure: A study of water disclosures by mining companies using the global reporting initiative framework. *Journal of Legal, Ethical and Regulatory Issues*, 18(2).

Dickson, M.A., 2018. *Better Buying Practices Purchasing Index*, Spring 2018; Purchasing Practices Performance in Apparel, Footwear and Household Textile Supply Chains. Available at www.betterbuying.org.

Doda, B., et al., 2016. Are corporate carbon management practices reducing corporate carbon emissions? *Corporate Social Responsibility and Environmental Management*, 23(5).

Donor Committee for Enterprise Development (DCED), 2017. 'Private sector engagement. Synthesis Note'. https://cdn.enterprise-development.org/wp-content/uploads/DCED-Private-Sector-Engagement-Synthesis-Note.pdf

Oxfam and Donor Committee for Enterprise Development, 2016. Does business structure influence social impact? Early insights and practical implications for donor agencies. Briefing Note, November.

Emel, J., Makene, M.H., & Wangari, E., 2012. Problems with reporting and evaluating mining industry community development projects: A case study from Tanzania. *Sustainability*, 4(2).

Enrique Bonsón, and Michaela Bednárová, 2015. CSR reporting practices of Eurozone companies. *Revista de Contabilidad*, 18(2), pp. 182–193, https://doi.org/10.1016/j.rcsar.2014.06.002.

Evans, A., 2018. The politics of pro-worker reforms. Available at: www.researchgate.net/publication/323259257_The_Politics_of_Pro-Worker_Reforms

Farag, H., Meng, Q., & Mallin, C., 2015. The social, environmental and ethical performance of Chinese companies: Evidence from the Shanghai stock exchange. *International Review of Financial Analysis*, 42, pp. 53–63. Available at: http://linkinghub.elsevier.com/retrieve/pii/S1057521914001951 [Accessed January 9, 2017].

Fatima, A.H.A., Abdullah, N. & Sulaiman, M., 2015. Environmental disclosure quality: Examining the impact of the stock exchange of Malaysia's listing requirements. *Social Responsibility Journal*, 11(4).

Ford, M., 2015. *The Rise of the Robot: Technology and the Threat of Mass Unemployment*. One-World Publications. Bloomsbury, UK.

FutureFit, 2018. Methodology guide. Release 2.0.4., February. Available at: http://futurefitbusiness.org

Gallego-Alvarez, I., 2008. Analysis of social information as a measure of the ethical behavior of Spanish firms. *Management Decision*, 46(4), pp. 580–599. Available at: www.emeraldinsight.com/doi/10.1108/00251740810865076 [Accessed January 9, 2017].

GRI, UNGC, WBCSD, 2015. SDG compass: The guide for business action on the SDGs.

Hong, H., & Kacperczyk, M., 2009. The price of sin: The effects on social norms on markets. *Journal of Financial Economics*, 93, pp. 15–36.

Horner, R., & Nadvi, K., 2018. Global value chains and the rise of the global South: Unpacking twenty-first century polycentric trade. *Global Networks*, 18(2), pp. 207–237. ISSN 1470-2266.

IDH, 2018. How we are making a difference: First insights into IDH's 2016–2020 contribution to public good impact. Available at: www.idhsustainabletrade.com/uploaded/2017/06/IDH-How-we-are-making-a-difference1-web.pdf

IDS, 2006. The ETI code of labour practice: Do workers really benefit? Report on the ETI Impact Assessment 2006, Part 1: Main Findings. Available at: www.ids.ac.uk/files/ETI_impact_1_main_get.pdf

IFC, 2003. 'Towards Sustainable and Responsible Investment in Emerging Markets. A Review and Inventory of the Social Investment Industry's Activities and Potential in Emerging Markets'. October.

ILO, 2016. Assessment of labour provisions in trade and investment arrangements'. Studies on Growth with Equity. ISBN 978-92-2-130375-6.

ILO, 2017. Purchasing practices and working conditions in global supply chains: Global survey results. INWORK Issue Brief No. 10.

Islam, M.A., & Jain, A., 2013. Workplace human rights reporting: A study of Australian garment and retail companies. *Australian Accountability Review*. 23(2), pp. 102–116.

Jamali, D., Lund-Thomsen, P., & Khara, N., 2017. CSR institutionalized myths in developing countries: An imminent threat of selective decoupling. *Business & Society*, 56(3), pp. 454–486, March.

KPMG, 2017. The road ahead: KPMG international survey of corporate responsibility reporting 2017. Available at: https://home.kpmg.com/xx/en/home/insights/2017/10/executive-summary-the-kpmg-survey-of-corporate-responsibility-reporting-2017.html

Lauwo, S.G., Otusanya, O.J., & Bakre, O., 2016. Corporate social responsibility reporting in the mining sector of Tanzania. *Accounting, Auditing & Accountability Journal*, 29(6), pp. 1038–1074. Available at: www.emeraldinsight.com/doi/10.1108/AAAJ-06-2013-1380 [Accessed January 9, 2017].

Locke, R.M., 2013. *The Promise and Limits of Private Power – Promoting Labor Standards in a Global Economy*. Cambridge Studies in Comparative Politics. Cambridge University Press. ISBN-10: 1107670888.

Mayer, C., 2016. Reinventing the corporation. *Journal of the British Academy*, 4, pp. 53–72.

McPhail, K., & Adams, C.A., 2016. Corporate respect for human rights: Meaning, scope, and the shifting order of discourse. *Accounting, Auditing and Accountability Journal*, 29(4).

Milberg, W., & Winkler, D., 2013. *Outsourcing economics: Global value chains in capitalist development*. Cambridge University Press, pp. 1–349.

Molenaar, J.W., Dallinger, J., Gorter, J., Heilbron, L., Simons, L., Blackmore, E., & Vorley, B., 2015. The role of VSS in scaling sustainability in smallholder dominated agricultural sectors. White Paper 4. Commissioned by IFC.

Momin, M.A., & Parker, L.D., 2013. Motivations for corporate social responsibility reporting by MNC subsidiaries in an emerging country: The case of Bangladesh. *The British Accounting Review*, 45(3), pp. 215–228.

Morali, O., & Searcy, C., 2013. A review of sustainable supply chain management practices in Canada. *Journal of Business Ethics*, 117(3).

Morhardt, J.E., 2009. General disregard for details of GRI human rights reporting by large corporations. *Global Business Review*, 10(2).

Mulyadi, M.S., & Anwar, Y., 2012. The impact of corporate social responsibility toward firm value and profitability. *The Business Review*, 19(2), Summer, Cambridge.

Nelling, E., & Webb, E., 2009. Corporate social responsibility and financial performance: The "virtuous circle" revisited. *Review of Quantitative Finance and Accounting*, 32, pp. 197–209.

Nelson, V., Flint, M., & Martin, A., (2017) Trade and global value chains: Final evaluation. Natural Resources Institute report commissioned by DFID. Chatham, UK.

Nelson, V., & Martin, A., 2013. Final technical report: Assessing the poverty impact of sustainability standards. NRI Report, Commissioned by the UK Department for International Development. Available at: https://www.nri.org/images/documents/development-programmes/sustainable_trade/AssessingThePovertyImpactOfSustainabilityStandards.pdf

Nelson, V., Martin, A., & Ewert, J., 2007. The impacts of codes of practice on worker livelihoods; Empirical evidence from the South African wine and Kenyan cut flower industries. *Journal of Corporate Citizenship*, 28, pp. 61–72, December.

Nelson, V., Tallontire, A., & Collinson, C., 2002. Assessing the potential of ethical trade schemes for forest dependent people: Comparative experiences from Peru and Ecuador. *International Forestry Review*, 4, pp. 99–110.

Nelson, V., & Tallontire, A., 2014. Battlefields of ideas: Changing narratives and power dynamics in private standards in global agricultural value chains. Special Issue of *Journal of Agriculture and Human Values*, June (Online). doi:10.1007/s10460-014-9512-8.

Nelson, V., & Phillips, D., 2018. Sector, landscape or rural transformations? Exploring the limits and potential of agricultural sustainability initiatives through a Cocoa Case study. *Business Strategy and the Environment*, 27, pp. 252–262. doi:10.1002/bse.2014.

Niforos, M., Ramachandran, V., & Rehermann, T., 2017. *Blockchain: Opportunities for Private Enterprises in Emerging Markets*. International Finance Corporation World Bank Group. Available at: https://www.ifc.org/wps/wcm/connect/publications_ext_content/ifc_external_publication_site/publications_listing_page/blockchain+report

Orlitzky, M., Schmidt, F.L., & Rynes, S.L., 2003. Corporate social and financial performance: A meta-analysis. *Organization Studies*, 24(3).

Oya, C., Schaefer, F., Skalidou, D., McCosker, C., & Langer, L., 2017. Effects of certification schemes for agricultural production on socio-economic outcomes in low-and middle-income countries: A systematic review. Campbell Collaboration, 3iE. Available at: https://campbellcollaboration.org/media/k2/attachments/Campbell_systematic_review-agricultural_ertification_schemes.pdf

Pérez-López, D., Moreno-Romero, A., & Barkemeyer, R., 2015. Exploring the relationship between sustainability reporting and sustainability management practices. *Business Strategy & the Environment*, 24, pp. 720–734. doi:10.1002/bse.1841.

Porter, M.E., & Kramer, M.R., 2011. Creating shared value. *Harvard Business Review*, January–February 2011 Issue

Principles for Responsible Investment, 2016. From poor working conditions to forced labour – What's hidden in your supply chain? A guide for investor engagement on labour practices in agricultural supply chains. Available at: www.unpri.org/download?ac=1652.

Raworth, K., 2017. *Doughnut Economics: Seven Ways to Think Like a 21st-Century Economist.* Random House Business.

Rockström, J., Steffen, W., Noone, K., Persson, Å., Chapin III, F.S., Lambin, E., Lenton, T.M., Scheffer, M., Folke, C., Schellnhuber, H., Nykvist, B., De Wit, C.A., Hughes, T., van der Leeuw, S., Rodhe, H., Sörlin, S., Snyder, P.K., Costanza, R., Svedin, U., Falkenmark, M., Karlberg, L., Corell, R.W., Fabry, V.J., Hansen, J., Walker, B., Liverman, D., Richardson, K., Crutzen, P., & Foley, J., 2009. A safe operating space for humanity. *Nature*, 46, pp. 472–475.

Said Business School, University of Oxford, 2016. State and direction of inclusive capitalism.

Salazar, J., Husted, B.W., & Biehl, M., 2012. Thoughts on the evaluation of corporate social performance through projects. *Journal of Business Ethics*, 105(2).

Sardinha, I.D., Reijnders, L., & Antunes, P., 2011. Using corporate social responsibility benchmarking framework to identify and assess corporate social responsibility trends of real estate companies owning and developing shopping centres. *Journal of Cleaner Production*, 19(13), pp. 1486–1493.

Sethi, S.P., & Schepers, D.H., 2014. United Nations global compact: The promise-performance gap. *Journal of Business Ethics*, 122(2).

Servigón Caballero, V., undated. *Compañías de Beneficio Público: El Nuevo Paradigma Societario (Parte I).* Ediciones Legales. http://academiab.info/bitstream/123456789/98/1/NJ134%20FORO.pdf

Shift and Mazars, 2015. UN guiding principles reporting framework with implementation guidance. Available at: www.ungpreporting.org/wp-content/uploads/2015/02/UNGuidingPrinciplesReportingFramework_withimplementationguidance_Feb2015.pdf.

Siroën, J.M., & Andrade, D., 2016. Regional trade agreements and the spread of international labour standards.

Sorensen, P., 2012. Sustainable development in mining companies in South Africa. *International Journal of Environmental Studies*, 69(1).

Standing, G., 2016. *The Corruption of Capitalism: Why Rentiers Thrive and Work Does Not Pay.* Biteback. ISBN: 9781785900440.

Starmanns, M., 2017. Purchasing practices and low wages in global supply chains: Empirical cases from the garment industry. Conditions of Work and Employment Series, No. 86, ILO Geneva.

Steffen, W., Richardson, K., Rockström, J., Cornell, S.E., Fetzer, I., Bennett, E.M., Biggs, R., Carpenter, S.R., de Vries, W., de Wit, C.A., Folke, C., Gerten, D., Heinke, J., Mace, G.M., Persson, L.M., Ramanathan, V., Reyers, B., Sörlin, S., 2015. Planetary boundaries: Guiding human development on a changing planet. *Science*, February, 347(6223). doi:10.1126/science.1259855.

Thorpe, J., & Prakash-Mani, K., 2003. Developing value: The business case for sustainability in emerging markets. *Greener Management International*, 44, pp. 17–32.

Toppinen, A., & Korhonen-Kurki, K., 2013. Global reporting initiative and social impact in managing corporate responsibility: A case study of three multinationals in the forest industry. *Business Ethics*, 22(2).

Topple, C., Donovan, J.D., Masli, E.K., & Borgert, T., 2017. Corporate sustainability assessments: MNE engagement with sustainable development and the SDGs. *Transnational Corporations*, 24(3), pp. 61–72.

Tsang, S., Welford, R., & Brown, M., 2009. Reporting on community investment. *Corporate Social Responsibility and Environmental Management*, 16(3), pp. 123–136. Available at: http://doi.wiley.com/10.1002/csr.178 [Accessed January 9, 2017].

UNRISD, 2017. Promoting social and solidarity economy through public policy. Chapter 4. in Transforming our world. Available at: www.unrisd.org/flagship2016-chapter4.

UNGC Accenture, 2013. Architects of a better world. https://www.accenture.com/_acnmedia/accenture/conversion-assets/dotcom/documents/about-accenture/pdf/3/accenture-13-1739-ungc-report-final-fsc3.pdf

UNGC/DNV, 2015. Impact. Transforming business. Changing the world. https://www.unglobalcompact.org/docs/publications/ImpactUNGlobalCompact2015.pdf

UNGC, 2017. 2017 United Nations Global Compact Progress Report: Business Solutions to Sustainable Development. https://www.unglobalcompact.org/library/5431

Wang, Q., Dou, J., & Jia, S., 2015. A meta-analytic review of corporate social responsibility and corporate financial performance: The moderating effect of contextual factors. *Business and Society*, 55(8), pp. 1083–1121. https://doi.org/10.1177/0007650315584317.

Winston, A.S., 2014. The big pivot: Radically practical strategies for a hotter, scarcer and more open world. *Harvard Business Review Press*; USA. ISBN 978-1-4221-6781-6.

World Economic Forum, 2015. Beyond supply chains: Empowering responsible value chains.

Yeung, H.W., & Coe, N.M., 2014. Toward a dynamic theory of global production networks. *Journal of Economic Geography*, 91(1), pp. 29–59.

9 Multistakeholder initiatives in global value chains

Opportunities and challenges for women workers

Ahmad Hassan

Introduction

In the process of globalization, the number of multistakeholder initiatives such as the Better Cotton Initiative (BCI, 2013), the United Kingdom–based Ethical Trading Initiative, and the Fairtrade Labelling Organization (FLO) have risen in recent years. As a response to the social and environmental problems in export-oriented industries in developing countries, these multistakeholder initiatives promote voluntary governance solutions (Hassan & Lund-Thomsen, 2016; Utting, 2015). Mena and Palazzo (2012) and define multistakeholder initiatives as "private governance mechanisms involving corporations, civil society organizations, and sometimes other actors, governments, academia or unions, to cope with social and environmental challenges across industries and on a global scale" (pp. 527–28). The proliferation of multistakeholder initiatives is taking place in a context of liberalization of international trade, deregulation of the economies of developing countries, privatization of state enterprises, and the rise of global value chains that link dispersed consumers and international buyers in developed countries with local producers and workers in the developing world (Bair & Palpacuer, 2015; Utting & Zammit 2009).

Multistakeholder initiatives are perceived to be more inclusive compared to corporate self-regulation because the local stakeholders, such as civil society organizations, suppliers/producers, local governments, etc., participate (Dolan & Opondo, 2005; Lund-Thomsen & Nadvi, 2010). The inclusion of various stakeholders both from public and private sectors in the process of standard making and execution presumably renders a higher degree of legitimacy (Cheyns & Riisgaard, 2014). Multistakeholder initiatives are seen to have the potential to find innovative solutions for problems arising from the economic, social, and environmental externalities related to the global value chains because they contribute to the expert knowledge and they connect resources among the stakeholders. Participants with diverse knowledge and skills can address environmental and social problems under the umbrella of multistakeholder partnership, specifically because several solutions need access to non-economic acquaintance (Utting, 2002). Finally, multistakeholder initiatives are acknowledged for their potential to create possibilities to pool finances, and their cooperative nature makes it possible to integrate the efforts of various stakeholders to enable long-lasting collaboration, dialogue, and continual interface that can lead to mutual respect, trust, and learning respect (Boström, 2006; Fransen, 2012; Fransen & Kolk, 2007).

These initiatives are acknowledged for their potential to legitimize and democratize decision-making processes in global value chains by putting pressure on the main decision makers such as the international buyers (Dingwerth, 2008), or to elucidate social expectations towards transnational corporations (Detomasi, 2007). However, we have less knowledge about how particular local challenges in developing countries are solved by the multistakeholder initiatives. In particular the gendered[1] aspects within developing countries stand as timely and extensive challenges, and it remains unclear whether, and if so, how multistakeholder initiatives can improve social and environmental conditions of the marginalized "fringe" stakeholders within global value chains women workers.

In a developmental perspective, women participation in global value chains is vital for the achievement of economic and social development, because this increases women's access to economic assets and prospects such as employment and skills development. In other words, to attain a sustainable economic and social development, the entire population must pool their abilities, creativeness, and innovative skills. Females make up around 40 percent of the worldwide labor force; they own 30 percent of the formal business, and they are liable for or effect around 80 percent of consumer expenditure. However, economies can only develop and grow if both men and women contribute. If, for example, females had equal access to the markets and other productive assets as males, they could raise revenues on their agricultural fields between 20 and 30 percent, and thus increase the overall agricultural yield between 2.5 and 4 percent in developing countries. Such growth in the production of food would possibly contribute to food for around 150 million people (FAO, 2010a). Similarly, the World Bank illustrates that the productivity per female worker could be improved between 25 and 40 percent by eliminating discrimination against female managers and workers. The significance of women regarding economic development has been highlighted in research conducted to support the World Bank's "Gender Mainstreaming Strategy" implemented in 2001. This research shows that societies that treat men and women more equally tend to experience a more rapid economic development and a reduction in poverty compared to societies that discriminate against females and males. Thus, it is argued that the disparities between men and women entail economically ineffective results; African countries could almost have doubled the per capita income in their region had they managed to close the gender gap in the fundamental schooling from 1960 to 1992 in comparison with East Asian countries (Dollar & Gatti, 1999).

Although there are significant motives to support women's economic and social development and to improve gender equality, there is still a substantial economic gap between males and females in most countries of the world, particularly in developing countries. For example, a report published by the International Labour Organization (ILO) indicates that females' wages as part of the paid labor workforce are overall 10 to 30 percent lower than that of males (ILO, 2008). The ratio of females in the labor force has risen gradually during the last two decades, but there are still significant differences in the workforce participation rates, because women involvement in the workforce is only one part of the overall scenario. We need to look into the details of the work conditions for these females, who are more often locked in lower-paying jobs compared to males. In developing countries, six out of ten working females work as informal factory workers under vulnerable conditions or they are unpaid workers in family businesses or farms (ibid). Furthermore, profitability margins and growth levels are higher in businesses controlled by men compared to businesses controlled by women, and generally men have higher positions when it comes to the management of businesses.

More specifically, a number of researchers have pointed out that it is difficult to improve gender inequalities in global value chains (Barrientos, Dolan, & Tallontire, 2003; Loconto, 2015; Pearson, 2007; Smith & Dolan, 2006). These inequalities are frequently described as (1) sexual, physical, and verbal harassment; (2) less appreciation for women's reproductive work; (3) unequal pay and contextual barriers that prevent women from contributing to social, economic, and political life; (4) poor health and safety conditions; etc. (Allen & Sachs 2012; Bain, 2010; Dolan, 2004; Islam, 2008). These gender inequalities hamper women's productivity and downgrade their roles in the agriculture sector and in the accomplishment of wider economic and social development goals. Gender inequality is a worldwide phenomenon; however, it is a pressing element in the developing countries, particularly as globalization and trade liberalization have inclined progress to equality backwards (Seguino, 2010; Walby, 2011). Also, Beath, Christia, and Enikolopov (2013) argue that promoting gender equality has proven to be particularly challenging in the developing countries, with long-lasting values and customs that endure discrimination against women in all areas of life. For example, females are mostly working in domestic activities and unpaid work. According to the ILO, females contribute to around 83 percent of domestic work activities globally. Female workers, specifically those involved in the agriculture sector and living in rural communities in developing countries, have limited access to training, education, and other resources such as capital and specialized knowledge in relation to connecting with commercial markets and updated information about available technologies compared to males. In other words, these obstacles to getting access to resources such as land, tools for implementing modern farming methods, pesticides, fertilizers, and commercial credits or start-up funds are key causes in relation to females' work and are part of an unseen informal economy. Also, women frequently face established institutional restraints, such as prejudiced legal systems that constrain their right to control or to possess productive assets and/or to participate in paid labor activities. In the majority of developing countries, local laws inhibit females from inheriting and possessing land; thus, their level of poverty is maintained and they are further discriminated against. These hurdles and conditions related to females are often not effectively addressed or exposed in governments' policy agendas, partially because of weak institutional capability and inadequate statistics about sex disaggregation. Even though in some cases where governments in developing countries have legally favored women, they are regularly challenged when trying to implement the legislation by tough norms of patriarchal land ownership (ILO, 2011).

Redressing such inequalities in global value chains would substantially benefit society by increasing the agricultural productivity, reducing hunger and poverty, and promoting economic growth (FAO, 2010a). In addition, to include women participation in global value chains may provide economic and social empowerment, a supplement to home labor, and may bring previously unimagined prospects. This advances that the viewpoints of women working in these chains are further nuanced (Said-Allsopp & Tallontire, 2015). Also, encouraging women participation in value chains, strengthening women's privileges, and making it easier for them to control their lives will produce the utmost returns on all development funds, because women generally spend a higher amount of their wages on their family members than men. So, an increase in women's income and their control of family expenditures can possibly lead to enhancements in child nutrition, health, and education. Also, improving women's economic conditions may directly promote their well-being and decrease their level of poverty, because a majority of the women in developing countries are poor.

In the context of multistakeholder initiatives, gender equality is 'the key to a sustainable, smart and inclusive society'; therefore, "gendering" global value chains is essential to understand the opportunities and limitations that multistakeholder initiatives may have on economic and social development goals in general, and gender equality in particular (Grosser, McCarthy, & Kilgour, 2016). However, so far researchers have not paid much attention to the challenges that the marginalized workers in global value chains face, particularly women, nor to the potential of addressing these issues by means of multistakeholder initiatives. In relation to development studies, it is vital to investigate how and if the economic, social, and environmental impact of multistakeholder initiatives reach the lowest rungs of global value chains (Lauwo, 2016; Mezzadri, 2014). The overall objective of this chapter can be summed up in the following research question:

How do multistakeholder initiatives provide opportunities and challenges for women workers in global value chains?

By exploring the opportunities and challenges that the multistakeholder initiatives provide for women workers in developing countries, the chapter contributes to the literature on multistakeholder initiatives by focusing on the interconnectedness between men's and women's household lives and the concepts of global value chains and global production networks. The chapter argues that the notions of global value chains and global production networks provide a well-founded conceptual framework for studying gender in the context of multistakeholder initiatives (Barrientos, 2014b). Thus, the significance of the intrahousehold bargaining over men and women's domestic lives in relation to global value chains is enormously significant in the context of gender. In empirical terms, this is one of the first independent studies which focuses on how the BCI seeks to address the women workers' concerns and problems in the global value chain in Pakistan. As such, the chapter has implications for both policymakers and academics working in the realm of multistakeholder initiatives and gender studies.

The remainder of the chapter is structured as follows. The second section explains the conceptual framework for this chapter aimed at explaining the concepts of global value chains, global production networks, and feminist economists in relation to gender studies. The third section seeks to elaborate the context of (1) women workers in the cotton value chain in Pakistan and (2) the evolution of the BCI. The fourth section focuses on the methodology comprising the selection of the case study and data collection methods. The fifth section analyzes the data and discusses the empirical findings. Finally, the conclusion section summarizes the main findings and the contribution of the chapter and provides implications for policymakers and for further research.

Conceptual framework

The global value chain approach argues that the connections among the producers, the distributors, and the consumers of goods and services can be theorized as a chain of processes and activities (Gereffi & Korzeniewicz, 1994). Gereffi (1994) initially described three dimensions of a global value chain: (1) the input–output structure, that is, the chains of value-adding activities in the manufacturing and consumption of a product; (2) the geographical coverage, that is, its territorial diffusion of stakeholders and events interrelated to a global value chain; and (3) the form of governance, that is, the distribution of power among various stakeholders, the authority, and the decision-making processes throughout the chain. Although the input–output structure and the geographical coverage remain largely descriptive concerns in the literature, the global value chain approach has mostly explored governance-related issues and sharing of economic rents particularly in buyer-driven value chains where global buyers play a central role (Gereffi & Lee, 2016).

The notion of governance in global value chains focuses on the power of the international lead buyers to control value chains, deciding what will be produced, in which quantity, the price of each product, the quality of the product, the location of the production, the timing of production and when the product will be delivered, the selection of the supplier(s), etc. (Lund-Thomsen & Lindgreen, 2014). This further connects to the decisions regarding what kind of standards are to be required for local suppliers in developing countries to achieve a certain level of product quality, the process of production, and possibly the distribution. The initial literature on the governance in global value chains makes a distinction between two forms of value chains:

(1) producer-driven value chains, which are typically found in technology and capital demanding businesses where governance of the value chains is executed by firms that own key technologies and production units, and (2) buyer-driven value chains, which are mainly found in labor demanding businesses where governance of the value chains is affected by larger international buyers such as brand-name retailers with no or very limited ownership of the production units (Gereffi, 1994). Particularly, in the buyer-driven form of global value chain governance, global retailers play a dominant part in the value chain's governance, which allows them to apply environmental and social standards as a prerequisite of supply. Later literature on global value chains has extended this narrow understanding of governance by distinguishing among five different forms of governance in relation to global value chains: market mechanisms on the one side and hierarchy on the other side with modular, captive, and relational linkages as distinct buyer-producer relations in between (Gereffi, Humphrey, & Sturgeon, 2005).

In the context of globalization, the global value chain approach is considered an essential framework adopted by global organizations such as the ILO for examining the economic development (Dolan & Humphrey, 2004). In addition, through the demonstration of interaction between international buyers and their local suppliers in developing countries and the display of their power irregularities, this approach has highlighted some inequalities inside the global production systems. For example, Barrientos (2001) argues that buyer-driven global value chains are extremely competitive and price conscious, where production orders could change weekly, or maybe daily, due to a "just-in-time" inventory strategy, thus forcing factory owners and landlords to hire or lay off workers as the orders dictate. Although the power- and governance-related issues are acknowledged in the global value chain approach, this approach is often limited to relationships and coordination mechanisms between economic factors and actors such as global buyers and local suppliers (Sturgeon, 2008).

Henderson et al. (2002) have extended the global value chain approach through more critical understandings of the value chains as global production networks. They argue that global value chains include a variety of stakeholders such as government agencies, labor unions, civil society organizations, and other related stakeholders that might influence the environments surrounding interfirm networks in the international economy. In other words, global value chain governance cannot just be reduced to a discussion on the comparative powers of global buyers and their local suppliers in developing countries but must also be considered in relation to the power of other stakeholders (Hess, 2008). Furthermore, a global production network analysis emphasizes that these networks are simultaneously local as well as global structures; they have specific institutional and physical features that form the production strategies and the interactions between nodules in a production network (Bartley & Egels Zandén, 2015; Coe, Dicken, & Hess, 2008a). Thus, global production network analysis goes beyond the vertical, interfirm emphasis that much of the literature has focused on when it comes to global value chains. Similarly, Neilson and

Pritchard (2010) discuss that the scope of the literature on global value chain governance is very limited in relation to institutions and governance. They argue that there are other important factors and players such as nongovernmental organizations (NGOs) and the local governments that may influence global value chain governance, and they have proposed a framework that goes further than the straight actors participating in the value chains, merging *horizontal* relationships (with regard to the institutional settings of producer countries) along with *vertical* powers (with regard to the global value chain governance). Finally, Yeung and Coe (2015) argue that these global production networks are regularly altering and developing, and are thus more active in nature than the static notion of interfirm relationships that is often predominant in the global value chain literature.

In short, the literature on global production networks complements the global value chain analysis with its focus on social arrangements and practices around production networks, and the directness to formal and informal corporations among various stakeholders within these networks. Nevertheless, the literature on global value chains and global production networks is in practice inclined to focus mainly on global buyers and their interactions with local suppliers, with very limited studies into collaborations, power relations, and decision-making processes within these firms (Coe et al., 2008b). Particularly, Barrientos (2013, 2014a, 2014b) has criticized global value chain studies and the global production networks studies for mostly remaining quiet on the opportunities and challenges for the gendered dimensions of women in the context of globalization. She explains that in order to integrate a gender viewpoint, it is very essential to expand the notion of the value chain beyond firms to the wide range of institutions and stakeholders that are involved in and affect the economic and social aspects of the value chain. The work of Tallontire (2007) is of specific significance in relation to this chapter. She has contributed to the literature on multistakeholder initiatives in global value chains and global production networks by differentiating among legislative governance (who decides the formulation process of these standards and how?), executive governance (how are these standards implemented in developing countries?), and judicial governance (how are these standards monitored?). In this chapter, I extend her contribution by linking an analysis of the implementing process (executive governance) to multistakeholder initiatives, looking into their impact on the conditions of women workers at the bottom of global value chains in developing countries.

In addition, feminist economists argue that gender views should be examined by involving wider societal and cultural practices such as intrahousehold struggles over income and labor-related activities. Females make several of the decisions, such as the children's education and health care, both of which determine a household's contribution to a society in general (Kasi, 2013). Because women spend most of their time taking care of children and carrying out other domestic duties, they do not have much time to participate in full-time job opportunities or other economic-generating activities. Unfortunately, most of the domestic responsibilities are not measured or considered formal income-producing occupations in national and regional economic statistics. Therefore, these domestic activities are degraded and perceived as economically immaterial but are yet vital to the overall well-being of rural families (Peterson, 2006). Thus, to be able to explore women's situation in a value chain and how changes in a value chain possibly affect gender discrimination, and the main restraints for women in relation to gain through participation in value chains, one needs to put gender into the setting of intrahousehold bargaining and into wider societal and cultural processes (see e.g., Wyrod, 2008). In other words, to understand the situation of women in global value chains and to improve their conditions are matters that also affect men/and are affected by men, and hence, it is crucial to focus on the native environment that may support or challenge gender empowerment (Kabeer, 2001; Riisgaard, Fibla, & Ponte, 2010). The focus of this chapter is on exploring the opportunities and challenges for women workers in the global value chains for the BCI in Pakistan. With this in mind, the next section offers a brief introduction to the particular context of the cotton industry in Pakistan, focusing on the problems and concerns related to women workers in the value chain and evolution of the BCI.

Cotton value chain in Pakistan and evolution of the Better Cotton Initiative

Pakistan is the fourth largest grower of cotton in the world, the third largest exporter of cotton textiles, and the second largest supplier of cotton yarn, with 26 percent share of the global market (Ataullah, Sajid, & Khan, 2014). Cotton is primarily grown in the Punjab and Sindh provinces. On average, the Punjab contribution is 75.40 percent area under cotton production with 75 percent of production. The Sindh contribution is 20.60 percent area to cotton with around 25 percent of production (USDA, 2016). Cotton is an important crop for the Pakistan economy; it is particularly a vital source of raw material to the textile industry, contributing 55 percent of total foreign exchange earnings (Ali, Aslam, & Ali, 2012).

In Pakistan, a vast majority of cotton farms are operated as family farms by owners/cultivators living in rural societies with a higher degree of illiteracy and lesser access to productive resources. Cotton farming is mainly dependent on manual labor, with nominal levels of mechanization in the cultivation cycle. This usually means that even small family farms are obliged to hire external labor inputs for specific key processes such as harvesting (Kouser & Qaim, 2017). The cotton growing community mainly includes cotton pickers and farmers. Farmers are mostly males involved in the sowing of the cotton seed, the groundwork on agricultural land, the irrigation, the selling of cotton crops, etc. Women act mainly as cotton pickers, employed in three to five waves from July to November every year. The employment of agriculture workers in cotton farming is mostly contract based. This comprises both skilled and unskilled workers hired on casual and regular terms of employment. Skilled workers are employed largely to supervise seasonal and casual workers on the farms for harvesting. Unskilled workers are mainly hired on a regular basis for seeding, fertilizing, soil softening, irrigating, etc. (International Cotton Advisory Committee, 2008). In recent years, however, gender disaggregation showed that the major growth in hired labor demand arises for women workers, as farmers largely hire female workers for harvesting and other labor-intensive jobs in the cotton production (Kouser & Qaim, 2017).

In Pakistan on average, the agriculture workers are paid Rs 6,221 (US$ 62.2) per month. However, women workers are grossly underpaid Rs 3,863 (US$ 38.6), whereas male workers receive Rs 7,873 (US$ 78.7). In addition, women workers, apart from receiving extremely low wages for their job of cotton picking, are also exposed to pesticides that harm their reproductive systems (Labour Force Survey, 2012–13). Some studies noted that insecticide remains greatly influence the health of cotton-picking female workers because pesticides affect the hormone levels of cotton pickers in Pakistan. Furthermore, despite the fact that women work in the cotton field which requires hard work and long working days (on average 10 to 12 hours per day), their domestic responsibilities of reproduction and caregiving are not accommodated or given any flexibility. Finally, women's employment at the bottom of the cotton value chain shows their nominal access to resources such as credit, land, and technology (Balagamwala, Gazdar, & Mallah, 2015; Reuters, 2015).

The multistakeholder initiative known as the BCI, primarily supported by a group of key multinational corporations such as Gap, Inc., Adidas, IKEA, and H&M, launched the Better Cotton global standard (the BCI standard) in 2009. The BCI "exists to make global cotton production better for the people who produce it, better for the environment it grows in and better for the sector's future, by developing Better Cotton as a sustainable mainstream commodity." The BCI designed the Better Cotton Standard System to encourage the scaling up of joint efforts and to communicate good practices among stakeholders to develop Better Cotton as a sustainable mainstream commodity. In line with the traditional understanding of sustainability, the BCI considers that sustainability of the global cotton production requires not only environmental but also social and economic concerns (BCI, 2016). This system covers six elements: (1) production principles and criteria, (2) capacity building, (3) assurance program, (4) chain of custody, (5) claims framework, and (6) results and impacts.

The production principles and criteria (P&C) of the BCI describe the worldwide definition of better cotton. The P&C was first established in 2010 based on contributions and discussions with the regional working groups in India, Pakistan, Brazil, and Central and West Africa; members of the Advisory Committee; Better Cotton Partners; and specialists. In accordance with the BCI Standard Setting and Revision Procedure, an inclusive review process of the P&C was developed in February 2015. This review process was launched in compliance with the "ISEAL Code of Good Practice for Setting Social and Environmental Standards (Public Version 6–0, December 2014) and under the guidance of ISO/IEC Guide 59 Code of Good Practice for Standardization (February 1994)." The P&C is a vital element of the Better Cotton Standard

System, with the purpose of increasing the economic development and livelihood in cotton-producing countries, as well as to decrease the environmental harms of cotton through the BCI theory of change. The P&C provides prescription and guidelines to farmers joining the BCI training programs on how to achieve the BCI goals related to social, economic, and environmental sustainability (BCI, 2016). According to the BCI home page, the P&C is composed of the following seven principles:

Principle 1: Better Cotton farmers minimize the harmful impact of crop protection practices
Principle 2: Better Cotton farmers promote water stewardship
Principle 3: Better Cotton farmers care for the health of soil
Principle 4: Better Cotton farmers enhance biodiversity
Principle 5: Better Cotton farmers care for and preserve the quality of fiber
Principle 6: Better Cotton farmers promote decent work
Principle 7: Better Cotton farmers operate an effective management system

In particular, principle 6 related to decent work is of significance to the situation of women workers in the cotton industry. The BCI considers decent work as the notion initiated by the ILO to describe work that gives prospects for men and women to work effectively in conditions of equity, freedom, human dignity, and security. For defining how work promotes inclusive, fair, and sustainable development, this notion of decent work facilitates the BCI to develop a wide-ranging and reliable method to the diversity of national and local contexts in which cotton is produced from family-based, small-scale producers to large-scale farms. The BCI understands the ILO, the United Nations (UN) expert organization on work and employment, to be the global specialist on labor-related issues. Although the decent work production principle of the BCI is phrased in specific expressions, the BCI has primarily referred to the ILO convention and to other private voluntary standards related to agriculture (BCI, 2016) when trying to explain the content of this production principle. The basic idea is that all Better Cotton producers must follow national and regional laws, unless those laws that regulate standards that are lower than the referenced global renowned standards and conventions such as the ILO convention, and if this is the case, the global standards prevail. This is particularly relevant to a country like Pakistan, where agriculture is not included in the labor laws.

The BCI is dedicated to these seven elements and reflects that each of these elements should work collectively in supporting the Better Cotton Standard System and the credibility of the initiative. The BCI as a standard implementing organization aims at helping workers and farmers to fulfill the guidelines of the standard system through a capacity-building approach. The BCI states that the focus on capacity building of farmers and workers can be distinguished with other multistakeholder initiatives whose emphasis is mainly on certification. In other words, to confirm compliance with the production codes written in a certain standard system instead of aiming on facilitating local producers to meet these practices through capacity building of on-farm workers and farmers. Therefore, the BCI relies on putting effort into the capacity building of workers and farmers to support them in producing better cotton that will then finally receive a Better Cotton license. The BCI coordinates this capacity-building approach via local implementing partners to assist workers and farmers to follow practices that are in accordance with the production principles of the standard system. These local implementing partners are crucial actors in relation to the execution of the Better Cotton standard system (including the capacity-building approach of the system), because they are intent on working with cotton workers and farmers and are in charge of helping farmers to harvest and sell Better Cotton (BCI, 2016).

In order to make sure that farmers regularly comply with their production principles and criteria, the BCI has introduced an assurance program, which targets at linking workers and farmers in continuous learning techniques that will support them to develop their production methods, productivity, and profitability. This assurance program also assesses whether farmers have the capability to grow Better Cotton, because the prerequisite for getting a license to produce Better Cotton is that the farmers need to meet a number of minimum demands which contain well-defined criteria for the use of pesticides, decent work, water management, data protection, participating in training sessions, and other aspects. The first step in the assurance program is the selection of the local implementing partners and their training. Each selected implementing partner will train a certain number of farmers. When training is given to farmers, the implementing partner will collect data such as the number of farmers trained and how the implementing partner has organized those farmers in group(s), etc. The local BCI staff and an independent third party then pay regular visits the farmers to measure compliance with the Better Cotton standard system. The assurance program has a specific emphasis on supporting the farmers' self-improvement. The evaluation is based on data collected by means of questionnaires, which the farmers have to fill out revealing what they know about the Better Cotton production principles and criteria. Based on their responses, the farmers obtain a certain score. If farmers get an adequately high score, they are qualified as Better Cotton farmers. Actually, the farmers will be licensed for a longer period if they get a relatively high score, and similarly, they will be licensed for a shorter period if they obtain a low score.

Methodology

Case study selection

To examine the opportunities and challenges that multistakeholder initiatives give women workers in global value chains, I employed a qualitative case-study methodology because this is acknowledged as an appropriate method when exploring "how" and "why" questions (Yin, 2013). A distinctive case was selected that fits the proposed profile, namely the case of the BCI in Pakistan, because it is the first initiative which established the Better Cotton global standards known as the Better Cotton P&C (details are presented in the earlier section). Some scholars argue that a single case study draws various issues related to the narrow generalizability of outcomes, the method of collecting qualitative data that does not allow vigorous critical procedures, and the overall inadequate level of reliability of the research processes (Yin, 2013). However, proponents of single case study research claim that through single case study, researchers may gain proximity to the phenomena under investigation, which is probably not possible with other methods of conducting research. Therefore, they have proposed several techniques to overcome the weaknesses related to the single case study research, such as mentioning all limitations for the research area, thus strengthening the validity of the research (Jasper, 1994); forming a series of evidence or review trail (Yin, 2013); and enabling the research procedure to offer further rationality to the study (Cronin, 2014). In addition, a case study method is particularly significant for this study because it makes it easier to understand the dynamic forces that exist within single locations, specifically when settings under study are stable (Eisenhardt, 1989). Several of the main stakeholders, first related to the BCI in Pakistan when it came into existence in 2010, were still working with the BCI when we collected data in late 2017 for this study, and they were happy to participate in the study and they were easily accessible for proving and disapproving the data.

Data collection

In 40 semi-structured, qualitative interviews conducted with key stakeholders from the global value chain for the BCI in Pakistan, I gained access to numerous understandings of the activities related to the BCI, comprising both positive and skeptical opinions. These stakeholders comprises the women and men workers working with the BCI in Punjab,[2] Pakistan, the implementing partners (NGOs) of the BCI, field facilitators, farmers' association, and BCI staff in Pakistan. This selection criterion shows that interviews were conducted with representatives from almost all important stakeholders involved in the BCI in Pakistan. As such, the focus was on the use of semi-structured interviews, because the purpose was to understand, explain, and discover the working conditions for women workers in the initiative (Saunders, Lewis, & Thornhill, 2009). Interviews with women workers were conducted to gain unique data on the specific settings in relation to the research question for this chapter, and the interviews with other key stakeholders were considered valuable to develop a better understanding of the phenomenon studied and to increase the value of the collected data (Stake, 2010). The selection process for conducting interviews with women workers was based on the aim to interview those workers who were likely to know the BCI, such as those joining the training sessions conducted by the implementing partners – training sessions meant to raise women workers' awareness in relation to promote decent work. Thus, as suggested by (Kvale, 1996), the emphasis was to select interviewees with extensive experience and awareness of the studied initiative. As a whole, the interviews gave me entrenched and context-dependent findings (see the later section on empirical analysis) regarding the opportunities and challenges for the women workers working with the BCI in Pakistan.

Before starting an interview, I asked for approval from the interviewees to record the interviews, and thus all interviews were recorded digitally. Interviews with workers and field facilitators were conducted in Punjabi, the native language of the interviewees, and interviews with other stakeholders were conducted in English. However, all interviews were transcribed in full and translated into English. The interviews each lasted between 25 and 60 minutes. An interview generally started with stating the overall objective of the research, a brief introduction of the interviewer, and explanations about the significance of the interviewees' viewpoints for this specific research project.

I developed a comprehensive interview guide before conducting the interviews, and this process helped me to uphold the overall purpose of the study and to enhance the possibility of successful data collection. All interviews were based on specific themes related to the research question for this chapter. In addition, I asked open questions that allowed the respondents to express their individual concerns through their particular ways of telling their own story as they observe it (Yin, 2011). Hence, the flexibility of semi-structured interviews gave me further insight into the relation to the women workers' conditions and the key stakeholders' specific viewpoints – insight that may not have been accessible otherwise (Kvale & Brinkmann, 2009). After collecting data from some interviews, I established abstract notes as part of the development of other interviews for exploring whether and how the BCI provides opportunities and constraints for women workers in Pakistan (Corbin & Strauss, 2008). This continual procedure helped me in refining my research question and the theoretical motivation for later interviews.

Empirical analysis

In the previous section I explained the key outlines of the fieldwork site and discussed the methodology for this chapter. In this section, I now turn my attention to apply the concepts outlined from conceptual framework, as well as the context overview, to analyze how the BCI does potentially provide opportunities and challenges for women workers in the cotton value chain in Pakistan.

Opportunities

First, I explore the overall women workers' conditions in the broader global value chain context in which the BCI is implemented, as well as analyze if the BCI has possibly improved working conditions for women workers in Pakistan. In various agriculture value chains, women make up the majority of workers (Barrientos et al., 2005). Women are favored instead of men for particular work, including picking cotton/fruit, harvesting, and packing of final products because they are perceived as obedient, hardworking, and careful, so as not to harm the crop. In addition, this type of work, perceived as light and unskillful, is believed to be jobs appropriate for females based on their gender characteristics, such as carefulness. Furthermore, employment for women workers in value chains tends to be short-term, part-time, seasonal, and without contracts. These job conditions allow employers to cut expenses in relation to salaries, as well as social benefits (WWW, 2007).

Nevertheless, the BCI recognizes that women workers in global value chains for cotton face various work challenges, including unskilled, part-time or seasonal work, and pesticide exposure (BCI, 2016). Therefore, through a capacity-building approach, the BCI – along with its implementing partners – conducts training sessions to raise workers' awareness of relevant concerns. This claim was supported by many interviewees in this study; as one woman worker put it: "I have been picking cotton for twenty-five years. During the last year, I was for the first time in my life trained two to three times" [from the BCI].

These training sessions are considered to be particularly valuable for bringing female cotton pickers into the value chain for the BCI, for example, a woman worker stated: "Before this training, only my husband was earning money. The female trainer was good. After the training, I began to pick cotton. Now we can easily manage our monthly expenses, previously it was hard to manage."

In addition, these training programs enable women cotton workers to group together and to bargain collectively for better wages. As a number of women workers explained in interviews: "We work in a group. It increases our bargaining power, the zamindar (farmers) are compelled to accept our demand. The group leader negotiates with farmers on our behalf, she then comes back to us (her team) and discuss the wages with us. We get better wages now."

Directly put by another woman worker:

> Before this training, the cotton picking rate in our village was RS 10 (around $ 0.10) per kg. In other villages, wages were increased to RS 15 (around $ 0.15) per kg. After the training, we as a group began to go to other villages for work, and they (farmers from our villages) then came and offered us the same amount (RS 15) for working in their fields.

Finally, in recent years, a proliferation of multistakeholder initiatives and ILO conventions on labor rights mean that the labor force is hypothetically more secure than ever in the global value chain. One specific issue related to women workers in the agricultural value chains is pesticides causing health problems. In the women's informal labor environment, they are usually not protected by multistakeholder initiatives or a law that oblige laborers to wear gloves and dress in a precautionary way or to keep away from treated fields for a certain period of time (Bain, 2010). In relation to cotton production, pesticides are normally used on cotton bolls to control pests, and the use of pesticides in the production of cotton causes numerous health dangers to farm laborers. In Pakistan, these conditions are even more awful, as workers are not very conscious about pesticide use and hardly protect themselves in any way. Workers and farmers do not attach great importance to health concerns and clearly undervalue the health hazard posed by the use of pesticides. Women workers are particularly at risk to pesticide exposure and other chemicals in the period of cotton picking because of their low financial independence in the society (Bakhsh, 2016). However, female workers benefit from the increased training and awareness by implementing partners of the BCI that promote decent work for women workers in Pakistan and showing some possible benefits for women workers. As some women workers said during interviews with them:

> This training has helped us a lot as the sister (the trainer) has shown us how best to pick cotton. Previously we were facing many problems; our clothes were damaged during picking, and we lost some of our hair. The trainer told us to wear a dupatta (shawl) tightly around our heads, and cover our nose and mouth with the shawl while picking cotton. After having been trained we have begun to wear cotton clothes when going to work and then the clothes is not damaged. And we no longer [lose] hair.

Another worker stated: "I had asthma and developed [an] allergy from spraying of pesticides. After having been trained, I became aware of precautionary measures such as to cover my body while working in the cotton fields and now I am doing fine. It has improved my health."

Challenges

Having outlined the potential opportunities for women workers through multistakeholder initiatives (in this case the BCI) in global value chains, I now move on to exploring the nature of global value chain analyses in the view of feminist economists who claim that although the productive economy (paid work) is vital for females, it is essential to keep in mind that females still carry out the majority of the reproductive economy (unpaid work) in their homes. Such work includes the primary obligation for child care and care of elderly people or vulnerable members of the family, as well as obligations for doing activities such as carrying firewood and water, cooking for the family, washing pots and pans and clothing, sweeping the house, etc. (Blackden & Wodon, 2006). According to the World Bank (2011), females spend almost double as much time as men on household work. Therefore, women in all parts of value chains face challenges when it comes to employment because of their domestic duties. So, women involved in salaried work usually have a double work day, as they are perhaps only permitted to work in the fields as long as their household activities are still satisfied (Kasente, 2012). This shows that women have a substantial time burden, and it could affect their well-being and health, and thus keep women out of the global market economies and limit their development (Carmona, 2013). In this study, this also came forward in many interviews with women workers. For example, one of the women workers stated: "Yes, I get tired, I do work at home, then go to fields and then return and do more work at home." She further explains: "I have to do all types of work, and work has increased over time. My husband's work is down as the looms are closed for two to three months. It creates problems for the entire family and I have to do all kinds of work to earn our livelihood."

Interviewer: *Do you get help from any male member in the household when you have*
 to manage all household activities along with picking cotton?
Respondent: *No, I have to manage all work at home and in the fields. It is difficult*
 to live, poor women have many problems, and we have to earn our own
 livelihood.

Another woman worker also argued along similar lines: "I have to work though my health is poor. I work to get some money for our children."

Conclusions

In this chapter, the author contributed to the emerging literature on multi-stakeholder initiatives by combining the notion of global value chains and global production networks with intrahousehold struggles over paid work, as women workers still do the bulk of unpaid work in their homes. The author argues that global value chain activities are connected to both the productive economy (paid work) and the reproductive economy (unpaid household work and caring of children and elderly people normally done by females) – the latter is considered necessary for the effectiveness of the productive economy through the reproduction of the labor force. In other words, to examine how multistakeholder initiatives potentially affect women workers in global value chains, it is crucial to combine insights from the global value chain and the global production network literature, specifically trying to understand women workers' involvement in income-generating activities, with insights from intrahousehold activities.

The empirical analysis in this chapter revealed that women cotton workers in the global value chain for the BCI in Pakistan are involved in the productive as well as the reproductive economy. Overall, this analysis indicates that the training sessions by implementing partners of the BCI have probably facilitated women workers to work together in groups, and this has potentially improved their collective bargaining power for getting better salaries, and thus have possibly increased their household income. These training programs also have an encouraging effect on the health conditions of women cotton workers. However, the programs do not overall have much effect on the position of women with regard to their role in household activities. Certainly, as this chapter has demonstrated, there is a strong possibility that putting excessive focus on women workers' participation in global value chains could increase their amount of work and thus possibly harm them, as they have to work in the fields but still have to carry out their household activities. Such issues must be carefully considered and highlighted in training programs aiming to "promote" decent work for women workers in global value chains through multistakeholder initiatives.

In terms of implications for the literature of the findings of this chapter, the author combines the concepts of global value chains and global production networks, thereby specifically understanding the involvement of women workers in income-generating activities, with intrahousehold bargaining over men's and women's domestic lives. In terms of policy implications, the author proposes that to promote decent work in global value chains, multistakeholder initiatives should strongly focus on concerns such as local gender customs and the balance between women workers' involvement in the reproductive and productive economies. In other words, attention needs to be paid to make sure that these training programs serve women's desires and embody their views when designing the programs, so that they are more likely to find appropriate solutions for their problems in a supportive way. In terms of implications for academics, we are obviously in need of further empirical studies that can explain the complexities of global value chains, particularly stressing the significance of gender equity and women's participation in the reproductive and productive economies. In addition, these studies should show the nuances in different cultures and contexts in relation to gender and explore how multistakeholder initiatives should conceptualize training programs to promote decent work for women workers in global value chains.

Notes

1 In this chapter, the term gender belongs to socially and culturally constructed beliefs in relation to the behavior and conduct of females and males. In this way, the term makes a distinction between the roles of men and women based on social norms and values and their mutual relations, as opposed to sex, thus relating to biologically dogged characteristics of being men and women.

2 Within Punjab, interviews were conducted in the districts of Toba Tek Singh and Layyah, because these are known as cotton growing districts.

References

Ali, H., Aslam, M., & Ali, H. (2012). Economic analysis of input trend in cotton production process in Pakistan. *Asian Economic and Financial Review, 2*(4), 553.

Allen, P., & Sachs, C. (2012). Women and food chains: The gendered politics of food. *Taking Food Public: Redefining Foodways in a Changing World,* 23–40.

Ataullah, M. A., Sajid, A., & Khan, M. R. (2014). Quality related issues and their effects on returns of Pakistan textile industry. *Journal of Quality and Technology Management, 10*(1), 69–91.

Bain, C. (2010). Structuring the flexible and feminized labor market: Global GAP standards for agricultural labor in Chile. *Signs: Journal of Women in Culture and Society, 35*(2), 343–370.

Bair, J., & Palpacuer, F. (2015). CSR beyond the corporation: Contested governance in global value chains. *Global Networks, 15*(1), 1–19.

Bakhsh, K., Ahmad, N., Kamran, M. A., Hassan, S., Abbas, Q., Saeed, R., & Hashmi, M. S. (2016). Occupational hazards and health cost of women cotton pickers in Pakistani Punjab. *BMC Public Health*, *16*(1), 961.

Balagamwala, M., Gazdar, H., & Mallah, H. B. (2015). Synergies or trade-off between agricultural growth and nutrition: Women's work and care. *The Pakistan Development Review*, *54*(4), 897–913.

Barrientos, S. (2001). Gender, flexibility and global value chains. *IDS Bulletin*, *32*(3), 83–93.

Barrientos, S. (2013). Corporate purchasing practices in global production networks: A socially contested terrain. *Geoforum*, *44*, 44–51.

Barrientos, S. (2014a). Gender and global value chains: Challenges of economic and social upgrading in agri-food. *Browser Download This Paper*. file:///C:/Users/AU575382/Downloads/SSRN-id2503391.pdf (accessed on March 6, 2017).

Barrientos, S. (2014b). Gendered global production networks: analysis of cocoa – chocolate sourcing. *Regional Studies*, *48*(5), 791–803.

Barrientos, S., Dolan, C., & Tallontire, A. (2003). A gendered value chain approach to codes of conduct in African horticulture. *World Development*, *31*(9), 1511–1526.

Barrientos, S., Kritzinger, A., Opondo, M., & Smith, S. (2005). Gender, work and vulnerability in African horticulture. *IDS Bulletin*, *36*(2), 74–79.

Bartley, T., & Egels-Zandén, N. (2015). Responsibility and neglect in global production networks: The uneven significance of codes of conduct in Indonesian factories. *Global Networks*, *15*(1), 21–44.

BCI. (2013). *Better cotton production principles and criteria explained*. http://bettercotton.org/wp-content/uploads/2014/01/Better-Cotton-Production-Principles-and-Criteria-Explained_Final-2013_eng_ext.pdf (accessed on February 15, 2017).

BCI. (2016). http://bettercotton.org/ (accessed on February 22, 2017).

Beath, A., Christia, F., & Enikolopov, R. (2013). Empowering women through development aid: Evidence from a field experiment in Afghanistan. *American Political Science Review*, *107*(3), 540–557.

Blackden, C. M., & Wodon, Q. (Eds.). (2006). *Gender, time use, and poverty in sub-Saharan Africa. (73)*. New York: World Bank Publications.

Boström, M. (2006). Regulatory credibility and authority through inclusiveness: Standardization organizations in cases of eco-labelling. *Organization*, *13*(3), 345–367.

Carmona, M. S. (2013). *Unpaid work, poverty and women's human rights*. New York: United Nations.

Cheyns, E., & Riisgaard, L. (2014). Introduction to the symposium. *Agriculture and Human Values*, *31*(3), 409–423.

Coe, N. M., Dicken, P., & Hess, M. (2008a). Global production networks: Realizing the potential. *Journal of Economic Geography*, *8*(3), 271–295.

Coe, N. M., Dicken, P., & Hess, M. (2008b). Global production networks: Debates and challenges. *Journal of Economic Geography*, *8*(3), 267–269.

Corbin, J., & Strauss, A. (2008). *Basics of qualitative research: Techniques and procedures for developing grounded theory*. Thousand Oaks, CA: Sage Publication.

Cronin, C. (2014). Using case study research as a rigorous form of inquiry. *Nurse Researcher*, *21*(5), 19–27.

Detomasi, D. A. (2007). The multinational corporation and global governance: Modelling global public policy networks. *Journal of Business Ethics*, *71*(3), 321–334.

Dingwerth, K. (2008). Private transnational governance and the developing world: A comparative perspective. *International Studies Quarterly*, *52*(3), 607–634.

Dolan, C. S. (2004). On farm and packhouse: Employment at the bottom of a global value chain. *Rural Sociology, 69*(1), 99–126.

Dolan, C. S., & Humphrey, J. (2004). Changing governance patterns in the trade in fresh vegetables between Africa and the United Kingdom. *Environment and Planning A, 36*(3), 491–509.

Dolan, C. S., & Opondo, M. (2005). Seeking common ground: Multi-stakeholder processes in Kenya's cut flower industry. *The Journal of Corporate Citizenship*, (18), 87.

Dollar, D., & Gatti, R. (1999). *Gender inequality, income, and growth: Are good times good for women?* (Vol. 1). Washington, DC: Development Research Group, The World Bank.

Eisenhardt, K. M. (1989). Agency theory: An assessment and review. *Academy of Management Review, 14*(1), 57–74.

FAO. (2010a). *Roles of women in agriculture.* Prepared by the SOFA team and Cheryl Doss. Rome.

Fransen, L. (2012). Multi-stakeholder governance and voluntary programme interactions: Legitimation politics in the institutional design of corporate social responsibility. *Socio-Economic Review, 10*(1), 163–192.

Fransen, L., & Kolk, A. (2007). Global rule-setting for business: A critical analysis of multi-stakeholder standards. *Organization, 14*(5), 667–684.

Gereffi, G. (1994). The organization of buyer-driven global commodity chains: How US retailers shape overseas production networks. *Commodity Chains and Global Capitalism.* 149 ABC-CLIO. 95–122.

Gereffi, G., Humphrey, J., & Sturgeon, T. (2005). The governance of global value chains. *Review of International Political Economy, 12*(1), 78–104.

Gereffi, G., & Korzeniewicz, M. (1994). *Commodity chains and global capitalism* (No. 149). ABC-CLIO.

Gereffi, G., & Lee, J. (2016). Economic and social upgrading in global value chains and industrial clusters: Why governance matters. *Journal of Business Ethics, 133*(1), 25–38.

Grosser, K., McCarthy, L., & Kilgour, M. A. (Eds.). (2016). *Gender Equality and Responsible Business: Expanding CSR Horizons.* Greenleaf Publishing.

Hassan, A. & Lund-Thomsen, P. (2016). Collaborative Governance and Corporate Social Responsibility (CSR) in Global Value Chains (GVCs): Towards an Analytical Framework and a Methodology. In Jamali, Dima. (Ed.), *Comparative Perspectives on Global Corporate Social Responsibility.* IGI Global.

Henderson, J., Dicken, P., Hess, M., Coe, N., & Yeung, H. W. C. (2002). Global production networks and the analysis of economic development. *Review of international political economy, 9*(3), 436–464.

Hess, M. (2008). Governance, value chains and networks: an afterword. *Economy and Society, 37*(3), 452–459.

International Cotton Advisory Committee. (2008). *Literature review and research evaluation relating to social impacts of global cotton production for ICAC expert panel on social, environmental and economic performance of cotton (SEEP).* Prepared by Ergon.

International Labour Organization. (2008). *Global wage report 2008–09: Minimum wages and collective bargaining, towards policy coherence.*

International Labour Organization. (2011). *Special focus discussion women's social and economic empowerment and gender equality.* 12th African Regional Meeting Johannesburg, South Africa, 11–14 October 2011. Available at: www.ilo.org/wcmsp5/groups/public/-ed_norm/-relconf/documents/meetingdocument/wcms_164291.pdf [Accessed on 23 May 2018].

Islam, M. S. (2008). From sea to shrimp processing factories in Bangladesh gender and employment at the bottom of a global commodity chain. *Journal of South Asian Development, 3*(2), 211–236.

Jasper, M. A. (1994). Issues in phenomenology for researchers of nursing. *Journal of Advanced Nursing, 19*(2), 309–314.

Kabeer, N. (2001). Conflicts over credit: Re-evaluating the empowerment potential of loans to women in rural Bangladesh. *World Development, 29*(1), 63–84.

Kasente, D. (2012). Fair trade and organic certification in value chains: Lessons from a gender analysis from coffee exporting in Uganda. *Gender & Development, 20*(1), 111–127.

Kasi, E. (2013). Role of women in sericulture and community development: A study from a South Indian village. *Sage Open, 3*(3), 2158244013502984.

Kouser, S., & Qaim, M. (2017). Bt cotton and employment effects for female agricultural laborers in Pakistan. *New Biotechnology, 34*, 40–46.

Kvale, S. (1996). *Interviews: An introduction to qualitative research interviewing.* Thousand Oaks, CA: Sage.

Kvale, S., & Brinkmann, S. (2009). *Interviews: Learning the craft of qualitative research interviewing.* Thousand Oaks, CA: Sage.

Labour Force Survey (2012–13). www.pbs.gov.pk/content/labour-force-survey-2012-13-annual-report [Accessed on 15 February 2017].

Lauwo, S. (2016). Challenging masculinity in CSR disclosures: Silencing of women's voices in Tanzania's mining industry. *Journal of Business Ethics*, 1–18.

Loconto, A. (2015). Can certified-tea value chains deliver gender equality in Tanzania? *Feminist Economics, 21*(3), 191–215.

Lund-Thomsen, P., & Lindgreen, A. (2014). Corporate social responsibility in global value chains: Where are we now and where are we going? *Journal of Business Ethics, 123*(1), 11–22.

Lund-Thomsen, P., & Nadvi, K. (2010). Clusters, chains and compliance: Corporate social responsibility and governance in football manufacturing in South Asia. *Journal of Business Ethics, 93*, 201–222.

Mena, S., & Palazzo, G. (2012). Input and output legitimacy of multi-stakeholder initiatives. *Business Ethics Quarterly, 22*(3), 527–556.

Mezzadri, A. (2014). Indian garment clusters and CSR norms: Incompatible agendas at the bottom of the garment commodity chain. *Oxford Development Studies, 42*(2), 238–258.

Neilson, J., & Pritchard, B. (2010). Fairness and ethicality in their place: The regional dynamics of fair trade and ethical sourcing agendas in the plantation districts of South India. *Environment and Planning A, 42*(8), 1833–1851.

Pearson, R. (2007). Beyond women workers: Gendering CSR. *Third World Quarterly, 28*(4), 731–749.

Peterson, V. S. (2006). How (the meaning of) gender matters in political economy. In *Key debates in new political economy* (pp. 87–113). London: Routledge.

Reuters. (2015). *Pakistan's women cotton pickers find power in uniting over wages.* www.reuters.com/article/us-pakistan-cotton-widerimage-idUSKCN0JJ1KX20141206 [Accessed on 28 February 2017].

Riisgaard, L., Fibla, A. M., & Ponte, S. (2010). *Evaluation study: Gender and value chain development.* Copenhagen: The Evaluation Department of the Danish Foreign Ministry.

Said-Allsopp, M., & Tallontire, A. (2015). Pathways to empowerment? Dynamics of women's participation in global value chains. *Journal of Cleaner Production, 107*, 114–121.

Saunders, M., Lewis, P., & Thornhill, A. (2009). *Research methods for business students* (5th edition). Harlow. Prentice Hall.

Seguino, S. (2010). The global economic crisis, its gender and ethnic implications, and policy responses. *Gender & Development, 18*(2), 179–199.

Smith, S., & Dolan, C. (2006). Ethical trade: What does it mean for women workers in African horticulture? In *Ethical Sourcing in the Global Food System*, 79–96. New York: Routledge.

Stake, R. E. (2010). *Qualitative research: Studying how things work*. Guilford Press.

Sturgeon, T. J. (2008). From commodity chains to value chains: Interdisciplinary theory building in an age of globalization. In *Frontiers of commodity chain research*. Stanford University Press.

Tallontire, A. (2007). CSR and regulation: Towards a framework for understanding private standards initiatives in the agri-food chain. *Third World Quarterly, 28*(4), 775–791.

United States Development of Agriculture (USDA). 2016. *Commodity intelligence report*. https://pecad.fas.usda.gov/highlights/2016/10/Pakistan/index.htm [Accessed on 28 February 2017].

Utting, P. (2002). Regulating business via multistakeholder initiatives: A preliminary assessment. In R. Jenkins, P. Utting, & R. A. Pino (Eds.), *Voluntary approaches to corporate responsibility: Readings and a resource -guide* (pp. 61–130). Geneva: United Nations Research Institute for Social Development (UNRISD).

Utting, P. (2015). Corporate accountability, fair trade, and multi-stakeholder regulation. In L. Raynolds & E. A. Bennett (Eds.), *Handbook of research on fair trade*. Cheltenham, UK: Edwar Elgar.

Utting, P., & Zammit, A. (2009). United nations business partnerships: Good intentions and contradictory agendas. *Journal of Business Ethics, 90*(1), 39–56.

Walby, S. (2011). Is the knowledge society gendered? *Gender, Work & Organization, 18*(1), 1–29.

Wyrod, R. (2008). Between women's rights and men's authority: Masculinity and shifting discourses of gender difference in urban Uganda. *Gender & Society, 22*(6), 799–823.

Women Working Worldwide. (2007). *Promoting women workers' rights in African horticulture: Overview of research into conditions on horticulture farms in Kenya, Zambia, Tanzania and Uganda*. Manchester: WWW.

World Bank. (2011). *World development report 2012: Gender equality and development*. Washington: World Bank.

Yeung, H. W. C., & Coe, N. M. (2015). Toward a dynamic theory of global production networks. *Economic Geography, 91*(1), 29–58.

Yin, R. K. (2011). *Qualitative research from start to finish*. New York: Guilford.

Yin, R. K. (2013). *Case study research: Design and methods*. Thousand Oaks, CA: Sage.

Part IV

International business, corporate social responsibility, and development

10 CSR in developing countries

Competing perspectives on businesses, their roles, and responsibilities

Sameer Azizi and Søren Jeppesen

Introduction

In this chapter, we shed light on corporate social responsibility (CSR) as a phenomenon that enables large firms in the developing world to take responsibility by engaging in development. We focus on businesses that can be categorized as large domestic firms or multinational corporations (MNCs) that are driven by for-profit motives and owned by private shareholders. Hence, we do not include small or micro-enterprises (Jamali, Lund-Thomsen, and Jeppesen 2017; Spence et al. 2018; Tran and Jeppesen 2016, 2018) or other ownership models of business (e.g., social enterprises, state-owned enterprises (Sánchez, Bolívar, and Hernández 2017), as these types of businesses have developed their own particular field in relation to the business development debates.

The roles and responsibilities of business in society are a result of ongoing debates in a given society (or national context) as well as globally – and as such are open to many, often contradictory, views. Hence, these roles and responsibilities are also often contested. Over the last number of years the perception of business and of the roles and responsibilities has evolved from a narrower understanding to a broader one. Historically, the emphasis has tended to be on the economic and legal responsibilities of and in(side) the firm (the narrow understanding), and any other practices have been viewed as doing more than necessary – something "extra" and philanthropic – by firms. Today, increasingly, the perception is that social and environmental issues outside of the firm also are part of what business should be responsible for, hence suggesting "the broader understandings." Some proponents argue that such practices have a strategic value to firms, and others emphasize the societal responsibility that business should take on in order to have a license to operate. The debates on how to understand such aspects of business have to a large extent been coined as CSR, though concepts like corporate citizenship, sustainability, and corporate philanthropy also have surfaced.

The contested nature of the concept can be illustrated by some of the numerous perspectives and definitions of the role and responsibilities of business that have been formulated. Carroll's distinction between the legal, economic, and philanthropic (Carroll 1979) is one influential perception of CSR in the academic literature. For practitioners, definitions by the World Business Council

for Sustainable Development and the European Commission have been important, as both institutions highlight the voluntary nature – though "going beyond
compliance" – of CSR (The European Commission 2018; WBCSD 2000).
A third influential perception of CSR for both academics and practitioners has
been the idea that CSR provides "shared value" and "win–win" situations for
business and society (see e.g. Porter and Kramer 2011). Finally, attempts to provide a kind of "umbrella term" definition of CSR have materialised, like Blowfield and Frynas, who have addressed the wider responsibilities not only relating
to what are taking place in the firms but also what is occurring in the relationship with other firms (suppliers, BTB customers) and for society at large,

> as companies having a responsibility: (a) for their impact on society and the
> natural environment, sometimes beyond legal compliance and the liability
> of individuals; (b) for the behaviour of others with whom they do business
> (e.g. within the supply chains); (c) to manage their relationship with the
> wider society, whether for reasons of commercial viability or to add value
> to society.
>
> (Blowfield and Frynas 2005, p. 503)

Displayed by a huge body of literature, the debates on CSR at first mainly
discussed the concept based on conditions in the Global North. Then growing
attention was drawn to CSR in the Global South or developing countries (as
the term that we will use in this chapter). Factoring CSR into the equation, the
"business in development field," which, among others, had a strong emphasis on
the role of MNCs, environmental management, and governance in developing
countries, led to intriguing analyses.

The growing attention directed to CSR in developing countries was critically instigated and marked by Blowfield and Frynas (2005).[1] With many
contributions delivered, including special issues (see e.g. Jeppesen and Lund-
Thomsen 2010), review articles (see e.g. Jamali and Karam 2016), and books
(see e.g. Banerjee 2008a; Jamali, Karam, and Blowfield 2015a; b), the academic
debate on business, CSR practices, and development (hereafter termed CSR-
development) is now showing emerging signs of maturity. In spite of the growth
in the number of contributions and the maturity displayed by different and
competing perspectives on CSR, we argue that though various perspectives
on the CSR-development relationship have been developed, these perspectives
have yet to be well explained and compared.

Given that some of the main puzzles in the CSR-development debates still
remain unsolved, debates still continue on whether (1) CSR is an "addition"
to the core effects of business or a part of business strategy and, either way,
(2) how can we assess the contribution of CSR to development. We argue that
there is not a simple understanding of the CSR-development relations, but
it is a matter of which theoretical, disciplinary perspective one puts on CSR,
development, and their interrelations. We seek to address the gap and contribute to the growing literature on CSR in developing countries by providing an

overview of three distinct perspectives (the business perspective, the development perspective, and the critical political economy perspective) based on the theoretical assumptions (views, focus, and the claims) put forward about CSR-development relations in each perspective. The overviews will be supported by empirical examples – if possible – of typical CSR practices undertaken and/or potential alternative views on CSR. Our aspiration is that clarifying the contribution of each perspective will give the reader a better understanding of the complexity of the debate on CSR-development relations.

The rest of the chapter is structured as follows. We continue with an introduction of three perspectives on CSR-development relations from the literature on business and CSR in developing countries. We then outline three dimensions of each perspective: (1) the theoretical foundation (business studies, development studies, political-economy studies); (2) views on CSR-development relations (inside-out, outside-in, and a question of structural contradiction), focus of study, and claims; and (3) the methodological focus, while we seek to illustrate the arguments through examples that support the CSR-development relations. In the discussion section, we then assess the similarities and differences between the perspectives relating to how each perspective views CSR, the focus of the studies, and claims about business–society relations within each perspective. We end with a discussion on the contribution to the field of business, CSR, and development, and we finally reflect on the future research needs in the field.

A categorization of perspectives on business, CSR, and development

The business, CSR, and development debates reflect different perspectives of the role and responsibilities of business to society. The first perspective we identified is what we refer to as "the business perspective" on how to understand the role and responsibilities of business in the developing world. Garriga and Melé (2004) and Azizi (2017a, p. 26) have labeled this literature as the "instrumental" or "mainstream" view on CSR. However, we extend the terminology to "the business perspective," as a key feature of the vast literature is the use of management and firm-level theories to conceptualize the role and responsibility of business in society. The key claim about the CSR-development relation in the business perspective is that CSR practices are "doing good while doing well" and that firms can explore and experience "win-win" situations beyond the firm extending to and benefitting workers, consumers, communities, and even developing country societies at large (Carroll and Shabana 2010; McWilliams and Siegel 2001, 2011; McWilliams, Siegel, and Wright 2006; Rahbek Gjerdrum Pedersen 2006).

The other two perspectives that we have identified are both critical to the business perspective, but with different theoretical lenses on the CSR-development relations. The second perspective is "the development perspective," which takes the point of departure in development studies and related social science disciplines (e.g., geography, area studies) to criticize the claims about win-win situations where businesses, per definition, are doing good for society. Instead, this perspective underlines the importance of context matters and local needs of a social and environmental nature when debating CSR–development relations (Jamali, Karam, and Blowfield 2015a, pp. 1–3). The third perspective takes the critical stance even further and questions and rejects that business can move beyond its own economic interests and contribute to (social and environmental) development also through CSR. By taking a point of departure in the critical political economy literature, this perspective argues that large, for-profit businesses are embedded in firm-level and macro-level structures, that are, the present neo-liberal regime and its economic and political rationales, preventing a meaningful contribution by business to social and environmental change in developing countries.

The business perspective on CSR–development

Businesses have for centuries engaged in societal issues through what is termed philanthropy, but the contemporary CSR literature has historically been developed in Anglo-Saxon contexts since the 1950s with Bowen's seminal work that initiated a debate about the responsibility of "the businessman" (Carroll 1999, 2008). The debate has its roots in the conditions of the capitalist society in Anglo-Saxon societies and particularly in the US context (Banerjee 2008a). Later, Friedman famously stated that

> there is one and only one social responsibility of business – to use its resources and engage in activities designed to increase its profits so long as it stays within the rules of the game, which is to say, engages in open and free competition without deception or fraud.
>
> (Friedman 1970, p. 6)

We argue that since the 1970s the business perspective on CSR has not developed contrary to Friedman's view, but is rather deeply rooted in Friedman's view on the social responsibility of business, as the interest of shareholders are taking precedence over any other stakeholder's interests. The theoretical foundation for the business perspective takes the theory of the firm as the point of departure to theorize the responsibility of business towards society and assessing the impact and contribution to society – irrespective of the contextual differences between Anglo-Saxon countries and developing countries. Like Friedman, we argue that given the corporate structures, responsible managers operate as agents with the sole social responsibility to maximize shareholder value in the corporate context of scarce resources, but not to promote social causes without any connection to profit maximization. The societal engagement of corporations seen through the business perspective is thereby aligned with Friedman's view, as any corporate engagement in society is for the long-term interest of the business, for example, to attract employees, reduce wage costs, enable tax reductions, and/or create goodwill for the corporation (Friedman 1970, p. 5). The business perspective has in other words mainly focused on the "business case" of

CSR as the dominant driver of CSR practices, and whether this business case is framed as "strategic" CSR or as enlightened self-interest is less important as long as the practices have profit-maximizing purposes.

The past decades of the business perspective on CSR have therefore primarily discussed whether, how, and when businesses can capitalize on CSR as an instrument for achieving economic benefits (Carroll and Shabana 2010). This has led debates in a large range of areas and business functions (whether HR, management, logistics, production, services, finance, and sales and marketing) of the potentials of CSR (Djursø and Neergaard 2006; Rahbek Gjerdrum Pedersen 2015). As an illustration, marketing has integrated terms like "green," "sustainable," "doing good," and more (Kotler and Lee 2005; Lantos 2001). Various other studies have measured the impact of CSR on corporate financial performance (Adewale and Rahmon 2014; Griffin and Mahon 1997; Orlitzky, Schmidt, and Rynes 2003) but remain inconclusive about the CSR-financial performance relations both in Anglo-Saxon contexts (Margolis and Walsh 2003; Perrini et al. 2011; Salzmann, Ionescu-somers, and Steger 2005; Vogel 2006) and in developing countries (Amini and Dal Bianco 2015; Aras, Kutlu, and Aybars 2010).

Another stream of interest has been on the strategic integration of CSR that was addressed in the initial stages of formalizing CSR as a management practice (Ansoff 1979) and continues to be debated in relation to the developing countries (Jamali, Karam, and Blowfield 2015a). The strategic CSR debate has focused on how to create a fit between corporate strategy and CSR (Burke and Logsdon 1996), and has led to various strategic arguments for the importance of CSR (Kurucz, Colbert, and Wheeler 2008) in terms of (1) cost and risk reduction, that is, utilizing CSR to mitigate potential threats from stakeholders in order to reduce costs and risks, for example, efficiency gains based on organizational improvements (Locke and Romis 2007); (2) competitive advantage, that is, utilizing CSR to adapt to and gain from opportunities in the external environment in order to improve competitive strategic positioning in the market (Roberts 2003); (3) reputation and legitimacy, that is, alignment with external expectations, utilizing CSR in accordance with the view that gaining legitimacy to operate and improving corporate reputation constitutes competitive advantage (Paine 2003); and (4) the creation of synergistic value, an approach that synthesizes diverse stakeholder interests and views to create synergy for both the corporation and stakeholders (Porter and Kramer 2011).

A key example of how firm theories build the foundations for the business literature on CSR is seen with the "shared value" and "win-win" arguments led by the engagement of management scholars (Porter and Kramer 2011; Salzmann, Ionescu-somers, and Steger 2005) into the CSR debates on developing countries (Jain and Jamali 2015; Jamali 2007; Kemp, Parto, and Gibson 2005; Pope, Annandale, and Morrison-Saunders 2004). Although the "shared value proposition" particularly gained popularity among businesses and practitioners (see e.g. McFalls 2007 on HP in South Africa), other CSR scholars criticized the originality and simplified the understanding of the role of business in society as assumed by the "shared value" argument (Crane et al. 2014).

In terms of methodology, the CSR debates on developing countries are mainly based on qualitative studies (Jamali and Karam 2016) in contrast to the quantitative studies traditionally seen in CSR studies on the Anglo-Saxon contexts (Aguinis and Glavas 2012). The latter analyses CSR in relation to financial and social performance (Amini and Dal Bianco 2015; van Beurden and Gössling 2008; Orlitzky et al. 2017; Perrini et al. 2011), but a growing trend is the usage of mixed methods (Jamali and Karam 2016). On that background, it is not surprising that we see more studies of firm-level conditions and to some extent on industry issues, while fewer seek to address macro-level and societal dimensions of the field (Jamali and Karam 2016; Jamali, Karam, and Blowfield 2015a, 2015b, pp. 3–4). The business perspective is the dominant view both in terms of the size of the literature and the influence on how to define and understand CSR in relation to development. The following two perspectives have emerged as a critique of the business perspective, but with two different points of critique.

The development perspective on CSR-development

The second perspective originated as a critique to the assumptions and claims by the business perspective when applied to the developing countries. Parallel to the spread of the CSR phenomenon across developing countries, and drawing on debates on MNCs and globalization, as well as on environmental management in developing countries, early contributions like Fox (2004) and the special issue of *International Affairs* (2005, vol. 81, issue 3) started questioning the key assumptions embedded in the business literature about the application and impact of CSR. The most recent and first systematic review of CSR in developing countries still points out that, in comparison to the business perspective on CSR, the characteristics, contextual dynamics, and implications of CSR in developing countries differ significantly and calls for further studies on these dimensions (Jamali and Karam 2016). Although the business perspective on CSR has triggered various critical responses from development scholars, we argue that the development perspective addresses two general points of critique against the business perspective.

First, the development perspective criticizes the theoretical underpinnings of the business perspective for being predominantly derived from (1) concepts and frameworks developed for Western contexts (Egri and Ralston 2008) and often (2) built on knowledge from large firms (in most cases MNCs headquartered in the Global North) (Blowfield and Frynas 2005). Several studies have highlighted the fact that business–society relations in developing countries are different from Anglo-Saxon contexts due to their economic, political, and social contexts (Jamali and Karam 2016). Utilizing the insights from development and area studies, a call for "South-centered" studies on CSR is promoted and emphasizes more a contextualized understanding of the nature, drivers, and societal implications of CSR in developing countries (Blowfield and Dolan 2008; Blowfield and Frynas 2005;

Dobers and Halme 2009; Idemudia 2008, 2011; Jamali, Lund-Thomsen, and Jeppesen 2017, Jamali and Sidani 2012; Jeppesen and Lund-Thomsen 2010; Prieto-Carrón et al. 2006).

In the same vein, other authors have argued the need for gaining an in-depth understanding of governance actors, structures, and incentives by focusing the analyses at the national, industry, and firm levels (Frynas 2008; Haufler 2010; Idemudia 2011; Jamali 2010, 2014; Jamali and Neville 2011). Lately, scholars have also capitalized on institutional theory for context-specific studies on national and regional contexts, such as studies of CSR in the Asian context (Chapple and Moon 2005, 2007), the Middle Eastern context (Jamali and Mirshak 2010; Jamali and Sidani 2008, 2012), and the African context (Amaeshi, Adegbite, and Rajwani 2016; Börzel and Hamann 2013; Hamann 2004; Muthuri, Moon, and Idemudia 2012). However, not all national and macro settings of the "developing world" are covered in the debate that has primarily focused on emerging markets and BRICS countries (Brazil, Russia, India, China, and South Africa).

Other context-based studies of CSR have also paid attention to the sector- and industry-specific conditions for CSR (Acutt, Medina-Ross, and O'Riordan 2004; Jeppesen and Lund-Thomsen 2010; Prieto-Carrón et al. 2006) and, not least, firm attributes such as size and ownership (Jamali, Zanhour, and Keshishian 2009; Jeppesen, Kothuis, and Tran 2012; Luetkenhorst 2004; Vives 2006). The focus has predominantly been on MNCs in global industries such as textiles, garments, automotive, electronics, and toys, as well as mining and extraction (Frynas 2001, 2005; Idemudia 2011), and in global manufacturing or production chains (Lund-Thomsen and Lindgreen 2014; Lund-Thomsen and Nadvi 2010a, 2010b). The less studied industries include the ones that are domestically oriented (often food processing, [local] beverages, construction, and services like tailors, hair dressers, traders, and transport), undertaken by developing country firms engaged in formal and informal sectors.

Second and as consequence of the first point, studies have highlighted that due to the heterogeneity of "developing countries," the simplified claims made in the business perspective about win-win situations and shared value are not realized. The development perspective calls for more focus on the "development case" of CSR and criticizes the business perspective for not dealing with issues and challenges pertinent in developing country contexts when corporate interests are aligned with societal interests through CSR (Nijhof and Jeurissen 2010). Taking natural resources (mining and extraction) as an example, Kemp, Owen, and Dejvongsa point out that "the community development contribution" needs to be clearly laid out when assessing the developmental role of a mining company (2015, pp. 49–50). Relating to the same industry, Littlewood and Russon argue that the developmental contributions are to be found within five areas (assets/infrastructure, people, community development, macroeconomic, and environmental practices (2015, pp. 119–22). In contrast, Yap proposes that such contributions should relate to three key areas (accountable and democratic governance, prudent resource and environmental management, and community resilience) (2015, pp. 138–9). Still with reference to the large-scale projects, now energy, Ramirez (2015) proposes that bringing in local needs through consultation with the local community affected is crucial. Clearly, the emphasis from these contributions is on the outside-in dimension, expressed by the local community needs to be addressed by the company if they are to contribute to development. A similar stance is found among contributions that focus more on conditions inside the company premises (e.g., in various manufacturing industries). A basic issue is the compliance with legislation (whether on waste handling, working environment, or labor conditions), but the development contribution is brought forward when the level of wages, working hours, social benefits are assessed (Huber and Gilbert 2015; Husain and Lund-Thomsen 2015). A key dimension is whether a minimum wage is sufficient or if MNCs should aim to pay a "decent" or living wage (see e.g. Chan 2003; Ngoc Tran 2007).

A recent literature review reveals the qualitative nature of CSR debates in developing countries, as single case studies on MNCs are dominant (Bolzani and Marabello 2015; Littlewood and Russon 2015; Mallin 2009; Ramirez 2015), and only a few multiple case studies are employed (Rahbek Gjerdrum Pedersen and Andersen 2006; Yap 2015). The development perspective contributes with two types of studies. One group of contributions is mostly conceptual, as they seek to present frameworks that can be applied for the study of the business' responsibilities in development (Blowfield 2012; Blowfield and Dolan 2014; Halme and Laurila 2009; McKague, Wheeler, and Karnani 2015). Some of these studies also bring in empirical data (qualitative, documentary, and archival), mainly of a single case study type. The other group of contributions is predominantly based on qualitative methods, which apart from including management also are involving (and in some cases only) workers/employees, community members, and other "nonmanagement" sources in the "case type types" of studies of individual firms as well as industries (Bolzani and Marabello 2015; Littlewood and Russon 2015; Ramirez 2015), whereas Yap (2015), for example, employs a multiple case study. Mixed-methods are increasingly being used (see e.g. Husain and Lund-Thomsen 2015; Uyan-Atay and Tuncay-Celikel 2015) to contribute with in-depth understanding of the developmental case of CSR and have built the foundation for the critique of the business perspective. However, the emphasis on the application of (single) case studies at industries and/or the firm level also leaves a gap, as the perspective lacks studies that are based on comparative methodological elements in order to address CSR-development issues at the national, industry, and/or firm levels. Finally, the contributions apply different perceptions of development, which results in a fragmented picture of how businesses can affect development through CSR.

The critical political economy perspective on CSR-development

Finally, we identify a third perspective addressing CSR-development relations that we frame as the "critical political economy" perspective. This strand has also emerged as a critique of the business literature on CSR, but with a critical political economy foundation. Instead of stressing the contextual differences for CSR-development relations, this perspective underlines that CSR debates are "missing the forest for the trees" (Jones 1996), because the ideological and political economic issues of CSR remain untouched with a particular reference to the business perspective (Hanlon and Fleming 2009; Jones 2009, 1998). It has a particular empirical focus on CSR by MNCs not only in developing countries but also as part of debating the role of MNCs in globalization. The theoretical lenses of political-economy are employed in various ways to criticize the assumptions and claims of the business perspective in terms of ideology, power relations, and the for-profit capitalist logic of CSR by MNCs in the era of globalization.

As an example, the ideological critique views CSR by MNCs as a neo-liberal tool used by MNCs and neo-liberal regimes (Shamir 2008), enabling privatization and marketization of public goods in both developed and developing countries (Harvey 2007). Other studies shed light on how the voluntary nature of CSR has emerged (Vallentin and Murillo 2012) and how CSR as voluntary private regulation in opposition to a mandatory regulation alternative serves the interests of MNCs (Banerjee 2008b, 2010). The win–win claims from the business perspective are criticized for neglecting the discursive and material power relations constructed by the undemocratic global governance structures of the various political supranational organizations (e.g., World Bank) and MNCs as private agents of the capitalist regime (Banerjee 2010, 2014). As a result, the voices of particular groups of people in developing countries become and remain marginalized in terms of calling for corporate accountability (Banerjee 2008a, 2008b; Newell 2005; Newell and Frynas 2007).

Finally, a spotlight is also put on the firm-level analysis of MNCs as an undemocratic and authoritarian organization with the sole purpose of profit maximization through any means possible. CSR in such businesses are embroiled in structural tensions and contradictions with-in corporations, with the primary goal of maximizing profit claims to promote societal and/or environmental development. From this position, corporations have used CSR as a smokescreen for the damage they cause to society and/or in order to legitimize private self-regulation so as to enable profit maximization throughout the world (Banerjee 2014). Instead, the debate about CSR is pointless unless the "parasitical" (Fleming and Jones 2013), "predatory" (Hanlon and Fleming 2009), and "necrocapitalist" (Banerjee 2008c) structures that enable corporations throughout the world to create and sustain social and economic inequality through CSR and core business activities are problematized.

Among the contributions to the critical political economy perspective, the critique of existing studies is often conducted from a theoretical and partly normative position. However, some studies have used qualitative methods to back up the contrasting findings highlighted in this debate. As an example, Banerjee studies native populations in Australia, Chile, Canada, etc., facing large corporations over controversies of land rights and access to land for business interests (Banerjee 2008a). Maher conducts a critical case study of the corporate–community relations in the mining industry in Chile (Maher 2018). In other cases, anecdotal (historical, documentary) data are used to support the argument that contradictions and paradoxes occur when businesses engage in development through CSR as, for example, Fleming and Jones 2013.

Given the focus on various underlying structural tensions and contradictions in which CSR by MNCs is embedded in, this perspective views "development" as a broader interrelated concept of the economic, social, and environmental issues. The CSR-development relations are thereby neither an inside-out or outside-in relation, but the focus is more on the contradictions and impossibilities of equally aligning business and society interests.

Table 10.1 illustrates the three perspectives and summarizes the arguments put forward on their respective views and focus on CSR and the CSR-development relations, which we discuss and relate to each other in the discussion section after the table. The presentation earlier shows that each of the three perspectives has different assumptions and claims about the CSR-development relations, though some commonalities and overlaps between some of the perspectives are also observed.

Discussion

We now address the issues of how each perspective views CSR, the focus of the studies, and claims about business–society relations within each perspective as summarized in Table 10.1 as a means to discuss the similarities and differences between the three perspectives. We also highlight our assumption regarding the theory-related nature of the perspectives and how this influences the understanding of the CSR-development relations.

Assessing the literature, it is clear that the majority of the contributions are related to the business perspective and how business can contribute to development through CSR. The business perspective has been utilizing business theories (e.g., strategy, business case, financial performance, value chain, etc.) to identify and conceptualize the roles and responsibilities for business in society from an inside-out process. The contributions present the improved conditions based on company activities and argue that win–win situations have taken place (and can be replicated). Traditionally, the business perspective has only perceived and viewed "development" through an economic lens on wealth creation (jobs, income, innovation, and more) that will happen "automatically" and hence that CSR activities will have a positive impact on workers and communities. This resembles a kind of "trickle-down" to the poor through core business activities. However, the increasing focus on CSR and relating CSR to a core business strategy has opened a window for businesses to claim an active role in solving or improving the economic livelihood of the poor (Blowfield and Dolan 2014; Halme et al. 2016; Halme, Lindeman, and Linna 2012; London and Hart 2010).

As opposed to the business perspective, the development perspective can offer an outside-in approach that stresses utilizing insights from development

Table 10.1 Overview of the three perspectives on CSR: development and view, focus, and claims

	View on CSR	Main focus of study	Claims about CSR–development relations	Examples of CSR impact on development
Business perspective	• CSR is voluntary and strategic corporate engagement in society to maximize profit within the rules of the game.	• How to show the contributions of business and CSR to development. • How to define and measure the impact of CSR on the strategic and financial performance of corporations. • Potential societal benefits.	• CSR enables business to "do good while doing well." • Enlightened self-interest creates win–win situations for business and society. • Generalizations based on "success stories"	• Improves working environment • Reduces pollution • Increases innovation • Ensure better products and services
Development perspective	CSR consists of both a business and a development case.	• How to redirect business from "doing harm" to "doing good" for social and environmental purposes in developing countries. • How to ensure that business addresses key development issues (local, community needs)	• CSR has potentials to enable social and environmental development and reduce the social and environmental harm caused by business. • Contextualization is key to enable the realization of the potentials of CSR "success stories," in developing countries	• If a company functions as a "development agent," the impact will be possible • If workers' needs are met and e.g. wages increased to a living wage, impact is possible • If community needs are met, impact is possible
Critical political economy perspective	• CSR is a neo-liberal smokescreen to deflect criticism and prevent regulatory pressures on corporations.	• How to problematize CSR from a political, economic, and ideological critique.	• CSR is embedded in the structural limitations of neo-liberal ideology and political economy and is thus a dead end. • Radical alternatives are needed to achieve sustainable development and democratic governance of business–society relations. • Failures of CSR–development are not reported	• Loss of land rights • Lack of fulfilment of "promises" • Private regulation by MNCs does not work

Source: The Authors, adapted from Azizi 2017a, p. 30

246 Sameer Azizi and Søren Jeppesen

and area studies to overcome the limitations of the managerial application of CSR and managing CSR-development relations. Furthermore, it problematizes dimensions of normativity embedded in the business perspective when theorizing about context and win-win claims of CSR based on Western-biased assumptions about business–society relations. The critique provided by the development perspective informs us, on one hand, that the business perspective simplifies the complexity of development and emphasizes, on the other hand, the lack of contextual understanding (e.g., national/industry/sector specificities). Therefore, the business perspective claims about CSR in relation to development lead to insufficient and unrealistic viewpoints on the possible (positive) outcomes of CSR. The development perspective criticizes the business perspective for making CSR a managerial tool for "solving" developmental issues through corporate logics without understanding the complexity of such societal developmental challenges (Blowfield and Frynas 2005; Fox 2004; Jenkins 2005; Newell and Frynas 2007; Reed and Reed 2009). Hence, a necessary distinction between the business case outcome of CSR (i.e., what a corporation gains from CSR) and the development case outcome of CSR (i.e., what beneficiaries [might] gain from CSR) is not made in the business perspective (Blowfield 2005). Moreover, some authors have argued that in reality the former (the business case) defines and reinvents the latter (the development case) (Blowfield 2005, 2007; Idemudia 2008; Newell 2008; Newell and Frynas 2007).

However, the development perspective still acknowledges that the private sector, and particularly MNCs, has enormous resources with which to enable social development in developing and least-developed countries (Frynas 2008, p. 275). The "development perspective" identifies barriers and opportunities for CSR-development relations by underlining the importance of contexts for both the business and the development case of CSR. The optimistic view is that a (possible) development contribution through CSR exists, if companies manage to integrate local needs and contextual opportunities in developing countries to improve CSR-development relations (Jamali 2014, 2015; Visser 2010). The more "skeptical" position argues that CSR "works sometimes, in some places for some certain issues, and for some groups of people" (Newell 2005, p. 556). This position underlines the lack of evidence for the contribution of CSR to development (Frynas 2005; Newell and Frynas 2007; Prieto-Carrón et al. 2006; Sagebien and Whellams 2010) and argues therefore that raising the bar for how to assess development beyond the business case is needed (Blowfield 2012; Blowfield and Dolan 2014; Utting and Marques 2010; Utting, Reed, and Mukherjee-Reed 2012).

In contrast to the critical views on CSR-development stands the critical political economy perspective, which we view as a new perspective that has not been categorized as a distinct perspective in the reviews on CSR-development relations (Blowfield and Frynas 2005; Jamali and Karam 2016; Newell and Frynas 2007; Prieto-Carrón et al. 2006). Although we acknowledge the contributions from the development perspective to underline the complexities of poverty and the contextual settings, the critical political economy perspective is distinct due to the emphasis on the structural contradictions between the business and development case of CSR. As seen earlier, the latter put an emphasis on the for-profit structure, logic, and motivation of large businesses. All three perspectives share commonalities in acknowledging that profit matters for business; however, the critical political economy perspective stresses that any firm engagement in economic development will only occur under the beneficial conditions for profit. In other words, the critical political economy perspective underlines that profit logic as the *raison d'être* of business will inevitable prioritize the business case over the development case. Debating CSR is therefore not only a matter of improving management practices or stakeholder relations (Fleming and Jones 2013) put forward by the business and to some degree the development perspective. Instead, a structural change of business is needed, and unless the ownership structure and international regulations are not questioned, there is no reason to "hope" for business to change to a balanced prioritization of the business and development case of CSR. In other words, the critical political economy perspective highlights that, ultimately, the business perspective on CSR has never served a societal interest, as "CSR research appears paralysed, unable to offer solutions" (Fleming and Jones 2013, p. 96) to the devastating global social and environmental outcomes produced by capitalist structures. Instead, the contributors to the third perspective argue that other types of regulation and alternative economic and political regimes are needed to ensure that the responsibility and role of business benefit societies.

CSR and development relations – and the theoretical/ disciplinary nature/foundation

These different perspectives are important to have in mind when debating business-development relations through CSR. Returning to the one of key question on how to assess the effects of (core) business activity on development vis-à-vis the effects of CSR activities on development, the perspectives provide different answers. We argue that the distinction between the business and development case of CSR and the weight/priority given to the business vis-à-vis the development case is the core differentiator of three perspectives.

From a business perspective CSR can be "an add-on tool" that contributes to development as a wealth-creating tool (Spence et al. 2018, p. 1) that provides jobs and income and stimulates entrepreneurship and innovation. In addition, the move towards integrating CSR into core business activities and strategy argues for an "enlightened self-interest" (Smith 2009) for businesses to become development agents (Blowfield and Dolan 2014). In other words, the CSR-development relations are driven by for-profit motivation, where the business case directs what responsibility and role are most beneficial for a firm to undertake in a society.

In contrast, the development perspective views CSR as a platform for discussing the role and responsibility of business beyond the economic view on "wealth-creating mechanisms." If businesses are to contribute, extended responsibilities are needed, for example, providing safe jobs, an income above the minimum level, promoting particular types of entrepreneurship, and innovation with social and environmental features included. Importantly, the demands regarding responsibilities need to come from workers, communities, and other local actors including pertinent local needs to be meet. The outside-in view of the developmental perspective adds an overarching social lens to development on top of the pure economic lens seen in the business perspective. We argue that these two perspectives indicate common assumptions about the role of business in society that is similar to the business perspective. Businesses are seen as social actors in a society that can utilize their resources and knowledge – under the right conditions – to enable development or to remove barriers to it.

The outside-in view by the development perspective, however, underlines that unless CSR practices by firms are not coordinated with relevant local actors (e.g., business associations, government entities, local civil society organizations) and other companies across an industry, little effect will materialize in terms of development (Azizi and Jamali 2016; Newell 2005; Newell and Frynas 2007; Utting and Marques 2010). This means that CSR practices tend to be presented as stand-alone activities in a particular setting and situation, like mining companies undertaking certain activities in a local area or a number of textiles and garment firms implementing codes of conduct among the workforce. If CSR practices are to make social and environmental improvements, they need to have a wider embedding in an area or an industry. Nevertheless the literature contains a few examples to suggest such a kind of "major" impact or just some noticeable changes in the social development indicators among the poor and marginalized groups in developing countries. Though individual improvements might have happened to some groups in some incidences, the overall picture from a development perspective is one of limited impact, fragmented and uncoordinated with other actors. Even if we look at best practices of business, for example, in improving the working environment or limiting the amount of waste, the reality is that far from all firms in the industry participate. The anecdotal examples provided by the business perspective will end up being a nice "case story" but also an isolated example. It is striking that very few studies report "success stories" (see Amini and Dal Bianco 2015 as one illustration), and most studies report a limited impact of CSR activities.

On the other hand, limited consensus is found among the contributions regarding what CSR in development entails, with numerous studies having a normative position emphasizing what business "should do." We argue that despite the intended emphasis on context, local social, economic, and environmental needs, including a Southern-led understanding of socioeconomic development, there is a lack of clear definition of what such development lens entails when debating CSR-development relations within the development perspective.

Finally, the critical economy perspective views CSR as smokescreen for continuing irresponsible engagements in societies throughout the world, as profit more than anything matters and drives large private-owned businesses. Hence, whether CSR is strategic or not is not important, but how CSR legitimizes the neo-liberal regime and allows businesses to exploit workers, the environment, and regulations is the key concern. However, it is also worth noting that although this perspective offers a substantial critique of CSR by firms, it does not elaborate on how to understand "development." Although no concrete solutions are provided for alternatives for CSR by the critical political economy perspective, we view the critique of the taken-for-granted profit logic and shareholder ownership model of business as point of departure for identifying alternative ways for understanding the role and responsibility of business in relation to socioeconomic and environmental issues and hence of interest to the debate.

Conclusions

The chapter has focused on CSR by large firms as means to address development in developing countries. We argue that the CSR literature has reached a level of maturity, as various theory-laden assumptions and claims have been put forward in the debate on the relationship between CSR and development, based on which we identify three perspectives that have distinct theoretical angles in order to show the spectrum of the debate. Depending on the theoretical perspective put on the CSR-development relations, one can have very different views, claims, and assumptions about business's role and responsibility in the development of society.

Our contribution is the categorization outlined and discussed which opens up a further assessment of the different perspectives on business, CSR, and development. The categorization and three perspectives presented give an overview of distinct and contrasting perspectives that will nuance the future debates. It is a conceptualization which can be further developed where, in particular, the interphases and overlaps between the perspectives are relevant to explore further. If we perceive the three perspectives as three circles with some overlapping areas, then precisely these areas of overlap are the foci areas to come.

Such research includes (1) providing more emphasis on development by employing more nuanced perceptions of it (poverty, the state, and more), including further exploration of the CSR phenomenon in so-called "least developed countries" (Azizi 2017b; Azizi and Jamali 2016), and (2) elaborating on the inherent contradictions that exist in CSR when firms address responsibility towards the corporate head (business case), while also addressing social responsibility and/or environmental responsibility towards noncorporate actors. We hope that work in these areas will assist in bringing the field forward.

Note

1 And the special issue in *International Affairs*, 2005, volume 81, no. 3, May.

References

Acutt, N. J.,V. Medina-Ross and T. O'Riordan (2004), "Perspectives on corporate social responsibility in the chemical sector: A comparative analysis of the Mexican and South African cases," *Natural Resources Forum,* 28 (4), 302–16.

Adewale, M. T. and T. A. Rahmon (2014), "Does corporate social responsibility improve an organization's financial performance? Evidence from Nigerian banking sector," *IUP Journal of Corporate Governance,* 13 (4), 52.

Aguinis, H. and A. Glavas (2012), "What we know and don't know about corporate social responsibility: A review and research agenda," *Journal of Management,* 38 (4), 932–68.

Amaeshi, K., E. Adegbite and T. Rajwani (2016), "Corporate social responsibility in challenging and non-enabling institutional contexts: Do institutional voids matter?" *Journal of Business Ethics,* 134 (1), 135–53.

Amini, C. and S. Dal Bianco (2015), "CSR and firm performance: New evidence from developing countries," in *Development-Oriented CSR,* M. Blowfield, Dima Jamali, and C. Karam, eds. Sheffield: Greenleaf Publishing.

Ansoff, H. I. (1979), Societal strategy for the business firm. *European Inst. for Advanced Studies in Management.*

Aras, G., O. Kutlu and A. Aybars (2010), "Managing corporate performance: Investigating the relationship between corporate social responsibility and financial performance in emerging markets," *International Journal of Productivity and Performance Management,* 59 (3), 229–54.

Azizi, S. 2017a), "Corporate social responsibility in Afghanistan," PhD Series, November. Copenhagen, Denmark: Copenhagen Business School.

Azizi, S. (2017b), "MNCs as political actors in contexts of anarchy: The case of mobile telecommunications industry in Afghanistan," Copenhagen, Denmark.

Azizi, S. and D. Jamali (2016), "CSR in Afghanistan: A global CSR agenda in areas of limited statehood," *South Asian Journal of Global Business Research,* 5 (2), 165–89.

Banerjee, S. B. (2008a), "Corporate social responsibility: The good, the bad and the ugly," *Critical Sociology,* 34 (1), 51–79.

Banerjee, S. B. (2008b), "The political economy of corporate social responsibility," in *Handbook of research on global corporate citizenship,* A. G. Scherer and G. Palazzo, eds. Cheltenham, UK: Edward Elgar, 454–75.

Banerjee, S. B. (2008c), "Necrocapitalism," *Organization Studies,* 29 (12), 1541–63.

Banerjee, S. B. (2010), "Governing the global corporation: A critical perspective," *Business Ethics Quarterly,* 20 (2), 265–74.

Banerjee, S. B. (2014), "A critical perspective on corporate social responsibility: Towards a global governance framework," *Critical Perspectives on International Business,* 10 (1–2), 84–95.

Blowfield, M. (2005), "Corporate social responsibility: Reinventing the meaning of development?" *International Affairs,* 81 (3), 515–24.

Blowfield, M. (2007), "Reasons to be cheerful? What we know about CSR's impact," *Third World Quarterly,* 28 (4), 683–95.

Blowfield, M. (2012), "Business and development: Making sense of business as a development agent," *Corporate Governance,* 12 (4), 414–26.

Blowfield, M. and C. Dolan (2008), "Stewards of virtue? The ethical dilemma of CSR in African agriculture," *Development & Change,* 39 (1), 1–23.

Blowfield, M. and C. S. Dolan (2014), "Business as a development agent: Evidence of possibility and improbability," *Third World Quarterly*, 35 (1), 22–42.

Blowfield, M. and J. G. Frynas (2005), "Editorial setting new agendas: Critical perspectives on corporate social responsibility in the developing world," *International Affairs*, 81 (3), 499–513.

Bolzani, D. and S. Marabello (2015), "Migrants' engagement in CSR: The case of a Ghanaian mirants' transnational social enterprise," in *Development-oriented CSR*, M. Blowfield, Dima Jamali, and C. Karam, eds. Sheffield: Greenleaf Publishing, 99–114.

Börzel, T. A. and R. Hamann (Eds.) (2013), *Business and climate change governance: South Africa in comparative perspective.* Houndmills, Basingstoke, Hampshire and New York: Palgrave Macmillan.

Burke, L. and J. M. Logsdon (1996), "How corporate social responsibility pays off," *Long Range Planning*, 29 (4), 495–502.

Carroll, A. B. (1979), "A three-dimensional conceptual model of corporate performance," *Academy of Management Review*, 4 (4), 497–505.

Carroll, A. B. (1999), "Corporate social responsibility: Evolution of a definitional construct," *Business & Society*, 38 (3), 268–95.

Carroll, A. B. (2008), "A history of corporate social responsibility," in *The Oxford handbook of corporate social responsibility*, A. Crane, A. McWilliams, D. Matten, J. Moon, and D. S. Siegel, eds. Oxford: Oxford university Press, 19–48.

Carroll, A. B. and K. M. Shabana (2010), "The business case for corporate social responsibility: A review of concepts, research and practice," *International Journal of Management Reviews*, 12 (1), 85–105.

Chan, A. (2003), "Racing to the bottom: International trade without a social clause," *Third World Quarterly*, 24 (6), 1011–28.

Chapple, W. and J. Moon (2005), "Corporate social responsibility (CSR) in Asia: A seven-country study of CSR web site reporting," *Business & Society*, 44 (4), 415–41.

Chapple, W. and J. Moon (2007), "CSR agendas for Asia," *Corporate Social Responsibility & Environmental Management*, 14 (4), 183–8.

Crane, A., G. Palazzo, L. J. Spence and D. Matten (2014), "Contesting the value of 'creating shared value'," *California Management Review*, 56 (2), 130–53.

Djursø, H. T. and P. Neergaard (Eds.) (2006), *Social ansvarlighed: Fra idealisme til forretningsprincip.* Aarhus, Denmark: Academica København.

Dobers, P. and M. Halme (2009), "Corporate social responsibility and developing countries," *Corporate Social Responsibility & Environmental Management*, 16 (5), 237–49.

Egri, C. P. and D. A. Ralston (2008), "Corporate responsibility: A review of international management research from 1998 to 2007," *Journal of International Management*, 14 (4), 319–39.

The European Commission (2018), "Corporate social responsibility (CSR)," [Available at http://ec.europa.eu/growth/industry/corporate-social-responsibility_en].

Fleming, P. and M. T. Jones (2013), *The end of corporate social responsibility crisis & critique.* London: Sage.

Fox, T. (2004), "Corporate social responsibility and development: In quest of an agenda," *Development*, 47 (3), 29–36.

Friedman, M. (1970), "The social responsibility of business is to increase profits," *New York Times*, September 13.

Frynas, J. G. (2001), "Corporate and state responses to anti-oil protests in the Niger Delta," *African Affairs*, 100 (398), 27–54.

Frynas, J. G. (2005), "The false developmental promise of corporate social responsibility: Evidence from multinational oil companies," *International Affairs*, 81 (3), 581–98.

Frynas, J. G. (2008), "Corporate social responsibility and international development: Critical assessment," *Corporate Governance: An International Review,* 16 (4), 274–81.

Garriga, E. and D. Melé (2004), "Corporate social responsibility theories: Mapping the territory," *Journal of Business Ethics,* 53 (1), 51–71.

Griffin, J. J. and J. F. Mahon (1997), "The corporate social performance and corporate financial performance debate twenty-five years of incomparable research," *Business & Society,* 36 (1), 5–31.

Halme, M., A. Kourula, S. Lindeman, G. Kallio, M. Lima-Toivanen and A. Korsunova (2016), "Sustainability innovation at the base of the pyramid through multi-sited rapid ethnography: Sustainability innovation through rapid ethnography at the BOP," *Corporate Social Responsibility and Environmental Management,* 23 (2), 113–28.

Halme, M., A. Kourula, S. Lindeman, G. Kallio, M. Lima-Toivanen, A. Korsunova and J. Laurila (2009), "Philanthropy, integration or innovation? Exploring the financial and societal outcomes of different types of corporate responsibility," *Journal of Business Ethics,* 84 (3), 325–39.

Halme, M., A. Kourula, S. Lindeman, G. Kallio, M. Lima-Toivanen, A. Korsunova, J. Laurila, S. Lindeman and P. Linna (2012), "Innovation for inclusive business: Intrapreneurial bricolage in multinational corporations," *Journal of Management Studies,* 49 (4), 743–84.

Hamann, R. (2004), "Corporate social responsibility, partnerships, and institutional change: The case of mining companies in South Africa," *Wiley Online Library,* 278–90.

Hanlon, G. and Prof P. Fleming (2009), "Updating the critical perspective on corporate social responsibility," *Sociology Compass,* 3 (6), 937–48.

Harvey, D. (2007), *A brief history of neoliberalism.* New York: Oxford University Press.

Haufler, V. (2010), "Governing corporations in zones of conflict: Issues, actors and institutions," *Who Governs the Globe,* 102–30.

Huber, K. and D. Gilbert (2015), "Political CSR and social development: Lessons from the Bangladesh garment industry," in *Development-oriented corporate social responsibility. Vol. 1: Multinational corporations and the global context,* D. Jamali, C. Karam and M. Blowfield, eds. Sheffield: Greenleaf Publishing, 228–46.

Husain, S. and P. Lund-Thomsen (2015), "CSR and sexual and reproductive health: A case study among women workers in the football manufacturing industy of Sialkot Pakistan," in *Development-oriented CSR,* M. Blowfield, Dima Jamali and C. Karam, eds. Sheffield: Greenleaf Publishing, 189–202.

Idemudia, U. (2008), "Conceptualising the CSR and development debate," *Journal of Corporate Citizenship,* (29), 91–110.

Idemudia, U. (2011), "Corporate social responsibility and developing countries," *Progress in Development Studies,* 11 (1), 1–18.

Jain, T. and D. Jamali (2015), "Strategic approaches to corporate social responsibility," *Development-Oriented Corporate Social Responsibility: Volume 2: Locally Led Initiatives in Developing Economies,* Sheffield: Greenleaf Publishing, 71.

Jamali, D. (2007), "The case for strategic corporate social responsibility in developing countries," *Business & Society Review (00453609),* 112 (1), 1–27.

Jamali, D. (2010), "The CSR of MNC subsidiaries in developing countries: Global, local, substantive or diluted?" *Journal of Business Ethics,* 93 (2), 181–200.

Jamali, D. (2014), "CSR in developing countries through an institutional lens," in *Corporate social responsibility and sustainability: Emerging trends in developing economies,* G. Eweje, ed. Sheffield: Greenleaf Publishing, 21–44.

Jamali, D. (Ed.) (2015), *Locally led initiatives in developing economies, development-oriented corporate social responsibility,* Sheffield: Greenleaf.

Jamali, D. and C. Karam (2016), "Corporate social responsibility in developing countries as an emerging field of study: CSR in developing countries," *International Journal of Management Reviews,* 20, 32–61, https://doi.org/10.1111/ijmr.12112

Jamali, D., C. Karam and M. Blowfield (Eds.) (2015a), *Development-oriented corporate social responsibility volume 1: Multinational corporations and the global context*, Sheffield: Greenleaf Publishing.

Jamali, D., C. Karam and M. Blowfield (Eds.) (2015b), *Development-oriented corporate social responsibility volume 2: Locally led initiatives in developing economies*. Sheffield: Greenleaf Publishing.

Jamali, D., C. Karam, M. Blowfield, P. Lund-Thomsen and S. Jeppesen (2017), "SMEs and CSR in developing countries," *Business & Society*, 56 (1), 11–22.

Jamali, D., C. Karam, M. Blowfield, P. Lund-Thomsen, S. Jeppesen and R. Mirshak (2010), "Business-conflict linkages: Revisiting MNCs, CSR, and conflict," *Journal of Business Ethics*, 93 (3), 443–64.

Jamali, D., C. Karam, M. Blowfield, P. Lund-Thomsen, S. Jeppesen, R. Mirshak and B. Neville (2011), "Convergence versus divergence of CSR in developing countries: An embedded multi-layered institutional lens," *Journal of Business Ethics*, 102 (4), 599–621.

Jamali, D., C. Karam, M. Blowfield, P. Lund-Thomsen, S. Jeppesen, R. Mirshak, B. Neville and Y. Sidani (2008), "Classical vs. modern managerial CSR perspectives: Insights from Lebanese context and cross-cultural implications," *Business & Society Review (00453609)*, 113 (3), 329–46.

Jamali, D., C. Karam, M. Blowfield, P. Lund-Thomsen, S. Jeppesen, R. Mirshak, B. Neville and Y. Sidani (2012), *CSR in the Middle East: Fresh perspectives*. New York: Palgrave Macmillan.

Jamali, D., C. Karam, M. Blowfield, P. Lund-Thomsen, S. Jeppesen, R. Mirshak, B. Neville, Y. Sidani, M. Zanhour and T. Keshishian (2009), "Peculiar strengths and relational attributes of SMEs in the context of CSR," *Journal of Business Ethics*, 87 (3), 355–77.

Jenkins, R. (2005), "Globalization, corporate social responsibility and poverty," *International Affairs*, 81 (3), 525–40.

Jeppesen, S., B. Kothuis and A. N. Tran (2012), *Corporate social responsibility and competitiveness for SMEs in developing countries: South Africa and Vietnam*, Paris: Agence Française de Développement.

Jeppesen, S., B. Kothuis, A. N. Tran and P. Lund-Thomsen (2010), "Special issue on 'New Perspectives on Business, Development, and Society Research'," *Journal of Business Ethics*, 93 (Supplement 2), 139–42.

Jones, C. (2009), "Poststructuralism in critical management studies," in *The Oxford handbook of critical management studies*, Oxford: Oxford University Press.

Jones, M. T. (1996), "Missing the forest for the trees: A critique of the social responsibility concept and discourse," *Business & Society*, 35 (1), 7–41.

Jones, M. T. (1998), "Blade runner capitalism, the transnational corporation, and commodification: Implications for cultural integrity," *Cultural Dynamics*, 10 (3), 287–306.

Kemp, D., J. R. Owen and V. Dejvongsa (2015), "Operational intent and development impact in mining," in *Development-oriented corporate social responsibility. Vol. 1: Multinational corporations and the global context*, D. Jamali, C. Karam and M. Blowfield, eds. Sheffield: Greenleaf Publishing, 49–61.

Kemp, R., S. Parto and R. B. Gibson (2005), "Governance for sustainable development: Moving from theory to practice," *International Journal of Sustainable Development*, 8 (1–2), 12–30.

Kotler, P. and N. Lee (2005), "Best of breed: When it comes to gaining a market edge while supporting a social cause, 'corporate social marketing' leads the pack," *Social Marketing Quarterly*, 11 (3–4), 91–103.

Kurucz, E., B. Colbert and D. Wheeler (2008), "The business case for corporate social responsibility," in *The Oxford handbook of corporate social responsibility*, A. Crane, A. McWilliams, D. Matten, J. Moon, and D. S. Siegel, eds. Oxford: Oxford University Press, 83–112.

Lantos, G. P. (2001), "The boundaries of strategic corporate social responsibility," *Journal of Consumer Marketing,* 18 (7), 595–632.

Littlewood, D. and J. Russon (2015), "CSR, mining and development in Namibia," in *Development-oriented corporate social responsibility. Vol. 1: Multinational corporations and the global context,* M. Blowfield, Dima Jamali and C. Karam, eds. Sheffield: Greenleaf Publishing, 116–33.

Locke, R. M. and M. Romis (2007), "Improving work conditions in a global supply chain," *MIT Sloan Management Review,* 48 (2), 54.

London, T. and S. L. Hart (2010), *Next generation business strategies for the base of the pyramid: New approaches for building mutual value,* New Jersey: FT Press.

Luetkenhorst, W. (2004), "Corporate social responsibility and the development agenda," *Intereconomics,* 39 (3), 157–66.

Lund-Thomsen, P. and A. Lindgreen (2014), "Corporate social responsibility in global value chains: Where are we now and where are we going?" *Journal of Business Ethics,* 123 (1), 11–22.

Lund-Thomsen, P., A. Lindgreen and K. Nadvi (2010a), "Global value chains, local collective action and corporate social responsibility: A review of empirical evidence," *Business Strategy & the Environment* (John Wiley & Sons, Inc), 19 (1), 1–13.

Lund-Thomsen, P., A. Lindgreen and K. Nadvi (2010b), "Clusters, chains and compliance: Corporate social responsibility and governance in football manufacturing in South Asia," *Journal of Business Ethics,* 93 (2), 201–22.

Maher, R. (2018), "Squeezing psychological freedom in corporate – community engagement," *Journal of Business Ethics,* 1–20.

Mallin, C. A. (2009), *Corporate social responsibility: A case study approach,* Cheltenham, UK: Edward Elgar Publishing.

Margolis, J. D. and J. P. Walsh (2003), "Misery loves companies: Rethinking social initiatives by business," *Administrative Science Quarterly,* 48 (2), 268–305.

McFalls, R. (2007), "Testing the limits of 'Inclusive Capitalism': A case study of the South Africa HP i-community," *The Journal of Corporate Citizenship,* (28), 85–98.

McKague, K., D. Wheeler and A. Karnani (2015), "An integrated approach to poverty alleviation: Roles of the private sector, government and civil society," in *The business of social and environmental innovation,* Cham: Springer, 129–45.

McWilliams, A. and D. Siegel (2001), "Corporate social responsibility: A theory of the firm perspective," *The Academy of Management Review,* 26 (1), 117–27.

McWilliams, A. and D. S. Siegel (2011), "Creating and capturing value: Strategic corporate social responsibility, resource-based theory, and sustainable competitive advantage," *Journal of Management,* 37 (5), 1480–95.

McWilliams, A., D. S. Siegel and P. M. Wright (2006), "Corporate social responsibility: Strategic implications," *Journal of Management Studies,* 43 (1), 1–18.

Muthuri, J. N., J. Moon and U. Idemudia (2012), "Corporate innovation and sustainable community development in developing countries," *Business & Society,* 51 (3), 355–81.

Newell, P. (2005), "Citizenship, accountability and community: The limits of the CSR agenda," *International Affairs,* 81 (3), 541–57.

Newell, P. (2008), "CSR and the limits of capital: CSR and the limits of capital," *Development and Change,* 39 (6), 1063–78.

Newell, P. and J. G. Frynas (2007), "Beyond CSR? Business, poverty and social justice: An introduction," *Third World Quarterly,* 28 (4), 669–81.

Ngoc Tran, A. (2007), "Alternatives to the 'race to the bottom' in Vietnam: Minimum wage strikes and their aftermath," *Labor Studies Journal,* 32 (4), 430–51.

Nijhof, A. H. J. and R. J. M. Jeurissen (2010), "The glass ceiling of corporate social responsibility: Consequences of a business case approach towards CSR," *International Journal of Sociology and Social Policy,* (J. Burchell, ed.), 30 (11–12), 618–31.

Orlitzky, M., F. L. Schmidt and S. L. Rynes (2003), "Corporate social and financial performance: A meta-analysis," *Organization Studies,* 24 (3), 403–41.

Orlitzky, M., C. Louche, J-P. Gond and W. Chapple (2017), "Unpacking the drivers of corporate social performance: A multilevel, multistakeholder, and multimethod analysis," *Journal of Business Ethics,* 144 (1), 21–40.

Paine, L. S. (2003), *Value shift: Why companies must merge social and financial imperatives to achieve superior performance,* New York: McGraw-Hill.

Perrini, F., A. Russo, A. Tencati and C. Vurro (2011), "Deconstructing the relationship between corporate social and financial performance," *Journal of Business Ethics,* 102, 59–76.

Pope, J., D. Annandale and A. Morrison-Saunders (2004), "Conceptualising sustainability assessment," *Environmental Impact Assessment Review,* 24 (6), 595–616.

Porter, M. E. and M. R. Kramer (2011), "The big idea: Creating shared value," *Harvard Business Review,* 89 (1), 2.

Prieto-Carrón, M., P. Lund-Thomsen, A. Chan, A. Muro and C. Bhushan (2006), "Critical perspectives on CSR and development: What we know, what we don't know, and what we need to know," *International Affairs,* 82 (5), 977–87.

Rahbek Gjerdrum Pedersen, E. (2006), "Making corporate social responsibility (CSR) operable: How companies translate stakeholder dialogue into practice," *Business and Society Review,* 111 (2), 137–63.

Rahbek Gjerdrum Pedersen, E. (2015), *Corporate social responsibility,* London: Sage.

Rahbek Gjerdrum Pedersen, E. and M. Andersen (2006), "Safeguarding corporate social responsibility (CSR) in global supply chains: How codes of conduct are managed in buyer-supplier relationships," *Journal of Public Affairs,* 6 (3–4), 228–40.

Ramirez, J. (2015), "Indigenous communities and mega-projects: Corporate social responsibility (CSR) and consultation-consent principles," in *Development-oriented corporate social responsibility. Vol. 1: Multinational corporations and the global context,* D. Jamali, C. Karam and M. Blowfield, eds. Sheffield: Greenleaf Publishing, 79–98.

Reed, A. and D. Reed (2009), "Partnerships for development: Four models of business involvement," *Journal of Business Ethics,* 90, 3–37.

Roberts, S. (2003), "Supply chain specific? Understanding the patchy success of ethical sourcing initiatives," *Journal of Business Ethics,* 44 (2–3), 159–70.

Sagebien, J. and M. Whellams (2010), "CSR and development: Seeing the forest for the trees," *Canadian Journal of Development Studies / Revue canadienne d'études du développement,* 31 (3–4), 483–510.

Salzmann, O., A. Ionescu-somers and U. Steger (2005), "The business case for corporate sustainability," *European Management Journal,* 23 (1), 27–36.

Sánchez, R. G., M. P. R. Bolívar and A. M. L. Hernández (2017), "Corporate and managerial characteristics as drivers of social responsibility disclosure by state-owned enterprises," *Review of Managerial Science,* 11 (3), 633–59.

Shamir, R. (2008), "The age of responsibilization: On market-embedded morality," *Economy and Society,* 37 (1), 1–19.

Smith, N. C. (2009), "Bounded goodness: Marketing implications of Drucker on corporate responsibility," *Journal of the Academy of Marketing Science,* 37 (1), 73–84.

Spence, L. J., J. G. Frynas, J. N. Muthuri and J. Navare (Eds.) (2018), *Research handbook on small business social responsibility, research handbooks in business and management,* Cheltenham: Edward Elgar Publishing.

Tran, A. N. and S. Jeppesen (2016), "SMEs in their own right: The views of managers and workers in Vietnamese textiles, garment, and footwear companies," *Journal of Business Ethics,* 137 (3), 589–608.

Tran, A. N. and S. Jeppesen (2018), "Industry matters: Comparative study of Vietnam's SME managers and workers on meaning and impacts of CSR in two manufacturing sectors," in *Research handbook on small business social responsibility, research handbooks in business and management,* L.J. Spence, J.G. Frynas, J.N. Muthuri and J. Navare, eds. Cheltenham: Edward Elgar Publishing Limited, 47–76.

Utting, P. and J. C. Marques (2010), *Corporate social responsibility and regulatory governance: Towards inclusive development?* International political economy series. New York: Palgrave Macmillan.

Utting, P., J. C. Marques, D. Reed, and A. Mukherjee-Reed (2012), *Business regulation and non-state actors: whose standards? Whose development?* Routledge studies in development economics. London and New York: Routledge.

Uyan-Atay, B. and A. Tuncay-Celikel (2015), "CSR practices in Turkey: Examining CSR reports," in *Development-oriented CSR,* M. Blowfield, Dima Jamali and C. Karam, eds. Sheffield: Greenleaf Publishing.

Vallentin, S. and D. Murillo (2012), "Governmentality and the politics of CSR," *Organization,* 19 (6), 825–43.

van Beurden, P. and T. Gössling (2008), "The worth of values – a literature review on the relation between corporate social and financial performance," *Journal of Business Ethics,* 82 (2), 407–24.

Visser, W. (2010), "The age of responsibility: CSR 2.0 and the new DNA of business," *Journal of Business Systems, Governance & Ethics,* 5 (2), 7–22.

Vives, A. (2006), "Social and environmental responsibility in small and medium enterprises in Latin America," *Journal of Corporate Citizenship,* (21), 39–50.

Vogel, D. (2006), *The market for virtue: The potential and limits of corporate social responsibility,* Washington, DC: Brookings Institution Press.

WBCSD (2000), *Corporate social responsibility: Making good business sense,* Geneva: World Business Council for Sustainable Development.

Yap, N. (2015), "CSR and the development deficit: Part of the solution or part of the problem?" in *Development-oriented corporate social responsibility. Vol. 1: Multinational corporations and the global context,* D. Jamali, C. Karam and M. Blowfield, eds. Sheffield: Greenleaf Publishing, 134–53.

11 The state of international business, corporate social responsibility, and development

Key insights and an application to practice

Ans Kolk, Arno Kourula, Niccolò Pisani,
and Michelle Westermann-Behaylo

Introduction

The role of international business in development has long been a source of interest and controversy, depending on one's views of companies and conceptualizations of the development notion.[1] The topic has attracted increasing attention from business scholars, while at the same time some companies are gradually taking a more (pro)active role in addressing some of the so-called grand societal challenges (Kolk 2016). This trend is also perceived to be controversial, as multinational enterprises (MNEs) are seen to possess more power and influence in determining the dominant discourses of international business and development (Banerjee 2014; Ruggie 2017). Over the years, business is increasingly seen as an actor that, in partnership with governments, nongovernmental organizations, and other stakeholders, participates in sustainable development. Most recently, the Sustainable Development Goals (SDGs), a set of aspirational goals spearheaded by the United Nations (UN), has become an influential initiative illustrating the call for companies to collaborate with other actors to achieve development. The SDGs are becoming a focal point of attention for the whole range of stakeholders involved, as well as, gradually, for international business academics (Kolk, Kourula, and Pisani 2017).[2] Although the need to deal with issues such as poverty, inequality, and climate change has long been understood, development has often been seen as the realm of governments, intergovernmental organizations, and international nongovernmental organizations. With the rise of corporate social responsibility (CSR), private governance, and multistakeholder initiatives, companies are more and more seen as appropriate partners, indeed even as direct actors, in addressing development.

Although international business scholars have long been interested in development, this broad area of inquiry, and specific themes within it, remain relatively under-researched. In this chapter, we argue that the field of international business (IB) has much to offer to development research given its interdisciplinary approach and knowledge of the key firms that operate across borders, and also very often in developing countries and/or in relation to relevant development issues.[3] It should be noted that our focus here is not on economic development as such, an area to which IB has paid attention also in relation to developing countries (see Fortanier and Kolk 2007; Kolk 2016), but a much broader notion including also the environmental and social dimensions, as explained earlier. The chapter first presents key trends in IB scholarship, including a review of recent relevant academic review articles on the theme (second section), and the geographical and thematic foci of investigation (in the third and fourth sections, respectively). Subsequently, the fifth section gives a short summary of the SDGs covered by existing IB research reviews. We then present frameworks for understanding ways in which organizations (can) engage with the SDGs into their strategy and activities, elucidated with a case example. The final section offers reflections, conclusion,s and recommendations for both researchers and practitioners.

An overview of relevant academic reviews

The past decade has seen quite some reviews on CSR in general, or, in a smaller number of cases, specifically concerning the role of international firms and/ or business in development. In a very recent review article, Pisani et al. (2017) provide a summarizing table with details of the most relevant ones to date (see Table 11.1), including the journals and periods covered, keywords addressed, key foci, concepts, and recommendations. Thereafter, Pisani et al. (2017) give an extensive analysis of almost 500 articles from 31 journals over a 31-year period, a dataset that we use here for the purpose of this chapter for an additional examination on how IB research on development and developing countries has evolved in the past three decades, relying on the relevant subset of articles.

As shown in Table 11.1, early reviews by Egri and Ralston (2008) and Kolk and Van Tulder (2010) identify several gaps within IB scholarship, including the lack of attention to developing countries. In this chapter, we argue that this call for research has yet to be properly answered. Nonetheless, some of the recommendations by Kolk and Van Tulder (2010), such as exploring the various institutional, industry, firm, and supply and demand drivers for CSR, have received a fair amount of attention already. Kolk (2016) and Pisani et al. (2017) provide more up-to-date and longer-term overviews of how international business scholarship has addressed development issues, typically from a CSR lens, while – in the process – also paying specific attention to IB activities in and implications for developing countries. Kolk (2016) describes how the field has moved from exploring ethics and the environment to emphasizing the CSR and sustainable development concepts. Thus, over time we see increased concern with development and, with particular issues of importance to least developed countries. Next, we will present and discuss the state of the art and key trends in more detail.

Table 11.1 Key features of the most relevant review articles (in chronological order per category)

Authors	Focus/context of article	(IB) journal sample[a]	Period covered	Search criteria to identify articles	Main analytical concepts and/or dimensions addressed	Recommendations for research(ers), and if applicable, research institutes, policy, business practice
IB-focused reviews						
Egri and Ralston (2008)	State of corporate responsibility (CR) research over a decade as introduction to a special issue	APJM, CCM, EMJ, IBR, IJCM, IJHRM, IJM, ISMO, JIBS, JIM (Mgt) JWB, MIR, TIBR	1998–2007 (10 years)	Search on CSR (16 key words), environmental (9), ethics (6), governance (4)	Level of emphasis on corporate responsibility research, primary content focus, predominantly theoretical or empirical, and how "international" in scope	Broadening of research away from merely wealthy nations, and from restricted variance in contexts and questions; Collecting local data in countries with largest CR problems; Studying internationalization of CR research in specialized CR journals.
Kolk and Van Tulder (2010)	Overview of research trends in four main IB journals, compared to earlier reviews, as introduction to special issue on IB, CSR and sustainable development	Focus on IBR, JIBS, JWB, MIR (with article counts compared to journals from general management (8), functional areas (5), CSR/ethics ("core" [3])	1990–2008 (19 years)	Search on key words CSR; sustainable development	Overview of numbers of articles published on the themes in the journals, specific consideration of trends and special issues, and comparison with earlier reviews (in IB, but also in management, marketing and specifically on Africa given observed dearth of studies on this region)	Moving away from predominant focus on US and some triad countries where larger-scale databases are more easily available; Moving research more to the mainstream in terms of outlets and links to/embeddedness in IB theories and themes; Building on innovative articles of the special issue (also on Africa); Conducting studies on institutional, industry, organizational, supply and demand drivers.

(Continued)

Table 11.1 (Continued)

Authors	Focus/context of article	(IB) journal sample[a]	Period covered	Search criteria to identify articles	Main analytical concepts and/or dimensions addressed	Recommendations for research(ers), and if applicable, research institutes, policy, business practice
Holtbrügge and Dögl (2012)	State of research on international aspects of corporate environmental responsibility	4 IB journals: JIM (Mgt), IBR, JIBS, JWB + 8 management journals: AMJ, AMR, ASQ, JM, JMS, MS, OSc, SMJ	1997–2010 (14 years), most likely[b]	11 key words regard the environment (including CER, green, and sustainability)	Corporate environmental responsibility (CER)	Designing further multicountry studies; Moving away from developed countries to include analyses of developing countries; Including more industries especially environmentally friendly ones and industry comparisons; Going beyond the resource-based view and institutional theory; Supporting interdisciplinary studies in universities; Developing more stringent environmental regulation in developing countries.
Doh and Lucea (2013)	Focus on extent to which international strategy articles integrate market and nonmarket aspects using a bibliographical analysis	Articles included in SSCI or A&HCI and classified as "business" or "management" by Web of Science	2001–2011 (11 years)	Search for combination of global/ international strategy and a nonmarket type of key word (including CSR, sustainability, stakeholder)	Relationship between nonmarket actors (governments and civil society organizations) and international strategy; focus on integration of market and non-market using different search terms	Integrating competitive, social and governmental aspects of the global environment in which firms operate; Increasing our understanding of MNE-NGO interaction, NGOs as actors, local and comparative issues and diffusion mechanisms, and individual level issues; Changing institutional arrangements in universities and intervening from scholars, journal editors, deans, and accreditation agencies to support complex and cross-disciplinary research.

Author (Year)	Description	Journals / Sources	Time period	Method	Themes / Focus	Future directions
Kolk (2016)	Quasi-historical review of overall trajectory of ethical, environmental and social concerns in IB and of MNEs' consideration of their sustainable development impacts	JWB and JIBS over the full period, plus other journals considered where relevant	1965–2014 plus all forthcoming articles per mid-2015 (50 years)	Manual screening of all JWB and JIBS issues/articles, plus author's expert view of the (sub) fields covered	Examination of three subthemes: the (green) environment; ethics, rights and responsibilities; poverty and sustainable development.	Studying MNEs' impact on sustainable development broadly defined (in post-2015 goals) through their foreign direct investment (FDI), trade and "pro-poor" activities, and where relevant in the interaction with local firms and other organizations; Considering specific issues (with people, justice, dignity clusters standing out); Reaching out to other disciplines where applicable; Being braver and opening to unconventional work in field journals.
Non-IB focused reviews						
Aguinis and Glavas (2012)	Review of the corporate social responsibility literature, not meant as an "exhaustive historical review," but to "offer a general theoretical framework that is broad" and "allows for inclusion of more variables in the future" [c]	AMJ, AMR, ASQ, B&S, BEQ, JAP, JBE, JM, JMS, JOOP, JOB, OBHDP, OS, OSc, PP, SMJ, IJMR, JIBS, JAMS, JM(kt). Content analysis restricted to 17 non-CSR journals: AMJ, AMR, ASQ, IJMR, JAMS, JAP, JIBS, JM, JM(kt), JMS, JOB, JOOP, OBHDP, OS, OSc, PP, SMJ	1970–2011 (41 years)	Keyword search ("corporate social responsibility") in 20 journals with content analysis restricted to 17 of them (combined with comparison with prior reviews; general author specific search; general keyword search in Web of Science of additional keywords of "corporate social performance" and "corporate citizenship"; inclusion of selected books and book chapters)	Institutional, organizational and individual levels of analysis; predictors of CSR, mediators and moderators of CSR–outcomes relationship, outcomes of CSR	Integrating theories and multiple levels of analysis (variables at different levels and relationships between them, multilevel modeling, theory pruning, bringing CSR contributions to other fields); Exploring the microfoundations of CSR (underlying mechanisms and individual-level processes, including micro-level variables as mediators, CSR implementation at the individual and team levels, role of training, recruitment, and supervisor communication, work); Developing methodologies (going beyond cross-sectional single-level designs, rethinking measurement approaches, nested data across hierarchies and time, multilevel quantitative and qualitative data).

(Continued)

Table 11.1 (Continued)

Authors	Focus/context of article	(IB) journal sample[a]	Period covered	Search criteria to identify articles	Main analytical concepts and/or dimensions addressed	Recommendations for research(ers), and if applicable, research institutes, policy, business practice
Frynas and Yamahaki (2016)	Review of theories used to explain the external and internal drivers of CSR	6 CSR journals (AAAJ, AOS, BEER, BEQ CG, JBE) and 7 management journals (AMJ, AMR, ASQ, BJM, HBR, JM, JMS)	1990–2014 (25 years)	Search for articles "related to social and environmental responsibilities of firms (e.g., environmental standards, corporate community involvement)"[d]	Theorizing external drivers (stakeholder theory, institutional theory, legitimacy theory, resource dependency theory), and internal drivers (resource-based view, agency theory)	Conducting multi-theory studies (combination of internal and external drivers for CSR, combination of, e.g., institutional, RBV, and agency perspectives); Designing multilevel studies (multiple levels, surpassing methodological weaknesses, studying illegal activities); Employing individual level analyses (theories of individual action, e.g., psychology, and rediscovering role of individuals in more mainstream theories).
Jamali and Karam (2016)	Focus on "how CSR in developing countries is commonly understood" and its expression and implementation there "in practice"[e]	Different sets considered but analysis of articles in a large variety of journals (impact-factor and nonimpact factor; business and many other areas)[f]	1990– 2014/2015 (25 years)[g]	Combination of keywords on CSR (4) and on developing countries (5 or 6 depending on search set)	Antecedents and consequences of CSR at the institutional, organizational and individual levels; plus "CSR thinking" and "CSR doing"	Examining CSR variation coming from national business system configurations and outside such configurations; Studying the salience of different actors involved in formal and informal governance; Exploring hybridized and other nuanced forms of CSR; Analyzing developmental and detrimental CSR consequences.

Source: Pisani et al. (2017). Adapted from the original table.

a AAAJ: Accounting, Auditing & Accountability Journal; AOS: Accounting, Organizations & Society; APJM: Asia Pacific Journal of Management; AMJ: Academy of Management Journal; AMR: Academy of Management Review; ASQ: Administrative Science Quarterly; BEER: Business Ethics: A European Review; B&S: Business & Society; BEQ: Business Ethics Quarterly; BJM: British Journal of Management; CCM: Cross Cultural Management; CG: Corporate Governance: An International Review; EMJ: European Management Journal;

HBR: Harvard Business Review; IBR: International Business Review; IJCM: International Journal of Commerce & Management; IJHRM: International Journal of Human Resource Management; IJM: International Journal of Management; IJMR: International Journal of Management Reviews; ISMO: International Studies of Management and Organization; JAMS: Journal of the Academy of Marketing Science; JAP: Journal of Applied Psychology; JBE: Journal of Business Ethics; JIBS: Journal of International Business Studies; JIM (Mgr): Journal of International Management; JM: Journal of Management; JM(kt): Journal of Marketing; JMS: Journal of Management Studies; JOB: Journal of Organizational Behavior; JOOP: Journal of Occupational and Organizational Psychology; JWB: Journal of World Business; MIR: Management International Review; MS: Management Science; OBHDP: Organizational Behavior and Human Decision Processes; OS: Organization Studies; OSc: Organization Science; PP: Personnel Psychology; SMJ: Strategic Management Journal; TIBR: Thunderbird International Review.

b The article uses different formulations for time periods/years, including "between 1997 and 2010" (Holtbrügge and Dögl, 2012, p. 180), "13-year time period from 1997 to 2009" (p. 181), "from 1997 to 2010" (p. 181), "from 1997 to 2011" (p. 193), "Limiting our time period to a 15-year frame" (p. 193), and – the phrasing that is most explicit and that we thus put in the table, "including all CER articles that were published until the end of 2010" (p. 18).

c Aguinis and Glavas (2012, p. 934).

d Frynas and Yamahaki (2016, p. 5).

e Jamali and Karam (forthcoming, p. 2).

f Looking at the full set of articles used (Appendix 3), it includes publications in well-known outlets (e.g. Aguinis & Glavas list, especially JBE), but also quite some unknown ones of which the quality is uncertain. Examples include Acta Commercii; Atatürk Üniversitesi İktisadiveİdari Bilimler Dergisi; BMC Public Health; Developing World Bioethics; International Journal of Cuban Studies; IUP Journal of Corporate Governance; Journal of Agricultural and Environmental Ethics; Journal of Efficiency and Responsibility in Education and Science; Journal of Health, Population & Nutrition; Kajian Malaysia; North Carolina Journal of International Law & Commercial Regulation; RAM – Revista de Administração Mackenzie; Review of Income and Wealth; SCMS Journal of Indian Management.

g The article refers to 2015 sometimes (e.g. Table 11.1), but the full list of journals included in their Appendix 3 reveals that there are only five articles from 2015, of which two seemingly forthcoming (seven others, in earlier years, also lack volume/issue numbers so appear to have been included as online doi versions, without necessarily being published in that specific year).

Key geographic trends in research

In their review of international CSR, Pisani et al. (2017) demonstrate a rise in research on this topic in the key journals in the most relevant fields of study. Figure 11.1 shows the same 494 articles published in 31 journals[4] over a period of 31 years to explore the focal countries of the studies. Although the literature has employed the labels "developing" and "emerging" countries in multiple ways, Pisani et al. (2017) use the World Bank's classification that distinguishes between low-income, middle-income, and high-income in order to group developing, emerging, and developed countries, respectively. Considering the extensive search for articles undertaken by Pisani et al. (2017) in a comprehensive list of journals, using a broad and inclusive range of keywords related to CSR, as well as indicating the international/global/transnational dimensions,[5] we argue that a majority of studies focusing on development is covered in our analysis. This is especially the case as only studies that combined these two types of aspects were included, also on closer inspection and going through them one by one.

Overall, we see a strong rise in scholarly interest in international CSR and development over the 31-year period, with a spike around 2009 and 2010 mostly due to a few more articles published in key outlets, as well as special issues on the theme. When analyzing in further detail the focal countries of the studies, we note a very strong emphasis on developed country contexts with a fairly steady rise of interest in emerging countries. It is worth considering the specific methodology used by Pisani et al. (2017) to classify studies according to their primary focus on developed, emerging, or developing countries. In

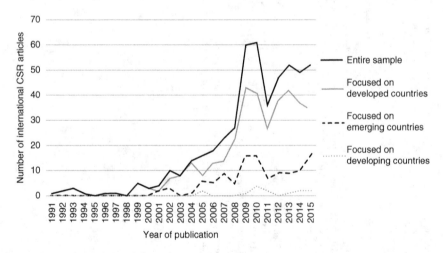

Figure 11.1 The evolution of international CSR research and its focus on developed, emerging, and developing countries

Source: Pisani et al. (2017). Adapted from the original figure.

Note: The number of articles considered is 494, i.e., the full set of articles used for the content analysis in Pisani et al. (2017)

fact, when a specific study covered countries belonging to more than one of the three categorizations (e.g., both developing and emerging countries), the authors classified it as being primarily focused on only one category based on the country categorization that was mostly represented in the sample. This implies that, although very few studies have indeed the primary (or sole) focus on developing countries as highlighted in Figure 11.1, the reality is that many more studies in the literature consider some developing as well as developed or emerging countries in their empirical settings. To this end, Table 11.2 offers the list of emerging and developing countries considered in the articles sampled by Pisani et al. (2017), documenting a relatively inclusive coverage of these countries in the literature, even if not as primary target countries.

Based on the same data and analysis used in Pisani et al. (2017), Figure 11.2 goes deeper into the home and host countries of international CSR studies providing such country-level information. These data indicate a strong

Table 11.2 Emerging and developing home and host countries investigated in international CSR research[a]

No.	Home country	No.	Host country
22	China	36	China
13	India	16	Nigeria
11	Brazil	14	India
7	Thailand	11	Mexico
5	Argentina, Malaysia, Mexico	9	South Africa
4	South Africa, Sri Lanka	8	Brazil, Pakistan
3	Hungary, Indonesia, Nigeria, Pakistan, Philippines, Vietnam	7	Indonesia
		6	Argentina
2	Bangladesh, Peru	5	Bangladesh, Turkey
1	Cambodia, Cameroon, Colombia, Ethiopia, Jordan, Kenya, Lebanon, Romania, Serbia, Syria, Tunisia, Turkey, Uruguay	4	Angola, Kenya, Lebanon, Myanmar
		3	Congo, Peru, Romania, Tanzania, Uruguay
		2	Colombia, Dem. Rep. of the Congo, Hungary, Malawi, Malaysia, Trinidad and Tobago, Zimbabwe
		1	Albania, Bermuda, Bosnia and Herzegovina, Burundi, Cambodia, Costa Rica, Ecuador, Egypt, Gambia, Haiti, Iraq, Kazakhstan, Nepal, Panama, Rwanda, Senegal, Somalia, Sri Lanka, Sudan, Uganda, Venezuela, Vietnam

Number of developing and emerging countries per group

5	Developing countries	30	Developing countries
105	Emerging countries	156	Emerging countries

Source: Pisani et al. (2017). Adapted from the original table.

a   The number refers to the number of papers in which a given country is considered in as either home or host country in the empirical analysis.

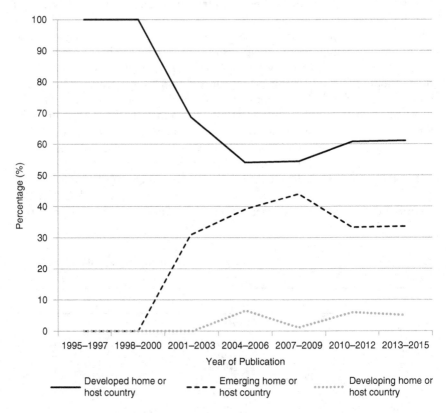

Figure 11.2 The distribution of international CSR articles over developing, emerging, and developed countries

Source: Pisani et al. (2017). Adapted from the original figure.

a The number of articles considered is 257, i.e., the articles that report information on the home and/ or host countries.

b The first year considered is 1995 due to the fact that the fist article that reported information on the home and/or host countries was published in 1996. Percentages are on the basis of 3-year averages per group.

rise in studies exploring CSR of companies based in or operating in emerging economies. This trend in research is reflective of the rise in corporate and media interest in Brazil, Russia, India, and China, as well as other emerging economies. To further elucidate the coverage of countries in the literature on international CSR in Table 11.2, we report the complete list of emerging and developing home and host countries investigated in the articles sampled by Pisani et al. (2017) (see the lower part of Table 11.2). We thus highlight the relatively large variety of both emerging and developing countries included in the empirical settings of these studies. The results reported in the table also substantiate the rise in coverage of emerging countries, with China leading both home- and host-country groupings. Whereas in the home-country grouping few developing countries have been considered (e.g., Ethiopia), their coverage in the host-country grouping is significantly larger. Looking more specifically at the subset of so-called "fragile and conflict affected" countries, these appear even less often in research, only in an incidental case as home country, and in a few more instances as host countries.

Key themes and findings

Moving from examining geography to a more thematic analysis also based on Pisani et al. (2017), Table 11.3 summarizes the broad themes and key findings in the international research focused on emerging and developing countries. In terms of antecedents in emerging and developing countries, existing studies highlight the contextual, firm, and individual drivers of international CSR engagement. Key contextual drivers that support and/or stifle CSR include pressure from intergovernmental organizations, regulatory agencies, financial markets, nongovernmental organizations, and local communities and institutions. At the firm level, industry, type of product and pollution caused, the customer, the ownership, and governance structure all have an impact on corporate engagement. At the individual level, studies have examined the role of employee participation and management commitment as drivers of international CSR engagement.

In terms of the CSR phenomenon, studies focusing on the home- and host-country contexts have examined topics as diverse as when firms invest in conflict regions; what the importance is of national histories in the globalization of the notion of CSR; and how philanthropy, resources, and ethical culture affect whether a company will collaborate or be assertive with a host government. Furthermore, depending on the institutional context, local vs. foreign firms adopt different priorities, and internal tools, such as codes of conduct, are seen to be more influential than external ones, such as globally certified management systems. Although firms often also use government-stakeholder relations strategically in foreign operations, it is still not seen to be very effective in getting new licenses and contracts. The types of CSR implemented locally and the subsidiary's strategic commitment have a large impact on firm value creation. Studies also examine the conditions under which CSR programs and partnerships can become successful and sometimes even warn against implementing symbolic partnerships with nongovernmental organizations and/or assuming supplier compliance to CSR programs.

In terms of consequences of international CSR, the institutional-level outcomes of CSR can be seen to be conflicting across studies. Local engagement and adaptation of CSR can lead to competitive advantage, reputational gains, and local empowerment, but it does not necessarily improve community relations in all cases and can lead to paternalistic practices with unintended consequences. A tension can also build between local adaptation and global regulation. At the firm level, MNEs can also take advantage of regulatory loopholes leading to substandard ethical practices. In fact, CSR is often framed only as compliance instead of taking a more proactive stance to regulatory requirements. Nonetheless, other

Table 11.3 Broad themes and key findings in international CSR research focused on emerging and developing countries [a,b,c]

Theme	Representative references	Key findings
Antecedents		
Contextual drivers	Adegbite, Amaeshi, and Nakajima (2013); Muthuri and Gilbert (2011); Mzembe and Meaton (2014)	• Three major stakeholders (international organizations, rating agencies, and local institutions) trigger the development of corporate governance practices in emerging economies and pull them in multiple directions. • *A firm's CSR agenda is strongly influenced by civil society activism, community expectations, public and private regulations, and pressure from financial markets.* • *Conditions that stifle CSR uptake, such as lack of government regulations, and the government's capacity and commitment to enforce regulation also play a role, especially in developing countries.*
Firm drivers	Perez-Batres et al. (2012); Tatoglu et al. (2014); Robertson (2009)	• Stakeholder pressures, perceived polluting potential, and customer focus are significant antecedents to the adoption of voluntary environmental management practices by foreign subsidiaries in emerging countries. • The type of industry and a firm's affiliation to a national sustainability program are strong antecedents of its decision to follow local sustainability initiatives transparently. • *A firm's ownership structure and corporate governance, as well as the openness of the economy to international investment and the role of civil society, trigger firms' local responsiveness of CSR.*
Micro-level drivers	Muller and Kolk (2010); Yu (2009)	• Workers' participation in the CSR movement against labor abuses have increased in the recent past. Although worker participation has positive impacts on codes implementation and labor standards improvement, many challenges remain before workers can play deeper and broader participative roles in pursuing a sustainable codes compliance model in emerging countries. • Management commitment to ethics is a dominant driver (compared to extrinsic drivers) of international CSR practices.
Phenomenon		
Home-country institutions	Driffield, Jones, and Crotty (2013)	• Firms based in home countries with weaker institutions and less concern about CSR, as well as firms characterized by more concentrated ownership, are more likely to invest in conflict regions.

Host-country institutions	Jamali and Neville (2011); Kolk and Lenfant (2010); Luo (2006)	• Global convergence in CSR practices may materialize in light of mimetic isomorphic pressures, but path dependencies are crucial in view of national history trajectories and sociopolitical configurations, especially in emerging countries. • MNEs face large CSR dilemmas in emerging and developing countries, especially in the presence of conflicts. These range from the level of contribution they can give to their attitude vis-a-vis ongoing conflicts. Whereas MNEs clearly see opportunities in these contexts, CSR reporting is fairly generic, and the specific context seems to have little impact on the type of CSR activities. • MNE's propensity to cooperate with the host government is positively related to its philanthropic contribution and resource accommodation, whereas its propensity to be assertive with the host government is positively related to its focus on ethics and organizational credibility. • When perceived corruption increases, an MNE's likelihood to cooperate and be assertive with host governments decreases.
International CSR engagement	Husted and Allen (2009); Khan and Nicholson (2014); Kolk, Hong, and Van Dolen (2010); Mijatovic and Stokic (2010); Xun (2013); Wiig and Kolstad (2010)	• Local and international firms show differences in their CSR reporting in emerging countries. In the retailing industry and focusing on China, Chinese retailers report more on economic dimensions, including philanthropy, whereas the international retailers more on product responsibility. Having said that, contentious labor issues and the environment seem to receive relatively limited attention in both groups. • Internal self-regulations such as statements of corporate values and codes of conduct have more influence on CSR practices than external self-regulations, such as the implementation of generic management system standards such as the ISO 14001 standard. • Global firms develop specific CSR strategies in emerging countries. Rather than adopting a canonical holistic CSR stakeholder model as typically observed in Western countries, these firms adopt a preferential stakeholder model using government-aimed CSR strategically. • Although companies use CSR strategically in emerging/developing countries, it is relatively unimportant in winning licenses and contracts. • Centrality, visibility, and voluntarism of CSR programs are important conditions under which CSR is related to firms' value creation.
Focus on subsidiaries	Reimann, Rauer, and Kaufmann (2015)	• In the interaction between suppliers and buyers, key relational, knowledge transfer, and operational factors need to be considered in three stages (evaluation, exploration, and interactive). • MNE subsidiaries' strategic commitment to CSR in emerging countries can vary depending on a range of factors. In particular, the greater the administrative distance between MNEs' home and host countries, the lesser the subsidiaries strategically commit to CSR. Moreover, the greater the administrative distance, the lesser the subsidiaries strategically commit to CSR.

(Continued)

Table 11.3 (Continued)

Theme	Representative references	Key findings
Phenomenon		
Focus on multiple stakeholders	Christmann and Taylo (2006); Jamali and Keshishian (2009); Lim and Phillips (2008); Rotter, Airike, and Mark-Herbert (2014); Wadham and Warren (2013)	• Partnerships between businesses and NGOs in the context of CSR have become more usual in the recent past, particularly in emerging countries. This said, many partnerships are symbolic and instrumental rather than substantive and integrative, showing a limited scope of activities, fluctuating investments of resources, simple processes, sporadic modes of communication, and low levels of engagement. • Many firms have adopted CSR practices to address criticisms of working and environmental conditions at subcontractors' factories. However, supplier compliance has been elusive, and even third-party monitoring has proven unsuccessful. Collaborative partnerships where the firm gives suppliers secure product orders and other benefits to incentivize CSR compliance may help. • Firms strategically select their level of compliance (substantive versus symbolic) depending on customer preferences, customer monitoring, and expected sanctions by customers. • *Cross-sector partnerships involve both instrumental and communicative encounters, usually with slow progress with occasional fast development of partners' understanding of themselves and the challenges they seek to address.* • *Firms harness their political influence in CSR practices via collaboration and dialog with stakeholders and civil society actors.*
Consequences		
Institutional effects of CSR outcomes	Fong, Li, and Du (2013); Gifford, Kesler, and Anand (2010); Mena et al. (2010); Newenham-Kahindi (2011); Nurunnabi (2015)	• Instead of relying on proven global capabilities to adapt existing business models, firms need to adopt a hybrid approach that balances local and global strategies when working in emerging countries. In this context, MNEs develop an institutional environment in the host country where those firms that do not provide substantial local assistance will be at a competitive disadvantage. • In a host-country market with low consumer animosity, reputation transfer of a local acquisition target is pronounced, whereas in a host country market with high consumer animosity, animosity will restrain or even exceed reputation transferability. • *Implementing global CSR policies to strike a balance between international business capabilities and localization strategies does not necessarily help local community relations.* • *Political institutional pressures can stand in the way of mimetic isomorphism and constitute negative forces that add further tension to global regulation.* • *Several innovative solutions in business and human rights can build on empowerment, dialogue, and constructive engagement.*

Firm outcomes	Maruyama and Wu (2015); Perry, Wood, and Fernie (2015); Tan (2009); Zeng et al. (2013)	• MNEs often adopt double standards in their operating policies and fail to uphold the CSR practices of their host countries in emerging and developing economies. The regulatory and preexisting ethical conditions in these countries have proven inadequate and contribute to this troubling phenomenon. This effect is compounded by an institutional environment that easily offers loopholes for MNEs to exploit. MNCs exploitation of these substandard ethical practices and institutional weaknesses, and instituting negligent management over their downstream supply chains, make the MNCs themselves responsible for these conditions. • Factory management perspectives on the implementation of CSR practices are particularly relevant in emerging and developing countries as they relate to the strategy balancing of ethical considerations against the commercial pressures of cost and lead time. In this context, factory managers often tend to frame CSR in terms of compliance, rather than going above and beyond regulatory requirements. • Contrary to expectations, CSR activities are not effective in mitigating the disadvantages of perceived importance of supporting domestic retailers faced by foreign retailers entering emerging countries. • The social dimension of societal marketing is most effective when it affects a firm's CSR image and legitimacy in an emerging country.
Irresponsible corporate behavior	Zhao, Tan, and Ho Park (2014)	• Firms' social adaptation activities have significant positive effects in mitigating public crises associated with their irresponsible behavior, whereas certain aspects of economic adaption, such as early entry into the host country, reliance on local leadership, and speedy expansion of local employees, lead to public crises.
Micro-level outcomes	Khan, Westwood, and Boje (2010); Wettstein (2012); *Belal and Roberts (2010)*	• Many Western-led interventions to eliminate child labor in emerging countries rest on universalistic, paternalistic, decontextualizing, and atomistic assumptions that bring negative unintended consequences. A postcolonial perspective insistent on an inclusive "bottom-up," "reversed-engineered" approach, wherein CSR problems are traced back to Western MNEs' policies and practices is needed. • Global businesses are confronted with the question of complicity in human rights violations committed by abusive host governments, and this is especially the case in emerging and developing countries. MNEs have a moral responsibility beyond the negative realm of doing no harm to help protect human rights by putting pressure on perpetrating host governments involved in human rights abuses. • *Stakeholder agents generally believe that the motivation and practice of CSR reporting develops in response to pressures from international markets and generates largely cosmetic responses.*

Source: Pisani et al. (2017). Adapted from the original table.

a The number of articles considered is 494, i.e., the full set of articles used for the content analysis.
b The key findings reported in regular font refer to studies that contain information on the home and/or host countries as either home or host countries.
c The key findings reported in italic and underlined font refer to studies that contain information on the home and/or host countries and focus on emerging countries as either home or host countries and focus on developing countries as either home or host countries.

articles suggest that CSR can improve operations and mitigate public crises for companies. Overall, several studies exploring the consequences of international CSR remain skeptical about cosmetic responses.

Our review as presented here provides a relatively comprehensive overview of existing insights, some of which have come to the fore elsewhere as well. The review by Jamali and Karam (2016), included in Table 11.1, focuses on CSR and developing countries. It describes the national business system related and international antecedents of CSR, the formal and informal elements of governance of business conduct, the new forms of CSR that emerge, and the positive and detrimental impacts of business in developing countries. They highlight the importance of a contextually sensitive and locally shaped form of CSR. Similarly, Jamali et al. (2017) also provide an overview of CSR in developing countries by exploring an institutional logics approach. They describe how implicit institutions such as the state, the market, corporations, professions, families, and religions interact with the local institutional context in terms of the translation and adaptation processes of CSR.

Attention for the UN SDGs: a further review of relevant reviews

As noted in the introduction, the past few years have seen increasing interest in the SDGs. Adopted by the UN General Assembly in 2015, the SDGs consist of 17 goals with 169 accompanying targets (see Table 11.4 for an overview of

Table 11.4 Number of targets and indicators for each SDG[a]

Sustainable Development Goal	Number of Targets	Number of Indicators
1. End poverty	7	9
2. Zero hunger	8	14
3. Ensure healthy lives	13	26
4. Quality education	10	11
5. Gender equality	9	14
6. Clean water and sanitation	8	11
7. Affordable and clean energy	5	6
8. Decent work and economic growth	12	17
9. Industry, innovation, and infrastructure	8	12
10. Reduced inequalities	10	11
11. Sustainable cities and communities	10	15
12. Responsible consumption and production	11	13
13. Climate action	5	7
14. Life below water	10	10
15. Life on land	12	14
16. Peace, justice, and strong institutions	12	23
17. Partnerships for the goals	19	25
Total	169	232

a The table includes the number of SDGs and targets mentioned in the text, and also the number of indicators per SDG. In the calculation of the total number of indicators, we have excluded duplicate targets that appear under more than one goal.

these 17 goals and the number of targets and indicators for each of them) that are to be realized by 2030. The quantitative and qualitative objectives which cover the social, economic, and environmental dimensions of sustainable development have also been categorized into five categories (the five Ps): people, planet, prosperity, peace, and partnership. Although the latter category is also an aim of the SDGs, partnership is at the same time the all-encompassing collaborative approach adopted throughout the process to achieve and implement what has been called "the plan for action" (UN 2015, p. 1). This fifth P remains in that sense somewhat ambiguous.

The SDGs have received much interest among policymakers and stakeholders and a range of researchers, thus far mostly those specialized in development studies and sustainability sciences. In a recent review, Kourula, Pisani, and Kolk (2017) explore how international business, management, and business and society literatures have addressed the 17 SDGs most recently. Overall, studies have focused on environmental and labor issues, with much less emphasis on human well-being and empowerment. Some SDGs (particularly SDGs 3, 4, 5, 6, 11, 14, 15, and 16) have received limited attention within this field. In another recent review article, Kolk, Kourula, and Pisani (2017) zoomed in on key themes, providing an overview of how particular SDGs, namely poverty and inequality, energy and climate change, and peace, have been addressed in IB scholarship in the past decade. The analysis suggests that poverty and inequality, as well as peace, have been underexamined. Remarkably, their search for articles related to peace and (post)conflict yielded results on conflict and terrorism, but not on peace, which thus seems a crucial gap. Although a multidisciplinary body of work on "business for peace" or "peace through commerce" has been emerging outside of IB, this deserves further attention within the field.

These reviews thus identify key gaps and also offer suggestions for interdisciplinary approaches to tackle them. Ultimately, much critical research is still necessary to understand the interconnectedness between SDGs and targets, and more importantly, of the SDGs and their systemic impacts. In addition to a need to investigate these interrelationships, it is crucial to discover the determinants affecting one or more specific SDGs. Interestingly, such an approach may provide insights that can subsequently be utilized and extended to better understand other SDGs as well, either similarities or differences in terms of drivers and consequences. In a recent review article, Kolk, Rivera-Santos, and Rufin (2018) present findings from business, economics, and policy, developing a cross-disciplinary framework to disentangle business, country, and industry effects influencing poverty alleviation (see Figure 11.3).

Several things are valuable for transferring to other SDGs. One is the multifaceted nature of many of the issues, be it one SDG or even sometimes one target. In this case, Kolk, Rivera-Santos and Rufin (2018) focus on absolute poverty and already distinguish, following World Bank definitions, five dimensions of that construct. Furthermore, they note that it is important to distinguish those type of activities that are typically and inherently part of pro-poor, CSR, or related types of trade and investment activities ("responsible globalization"),

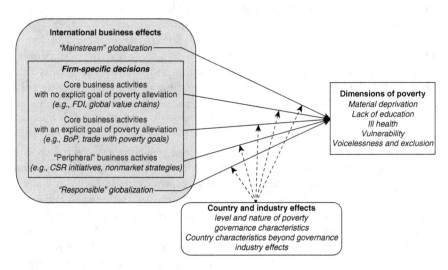

Figure 11.3 Modeling the links between international business, MNEs, and poverty
Source: Kolk et al. (2018), p. 98.

for example, fair trade or social entrepreneurship. Furthermore, "mainstream" globalization entails core activities with or without the explicit goal of, in this case, poverty alleviation, and what are called "peripheral" activities (or non-core), which are not inherently related to core business functions but are part of separate philanthropy, corporate citizenship, or social responsibility policies. In the next section, we present further frameworks based on a similar categorization of core business with a specific SDG goal, core business activities without such a goal, and peripheral business activities to guide research and practice.

Frameworks for SDGs in research and practice, and an application

Figure 11.4 presents a framework that can be used to guide further research on international business and the SDGs, distinguishing between different types of business activities (explained in the previous section), and including key dimensions of MNEs, that is, the "parent" firm, on the one hand, and their relationships with local entities in the developing country of activity, on the other. It also includes the links to the people, planet, peace, and prosperity categories discussed in the previous section.

After providing our assessment of the state of IB research on CSR and development and possible frameworks that can be used for further investigation, we now, lastly, turn to exploring how companies can participate in development. Figure 11.5 provides a practically oriented overview of a process that different types of organizations may use to engage with the SDGs. Step 1 consists

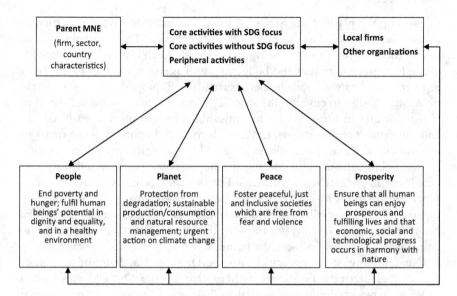

Figure 11.4 Framework for analyzing MNEs' impact on sustainable development

Source: Adapted from Kolk (2016), Kolk et al. (2017, 2018)

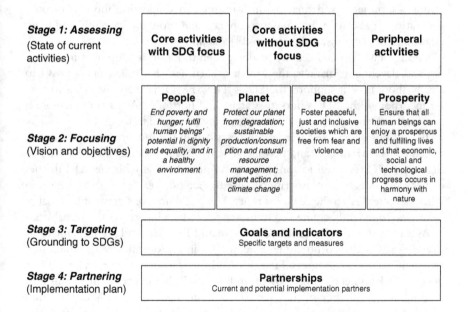

Figure 11.5 An engagement framework for SDGs

Sources: Adapted from Kolk (2016); Kolk et al. (2017); Kolk et al. (2018)

of assessing the place of the SDGs in general, or individual ones in particular, in the overall set of the activities of the organization. This can help to provide a good insight into the relative importance, which may help to assign, for example, concomitant staff and budgets, as well as streamline communications to internal and external stakeholders, particularly to properly manage expectations. Step 2 helps to envision the specific "P" on which to focus, and the third step fine-tunes in terms of the identification of more specific goals, targets, and indicators for measurement. Although focus is important, it is crucial to remember the interconnectedness of the SDGs and that promoting specific goals should not be used to hide negative impacts on other goals. The final step entails the implementation with regard to the need or desire to reach out to other organizations to help realize the best engagement strategy. It should be noted that all of this will be very organization-specific and depend on history, characteristics, and contexts (see the seventh section). Next, we will discuss one company case to illustrate how the framework may be applied in practice.

Our illustrative case concerns FMO, the Development Bank of the Netherlands ("Nederlandse Financierings-Maatschappij voor Ontwikkelingslanden N.V.," or as put on the front page of their 2017 annual report, "Entrepreneurial Development Bank"). It is owned 51 percent by the Dutch state and 42 percent by Dutch private banks, with small shares owned by other groups. FMO aims to make a positive difference in emerging economies by empowering entrepreneurs to build a better world. FMO does this by investing in emerging market businesses, projects, and financial institutions and supporting job and income generation. It also helps businesses to operate and grow transparently and in an environmentally and socially responsible manner.

Though FMO's main activity has long been to foster development in emerging and developing markets, the Dutch government has called upon FMO to clearly show how it supports the SDGs. Thus, FMO has been working to better incorporate the SDGs into its strategy and portfolios. As its core purpose is development, and all its activities can generally be related to themes of the SDGs, FMO did not undertake the first step described in the model earlier of assessing which of its current core and peripheral activities are relevant to the SDGs. The first step FMO took was to connect its mission and vision with the SDG themes of people, planet, and prosperity. Similar to our note earlier regarding gaps in scholarship related to the SDG for peace, FMO did not consider that the goal of peace was sufficiently connected to its strategy to be addressed at this initial stage.

As a next step FMO identified three main SDGs particularly relevant to its overall goals at the corporate level, as well as indicators and measurements by which it can assess progress. First, FMO directly contributes toward SDG 8, decent work and economic growth, and sets itself the objective under this goal to double the number of jobs supported by its investments. FMO also finds that SDG 10, reduced inequalities, is highly relevant to its development activities and will seek to increase its investments labeled as reducing inequality to achieve this goal. Finally, FMO focuses on SDG 13, climate action, as related to its core business, particularly its investments in renewable energy. FMO will measure its progress toward SDG 13 by measuring the amount of greenhouse gas avoided as a result of its investments and increasing the share of its green investments (under its green label).

FMO also works to identify SDGs that are relevant to its sector portfolios. As FMO has a significant amount of investments in the agribusiness value chain, SDG 2 for no hunger is highly relevant. Given its significant investments in renewable energy and energy efficiency, FMO identifies SDG 7 for affordable and clean energy as another significant goal. FMO also focuses on SDG 5 for gender equality, through a variety of investments, such as those that promote capacity development for women-owned businesses. Finally, as much of its investing is through blended structures joined by other financing parties, there is a natural connection to SDG 17, partnerships. Figure 11.6 details how

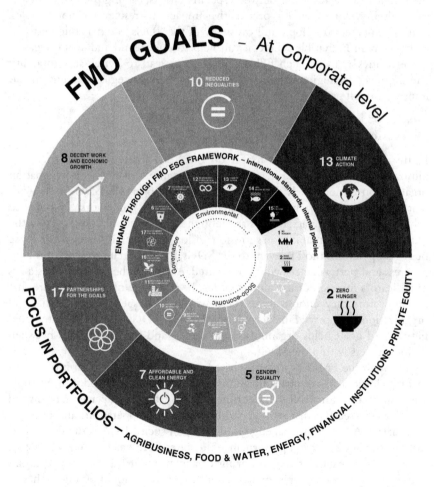

Figure 11.6 FMO goals

Source: FMO (2017), p. 16

FMO has envisioned its strategy related to the goals. In order to ensure that the company makes progress toward these goals, it identifies specific targets and ambitions in order to be able to measure its achievements.

FMO has made great progress in linking its vision and strategy to the SDGs and finding ways to measure implementation. However, one limitation inherent to drilling so deep into specific goals makes it difficult to see the SDGs as a systemic and interactive network, with overarching synergies and tensions between the goals. FMO maintains attention to the SDG trade-offs and synergies by listing all the SDGs in the inner circle of Figure 11.6 and includes them in environment, social, and governance (ESG) management. Understanding the interconnectedness between the SDG targets can help see how progress (or regression) on one target can have spillover effects on other targets. Further, there can be feedback loops between specific targets, leading positive feedback to result in virtuous circles, or negative impacts to result in vicious circles. When companies develop a full overview of the SDGs as a dynamic network making up an indivisible whole, it can help to understand and avoid negative "externalities." Finally, such fuller planning can lead to better accountability and improved strategic planning to point out where strategic intervention can improve overall progress.

Discussion and conclusions

In this final section, we first reflect on the SDG framework presented and illustrated with the case earlier. Overall, the example of FMO shows that an organization is more likely to be proactive in promoting the SDGs in its work if it follows an approach demonstrated in the SDG framework. In order to achieve the fullest impact, leaders at the highest level should consider how the SDGs fit into the organization's mission, vision, and overall strategy. For those business operations most relevant to the SDGs, it is important to work out how progress and performance will be measured. Although the UN provides a list of indicators for each of the targets under the goals, the firm must ensure that the indicators they choose make sense within their specific operational and organizational contexts. Finally, understanding the SDGs as a wholly integrated network of goals helps organizations to understand the interactions between various targets within the SDGs.

Although the FMO is primarily based in the Netherlands with investments in firms located in countries throughout the developing world, this example seems illustrative for MNEs (and/or the specific category of partly state-owned enterprises – see the first section) with international operations and multiple subsidiaries. A common challenge in the case of such MNEs is the dissemination of strategic goals and performance measures from headquarters to foreign subsidiaries, as well as the monitoring of achievements in different locations and bringing them together in a coherent manner. It should be noted that, as development bank, FMO typically has core activities with SDG focus (the first category in the box in the upper middle of Figure 11.4), which may be very different for other trade- or investment-oriented firms. Still, for them as well, and even in the case of "peripheral," CSR-oriented SDG activities, it is key to clearly assess beforehand which SDGs are most relevant and go through the focusing, targeting, and partnering steps included in Figure 11.5.

As mentioned earlier, the debate on business and development seems to show a certain tendency to be fully channeled, or some might say, "narrowed down" to the SDGs. This may, for example, give rise to research focusing on which SDGs are adopted most or least often by firms, as reported or perceived by these firms themselves, based on corporate communications or surveys (cf. Van Zanten and Van Tulder 2018). Although valuable as such, resulting debates might merely concentrate on the self-perceived activities or intentions of firms and/or shaped by them. Importantly, although the SDGs are very broad and comprehensive, there is more to development than how they are framed in this UN-led initiative, as valuable as it is. More critical notions related to, for example, empowerment or inclusiveness (cf. Pouw and Gupta 2017) can easily be forgotten if one exclusively focuses on the SDGs.

In addition, it is crucial to take firm characteristics peculiar to IB that operates across borders into account (see Figure 11.4, left-hand box). IB scholarship has much to offer to explicate drivers and better understand the why and how of firm behavior and consequences, and thus also how these can be influenced by policymakers and other stakeholders, as well as industry dynamics. As noted earlier in this chapter, review studies have concluded that a research agenda on sustainable development is emerging in IB, which can contribute many insights at the firm level as well as the impacts of firms on their environment. At the same time, as shown in the first half of this chapter, the field has its limitations, with several "blind spots," despite all its contributions. We want to mention at least three of them here, which are related to lack of geographical scope, selective attention to topics, and limited interdisciplinarity.

Blind spot 1: Dearth of research on least developed and fragile countries.

Blind spot 2: Too much focus on specific topics, at the cost of other topics and systemic impacts.

Blind spot 3: Too limited interaction across disciplines.

First, as Figures 11.1 and 11.2 indicate, the focus of research has been on developed countries with only a recent increase in studies examining emerging countries. In terms of the latter, most of the literature in IB is on a rather small subset of high-growth emerging countries. The context of developing countries receives scarce attention in comparison. This opens a new research agenda for IB on least developed and fragile countries. IB scholars are especially well positioned to address this call for research due to extensive cross-national expertise and an in-depth understanding of corporate impacts, both direct positive and negative, as well as indirect spillovers.

Second, as is clear from our literature review and the thematic analysis of Table 11.3, the focus of business in development research tends to be on particular themes or SDGs, such as poverty, responsible consumption and production, climate action, and partnerships (Kolk, Kourula, and Pisani, 2017; Kolk, Rivera-Santos, and Rufin, 2018; Kourula, Pisani and Kolk, 2017). This means that a spotlight effect makes a handful of themes receive much of the attention, while other important and interconnected topics receive little attention from IB scholars. In addition, the spotlight effect also makes it more difficult to identify the interconnectedness between themes and sustainable development goals and the systemic impacts. Both our thematic analysis and illustrative case provide insights into how we could understand and manage these systemic impacts.

Finally, as our analysis of IB and SDGs implies and as Kolk, Kourula, and Pisani (2017) and Kourula, Pisani, and Kolk (2017) point out, there are many unused opportunities to gain insights and inspiration from other disciplines beyond business studies. Development studies, political science, and environmental/sustainability science, among other fields, are particularly interesting as complementary or even contradictory perspectives to business studies. Although environmental/sustainability sciences are particularly well suited to support SDGs related to the biosphere (life on land, life below water, clean water and sanitation, and climate action), political science, development studies, economics, engineering, and medical sciences often tackle societal SDGs (poverty, sustainable cities, peace, clean energy, health, education, gender, and hunger). IB and other business scholars' insights are particularly relevant to and can lead the way in exploring economic goals (decent work and economic growth, industry innovation and infrastructure, reduced inequalities, and responsible consumption and production). Nonetheless, all biosphere and societal goals also include elements where international business studies can offer rigorous analysis and perceptive theorizing. For instance, it would be good, as shown by Kolk and Rivera-Santos (2018) and Kolk, Rivera-Santos and Rufin (2018), to also consider macro-level insights from economics and especially their empirical approaches. By combining levels of analysis, these multiple fields can achieve a better picture of the role of business in development and its positive and negative impacts.

Notes

1 An extensive treatment of definitions is beyond the scope of this chapter; it has also received ample scholarly attention already. For our purposes, we follow a broad approach popularized by the Brundland commission in which the social, economic, political, technological, and cultural aspects of societal change and human "progress" are judged on their ability to meet "the needs of the present without compromising the ability of future generations to meet their own needs" (WCED 1987, p. 43). Often specified as sustainable development, it takes the three dimensions of environmental integrity, social equity, and economic prosperity into account and notes that: "Two conditions must be satisfied before

international economic exchanges can become beneficial for all involved. The sustainability of ecosystems on which the global economy depends must be guaranteed. And the economic partners must be satisfied that the basis of exchange is equitable" (WCED 1987, p. 67).

2 See the special issue of *Transnational Corporations* published in 2017, available at <http:// unctad.org/en/PublicationsLibrary/diaeia2017d4_en.pdf>, and forthcoming special issues of *Journal of International Business Policy*, resulting from a call for papers launched in the second half of 2018, and a more generic, not international business focused one per se, of *Academy of Management Discoveries*.

3 Although IB most often focuses on profit-making entities (firms/companies) active in more than one country, it never excluded state-owned enterprises (SOEs), which are partly or sometimes even fully owned by governments and operate in sectors or areas in which for-profit organizations are (or could have been) playing a role; in recent years, attention for SOEs has grown further in the international business and management literature.

4 Pisani et al. (2017) included journals widely considered to be the leading publishers in three distinct subcategories to secure the comprehensiveness of their coverage of high-quality research focused on international CSR. For the first subcategory – generic management journals – they considered *Administrative Science Quarterly, Academy of Management Journal, Academy of Management Review, Human Relations, Journal of Applied Psychology, Journal of Management, Journal of Management Studies, Journal of Occupational and Organizational Psychology, Journal of Organizational Behavior, Management Science, Organizational Behavior and Human Decision Processes, Organization Science, Organization Studies, Personnel Psychology*, and *Strategic Management Journal*. For the second subcategory – specialized CSR journals – they included *Business & Society, Business Ethics Quarterly, Business Ethics: A European Review, Business, Strategy and the Environment, Corporate Governance: An International Review, Corporate Social Responsibility and Environmental Management, Journal of Business Ethics*, and *Organization & Environment*. For the third subcategory – specialized IB journals – they considered *Global Strategy Journal, International Business Review, International Marketing Review, Journal of International Business Studies, Journal of International Management, Journal of International Marketing, Journal of World Business*, and *Management International Review*.

5 Pisani et al. (2017, p. 591) follow Aguinis's definition for CSR, comprising "context-specific organizational actions and policies that take into account stakeholders' expectations and the triple bottom line of economic, social, and environmental performance." Their keywords include these three dimensions as well, thus also covering what Bansal (2005) named "corporate sustainable development," a translation of the social equity, environmental integrity, and economic prosperity notions of the Brundtland commission to the business realm. Interestingly, she finds international experience, a typical IB feature, to be important for enabling such an application of generic sustainable development to corporate reality.

References

Adegbite, Emmanuel, Kenneth Amaeshi, and Chizu Nakajima (2013), "Multiple Influences on Corporate Governance Practice in Nigeria: Agents, Strategies and Implications," *International Business Review*, 22 (3), 524–538.

Aguinis, Herman, and Ante Glavas (2012), "What We Know and Don't Know About Corporate Social Responsibility: A Review and Research Agenda," *Journal of Management*, 38 (4), 932–968.

Banerjee, Subhabrata B. (2014), "A Critical Perspective on Corporate Social Responsibility: Towards a Global Governance Framework," *Critical Perspectives on International Business*, 10 (1–2), 84–95.

Bansal, Pratima (2005), "Evolving Sustainably: A Longitudinal Study of Corporate Sustainable Development," *Strategic Management Journal*, 26 (3), 197–218.

Belal, Ataur R., and Robin W. Roberts (2010), "Stakeholders' Perceptions of Corporate Social Reporting in Bangladesh," *Journal of Business Ethics*, 97 (2), 311–324.

Christmann, Petra, and Glen Taylor (2006), "Firm Self-Regulation Through International Certifiable Standards: Determinants of Symbolic Versus Substantive Implementation," *Journal of International Business Studies*, 37 (6), 863–878.

Doh, Jonathan P., and Rafael Lucea (2013), "So Close Yet So Far: Integrating Global Strategy and Nonmarket Research," *Global Strategy Journal*, 3, 171–194.

Driffield, Nigel, Chris Jones, and Jo Crotty (2013), "International Business Research and Risky Investments, an Analysis of FDI in Conflict Zones," *International Business Review*, 22 (1), 140–155.

Egri, Carolyn P., and David A. Ralston (2008), "Corporate Responsibility: A Review of International Management Research from 1998 to 2007," *Journal of International Management*, 14 (4), 319–339.

FMO (2017). *Annual Report 2017: Investing in Local Prosperity*. The Hague, The Netherlands.

Fong, Cher-Min, Chung-Ling Lee, and Yunzhou Du (2013), "Target Reputation Transferability, Consumer Animosity, and Cross-Border Acquisition Success: A Comparison Between China and Taiwan," *International Business Review*, 22 (1), 174–186.

Fortanier, Fabienne, and Ans Kolk (2007), "On the Economic Dimensions of CSR: Exploring Fortune Global 250 Reports," *Business and Society*, 46 (4), 457–478.

Frynas, Jędrzej George, and Camila Yamahaki (2016), "Corporate Social Responsibility: Review and Roadmap of Theoretical Perspectives," *Business Ethics: A European Review*, 25 (3), 258–285.

Gifford, Blair, Andrew Kestler, and Sharmila Anand (2010), "Building Local Legitimacy into Corporate Social Responsibility: Gold Mining Firms in Developing Nations," *Journal of World Business*, 45 (3), 304–311.

Holtbrügge, Dirk, and Corinna Dögl (2012), "How International Is Corporate Environmental Responsibility? A Literature Review," *Journal of International Management*, 18 (2), 180–195.

Husted, Bryan W., and David B. Allen, (2009), "Strategic Corporate Social Responsibility and Value Creation," *Management International Review*, 49 (6), 781–799.

Jamali, Dima, and Charlotte Karam (2016), "Corporate Social Responsibility in Developing Countries as an Emerging Field of Study," *International Journal of Management Reviews*, 20 (1), 32–61.

Jamali, Dima, Charlotte Karam, Juelin Yin, and Vivek Soundararajan (2017), "CSR Logics in Developing Countries: Translation, Adaptation and Stalled Development," *Journal of World Business*, 52(3), 343–359.

Jamali, Dima, and Tamar Keshishian (2009), "Uneasy Alliances: Lessons Learned from Partnerships Between Businesses and NGOs in the Context of CSR," *Journal of Business Ethics*, 84 (2), 277–295.

Jamali, Dima, and Ben Neville (2011), "Convergence versus Divergence of CSR in Developing Countries: An Embedded Multi-Layered Institutional Lens," *Journal of Business Ethics*, 102 (4), 599–621.

Khan, Farzad R., Robert Westwood, and David M. Boje (2010), "'I Feel Like a Foreign Agent': NGOs and Corporate Social Responsibility Interventions into Third World Child Labor," *Human Relations*, 63 (9), 1417–1438.

Khan, Zaheer, and John D. Nicholson (2014), "An Investigation of the Cross-Border Supplier Development Process: Problems and Implications in an Emerging Economy," *International Business Review*, 23 (6), 1212–1222.

Kolk, Ans (2016), "The Social Responsibility of International Business: From Ethics and the Environment to CSR and Sustainable Development," *Journal of World Business*, 51 (1), 23–34.

Kolk, Ans, Pan Hong, and Willemijn Van Dolen (2010), "Corporate Social Responsibility in China: An Analysis of Domestic and Foreign Retailers' Sustainability Dimensions," *Business Strategy and the Environment*, 19 (5), 289–303.

Kolk, Ans, Arno Kourula, and Niccolò Pisani (2017), "Multinational Corporations and the Sustainable Development Goals: Perspectives on a Collaborative Agenda," *Transnational Corporations*, 24 (3), 9–32.

Kolk, Ans, and François Lenfant (2010), "MNC Reporting on CSR and Conflict in Central Africa," *Journal of Business Ethics*, 93, 241–255.

Kolk, Ans, and Miguel Rivera-Santos (2018), "The State of Research on Africa in Business and Management: Insights from a Systematic Review of Key International Journals," *Business & Society*, 57 (3), 415–436.

Kolk, Ans, Miguel Rivera-Santos, and Carlos Rufin (2018), "Multinationals, International Business, And Poverty: A Cross-Disciplinary Research Overview and Conceptual Framework," *Journal of International Business Policy*, 1 (1), 92–115.

Kolk, Ans, and Rob Van Tulder (2010), "International Business, Corporate Social Responsibility and Sustainable Development," *International Business Review*, 19 (2), 119–125.

Kourula, Arno, Niccolò Pisani, and Ans Kolk (2017), "Corporate Sustainability and Inclusive Development: Highlights from International Business and Management Research," *Current Opinion in Environmental Sustainability*, 24 (1), 14–18.

Lim, Suk-Jun, and Joe Phillips (2008), "Embedding CSR Values: The Global Footwear Industry's Evolving Governance Structure," *Journal of Business Ethics*, 81 (1), 143–156.

Luo, Yadong (2006), "Political Behavior, Social Responsibility, and Perceived Corruption: A Structuration Perspective," *Journal of International Business Studies*, 37 (6), 747–766.

Maruyama, Masayoshi, and Lihui Wu (2015), "Overcoming the Liability of Foreignness in International Retailing: A Consumer Perspective," *Journal of International Management*, 21 (3), 200–210.

Mena, Sébastien, Marieke de Leede, Dorothée Baumann, Nicky Black, Sara Lindeman, and Lindsay McShane (2010), "Advancing the Business and Human Rights Agenda: Dialogue, Empowerment, and Constructive Engagement," *Journal of Business Ethics*, 93 (1), 161–188.

Mijatovic, Ivana S., and Dusan Stokic (2010), "The Influence of Internal and External Codes on CSR Practice: The Case of Companies Operating in Serbia," *Journal of Business Ethics*, 94 (4), 533–552.

Muller, Alan, and Ans Kolk (2010), "Extrinsic and Intrinsic Drivers of Corporate Social Performance: Evidence from Foreign and Domestic Firms in Mexico," *Journal of Management Studies*, 47 (1), 1–26.

Muthuri, Judy N., and Victoria Gilbert (2011), "An Institutional Analysis of Corporate Social Responsibility in Kenya," *Journal of Business Ethics*, 98 (3), 467–483.

Mzembe, Andrew N., and Julia Meaton (2014), "Driving Corporate Social Responsibility in the Malawian Mining Industry: A Stakeholder Perspective," *Corporate Social Responsibility and Environmental Management*, 21 (4), 189–201.

Newenham-Kahindi, Aloysius M. (2011), "A Global Mining Corporation and Local Communities in the Lake Victoria Zone: The Case of Barrick Gold Multinational in Tanzania," *Journal of Business Ethics*, 99 (2), 253–282.

Nurunnabi, Mohammad (2015), "Tensions Between Politico-Institutional Factors and Accounting Regulation in a Developing Economy: Insights from Institutional Theory," *Business Ethics: A European Review*, 24 (4), 398–424.

Perez-Batres, Luis A., Van V. Miller, Micheal J. Pisani, Irene Henriques, and Jose A. Renau-Sepulveda (2012), "Why Do Firms Engage in National Sustainability Programs and

Transparent Sustainability Reporting? Evidence from Mexico's Clean Industry Program," *Management International Review*, 52 (1), 107–136.

Perry, Patsy, Steve Wood, and John Fernie (2015), "Corporate Social Responsibility in Garment Sourcing Networks: Factory Management Perspectives on Ethical Trade in Sri Lanka," *Journal of Business Ethics*, 130 (3), 737–752.

Pisani, Niccolò, Arno Kourula, Ans Kolk, and Renske Meijer (2017), "How Global Is International CSR Research? Insights and Recommendations from a Systematic Review," *Journal of World Business*, 52 (5), 591–614.

Pouw, Nicky, and Joyeeta Gupta (2017), "Inclusive Development: A Multi-Disciplinary Approach," *Current Opinion in Environmental Sustainability*, 24, 104–108.

Reimann, Felix, Johan Rauer, and Lutz Kaufmann (2015), "MNE Subsidiaries' Strategic Commitment to CSR in Emerging Economies: The Role of Administrative Distance, Subsidiary Size, and Experience in the Host Country," *Journal of Business Ethics*, 132 (4), 845–857.

Robertson, Diana C. (2009), "Corporate Social Responsibility and Different Stages of Economic Development: Singapore, Turkey, and Ethiopia," *Journal of Business Ethics*, 88, 617–633.

Rotter, Julia P., Peppi-Emilia Airike, and Cecilia Mark-Herbert (2014), "Exploring Political Corporate Social Responsibility in Global Supply Chains," *Journal of Business Ethics*, 125 (4), 581–599.

Ruggie, John Gerard (2017), "Multinationals as a Global Institution: Power, Authority and Relative Autonomy," *Regulation & Governance*, doi 10.1111/rego.12154.

Tan, Justin (2009), "Institutional Structure and Firm Social Performance in Transitional Economies: Evidence of Multinational Corporations in China," *Journal of Business Ethics*, 86, 171–189.

Tatoglu, Ekrem, Erkan Bayraktar, Sunil Sahadev, Mehmet Demirbag, and Keith W. Glaister (2014), "Determinants of Voluntary Environmental Management Practices by MNE Subsidiaries," *Journal of World Business*, 49 (4), 536–548.

United Nations (2015), *Resolution Adopted by the General Assembly on 25 September 2015*. A/RES/70/1, United Nations. https://sustainabledevelopment.un.org/post2015/transformingourworld.

Van Zanten, Jan A., and Rob Van Tulder (2018), "Multinational Enterprises and the Sustainable Development Goals: An Institutional Approach to Corporate Engagement," *Journal of International Business Policy*, 1(3–4), 208–233.

Wadham, Helen, and Richard Warren (2013), "Inspiring Action, Building Understanding: How Cross-Sector Partnership Engages Business in Addressing Global Challenges," *Business Ethics: A European Review*, 22 (1), 47–63.

Wettstein, Florian (2012), "Silence as Complicity: Elements of a Corporate Duty to Speak Out Against the Violation of Human Rights," *Business Ethics Quarterly*, 22 (1), 37–61.

Wiig, Arne, and Ivar Kolstad (2010), "Multinational Corporations and Host Country Institutions: A Case Study of CSR Activities in Angola," *International Business Review*, 19 (2), 178–190.

World Commission on Environment and Development. (1987), *Report of the World Commission on Environment and Development: Our Common Future*. World Commission on Environment and Development.

Xun, Jiyao (2013), "Corporate Social Responsibility in China: A Preferential Stakeholder Model and Effects," *Business Strategy and the Environment*, 22 (7), 471–483.

Yu, Xiaomin (2009), "From Passive Beneficiary to Active Stakeholder: Workers' Participation in CSR Movement Against Labor Abuses," *Journal of Business Ethics*, 87, 233–249.

Zeng, Fue, Ji Li, Hong Zhu, Zhenyao Cai, and Pengcheng Li (2013), "How International Firms Conduct Societal Marketing in Emerging Markets," *Management International Review*, 53 (6), 841–868.

Zhao, Meng, Justin Tan, and Seung Ho Park (2014), "From Voids to Sophistication: Institutional Environment and MNC CSR Crisis in Emerging Markets," *Journal of Business Ethics*, 122 (4), 655–674.

12 Corporate social responsibility and development

The case of international business firms in emerging economies

Dima Jamali, Georges Samara, and Mohamad Hossary

Introduction

Corporate social responsibility (CSR) has caught traction in recent years, and the increased interest in the topic is evident through the changing business CSR arena and the explosion of written content on CSR in books, journals, reports, and published works by scholars, researchers, managers, and practitioners. The European Commission defines CSR as the voluntary actions taken by the company to integrate social and environmental challenges with core business strategies, operations, and interactions (Commission of the European Communities, 2002), and the World Economic Forum (WEF, 2002) defines CSR as the contribution a company generates towards society through its core business activities, philanthropic investments, social investments, and public policy engagements. Through this paradigm, a company is considered a member of society, and the relationships formed by the management with society, environment, economy, and all other internal and external stakeholders are essential to its involvement in socially responsible business practices and sustainable development (WEF, 2002).

CSR first originated in regard to a professional understanding in Western contexts, and therefore in its nature, it carries Western connotations, understandings, and practices. This western-based outlook on CSR is referred to as Western assumptive logics, as evident in mainstream business literature that researches, analyzes, and discusses CSR. However, this understanding or outlook on CSR varies greatly as it is transferred to other parts of the world; each country will result in nuanced expressions of CSR and a unique local CSR arena. Therefore, its logics are not static entities, but are dependent on the local contexts and systems of meaning in which concepts are understood and practiced. The aim of this chapter is to understand the degree, efficiency, and scope of the impact of CSR activities on sustainable development, particularly in developing countries.

Country categorization schemes are not a science, and although they make analysis easier, they carry a set of limitations and biases; this is especially true with a two-dimensional categorization of the world. Development categorization is based on income classification; the World Bank has used low, lower-middle, upper-middle, and high income groups, where the high-income group is called the developed world and the other three categories are clumped under the umbrella term developing countries (World Bank, 2015). The term "developing countries" is misleading, as the world no longer conforms to a dichotomous split in country categorization between the North and the South. The scale of development of the world is fluctuating, and countries categorized as developing are usually not comparable to each other and are completely heterogeneous. The World Bank even stopped using the term developing countries in its categorization frameworks since the "2016 World Development Indicators" publication that no longer distinguishes between developing and developed nations; instead, they opt for geographical categorization such as East Asia, Central Asia, Europe, North America, etc. (World Bank, 2016). Hence, a more appropriate representation for development would be a continuum, where the lowest group is labeled as a frontier market, the middle group is labeled as an emerging market, and the top group is referred to as developed markets (M.C.S.I (2014)). This classification improves on the older model by providing a more representative nomenclature and thus a better tool for analysis.

Development frameworks are themselves changing and are now focused on development contributions in every single nation, rather than on developing countries. The United Nations (UN) development agenda has switched from Millennium Development Goals (MDGs) to Sustainable Development Goals (SDGs) (United Nations, 2015). The outdated development categorization was more relevant with the MDGs, as MDG goals 1 to 7 were relevant for the developing world and MDG goal 8 was relevant to developed nations. The 17 SDGs for the period 2016–2030 include 169 targets that marked a changing scope and ambition for development in the world, altered the global discourse and debate about development, and set new standards for progressing development policies and practices. Although the need to promote inclusive development for the less developed nations is still needed, the applicability of the new goals set by the UN General Assembly in 2015 is universal and has reformed the development dialogue, as now every country is accountable and responsible for the defined development targets. All regions are required to cooperate and enhance partnerships to aid the achievement of inclusive sustainable development; this entails the cooperation of private sector, states, and civil societies, as they all are responsible for setting a route for a sustainable future. Therefore, a development-oriented CSR agenda ought to conform to the SDGs set forth by the UN for a sustainable future, making developmental CSR relevant and applicable in all countries and following global goals while focusing on local challenges and contexts. Keeping this in mind and the heterogeneity of developing contexts, we will focus on emerging economies in regard to our CSR analysis, where the development of the CSR concept is transformed and adapted to the non-Western frameworks. In analyzing the targets of CSR strategies, the SDGs will act as a framework of efficiency analysis for the CSR activities and outcomes.

International firms are in a strong position to contribute greatly in achieving a sustainable future, as they are considered a source of wealth to local communities and economies. Their harmful practices substantially add to the negative externalities on people and the environment, hindering the attainment of a sustainable and inclusive future. The role of the private sector allows for specific strengths in its contribution to the SDGs, including research and development, innovation, responsiveness, and providing efficient delivery of services. The UN Global Compact released a white paper in 2014 discussing the role of business in supporting the 2030 Agenda; in it, they draw attention to the significance of the private-sector contribution in the achievement of the development goals and the importance of the SDGs in ensuring a long-term success for businesses (UN Global Compact, 2014). This chapter will discuss the merger of CSR strategies of corporations with the SDGs and the pathways that need to be built by businesses to reach sustainable development. The current state of multinational corporations' (MNC) strategies for CSR in emerging economies will be analyzed in three countries, namely India, Nigeria, and Lebanon; to infer on the intent and outcomes of CSR activities of international firms in emerging economies.

Literature review

Many theoretical frameworks have been used to explain the concept of CSR; these include a resource-based view, resource dependence theory, institutional theory, agency theory, legitimacy theory, and stakeholder theory (Frynas & Yamahaki, 2016). Carroll (1991) also defines a theoretical concept of CSR in the CSR pyramid; it includes economic, legal, ethical, and philanthropic paradigms that are defined through four main categories constituting wealth maximization, policy and regulations, ethical decision making, and social welfare. Corporations usually start their CSR activities and practices in response to public criticism regarding harmful practices to society and the environment, and by following these four paradigms, the strategies may become integrated with core business practices and aimed at aiding local development. The UN Global Compact provides a multifaceted view on CSR with an orientation towards sustainability through financial, environmental, ethical, and social standards. There is a minimum responsibility for businesses to respect universal standards, and additionally support them. Respect for universal standards means that firms ought not to cause any kind of harm to society and the environment (for example, reducing human rights violations, ecosystem degradation, and pollution); these are outlined through the triple bottom line, ISO 14000, and UN Global Compact; additionally they can supportively aid the achievement of sustainable development goals, and this can be done through "their core business, philanthropy, collective action, and public policy advocacy" (UN Global Compact, 2014, p. 3). However, the supportive action of firms is not a substitute for respecting universal standards. Philanthropic activities are no longer sufficient for corporations to partake in; they must initially integrate social and environmental challenges into their core business operations and strategies and avoid any harmful impacts.

CSR in emerging economy contexts is a growing field of interest geared by public pressure, the role of media, international treaties, governmental regulations, and market competition (Raimi, Yekini, & Adelopo, 2015). Research on CSR has been mainly focused on the nature and perceptions of CSR rather than its tangible developmental outcomes and impact on local communities (Windsor, 2015). Through analyzing the results of CSR activities in emerging economies, inferences can be made on whether businesses in this context act as effective developmental agents. CSR in this sense becomes a political tool that is used by corporations to participate in developmental change and complement the role of states, specifically in emerging economies contexts characterized by institutional voids where corruption, unemployment, lack of inclusiveness, and bad governance are generally salient. Political CSR is a growing concept fueled by "globalization pressure, a need for inclusiveness in governance, socio-political risk management and pervasive infrastructural deficits in developing nations" (Raimi et al., 2015, p. 31). Through political CSR, roles that are conventionally assigned to governmental bodies are now also part of the social responsibilities of business actors or civil society groups.

MNCs are one of the most powerful social constructs of the time and have the potential to contribute greatly to the development goals in emerging economies where they operate and, through that, perform or complement the role of governments. Specifically in these contexts, MNCs sometimes report annual revenues that are substantially higher than a country's gross domestic product (GDP) where they operate; in emerging economies MNCs have the prospective to participate in public goods issues and global regulations, ultimately shifting the local geopolitical and economic affairs (Jamali, 2010). Therefore, expectations for social contributions from MNCs are high, particularly when operating in emerging or low-income economy contexts where they are considered a source of finance and can have substantial developmental influences (Barsoum & Refaat, 2015).

Globalization is an unstoppable dynamism, constantly driving the discourse on political CSR forward, and it has been used by international firms to go beyond the business domain of activities and create change and transformations in institutions, ethics, and practices of local economies. MNCs are not individual corporations but are formed with complex structures of separate entities and processes. Each MNC subsidiary has its individual strategies and a specific framework of operation, and the collective complex of all these units make up the transnational structure of international business firms (Jamali, 2010); this assembly makes CSR analysis of MNC subsidiaries a challenging task. The political activity of MNCs in their developmental CSR strategies complements the role of the state in social development. Governance is an essential aspect of development, and to serve as an effective development actor, corporations should act to bridge governance gaps where they operate. Raimi et al. (2015) assert that business actors ought to bridge governance gaps where they exist as part of their developmental CSR agenda, and civil society actors ought to act as pressure groups to lobby corporations to get involved in socioeconomic affairs.

However, through business–society literature, MNCs have been criticized for having a "global legal vacuum," a phenomenon that entails accountability and distortion of governance issues in emerging economy contexts (Jamali, 2010). The literature also points that MNC subsidiaries tend to cherry-pick only those social activities that serve their own interests, such as activities pertaining to risk management and reputational gains, rather than addressing pressing development needs and targets. MNCs usually seek to participate in the public policy arena to shape the social and political conditions to their benefit. "Regulatory arbitrage" is also attributed to MNC operations; it points to the accountability gaps in the transnational space within which MNCs function, particularly in feeble government bodies with weak or nonexistent environmental and human and labor rights policies (Jamali, 2010).

There are many examples of MNCs that have been responsible for negative externalities, such as ecosystem degradation, improper industrial waste systems, oil spillages, chemical diffusion, CO emissions, and others. MNCs instill a myriad of negative impacts on the local and the global society and the environment; their operations cause harm to communities, and this harm cannot be offset by doing corporate "good deeds" elsewhere. In the form of CSR activities, MNCs often try to compensate on negative impacts elsewhere in their operational processes. Therefore, CSR strategies of MNCs need to be framed under the universal development agenda and through a broad scope of CSR where philanthropy and sponsorship activities (even if they might meet targets of SDGs) are analyzed as secondary CSR; mainly firms ought to avoid any harmful impacts and integrate developmental targets into core business operations. The intent and outcome of MNC CSR strategies give an idea about the extent of developmental benefits and positive impact ensued and the efficiency in providing societal value through local development. It has been highlighted in the literature that the CSR discourse lacks assessments of their development contributions and effectiveness in instilling social, economic, and environmental change (Jenkins, 2005; Blowfield, 2012).

Political factors salient through MNC networks could also have a potential role in shaping CSR strategies, affecting the coordination and integration in subsidiary political activities (Jamali, 2010). The political risk and bargaining power literatures discuss how MNC subsidiaries face different political, regulative, and resource ownership in different nations and have different strategic roles in their MNC network, which might call for more localized strategies (Jamali, 2010). Moreover, resource dependence theory identifies factors that influence the management of cross-border political imperatives, such as a subsidiary's economic competitiveness, market attractiveness, and economy integration with other national economies, and structural theories of political behavior also identify strategic factors such as the subsidiary strategic significance and strength within the MNC network, geographic distance, and downstream competence (Jamali, 2010).

CSR is a field that operates through social and political undercurrents; in the social paradigm, it is used as a tool to support society and the challenges societies face, providing positive outcomes to the surrounding communities. However, this concept is transforming as corporations, particularly MNCs, continue to use it as a political tool with underlying agendas aimed for imperialistic and exploitative goals (Raimi et al., 2015). This is more salient in contexts where poor governance and feeble policies prevail, such as in emerging economies; through their CSR strategies, MNCs try to cover up the negative externalities they have created. Offsetting negative impacts with CSR is merely a political strategy to garner legitimacy and gain reputational gains. However, operational impact and development contribution cannot be viewed in isolation; CSR is a contribution that occurs through core business activities and through its integration with internal processes and stakeholder engagement. As members of society, corporations also reflect their CSR strategies through stakeholder relationships with society, environment, economy, and all other internal and external stakeholders (WEF, 2002).

Methodology

To analyze the efficiency of CSR and its differential impact on development in emerging economies, this chapter chooses to analyze three emerging countries through a selective review of literature. Although nonexhaustive, this selective review allows us to disentangle how MNCs CSR/SDGs practices seem to vary between countries, therefore providing implications on the impacts and intents of CSR strategies of MNC subsidiaries in the local and global context. By examining the CSR practices in three countries, the various CSR initiatives can be documented and better understood within their context. After reviewing the contextualized CSR, deductions can be made regarding how and why MNCs focus on different SDGs. The choice of countries for the analysis was according to the Human Development Index (HDI) reported in the UN Human Development Report 2016. HDI is a measure that symbolizes the level of human development in a country; it includes factors such as health, living standards, and education. In this report, countries are categorized in an HDI ranking with very high, high, medium, and low categories. The scope of this chapter is on emerging economies, and for the purpose of providing accurate results, countries from high, medium, and low HDI ranks were chosen, namely Lebanon, India, and Nigeria, respectively. This implies heterogeneous variations in socioeconomic contexts and a broad scope of analysis with regard to local development levels, with the aim of precise conclusions and generalizations on CSR activities of MNC subsidiaries in emerging economies. Table 12.1 outlines quantitative data about the countries of focus in this chapter and helps guide the evaluation by giving an understanding of each country's local context and development needs. According to the measures outlined in Table 12.1, the

Table 12.1 Country-level indicators for Lebanon, India, and Nigeria

	Lebanon	India	Nigeria
Human Development Index (HDI), 2016[4]	0.763	0.624	0.527
Population (million), 2014[1]	6.01	1,324	186
GDP per capita (US$), 2016[1]	8,257	1,710	2,176
GDP growth (annual %), 2016[1]	2.0	7.1	-1.6
GDP (PPP) as a share (%) of world total, 2015[2]	0.07	6.97	0.95
Global Competitiveness Index (GCI) (Rank 1–7), 2015[2]	3.8	4.3	3.5
Subindex A: Basic Requirements (Rank 1–7), 2015[2]	3.7	4.4	3.2
Institutions	3.2	4.1	3.2
Public institutions	3.0	4.0	2.9
Infrastructure	2.7	3.7	2.1
Macroeconomic environment	2.6	4.4	4.6
Health and primary education (Rank 1–7), 2015[2]	6.3	5.5	2.9
Subindex B: Efficiency Enhancers (Rank 1–7), 2015[2]	4.0	4.2	3.9
Higher education and training	4.5	3.9	2.8
Goods market efficiency	4.4	4.2	4.1
Labor market efficiency	3.8	3.9	4.5
Financial market Development	3.8	4.1	3.8
Technological readiness	4.0	2.7	3.0
Market size	3.6	6.4	5.1
Subindex C: Innovation and sophistication factors (Rank 1–7), 2015[2]	3.6	3.9	3.2
Business sophistication	4.1	4.2	3.7
Innovation	3.1	3.6	2.8
Corruption perception index (Rank out of 168), 2015[3]	123	76	136

1 World Development Indicators (World Bank, 2016)
2 1=worst rank, 7=best rank (World Economic Forum, 2015)
3 Corruption Perceptions Index (Transparency international, 2015)
4 Human Development Report (UNDP, 2016)

institutional, social, and business realities of each of the three countries can be inferred, which aids the evaluation of CSR activities in regard to their attunement to the local context.

Lebanon has a high HDI (0.763), followed by India with a medium HDI (0.624), and Nigeria with a low HDI (0.527). India has a population of 1,324 million people, which contributes to its low GDP per capita compared to Lebanon and Nigeria, but it has experienced the highest GDP growth in 2017 of 7.1 percent. India also ranked highest on global competitiveness above the median and the highest on all subindexes, followed by Lebanon and then Nigeria that rank below the Global Competitiveness Index (GCI) median (World Economic Forum, 2015). Lebanon has a population of 6.01 million, experienced a 2 percent annual GDP growth in 2016, and ranked highest on GDP per capita, followed by Nigeria and then India; Lebanon also had the highest rank on health and primary education, higher education and training, goods market efficiency, and technological readiness. Nigeria has a population of 186 million people, ranked lowest among the sample on HDI and GCI, and experienced a decrease in GDP in 2016 by 1.6 percent. In terms of the GCI factors, Nigeria ranked highest in labor market efficiency and macroeconomic environment. In terms of corruption perception index, all countries seem to have high levels of corruption; the highest is Nigeria, with a comparable ranking to Lebanon, followed by the lowest corruption among the sample in India.

The evaluation criteria of MNC subsidiaries and their CSR strategies needs to be outlined, and this is done through a framework linking each of the 17 SDGs with the corresponding needed corporate strategies to fulfill these goals operationally and further contribute through philanthropic CSR. Journal articles discussing the CSR of MNC subsidiaries in Lebanon, India, and Nigeria were downloaded; three folders were created for each country, and through content analysis of qualitative and quantitative data presented in research, results on the impact of CSR activities on local and global sustainable development are outlined. Furthermore, the focus on the CSR targets needs to take the local context into consideration for effective developmental impacts. The papers were filtered based on their explicit mentions of CSR and MNCs. The literature was then resynthesized to reflect the different findings in each geographical context. Each country has different levels of development in regard to each development goal. Data on the current local context of each country are outlined in Table 12.2 using 2015 data on each country's progress in achieving MDG targets. Tables 12.1 and 12.2 will aid the analysis of CSR activities in each country by providing a strong framework of evaluation.

Table 12.2 Country MDG progress levels

	India[1]	Lebanon[2]	Nigeria[3]
MDG 1. Poverty and Hunger	Moderate	Slow	Slow
MDG 2. Primary Education	Moderate	On Track	Slow
MDG 3. Gender Equality	On Track	Moderate	Moderate
MDG 4. Reduce child mortality	Moderate	On Track	Moderate
MDG 5: Improve maternal health	Slow	On Track	Slow
MDG 6: Combat diseases	Moderate	Moderate	Slow
MDG 7: Environmental sustainability	Slow	Slow	Slow
MDG 8: Global partnerships	On Track	Slow	Moderate

1 UNDP, 2015a, 2015b
2 UNDP, 2013
3 UNDP, 2015a

Juxtaposing CSR strategies and the SDGs

The authors have discussed the possibility of achieving the UN SDGs in the context of current neoliberal market frameworks, especially in low and medium developed nations. Hence, it is inferred that serious reforms are needed to policies and state and economy structures. Policy change needs to address the distribution of power in emerging economies, giving more participation to low-income populations in strategizing the pathway to development goals (Mulky, 2017). This suggests an inclusive participation plan involving all sectors, such as national and local states, private sector, international financial institutions, development agencies, civil society, and academia.

Many political and socioeconomic factors affect the CSR strategies of MNC subsidiaries in emerging economies and participate in forming the intent of international businesses in CSR activities. However, to fully evaluate CSR strategies of MNC subsidiaries, their impact and contribution to the SDGs need to be analyzed, as they are the current universal framework for a pathway to a sustainable future for all. Research juxtaposing CSR and SDGs is still scarce, and this chapter will add to the knowledge base for future research and for MNCs and policymakers in studied countries and in low and medium developed nations in general. Accordingly, the merger of the 17 SDGs and CSR business strategies need to be understood in order to build a comprehensive evaluation framework for MNC activities in the countries of interest. Table 12.3 outlines this evaluation framework and is based on an extensive analysis of the UN reports titled *Transforming Our World: The 2030 Agenda for Sustainable Development* and '*The Sustainable Development Goals Report 2016*. The SDG goals were extracted from the Agenda for Sustainable Development along with the breakdown of each goal into its various objectives. The Sustainable Development Goals Report was then read and coded and juxtaposed to the CSR literature. Possible CSR strategies for each objective were recorded or deduced from the text to ensure that the different facets of each goal were properly addressed. Finally, the recorded strategies for each objective were compiled into one paragraph that represented the translation to CSR. Our analysis aims to create a direct correlation between each of the 17 SDGs and the corresponding CSR business strategies to fulfill in core business operations and further philanthropic activities that contribute to the achievement of sustainable development.

Results

India

India has the second highest population in the world with over 1.3 billion people, with 23 percent of the population living under $1.25 a day, low life expectancy of 68 years at birth, and low expected years of schooling at 11.1 years (Mulky, 2017). India has made dramatic progress in extreme poverty reduction

Table 12.3 SDGs and CSR strategies

SDG goals	Description	Translation to CSR
1. Poverty	End all kinds of poverty in the world, i.e., all people are to live above the current poverty line of $1.25 per day. This includes implementing programs for social protection benefits and ensuring conflict affected people receive proper support to access basic services and standards of living.	Goal 1 addresses macro-level challenges and thus is the sole responsibility of governments. However, corporations can support governmental social protection programs and labor market programs in the form of finances, food and education assistance, maternity benefits, disability pensions, unemployment insurance, skills training, and wage subsidies.
2. Hunger and food security	End hunger and improve nutrition through sustaining food security and sustainable agriculture and food production. This entails increased investments for improving production, efficient food markets, promoting equal land access, and innovative technologies.	International businesses can support productive capacity, small-scale agriculture, and farmers in emerging economies; child nutrition and access to food; and the preservation of agricultural ecosystems. Corporations in the food sector can focus mainly on this goal operationally to aim for collaboration in the sector for more sustainable practices in agriculture, production, shipping, and sales.
3. Health and well-being	Ensure healthy lives through enhancing reproductive, maternal and child health; focusing on infectious, noninfectious, and environmental diseases; and ensuring a universal health coverage and access to affordable medicine and vaccination.	Corporations ought to avoid contributing to pollution of the environment. They can also support research and development, health financing, and capacities to reduce and manage health risks in emerging economies. They can invest in providing health benefits in the form of insurance to their workers' families to help increase health coverage, as well as maternal benefits. They can also support programs that deal with child mortality, communicable diseases, family planning, and substance abuse.
4. Quality education	Ensure inclusive and equitable access to quality education at all levels, including technical, vocational, higher education, and other forms of lifelong learning and training opportunities.	Corporations can support and promote access to technical and vocational education and training (TVET), skills training, illiteracy programs, educational gender disparity programs, and other forms of education that give the knowledge, skills, and values for a proper functioning society.

(Continued)

Table 12.3 (Continued)

SDG goals	Description	Translation to CSR
5. Gender equality and women's empowerment	Empower women and girls; and eliminate gender-based discrimination, violence, and unsafe practices. Ensure their access to sexual and reproductive health, reproductive rights, productive resources, paid employment, and equal participation in public domains.	Corporations ought to promote gender equality in the workspace and equal pay and participation and provide employment programs targeting women. Additionally, they can support women empowerment programs, women reproductive health programs, and reproductive rights programs.
6. Clean water and sanitation	Ensure access to drinking water, sanitation, hygiene; address the sustainability, efficiency, and management of water resources.	Corporations ought to ensure the preservation of natural resources with operational standards and safe disposal of industrial waste in water resources; invest in sustainable water management programs and cooperation, including implementation of integrated water resources management (IQRM); and support drinking water and sanitation programs.
7. Affordable and clean energy	Ensure access to sustainable and affordable, modern, and clean energy; improve energy efficiency and share of clean energy sources.	Investing in renewable energy programs internally and externally and in promoting energy technologies and investing in energy innovative ideas, as well as implementing energy efficiency regulations. Corporations in the energy sector can focus primarily on their contribution to this goal.
8. Economic growth	Promote sustainable and inclusive economic growth, decent employment, labor rights, sustainable tourism, and access to financial services.	Corporations can support the achievement of this goal by financing skill development programs, entrepreneurship programs, and ensuring proper labor rights practices internally.
9. Infrastructure and industrialization	Build robust infrastructure and promote innovation and sustainable industrialization.	Corporations can support international and local financial, technological, and technical support programs, including research and innovation, as well as support to infrastructure development, and integrating small and medium-sized enterprises (SMEs) to global supply chains.
10. Inequality	Reduce inequality in income, including gender, age, disability, race, class, ethnicity, and religion-based inequalities, including the decision-making power of emerging economies in global discourse.	Corporations can support governmental programs towards achieving this goal. They can also promote income growth for the poorest people through increased benefits and better working conditions, as well as avoiding discriminatory actions in their organizational behavior and providing employment programs for minority groups, such as women, disabled people, etc.

11. Cities	Ensure cities and settlements are safe, inclusive, and sustainable; for greater community cohesion and personal security, promoting employment and innovation	Corporations should avoid air pollution and hazardous particulate matter; proper industrial waste management. They can support local city and community renewal and planning to foster community cohesion; in addition to affordable housing programs, transport, and cultural and natural heritage, and green public space preservation, as well as supporting disaster management schemes.
12. Sustainable consumption and production	Promote sustainable consumption and production and policies for the management of hazardous and toxic materials to humans and the environment	Minimize the natural resources used for production by efficient resource management, and work to stop using and producing toxic materials. Minimize hazardous practices and chemical outputs throughout the entire consumption and production cycles and improve operational waste management programs; promote efficient and sustainable cycles, reduce food loss throughout the supply chains, and promote and communicate on sustainable lifestyles.
13. Climate change	Urgent procedures are needed to combat climate change and its impact, as well as to enhance resilient responsiveness to climate-related hazard and disasters.	Reduce carbon emissions, preserve green spaces, and avoid deforestation activities and any activities contributing to climate change. Invest in awareness schemes, climate change mitigation programs, and disaster risk management programs.
14. Oceans	Promote the conservation of marine life and costal ecosystems; prevent its pollution.	Corporations ought to avoid polluting the marine environment, invest in developing marine technology; provide market access to small-scale fisheries, and support marine conservation schemes.
15. Biodiversity, forests, and desertification	Promote sustainable management of forests, restore degraded ecosystems, ensure protection of biodiversity, and combat desertification.	Corporations are to promote sustainable forestry; ensure no harm to ecosystems in their operations.
16. Peace, justice, and strong institutions	Promote inclusive and peaceful societies; enhance the existence and accountability of institutions to provide access to equal justice and transparent information, and other basic human freedoms.	Corporations ought to avoid any forms of corruption, extortion and bribery; invest in accountability schemes; enhance corporate transparency; follow best practices for corporate governance; and promote labor rights, such as the freedom of association and collective bargaining.
17. Partnerships	Enhance international partnerships and cooperation between all sectors, including governments, private sector, civil society, and other actors. This means an enhanced support to least developed countries (LDCs) and landlocked countries and small island states.	Corporations need to be transparent and promote collaboration and cooperation with all sectors.

in recent years, but it remains a pressing issue; apart from international aid inflows to India, it is the largest recipient of remittances in the world totaling $70 billion (3.4 percent of gross national income [GNI]) only in 2014, which is only slightly lower than net inflows of debts and foreign direct investments (World Bank, 2016a, 2016b). Sustainable development is a pressing issue and need for India, and this chapter will help add to the development research in the country.

Indian firms are shifting to the stakeholder model in the hopes to become more attuned to the demands of their stakeholders. Despite the advent of globalization and the resulting increase in pressures to become more competitive and profitable, Indian managers still view CSR primarily from a philanthropic mentality rather than a profit-driven one (Arevalo & Aravind, 2011). However, lack of resources, difficulty of implementing CSR, and lack of management support at both top and middle levels have hindered CSR practices.

MNCs in India are particularly active in environmental marketing, climate change, and social issues (Narwal & Singh, 2013). In terms of communication, MNCs seem to be ahead of regular organizations in India. Only large organizations with overseas operations are on par with MNCs in this domain (Tewari & Dave, 2012). However, the institutional environment still features a weak civil society and an underdeveloped regulatory system that allows or incentivizes organizational misconduct. On the other hand, the continuous legislative efforts by the government, the diversification of grassroots stakeholders, and the increase of stakeholder challengers have started creating substantial pressures on business misconduct (Zhao, Tan, & Park, 2014). The Indian government has made efforts to involve the public and private sector in CSR activities. In 2010 the Indian government passed new regulations that made it mandatory for the public sector to get involved in CSR activities. This was followed in 2013 with reforms that made it obligatory for private companies to contribute through CSR; specifically, companies that have a high net worth or profit are expected by law to spend at least 2 percent of their net profits on CSR activities (Mulky, 2017). These regulations also provide guidelines for CSR where activities need to address specific local challenges, including poverty, human rights, health, education, environment, unemployment, and donations to governmental social and economic development projects (Ray, 2013). Further governmental guidelines are concerned with the implementation processes of CSR activities that ought to be managed by a CSR committee (Shin et al., 2015). These committees must have independent directors and disclose a detailed plan of the CSR activities and their implementation processes, including type of activities, targets, budgets, responsibilities of different stakeholders, and monitoring and evaluation of implementation. CSR strategies outlined by the CSR committee are approved by the company board and published in annual reports and online on company websites (Mulky, 2017).

Supported by governmental initiatives, Indian environmentalists and consumer activists started organizing and educating illiterate villagers to help defend their lands from encroachment by large organizations. By backing stakeholder claims that were previously not protected by the law, CSR legislation is making stakeholder accusations cheaper, easier, and processed faster. These factors have put MNCs under increasingly intensive government scrutiny (Zhao, Tan, & Park, 2014). Additionally, the increase in grassroots movements, including labor unions, green nongovernmental organizations (NGOs), and individual stakeholders, all connected through social media, has driven organizational crises occurrences. These factors point to a shift towards an updated stakeholder–MNC relationship within leading emerging markets, including India (Zhao, Tan, & Park, 2014).

Nigeria

Nigeria is an oil-rich country that still struggles with poverty. The Niger Delta, a region that accounts for more than 90 percent of Nigeria's export earnings and up to 70 percent of federal earnings, still faces pervasive issues ranging from poverty to providing health care to an increasingly growing population (Ite, 2004). Perhaps the most common type of multinational companies in Nigeria are the extractive MNCs (Pesmatzoglou et al., 2014). Companies like Shell, Exon Mobil, and Total have been operating within the Niger Delta for a long time (Adewuyi and Olowookere, 2010; Eweje, 2007; Idemudia, 2009; Ogula, Rose, & Abii, 2012). Given their long history, the development issues within the Niger Delta, and the effects of resource extraction on the communities and the environment, CSR is being used to garner a "social license" to operate within that region (Wopara, 2015; Olufemi, 2010; Pesmatzoglou et al., 2014; Ako, 2012).

Extractive MNCs have conducted many different forms of CSR in Nigeria. An early strategy for these MNCs was to provide one-time contributions to the communities. This strategy is referred to as community assistance. Multinational oil companies have restored schools, built hospitals, and paved roads under this style of CSR (Ite, 2004). However, this approach was later supplanted by community development that emphasizes partnership, especially with the local communities. This change was brought on by the conflicts in the region and the increasing pressure from the local communities (Olufemi, 2010; Idemudia, 2009). Organizations now form partnerships that set goals and targets in collaboration with local communities (Ite, 2005; Idemudia, 2009).

In Nigeria, the discourse surrounding the effectiveness of CSR targeting community development is still split, with one side arguing that MNCs are making considerable contributions to community development, while the other side argues that the contributions are lacking. Community development partnerships can empower local communities and provide much-needed infrastructure. Additionally, the facilities provided can serve as informal and formal conflict resolution centers (Idemudia, 2009; Amaeshi and Amao, 2009). However, these CSR practices do not address the negative externalities that result from those MNCs' core business. It is also argued that oil MNCs tend to prioritize CSR that focuses on social infrastructure provision. These organizations are so focused on micro-level issues that serve their own interests that they do not end up targeting the real problems that communities face (Idemudia, 2011).

One common point that is brought up in the literature is the need for governmental support and intervention (Pesmatzoglou et al., 2014). Ite (2005) argued that the job of MNCs is to produce wealth, while the government's main duty is to represent society in wealth distribution and to ensure that various groups in society receive equitable treatment. Okoye (2012) further argued that although CSR is a consensual and voluntary process for businesses, it does not dismiss the use of obligatory instruments by governments.

The limited effectiveness of oil MNCs' CSR is largely attributed to the failure of governmental policies and actions (Olufemi, 2010; Okoye, 2012; Idemudia, 2011; Amadi & Abdullah, 2012; Ite, 2005; Gonzalez, 2016; Ako, 2012). For instance, Wopara (2015) criticized the government for its failure to provide local communities with opportunities to seek reparations for the damages caused by oil MNCs. Additionally, the author noted that the government used the military to suppress the environmental demands of agitating communities. As a result of these failures, Ite (2004) concluded that there is a direct and indirect reliance on oil MNCs for the development of the region.

Lebanon

Lebanon is a Middle Eastern country on the eastern shore of the Mediterranean. Social issues are prevalent in Lebanon, particularly the economic divide between the rich and the poor (Jamali, 2010). The underprivileged segment of the population was hit hard by the increasing costs that resulted from the Lebanese civil war and the more recent 2006 war. Their situation is further exasperated by the low-cost housing crises resulting from the aftermath of the war. The poor also struggle with limited access to health care in the country. Given all of these issues, the government adopted a social action plan that attempts to address social issues through a coordinated approach.

Companies in Lebanon have recently regained focus after a civil war that lasted 15 years. Globalization further shifted the priorities of different sectors to increased competitiveness rather than sustainability (Jamali, Mezher, & Bitar, 2006). However, globalization has also led to increased exposure of businesses to CSR (Jamali, Sidani, & El-Asmar, 2008). Lebanese managers have mostly adopted modern and philanthropic views to CSR, where organizations perceive added value in serving a wider range of societal needs, or where organizations have a broader view of social responsibility, even if the actions taken are perceived as a net cost (Jamali, Mezher, & Bitar, 2006; Jamali & Sidani, 2008).

Subsidiaries of multinational organizations in Lebanon also take an active role in CSR. They tend to generate CSR initiatives based on MNC directives (Jamali & Neville, 2011). MNCs have the added benefit of high levels of formalization, integration, and standardization in their CSR practices when compared to local SMEs (Jamali, Zanhour, & Keshishian, 2009). However, it was noted that this level of sophistication does not necessarily indicate a stronger commitment to CSR. Given the centralized decision making of MNC sub-sidiaries, CSR efforts tend to be generic compared to that of SMEs (Jamali & Neville, 2011). It was identified that the limited size of the market and the subsidiary and the downstream competence have led to the standardized CSR initiative as stronger subsidiaries in the MNC network dominate the decision making. This limited responsiveness is further exemplified in the limited budgets and institutionalization of CSR by MNCs. As a result, the diffusion of global rhetorical CSR mandate tends to get diluted at the level of implementation (Jamali, 2010).

One common theme that was apparent from the literature is that key institutional actors still do not have full awareness of their respective roles and responsibilities in the context of a national CSR agenda (Jamali & Neville, 2011). This is particularly applicable to the government. The local government has shown limited efforts to incentivize and regulate CSR (Jamali & Neville, 2011).

Discussion

Given their size and potential societal impact, MNCs have a primary role in contributing to the UN SDGs. MNCs in the context of the three emerging economies seem to be active in their CSR. Their initiatives target some of the countries' prevalent issues, such as health and well-being, quality education, and economic growth (Table 12.4). At the same time, some challenges remain for MNCs to realize their full potential in contributing to SDGs. Those challenges are mostly related to institutional voids that characterize emerging economies, especially with regard to the role of the government in incentivizing the realization of SDGs. In this chapter, we show that the taken-for-granted assumption that, to a certain extent, CSR/SDG practices will be homogenous across the three countries should be met with some skepticism. As Table 12.4 shows, although there are some signs of homogeneity, CSR/SDG practices seem to vary substantially across the three emerging countries. This observed variation will be discussed further next.

In the case of Nigeria, oil MNCs work on initiatives that deal with poverty, education, economic growth, and health care. There is an apparent focus on SDG 3 targeting health and well-being, SDG4 targeting quality education, and SDG 9 targeting infrastructure and industrialization. This is not surprising given Nigeria's very low score of 2.9 (out of 7) on the Health and Primary Education index, as well as their low score of 2.1 on Infrastructure. In the case of Lebanon, the Infrastructure index is 2.7; however, MNC initiatives do not address this issue. This is where the limited size of the market and subsidiary and the downstream competence limit the possibility of CSR investments and initiatives. The MNCs in Nigeria are mostly in the lucrative oil industry; thus, these subsidiaries are dominant in their respective networks allowing for larger initiatives and more investments. In the Indian context, MNCs conduct substantial forms of CSR targeted towards infrastructure and development, including the construction of gas pipelines and other infrastructure-related investments.

Table 12.4 Summary of results

SDGs	India [2]	Lebanon	Nigeria
1. Poverty	No MNC initiative that targets this SDG	– Micro-finance programs – Building homes for the displaced	No MNC initiative that targets this SDG
2. Hunger and food security	– Child nutrition and access to food	– Donations to charities	No MNC initiative that targets this SDG
3. Health and well-being	– Access to medical care – Building hospitals and clinics in rural areas – Health awareness campaigns – Support for surgery	– Youth smoking prevention campaigns – Financing entertainment for children hospitals	– Construct and renovate health centers – Donate medical equipment and medicines – Funding program for treating Malaria – Renovation and refurbishment of abandoned health care center
4. Quality education	– Student scholarships – Training for public school teachers – Computer education – Other education programs	– Student scholarships – Child labor prevention programs – Improving IT access for children	– Construction and renovation of classroom blocks – Donation of science equipment – Provision of financial incentives for teachers – Renovation of classroom – Donation of science equipment – Training youth – Scholarships
5. Gender equality and women's empowerment	– Skill training for women – Psychosocial support and women empowerment programs	No MNC initiative that targets this SDG	No MNC initiative that targets this SDG
6. Clean water and sanitation	– Public toilets – Sanitation systems – Cleanliness campaigns	No MNC initiative that targets this SDG	No MNC initiative that targets this SDG
7. Affordable and clean energy	– Funding gas connections – Promoting sustainable energy systems	No MNC initiative that targets this SDG	No MNC initiative that targets this SDG
8. Economic growth	– Skills development programs – Employee training programs – Training local farmers	– Entrepreneurship award – IT skill development programs for rural villages	– Micro-credit scheme for corporate and individuals to boost small-scale enterprise – Support and training entrepreneurship program – Growing business foundation – Construction of market stalls

SDG			
9. Infrastructure and industrialization	– Infrastructure development	No MNC initiative that targets this SDG	– Provision of social infrastructures like tap water – Paving roads
10. Inequality	– Employment generation for disabled people	No MNC initiative that targets this SDG	No MNC initiative that targets this SDG
11. Cities	– Waste recycling – Pollution control	No MNC initiative that targets this SDG	No MNC initiative that targets this SDG
12. Sustainable consumption and production	– Water conservation schemes – Consumer awareness campaigns – Quality control measures	– Consumer protection laws (regarding tobacco law)	No MNC initiative that targets this SDG
13. Climate change	– Help to victims of natural disasters – Providing drinking water to drought-affected areas	No MNC initiative that targets this SDG	No MNC initiative that targets this SDG
14. Oceans	No MNC initiative that targets this SDG	No MNC initiative that targets this SDG	No MNC initiative that targets this SDG
15. Biodiversity, forests, and desertification	– Environmental awareness programs – Planting trees – Natural resource preservation measures	– Supporting environmental campaigns	No MNC initiative that targets this SDG
16. Peace, justice, and strong institutions	No MNC initiative that targets this SDG	– Anti-illicit trade campaign – Advisory for a local NGO	No MNC initiative that targets this SDG
17. Partnerships	No MNC initiative that targets this SDG		– Partnership to provide healthcare – Joint venture between companies and government to provide energy to people – Agricultural partnership – Partnership with Africare to combat malaria – Partnership with government to combat HIV/AIDS – Partnership with government to provide immunization

These contributions also further demonstrate the effects of dominant network subsidiaries and markets, especially given India's strategic importance in the software and technology space. The literature also revealed additional pressures that incentivized these CSR activities. In the case of Nigeria, civil unrest and social pressures arose as the local communities were struggling with poverty while oil MNCs were generating substantial profits. In the case of India, institutional pressure came from the government through regulations that make CSR a mandatory practice. This process of adoption of CSR may be criticized given that organizations are pressured into adopting these practices, but the literature indicates that corporations usually start their CSR activities and practices in response to public criticism regarding harmful practices to society and the environment and, at a later stage, CSR strategies become integrated with core business practices (Carroll, 1991).

A key idea that was extracted from the findings is the reliance on MNCs as developmental agents. As the literature had suggested, CSR can be used as a tool to fill the institutional void created by weak state institutions (Samara et al., 2018). This concept is clear in Nigeria where state corruption and poverty are prevalent. Oil MNCs in Nigeria have taken several different initiatives to provide health care, education, and overall economic growth of the country. In fact, Ite (2004) stated outright that there is a direct and indirect reliance on oil MNCs for the development of the region. In the literature, it is noted that CSR used to create effective development becomes a political tool that is used by corporations to participate in developmental change and complement the inefficient role of states, specifically in emerging economies contexts characterized by institutional voids where corruption, unemployment, lack of inclusiveness, and bad governance are generally salient. Nigeria is not the only country where political CSR is present. The initiatives carried out in the Indian context supplement and sometimes replace the government initiatives through various projects that tackle the environment, health care, education, and infrastructure development goals. In the Lebanese context, the initiatives carried out also supplement government actions. However, as shown earlier, the degree to which these initiatives are effective is dependent on the size of the market.

CSR efforts of MNCs were criticized for several different issues. In the Lebanese context, it was found that global CSR directives tend to be diluted as they diffuse into the local context into practical projects. These initiatives materialized as a way for MNCs to garner symbolic legitimacy, thus limiting their societal impact. In the Nigerian context, the literature reveals similar criticism whereby MNCs were criticized for providing one-time donations and for basing their initiatives on their own value systems, thus marginalizing the communities that they aimed to support and limiting the potential impact of their efforts while garnering a social license to operate. More importantly, MNCs in Nigeria were criticized for selecting CSR activities that benefit their own operations. The focus on building infrastructure benefited oil MNCs by supporting their extractive operations in the Niger Delta and garnering them a social license through positive perceived relationship with their stakeholders.

These actions fall in line with the literature, as it was found that MNC subsidiaries tend to cherry-pick those social activities that serve their own interests, such as activities pertaining to risk management and reputational gains, rather than addressing pressing development needs and targets. It was additionally noted that MNCs in Nigeria don't seem to address their own negative externalities, but rather focus on other CSR activities that target the population directly. In the Indian context, although organizations do seem to target various SDGs, including the environment, the findings do not link the CSR to negative externality reduction or greenwashing. This may be due to the simplistic understanding of CSR as complying with governmental rules and regulations, therefore reflecting a lack of actual drive from the organizations themselves to address the negative results from their own operations. These findings fall in line with expectations from the literature, as MNCs in general are found to cause a range of negative impacts on the societies where they operate, yet they chose to compensate on negative impacts elsewhere in their operational processes.

In the SDG document created by the UN Global Compact, the achievement of SDGs can be done in partnership with the private sector through "core business, philanthropy, collective action, and public policy advocacy" (UN Global Compact, 2014, p. 3). However, our findings show that conducting philanthropic activities is a necessary, albeit not sufficient, requirement to realize the SDGs, especially in emerging countries. Country-specific institutional idiosyncrasies must be closely scrutinized and accounted for in any effort aimed to incentivize the private sector to contribute to SDGs. This shift is evident in the case of MNCs in Nigeria that responded to community pressures by adopting a community development approach to CSR. This approach emphasizes partnership in their CSR strategy rather than the traditional philanthropic approach. Some MNCs in Lebanon seem to also conduct community development by partnering with NGOs, whereas MNCs in India still focus on one-time donations rather than partnerships.

One common point that is reiterated throughout the literature for all three contexts is the need for governmental support and intervention as the primary source for ensuring social equity and adequate wealth distribution. In the Nigerian context, the government had not supported the communities that were seeking to get reparations for the damages caused by the oil MNCs. In the Lebanese context, the government has been criticized for its limited efforts to incentivize and regulate CSR. And in the Indian context, the institutional environment still features a weak civil society and an underdeveloped regulatory system; it seems that the Indian government has made gradual progress in terms of improving regulations, as Zhao et al. (2014) have indicated.

Conclusions

This chapter examined the CSR efforts of MNCs in the context of three emerging economies. To ensure some variability in our selection process, Lebanon, India, and Nigeria were chosen based on their HDI scores. Content

analysis has been done on journal articles that discuss CSR of MNCs in Lebanon, India, and Nigeria. The results show that MNCs engage in different types
of CSR activities that target multiple SDGs. MNCs, however, were criticized
for cherry-picking CSR activities that serve their own interest, therefore limiting the effectiveness and scope of these initiatives. MNCs were also criticized
for having centralized decision making that affected which CSR efforts were to
be initiated. This centralized decision making was found to have caused dilution
when the CSR efforts were converted into practical initiatives.

This chapter offers important contributions to the international CSR literature. This chapter developed an evaluation framework to link current CSR strategies to the SDGs, particularly in an emerging countries context. This framework
allows for a deeper analysis of the current CSR practices by organizations. After
analyzing the CSR activities of MNCs within three countries, different SDG
orientations were observed across the sampled nations. Although we have found
few common trends among the three countries explored, our analysis suggests
that each country is characterized by institutional peculiarities that shape the
contributions of MNCs to CSR. For example, extractive MNCs operating in
oil-producing countries have been concerned with building partnerships with
their communities and with contributing to the health and welfare of the population in an attempt to legitimize their oil-extracting operations and to get support from the community in which they operate. Whereas in Lebanon, the focus
of MNCs was on philanthropic activities targeting the reduction of poverty and
the provision of quality education to an increasingly growing young population,
therefore increasing the reputational benefits they gain from CSR. In this way,
another important contribution that this chapter makes is that it shows that the
main driver for MNCs CSR activities was instrumental. Our analysis shows that
MNCs are only contributing to SDGs that can grant them positive spillovers
in terms of their business operations. The role of the government in all three
emerging economies remains weak, and there is an urgent need to improve government interventions through legislations and policies that aim to incentivize
MNCs to address SDGs that do not necessarily affect their business operations.

Finally, it is our hope that this chapter will offer a step forward toward raising
awareness about the peculiarities of emerging economies and in fostering the
awareness of MNCs about their role and potential to contribute to the achievement of SDGs 2030.

References

Adewuyi, Adeolu O., and Afolabi E. Olowookere. (2010). Corporate social responsibility
of a Nigerian polluter: the West African Portland Cement (WAPCO) Nigerian PLC's
case." *Social Responsibility Journal*, 6(1), 108–125.
Amadi, Bede Obinna, and Haslinda Abdullah. (2012). Poverty alleviation through corporate
social responsibility in Niger Delta, Nigeria. *Asian Social Science*, 8(4), 57.
Amaeshi, Kenneth, and Olufemi O. Amao. (2009), Corporate social responsibility in transnational spaces: exploring influences of varieties of capitalism on expressions of corporate
codes of conduct in Nigeria. *Journal of Business Ethics*, 86(2), 225–239.

Arevalo, Jorge A., and Deepa Aravind. (2011). Corporate social responsibility practices in India: approach, drivers, and barriers. *Corporate Governance*, 11(4), 399–414.

Barsoum, Ghada, and Sara Refaat. (2015). "We don't want school bags" discourses on corporate social responsibility in Egypt and the challenges of a new practice in a complex setting. *International Journal of Sociology and Social Policy*, 35(5–6), 390–402. doi:10.1108

Blowfield, Micheal. (2012). Business and development: making sense of business as a development agent. *Corporate Governance: The International Journal of Business in Society*, 12(4), 414–426. doi:10.1108/14720701211267775

Carroll, Archie B. (1991). The pyramid of corporate social responsibility: toward the moral management of organizational stakeholders. *Business Horizons*, 34(4), 39–48.

Commission of the European Communities (2002). *Communication from the commission concerning corporate social responsibility: a business contribution to sustainable development*, COM(2002) 347 final, Brussels, 2nd July.

Eweje, Gabriel. (2007). Multinational oil companies' CSR initiatives in Nigeria: the skepticism of stakeholders in host communities. *Managerial Law*, 49(5–6), 218–235.

Frynas, Jędrzej George, and Camila Yamahaki. (2016). CSR: review and roadmap of theoretical perspectives. *Business Ethics: A European Review*, 25(3), 258–285.

Gonzalez, Adrian. (2016). Poverty, oil and corruption: the need for a quad-sector development partnership (QSDP) in Nigeria's Niger Delta. *Development Policy Review*, 34(4), 509–538.

Idemudia, Uwafiokun. (2009). Oil extraction and poverty reduction in the Niger Delta: a critical examination of partnership initiatives. *Journal of Business Ethics*, 90(1), 91–116.

Idemudia, Uwafiokun. (2011). Corporate social responsibility and developing countries: moving the critical CSR research agenda in Africa forward. *Progress in Development Studies*, 11(1), 1–18.

Ite, Uwem E. (2004). Multinationals and corporate social responsibility in developing countries: a case study of Nigeria. *Corporate Social Responsibility and Environmental Management*, 11(1), 1–11.

Ite, Uwem E. (2005). Poverty reduction in resource-rich developing countries: what have multinational corporations got to do with it?. *Journal of International Development*, 17(7), 913–929.

Jamali, Dima. (2010). The CSR of MNC subsidiaries in developing countries: global, local, substantive or diluted? *Journal of Business Ethics*, 93(S2), 181–200. doi:10.1007/s10551-010-0560-8

Jamali, Dima, Toufic Mezher, and Hiba Bitar. (2006). Corporate social responsibility and the challenge of triple bottom line integration: insights from the Lebanese context. *International Journal of Environment and Sustainable Development*, 5(4), 395–414.

Jamali, Dima, and Ben Neville. (2011). Convergence versus divergence of CSR in developing countries: an embedded multi-layered institutional lens. *Journal of Business Ethics*, 102(4), 599–621. doi:10.1007/sl0551-011-0830-0

Jamali, Dima, and Yusuf Sidani. (2008). Classical vs. modern managerial CSR perspectives: Insights from Lebanese context and cross-cultural implications. *Business and Society Review*, 113(3), 329–346.

Jamali, Dima, Yusuf Sidani, and Khalil El-Asmar. (2009). A three country comparative analysis of managerial CSR perspectives: insights from Lebanon, Syria and Jordan. *Journal of Business Ethics*, 85(2), 173–192.

Jamali, Dima, Mona Zanhour, and Tamar Keshishian. (2009). Peculiar strengths and relational attributes of SMEs in the context of CSR. *Journal of Business Ethics*, 87(3), 355–377.

Jenkins, Rhys. (2005). Globalization, corporate social responsibility and poverty. *International Affairs (Royal Institute of International Affairs 1944-)*, 81(3), 525–540. doi:10.1111/j.1468-2346.2005.00467.x

Mulky, Avinash. (2017). *Are CSR activities directed towards sustainable development goals? A study in India.* 5th International OFEL Conference on Governance, Management and Entrepreneurship: The Paradoxes of Leadership and Governance in the Postmodern Society, 266–279.

Narwal, Mahabir, and Rajinder Singh. (2013). Corporate social responsibility practices in india: a comparative study of MNCs and Indian companies. *Social Responsibility Journal,* 9(3), 465–478. doi:10.1108/SRJ-11-2011-0100.

Ogula, David, Jonathan Rose, and Francesca E. Abii. (2012). A phenomenological study of corporate social responsibility in the Niger delta, Nigeria. *Journal of Leadership Studies,* 6(2), 32–47.

Okoye, Adaeze. (2012). Exploring the relationship between corporate social responsibility, law and development in an African context: should government be responsible for ensuring corporate responsibility? *International Journal of Law and Management,* 54(5), 364–378.

Olufemi, Okoji. (2010). Corporate social responsibility of multinational oil corporations to host communities in Niger Delta Nigeria. *IFE PsychologIA: An International Journal,* 18(2), 21–34.

Pesmatzoglou, Dimitrios, Ioannis E. Nikolaou, Konstantinos I. Evangelinos, and Stuart Allan. (2014). Extractive multinationals and corporate social responsibility: a commitment towards achieving the goals of sustainable development or only a management strategy? *Journal of International Development,* 26(2), 187–206.

Raimi, Lukman, Kemi Yekini, and Ismail Adelopo. (2015). Bridging the governance gap with political CSR. In Jamali, Dima, Charlotte Karam, and Micheal Blowfield, *Development-oriented corporate social responsibility* (pp. 29–48). Sheffield: Greenleaf Publishing.

Ray, Subhasis. (2013). linking public sector corporate social responsibility with sustainable development: lessons from India. *Revista De Administração Mackenzie,* 14(6), 112–131.

Samara, Georges, Dima Jamali, Vicenta Sierra, and Maria Jose Parada. (2018). Who are the best performers? The environmental social performance of family firms. *Journal of Family Business Strategy,* 9(1), 33–43.

Shin, Jin Young, Moosup Jung, Kyung-il Khoe, and Myung-Su Chae. (2015). Effects of government involvement in corporate social responsibility: an analysis of the Indian companies act, 2013. *Emerging Markets Finance and Trade,* 51(2), 377–390. doi:10.1080/15404 96X.2015.1021600

Temitope Ako, Rhuks. (2012). Re-defining corporate social responsibility (CSR) in Nigeria's post-amnesty oil industry. *African Journal of Economic and Management Studies,* 3(1), 9–22.

Tewari, Ruchi, and Darshana Dave. (2012). Corporate social responsibility: communication through sustainability reports by Indian and multinational companies. *Global Business Review,* 13(3), 393–407. doi:10.1177/097215091201300303

Transparency International. (2015). *Corruption perceptions index 2015* (Rep). Retrieved from www.transparency.org/cpi2015

United Nations (UN). (2015). *Transforming our world: the 2030 agenda for sustainable development.* Sustainable Development UN. Retrieved from https://sustainabledevelopment. un.org/post2015/transformingourworld/publication

United Nations (UN) Global Compact. (2014). *The role of business and finance in supporting the post-2015 agenda.* Retrieved from www.unglobalcompact.org/docs/news_events/9.6/ Post2015_WhitePaper_2July14.pdf

UNDP. (2013). *Lebanon millennium development goals report 2013.* Retrieved from www.undp. org/content/dam/undp/library/MDG/english/MDG%20Country%20Reports/Lebanon/ MDG%20English%20Final.pdf

UNDP. (2015a). *Nigeria 2015 millennium development goals end-point report*. Retrieved from www.undp.org/content/dam/undp/library/MDG/english/MDG%20Country%20 Reports/Nigeria/Nigeria_MDGs_Abridged_Sept30.pdf

UNDP. (2015b). *Millennium development goals India overview*. Retrieved January 5, 2018, from www.in.undp.org/content/india/en/home/post-2015/mdgoverview.html

UNDP. (2016). *Overview human development report* (Rep.). Retrieved from http://hdr.undp. org/sites/default/files/HDR2016_EN_Overview_Web.pdf

WEF (World Economic Forum). (2002). *Global corporate citizenship initiative*. Retrieved from weforum: www.weforum.org/pdf/GCCI_CEO_Questionnaire.pdf

Windsor, Duane. (2015). A corporate social responsibility calculus. In Jamali, Dima, Charlotte Karam, and Micheal Blowfield. *Development-oriented corporate social responsibility* (pp. 13–28). Sheffield: Greenleaf Publishing.

Wopara, Goodness Ruhuoma. (2015). *Corporate social responsibility as a mechanism of community development: a study of the Nigeria liquefied natural gas limited's CSR for Bonny Kingdom, Niger Delta Nigeria* (Master's thesis, Universitetet i Agder; University of Agder).

World Bank. (2015). *World development indicators 2015* (Rep.). Washington, DC: World Bank Group.

World Bank. (2016a). *World bank indicators*. Retrieved December 12, 2017, from http:// databank.worldbank.org/data/reports.aspx?source=world-development-indicators

World Bank. (2016b). *World development indicators 2016* (Rep.). Washington, DC: World Bank Group.

World Economic Forum. (2015). *The global competitiveness report 2015–2016*. Retreived December 12, 2017, from http://reports.weforum.org/global-competitiveness-report-2015-2016/

Zhao, Meng, Justin Tan, and Seung Ho Park. (2014). From voids to sophistication: institutional environment and MNC CSR crisis in emerging markets. *Journal of Business Ethics*, 122(4), 655–674.

Zyglidopoulos, Stelios, Peter Williamson, and Pavlos Symeou. (2016). The corporate social performance of developing country multinationals. *Business Ethics Quarterly*, 26(3), 379–406.

13 Analysis of MNEs' social practices in Latin America

Implications for development studies research

Anabella Davila

Introduction

It is traditional to start the study of corporate social responsibility (CSR) acknowledging the thorough discussion in the literature on the issues that should be covered within the CSR concept (Carroll 1999; Dahlsrud 2008; Lee 2008). This chapter is not the exception, and it departs from a broad, but well-known, definition in which CSR refers to the responsibilities of the companies toward society (Bowen 1953, in Carroll 1999).

While the CSR concept expands the research for understanding how and why organizations should respond to the society, the challenges to multinational enterprises' (MNE) CSR policies and practices increase in their international operations. Developed countries' MNE subsidiaries that operate in developing countries need to discern what CSR activities and practices to implement: either those standardized globally across the company or those demanded by local stakeholders. Research on MNEs' CSR shows that, and for diverse reasons, international subsidiaries tend to follow their home headquarters' global standardized CSR practices, therefore favoring their alignment to the corporate principles and business scope (Bondy and Starkey 2014; Husted and Allen 2006), ignoring local issues which make CSR relevant (Bondy and Starkey 2014). Research also shows how local CSR issues acquire considerable importance given the emphasis on developmental challenges (Egri and Ralston 2008; Eweje 2006; Gulbrandsen and Moe 2007; Idemudia 2011; Visser 2008). That is, in developing countries, the social infrastructure for human development tends to be precarious, and governments either do not have the resources to provide it or have lost their capacity to build the appropriate conditions for an acceptable living standard. It is contradictory to observe how some developing countries have been able to attract foreign direct investment (FDI) and develop a vigorous export economy but have not been able to build the infrastructure for development. Therefore, there is a high expectation from local societies in developing countries for MNEs to engage and invest in the development of such social infrastructure (Eweje 2006; Gulbrandsen and Moe 2007).

The case of the Latin American countries presents an opportunity to advance CSR knowledge based on their distinctive development characteristics, and because foreign economic actors (e.g., investors and firms) are expected to assume the responsibility to contribute to local and regional social development (UNCTAD 2010). Such expectations are based, first, on the fact that FDI is highly concentrated in commodity export sectors, which have been key to the development of the region and continue to play a central role (UNCTAD 2010; 2018). Second, the region continues to attract FDI in the extractive and raw materials sectors that do not necessarily translate into better jobs or social infrastructure (ECLAC 2013). Third, empirical studies that contrast the Latin American and US CSR activities acknowledge that in Latin America the emphasis is on community investment (Contreras 2004). Thus, expectations can be summarized in that MNEs receive resources from the communities and they are expected to reciprocate by returning other resources to the communities (Davila and Elvira 2012).

In this regard, international corporations will play an even more important role as significant stakeholders in development. However, we know minimal how CSR is understood and implemented in Latin America by MNEs' subsidiaries operating in the region and how these companies are addressing the overall needs of the society, in particular, those of the local communities. Therefore, the purpose of this chapter is to analyze the CSR activities and practices of Latin American MNEs' subsidiaries to draw implications for development studies research. Based on the literature reviews on CSR research and empirical studies of MNEs operating in the region, the chapter proposes an analytical framework to identify patterns on how MNEs understand and implement CSR in this region. This chapter contributes to the development studies area by analyzing the CSR agenda of MNEs in Latin America with regard to its developmental impact.

This chapter is structured in two main sections. The first section synthetically reviews the mainstream literature on CSR and the central elements of CSR in developing countries to suggest an analytical framework to explain how CSR is understood and implemented by MNEs in Latin America. The second section presents implications for development studies research.

CSR, CSR in developing countries, and MNEs in Latin America

The concept of CSR is as popular in Latin America as it is in the international academic and practitioner communities (e.g., *Fundación PROhumana* in Chile; Lindgreen and Córdoba 2010). However, to understand what is unique about CSR in relation to Latin America, there is a need to review how local companies respond to societal expectations for development. Research shows that international Latin American corporations (also known as Multilatinas) have a long history of a unique commitment to social development in the Latin American region (Logsdon, Thomas, and Van Buren III 2006) and have invested in community development (Davila, Rodriguez-Lluesma, and Elvira 2018).

In a recent study, the author analyzed the social section of the public sustainability corporate reports of ten of the most internationalized Latin

American companies according to the *AmericaEconomía* Multilatinas 2015 ranking (Davila 2018). The analysis shows that CSR activities and practices present highly homogenous patterns. These companies report implementing social practices along various themes such as education at all levels, employability skills and housing for the community, and, to a lesser extent, health services. Moreover, Multilatinas established a CSR path in the implementation of their social practices: they take care of their workers, providing them with appropriate training, offering health and other personal services, and extending these practices to employees' families and members of the local community. Additionally, Multilatinas report how some of the social practices were converted into social institutions to empower the community for human development, reinforcing their long-term commitment to the social development of the region. These institutions include schools, colleges, and community centers; water and power systems; and health care programs, among others. For example, Argentinean Ternium (steel) donated $15.9 million to build the Roberto Rocca Technical School in Northern Mexico. The first school of its kind in the country, with 252 students in its second year of operation, offers specializations in electromechanics and mechatronics, as well as scholarships for all students (Ternium 2017).

The analysis also shows how Multilatinas extend their social practices to communities that do not necessarily surround the company's operations (Davila 2018). The next example illustrates practices that often follow patterns more congruent with the needs and expectations of the local stakeholders and the community. The CEO of the Mexican multinational FEMSA (beverage, convenience stores, and logistics) asked former Colombian President Uribe what FEMSA could do for Colombia. Without hesitation, Uribe asked him to help in the social and economic reintegration process of the low-intensity groups of the civil war (Cornejo 2013). The Colombian government had several reintegration programs, which were failing because no one wanted to hire a demobilized member of a guerrilla group. FEMSA introduced an entrepreneurship program managed by volunteers that would donate their time to train former members of guerrilla groups in new businesses. FEMSA offered the graduates of its program to become its suppliers. The company's program started by including 35 micro-entrepreneurs as its suppliers in textile, wooden pallets, and promotional items. FEMSA became the first private-sector company to aid in the peace process that sought to reintegrate demobilized members into society (Cornejo 2013).

Despite Multilatinas' CSR efforts, the region suffers from a pervasive social and economic inequality. There is a need to invest in the most disadvantaged people to close the skill and entrepreneurship opportunity gaps and ultimately to reduce income inequality. Latin American societies are socioeconomically diverse, partly due to their history and partly due to unsuitable socioeconomic policies (OECD/ECLAC/CAF 2016). Thus, one can observe how Multilatinas participate in other spheres of society and seem to be particularly active in establishing the CSR agenda in this region, although we know little regarding how other MNEs that operate in the region implement their CSR activities and practices.

To analyze extant research on the Latin American MNEs' subsidiaries' CSR activities, the chapter presents an analytical framework based on the theoretical developments of the CSR concept. From any angle, CSR is a complex phenomenon and sometimes even diffuse. There have been many proposals, criticisms, and attempts to clarify and define the concept. These efforts and the increase in studies about CSR, specifically in the US and European countries, have generated a series of theoretical positions that, for the moment, take the form of two broad contesting research paths: mainstream CSR research and CSR research in developing countries. The central elements identified in each path conform an analytical framework that seeks to help us to clarify and understand the CSR concept and its research applications.

For this review, the selected studies focus on the social dimension of CSR that tends to be understudied (Egri and Ralston 2008; Lockett, Moon, and Visser 2006; Pfeffer 2010) and generally includes categories on employees and community development as well as product responsibility. Among these categories, community development is suitable for analysis within Latin American MNEs' subsidiaries' overall CSR activities because of the vulnerability of the surrounding communities in which these companies operate (Gifford and Kestler 2008). Studies targeting natural resources or environmental conservation activities and practices, which are important topics for CSR, were not considered in this chapter. Thus, the chapter turns next into a synthesis on CSR as it is driven in the mainstream literature and in developing countries following a group of studies that portray patterns of CSR activities and practices in the region.

Level of analysis in the CSR definition. Scholars emphasize that the definition of CSR has multiple interpretations by both academia and practitioners, and this causes an impact on the way the research on CSR has evolved (Carroll 1999) and how companies formulate and implement their CSR actions (Carroll and Shabana 2010). The discussion on what CSR means for a given organization requires a serious reflection on its responsibilities, namely, economic, legal, and ethical, as well as acting as a good corporate citizen with rights and duties (Carroll 1999). How much weight is given to a certain responsibility is what determines the CSR orientation of a given company. Research that builds on this CSR definition takes the organizational level of analysis emphasizing the impact of CSR on the organization's performance, influencing at the same time the CSR policies (Carroll and Shabana 2010). In contrast, the discussion on what CSR means for the society is to be found in the analysis of the business–society social contract. This perspective, characteristic of developing countries research, derives from the congruence on prescriptive, normative, and societal values about the role of businesses in the development of a given country (Jamali and Karam 2018). Thus, CSR research in developing countries integrates the contextual characteristics into the study of CSR, adding development to the business social responsibilities (Idemudia 2011). In this vein, it is important to distinguish when

MNEs orient their CSR policies and practices to micro-level or macro-level issues in the countries in which they operate. For example, micro-level CSR issues include small-scale projects that target only local community in basic areas of health or education. In contrast, CSR macro-level issues tend to be related to the development of broader societal issues such as human rights, good governance, and social development (Gulbrandsen and Moe 2007).

Both levels of analysis in the CSR definition, societal and organizational, seem to be mutually exclusive, although more research needs to be done to understand under what circumstances both levels can be integrated. Nevertheless, the general orientation of the CSR definition is a starting point to inquire about Latin American MNEs' subsidiaries' CSR activities and practices. The next study illustrates how two MNEs that operate in the same context and industry in Chile follow the two different levels of definition in their CSR practices.

MNEs in Latin America. Two Norwegian firms operating in Chile faced the challenge of deploying a global CSR approach in the socioeconomic context of Chile. The dilemma was for the managers of the Chilean subsidiaries that encounter a double identity: the Norwegian way of doing business and the reality of the economic conditions of the Chilean workers (Huemer 2010). Although both subsidiaries followed the core principles of the headquarters, how they were translated into practices was different. One of the subsidiaries maintained the global CSR core principles expressed in long-term obligations focusing on business-mindedness and shareholder interests. Huemer (2010) reported a low impact of this subsidiary's CSR practices, addressing only better working conditions and a commitment to maintain manual labor to keep salaries low and, in the same way, sporadically sponsoring local schools and cultural events.

The other subsidiary followed a societal approach, providing benefits such as education and health services for the employees and their families. In fact, Huemer (2010) identified that the CSR practices in this Chilean subsidiary were more developed there than elsewhere (e.g., the Canadian subsidiary).

Research focus. Although different disciplinary perspectives offer a set of theoretical foundations to advance the research on CSR, there still is a call for integrative approaches (Garriga and Melé 2004). Various literature reviews seek to respond to this call, analyzing research advances according to the focus of the CSR level of analysis: societal/institutional, organizational, and individual (Aguinis and Glavas 2012; De Bakker et al. 2005; Lee 2008). Although this research focuses seem to be contesting alternatives to guide CSR research, the literature constantly stresses that they can be integrated, producing a comprehensive but complex phenomenon (e.g., Jamali and Neville 2011).

In mainstream theoretical developments, when CSR studies take the societal level of analysis, the elements that are analyzed correspond to the institutional business environment, generally referring to the regulations or standards in a given context and that influence the types of CSR policies that firms implement (Aguinis and Glavas 2012). A counterpoint with this approach is that some studies have concluded that when firms' CSR actions and policies are not genuine, regulatory or standards forces can often lead to symbolic CSR that tend to calm stakeholder demands or to make the company conform with the minimum requirements of local standards (Aguinis and Glavas 2012). In developing countries, the institutional level of analysis refers mainly to the geopolitical landscape and the cultural system of the country as antecedents of the companies' CSR actions (Jamali and Karam 2018). Then, in developing countries, the contextual paradigm used in comparative studies "of what is contextually unique and why" (Brewster 1999, p. 215) emerges as an important dimension for CSR research.

Thus, beyond regulations and standards, the contextual approach to CSR research is highly relevant in developing countries mainly because of the internationalization of the concept, along with the rapidly changing of the socioeconomic and political landscape in these countries. Additionally, there is a need to position the CSR actions in their respective historical context of the country (Logsdon, Thomas, and Van Buren III 2006) to understand its evolution. Idemudia (2011) states that it is not realistic to assume that CSR means the same thing in developing countries because development has been added to the businesses' social responsibilities.

At the organizational level of analysis, the mainstream CSR research shows consistent findings on how firms engage primarily in CSR activities due to instrumental reasons seeking for a positive impact on organizational performance (e.g., financial and nonfinancial outcomes) (Aguinis and Glavas 2012). However, research also indicates that some firms engage in CSR activities for normative reasons based on their values (Aguinis and Glavas 2012). In developing countries, research also shows that organizations with diverse types of ownership (e.g., MNEs, local firms) and structures (e.g., corporate governance) engage in CSR activities seeking to meet the expectations of the local populations in terms of their basic needs such as health care services, sanitation, basic education, or roads, as well as those expectations of powerful local groups (Jamali and Karam 2018).

Thus, CSR research at the organizational level in developed countries might be understood under the umbrella of corporate social performance (CSP), or corporate social policy, in order to respond to stakeholders' pressures. In developing countries, in contrast, CSR research seeks to fulfill the social contract between the company and the expectations of the society. Once more, the contextual approach to CSR continues to be relevant at this level of analysis, although it can take the narrow form of the surrounding community or the broader developmental approach. The following studies analyze how MNEs take an organizational view in their CSR actions and clearly follow their headquarters' CSR policies.

MNEs in Latin America. Newell and Muro (2006) noted how MNEs tend to have become involved in several disputes in Argentina with local groups such as indigenous communities, mainly due to the lack of regulations on CSR issues. The authors argued that these companies seem to respond more to the pressures from their headquarters and supply chain pressures or market entry requirements when implementing their CSR practices than from local pressures; an exception is the social movements. In addition, the authors stated that MNEs' CSR strategies clearly reflect European or North American priorities without considering the needs of the local communities.

The mining sector in Latin America has been the center of many company–community controversies, but an interesting approach to solve these confrontations is to know how MNEs negotiate CSR issues with local stakeholders according to their expectations (Yakovleva and Vazquez-Brust 2012). Thus, in a study of the CSR orientation of mining MNEs in Argentina, it was identified that companies negotiate the economic, environmental, and legal CSR responsibilities with the government; philanthropic responsibilities with the communities and ethical responsibilities, defined by the headquarters, were not negotiated locally (Yakovleva and Vazquez-Brust 2012). However, Yakovleva and Vazquez-Brust's (2012) analysis revealed that for the society at large, the environmental duty is the critical element of CSR in the mining sector in Argentina, although it was not included in the mainstream models of CSR that they used in the study. Nevertheless, this study distinguishes the particular CSR issues in which MNEs' subsidiaries require flexibility from headquarters' CSR policies to operate globally in an effective manner.

The case of the Brazilian DuPont subsidiary (US MNE chemical company) also presents evidence on how its CSR actions are aligned to the corporate policies, responding only to salient stakeholder demands and not because they were the company's initiatives (Griesse 2007a). Since the company started operations in 1937, its CSR activities and practices have been limited to comply with local labor laws. However, the company worldwide is receiving international societal and governmental demands because of the genetically modified seeds that it produces. DuPont created an external advisory board to assess the company's CSR programs and to provide advice on all the aspects of the product. In Brazil, the subsidiary deployed the same strategy and created the Biotechnology Information Council, which networked with other international councils. The purpose of the council was the diffusion of scientific information on biotechnologies in the region. Thus, the case presents evidence on how the MNE aligned its response to the central corporate social policies.

Torres-Baumgarten and Yucetepe (2009) analyzed the CSR website section of the ten largest US MNEs[1] with operations in Latin America, concluding the limited information on community social investment that the companies provide for the region compared to other regions such as Africa, Asia, and Europe. Most of the companies have had operations for a long time in many countries in the region, and the information that they provide is about the support of local programs in the areas of entrepreneurship, financial, educational, or cultural, although General Electric is differentiated from the rest because it sponsors a great range of CSR initiatives in the region. However, the authors questioned the role of MNEs in society, as well as the local subsidiaries' understanding of CSR actions in the region.

Although, in these cases, researchers inquired about a broad view of CSR to identify particularities of the studies, what is common in all of them is that the MNEs' subsidiaries implement their CSR actions in compliance with corporate policies. The implementation of CSR practices meets minimally the local expectations for social development.

Stakeholders. Scholarly works that grant the actions and influence of organizational stakeholders are important elements that firms consider for their engagement to CSR and to particular actions and policies. Then, the literature suggests that CSR actions should be designed to satisfy key stakeholders' demands (Aguinis and Glavas 2012). The debate here is to identify who the stakeholders are. The mainstream literature proposes that the organization responds to those stakeholders that have salient attributes such as legitimacy, power, or urgency because those stakeholders are the ones that can affect organizational objectives (Mitchell, Agle, and Wood 1997). Overall, salient stakeholders are categorized as primary stakeholders and are usually consumers, managers, employees, and shareholders.

Under the stakeholder perspective of the organization, studies on mainstream CSR research seek to identify the forms of organization–stakeholder relationships toward specific organizational outcomes, such as legitimacy, reputation, perception, or trust from any of the stakeholders toward the organization (Aguinis and Glavas 2012). Research also suggests that organizations engage in CSR projects when they are under greater scrutiny by their external stakeholders, affecting the organizations' social performance (Chiu and Sharfman 2011). Thus, organizations and stakeholders, under certain conditions, exert mutual influence toward corporate social performance issues and, therefore, corporate CSR policies.

Research on CSR in developing countries indicates that organizations tend to engage with multiple stakeholders that are the beneficiaries of CSR, including children, women, farmers, laborers, workers, miners, manufacturers, local communities and rural poor, disadvantaged communities, or low-income consumers (Jamali and Karam 2018). Davila and Elvira (2009) introduced the term "silent stakeholders" to refer to those individuals or groups that have a lack of legitimacy or power and may lack resources to defend their interests and thus may be ignored by business organizations (Tavis 1994). These silent stakeholders are even invisible to the organization-stakeholder network, but they are part of the socioeconomic sector (Davila and Molina 2017).

MNE in Latin America. The case of Newmont (US mining company) that operates in Peru has a long history of tensions with its surrounding community. The case shows how Newmont's Latin American subsidiary had to interact with multiple stakeholders beyond its primary stakeholders. Gifford and Kestler (2008) analyzed how this company had to acquire an in-depth knowledge of the conditions of deprivation in which the individuals of the community were living. Based on the advice of a group of social scientists, the company worked together with the community representatives on identifying the most urgent needs and offered a health infrastructure to help the community in other health issues. Thus, the case illustrates that in Latin America, diverse stakeholders coexist with organizations and expect to participate in the community's development efforts, seeking social integration. One important question here is how to bridge the gap among diverse societal groups' expectations or needs, organizations' interests, and governmental duties and responsibilities.

Bridging mechanisms: society–organizations–government. Stakeholder engagement is a major concern among CSR scholars and practitioners because of the need organizations have to make a social impact in the society. Whether this need is part of the organization's essence or the result of environmental pressures, organizations require the involvement of their stakeholders to succeed in their CSR efforts. The literature defines stakeholder engagement in general terms as those practices that an organization implements to involve its groups of interest positively in its social actions or decision making (Greenwood 2007). Because of the diversity of organizational stakeholders, the mainstream literature on CSR identifies central mechanisms for stakeholder engagement such as dialogue, partnership, and employee volunteering (e.g., Bowen, Newenham–Kahindi, and Herremans 2010; Erdiaw-Kwasie, Alam, and Shahiduzzaman 2017). Although the purpose of the engagement mechanisms is to promote the involvement of the stakeholders in the social activities of the organization, they also help the company in bridging the expectations of the societal actors such as organizations and other powerful stakeholders' groups, for example, governments (Davila, Rodriguez-Lluesma, and Elvira 2018).

In developing countries, research finds similar stakeholder engagement mechanisms but with nuanced features. For example, research indicates that such mechanisms need to be oriented to the local needs of the community in which the company operates (Jamali and Karam 2018). Partnerships between MNEs and nongovernmental organizations (NGOs) in that context of CSR have incipient performance mainly due to the lack of interest of the headquarters (Jamali and Keshishian 2009). However, recent research indicates four mechanisms Latin American companies use to engage with the local communities: (1) close relationships with local community social/governmental organizations; (2) continuous dialogue with members of the community; (3) networks of volunteers to help perform the social activities of the companies; and (4) creation of social infrastructure institutions (Davila, Rodriguez-Lluesma, and Elvira 2018). The next study shows how an MNE in Latin America implemented stakeholder engagement mechanisms because of external pressures more than for intrinsic reasons.

MNEs in Latin America. A longitudinal case study of Caterpillar (US MNE engine and tractor manufacturing firm) in Brazil shows how the strong alignment of the companies to the central headquarters' CSR policies prevent them from engaging with local communities and fulfilling their expectations. Despite that the companies reported compliance with the local legal requirements and offered good pay and comprehensive benefits to their employees, Griesse (2007b) documented how the surrounding communities complained about the minimal commitment of the MNE's CSR in the community.

Caterpillar, which started operations in Brazil in 1976, maintained minimal interactions with its surrounding community despite its poor conditions and lack of urban infrastructure. The company started to interact with the community in the 1990s because it was being threatened by environmentalists who criticized how the Caterpillar tractors were being used to deforest the Amazonian region. The case describes several stakeholder engagement mechanisms that the company used to reconcile with the community, such as developing a sustainable forest management program for indigenous groups and donating its employees' time to lead the city of Piracicaba toward the United Nations (UN) Agenda 21 on globally sustainable goals. Additionally, the company implemented philanthropic and cultural activities for the community that, according to the case, did not improve its weak position within the community. Despite all the efforts made by the company to engage with salient stakeholders, the considerable time that the company took to become concerned and, ultimately, to identify the community needs and learn about its demands is evident (Griesse 2007b).

Outcomes. Some scholars advocate in favor of MNEs' subsidiaries when they do not implement the right CSR actions and blame academia for providing so many new constructs and definitions that might make difficult the translation to practitioners (e.g., De Bakker et al. 2005). This causes organizations to receive mixed messages about what is the appropriate thing to do in the local and international contexts. However, the CSR outcomes tend to be divided into two general categories: first, there are firms' related benefits as the main outcomes, such as reputation, consumer satisfaction, financial performance, and firm capabilities, among others (Aguinis and Glavas 2012). Second is that MNEs' CSR subsidiaries follow and comply with what is established by the local laws, and when MNEs invest further, it is to compensate for the institutional voids of the business environment (Khanna and Palepu 2010). However, this outcome has been criticized simply because MNEs cannot operate under the conditions of a poor human and physical infrastructure (Visser 2008).

In developing countries, the literature discusses the outcomes of the CSR actions at different levels of analysis, but mainly the outcomes are related to the developmental impact of CSR. When organizations seek a systematic change at the societal level through the CSR actions, MNEs develop a social embeddedness capability, which includes developing relationships with nontraditional partners, co-inventing custom solutions, and building local capacity (London and Hart 2004). Recent studies show that building local capability through CSR actions or philanthropy in some particular countries refers to building schools or universities, health clinics or hospitals, and even housing. In other words, it is about investing in social infrastructure for human development (e.g., Davila and Elvira 2018; Davila, Rodriguez-Lluesma and Elvira 2018). Among the few studies on the CSR of MNEs operating in Latin America, the next study exemplifies how the MNEs seek legitimacy.

MNEs in Latin America. Lopez and Fornes (2015) analyzed the CSR initiatives of the Latin American subsidiaries of the eight largest Spanish MNEs in the service industries, concluding that such initiatives were used as a strategic tool to achieve economic objectives and protect their investments. That is, the study presents evidence on how the Spanish MNEs implemented CSR activities and practices seeking financial and nonfinancial outcomes such as global reputation and legitimacy, addressing their host country's challenges little. The engagement with local stakeholders was attributed to protecting the MNEs investment in the region.

Theoretically, the proposed analytical framework is structured around the central elements identified in the literature on CSR: level of analysis of the CSR definition, research focus, stakeholders, bridging mechanisms, and outcomes. The five elements are summarized schematically in Figure 13.1. The elements are arranged in a linear form but could represent a causal relationship among them. The position chosen on the level of analysis about the CSR definition is what determines, in a certain way, some of the positions of the other elements. The framework presents two broad paths that emerged from the review of the literature on the mainstream CSR theory and that from developing countries. In addition, the framework illustrates the existence of evidence that shows a dispersion in causality with respect to the research focus and outcomes.

The analytical framework presented here aims to be a tool to support the study of MNEs' subsidiaries' CSR in developing countries, although it is reductionist. Reality is complex, and any attempt to fragment it, as represented by the proposed framework, tends to limit and reduce it. In other words, most of the studies do not make sharp distinctions in terms of the content of the concept, and sometimes, researchers propose several explanations for the same phenomenon; thus, the paths are not necessarily mutually exclusive. For example, MNEs can take an organizational approach to CSR adhering to corporate policies that promote societal development in their international operations. This might be translated into CSR actions and practices beyond compliance with local regulations and invest in social infrastructure.

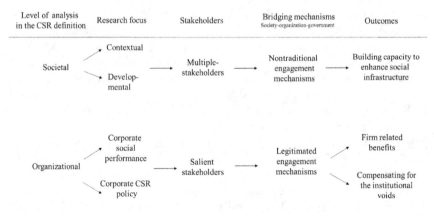

Figure 13.1 Analytical framework to study CSR in Latin America

The next section follows the implications of Latin American MNEs' subsidiaries' CSR research for development studies research in the region.

Implications for development studies research

This chapter analyses the CSR activities and practices of Latin American MNEs' subsidiaries in order to identify implications for development studies research. An analytical framework was developed to identify patterns on how MNEs understand and implement CSR in the region. Empirical studies on the social practices of MNEs operating in the region indicate two distinctive patterns: first is the alignment of their local CSR practices to their headquarters' global CSR policies, and second is the evident distance of the international subsidiaries from the surrounding community. Next follows a discussion on the patterns from the development studies perspective along the elements of the analytical framework.

Level of analysis in the CSR definition. Idemudia (2008) argued that in order to contribute to the CSR-development nexus, there is a need to reach a consensus on the definition of both concepts. However, the business literature has already addressed this discussion with a comprehensive analysis of the CSR concept (e.g., Carroll 1999). Based on the earlier analysis, this section presents emerging themes for the advancement of the CSR-development nexus.

Huemer's (2010) study concluded that when CSR is related to the ethos of organizations, CSR research should then focus on the purpose of the organizations. In this vein, there is a need to do research on what stops or obstructs an MNE from taking the CSR societal approach in Latin America, which ultimately will have an impact on social development and fulfilling societal expectations of MNEs.

Societal expectations come from diverse groups of interest. Beyond the traditional Latin American politicians' position of expecting that MNEs increase salaries and improve working conditions, unions also require having the same working conditions that their counterparts abroad have. That was the case in Norwegian MNEs in Chile, when Norwegian unions visited Chile expecting to find the same standards in the working conditions and work environment in the facilities in Chile as in Norway (Huemer 2010). However, it might be difficult to fulfill such expectations without a CSR societal-level approach.

Moreover, research has identified an additional responsibility in the CSR domain, that of job creation in Mexico (Husted and Allen 2006) and in Brazil (Griesse 2007b) by both countries' governmental officials and in Mexico by business leaders as well (Husted and Allen 2006). According to Husted and Allen (2006), this element has a singular interpretation by Mexican business leaders because of the impact that unemployment has on the welfare of families, crime, and other social problems. According to the authors, job creation is not declared as an issue in international developmental initiatives such as the Global Compact, but it acquires particular importance for Latin American economies. Thus, emerging themes for development studies research derived from the level of analysis on the CSR definition in the context of Latin America are what obstacles impede or stop MNEs' CSR from taking the societal- or contextual-level approach, the international influence of MNEs' unions in the implementation of CSR practices abroad, and the social impact on job creation.

Research focus. The deregulation and opening of the Latin American economies at the end of the 1980s raised the levels of FDI, meaning that developed MNEs with existing CSR programs started to invest in the region (Newell and Muro 2006). In particular, FDI was invested in certain industries such as energy, natural resources, financial services, and telecommunications (Casanova 2005), all key industries for development. In this regard, governments struggle between attracting FDI and regulating CSR for development (Newell and Muro 2006). In this vein, Idemudia (2011) stresses the lack of research on the role of governments in developing countries to regulate companies' CSR actions for community development. Puppim de Oliveira (2006) argues that because governments in Latin America lag in terms of accountability and human development provision, companies receive the demands to provide for social investments. This distracts society's attention from other important issues of corporate citizenship, such as corruption and tax avoidance, which have a significant impact on development.

What we already know is that governments exert more regulations on Latin American MNEs' subsidiaries according to the size of the country and when the subsidiary is oriented to the internal market, and regulations are lower when the companies are technology driven, larger in size, and export oriented (Grosse 1996). Moreover, it was only recently that international trade agreements included a provision on CSR aimed at ensuring more responsible and regulated investment activities through reference to global standards (UNCTAD 2018). Thus, from the development studies perspective, this line of research could help to analyze what factors of the FDI local governments pay more attention to and why and, more importantly, how regulations affect host countries social development, thus influencing MNEs to balance their CSR actions to corporate policies and host country development.

In Latin America, it is difficult to define CSR activities and practices as in the international mainstream literature because of the long tradition of the philanthropic engagement of the local corporations and businesspeople toward community development (Logsdon, Thomas, and Van Buren III 2006; Sanborn 2005). The research focus also requires refinement in terms of the relatively recent introduction of the CSR concept in the Latin American business environment (the 1980s). Agüero (2005) argues that the CSR concept was transferred to Latin America by the globalization movement with a significant strategic focus, reinforcing the performance-oriented level of research. Moreover, to promote the concept, there was a need to create the corresponding infrastructure of research centers, businesses and industry associations, businesspeople councils, governmental agencies, and NGOs, among others. Then, development studies research has the opportunity to inquire about the impact of MNEs' CSR performance-oriented approach on the philanthropic tradition of the regional businesses and the transforming expectations of the local societies.

Stakeholders. The definition of CSR guides companies to identify who their stakeholders are. The mainstream literature on stakeholder management proposes that managers pay more attention to those stakeholders that have salient attributes in their claims or demands (Agle, Mitchell, and Sonnenfeld 1999; Mitchell, Agle, and Wood 1997).

The "silent" term for stakeholders that lack legitimacy or power before the focal organization is a fruitful proposal for development studies research. The literature identifies two instances in which silent stakeholders make themselves visible to the focal organization: first, during land ownership disputes, which are characteristic of Latin America, in particular, disputes with MNEs (Davila and Elvira 2009). An example is the case of Benetton (fashion, Italian) in Argentina that bought upland areas of the Patagonia to raise flocks of sheep and to develop other agribusinesses, although the land was originally owned by the Mapuche ethnic group, causing serious conflicts among the indigenous groups, civil society, and governmental officials (Newell and Muro 2006). The conflict prevails currently, and Soria (2016), an Argentinean activist, critiques the case with an add that pictures Mapuche children with the label "Invisible peoples of Benetton." Another instance in which an organization can identify its silent stakeholders is through the analysis of the ultimate target population of the CSR activities or practices. For example, the case of Newmont in Peru describes the community-oriented activities that the company sponsored through a third party that helped the company to understand the unknown local context and the real needs of the community.

The dilemma here is how MNEs can identify their silent stakeholders and how research can inform MNEs about silent stakeholder identification beyond their involvement in conflict-ridden contexts. Although there are many instances in which local conflicts reach global attention, facilitating research attention for theoretical developments, there are other controversies that remain local and out of global sight (Newell and Muro 2006). In this vein, Idemudia (2011) suggests that governments or other societal agents should strengthen the capabilities of local civil societal groups to be able to monitor and demand such companies' CSR initiatives. This was the case of a longitudinal study of small coffee producers in southern Mexico, who formed a cooperative and developed saliency within their stakeholder network through the replacement of bureaucratic stakeholder relationships (i.e., those based on inequality, transactions, and hierarchy) with relationships characterized by strong moral commitment to stakeholders' claims (in this case, the improvement of the community's economic and social welfare), which enabled independent farmers to transform into an integrated, solid, and worldwide competitive group of coffee producers (Davila and Molina 2017). Thus, for development studies, there is an opportunity to build on the silent term within the stakeholder management perspective.

Bridging mechanisms: society–organization–government. Because of the silent attribute of many local stakeholders, studies in the region identify that the stakeholder needs rather than demands should be placed at the center of any CSR-development efforts (Davila and Elvira 2018; Davila, Rodriguez-Lluesma and Elvira 2018).The literature on CSR in developing countries also stresses that there should be stakeholder reciprocal responsibility on development initiatives (Idemudia 2011). Otherwise, a relationship of subordination could prevail, and this, in turn, would reinforce the dependency logic that currently characterizes many Latin American management relationships (Davila and Hartmann 2016). Idemudia (2011) notes that this issue of the stakeholder reciprocal responsibility has received inadequate research attention. Thus, there is another opportunity for development studies research to explore the topic further.

Outcomes. One of the main themes of research on MNEs' CSR is to question its contribution to developmental priorities in developing countries, mainly because the CSR construct was introduced in the United States and tends to be driven more for instrumental reasons on the impact of CSR on the organization's performance (Yakovleva and Vazquez-Brust 2012). Firms might not overcome their liability of foreignness if they do not build a capacity and sensitivity on how to create social value or to become locally embedded within the social infrastructure that prevails in developing countries (London and Hart 2004). There is a need to understand the relative position of Latin American communities when comparing them with other world regions. Because of the scarcity of reliable institutions to provide for human development, communities place greater trust in firms. MNEs need to contend with complex and dynamic institutional and physical contexts, characterized by institutional voids (Khanna and Palepu 2010), and such voids also emerge when economic growth advances faster than social and institutional structures (Rodrigues 2013).

Finally, the outcomes derived from the MNEs' CSR-development nexus should also be compared to other forms of developments paths such as those provided by local firms (e.g., emerging multinationals, indigenous cooperatives, or social enterprises) and to critically assess their contribution to development (Idemudia 2011). For example, in the case of Multilatinas' CSR activities and practices, a pending issue observed in the reports is the lack of information on methodologies to assess procedural compliance and to assess the impact of such CSR activities on the communities. In general, Multilatinas' reports specify the number of beneficiaries of their social activities as an indicator of social performance (e.g., students, schools, unskilled or jobless workers, etc.). In the context of the region, it has been suggested that corporate social performance informs on the improvement of the human development dimensions or the poverty reduction for the company's stakeholders and communities (Davila 2018).

In conclusion, this chapter provides a framework to analyze CSR activities and practices in Latin America of MNEs that operate in the region to draw implications for development studies research. In general, the analysis portrayed MNEs as distinct from their Latin American communities in contrast to what local companies report. However, the pressing developmental issues of the region threaten any corporate CSR policies, particularly those of MNEs that face the societal expectation to commit to the community development. Thus, to include the participation of businesses in development, there is a need to require agreements between companies, communities, governments, and society as a whole.

Note

1 Walmart, Exxon Mobil, General Motors, Chevron, Conoco Phillips, General Electric, Ford Motor, Citi Group, Bank of America Corp., and American International Group.

References

Agle, Bradley R., Ronald K. Mitchell, and Jeffrey A. Sonnenfeld (1999), "Who Matters to CEOs? An Investigation of Stakeholder Attributes and Salience, Corporate Performance and CEO Values," *Academy of Management Journal*, 42(5), 507–525.

Agüero, Felipe (2005), "The Promotion of Corporate Social Responsibility in Latin America" (pp. 103–134), in C. Sanborn and F. Portocarrero (Eds.). *Philanthropy and Social Changes in Latin America*. Boston: The David Rockefeller Center Series on Latin American Studies, Harvard University.

Aguinis, Herman, and Ante Glavas (2012), "What We Know and Don't Know About Corporate Social Responsibility: A Review and Research Agenda," *Journal of Management*, 38(4), 932–968.

AmericaEconomía (2015), "*Ranking de Multilatinas*" [Multilatinas Ranking]. Sep.–Oct., 36–42.

Bondy, Krista, and Ken Starkey (2014), "The Dilemmas of Internationalization: Corporate Social Responsibility in the Multinational Corporation," *British Journal of Management*, 25(1), 4–22.

Bowen, Frances, Aloysius Newenham–Kahindi, and Irene Herremans (2010), "When Suits Meet Roots: The Antecedents and Consequences of Community Engagement Strategy," *Journal of Business Ethics*, 95(2), 297–318.

Brewster, Chris (1999), "Different Paradigms in Strategic HRM: Questions Raised by Comparative Research" (Supplement 4: 213–238), in Patrick M. Wright, Lee D. Dyer, John W. Boudreau and George T. Milkovich (Eds.). *Strategic Human Resource Management in the Twenty-First Century: Research in Personnel and Human Resource Management*. Stamford, CT: JAI Press.

Carroll, Archie B. (1999), "Corporate Social Responsibility: Evolution of a Definitional Construct," *Business and Society*, 38(3), 268–295.

Carroll, Archie B., and Kareem M. Shabana (2010), "The Business Case for Corporate Social Responsibility: A Review of Concepts, Research, and Practice," *International Journal of Management Reviews*, 12(1), 85–105.

Casanova, Lourdes (2005), "Latin America: Economic and Business Context," *International Journal of Human Resource Management*, 16(12), 2173–2188.

Chiu, Shih-Chi, and Mark Sharfman (2011), "Legitimacy, Visibility, and The Antecedents of Corporate Social Performance: An Investigation of the Instrumental Perspective," *Journal of Management*, 37(6), 1558–1585.

Contreras, Manuel E. (Ed.) (2004), *Corporate Social Responsibility in the Promotion of Social Development Experiences in Asia and Latin America*. Washington: Inter-American Development Bank, (accessed March 30, 2016), https://publications.iadb.org/handle/11319/206

Cornejo, David (2013), "Cura de Tiempo ¿Puede Convertirse un Ex Miembro de la Guerrilla Colombiana en un Emprendedor? Coca-Cola FEMSA Propone la Respuesta" [Healing

Time, Can a Former Colombian Guerilla Member Become an Entrepreneur? Coca-Cola FEMSA Provides the Answer], *AmericaEconomia*, (accessed March 25, 2016), www.americaeconomia.com/revista/los-esfuerzos-del-sector-privado-en-colombia-para-ayudar-reintegrar-ex-guerrilleros

Dahlsrud, Alexander (2008), "How Corporate Social Responsibility Is Defined: An Analysis of 37 Definitions," *Corporate Social Responsibility and Environmental Management*, 15(1), 1–13.

Davila, Anabella (2018), "Multilatinas' CSR Activities and Practices: Implications for CSR Management Education" (pp. 73–96), in A. Stachowicz-Stanusch, G. Amann, and W. Amann, (Eds.). *Management Education for Corporate Social Performance*. Charlotte, NC: Information Age Publishing (IAP).

Davila, Anabella, and Marta M. Elvira (2009), "Theoretical Approaches to Best HRM in Latin America" (pp. 180–188), in Anabella Davila and Marta M. Elvira (Eds.). *Best Human Resource Management Practices in Latin America*. Oxford, UK: Routledge.

Davila, Anabella, and Marta M. Elvira (2012), Humanistic Leadership: Lessons from Latin America. *Journal of World Business*, 47(4), 548–554.

Davila, Anabella, and Marta M. Elvira (2018), "Revisiting the Latin American HRM Model" (pp. 393–407), in Chris Brewster, Wolfgang Mayrhofer, and Elaine Farndale (Eds.). *Handbook of Research in Comparative Human Resource Management*, 2nd. Ed. UK: Edward Elgar Publishing.

Davila, Anabella, and Andreas Hartmann (2016), "Traditional and Modern Aspects of Mexican Corporate Culture" (pp. 26–37), in Carlos M. Coria-Sanchez and John T. Hyatt (Eds.). *Mexican Business Culture: Essays on Tradition, Ethics, Entrepreneurship and Commerce and the State*. Jefferson, NC: McFarland and Company, Inc.

Davila, Anabella, and Christiane Molina (2017), "From Silent to Salient Stakeholders: A Study of a Coffee Cooperative and the Dynamic of Social Relationships," *Business and Society*, 56(8), 1195–1224.

Davila, Anabella, Carlos Rodriguez-Lluesma and Marta M. Elvira (2018), "Engaging Stakeholders in Emerging Economies: The Case of Multilatinas," *Journal of Business Ethics*, https://doi.org/10.1007/s10551-018-3820-7

De Bakker, Frank G. A. De, Peter Groenewegen, and Frank Den Hond (2005), "A Bibliometric Analysis of 30 Years of Research and Theory on Corporate Social Responsibility and Corporate Social Performance," *Business and Society*, 44(3), 283–317.

ECLAC (2013), *Natural Resources: Status and Trends Towards a Regional Development Agenda in Latin America and the Caribbean*, (accessed June 7, 2018), https://repositorio.cepal.org/bitstream/handle/11362/35892/1/S2013808_en.pdf

Egri, Carolyn P., and David A. Ralston (2008), "Corporate Responsibility: A Review of International Management Research from 1998 to 2007," *Journal of International Management*, 14, 319–339.

Erdiaw-Kwasie, Michael Odei, Khorshed Alam, and Md Shahiduzzaman (2017), "Towards Understanding Stakeholder Salience Transition and Relational Approach to 'Better' Corporate Social Responsibility: A Case for a Proposed Model in Practice," *Journal of Business Ethics*, 144(1), 85–101.

Eweje, Gabriel (2006), "The Role of MNEs in Community Development Initiatives in Developing Countries: Corporate Social Responsibility at Work in Nigeria and South Africa," *Business and Society*, 45(2), 93–129.

Garriga, Elisabet, and Domènec Melé (2004), "Corporate Social Responsibility Theories: Mapping the Territory," *Journal of Business Ethics*, 53(1–2), 51–71.

Gifford, Blair, and Andrew Kestler (2008), "Toward a Theory of Local Legitimacy by MNEs in Developing Nations: Newmont Mining and Health Sustainable Development in Peru," *Journal of International Management*, 14(4), 340–352.

Greenwood, Michelle (2007), "Stakeholder Engagement: Beyond the Myth of Corporate Responsibility," *Journal of Business Ethics*, 74(4), 315–327.

Griesse, Margaret Ann (2007a), "Developing Social Responsibility: Biotechnology and the Case of DuPont in Brazil," *Journal of Business Ethics*, 73(1), 103–118.

Griesse, Margaret Ann (2007b), "Caterpillar's Interactions with Piracicaba, Brazil: A Community-Based Analysis of CSR," *Journal of Business Ethics*, 73(1), 39–51.

Grosse, Robert (1996), "The Bargaining Relationship Between Foreign MNEs and Host Governments in Latin America," *The International Trade Journal*, 10(4), 467–499.

Gulbrandsen, Lars H., and Arild Moe (2007), "BP in Azerbaijan: A Test Case of the Potential and Limits of the CSR Agenda?" *Third World Quarterly*, 28(4), 813–830.

Huemer, Lars (2010), "Corporate Social Responsibility and Multinational Corporation Identity: Norwegian Strategies in the Chilean Aquaculture Industry," *Journal of Business Ethics*, 91, 265–277.

Husted, Bryan W. and David B. Allen (2006), "Corporate Social Responsibility in the Multinational Enterprise: Strategic and Institutional Approaches," *Journal of International Business Studies*, 37(6), 838–849.

Idemudia, Uwafiokun (2008), "Conceptualizing the CSR and Development Debate: Bridging Existing Analytical Gaps," *Journal of Corporate Citizenship* 29, 91–110.

Idemudia, Uwafiokun (2011), "Corporate Social Responsibility and Developing Countries: Moving the Critical CSR Research Agenda in Africa Forward," *Progress in Development Studies*, 11(1), 1–18.

Jamali, Dima, and Charlotte Karam (2018), "Corporate Social Responsibility in Developing Countries as an Emerging Field of Study," *International Journal of Management Reviews*, 20(1), 32–61.

Jamali, Dima, and Tamar Keshishian (2009), "Uneasy Alliances: Lessons Learned from Partnerships Between Businesses and NGOs in the Context of CSR," *Journal of Business Ethics*, 84(2), 277–295.

Jamali, Dima, and Ben Neville (2011), "Convergence Versus Divergence of CSR in Developing Countries: An Embedded Multi-Layered Institutional Lens," *Journal of Business Ethics*, 102(4), 599–621.

Khanna, Tarun, and Krishna G. Palepu (2010), *Winning in Emerging Markets: A Roadmap for Strategy and Execution*. Boston: Harvard Business Press.

Lee, Min-Dong Paul (2008), "A Review of the Theories of Corporate Social Responsibility: Its Evolutionary Path and the Road Ahead," *International Journal of Management Reviews*, 10(1), 53–73.

Lindgreen, Adam, and José-Rodrigo Córdoba (2010), "Corporate Social Responsibility in Latin America," *Journal of Business Ethics*, 91(2), 167–170.

Lockett, Andy, Jeremy Moon, and Wayne Visser (2006), "Corporate Social Responsibility in Management Research: Focus, Nature, Salience, and Sources of Influence," *Journal of Management Studies*, 43(1), 115–136.

Logsdon, Jeanne M., Douglas E. Thomas, and Harry J. Van Buren III (2006), "Corporate Social Responsibility in Large Mexican firms," *Journal of Corporate Citizenship*, 21(6), 51–60.

London, Ted, and Stuart L. Hart (2004). "Reinventing Strategies for Emerging Markets: Beyond the Transnational Model," *Journal of International Business Studies*, 35(5), 350–370.

Lopez, Belen, and Gaston Fornes (2015), "Corporate Social Responsibility in Emerging Markets: Case Studies of Spanish MNCs in Latin America," *European Business Review*, 27(2), 214–230.

Mitchell, Ronald K., Bradley R. Agle, and Donna J. Wood (1997), "Toward a Theory of Stakeholder Identification and Salience: Defining the Principle of Who and What Really Counts," *Academy of Management Review*, 22(4), 853–886.

Newell, Peter, and Ana Muro (2006), "Corporate Social and Environmental Responsibility in Argentina," *Journal of Corporate Citizenship*, 24(December), 49–68.

OECD/ECLAC/CAF (2016), *Latin American Economic Outlook 2017: Youth, Skills, and Entrepreneurship*. Paris: OECD Publishing, http://dx.doi.org/10.1787/leo-2017-en

Pfeffer, Jeffrey (2010), "Building Sustainable Organizations: The Human Factor," *Academy of Management Perspectives*, 24(1), 34–45.

Puppim de Oliveira, Jose Antonio (2006), "Introduction," *The Journal of Corporate Citizenship*, 21, 17–20.

Rodrigues, Sonia B. (2013), "Understanding the Environments of Emerging Markets: The Social Costs of Institutional Voids," *Farewell Addresses Research in Management Series*. Erasmus Research Institute of Management – ERIM, (accessed January 3, 2016), http://repub.eur.nl/pub/40429/

Sanborn, Cynthia A. (2005), "Philanthropy in Latin America: Historical Traditions and Current Changes" (pp. 3–29), in Cynthia Sanborn and Felipe Portocarrero (Eds.). *Philanthropy and Social Changes in Latin America*. Boston: The David Rockefeller Center Series on Latin American Studies, Harvard University.

Soria, Federico (2016), "Benetton Group is the Greatest Landholder of Argentina," *The Dawn News*, July, 7, (accessed March 3, 2018), www.thedawn-news.org/2016/08/03/benetton-group-is-the-greatest-landholder-of-argentina/

Tavis, Lee (1994), "Bifurcated Development and Multinational Corporate Responsibility" (pp. 255–274), in W. Michael Hoffman, Judith Brown Kamm, Robert E. Frederick, and Eedward S. Petry (Eds.). *Emerging Global Business Ethics*. Westport, CT: Quorum Books.

Ternium (2017), *Annual Report* (accessed June 11, 2018), https://terniumcomprod.blob.core.windows.net/wp-content/2018/03/Annual-Report-Ternium-2017.pdf

Torres-Baumgarten, Gladys, and Veysel Yucetepe (2009), "Multinational Firms' Leadership Role in Corporate Social Responsibility in Latin America," *Journal of Business Ethics*, 85, 217–224.

UNCTAD (2010), *Corporate Social Responsibility in Latin America. A Collection of Research Papers from the Virtual Institute Network* (accessed March 16, 2016), http://unctad.org/en/Docs/dtlktcd20102_en.pdf

UNCTAD (2018), *World Investment Report 2018* (accessed June 7, 2018), http://worldinvestmentreport.unctad.org/world-investment-report-2018/

Visser, Wayne (2008), "Corporate Social Responsibility in Developing Countries" (pp. 473–479), in Andrew Crane, Dirk Matten, Abagail McWilliams, Jeremy Moon, and Donald S. Siegel (Eds.). *The Oxford Handbook of Corporate Social Responsibility in Developing Countries*. Oxford, UK: Oxford University Press.

Yakovleva, Natalia, and Diego Vazquez-Brust (2012), "Stakeholder Perspectives on CSR of Mining MNEs in Argentina," *Journal of Business Ethics*, 106(2), 191–211.

14 Business, development, and human rights

Joanne Bauer and Erinch Sahan

Introduction

Now more than ever transnational business plays a critical role in determining the fate of the poor in developing countries. Leaders of developing countries increasingly look to foreign capital to lift their countries out of poverty. At $765 billion, private investment and trade with developing countries dwarfs the $135 billion in official development assistance (ODA) of developed countries (UNCTAD, 2016). Just as the efficacy of development aid has been scrutinized, since the earliest days of international trade and commerce, controversy has surrounded private investment in developing countries. Human rights harms are a big part of that story.

Starting in the colonial era with King Leopold's reign of terror in the Congo (Hochschild, 1998), there have been alarming incidents of plunder associated with investment in developing countries. Over the past two decades human rights advocates have pulled back the curtain to expose the human rights harms to development in all sectors: the global sourcing of electronics, apparel, and agricultural products from "sweatshop" farmlands and processors, where workers toil long hours with little pay in unsafe working conditions, drastically reducing costs for multinational brands and bringing cheap goods to Western consumers; pollution, displacement, and often violence accompanying natural resource extraction by mining, logging, and oil and gas companies in the farthest reaches of the world's poorest countries; and the pharmaceutical sector, which despite its humanitarian goals, often fails to reach the world's poor as high prices and bottom-line-driven research and development (R&D) agendas limit access to lifesaving medicines.

At the same time, foreign direct investment (FDI), which represents 60 percent of global capital flows to developing countries (World Bank, 2013), has delivered on many of its development promises. It is credited with a drop in the share of the population in developing countries living below the poverty line from 43 percent in 1990 to 21 percent by 2010 – a reduction of almost 1 billion people.[1] Over the years the international community has learned much about what it means to promote pro-poor investment that not only supports broad-scale economic growth but also channels that growth to places and people who are otherwise left behind. When investment is inclusive and respects rights, it can provide much-needed goods, services, and opportunities to the nation's poorest. Moreover, international standards of corporate responsibility that delineate what business must do to avoid harm have been established, most notably the United Nations (UN) Guiding Principles on Business and Human Rights, which have received widespread support from business, governments, and nongovernmental organizations (NGOs).

Although public trust in big business is at an all-time low in the Global North (Confino, 2015), development professionals remain enthusiastic about leveraging the power of the private sector to generate economic development (Greening, 2014).[2] Driven by the enthusiasm of donors and business alike, initiatives have proliferated that promote inclusive investment and minimize the negative impacts of business. These include Creating Shared Value (Harvard Business School, n.d.), Impact Investing (Global Impact Investing Network, n.d.), Making Markets Work for the Poor (Swiss Agency for Development Cooperation, 2015), and Inclusive Business (World Business Council on Sustainable Development, n.d.).

Multinational enterprises have also become more central to global policy-making on sustainable development and human rights. On the occasion of the adoption of the Sustainable Development Goals (SDGs) in New York in September 2015, UN Secretary-General Ban Ki-moon declared, "I am counting on the private sector to drive success" (UN News Centre, 2015). A central role for business has been welcomed by some, but others have highlighted concerns. According to one report on the SDGs by a group of civil society organizations during the heat of the negotiations: "The corporate sector is benefiting from privileged channels to influence the report of the Secretary-General and the Post-2015 process more generally" (Pingeot, 2014, p 25). Amidst widespread enthusiasm within governments, corporations, and civil society for attracting more investment, trade, and growth through the private sector to achieve the SDGs, human rights advocates are sounding the alarm that the emphasis on the private-sector role can also lead to harms if it neglects human rights.

Another aspect of the current narrative on business, development, and human rights is the notion of shared value: that companies can both satisfy the needs of their stakeholders – including rights holders – and also return strong profits to their shareholders (Kramer and Porter, 2011). There are many examples of companies "doing well by doing good," where the commercially optimal decision is also the one that benefits many stakeholders and respects human rights. It is far from proven, however, that companies can *always* increase profits from paying attention to human rights. Many major and otherwise widely respected companies have delivered handsome profits by neglecting labor, land, livelihood, and other rights. The focus on win-win solutions often ignores scenarios where social and human rights interests do not align with maximizing shareholder returns.

In this chapter, we describe the impact of business activity on development and human rights, focusing primarily on transnational corporations, and analyze the legal, policy, and normative developments guiding better business practice. The chapter begins with an analysis of the competing visions of the role of business in developing countries. Next, we explore the drivers of human rights violations in developing countries, followed by an analysis of the iconic cases of corporate abuses in developing countries that gave rise to the business and human rights movement. We then analyze the literature on the track record of business in developing countries overall, in terms of both positive and negative impacts, before focusing our attention on one pervasive business and human rights issue: global labor supply chains. Next, we look at the potential for a change in the trajectory by examining fledgling efforts to create companies with alternative business models with a more balanced approach to the stakeholders they affect, countering pressures to maximize returns only to shareholders and creating the space and incentive for managers to give more weight to human rights considerations. The chapter examines these alternatives with a particular focus on their impact on economic inequality, which can have severe human rights implications. The chapter concludes by noting several emerging human rights concerns relating to business and development that are not the focus of this chapter, the role and impact of the informal sector and companies developing from emerging economies, and ends with an observation that addressing power asymmetries is the focus for many of the approaches covered in this chapter.

The role of business in developing countries

Business investment in developing countries brings the promise of good jobs and better livelihoods, education, training and advancement, capital and tax revenues, new technology, and better infrastructure – all of which can in theory support development. Former UN Secretary General Kofi Annan was a prominent public voice in recognizing that business holds a key to changing the odds for many countries that are condemned to cycles of poverty and violence. In a UN press release published in 2002 on the need to strengthen UN–business partnerships, Annan said:

> In an age of interdependence, global citizenship – based on trust in a sense of shared responsibility – is a crucial pillar of progress. At a time when more than 1 billion people are denied the very minimum requirements of human dignity, business cannot afford to be seen as the problem. Rather, it must work with governments and all other actors in society to mobilize global science, technology and knowledge to tackle the interlocking crises of hunger, disease, environmental degradation and conflict that are holding back the developing world.
>
> (United Nations, 2002)

A few years later, in 2005 when the UN Human Rights Commission created a mandate for a Special Representative on Transnational Corporations and
Other Business Enterprises to be appointed by the UN Secretary General,
Annan approached Harvard professor John Ruggie. Ruggie had worked with
Annan in the lead-up to the launch in 2000 of the Millennium Development Goals to conceive the UN Global Compact, an initiative to engage business in contributing to the UN's mission of global peace, poverty reduction,
and human rights.[3] In his first report as UN Special Representative, Ruggie
famously described the problem of corporate impunity for human rights harms
as stemming from "governance gaps between market forces and the capacity
of societies to manage their adverse consequences" (United Nations Human
Rights Council, 2008, p 3). Although government action is necessary to fill the
gaps, Ruggie saw that business also had to be part of the solution:

> Yet a third rationale for engaging the transnational corporate sector ... [is]
> the sheer fact that it *has* global reach and capacity, and that it is capable
> of acting at a pace and scale that neither governments nor international
> agencies can match. Other social actors increasingly are looking for ways
> to leverage this platform in order to cope with pressing societal problems –
> often because governments are unable or unwilling to perform their func-
> tions adequately.
>
> (Ruggie, 2006, para 16)

Such pronouncements are not new. For decades, economists and management
experts have opined on the role of business in society (Friedman, 1970). Among
them, are management guru Peter Drucker and labor economist Robert Reich,
who each penned a journal article under the identical title "The New Meaning
of Corporate Responsibility" (Drucker, 1984; Reich, 1998). The two articles
reveal distinctly different ideas of corporate responsibility, with Drucker under-
scoring the business opportunity of meeting society's needs where less agile
government cannot, and Reich pointing out the need to have regulation by
government, not self-regulation or oversight by civil society, in order to make
companies accountable for social harm they inflict on communities.

Besides approaching the question from different professional perspectives,
the differences between the two interpretations of "the new meaning" could be
understood in light of the time lag between Drucker's publication in 1984 and
Reich's in 1998. Accelerated by the end of the Cold War and the opening up
of new markets, those 14 years marked a period of rapid globalization, a further
decline of economic nationalism, improvements in the information technology sector, which helped to standardize business practices, and the birth of
what former IBM CEO Samuel Palmisano has called, "the globally integrated
enterprise" (Palmisano, 2006, p 3). During this time, growing concern about
the harmful impacts of transnational corporations on workers and communities around the world led to the creation of business and human rights divisions
at Human Rights Watch and Amnesty International, as well as the genesis of

NGOs across the Global South focused on human rights and development, supported by philanthropy from the Global North. This global network of advocates has turned its attention to transnational business, with the goal of exposing the linkages between transnational business operations and human rights violations and achieving redress for harms.

Nonetheless, Drucker's argument that business can be part of the solution – a win-win for corporations and the poor – remains a compelling piece of the business and development narrative. The argument became even more prevalent in the 1990s with the opening of large new factories in the cities of Dhaka, Dongguan, Ho Chi Minh City, San Pedro Sula, and elsewhere and with them, the real promise of a better life for workers. In 2011 the argument was revived and popularized by Porter and Kramer as "Creating Shared Value" (Kramer and Porter, 2011). Today, a major emphasis of the Financing for Development agenda to implement the SDGs is how governments can stem the decline in FDI flows to developing countries by attracting private investment that can support the SDGs (United Nations Economic and Social Council, 2017, p 6).

Drivers of human rights violations in developing countries

Corruption and weak rule of law in many developing countries also leads to governments that are too often ready to the sell the rights of their citizens in exchange for capital. As George Soros has written,

> Perhaps the greatest threat to freedom and democracy in the world today comes from the formation of unholy alliances between government and businesses. This is not a new phenomenon. It used to be called fascism . . . The outward appearances of the democratic process are observed, but the powers of the state are diverted to the benefit of private interests.
>
> (Soros cited in Korten, 2015, p 19)

We see this phenomenon in bilateral investment treaties (BITs), which are concluded, often between a developed state and a developing state, for the purposes of enabling better market access in the developing state, grants strong protections to investors. Under a prevalent BIT provision, a foreign investor can pursue investor state dispute settlement (ISDS) proceedings against a host state for any change in that state's law or policy to protect the environment or public health, deal with social and financial crises, or promote social or cultural rights. And whereas a company can sue a state, the state may not sue the company.

There is evidence to indicate that the tendency of developing country governments to sell short the human rights of workers and communities in return for foreign investment is even greater in economic downturns. In the first year of the global financial crisis of 2008, FDI flows declined by 50 percent, creating greater competition among states to offer the most attractive markets for investors. According to a 2009 UNCTAD report:

> Countries have refrained from introducing restrictive policy measures towards both inward and outward FDI, and in several cases they have even taken steps to further ease the access of foreign investors to their economies and to promote outward FDI from domestic firms. This overall positive trend in national policies is mirrored by the marked increase in international investment agreements recently.
>
> (UNCTAD, 2009)

A lack of transparency surrounding concession agreements between governments and mining, gas, and oil companies to extract natural resources presents another human rights risk of foreign investment in developing countries. In theory, concession agreements are long-term contracts that grant the selected company rights to invest in the development of a resource. In return the government and its people benefit through job creation, royalty payments from the sale of resources, tax revenue, contribution to community initiatives such as schools and hospitals, and other economic activities resulting from the concession activities. As indicated earlier, the reality can be altogether different.

The rise of the business and human rights movement

With greater global integration has come more heightened awareness of corporate impacts across a range of sectors in developed and developing country contexts. The business and human rights (BHR) movement was a response to a series of high-profile, corporate-related tragedies in the 1990s concentrated in the apparel and oil and gas sectors. Among the notable cases are the poisoning of the Lago Agrio community in the Ecuadorian Amazon by oil and gas giant Texaco (bought by Chevron in 2001); Shell's role in the Nigerian military government's execution of the "Ogoni Nine," a group of environmental activists from the Niger Delta who had peacefully protested the polluting effects of the oil company's operations in the region; and the global boycott of Nike following the discovery of child labor in the company's Southeast Asian supplier factories. These were not the first such atrocities linked to multinational corporations; a decade earlier a gas explosion at a Union Carbide plant in Bhopal, India, killed an estimated 4,000 people and injured half a million. Even earlier, in the 1970s, a protest movement rose up against Nestlé for its unethical marketing of baby milk formula to poor women in developing countries that endangered babies. Despite the failure of earlier efforts within the UN to develop a code of conduct for multinational corporations (Sauvant, 2015), public outrage spurred human rights, development, and social justice organizations to mobilize again to address the unchecked power and reach of business.

From the beginning, the BHR movement made a strategic decision to emphasize national and international law and policy to regulate business behavior. It sought to build a system of corporate accountability by establishing the norm that business should not violate the rights, as clearly defined by the International Bill of Human Rights and the Core Conventions of the International Labour Organization (ILO). The strategy was "bottom-up," focusing on "rights-holders" – the individuals and communities harmed or potentially harmed by corporate activity (Bauer, 2014). In this way, advocates have sought to address the shortcomings of corporate social responsibility (CSR), a "top-down" process driven by companies, where management is concerned primarily with risks (mostly reputational) to the company, and regard the CSR program decisions as discretionary. A hazard of CSR programs is that companies regularly use them to deflect attention from socially irresponsible corporate practices – or to carry out their chosen CSR programs without also making serious efforts to track and address their broader human rights impacts.

The locus of activity for the BHR movement has been the UN, specifically its main human rights governing body, the Human Rights Council. Whereas the articulation of corporate responsibility had been previously attempted at the UN through a voluntary code of conduct, the effort to *require* corporations to observe international human rights standards and potentially be held legally liable for violations began in 1998. It was that year that a Sub-Commission of the UN Commission on Human Rights (the precursor to the Human Rights Council), under pressure from human rights NGOs, established a working group to study the problem and devise a set of standards. In 2003, the Sub-Commission adopted the Draft Norms on the Responsibilities of Transnational Corporations and Other Business Enterprises with Respect to Human Rights and presented the text for approval to the commission. Many understood the Draft Norms to be an attempt to lay the groundwork for a treaty, which would constitute a "'non-voluntary' international system for corporate violations of human rights." That proposal was set aside by the commission, which opted instead in 2005 to create a mandate for a Special Representative to be appointed by then UN Secretary General Kofi Annan.

The mandate called for an expert to identify and clarify existing human rights standards that apply to business conduct and to the role of the state in regulating business. Annan appointed Ruggie to the post, and Ruggie's first action was to abandon the UN Draft Norms. He moved instead to develop a voluntary standard, which was unanimously adopted by the Human Rights Council as the UN Protect, Respect and Remedy Framework (2008), and following the council's renewal of his mandate, Ruggie elaborated the operationalization of the framework as the UN Guiding Principles on Business and Human Rights (UNGP) (United Nations, 2011). The principles do not create new obligations under international law, but instead elaborate "the implications of existing standards and practices for States and businesses." The second of the three pillars of the framework outlines corporate responsibility to respect: namely, that businesses should "avoid infringing" on human rights and "should address adverse human rights impacts with which they are involved." This can be achieved only through a process of "human rights due diligence," in which companies establish policies and systems to identify, prevent, mitigate, and account for their human rights impacts and then publicly communicate these measures – and, ideally, the outcomes of the measures. Significantly, the UNGPs language of human rights "impacts" sees companies as duty bearers toward rights-holders, whereas the CSR movement focuses on companies as managers of risk to the company itself.

Following the launch of the SDGs there have been several efforts to make sense of the implications of the business and human rights standard established by the UNGPs in relation to the expectations of business with respect to the SDGs. A report by the NGO Shift written for the Business and Sustainable Development Commission emphasizes the centrality of business respect for human rights in its value chains as the greatest contribution it can make to the SDGs:

> There is no more pressing or more powerful way for business to accelerate social development than by driving respect for human rights across their value chains. The proposition that all companies not only can contribute at scale to development through these networks of business relationships, but that they have a responsibility to do so, is the quiet revolution that sits at the heart of the UN Guiding Principles on Business and Human Rights.
>
> (Shift, 2016, p 6)

The SDG Compass, a collaboration of the Global Reporting Initiative, the UN Global Compact, and the World Business Council for Sustainable Development, stresses that businesses should not ignore their baseline responsibilities under the UNGPs in their plans to implement the SDGs. In other words, they must undertake human rights due diligence to ensure that they "do no harm" and that any effort to positively realize human rights or promote them cannot offset that responsibility (Global Reporting Initiative et al., 2015, p 10).

The track record of business in developing countries

The literature on the positive and negative impacts of business in the developing country societies in which they operate is extensive. In *Distortion or Development: Contending Perspectives on the Multinational Corporation* published in 1978, economist Thomas Biersteker addressed a debate well underway at the time over the impact of multinational investment. His work has been summarized in a chart, "Seven Key Disputed Issues about the Role and Impact of Multinational Corporations in Developing Countries," which contains a checklist of questions about specific impacts of investments that determine its positive and negative impacts, which are often neglected: impacts on capital movements (including tax), indigenous production, technology transfer, patterns of consumption, social structure and stratification (e.g., higher wages to allied social groups), and distribution and dualistic development, including on inequality (Todaro and Smith, 2015).[4] This framework remains relevant today:

with widening economy inequality,[5] foreign investors who want to claim the mantel of social responsibility would do well to ask themselves the questions that Bierstecker posed 40 years ago.

In 1998 then Harvard Business School professor Deborah Spar weighed in on the debate on multinational private investment, asking, "Does it improve the plight of recipient states, or merely exploit them?" (Spar, 1999, p 56). In her article, Spar sets out to explore whether in fact foreign investment improves the human rights situation of developing countries either as a direct result of investment or indirectly through improved conditions that result from the investment. While conceding that the mining, oil, and gas sector has tended to support repressive governments in exchange for the rights to extract natural resources from the host country, in terms of overall investment, she noted that the "relative importance of these industries is declining," with the service sector dramatically overtaking it (p 61). Spar's three broad conclusions support the case that business brings improvement. First, FDI leads to gradual wage increases as a result of supply and demand. "Rarely, if ever, do repressive governments institute a mandatory wage ceiling to suppress this rise," she observes. Second, low labor costs are no longer a determinant for investment decisions. Instead, brands place priorities on a stable, well-trained labor pool, and therefore invest in countries with *better* labor standards and well-trained work force. And finally, companies export their standard operating procedures rather than conform to local standards, thereby upholding better, more rights-respecting standards. In 2006, writing in *Foreign Affairs*, Palmisano concurred: "The integration of the workforce in developing countries into global systems of production is already raising living standards, improving working conditions, and creating more jobs in those countries" (p 127).

Yet foreign investment has fallen short of these promises. Instead of decent work, jobs in supplier factories to electronics, apparel, and toy brands are too often sweatshop jobs – where poor young female workers toil long hours on the factory floors or in the fields, in unsafe conditions, with abusive managers, the threat of sexual violence, and pay that does not amount to a living wage (Clean Clothes Campaign, 2014). The argument that foreign firms operate at higher standards when operating abroad was severely undercut by the 2006 revelation of interference by European and American business associations in the revision of the labor contract law in China. According to a report by Global Labor Strategies, the American Chamber of Commerce, the European Chamber of Commerce, and the US-China Business Council, whose large memberships includes Walmart, Microsoft, Intel, Shell, Erikson, and Tesco, lobbied the Chinese government to weaken a law that would introduce greater protections for workers. The companies pressured the government by threatening to take their business elsewhere should these provisions, including a greater say for workers in their own working conditions, make their way into the law.[6]

The record in the extractive sector – oil, gas, and mining – is even more sobering. Because extractive projects require a large amount of capital up-front, they are typically carried out by large multinationals from the Global North as well as increasingly from China, India, and other emerging markets. These companies set up operations where geology dictates (i.e., where the resources are), which increasingly means remote and poor areas and often lands belonging to indigenous peoples in places like Colombia, Ecuador, Peru, Myanmar, the Niger Delta, and Zimbabwe (Accenture, 2011). Unprepared or unwilling to carry out adequate stakeholder engagement with these vulnerable complications, extractive companies have been implicated in the worst corporate violations of human rights, including forced labor, torture, death, displacement, gender exclusion, and loss of livelihood (Earth Rights International, 2009). Moreover in the case of oil and gas projects, the promise of many jobs is rarely met because once a pipeline is laid, labor needs are low.

There have been a number of empirical studies on the impacts of FDI which has implications for human rights. Chilean economists Manual Agosina and Ricardo Mayer (2000) carried out a study for the United Nations Conference on Trade and Development (UNCTAD) to find out whether foreign investment "crowded out" or "crowded in" domestic investment. They found that "[t]he positive impacts of FDI on domestic investment are not assured. In some cases, total investment may increase much less than FDI, or may even fail to rise when a country experiences an increase in FDI" (Agosin and Mayer, 2000, p 14).

In their review of the literature on the impacts of the private sector on development, Kolk et al. (2017) find mixed results. On the one hand, increased international trade and investment has yielded positive impacts on development – such as higher employment, greater international cooperation leading to a decrease in conflict, and the creation of an opening for collaborative solutions to intractable problems such as climate change. With a nod to the SDGs, the authors note the market opportunity of serving the lowest-income consumers through "base of the pyramid" schemes and building a positive reputation through investments into sustainable and responsible production. However, they also identify a number of studies that highlight the negative impacts of foreign investors (echoing Bierstecker), such as when investors draw talent from domestic firms, when they commercialize microfinance initiatives that lead to mission drift, or when they divert local government resources away from essential infrastructure investments.

The positive and negative impacts of corporations in developing countries are rarely assessed holistically. Oxfam International tried to do so by creating a poverty footprint tool to focus on supply chains of multinational enterprises (MNEs). The tool measures the potential impacts of MNEs in relation to five poverty dimensions (livelihoods, empowerment, health and well-being, security and stability, and diversity and gender inequality) across five dimensions of corporate activity (value chain, macro-economy, institutions and policy, social implications of environmental practices, and product development and marketing) (Oxfam International, 2009). From 2002 to 2013 Oxfam partnered with Unilever, Coca Cola/SABMiller, and Asda/Walmart to study the "poverty footprint" of each company's operations within selected countries.[7] The studies revealed a range of complex impacts, including shaping local norms and governance and reducing the availability of natural resources for other economic activities, such as water and land for agriculture. One common thread across these studies is that workers and farmers producing for MNEs often struggle to earn enough to meet their basic needs. When asked about what matters most to them, people in developing countries who depend on MNEs and their supply chains for a livelihood consistently put wages and incomes as the most important issue (Wilshaw, 2015). This issue is explored in more detail later.

Revelations of pervasive negative impacts of tax avoidance on national development programs has transformed an accepted business practice into a human rights issue. Distinct from illegal tax evasion, tax avoidance is the act of using agreements with governments, tax havens such as shell companies in Panama, loopholes, transfer pricing, and other creative accounting practices to avoid paying one's fair share of taxes and royalties. Developing countries rely more on corporate tax revenues than rich countries: according to the International Monetary Fund (IMF), corporate taxes make up 16 percent of government revenues compared to 8 percent in higher-income countries (Christian Aid et al., 2015). Therefore, when businesses avoid paying fair taxes, they deprive the host government of revenue much needed to deliver to citizens' health care, education, housing, clean water, and other human rights (World Economic Forum, 2016).

Nearly a decade before the 2016 leak of the "Panama Papers," revealing the tax avoidance practices of a raft of high-profile individuals and companies, NGOs in Africa began sounding the alarm. The Tax Justice Alliance for Africa was launched to call out practices and policies that promote illicit resource outflows. In 2008, the NGO Christian Aid calculated that in that year the loss of corporate taxes to the developing world was at US$160 billion a year, more than one and a half times the combined aid budgets of the developing world (Christian Aid, 2008). Action Aid, a South African–headquartered NGO that has been particularly active on this issue, published a report in 2013 alleging that the Zambian subsidiary of Associated British Foods had generated $123 million in profits but had paid "virtually no taxes" (Action Aid, 2013). Following the Panama Papers leak, the World Economic Forum made the link between tax havens and the resource course, reporting that tax avoidance is a key driver of the resource curse (Kende-Robb, 2016). The problem is getting worse with the use of tax havens having gone up fourfold between 2001 and 2014 (Oxfam, 2016). Today, the use of tax havens cost poor countries at least $170 billion in lost tax revenues each year. Nearly a third of rich Africans' wealth – a total of US$500 billion – is held offshore in tax havens (Ibid.). It is estimated that this costs African countries US$14 billion a year in lost tax revenues. This is enough money to pay for health care that could save the lives of 4 million children and employ enough teachers to get every African child into school (Ibid.). According to a 2013 report by the International Bar Association, the facilitation of tax avoidance strategies, such as use of tax havens, could constitute a violation of international human rights law (Cohn, 2013).

Work, wages, and poverty

In the previous sections we explored some of the wide-ranging impacts of business on development and human rights. In this section, we focus on two key debates around business conduct that particularly affects workers: sweatshops and living wages. These issues are a particular focus of the ILO, the UN body tasked with driving solutions and balancing perspectives through its Decent Work agenda.

The sweatshop debate

In 1997 MIT professor and *New York Times* columnist Paul Krugman penned an article in *Slate* magazine entitled, "In Praise of Cheap Labor." In it he defended an op-ed he had written for the paper, arguing that as appalling as sweatshop conditions in the new export industries are, they are a big improvement over rural poverty. The op-ed generated considerable moral outrage from readers (Krugman, 1997). Yet Krugman stood his ground, arguing that the new exporting facilities paid higher wages to attract workers from rural areas, and in turn the decline in pressure on the land caused rural wages to also rise. The result was a net positive effect on the economy and on people's lives. Three years later, *The New York Times Magazine* featured Nicholas Kristof and Sheryl WuDunn's article, "Two Cheers for Sweatshops" echoing the arguments of Krugman's article (Kristof and WuDunn, 2000). The headline speaks for itself.

The arguments were and remain iconoclastic and a direct challenge to the labor rights movement. Five years earlier David Korten had written *When Corporations Rule the World*, now considered a modern classic (Korten, 2015). There he coined the term "race to the bottom," which he described in the following way:

> What the corporate libertarians call "becoming more globally competitive" is more accurately described as a race to the bottom. With each passing day it becomes more difficult to obtain contracts from one of the mega-retailers without hiring child labor, cheating workers on overtime pay, imposing merciless quotas, and operating unsafe facilities. If one contractor does not do it, his or her prices will be higher than those of another who does. With hundreds of millions of people desperate for any kind of job the global economy may offer, there will always be willing competitors. Faced with its own imperatives, the core corporations can do little more than close their eyes to the infractions and insist that they have no responsibility for the conditions of their contractors.

(p 156)

The 1990s had been marked by labor scandals involving the world's most respected brands, including Nike, Gap, Disney, and Walmart. Arguably the most famous is the case of Nike, then the leading athletic footwear brand. A series of reports by American labor rights activists revealed that Nike had contracted with supplier factories in Vietnam, China, and Indonesia with abusive labor conditions. Later it was revealed that a supplier in Pakistan was using child labor (Schanberg and Dorigny, 1996). The decision to move production from South Korea and Taiwan was calculated: labor unions are prohibited in China, Vietnam, and Indonesia. The allegations set off a strong reaction in the United States in the form of a highly publicized boycott of Nike products and widespread vilification of the Nike "swoosh" logo. After years of denying the claims, in the late 1990s, Nike finally owned up to its responsibility and put in place policies and procedures that are considered to be good practice in the field (Boggan, 2001). Nonetheless, the stain on its public reputation may never completely fade.

In *Labor Rights as Human Rights*, Philip Alston puts the pro-sweatshop argument in historical perspective by recounting an early controversy over sweatshops in the United States that wound up in the Supreme Court: the landmark case of *Lochner v. New York* in 1905 (Alston, 2005). The case challenged a New York law that limited the number of hours a baker could work. By a 5–4 margin the court rejected "the notion that the law was necessary to protect the health of the bakers and maintained that it violated the right of workers and employers to freely enter into contract."

Although the Lochner era ended in 1937, with a new ruling that reinstated the state power to regulate working hours, some scholars, have argued that the *Lochner* decision was correct – in allowing for workers and their employers to set their own terms, uninhibited by the state, *Lochner* was favorable to new immigrants. Alston cites Christopher Wonnell:

> [Lochner] allowed greater room for workers and their employers to create hours of work that suited their concrete situations. Long and painful hours would decline when advances in productivity made them unnecessary, but it does not follow that good things would come from forcing those hours to fall before such advances took place.
>
> (p 97)

Like Krugman and Kristoff and WuDunn, these critics of the labor rights movement claim that regulation promoted by labor rights activists may limit opportunities for work. As Alston notes, "there is no shortage of voices playing down the utility of labor rights" and promoting "market flexibility" and "economic growth" as the most realistic way to move towards an adequate standard of living. This stance sidesteps the utilitarian argument for regulating working hours put forward by labor rights promoters such as Denis Arnold and Norman Bowie that

> workers whose minimum daily dietary requirements are met, and who have basic nonfood needs met, will have more energy and better attitudes at work, will be less likely to come to work ill, and will be absent with less frequency. Workers are thus likely to be more productive and loyal.
>
> (2003, p 620)

One only need look as far as the tragic events of the Rana Plaza building collapse in Bangladesh April 2013, which killed over 1,000 workers who were forced to work in a building they knew was unsafe, to know that the business case for protecting labor rights is often not strong enough to prevent abuses. The reason why protecting labor rights cannot be seen as the cost of doing business is that the market will not allow it.

Living wage

The Rana Plaza disaster also brought the issue of poverty wages and cost cutting into the public eye. Previously, labor rights advocates had been calling attention to the fact that the prices retail brands pay to their suppliers often make it impossible for supplier factory and farm workers to earn a living wage. Living wages are implied in Article 25(1) of the Universal Declaration of Human Rights (UDHR), which states:

> Everyone has the right to a standard of living adequate for the health and well-being of himself and of his family, including food, clothing, housing and medical care and necessary social services, and the right to security in the event of unemployment, sickness, disability, widowhood, old age or other lack of livelihood in circumstances beyond his control.

In order to achieve an adequate standard of living, wages must not only be sufficient to ensure the rights to food, shelter, education and health care but also to provide discretionary income to help improve workers' lives. Typically, minimum wages established by local law fall short of the cost of living; moreover, in developing countries, as governments compete for investment in a global market, the laws are often not enforced, keeping workers trapped in a cycle of poverty (Wilshaw, 2014). Gender plays a key role, with women workers receiving 25 to 30 percent less pay than men on average for the same work (Ethical Trading Initiative, 2016).

Until recently, the objection to a living wage was that it was too hard to calculate, particularly because living costs vary and households and individuals can have several sources of income. In 2009 the grassroots Asia Floor Wage campaign took the debate up a level by proposing a formula approach (Wilshaw, 2014). Based on a typical number of earners and dependents, it published benchmarks for Asian countries covering 80 percent of global garment production. In 2014, the NGO Labour Behind the Label reinforced the case for action by publishing assessments of the wages paid by the suppliers of 50 major brands against the Asian Floor Wage (McMullen, 2014).

Spain-based Inditex became one of the first corporate movers when in 2007 it signed an International Framework Agreement with the garment union, which included a reference to a living wage: "Wages should always be enough to meet at least the basic needs of workers and their families and any other which might be considered as reasonable additional needs"

(IndustriALL, 2014). In 2010, Marks & Spencer included in its corporate plan a commitment to pay prices that enable a "fair living wage" to be paid to workers of suppliers in Bangladesh, India, and Sri Lanka. Since then labor rights groups have pushed companies to look beyond changes in wage levels and overtime pay at the factory level to scaling up improvements. H&M's Roadmap to a Living Wage, for example, outlines a role for governments, trade unions, and employers, as well as stating its willingness to pay more to suppliers in order to ensure wages reach that of a living wage (Wilshaw, 2014). In 2016, a coalition of labor rights groups found that although some progress had been made since commitments by H&M and Marks & Spencer, workers in factories supplying both companies in Bangladesh, India, Sri Lanka, and Cambodia still earned below a living wage (McMullen and Majumber, 2016). Often, the low prices paid to suppliers can be a barrier to suppliers paying workers a living wage. Despite Marks & Spencer and H&M including a focus on prices they pay to their suppliers in their commitments, few other companies have brought their ethical sourcing goals in line with the way they negotiate pricing.

One way out of these dilemmas is through trade agreements that incentivize countries to enact and enforce international labor standards by linking their performance on labor to trade privileges. Another approach is to develop multistakeholder initiatives (MSIs), such as the Bangladesh Accord on Fire and Building Safety (the Accord). Brokered by two major labor unions, UNI Global Union and IndustriALL, the Accord is innovative for legally binding its corporate members to adherence to the standards. The Accord includes a provision for fair prices as well as worker participation. Corporate signatories agreed to four principles for a living wage: (1) enabling employees' freedom of association and collective bargaining; (2) working on wage systems that reward skill and productivity; (3) adjusting purchasing practices in line with wage policies; and (4) influencing governments. Since the Accord was formed, five new collective bargaining agreements were finalized and Bangladesh increased the minimum wage.

Business models and their impacts on development and human rights

A newer issue that has only started to be explored is how to address the problem of the mainstream business model designed to provide increasing returns to shareholders, known as "maximizing shareholder value." Share buybacks, whereby the company repurchases its stock with the extra cash it has on hand, which returns money to shareholders, together with dividends represent over 85 percent of profits for US companies today, up from 50 percent in 1970 (Purpose of the Corporation, 2016). In the UK, the trend to transfer profits to shareholders is even more stark – dividends paid to shareholders have gone from 10 percent of profits in 1970 to 70 percent today (Purpose of the Corporation, 2016). Alongside publicly listed companies, there are also private and family businesses that may be structured to prioritize shareholder returns in commercial decisions.

A business model emphasizing large, short-term returns to shareholders means that human rights and the environmental are often neglected. According to the chief economist of the Bank of England, when companies have a singular focus on maximizing profits, they often do so at the expense of other stakeholders, including workers, communities, and consumers (Haldane, 2015).

More recently, there has been an uptick in the number of enterprises opting for an alternative form of ownership and governance structures that take a more balanced approach that also emphasizes other stakeholder interests, including human rights (Sahan, 2016b). These alternative models include consumer (Saxena and Craig, 1990, pp 489–518) and producer cooperatives (Carney et al., 2015); worker-owned enterprises (Huertas-Noble, 2016, p 325); mission-led business models, like benefit corporations (Bauer and Umlas, 2017); Fair Trade Enterprises built around benefiting producers (World Fair Trade Organization); and zero-loss, zero-return social businesses (Yunus Social Businesses, 2007). Across the world, there are now a broad range of social enterprise and mission-led models, many of which are certified and verified by organizations like the World Fair Trade Organization and B Lab, the nonprofit promoting the benefit corporations model. Alternative structures don't automatically deliver higher wages and human rights improvements. Yet the new forms provide ways to build corporate respect for human rights as a design feature of businesses without being confined to situations where respecting rights also happens to be the path to maximum profits (e.g., Bauer and Umlas, 2017).

One area where the impacts of different business models is very clear is the phenomenon of growing inequality. As noted by the Center for Economic and Social Rights, extreme inequality is "a consequence as well as a cause of human rights deprivations" ("Inequality: can human rights make a difference?" n.d.). Businesses play a central role in creating and distributing the "fruits of an economy," and their approach to wages, taxes, and supplier pricing can determine who benefits from economic growth and the level of inequality within society (Sahan, 2016a). Profit-maximizing companies are wired to capture as much value as possible through all commercial activities, and overall they have dramatically increased the percentage of profits that is transferred to shareholders and other capital investors. In his best-selling book, *Capital in the Twenty-First Century* (Piketty, 2014), Thomas Piketty demonstrates how returns for the owners of capital have grown at a faster rate than general economic growth, meaning that workers are capturing a declining share of the gains from growth (Hardoon, 2017).

According to a survey of business leaders conducted by Pricewaterhouse-Coopers (PWC), just over 5 percent of business representatives surveyed saw inequality as a key impact or opportunity area for their business, ranking second to last in priority for businesses among the 17 SDGs (Price Waterhouse Coopers, 2015). Inevitably, inequality puts the spotlight on the prices paid to farmers, wages paid to workers, taxes paid to government, and prices charged to consumers (Sahan, 2016b). Acting on these areas almost inevitably hits the bottom line.

There are examples of how alternative business models can make a difference in reducing inequality. For instance, at the Kenyan Tea Development Agency, a business owned by 550,000 small-scale tea farmers with 66 tea processing factories, farmers receive over 75 percent of the final tea price (International Finance Corporation, 2014). Meanwhile, tea farmers in nearby Rwanda, without a similar business model, only earn 25 percent (Gatsby, n.d.). Other models share value further up the supply chain with farmers, allowing them to benefit beyond the farm gate. The fair trade chocolate business Divine Chocolate is one such example. As a business that captures value from branding, it uses a combination of financial flows to benefit farmers, including through sharing profits (Wills, 2015). These are examples of business and supply chain models where activities (e.g., tea processing, branding) are structured to channel additional value to farmers and workers. Such models that share value and power more with farmers and plantation workers are particularly important since according to the Food and Agriculture Organization of the United Nations, 2.5 billion people depend on agriculture for a livelihood (FAO, 2016). As the sector on which the livelihoods of many of the world's poorest depends, business models that channel greater value to smallholder farmers and plantation workers is critical to reversing the trend of growing inequality.

There are many other examples of business models where greater power and value is shared with workers and farmers. At production level, for instance, Muhanga Food Processing Industries in Rwanda is a food processing company, majority owned by a women-only cooperative, where farmer interests are represented on the enterprise's board and in executive committee (Jennings et al., 2018). In garment production, Creative Handicrafts in India is controlled by the women workers it provides livelihoods to, with a board that is largely made up of their representatives (Creative Handicrafts, Annual Report 2016–17). At importer and distribution levels, there are models like El Puente in Germany, which shares ownership and representation with producers in developing countries (WFTO Europe, 2014). At brand level, models like Café Direct are partly owned by coffee farmers and the board includes their representatives (Jennings et al., 2018). At retail level, there are employee-owned models like John Lewis (John Lewis Partnership, n.d.) in the UK and multistakeholder models like Biocoop in France, where farmers and small shop operators share profits and governance (Biocoop, Governance and Organisation, n.d.).

All these models exist across different parts of the value chain and deploy a range of ownership and governance that disperse power and value differently from mainstream models that only maximize returns to shareholders. In assessing business impacts on development and human rights, it is important to consider the way power and priority are directed in the structure of that business.

Conclusions

This chapter has focused principally on the human rights implications of Western multinationals with operations and supply chains in developing countries. Yet many of the issues presented can also be applied to growing businesses based in emerging markets, including Brazil, Russia, India, China, South Africa, Mexico, Indonesia, and Turkey. Enterprises based in these countries are fast increasing their economic and human rights footprints, both at home and abroad, and are in turn increasingly subject to scrutiny. Likewise, the informal sector, where the vast majority of the world's populations earn their living and which often encompasses the poorest of the poor,[8] also demands the attention of the business and human rights movement. For instance, workers in the informal sector often lack a contract, are less likely to have state protection of their labor rights, have less job security, and lack power to negotiate employment terms (International Labour Organization, 2012). Because the informal sector is, by definition, where government regulation is missing (International Institute for Environment and Development, n.d.), the adverse impacts of economic activity on marginalized populations often goes unnoticed.

The chapter has also focused on the more direct and tangible impacts of businesses on human rights and development, but their impacts can also be indirect. Companies, particularly large ones, play a key role in shaping not just business norms but also social norms. When globally recognized brands do business with corrupt officials or turn a blind eye to injustices, they lend credibility to those individuals and practices. In this way companies can entrench power inequities and legitimize discrimination, corruption, and even violence. As nations compete for much-needed investment, businesses seeking the cheapest means of production or access to land and resources can trigger a "race to the bottom" by gaining market access without expectations of respecting labor, land, and natural resource rights.

Underlying this discussion is a fundamental problem of profound power asymmetries and the potential for exploitation. Whether it is workers, farmers, consumers, or communities defending their rights against a corporation or a business in the informal economy, the critical factor is their level of power. People who are desperate for employment will accept lower wages and poorer conditions because they lack negotiating power. Farmers who are trapped in poverty and have just harvested perishable crops may have no choice but to accept prices for their produce that trap them and their families in a cycle of poverty. Without strong government intervention, business models that are designed to distribute power or enforcement of collective power – for example, through unions, cooperatives, or community organizations – power imbalances will exacerbate the human rights harms of business activity, overshadowing the potential gains to developing societies.

Notes

1 China is responsible for three-quarters of this drop in poverty, an achievement that many argue was fueled by investment and trade-led growth: "The world's next great leap forward: Towards the end of poverty," 2013.
2 A 2015 study of donor policies reported that the private sector features among the main priorities and objectives for 19 out of the 23 donor development policies examined (ITUCE et al, 2015).
3 Officially launched in July 2000, under the mandate of the UN General Secretary, today the Global Compact is composed of just over 13,000 members, roughly 9,000 of which are businesses: www.unglobalcompact.org/what-is-gc/participants.
4 The chart credits Thomas Biersteker, *Distortion or Development? Contending Perspectives on the Multinational Corporations*, Cambridge: MIT Press, 1978. Chapter 3.
5 According to the World Bank, increasingly inequality is rising within, not between, countries. Verbeek and Rodarte, 2015.
6 The organization issued two reports: "Behind the Great Wall of China – U.S. Corporations Opposing New Rights for Chinese Workers" in 2006 and "Undue Influence: Corporations Gain Ground in Battle over China's New Labor Law." The company responses to these reports can be found here: www.business-humanrights.org/Documents/China labourlawreform
7 In 2014, Oxfam and the UN Global Compact partnered to roll out a model of poverty footprinting that could be more easily adopted by a wider range of companies, including UN Global Compact's 8,000 corporate members. See: Oxfam and UN Global Compact, "Poverty Footprint: A people-centered approach to assessing business impacts on sustainable development," 2015, www.unglobalcompact.org/library/3131
8 According to the ILO, informal employment represents at least two-thirds of nonagricultural employment in 11 of 44 low- and middle-income countries it studied: International Labor Organization, "Statistical Update on Employment in the Informal Economy," 2011, http://laborsta.ilo.org/applv8/data/INFORMAL_ECONOMY/SU-2011-06-Informal_Economy.pdf

References

Accenture (2011). "Global Operating Models for Mining Companies: Adding Value Beyond the Individual Assets." www.accenture.com/t20150527T211403__w__/jp-ja/_acnmedia/Accenture/Conversion-Assets/DotCom/Documents/Local/ja-jp/PDF_2/Accenture-Mining-Global-Operating-Models-POV-FINAL.pdf

Action Aid (February 2013). "*Sweet Nothings: The Human Cost of a British Sugar Giant Avoiding Taxes in southern Africa.*" www.actionaid.org.uk/sites/default/files/publications/sweet_nothings.pdf

Agosin, Manuel R. and Ricardo Mayer (February 2000). "Foreign Investment in Developing Countries: Does it Crowd in Domestic Investment?" UNCTAD/OSG/DP/No. 146.

Alston, Philip (2005). "Labour Rights as Human Rights: The Not So Happy State of the Art," in Philip Alston (ed), *Labour Rights as Human Rights*. Oxford: Oxford University Press; Wonnell, Christopher T. and Lochner V. New York as Economic Theory (September 2001). *U of San Diego Public Law Research* Paper No. 24. SSRN: https://ssrn.com/abstract=285433 or http://dx.doi.org/10.2139/ssrn.285433

Arnold, Denis G. and Norman E. Bowie (2003), "Sweatshops and Respect for Persons," *Business Ethics Quarterly* (13).

Bauer, Joanne (December 17, 2014). "The Problem with Corporate Social Responsibility," *Open Democracy*. www.opendemocracy.net/joanne-bauer/problem-with-corporate-social-responsibility

Bauer, Joanne and Elizabeth Umlas (September 2017), "Making Corporations Responsible: The Parallel Tracks of the B Corp Movement and the Business and Human Rights Movement," *Business and Society Review* 122:3 285–325.

Biocoop, Governance and Organisation. www.biocoop.fr/Biocoop/Organisation/gouvernance-et-organisation

Boggan, Steve (October 20, 2001). "'We Blew It': Nike Admits to Mistakes Over Child Labor." *The Independent*.

Carney, Brent, David Haines and Stephen King (2015). "Farmer Cooperatives and Competition: Who Wins, Who Loses and Why?" http://ssrn.com/abstract=2673396

Centre for Economic and Social Rights, "Inequality: Can Human Rights Make a Difference?" www.cesr.org/inequality-can-human-rights-make-difference-0

Christian Aid (May 2008). "Death and Taxes: The True Toll of Tax Dodging." www.christianaid.org.uk/images/deathandtaxes.pdf

Christian Aid, Oxfam, Action Aid (November 2015). "Getting to Good – Towards Responsible Corporate Tax Behaviour." www.oxfam.org/sites/www.oxfam.org/files/file_attachments/dp-getting-to-good-corporate-tax-171115-en.pdf

Clean Clothes Campaign (April 29, 2014). "Gender: Women Workers Mistreated." https://cleanclothes.org/issues/gender

Cohn, Michael (October 11, 2013). "Tax Avoidance Seen as a Human Rights Violation," *Accounting Today*. www.accountingtoday.com/news/Tax-Avoidance-Human-Rights-Violation-68312-1.html

Confino, Jo (January 21, 2015). "Public Trust in Business Hits Five-Year Low," *The Guardian*. www.theguardian.com/sustainable-business/2015/jan/21/public-trust-global-business-government-low-decline

Creative Handicrafts, Annual Report 2016–17. https://creativehandicrafts.org/wp-content/uploads/2018/01/CH-Annual-Report-2016-2017.pdf

Drucker, Peter (Winter 1984). "The New Meaning of Corporate Social Responsibility," *California Management Review* 26:2.

Earth Rights International (2009). "Total Impact: The Human Rights, Environmental, and Financial Impacts of Total and Chevron's Yadana Gas Project in Military-Ruled Burma (Myanmar)." www.earthrights.org/publication/total-impact

Ethical Trading Initiative (May 18, 2016). "Base Code Guidance: Living Wages." www.ethicaltrade.org/sites/default/files/shared_resources/eti_living_wage_guidance_2.pdf

Food and Agriculture Organization (May 2016). "Increasing the Resilience of Agricultural Livelihoods." www.fao.org/3/a-i5615e.pdf

Friedman, Milton (September 13, 1970). The Social Responsibility of Business Is to Increase Its Profits. *The New York Times Magazine*, 122–126.

Gatsby. "Rwandan Tea Sector." www.gatsby.org.uk/africa/programmes/rwandan-tea-sector

Global Impact Investing Network (n.d.). "What Is Impact Investing?" https://thegiin.org/impact-investing/need-to-know/#what-is-impact-investing

Global Reporting Initiative, UN Global Compact, WBCSD (December 2015). "SDG Compass: The Guide for Business Action on the SDGs." https://sdgcompass.org/wp-content/uploads/2015/12/019104_SDG_Compass_Guide_2015.pdf

Greening, Justin (January 27, 2014). "Smart Aid: Why It's All About Jobs," Speech to the London Stock Exchange. www.gov.uk/government/speeches/smart-aid-why-its-all-about-jobs

Haldane, Andrew G. (2015). "Who Owns a Company?" Speech at University of Edinburgh Corporate Finance Conference. www.bankofengland.co.uk/-/media/boe/files/speech/2015/who-owns-a-company.pdf

Hardoon, Deborah (2017) "An Economy for the 99%: Its Time to Build a Human Economy That Benefits Everyone, Not Just the Privileged Few." Oxfam Briefing Paper. www.oxfam.org/en/research/economy-99

Harvard Business School (n.d.). "Creating Shared Value." www.isc.hbs.edu/creating-shared-value/Pages/default.aspx

Hochschild, Adam (1998) *King Leopold's Ghost: A Story of Greed, Terror, and Heroism in Colonial Africa*. New York: First Mariner Books.

Huertas-Noble, Carmen (2016), "Worker-Owned and Unionized Worker-Owned Cooperatives: Two Tools to Address Income Inequality," *Clinical Law Review* 22.

IndustriALL Global Union (July 8, 2014), "IndustriALL Renews Agreement with World's Largest Fashion Retailer." www.industriall-union.org/industriall-renews-agreement-with-worlds-largest-fashion-retailer

International Finance Corporation (June 2014), "Inclusive Business Case Study: Kenya Tea Development Agency Ltd. (KTDA)." www.ifc.org/wps/wcm/connect/5fa58180445b4102a1dbadc66d9c728b/KTDA.pdf?MOD=AJPERES

International Institute for Environment and Development. "The Informal Economy and Sustainable Development." www.iied.org/informal-economy-sustainable-development

International Labour Organization (2011), "Statistical Update on Employment in the Informal Economy." Pp 2–3. http://laborsta.ilo.org/applv8/data/INFORMAL_ECONOMY/SU-2011-06-Informal_Economy.pdf

International Labour Organization (2012), "From Precarious Work to Decent Work: Outcome Document to the Workers' Symposium on Policies and Regulations to Combat Precarious Employment." www.ilo.org/wcmsp5/groups/public/-ed_dialogue/-actrav/documents/meetingdocument/wcms_179787.pdf

International Trade Union Confederation and Eurodad (July 9, 2015), "Business Accountability for Development." www.ituc-csi.org/business-accountability-for-development

Jennings, Steve, Erinch Sahan and Alex Maitland (April 2018), "Fair Value: Case Studies of Business Structures for a More Equitable Distribution of Value in Food Supply Chains." Oxfam Discussion Paper. https://policy-practice.oxfam.org.uk/publications/fair-value-case-studies-of-business-structures-for-a-more-equitable-distributio-620452

John Lewis Partnership, Employee Ownership. www.johnlewispartnership.co.uk/work/employee-ownership.html

Kende-Robb, Caroline (May 17, 2016), "Africa Is Rich in Resources – But Tax Havens Are Keeping Its People Poor." World Economic Forum. www.weforum.org/agenda/2016/05/africa-is-rich-in-resources-but-tax-havens-are-keeping-its-people-poor

Kolk, A., A. Kourula and N. Pisani (2017). "Multinational Enterprises and the Sustainable Development Goals: What Do We Know and How to Proceed?" *Transnational Corporations*, 24(3), 9–32.

Korten, David C. (2015). *When Corporations Rule the World*. Oakland, CA: Berrrett Koehler Publishers.

Kramer, Mark and Michael Porter (January–February, 2011). "Creating Shared Value," *Harvard Business Review*, 89(1–2), 62–77.

Kristof, Nicholas and Sheryl WuDunn (September 24, 2000). "Two Cheers for Sweatshops," *The New York Times*.

Krugman, Paul (March 21, 1997). "In Praise of Cheap Labor," *Slate Magazine*, 6, 70.

McMullen, Anna (March 2014). "Tailored Wages," *Ethical Consumer*. www.ethicalconsumer. org/commentanalysis/humanrights/tailoredwages.aspx

McMullen, Anna and Sanjita Majumder (February 15, 2016). "Do We Buy It? A Supply Chain Investigation into Living Wage Commitments from M&S and H&M," Labour Behind the Label, Cividep, SUM, Heather Stilwell and CLEC. http://labourbehindthe-label.org/dowebuyit/

Oxfam (January 18, 2016). "An Economy for the 1%: How Privilege and Power in the Economy Drive Extreme Inequality and How This Can Be Stopped." www.oxfam.org/sites/www.oxfam.org/files/file_attachments/bp210-economy-one-percent-tax-havens-180116-en_0.pdf

Oxfam International (November 17, 2009), *Oxfam Poverty Footprint: Understanding Business Contribution to Development*, Briefings for Business No. 4. https://d1tn3vj7xz9fdh.cloud-front.net/s3fs-public/file_attachments/oxfam-poverty-footprint_3.pdf

Oxfam and UN Global Compact (2015), "Poverty Footprint: A People-Centered Approach to Assessing Business Impacts on Sustainable Development." Pp. 9–19. www.unglobalcom-pact.org/library/3131

Palmisano, Samuel (May–June 2006). "The Globally Integrated Enterprise," *Foreign Affairs* 85:3.

Piketty, Thomas (2014), *Capital in the Twenty-First Century*. Cambridge: Harvard University Press.

Pingeot, Lou (January 2014). "Corporate Influence in the Post-2015 Process," Miserior, Bread for the World, and Global Policy Forum. www.misereor.org/fileadmin//user_upload/misereor_org/Publications/englisch/working-paper-corporate-influence-in-post-2015-process.pdf

Price Waterhouse Coopers (2015), "Make It Your Business: Engaging with the Sustainable Development Goals." www.pwc.com/gx/en/sustainability/SDG/SDG%20Research_FINAL.pdf

Purpose of the Corporation (2016), "Behind the Purpose of the Corporation Info-graphic." www.purposeofcorporation.org/en/news/5009-behind-the-purpose-of-the-corporation-infographic/

Reich, Robert (1998). "The New Meaning of Corporate Social Responsibility," *California Management Review* 40:2.

Ruggie, John (2006). "Interim Report of the Special Representative of the Secretary-General on the Issue of Human Rights and Transnational Corporations and Other Business Enterprises." U.N. Doc. E/CN.4/2006/97

Sahan, Erinch (March 31, 2016a). "Tackling Inequality Is a Game-Changer for Business and the Private Sector, Which Is Why Most of Them Are Ignoring It," From Poverty to Power Blog. http://oxfamblogs.org/fp2p/tackling-inequality-is-a-game-changer-for-business-and-private-sector-development-which-is-why-most-of-them-are-ignoring-it/

Sahan, Erinch (2016b). "Does Business Structure Influence Social Impact? Early Insights and Practical Implications for Donor Agencies," *Donor Committee for Enterprise Development Briefing Note*. www.enterprise-development.org/wp-content/uploads/Does-business-structure-influence-social-impact-OxfamDCED-Briefing-Note.pdf

Sauvant, Karl. P. (2015). "The Negotiations of the United Nations Code of Conduct on Transnational Corporations Experience and Lessons Learned," *The Journal of World Investment & Trade* 16.

Saxena, Suren and John Craig (1990). "Consumer Cooperatives in a Changing World: Annals of Public and Cooperative Economics," *Annals of Public and Cooperative Economics* 61.

Schanberg, Sydney and Marie Dorigny (June 1996). "Six Cents and Hour," *Life*.

Shift (November 2016). "Business, Human Rights, and the Sustainable Development Goals: Forging a Coherent Strategy." http://s3.amazonaws.com/aws-bsdc/BSDC-Biz-HumanRights-SDGs.pdf

Spar, Deborah (January–February 1999). "Foreign Investment and Human Rights," *Challenge*, 42.

Swiss Agency for Development Cooperation (August 2015). *The Operational Guide for the Making Markets Work for the Poor (M4P) Approach*, Second Edition. Durham: The Springfield Centre.

Todaro, Michael and Stephen C. Smith (2015). *Economic Development*. New York: Pearson.

UNCTAD (June 23, 2009). "Global FDI Flows Halved in 1st Quarter of 2009 UNCTAD Data Show; Prospects Remain Low for Rest of Year," UNCTAD/PRESS/PR/2009/024. http://unctad.org/en/pages/PressReleaseArchive.aspx?ReferenceDocId=11666

UNCTAD, "World Investment Report 2016." www.worldbank.org/en/news/feature/2015/07/10/financing-the-end-of-poverty

United Nations (2011). *Guiding Principles on Business and Human Rights: Implementing the United Nations "Protect, Respect and Remedy" Framework*, HR/PUB/11/04. www.ohchr.org/Documents/Publications/GuidingPrinciplesBusinessHR_EN.pdf

United Nations Economic and Social Council (May 22–25, 2017). Report of the Economic and Social Council Forum on Financing for Development Follow-Up. www.un.org/esa/ffd/ffdforum/wp-content/uploads/sites/3/2017/10/Report-of-the-ECOSOC-Forum-on-FfD-followup_E-FFDF-2017-3.pdf

UN Global Compact. www.unglobalcompact.org/what-is-gc/participants

United Nations Human Rights Council (April 7, 2008). "Protect, Respect and Remedy: A Framework for Business and Human Rights," A/HRC/8/5. www.reports-and-materials.org/Ruggie-report-7-Apr-2008.pdf

Universal Declaration of Human Rights, United Nations. www.un.org/en/universal-declaration-human-rights/

United Nations Information Service (October 31, 2002). "In Message to Regional Meeting of International Chamber of Commerce, Secretary-General Stresses Strengthening Un/Business Partnerships," UNRIS Press Release. www.unis.unvienna.org/unis/en/pressrels/2002/sgsm8466.html

UN News Centre (September 26, 2015). "UN Forum Highlights 'Fundamental' Role of Private Sector in Advancing New Global Goals." www.un.org/sustainabledevelopment/blog/2015/09/un-forum-highlights-fundamental-role-of-private-sector-in-advancing-new-global-goals/

Verbeek, Jos and Israel Osorio Rodarte (October 2, 2015). "Increasingly, Inequality Within, Not Across, Countries Is Rising," *Let's Talk Development*, World Bank. http://blogs.worldbank.org/developmenttalk/increasingly-inequality-within-not-across-countries-rising

Wills, Jackie (April 2015). "Cocoa Farmers Spread the Taste for Divine Chocolate," *Guardian*. www.theguardian.com/sustainable-business/2015/apr/30/cocoa-farmers-spread-the-taste-for-divine-chocolate

Wilshaw, Rachel (December 10, 2014). "Steps Towards a Living Wage in Global Supply Chains." Oxfam International Policy Paper. http://policy-practice.oxfam.org.uk/publications/steps-towards-a-living-wage-in-global-supply-chains-336623

Wilshaw, Rachel (September 29, 2015). "In Work but Trapped in Poverty: A Summary of Five Studies Conducted by Oxfam, with Updates on Progress Along the Road to a Living Wage," Oxfam International. https://policy-practice.oxfam.org.uk/publications/in-work-but-trapped-in-poverty-a-summary-of-five-studies-conducted-by-oxfam-wit-578815

World Bank Group (October 2013). "Financing for Development Post-2015." www.worldbank.org/content/dam/Worldbank/document/Poverty%20documents/WB-PREM%20financing-for-development-pub-10-11-13web.pdf

World Business Council on Sustainable Development(n.d.). "Inclusive Business Insights." www.inclusive-business.org/

World Economic Forum (May 17, 2016). "Africa Is Rich in Resources – but Tax Havens Are Keeping Its People Poor." www.weforum.org/agenda/2016/05/africa-is-rich-in-resources-but-tax-havens-are-keeping-its-people-poor

World Fair Trade Organization. www.wfto.com

"The World's Next Great Leap Forward: Towards the End of Poverty," *The Economist*, June 1, 2013. www.economist.com/news/leaders/21578665-nearly-1-billion-people-have-been-taken-out-extreme-poverty-20-years-world-should-aim

WFTO Europe (March 11, 2014). "Member of the Month." https://wfto-europe.org/news/member-of-the-month-el-puente/

Yunus, Muhammad (2007). "Social Business." Yunus Centre. www.muhammadyunus.org/index.php/social-business/social-business

15 Impacts of neoliberal wind energy investments on environmental justice and human rights in Mexico

Jacobo Ramirez

Introduction

In postcolonial countries such as those in Latin America and the Caribbean (LAC), preventing changes to one's livelihood and territory appears to be one rationale for resistance against wind energy projects (Diego Quintana, 2015; Terwindt and Schliamann, 2017) and a cause of confrontation between governments and business, on the one hand, and indigenous people's vision of the environment (Agyeman, 2014; Martinez-Alier et al., 2016; Sikor and Newell, 2014), on the other. Indigenous people's concerns move beyond the NIMBY (not in my backyard) aesthetic rationale (Aitken, 2010) for opposing wind energy investments. One source of confrontation may be the inappropriate application of the free, prior, and informed consent (FPIC) principle (Colchester and Farhan Ferrari, 2007; Dunlap, 2017a). Regional development projects in wind energy require an extensive use of land, which appears to be a problem around the world, particularly for indigenous communities who have strong place-based attachments to the vision of their environment and territory (Cass and Walker, 2009; Dunlap, 2017b; Escobar, 2008; Martin, 2005; Nolte, 2016).

Opposition against governmental and multinational corporations (MNCs) seeking to implement sustainable energy solutions might appear retrograde to global strategies for reducing carbon emissions in the fight against climate change, such as the Paris Agreement (UNFCCC, 2019). Governments and MNCs present their investments in wind energy by strategically selecting aspects of perceived reality (Entman, 1993), such as key strategies that contribute to developing local communities in order to reduce poverty or fight climate change (e.g., FEMSA, 2017; IADB, 2011). MNCs' investments in wind energy are developed in Mexico based on the neoliberal principle (Diego Quintana, 2015; Williamson, 2008). However, little is known about indigenous people's environmental visions, which might clash with neoliberal principles and efforts to foster wind energy investments in postcolonial countries (Dunlap, 2018; Martin, 2005).

Neoliberal principles in wind energy investments rest on the superiority of market-based solutions over governmental ones. For example, the Swedish government has opted for "a get-others-to-do rather than a do-it-yourself policy" in wind energy (Corvellec, 2007: 131). In the case of Mexico, neoliberal development policies have been implemented since the 1980s following the Washington Consensus (Williamson, 2008). These policies facilitated private investments in wind energy parks (Juárez-Hernández and León, 2014), but they have also been associated with an increase in social inequalities and exclusion (Gonzalez Casanova, 1965; Martin, 2005; Olzak, 1983). In 2013, Mexico approved an energy reform based on the neoliberal principle of supporting national and international private investors in renewable energy. However, since the 1990s, private investors have constructed wind energy development projects in the Isthmus of the Tehuantepec region (Diego Quintana, 2015), which is located in Oaxaca State in Mexico. The Isthmus of Tehuantepec region possesses one of the most powerful wind resources in the world (Elliott et al., 2004). However, indigenous people in this region lack access to basic infrastructure, such as electricity (INEGI, 2015; Leyva Hernández et al., 2017). This region is where marginalized indigenous people continue their long tradition of struggles against local and foreign invasions and fight to bring development to their region (Campbell et al., 1993; Diego Quintana, 2015).

In postcolonial countries, there is a long tradition of studying indigenous people's mobilization against corrupt governments, inefficient regional economic development projects, and the fallout from neoliberal development policies (Bardhan, 2000; Campbell et al., 1993; Costanza, 2016; Davis and Rosan, 2004; Rubin, 1994, 2004). There is also a lack of knowledge regarding fairness and (in)justice, human rights abuses, environmental impacts, and land disputes (Agyeman, 2014; Martinez-Alier et al., 2016). The pattern of oppression, repression, and violation in postcolonial countries is considered internal colonialism (Gonzalez Casanova, 1965; Love, 1989). Internal colonialism is defined as a "geographically based pattern of subordination of a differentiated population located within the dominant power of country" (Pinderhughes, 2010: 2385–2386). Internal colonialism is the theoretical lends through which I discuss exclusion and environmental (in)justice in neoliberal wind energy investments (Aitken, 2010; Toke and Lauber, 2007).

Based on qualitative longitudinal research (2013–2018), I discuss internal colonialism at the Isthmus of Tehuantepec, integrating insights from the environmental justice literature. The findings suggest that MNCs and governments appear to neglect oversee the particularities of the history of struggles and resilience of local indigenous people (particularly the Zapotecas and Ikoojts) against local and foreign invasions, invasions that have further exacerbated the social exclusion, inequalities, environmental (in)justice, and human rights abuses that indigenous people have suffered in relation to wind energy projects. This study advances our understanding of how sustainable energy development projects negatively affect indigenous communities. This specific case proposes the argument that indigenous people in developing countries and white men in developed countries, who feel left behind in the march for neoliberalism (Edwards et al., 2017; Inglehart and Norris, 2016), tend to endorse anti-neoliberal mobilizations.

The chapter is structured as follows. First, the chapter develops a theoretical framework on internal colonialism and environmental justice. Second, the chapter introduces the developed methodology. In the third section of the chapter, the findings are presented, while also integrating past research at the Isthmus of Tehuantepec. The final section presents a discussion and the implications of the study, thus contributing to development studies in relation to sustainable green energy and indigenous people.

Theoretical background

Internal colonialism theory

Internal colonialism refers to a process of unequal development among regions in a given country and a lack of access to economic and social benefits; these problems are seen to result from the implementation of an economic development model (Gonzalez Casanova, 1965; Hechter, 2017). Internal colonialism has gained acceptance in the social science literature since the 1960s with the work of the Mexican sociologist Pablo González Casanova (Hind, 1984), who emphasized ethical elements of internal colonialism and built into his definition "the historical fact of conquest of members of one civilization by another" (Love, 1989: 906). Since then, internal colonialism has been used in the context of ethno-regional studies in Europe and the United States, as seen in studies of Great Britain (e.g., Hechter, 2017; Love, 1989).

Internal colonialism involves the exploitation of people and land; it applies to spatially differentiated groups within states (Love, 1989). During the European period of classic colonialism in the Global South, the following patterns (among others) occurred: (1) physical and/or psychological violence; (2) economic exploitation; (3) poverty; (4) illiteracy; (5) lawlessness; and (6) stealing and crime (Gonzalez Casanova, 1965; Pinderhughes, 2010). In contrast to classic colonialism, internal colonialism represents a condition in which both the dominant and the subordinate groups coexist as natives of the same society (Steady, 2009).

In this research, internal colonialism is understood as a "geographically based pattern of subordination of a differentiated population, located within the dominant power or country" (Pinderhughes, 2010: 235–236). Place-based attachments, identities, meanings, and values (Cass and Walker, 2009) are present in indigenous communities, for example, in festivities, food, and indigenous languages. Place-based attachments are a conscious process in which internal colonialism might not necessarily be consciously implemented (Love, 1989). For example, the collapse of oil prices in the 1970s, among other factors, resulted in Mexico's economic crisis, which is known as a debt crisis. In the 1980s, Mexico implemented the neoliberal development model as an alternative to the import substitution industrialization (ISI) development model to decrease dependence on oil revenues (Martínez Rangel and Reyes Garmendia, 2012). Neoliberal economic policies offer free play and open the economy (Hechter, 2017) to foreign direct investments (FDI), among other measures (Williamson, 2008), but these practices can have unintended distributional consequences (Hechter, 2017) in Mexico, especially for indigenous people (McAfee and Shapiro, 2010).

Studies of disparities in regional development in the rural areas of Mexico inhabited by indigenous people report that 70 percent are poor (APROMECI, 2016). In the State of Oaxaca, 70.4 percent of the population is poor (CON-AVAL, 2017). Uneven social contentions between developed and underdeveloped groups rest on access to basic human rights (e.g., health, education, food, water, freedom) and income inequalities (OECD, 2015). According to the Organisation for Economic Co-operation and Development (OECD), in Mexico, the incomes of the richest are more than 25 times those of the poorest (OECD, 2015). Internal colonialism serves as a theoretical framework for examining social unrest in the Global South, focusing specifically on the conflict between wind energy investments and indigenous people's place-based attachments to their territory (e.g., Cass and Walker, 2009) as related to environmental justice, a concept that is presented in the following section.

Environmental justice

Justice is a combination of ensuring and recognizing the basic equal worth of all people, referred to as the basic principle of human rights, together with a commitment to the "distribution of good and bad things" (Campbell, 2010). An ethical-normative approach to energy justice holds that energy justice "aims to provide all individuals, across all areas, with safe, affordable and sustainable energy" (McCauley et al., 2013: 1). This definition can be interpreted as stating that all individuals are equal (United Nations, 1948), in the sense of all ethnic groups belonging to a single community based on a collective morality, referred to as energy for all (McCauley et al., 2013).

Environmental justice has been defined as the fair treatment and meaningful involvement of all people – regardless of race, color, national origin, or income – in the development, implementation, and enforcement of environmental policies (Bullard and Johnson, 2002). Environmental justice calls for the meaningful involvement of different social groups, which implies procedural questions about the ability of different social groups to engage in and exert influence over environmental decision making (Agyeman, 2014). This vision is presented in Goal 7 of the Sustainable Development Goals (SDGs), which states: "Ensure access to affordable, reliable, sustainable and modern energy for all" (United Nations, 2015).

The first National People of Color Environmental Leadership conference in 1991 adopted a manifesto that defined environmental justice in 17 clauses (Environmental Justice/Environmental Racism, 1991). I highlight the following:

• Environmental justice affirms the sacredness of Mother Earth, ecological unity and the interdependence of all species, and the right to be free from ecological destruction.

- Environmental justice mandates the right to ethical, balanced, and responsible uses of land and renewable resources in the interest of a sustainable planet for humans and other living things.
- Environmental justice demands the right to participate as equal partners at every level of decision making, including needs assessment, planning, implementation, enforcement, and evaluation.

These clauses are derived in response to communities, such as indigenous people, who lack empowerment and access to energy resources. Respect for indigenous people's perceptions of the protection of Mother Earth appear to be at the center of disputes in environmental (in)justice. Sikor and Newell (2014: 152) echo Martinez-Alier et al. (2016), stating that poor people's claims

> are not only about the distribution of environmental goods and bads, but also about whose visions of the environment are recognised, who participates in environmental decision-making and democracy, and what kinds of values come to matter – all of which are central matters of justice.
>
> (Sikor and Newell, 2014: 152)

The debate about environmental justice has become more significant because of "observations that poorer and more deprived communities are often excluded from exerting influence in the decisionmaking processes that affect them and that they are disproportionately affected by negative social and environmental outcomes" (Gouldson, 2006: 402).

In the Global South, efforts at environmental justice are unclear regarding how democratic governance that integrates communities "to participate as equal partners at every level of decision making" are instrumented in renewable energy investments (e.g., Environmental Justice/Environmental Racism, 1991). A critical issue in these ethical dilemmas is how to evolve from a situation of political and business exclusion to the integration of indigenous communities in the process of the planning and development of renewable energy projects (Zografos and Martinez-Alier, 2009). A key foundation of such ethical dilemmas is the question of why indigenous communities were "devalued" (Schlosberg, 2013) and excluded in the first place, which is a pattern of internal colonialism (Gonzalez Casanova, 1965). Thus, environmental justice is about reversing past colonial repression, oppression, and practices that have violated Mother Earth, all of which place burdens on indigenous people in postcolonial countries. Thus, environmental justice cannot be achieved unless the environmental movement itself becomes democratic. As a result, an energy justice movement (Martinez-Alier et al., 2016) has emerged in Global South, seeking to create opportunities to destabilize power relations; reverse histories of dispossession, marginalization, and social and environmental (in)justice; and "replac[e] monopolized fossil fuel energy systems with democratic and renewable structures" (Burke and Stephens, 2017: 36).

Territory is a particular component of social justice in the Global South. The concept of territory encompasses the history of place, which is the shared sense of meaning that is connected to history, culture, landscape, and social life in a specific place (Escobar, 2008: 62). A lack of knowledge of territory may stem from improperly applying the FPIC principle (Colchester and Farhan Ferrari, 2007). The FPIC principle is based on the International Labour Organization's (ILO's) Convention on Indigenous and Tribal Peoples in Independent Countries – 169/1989 (International Labour Organization, 2016). The ILO 169 Convention was ratified by Mexico on September 5, 1990. The FPIC principle lays the groundwork for fair compensation to local communities as part of the land transfer process in, for example, sustainable energy development projects. The relation between the FPIC principle and human rights is related to Principle 13 of the United Nations' Guiding Principles on Business and Human Rights (UNGPs): "Principle 13: The responsibility to respect human rights requires that business enterprises: a) Avoid causing or contributing to adverse human rights . . ., b) Seek to prevent or mitigate adverse human rights impacts that are directly linked to their operations" (United Nations, 2011: 14). The FPIC principle is expected to be reached through political freedom, freedom of speech, and transparency between local communities and MNCs. This expectation suggests that to ensure business success, businesses should be proactive "respect for applicable legislation, and for collective agreements between social partners, is a prerequisite for meeting that responsibility" (The European Commission, 2011: 6).

The challenge that MNCs face when trying to operate in contexts with persistent corruption, rule of law, and the presence of organized crime and violence suggests that it is MNCs' responsibility to build healthy institutional settings in order to create legitimacy and respect for different visions of environmental justice. Based on the theoretical framework and previous research, I formulated the following research question: How do wind energy development investments affect indigenous peoples' environmental justice claims? To answer this research question, I developed a qualitative study, which is presented in the following section.

Methods

This qualitative longitudinal study began in 2013 when newspapers in Mexico and Denmark presented the Zapotecas and Ikoojts in Mexico protesting at the Danish Embassy and the headquarters of the Danish wind firm, Vestas. The protests were against the imminent construction of the *Mareñas Renovables* wind energy project at the Isthmus of Tehuantepec. In 2013, I developed desk research to identify key actors in the *Mareña Renovable* project and to begin to understand the context (Alvesson and Deetz, 2000; Yin, 2016) of the Zapotecas and Itkoojts' social movement against the wind farm projects. Over time, this longitudinal study evolved from the specific *Mareñas Renovables* project to an examination of internal colonialism at the Isthmus of Tehuantepec in relation to wind energy investments. Empirical material was collected over five years (2013–2017) based on archival data, in-depth interviews, focus groups, and participatory observation.

Access to resistance groups fighting the wind energy projects was achieved thanks to a key informant, a Zapoteca who was raised in Juchitán, and with whom I have a close, long-term, ongoing unexplored relationship. I developed several conversations with the key informant to more broadly understand the Zapotecas' traditions, culture, struggles, and resilience. Participant observations occurred at assemblies and weekly meetings at different locations in the Isthmus of Tehuantepec. In-depth interviews were performed with indigenous people, as well as governmental, MNC, and nongovernmental organization (NGO) representatives. Indigenous people and governmental officials requested to not be recorded, but they agreed that I could take notes. All semi-structured interviews with MNCs and NGOs were taped and transcribed verbatim, and notes were taken. The interviews lasted an average of 80 minutes. Semi-structured interviews consisted of questions to identify Mexico's national plan for wind energy and firms' strategies for investing in wind farm projects, as well as indigenous people's positions on these investments in the territories and human rights issues in Mexico.

I was careful not to promise anything to my informants, such as positive or negative writings in relation to the wind energy projects in the Isthmus of Tehuantepec. Governmental and NGO officials were eager to emphasize the official positions presented on social media and news reports of the benefits of wind energy in general (diary notes).

To ensure the quality of the empirical material, I implemented two strategies: (1) empirical material was organized with Nvivo11 (qualitative software) and was coded in accordance with the evoked texts (Gioia et al., 2013), which referred to the impacts of wind energy projects on internal colonialism at the Isthmus of Tehuantepec, and (2) a detachment procedure (Campbell, 2001), through which I aimed to step back from the key informants' and individuals' life experiences and feelings (Davies, 2010) in order to avoid magnifying their accounts (Gioia et al., 2013). I triangulated the empirical materials in Nvivo 11 with previous research on the Isthmus of Tehuantepec's indigenous people (e.g., Campbell et al., 1993; Diego Quintana, 2015; Juárez-Hernández and León, 2014; Rubin, 1994, 2004). These strategies prevented pre-explanations of the current conflict in relation to wind energy parks and decreased the impartiality of the reality found at the Isthmus of Tehuantepec.

The analysis of the empirical material moved from the general perspectives of the findings to contrasts with theory and research on internal colonialism. Developing this approach allowed me to develop a systematic analysis of the empirical material to focus on the strategies that were implemented by the MNCs' representatives, governmental officials, and indigenous people rather than myths on indigenous people and wind energy projects. The following section presents the findings, which triangulate the empirical material with previous research and reports on wind energy investment in Oaxaca. The section begins with a presentation of the research context.

Framing the Isthmus of Tehuantepec's neoliberal wind energy investment landscape

Institutional context

The Isthmus of Tehuantepec is located on a peninsula of the Atlantic Ocean and the Gulf of Mexico, which makes the territory a natural corridor for wind from both sides. Given this physical geography, the Isthmus of Tehuantepec has been a geopolitical territory since colonial times, given its potential to shorten the distance between the Atlantic and Pacific Oceans (Martin, 2005). This region has been "rediscovered" as a result of its proven natural wind resources, which are seen as ideal for building wind energy farms (Elliott et al., 2004).

The Heroic City of Juchitán de Zaragoza (hereafter Juchitán) is the head of the municipality of the Isthmus of Tehuantepec. This adjective, *heroic*, encompasses the current reality of the local indigenous people. The Zapotec race inherits rebelliousness and detests subjugation, and the Zapotec people have been marked by centuries of struggle and resilience against national and foreign invasions (Matus, 1993).

In the 19th century, the Zapotecas' capacity to defend their resources and autonomy via armed rebellion led to their reputation as criminal and barbaric (Rubin, 1996). Zapotecas expelled the French from their territory in 1888. In the 20th century, after the Mexican revolution (1920), the Zapotecas developed Juchitán and constructed schools, clinics, and roads during the 25 years of cacique rule by General Heliodoro Charis (1896–1964). During the ruling years of Charis, the Zapotecas demonstrated their ability to resist the hegemony of the national urban culture by maintaining their indigenous language, festivities such as *Velas*, clothes, and food. In the 1970s, students in Juchitán formed an activist grassroots movement, which became the *Coalición Obrera Campesina Estudiantil del Istmo* (COCEI), to democratically fight against failed economic development in the Isthmus of Tehuantepec that resulted in widespread poverty and political corruption (Rubin, 1996). A former member of the COCEI and a current human rights defender in Juchitán commented on one of these mobilizations: "I was in secondary school when, together with my classmates, we marched to Juchitán's town-hall to demand public transportation to the school" (Interview).

In the 1970s and 1980s, during a period in the Zapotecas' history that coexisted with the Oaxaca state and the rest of Mexico, COCEI presented its mobilization for Zapotec culture as a discourse for a poor people's movement and ethnicity, which were collectively defined as a multiclass pueblo (Rubin, 1996). COECEI also fought – with considerable success – for rural land and agricultural opportunities, urban wages and benefits, and municipal sovereignty, and the group overcame violent repression in the process (interviews). In the 1980s, the Zapotecas surprised Mexicans and foreigners, as Juchitán democratically won an election with a Socialist Party, which sent a strong message that opposed the technocratic, market-oriented *Partido Revolucionario Institucional*

(PRI) party that had uninterruptedly ruled Mexico's local municipalities and state governments between 1929 and 1989 and the federal government from 1929 through 2000.

The neoliberal development model was legitimatized by the technocratic market-oriented Mexican president, Carlos Salinas de Gortari (1988–1994), of the PRI party. The neoliberal development model was implemented in Mexico through changes in the Mexican constitution and laws. President Salinas de Gortari pushed through reform of Article 27 of the Mexican Constitution, which ended the program of land redistribution and enabled the sale and purchase of previously inalienable communal landholdings, known as *ejidos* (*ejidos* were parcels of land given to landless peasants). In Oaxaca, this land tenure regime existed alongside communal landholdings, which indigenous communities were given title to by the Spanish Crown (Martin, 2005: 208). In the 1990s, the energy sector, including electricity commercialization and distribution, constitutionally remained exclusive to the Mexican government. However, in 1992, a constitutional reform changed the law to public service electricity, *Ley del Servicio Público de Energía Eléctrica* (LSPEE), which allows private-sector participation in generating electricity for consumption and/or sale to third parties.

In the mid-1990s, Mexican President Ernesto Zedillo (1994–2000) launched a megaproject for the "development" of the Isthmus of Tehuantepec through investments in infrastructure (new roads, rail, canals, and airports) and industry (Reyes, 2011). The former Mexican President Vicente Fox (2000–2006) incorporated Mexico's "development" into a broader framework called *Plan Puebla Panama*, announced in 2001. The *Plan Puebla Panama* seeks to speed up development and integration among Central America's nations and Mexico's southern and southeastern states through sustainable and participatory projects (Martin, 2005). The development plan was intended to enable the construction of large-scale telecommunications, energy, and transportation networks reaching from the Mexican state of Puebla to the country of Panama (IADB, 2001). The *Plan Puebla Panama* has financial support from multilateral lending agencies such as the Inter-American Development Bank (IADB) for the purpose of investing in wind energy farms (IADB, 2011). The state of Oaxaca is part of the *Plan Puebla Panama* mega-project to open up the state for foreign investment as a means to address what former President Fox called the abandoned and underdeveloped Oaxaca state (Aznarez, 2001; Reyes, 2011).

In the march toward neoliberal development policies in Mexico, under the administration of the former president, Felipe Calderon (2006–2012), Mexico joined the Clean Technology Fund (CTF) investment plan. The CTF is a "business plan" agreed upon and owned by the government of Mexico for the International Bank for Reconstruction and Development (IBRD), the IADB, and the International Finance Corporation (IFC); the goal is to provide support for the low-carbon objectives contained in Mexico's 2007–2012 national development plan, its national climate change strategy and special climate change program (The World Bank, 2009). During that time period,

Mr. Calderón promoted wind energy projects in Mexico. In 2012, Mr. Calderón, accompanied by Spanish executives, inaugurated the wind parks La Venta I, II, and III, which were projects developed by Iberdrola (Presidencia de la República, 2012).

In 2013, Mexican President Enrique Peña Nieto (2012–2018) launched constitutional energy reform. The Energy Reform aims at increasing renewable energies and facilitating private investment in energy in Mexico. In 2014, a package of laws that governed Mexico's energy sector for private investors came into force. Under the new laws, project developers must inform both the property owners and the Mexican Energy Secretary of their proposed plans for energy development. Then developers can negotiate with the landowner to determine whether the land will be bought, leased, or subject to temporary use and how much the owner will receive in exchange (Terwindt and Schliamann, 2017).

In the 21st century, indigenous people at the Isthmus of Tehuantepec continue to contest the neoliberal policies that are implemented in Mexico. Although different human rights abuses have been registered and there have been protests for structural reforms in Mexico, the march toward neoliberalism continues. The neoliberal policies implemented in Mexico signified that the government was not the motivator for development and investment; rather, it appeared that the government's role was to create the conditions for private, large-scale investments (e.g., Aitken, 1996; Özen and Özen, 2017). The following section presents wind energy investments at the Isthmus of Tehuantepec.

Wind energy farms at the Isthmus of Tehuantepec

The geographical location of the Isthmus of Tehuantepec has attracted private wind energy investors who seek to exploit the area's proven wind resources. According to the Wind Resource Map of Oaxaca (Elliott et al., 2004), the area of San Mateo del Mar in the Isthmus of Tehuantepec, where the Ikootjs indigenous people live, has among the world's best wind resource potential. This area is estimated to have Class 7+ wind resources, which are measured at > 800 wind power density at 50 m W/m^2.

MNCs have constructed wind parks in the Isthmus of Tehuantepec primarily under the self-supply model – energy that is exclusively produced for customers. The wind parks were developed in the Isthmus of Tehuantepec as part of the United Nations (UN) Clean Development Mechanism (UNFCCC, 2016). This mechanism allows MNCs to compensate for their damage to the environment by purchasing carbon credits (McAfee and Shapiro, 2010).

Several wind energy farms have been constructed in the Isthmus of Tehuantepec since the 1990s, and other projected wind parks are in dispute. For example, *Mareña Renovables* was the name of a wind energy project started in 2004 by the Spanish renewable energy developer, Preneal (McGovern, 2012). It was planned that the electrical power produced by the wind power project would be purchased (with a 20-year power-purchasing agreement) by the beer producer Cuauhtémoc Moctezuma, which is an operating company of Heineken NV and a subsidiary of FEMSA (FEMSA, 2011). On August 29, 2012, the IADB announced the approval of a loan for 75 million USD to fund the project (IADB, 2011). FEMSA, through wind energy projects, has a primary role in proving the business case for an innovative multistakeholder investment scheme for sustainable green energy (FEMSA, 2017). An executive from the Dutch pension fund PGGM explained in an interview that PGGM's "adventure," as the executive described the *Mareña Renovables* project, was motivated to invest pension money in green energy projects. One of the challenges in wind energy investment is the consultation process with local communities.

Public consultation

An important aspect of making wind energy projects successful is the participation of local people:

> The critical point is participation. People want to participate directly in decision making, planning, implementation and managing.
>   (Interview, State Governmental Official at Oaxaca City)

However, the Ikoots, the indigenous people of San Mateo del Mar, and the Zapotecas, the indigenous people at Juchitán, have experienced the construction of wind energy parks in their territory without being consulted. The Zapotec entered an alliance with the Ikoojts to oppose the *Mareña Renovables* project. As a resident of San Mateo del Mar explained:

> The Zapotecas wanted to share their experiences with regard to the 16 wind parks [in 2013] that were already operating in the region. They [the Zapotecas] want to prevent us [the Ikoojts] from making the same mistakes that they made.
>   (Interview with Huave resident of San Mateo del Mar, Oaxaca)

Indigenous member of the Communal Assembly, Juchitán Oaxaca, commented:"In Mexico, wind energy project investments were traditionally developed without properly following the statutes in Convention 169 ILO" (Focus Groups at Juchitán). This statement was framed as "the cost of development" by a member of the Working Group on Human Rights at the UN (Interview).

The desk research developed does not provide evidence for considering the UNGPs' Principle 13 for public consultation in relation to the *Mareña Renovables* project or wind energy parks built at the Isthmus of Tehuantepec. Principle 13 appears to be relevant for *ejidos* or communal lands, as it suggests that developers must negotiate a land-lease payment that is fair and convenient for both parties.

According to Mexican Agrarian Law (Ley Agraria, 2012), when modifying and cancelling the collective farm system, at least three-quarters of the *ejidatarios*, or "members of the communal assembly," must be present for the valid installation of the assembly that will decide the land use. The territory on which the project was to be constructed was *ejidos*, which are communal agricultural lands. Construction of the *Mareña Renovables* project implied a change in the use of the land from agricultural to industrial.

Changes to the Mexican constitution in 2011 recognize the right to consultation, as Article 2, section IX states: "Consult indigenous peoples in the preparation of the National Development Plan and the state and municipal levels and, where appropriate, incorporate the recommendations into the proposals" (Cámara de Diputados del H. Congreso de la Unión, 2011: 4).

The desk research developed in 2013 reveals that in 2011, those responsible for the *Mareña Renovables* project organized events in public places to present and discuss the "myths and reality of wind energy" with local people; they also sponsored public seminars on the benefits of wind energy farms (Websites – wind energy firms and IADB, 2011). However, a recurrent statement of the Ikoots and Zapotecs concerning these initiatives is presented in the following quote:

> [T]heir "capitalist model" failed to take "the spiritual and social" ties between the indigenous rural communities and the land into account.
> (Focus groups in Juchitán and San Mateo del Mar)

Mareña Renovables investors called such events public at the San Dionisio del Mar consultations in 2011. However, the IADB reported that such consultations lacked the necessary audience that was required by Mexican law for the assembly to be legal (an attendance of at least 50 percent), (IADB, 2011). Zapotecas and Ikoots claim that "[i]t [2011 consultations] was not a consultation as it did not comply with Agrarian Law" (Focus Groups at San Mateo del Mar).

The Mexican Agrarian Law Article 23 states that attendance must exceed three-quarters of the *ejidatarios*, rather than the 50 percent that was highlighted in the IADB's report (IADB, 2011). A government official commented on this:

> The consultations were characterized by a lack of coherence and adequate dialog, given the formal institutions that were established by the government to protect the local communities. For example, the consultations failed to consider the current [2011] Agrarian Law.
> (Interview – Mexican Government official)

In 2014, for the first time in the history of Mexico, a public consultation with members of communal assembly at Juchitán was developed in relation to the *Mareña Renovables* project. Zapotecas and NGOs argue that:

> Consultations have been developed without following the guiding principles of business and human rights. MNCs and Governmental representatives,

for example, have scheduled public consultations at the period of the Velas, which is one of the most important festivities in the region. For example, there was a community assembly at the House of Culture in the city of Juchitán on July 30, 2015, at 5:00 p.m., with a large number of attendees and a delay of 40 minutes. The NGO PODER calculated that there was a capacity of more than one thousand people, and official reports estimated approximately 1500 people. This assistance decreased throughout the five and a half hours of the assembly, which is why at the time of an impromptu vote, there were less than half of the attendees as those who raised their hands constituted 25% of the initial figure, even though the official attendance lists say something else.

(PODER, 2015; Social Media Communal Assembly at Juchitán, Oaxaca)

Zapotecas and Ikoojs explained that business representatives failed to consider the equal involvement of indigenous communities in decisions regarding the ethical use of their communal land, where the project was to be built. Yet according to the communities, the project affects their land (Conversations).

The following section presents the impact of wind energy parks in the Isthmus of Tehuantepec.

Environmental (in)justice

The focus groups developed in 2013 indicate that opposition to the *Mareñas Renovables* project was focused on concerns about ecological destruction. Zapotecs and Ikoots argued that installing 132 V90–3.0 MW turbines on the *Barra* (Key) would have an adverse "environmental impact" (conversations). The *Barra* (Key) is located between *Laguna Superior* (Upper Lagoon) in the Municipality of San Dionisio del Mar and *Laguna Inferior* (Lower Lagoon) in the Municipality of San Mateo del Mar. Fishermen explained the following:

> We live by catching shrimps at *Laguna Inferior* [Lower Lagoon], the shrimps eat from the leaves that fall from the trees at the *Barra* [Key], if they [wind firm] install these *ventiladores* [wind turbines], there will be no more trees … and so no more shrimps.
>
> (Fishermen at San Mateo del Mar)

According to conversations with local residents, in certain circumstances, constructing wind energy parks might destroy sacred sites. In Mexico, as in many cultures, death is a cultural festivity that has a specific connotation for cemeteries, which are sacred for the Zapotecas and Ikoojts (Field notes). The webpage of wind energy investors in Oaxaca states the following:

> [T]he installation of wind power turbines in the park would not affect the daily activities of the local communities, such as agriculture and fishing.
>
> (Secondary Material, Webpages)

In 2013, there were disputes among indigenous people, *Mareñas Renovables* representatives, and government officials when engineers from the firm Vestas, responsible for building the *Mareñas Renovables* project, planned to drive trucks from the town of Alvaro Obregon to *Barra* Key. The firm Vestas attempted to initiate its work to install 102 wind turbines on the key and 30 wind turbines in Santa María del Mar, which is located in San Mateo del Mar (conversations in Juchitán and San Mateo del Mar). Indigenous people explained the reason for their dispute:

> Wind farms have contaminated lagoons with fuel waste, which has affected fishing. It is clear that large foreign companies, such as Iberdrola or Vestas Wind Systems, are those that have earned millions in profits at the expense of our land.
>
> (Conversations – Representative of the Communal Assembly at Juchitán)

Given the social unrest and the cancelation of the *Mareñas Renovables* project by a judge of the state of Oaxaca in 2013, the *Mareñas Renovables* project was renamed *Eólica del Sur* in 2015. However, the Dutch pension fund PGGM decided to cancel its participation in the renamed *Eólica del Sur* project. An executive from PGGM commented:

> PGGM trusted that all stakeholders in the project followed standard procedures for constructing the wind energy farm. However, this project is too controversial . . . so we decided to leave.
>
> (conversation with a PGGM executive in 2017)

In a follow-up focus group developed in 2015, indigenous communities present more sophisticated arguments in relation to the cost of development and environmental (in)justice:

> The biggest environmental impact of wind power is evident to the naked eye. As wind farms grow, a country needs to pay more attention to the landscape and to environmental, historical, cultural and tourist-related impacts.
>
> (Conversations with indigenous people at San Mateo del Mar)

Although the Zapotecas and Ikoojts argued for different negative impacts in relation to the wind parks, they had no scientific evidence to support their arguments. I interviewed an engineer in Denmark who worked on wind energy projects, who explained that the wind turbine itself does not damage the environment. The engineer explained that there is a risk of land ionizing radiation in relation to the transmission lines from the wind turbine to the electrical substation. This risk could be technical due to the quality of material and maintenance or external factors (Interview). For example, land ionizing radiation could register due to natural disasters. On September 7, 2017, the strongest earthquake to hit Mexico in over 100 years (8.2 in magnitude) destroyed thousands of buildings, specifically in the city of Juchitán. According to newspaper reports, 21 wind parks, which have a total of 1,186 wind turbines in the Isthmus of Tehuantepec, were affected by the earthquake, and each park has an electrical substation (Rasgado and Hernández, 2017). The Federal Electricity Commission (CFE) has three electrical substations in which all wind parks in the Isthmus of Tehuantepec provide electricity for firms and private users. There is not an official report about the consequences of the earthquake on the potential for land ionizing radiation in the Isthmus of Tehuantepec in relation to the wind parks in the region. The CFE only reported that the electrical substation Juchitán II was operating normally after the earthquake (Quadratín, 2017). An Ikoojts commented on the different reports in the aftermath of the earthquake as follows:

> [W]e never will read or hear the reality of the negative impacts of the earthquakes on our land. The government and firms always hide information, as they have done when assigning wind park construction to firms without our consultation.
>
> (Fisherman in San Mateo del Mar)

In response to the earthquake, wind energy firms, through the Mexican Wind Power Association (AMDEE) and in coordination with the federal, state, and local governments transported water, food, and essential medicines, in addition to providing personnel and machinery to remove debris and performing the first reconstructive work, including support to recover normal water and electricity supplies (Asociación Mexicana de Energía Eólica, 2017).

In an interview with local residents in Juchitán and Huamuchil, they explained that houses of residents who were in favor of wind energy parks or that leased their land were the first visited to evaluate the earthquake damage. A local resident from Huamichil explained as follows:

> Government official visited house by house in the Isthmus of Tehuantepec after the earthquake and assigned a folio to the house. The folio, the number painted outside the house, shows the private wind energy firm associated with the AMDEE when the firm's machinery should overthrow the houses. Residents in favour of wind energy parks got the first numbers.
>
> (Interview, member of the communal assembly in
> San Dionisio del Mar)

I will now focus on human rights stemming derived from wind energy investments on the Isthmus of Tehuantepec.

Human rights abuses

For business and human rights, in the "Global Agreement" between the European Union (EU) and Mexico, which took effect in 2000, Article 39 states: "The Parties may conduct joint projects in order to strengthen cooperation between their respective electoral bodies," and the incise C establishes: "the promotion of human rights and democratic principles" (European Union, 2000). However, it was not until 2015 that the Mexican government publicly committed to developing a national program for business and human rights. In April 2016, the Danish Institute for Human Rights signed a Memorandum of Understanding (MoU) with Mexico to develop the country's National Action Plan (NAP) on Business and Human Rights (The Danish Institute for Human Rights, 2016). In September 2016, Mexico invited the UN Working Group on Business and Human Rights to assess Mexico. After the visit (September 2016), the group made the following conclusion:

> Although the Mexican government has committed to moving forward on the human rights and business agenda, businesses continue to exhibit worrisome behaviour.
>
> (Interview – Member of the Working Group on HR at UN)

The president and chief executive officer at the European green-energy firm in 2014 declared:

> [Our Organization] expects its business partners to respect human rights, and will take measures to promote responsible practices by its business partners in relation to the our organization value chain. Our firm will identify and consult with stakeholders whose human rights might be impacted by our organization's operations, including engaging in dialogue with local communities to identify and address any human rights risks and opportunities of our organization's operations.
>
> (European wind energy firm's internal document)

This statement illustrates the compromise made by a European firm in relation to the basic principles of human rights. However, human rights abuses continue to mark wind energy projects in the Isthmus of Tehuantepec. For example, Héctor Regalado Jiménez, a member of the Asamblea Popular del Pueblo Juchiteco (APPJ), was assassinated in 2013 in relation to opposing the construction of a wind park, Bii Hioxho, by the Spanish firm, Gas Natural Fenosa (FIDH and OMCT, 2014).

> On 21 July 2013, hitmen working for the Spanish company Gas Natural Fenosa attacked, with gunfire, members of the Popular Assembly of the People of Juchiteco (APPJ), leaving fisherman Héctor Regalado Jiménez with six bullet wounds. Regalado Jiménez died from that attack on 1 August, according to a statement from the APPJ.
>
> (Blog SIPAZ, 2013; Kaos, 2013)

According to the *Centro Mexicano de Derecho Ambiental, A.C.* (CEMDA), between July 2015 and July 2016, 35 attacks have been registered as threats against human rights defenders at mega-projects in Oaxaca. For the wind energy project, there were eight human rights violations in 2015; CEMDA registered another assassination in relation to wind parks in the Isthmus of Tehuantepec, and four were reported to CEMDA in June 2016 (Leyva Hernández et al., 2017; Presbítero et al., 2015).

Zapotec and Ikoots communities have witnessed disputes over (uso y costumbres) customary rights, faced threats and physical violence, faced death threats in person and by phone, had guns fired in front of their homes, and experienced attempted kidnappings and assassinations related to wind energy investments (Dunlap, 2018; interviews). In relation to the *Eólica del Sur* project, Mr. Rolando Crispín López, a member of the communal assembly at Alvaro Obregón, was assassinated on July 24, 2018 (Manzo, 2018). Next, I discuss the findings in relation to internal colonialism and environmental justice.

Discussion

Over the years, Mexico's neoliberal development reforms appear to have emphasized the normative value of the capitalist free market (O'Toole, 2003). Neoliberalism has been implemented in Mexico through constitutional changes, new laws, and the signing of international conventions. Mexico's neoliberal development model has underpinned a "radical reconstruction of Mexican economy and society" (Martin, 2005: 204), which is presented in this chapter, particularly in wind energy investments at the Isthmus of Tehuantepec.

The neoliberal wind energy investment model implemented in Mexico is based on the assumption of the private sector's supremacy over state-owned investments (Corvellec, 2007). Neoliberalism might be the intuitive procedure with which to place Mexico at the forefront in, for example, wind energy and to fight against climate change (UNFCCC, 2015). This rationale is based on the assumption that MNCs, in contrast to some governments, have the latest renewable energy technology and access to financing (IADB, 2001). It seems intuitive to assume that indigenous people would support wind investments that, unlike fossil fuel investments, "theoretically" do not involve environmental (in)justice. However, a nonintuitive outcome is that the environmental vision of indigenous people clashes with neoliberalism in the context of wind energy investment. The findings support the view that the supremacy of wind turbine technology and the notion of "development" in the Isthmus of Tehuantepec within the *Plan Puebla Panama* mega-project (1) threaten local traditions, (2) entail environmental (in)justices, and (3) contribute to human rights abuses. These outcomes suggest that reaching the SDGs, particularly Goal 7, through wind energy investments, is naïve, given the failure to properly consider the fundamental place-based attachments to the environmental and territorial vision of indigenous communities (Escobar, 2008; Martin, 2005; Nolte, 2016). Thus, how do wind energy development investments affect indigenous peoples' environmental justice claims?

The history of the struggle of the indigenous people of the Isthmus of Tehuantepec to bring "development" to their region represents one example of the sophisticated political, cultural, and environmental visions that contrast with Mexico's neoliberal development model. The Zapotecas' and Ikoojts' visions of development are based on their consciousness of and pride in their history of constant fighting to bring to their communities basic access to education and respect for their human right of self-determination.

The wind energy farms built at the Isthmus of Tehuantepec visually present how neoliberal development projects become materialized, which alters the territories of indigenous people and alters and confronts their environmental visions. In contrast to protests, such as NIMBY, or the absence of protests against wind parks in developed countries (The Local. DK, 2017), Zapotecas and Ikoojts strategically interweave their opposition against wind energy projects with a framework that includes respect for territory (Escobar, 2008), human rights (Chenoweth et al., 2017), and cultural heritage (Haarstad and Fløysend, 2007).

The findings suggest that the Zapotecas and Ikoojts, on the one hand, and governmental and MNCs, on the other, have adopted different understandings of regional development through wind energy investments. It might be argued that the MNCs are attempting to implement their business models at the Isthmus of Tehuantepec, and in doing so, they seem to overlook the basic principles of environmental and human rights. Consultation and consent interactions with stakeholders on a voluntary basis (according to the principles Convention OLI 169) seem to be the origin of the conflict between MNCs and indigenous people. These conflicting views pose a dilemma for private investors in wind energy aiming to foster positive community relations (Aitken, 2010).

These findings present a concrete example of indigenous communities' continuous pattern of subordination in a system of inequality (Pinderhughes, 2010), understood in this chapter as internal colonialism (Gonzalez Casanova, 1965; Pinderhughes, 2010). In the institutional context, the lawlessness of human rights abuses in wind energy investments fosters environmental (in)justice and therefore social unrest. Equal access to renewable energy for all, as well as equal recognition and participation in the use of land and wind energy resources (Cass and Walker, 2009), appear to be at the center of environmental (in)justice related to neoliberal wind energy investments on the Isthmus of Tehuantepec. The findings presented here evolve from the struggles of exclusion in the consultation process and the negative environmental impacts of wind energy investment on human rights. However, rights struggles tend to be difficult when the claim threatens major economic interests (Chenoweth et al., 2017). Scholars and NGOs claim that governments implementing neoliberal development policies overlook human rights abuses perpetrated by foreign investors because FDI satisfies neoliberal policies (McAfee and Shapiro, 2010; Terwindt and Schliamann, 2017).

Neoliberal wind energy investments built in Mexico worsen internal colonialism (González Casanova, 1965; Hechter, 2017). In the state of Oaxaca,

5 percent of the population lacks electricity (INEGI, 2015), and 70 percent of the indigenous people at the Isthmus of Tehuantepec are poor (CONAVAL, 2017). The communities visited, such as San Mateo del Mar and Huamichil, do not have access to purified water, public drains, and sanitation. Governments and MNCs portray investments in wind energy as the development of sustainable energy, which aims to reduce carbon emissions. An aspirational talk (Christensen et al., 2013) connected MNCs with Mexican politicians, such as Mr. Calderón Hinojosa, who promoted Mexico as an ideal destination for green energy investments (e.g., McAfee and Shapiro, 2010). However, MNCs and government representatives fail to disseminate in a timely manner evidence on the impact of wind energy farms to indigenous people who are directly affected by Mexico's energy reform and rules of law that affect the struggle for human rights advocacy. Where the rule of law is weak, as reflected through corruption or a lack of accountability in security forces or judicial sectors, the protection of human rights almost universally suffers (Haugen and Boutros, 2010).

The Zapotecas and Ikoojts have been portrayed as a "rebel" people in Mexico in their response to wind energy, and other development investments continue to market the history of the Zapotecas and Ikoojts with this tone. Dante Pesce (ONUDH, 2016) stated in this regard: "*[Mexican] society and Government officials seem to live in a different planet – in particular the political Élites, they [Élite groups] do not have anything in common with indigenous people*". This statement reflects the different understandings of so-called "civilized" people (whites) and "natural" people (Indians) in the emergence of neoliberalism in Mexico. I posit that neoliberalism in wind energy investments is connected to internal colonialism (Gonzalez Casanova, 1965). Race and culture are legacies of the Spanish domination that emphasized greater purity, expressed in religion as well as the purity of blood: the conflicts between *Gente de razón* (civilized people – whites) and *naturales* (natural people – Indians) (Aitken, 1996) are replicated in wind energy investments at the Isthmus of Tehuantepec.

This research advances earlier arguments that it is time for business and government officials to move away from the connotation of the moral (e.g., Wettstein, 2009) or voluntary engagement of companies in relation to human rights as a legal obligation. Mexico has made advances in promulgating law and regulations for energy investments and protecting human rights. Mexico is currently (as of January 2018) developing the NAP on Business and Human Rights in collaboration with the Danish Institute of Human Rights. However, the role of current Mexican legislation and the eventual Mexican NAP on human rights in the "protect, respect, and remedy" framework is unclear. It might be time for MNCs to enforce this framework solely in institutional settings where local and national governments cannot protect, respect, and provide a remedy for civil society's human rights abuses. The empirical material indicates that indigenous people in the Isthmus of Tehuantepec fight against their local, state, and national government officials, who fail to implement current law and regulations in Mexico (e.g., Crippa, 2012). At the same time, the MNCs involved in the conflict have other resources with which they could "fight" indigenous people. For example, MNCs can protect their investments through contracts with Mexican officials. In addition, MNCs have access to tools, procedures, and even coaching from external stakeholders such as the United Nations, the IADB, or the ILO to assist in the implementation of such principles as ILO Convention 169, particularly with regard to consultations with and consent of local communities. One might wonder why MNCs do not utilize these tools. This observation challenges the assumption that foreign MNCs have transferred their management policies and practices, creating a mimetic effect in Mexican firms. Why do those who control FDI not apply their own policies from home in their FDI? It seems that these complexities tend to be more evident in wind energy projects. MNCs that have been invited by the Mexican federal government to invest in Mexico should exercise caution in, for example, due diligence exercises when engaging with local actors in institutional settings that challenge the rule of law.

The findings and discussion presented could help develop an agenda with a development orientation in which governmental officials function by public consent. MNCs are expected to constructively serve the needs of society (CED, 1971). However, based on the results presented, it could be argued that MNCs could function as a platform not only for job creation but also to remedy and reinstall basic FPIC principles aimed at sustainable development. Surprisingly, the Zapotecas and Ikoojts are fighting to reinstall the basic FPIC principles in their territories. Thus, remediation could also be a strategy developed by micro-level actors – indigenous people. MNCs and ingenuous people could function as key actors in host countries without governmental capacity to "protect, respect, and remedy" human rights and environmental justice.

Although the research setting presents unique particularities in the Isthmus of Tehuantepec, the Zapotecas' and Ikoojts' struggles echo the silent voices of developed countries. Silent voices are people who feel left behind due to neoliberalism, experience an increase in inequalities, and start to mobilize and trigger other political consequences, as seen in the United Kingdom (Hechter, 2017). The fine-grain empirical material shows concrete human rights abuses and the negative effects of neoliberal wind energy development investments.

Conclusions

Wind energy investments have also provoked internal colonialism in the Isthmus of Tehuantepec. It is clear that governments from emerging and developed countries have made efforts to integrate the Universal Declaration of Human Rights (UDHR) (United Nations, 1948) into their internal and foreign policy agendas. However, social mobilizations from indigenous people in different regions of the world (e.g., Bebbington et al., 2008) who demand protection of their basic human rights continue to characterize territorial conflicts (Banerjee, 2000) that directly and indirectly include business investments. Future research could examine how MNCs and governments manipulate national laws and international conventions to gain investments in wind energy and development projects. This study empirically presents how a government can be a strong connection that facilitates MNCs' FDI while simultaneously failing to protect local people's basic human rights.

References

Agyeman J (2014) Global environmental justice or Le droit au monde? *Geoforum* 54: 236–238.

Aitken M (2010) Why we still don't understand the social aspects of wind power: a critique of key assumptions within the literature. *Energy Policy* 38(4): 1834–1841.

Aitken R (1996) Neoliberalism and identity: redefining state and society in Mexico BT – dismantling the Mexican state? In: Aitken R, Craske N, Jones GA, et al. (eds) *Latin American Studies Series, Dismantling the Mexican State?* London, UK: Palgrave Macmillan, pp. 24–38.

Alvesson M and Deetz S (2000) *Doing Critical Management Research*. London, UK: Sage Publications Ltd.

APROMECI (2016) Afirma INEGI 70% de indígenas viven en la pobreza. Available at: http://apromeci.org.mx/2016/08/15/afirma-inegi-70-de-indigenas-viven-en-la-pobreza/ (accessed 20 December 2017).

Asociación Mexicana de Energía Eólica (2017) Asociación Mexicana de energía eólica. Available at: www.amdee.org/ (accessed 23 December 2017).

Aznarez JJ (2001) México crea el espacio centroamericano. Available at: https://elpais.com/diario/2001/06/23/internacional/993247218_850215.html (accessed 8 November 2018).

Banerjee SB (2000) Whose land is it anyway? National interest, indigenous stakeholders, and colonial discourses. *Organization & Environment* 13(1): 3–38.

Bardhan P (2000) The nature of institutional impediments to economic development. In: Olson M and Kähköhnen S (eds) *A Not-so-Dismal Science*. Oxford: Oxford University Press, pp. 245–267.

Bebbington A, Abramovay R and Chiriboga M (2008) Social movements and the dynamics of rural territorial development in Latin America. *World Development* 36(12): 2874–2887.

Blog SIPAZ (2013) Oaxaca: fallece por heridas de bala opositor a proyecto eólico de la multinacional Gas Natural Fenosa. Available at: https://sipaz.wordpress.com/2013/08/06/oaxaca-fallece-por-heridas-de-bala-opositor-a-proyecto-eolico-de-la-multinacional-gas-natural-fenosa/ (accessed 22 December 2017).

Bullard RD and Johnson GS (2002) Environmentalism and public policy: environmental justice: grassroots activism and its impact on public policy decision making. *Journal of Social Issues* 56(3): 555–578.

Burke MJ and Stephens JC (2017) Energy democracy: goals and policy instruments for sociotechnical transitions. *Energy Research & Social Science* 33: 35–48.

Cámara de Diputados H. Congreso de la Unión (2011) Constitución política de los Estados Unidos Mexicanos. Available at: http://transparencia.uaz.edu.mx/documents/70010/ea9cb1cb-4cde-4c60-a50c-e2d9ee4bb29b. (accessed 10 July 2013)

Campbell H, Binford L, Bartolomé M, et al. (1993) *Zapotec Struggles: History, Politics, and Representations from Juchitán, Oaxaca*. Washington, DC: Smithsonian Institution Press.

Campbell JR (2001) Participatory rural appraisal as qualitative research: distinguishing methodological issues from participatory claims. *Human Organization* 60(4): 380–389.

Campbell T (2010) *Justice*. Hampshire: Palgrave Macmillan.

Cass N and Walker G (2009) Emotion and rationality: the characterisation and evaluation of opposition to renewable energy projects. *Emotion, Space and Society* 2(1): 62–69.

CED (1971) Social responsibilities of business corporations. Available at: www.ced.org/reports/single/social-responsibilities-of-business-corporations (accessed 10 October 2014).

Chenoweth E, Hunter K, Moore P, et al. (2017) Struggles from below: literature review on human rights struggles by domestic actors. Available at: www.usaid.gov/sites/default/files/documents/2496/Struggles_from_Below_-_Literature_Review_on_Human_Rights_Struggles_by_Domestic_Actors.pdf. (accessed 26 June 2018).

Christensen LT, Morsing M and Thyssen O (2013) CSR as aspirational talk. *Organization* 20(3): 372–393.

Colchester M and Farhan Ferrari M (2007) Making FPIC – free, prior and informed consent – work: challenges and prospects for indigenous people. Available at: www.forestpeoples.org/topics/civil-political-rights/publication/2010/making-fpic-free-prior-and-informed-consent-work-chal (accessed 20 March 2017).

CONAVAL (2017) CONEVAL informa la evolución de la pobreza 2010–2016. Available at: www.coneval.org.mx/SalaPrensa/Comunicadosprensa/Documents/Comunicado-09-Medicion-pobreza-2016.pdf. (Accessed 11 November 2018)

Corvellec, H. (2007). Arguing for a license to operate: the case of the Swedish wind power industry. *Corporate Communications: An International Journal*, 12(2), 129–144.

Costanza JN (2016) Mining conflict and the politics of obtaining a social license: insight from Guatemala. *World Development* 79: 97–113.

Crippa LA (2012) Acerca del proceso de verificación de la observancia del MICI. Available at: http://indianlaw.org/sites/default/files/ME-MICI002-2012_INFORME_DE_VERIFICACIÓN_DE_LA_OBSERVANCIA_DEL_CASO_PROYECTO_MAREÑA_RENOVABLES_(ME-L1107)_Versiónfinal_español.pdf. (accessed 10 July 2013).

The Danish Institute for Human Rights (2016) New agreement for cooperation with Mexico. Available at: www.humanrights.dk/news/new-agreement-cooperation-mexico (accessed 3 August 2017).

Davies J (2010) Introduction: emotions in the field. In: Davies J and Spencer D (eds) *Emotions in the Field: The Psychology and Anthropology of Fieldwork Experience*. Stanford, CA: Stanford University Press, pp. 1–31.

Davis D and Rosan C (2004) Social movements in the Mexico City airport controversy: globalization, democracy, and the power of distance. *Mobilization: An International Quarterly* 9(3): 279–293.

Diego Quintana RS (2015) Energía limpia o energía perversa: actores sociales y parques eólicos en Dinamarca y en el Istmo de Tehuantepec. Available at: https://consultaindigenajuchitan.files.wordpress.com/2015/01/2015-enero-roberto-diego.pdf. (accessed 16 September 2016).

Dunlap A (2017a) "A bureaucratic trap": free, prior and informed consent (FPIC) and wind energy development in Juchitán, Mexico. *Capitalism Nature Socialism*: 1–21. doi:10.1080/10455752.2017.1334219.

Dunlap A (2017b) Wind energy: toward a "sustainable violence" in Oaxaca. *NACLA Report on the Americas* 49(4): 483–488.

Dunlap A (2018) Insurrection for land, sea and dignity: resistance and autonomy against wind energy in Álvaro Obregón, Mexico. *Journal of Political Ecology* 25(1): 120.

Edwards J, Haugerud A and Parikh S (2017) Introduction: the 2016 Brexit referendum and Trump election. *American Ethnologist* 44(2): 195–200.

Elliott D, Schwartz M, Scott G, et al. (2004) Atlas de recursos eólicos del estado de Oaxaca (The Spanish version of wind energy resource atlas of Oaxaca). Available at: www.nrel.gov/docs/fy04osti/35575.pdf (accessed 10 July 2013).

Entman RM (1993) Framing: toward clarification of a fractured paradigm. *Journal of Communication* 43(4): 51–58.

Environmental Justice/Environmental Racism (1991) The principles of environmental justice (EJ). Available at: www.ejnet.org/ej/principles.pdf. (accessed 10 July 2013).

Escobar A (2008) Place. In: Escobar A (ed) *Territories of Difference: Place, Movements, Life, Redes*. Durham, NC: Duke University Press, pp. 28–64.

The European Commission (2011) *Communication from the Commission to the European Parliament, the Council, the European Economic and Social Committee and the Committee of the Regions: A renewed EU strategy 2011–2014 for Corporate Social Responsibility*. Brussels: European Commission.

European Union (2000) Economic partnership, political coordination and cooperation agreement between the European community and its member states, of the one part, and the United Mexican states, of the other part. *Official Journal of the European Communities* L 276: 45–61.

FEMSA (2011) FEMSA y MMIF adquieren proyecto de energía eólica de 396 megawatts. Available at: www.femsa.com/es/medios/femsa-y-mmif-adquieren-proyecto-de-energia-eolica-de-396-megawatts/ (accessed 17 December 2017).

FEMSA (2017) Coca-cola FEMSA. Available at: www.coca-colafemsa.com/index.html. (accessed 11 November 2018).

FIDH and OMCT (2014) "No tenemos miedo" Defensores del derecho a la tierra: atacados por enfrentarse al desarrollo desenfrenado. Available at: www.omct.org/files/2014/12/22918/obs_2014_sp_web2.pdf (accessed 16 September 2018).

Gioia DA, Corley KG and Hamilton AL (2013) Seeking qualitative rigor in inductive research. *Organizational Research Methods* 16(1): 15–31.

Gonzalez Casanova P (1965) Internal colonialism and national development. *Studies in Comparative International Development* 1(4): 27–37.

Gouldson A (2006) Do firms adopt lower standards in poorer areas? Corporate social responsibility and environmental justice in the EU and the US. *Area* 38(4): 402–412.

Haarstad H and Fløysand A (2007) Globalization and the power of rescaled narratives: a case of opposition to mining in Tambogrande, Peru. *Political Geography*, 26(3), 289–308.

Haugen G and Boutros V (2010) And justice for all: enforcing human rights for the world's poor. *Foreign Affairs*, 89(3), 51–62.

Hechter M (2017) *Internal Colonialism: The Celtic Fringe in British National Development*. Abingdon, Oxon: Routledge.

Hind RJ (1984) The internal colonial concept. *Comparative Studies in Society and History* 26(3): 543–568.

IADB (2001) Mexico, Guatemala agree on power system interconnection under Puebla-Panama Plan. Available at: www.iadb.org/en/news/news-releases/2001-12-19/mexico-guatemala-agree-on-power-system-interconnection-under-puebla-panama-plan%2C1121.html (accessed 8 November 2018).

IADB (2011) Inter-American development bank Mexico mareña renovables wind power project (Me-L1107) environmental category: an environmental and social management report (Esmr). Available at: http://idbdocs.iadb.org/wsdocs/getdocument.aspx?docnum=36537741 (accessed 8 November 2018).

INEGI (2015) Viviendas. Available at: http://cuentame.inegi.org.mx/monografias/informacion/oax/poblacion/vivienda.aspx?tema=me&e=20 (accessed 8 November 2018).

Inglehart RF and Norris P (2016) *Trump, Brexit, and the Rise of Populism: Economic Have-Nots and Cultural Backlash*. Faculty Research Working Paper Series (No. RWP16–026). Cambridge, MA: Harvard University.

International Labour Organization (2016) Ratifications for Mexico. Available at: www.ilo.org/dyn/normlex/en/f?p=1000:11200:0::NO:11200:P11200_COUNTRY_ID:102764 (accessed 11 August 2017).

Juárez-Hernández S and León G (2014) Wind energy in the isthmus of tehuantepec: development, actors and social opposition. *Problemas del Desarrollo* 45(178): 139–162.

Kaos (2013) Fallece opositor a proyecto eólico que fue baleado por sicarios de Gas Natural Fenosa. Available at: www.wind-watch.org/news/2013/08/07/fallece-opositor-a-proyecto-eolico-que-fue-baleado-por-sicarios-de-gas-natural-fenosa/ (accessed 22 December 2017).

The Local. DK (2017) *Few Danes Complain About Wind Turbines: Group.* Copenhagen: The Local. DK

Ley Agraria [Agrarian Law] (2012) Cámara de Diputados del H. Congreso de la Unión, Estados Unidos Mexicanos [Chamber of Deputies of the H. Congress, United MexicanStates], DOF 09–04–2012), www.diputados.gob.mx/LeyesBiblio/pdf/13.pdf, accessed 5 June 2013.

Leyva Hernández A, Ulisse Cerami AD, Romero Bartolo F, et al. (2017) Informe sobre la situación de las personas defensoras de los derechos humanos ambientales en México 2016. Available at: www.cemda.org.mx/wp-content/uploads/2011/12/Informe-defensores-ambientales-2016.pdf. (accessed 8 November 2018).

Love JL (1989) Modeling internal colonialism: history and prospect. *World Development* 17(6): 905–922.

Manzo D (2018) La Jornada: Asesinan a Rolando Crispín López, activista de pueblos indígenas. *La Jornada,* p. 14. Available at: www.jornada.com.mx/2018/07/24/politica/014n1pol

Martin PM (2005) Comparative topographies of neoliberalism in Mexico. *Environment and Planning A* 37(2): 203–220.

Martinez-Alier J, Temper L, del Bene D, et al. (2016) Is there a global environmental justice movement? *The Journal of Peasant Studies* 43(3): 731–755.

Martínez Rangel R and Reyes Garmendia E (2012) El Consenso de Washington: la instauración de las políticas neoliberales en América Latina. *Política Y Cultura* 37: 35–64.

Matus M (1993) Juchitán political moments. In: Campbell H, Binford L, Bartolomé M, et al. (eds) *Zapotec Struggles -Histories, Politics, and Representations from Juchitán, Oaxaca.* Washington, DC: Smithsonian Institution Press, pp. 125–128.

McAfee K and Shapiro EN (2010) Payments for ecosystem services in Mexico: nature, neoliberalism, social movements, and the state. *Annals of the Association of American Geographers* 100(3): 579–599.

McCauley DA, Heffron RJ, Stephan H, et al. (2013) Advancing energy justice: the triumvirate of tenets. *International Energy Law Review* 32(3): 107–110.

McGovern M (2012) Developers face escalating militant opposition in Oaxaca. Available at: www.windpowermonthly.com/article/1124476/developers-face-escalating-militant-opposition-oaxaca. (accessed 16 September 2018).

Nolte C (2016) Identifying challenges to enforcement in protected areas: empirical insights from 15 Colombian parks. *Oryx* 50(02): 317–322.

O'Toole G (2003) A new nationalism for a new era: the political ideology of Mexican neoliberalism. *Bulletin of Latin American Research* 22(3): 269–290.

OECD (2015) Inequality. Available at: www.oecd.org/social/inequality.htm (accessed 20 December 2017).

Olzak S (1983) Contemporary ethnic mobilization. *Annual Review of Sociology* 9(1): 355–374.

ONUDH (2016) Conclusiones Preliminares del Grupo de Trabajo de la ONU sobre empresa y derechos humanos [Preliminary conclusions of the Working Group on the issues of human rights and transnational corporations and other business enterprises]. Available at www.youtube.com/watch?v=JZQb_9NCMCI (Accessed 8 September 2016)

Özen H and Özen Ş (2017) What makes locals protesters? A discursive analysis of two cases in gold-mining industry in Turkey. *World Development* 90: 256–268.

Pinderhughes C (2010) How black awakening in capitalist America laid the foundation for a new internal colonialism theory. *The Black Scholar* 40(2): 71–78.

PODER (2015) *Cuarto Reporte de la Misión de Observación Sobre el Proceso de Consulta Indígena Para la Implementación de un Proyecto Eólico en Juchitán, Oaxaca.* Mexico: PODER.

Presbítero A, Cerami A and Romero F (2015) *Informe Sobre La Situación de Los Defensores Ambientales en México 2015.* México: CEMDA.

Presidencia de la República (2012) El presidente calderón en la inauguración de las centrales eólicas Oaxaca i y la venta III. Available at: http://calderon.presidencia.gob.mx/2012/10/el-presidente-calderon-en-la-inauguracion-de-las-centrales-eolicas-oaxaca-i-y-la-venta-iii/ (accessed 27 October 2018).

Quadratín (2017) *Opera con Normalidad Servicio de Energía Eléctrica en el Istmo.* Oaxaca: Quadratín.

Rasgado R and Hernández CA (2017) *Paraliza sismo 21 Parques Eólicos en el Istmo, Oaxaca.* Juchitán de Zaragoga, Oaxaca: El Imparcial Del Istmo.

Reyes O (2011) *Power to the People? How World Bank Financed Wind Farms Fail Communities in Mexico.* London, UK: World Development Movement.

Rubin JW (1994) COCEI in Juchitán: grassroots radicalism and regional history. *Journal of Latin American Studies* 26(1): 109–136.

Rubin JW (1996) Decentering the Regime: Culture and Regional Politics in Mexico. *Latin American Research Review*, 31(3), 85–126.

Rubin JW (2004) Meanings and mobilizations: a cultural politics approach to social movements and states. *Latin American Research Review* 39(3): 106–142.

Schlosberg D (2013) Theorising environmental justice: the expanding sphere of a discourse. *Environmental Politics* 22(1), 37–55.

Sikor T and Newell P (2014) Globalizing environmental justice? *Geoforum* 54: 151–157.

Steady FC (2009) *Environmental Justice in the New Millennium: Global Perspectives on Race, Ethnicity, and Human Rights.* Basingstoke: Palgrave Macmillan.

Terwindt C and Schliamann C (2017) Mexico's energy: a tale of threats, intimidation, and dispossession of indigenous peoples. In: Foundation HB (ed) *Tricky Business: Space for Civil Society in Natural Resource Struggles.* Berlin: ARNOLD Group, pp. 46–51.

Toke D and Lauber V (2007) Anglo-Saxon and German approaches to neoliberalism and environmental policy: the case of financing renewable energy. *Geoforum* 38(4): 677–687.

UNFCCC (United Nations Framework Convention on Climate Change) (2015).

UNFCCC (United Nations Framework Convention on Climate Change) (2016) Clean development mechanism. Available at: http://unfccc.int/kyoto_protocol/mechanisms/clean_development_mechanism/items/2718.php (accessed 23 December 2017).

United Nations (1948) *Universal Declaration of Human Rights.* Paris: United Nations.

United Nations (2011) *Guiding Principles on Business and Human Rights.* New York, NY: United Nations.

United Nations (2015) Sustainable development goals. Available at: www.undp.org/content/undp/en/home/sustainable-development-goals.html (accessed 19 June 2018).

Wettstein F (2009) Beyond voluntaries, beyond CSR: Making a case for human rights and justice. *Business and Society Review*, 11(4), 125–152.

Williamson J (2008) A short history of the Washington consensus. In: Serra N and Stiglitz JE (eds) *The Washington Consensus Reconsidered: Towards a New Global Governance.* Oxford: Oxford University Press, pp. 14–30.

The World Bank (2009) *Clean Technology Fund Investment Plan for Mexico.* Washington, DC: The World Bank.

Yin RK (2016) *Qualitative Research from Start to Finish.* New York, NY: The Guilford Press.

Zografos C and Martinez-Alier J (2009) The politics of landscape value: A case study of wind farm conflict in rural Catalonia. *Environment and Planning A*, 41(7), 1726–1744.

Part V

Local firms, organizations, and development

16 When do businesses innovate in a developing country?[1]

An empirical investigation of determinants of innovative performance for Ugandan micro and small businesses

Giacomo Solano and Gerrit Rooks

Introduction

In developing countries, particularly in sub-Saharan Africa, dynamic and innovative entrepreneurship is a key factor contributing to economic growth (Ahlstrom 2010; Crespi and Zuniga 2012; Gries and Naudé 2010; Szirmai 2008). Unfortunately, dynamic entrepreneurship is uncommon in sub-Saharan African countries. Although a relatively high number of people attempt to start a business, many fail, and only very few businesses manage to grow (Balunywa et al. 2012). A major reason why businesses show limited growth is the low level of innovation (Rosenbush et al. 2011). Innovation refers to the introduction of new products/services, new ways of producing/offering them, and regular investment in business premises and machineries/tools.

Innovation has been extensively analyzed, but mainly in developed countries (Love and Roper 2015). Although an increasing number of studies address small business innovation in developing countries (see for example, De Jong and Vermeulen 2006), there is no established consensus on the factors fostering or hindering business innovation in nonadvanced economies (Radas and Božić 2009; Szirmai et al. 2011; Zanello et al. 2016). Furthermore, the studies that have been conducted in developed countries cannot really be generalized to the context of developing countries (Barasa et al. 2017; Bradley et al. 2012).

Businesses in developing countries, in Africa especially, are most often microenterprises. In Uganda, where we conducted our empirical research, businesses are mostly single proprietorships with two employees on average (Uganda Bureau of Statistics 2012). Despite this, most studies on business innovation in developing countries are focused on the firm level (e.g., Dohnert et al. 2017; Gebreeyesus and Mohnen 2013), and the individual level has received scant attention (Robson et al. 2009; Zanello et al. 2016). Furthermore, the majority of previous studies have considered only one particular set of factors (most often the firm level), without adopting a more comprehensive approach, including factors from different levels (individual characteristics, contextual factors, etc.).

In this chapter, we present the results of a large-scale survey conducted among rural and urban micro and small business owners in Uganda (sub-Saharan Africa). We take a multilevel perspective that combines the entrepreneur's individual level with a firm-level analysis, which was the focus of most previous research. By addressing urbanization, we also include the contextual level. The chapter reads as follows. In the theory section, we discuss innovation and possible factors influencing it. In the methodological and results section, we present our research on Ugandan entrepreneurs and we test our hypotheses. Finally, we discuss our findings and we address research and policy implications.

Theory: innovation in developing countries

The importance of innovation for business development has been widely recognized, especially in developing countries (OECD 2012; Prahalad 2012; Zanello et al. 2016). In particular, innovation is an important source for both economic development and business growth (Ahlstrom 2010; Bogliacino et al. 2012; Crespi and Zuniga 2012; Fagerberg et al. 2010; Gries and Naudé 2010; Szirmai 2008; Szirmai et al. 2011). However, creating and expanding innovations in developing countries are costly and contingent on appropriate institutional and environmental conditions (Fu and Gong 2011; Keller 2004).

Researchers have identified a number of factors that boost or hinder innovation (Love and Roper 2015). However, studies conducted in developed countries cannot be generalized to developing countries (Barasa et al. 2017; Bradley et al. 2012). Developing countries normally have underdeveloped institutional, legal, and financial systems, as well as a less diversified and specialized sectoral composition (Altenburg 2009; Zanello et al. 2016). Furthermore, social and cultural norms and attitudes differ between developing and developed countries. An example is the widespread use of "informal" arrangements in economic transactions in developing countries (Solano and Rooks 2018). Finally, businesses in developing countries, particularly in Africa, are most often micro and survival enterprises (Rooks et al. 2010; Sserwanga 2010).

The acknowledged importance of innovation for business growth and innovation, as well as the peculiarity of innovation in developing countries, has led to the establishment of a new subfield of research where business studies and development studies intersect. Innovation in developing countries – sometimes referred to as inclusive innovation (Chataway et al. 2014) – refers to "the production or delivery of new products and services for and/or by those people that so far were largely excluded by markets" (Zanello et al. 2016: 880).

This also links with the topic of frugal innovation (Knorringa et al. 2016; van Beers et al. 2014), which was developed around the idea of a different kind of innovation emerging from low-income settings and constrained environments (van Beers et al. 2014). Although the focus has mainly been on poor customers and implementation of innovations by medium-size companies (Knorringa et al. 2016; Zeschky et al. 2014), frugal innovation is also linked to small business innovation in a resource-constrained environment (Ray and Ray 2010).

Despite this increased interest in the topic of innovation in developing countries, there is still no established consensus on the factors fostering or hindering business innovation in nonadvanced economies (Barasa et al. 2017; Radas and Bozic 2009; Zanello et al. 2016). There is a wide range of studies dealing with the determinants of business innovation in developing countries (Fagerberg and Verspagen 2009; Zanello et al. 2016), but past research often addressed these factors as isolated causes (e.g., firm characteristics only) and/or focused less on other factors (e.g., the entrepreneur's individual characteristics, contextual characteristics).

Furthermore, most studies on business innovation in developing countries focused on the firm level (Dohnert et al. 2017; Gebreeyesus and Mohnen 2013). For example, innovation has been linked with the firm's size and age (Barasa et al. 2017; Chudnovsky et al. 2006; Gebreeyesus & Mohnen 2013; Radas and Bozic 2009; Robson et al. 2009).

As a consequence, the individual has received little attention (Robson et al. 2009; Zanello et al. 2016). In studies where the focus is on individual factors, most often only one type of factor is addressed – usually education (see for example, Gebreeyesus and Mohnen 2013; George et al. 2016). Other individual factors have not been considered very often. In particular, although it has been acknowledged that the personality of the entrepreneur is an important factor for business development (Frese and Gielnik 2014; Rauch et al. 2009; Zhao et al. 2010), this factor has largely been neglected as a determinant of business innovation.

Given the aforementioned trends and limitations, and following Hadjimanolis and Dickson (2000), Robson et al. (2009), and Romero and Martínez-Román (2012), this chapter adopts a multilevel approach. Whereas the majority of previous studies focus only on one factor or level, a multilevel approach is particularly suitable to produce a more in-depth understanding of entrepreneurial processes and the adoption of innovation (Baum et al. 2001).

Starting from previous research and models (Baum et al. 2001; Robson et al. 2009; Romero and Martínez-Román 2012; Rooks et al. 2016), we distinguish and develop hypotheses regarding three main sets of factors (or levels): *the individual level*, which includes the entrepreneur's personal traits, predispositions, and skills; *the firm level*, namely features of the business itself (business age, business size); and *the contextual level*, which refers to the general context where business is conducted (urban or rural area).

Hypotheses

The entrepreneur's individual characteristics

Education. Education – and the knowledge and skills acquired through it – is an important factor for micro and small business innovation. Entrepreneurs with a better education are more efficient in managing their businesses and in implementing innovations successfully (Romero and Martínez-Román 2012). This is particularly true in developing countries, as shown by a relevant number of studies (Gebreeyesus and Mohnen 2013; George et al. 2016; Mahemba and De Bruijn 2003; Oyelaran-Oyeyinka and Lal 2006; Radas and Božić 2009; Robson et al. 2009). For example, in their analysis of Ghanaian businesses, Robson et al. (2009) found that innovation was associated with higher education degrees (high school or higher).

Hypothesis 1: Education has a positive effect on business innovation.

Personality traits. Prior research suggests that personality traits, and in particular *proactivity* and *self-efficacy*, are particularly relevant personality traits for entrepreneurship (Boso et al. 2013; Frese and Gielnik 2014; Rauch et al. 2009; Zhao et al. 2010). *Proactivity entails anticipatory, change-oriented, future-focused behaviors* (Grant and Ashford 2008). *Proactive people have a* long-term view; they do not simply wait and react to external events, but rather they anticipate those events (Fay and Frese 2001; Grant and Ashford 2008). *Self-efficacy refers to one's* confidence in performing activities and executing tasks successfully (Bandura 1978; Chen et al. 1998). This influences how people approach tasks and challenges; those who are higher in self-efficacy are more likely to be confident when it comes to taking risks or facing challenges and problems.

Proactivity and self-efficacy positively affect business performance (Frese and Gielnik 2014; Lumpkin and Dess 1996; Rauch et al. 2009; Zhao et al. 2010). However, the effects of these two personality traits on innovation have not been studied extensively, particularly in developing countries. The few studies that did address the effects of proactivity (Oly Ndubisi and Iftikhar 2012; Rooks et al. 2016; Wang and Juan 2016) and self-efficacy (Ahlin et al. 2014; Kumar and Uzkurt 2011) on innovation underlined the fact that these two factors had a positive influence. They emphasized that these traits seem especially useful to overcome barriers in a constrained environment, as are Uganda and, more generally, developing countries. Therefore, we propose the following hypotheses:

Hypothesis 2: Proactivity has a positive effect on business innovation.
Hypothesis 3: Self-efficacy has a positive effect on business innovation.

Firm characteristics

Business size. At the firm level, innovation has been associated with business size. The idea that larger companies are more likely to innovate than smaller ones originates from Schumpeter (1942). In comparison with small businesses, large companies have more financial power. They can spread the cost of introducing new technologies over a larger sale base; they also have knowledge and expertise that are more difficult to access for small businesses (Robson et al. 2009; Rogers 2004). However, smaller companies are more flexible (due to less rigid structures and easier internal communications), and this can facilitate innovation (Bhattacharya and Bloch 2004; Rogers 2004).

Previous research in developing countries seems to corroborate Schumpeter's idea that larger companies are more innovative than smaller ones (Barasa et al. 2017; Chudnovsky et al. 2006; Wignaraja 2002; Zanello et al. 2016), due to resource constraints and the "subsistence" condition of most of businesses in developing countries. Therefore, we propose the following hypothesis:

Hypothesis 4: Business size has a positive effect on business innovation.

Business age. Business age can affect innovation in two opposite ways. On the one hand, the ability to innovate increases over time, due to an increasing knowledge of the sector where the business operates. Furthermore, by and large, older businesses have greater financial capital, which gives them an advantage compared to newer businesses (Balasubramanian and Lee 2008). In developing countries, this might be linked to the fact that entrepreneurs face many financial constraints and have difficulties in accessing finances (Solano and Rooks 2018). On the other hand, older businesses may suffer from "organizational inertia" (Hannan and Freeman 1984), because older businesses are often less keen to modify their products and services or the way in which they produce and offer them.

There is no consensus among scholars regarding the relation between firm age and innovation level in developing countries. Some researchers found that longer-established businesses are more innovative (Deraniyagala and Semboja 1999; Wignaraja 2002), whereas others did not find any such effect (Radas and Božić 2009; Robson et al. 2009), or found a negative effect (Gebreeyesus and Mohnen 2013). Given this lack of consensus, we formulate two contrasting hypotheses:

Hypothesis 5a: Business age has a positive effect on business innovation.
Hypothesis 5b: Business age has a negative effect on business innovation.

Urbanization

Rural and urban areas differ considerably in Africa. Urban areas are more dynamic than rural areas. In urban environments, markets are livelier, and customer preferences change at a quicker pace. Furthermore, urban areas are characterized by rapidly changing technologies (Bell and Abu 1999; Sserwanga 2010). In such a dynamic environment, opportunities for innovation arise. On the contrary, rural areas are more static environments; consequently, there are fewer opportunities to innovate (Casson and Wadeson 2007).

Large, densely populated cities make it easier to interact and to exchange information with different people. This can lead to new ideas and to innovation. One of the few studies comparing innovation in urban and rural settings supports the finding that urbanization is associated with innovation (Robson et al. 2009). In their research on Ghana, the authors found that businesses located in bigger cities were more innovative than businesses in smaller towns. Therefore, we formulate the following hypothesis:

Hypothesis 6: Urbanization has a positive effect on business innovation.

Methodology

Background to the study

Uganda has a population of about 34 million people, 7.4 million of whom live in urban areas (22 percent). A reported 1.5 million people live in the country's capital, Kampala. Twenty percent of the population live in poverty – with worse conditions in rural areas (Uganda Bureau of Statistics 2017). The total employed population is estimated at 7.9 million people, 48 percent of the working age population (Uganda Bureau of Statistics 2017). Among employed people, about 52.6 percent are self-employed (Uganda Bureau of Statistics 2017). Estimates from the Global Entrepreneurship Monitor (Balunywa et al. 2012) confirm that entrepreneurial activity in Uganda is high, and they underline that Uganda is one of the most entrepreneurial countries (together with other sub-Saharan countries). The entrepreneurship rate is higher among women, in the younger part of the population (18 to 34 years old), as well as in the better-educated members of society (Balunywa et al. 2012).

There are approximately 460,000 businesses in Uganda; the majority of them are in the Central Region of the country (59 percent of the total number of businesses in Uganda). Many businesses are in the trade (50 percent) or service (31 percent) sectors (Uganda Bureau of Statistics 2011). Almost all businesses (94 percent) are owned by one person only (sole proprietorship). High levels of entrepreneurship do not seem to correspond to high quality. Previous literature reports that the quality of entrepreneurship in Uganda is low (Balunywa et al. 2012; Sserwanga 2010), and statistics support this. Despite the high number of businesses and high percentage of self-employed people, Ugandan businesses are rather small (two employees on average). They are also young, as more than 50 percent of businesses were less than six years old, and 45 percent were less than five years old (Uganda Bureau of Statistics 2011). Furthermore, Ugandan businesses face a great risk of failure, as many of them fail within the first year, and only very few businesses manage to grow (Balunywa et al. 2012; Uganda Bureau of Statistics 2012).

A major reason why businesses show limited growth is a low level of dynamism and innovation. Rooks and colleagues (Rooks et al. 2010) found that only a small part of the interviewed Ugandan entrepreneurs showed any degree of dynamism and growth. Most entrepreneurs were survival entrepreneurs, who operated their own businesses for lack of other options. The authors also found that businesses were not very innovative and that the kinds of innovation introduced were new only to the firm, not to the domestic or international market.

This lack of innovation may be linked to institutional and cultural factors. Like other developing countries, Uganda still has underdeveloped institutional, legal, and financial systems (Sserwanga 2010). As a consequence, financial resources are a critical issue (Beck and Demirguc-Kunt 2006; Cook 2001). Entrepreneurs face many difficulties in accessing financial resources, especially in Ugandan and sub-Saharan Africa, where the formal borrowing rate is lower compared to other developing areas (Siba 2016 – elaboration on World Development Indicators). This can affect the degree of innovation.

Furthermore, Ugandan entrepreneurs are embedded in a series of relationships (kinship, clan relationship, etc.) that are both an asset and a liability. Entrepreneurs face distributive obligations; further growth may be hindered because entrepreneurs are expected to support relatives, friends, and community members. For example, Solano and Rooks (2018) showed that relatives are more likely to provide access to financial resources, but they are also more likely to ask for financial support.

All of these factors may hinder business innovation and business development.

Data collection and sample

We conducted a survey in January 2016. We pre-tested the questionnaire (specifically the scales concerning personality traits and innovation) during a pilot study carried out in Kampala in May 2015.

In the survey we randomly selected 608 respondents from a list of the 2011 Census of Business and Establishments (COBE) from the Uganda Bureau of Statistics (UBOS), which is the most recent list available. This COBE was conducted in 2010–2011 and covered all businesses with fixed establishments, irrespective of their degree of formality – UBOS worked autonomously from the Uganda Revenue Authority – (Uganda Bureau of Statistics 2011). The list displayed the location of the businesses, but not the description of the businesses themselves. Only in about 1 percent of cases did we go to the indicated location and found that there was no business present. Almost every person who was contacted agreed to participate in the study. Our response rate was 98.3 percent. This very high response rate is consistent with previous studies in the Ugandan context (Blattman et al. 2014; Kiconco et al. 2018; Rooks et al. 2016; Tushabomwe-Kazooba 2006).

When it was not possible to reach a business or when the person contacted refused to participate, we replaced it with the geographically closest alternative (first on the opposite side of the street, or, if this was not possible, on the same side).

We selected entrepreneurs from two sampling sites: an urban district and a rural district. Then, we randomly selected entrepreneurs from two of the COBE lists, one for the urban district and one for a rural district. We selected entrepreneurs from the capital Kampala (N = 294), and from the Nakaseke district (N = 314), a rural area located in the Central Region of Uganda and approximately 150 km away from the capital. We decided to focus on the Central Region because, according to UBOS statistics (Uganda Bureau of Statistics 2011), this is the region where the majority of businesses are located; 59 percent

Table 16.1 Business sectors: comparison between survey
sample and UBOS statistics (%)

	Survey Sample (2016)	UBOS (2011)
Trade	50.2	61.5
Service	30.8	29.4
Production	11.7	7.3
Agriculture	7.3	1.8
Total	100	100
N	608	454,766

of the total number of businesses in Uganda are located there (30 percent if we
do not consider Kampala).

A team of eight research assistants conducted the interviews. They attended
a three-day training session and conducted a number of pilot interviews to get
acquainted with the questionnaire and the data collection software (Question-
Pro). Respondents were interviewed on their business premises. The interviews
lasted 25 to 35 minutes.

Respondents were 34 years old on average and had nine years of education,
with a majority of female entrepreneurs (53 percent) making up the sample.
The age, education, and gender characteristics of our sample are consistent with
the most recent Global Entrepreneurship Monitor (GEM) report for Uganda
(Balunywa et al. 2012). Furthermore, businesses in our sample were mainly in
trade-related industries or services. Together, these represent more than 80 percent of all the businesses in our sample. The comparison with UBOS figures
(Uganda Bureau of Statistics 2011) shows that our sample is in line with the
reference population (see Table 16.1).

Dependent variable: innovation

Innovation refers to "a new or improved product or process (or combination
thereof) that differs significantly from the unit's previous products or processes
and that has been made available to potential users (product) or brought into
use by the unit (process)" (OECD 2018, 60).

Based on previous research on innovation of small businesses in developing countries (Rooks et al. 2005; Rooks et al. 2012), we used a set of four
dichotomous items to measure degree of innovation in our respondents. We
tested those items in a pilot study conducted in May 2015. In particular, we
asked questions regarding the introduction of new products/services (or new
ways of producing/offering them) *and* questions about investments in business
premises and machineries/tools (Table 16.2). In line with the recent debate on
frugal innovation, which underlines that innovations in developing countries
consist of "new or significantly improved products (both goods and services),
processes, or marketing and organizational methods that seek to minimize the

Table 16.2 Innovation items

Innovation items	Mean	Range	Mokken H
In the last three years, has your business introduced new products or services, or improved the existing ones?	.62	0–1	.57
In the last three years, has your business improved the way or implemented any new way to produce or offer your products and services?	.60	0–1	.58
In the last three years, have you invested resources to improve your (business) premises?	.41	0–1	.44
In the last three years, have you invested resources to improve your (business) machineries or tools?	.55	0–1	.44
Innovation	2.17	0–4	–

use of material and financial resources (. . .) with the objective of significantly reducing the total cost of ownership and/or usage" (Tiwari and Herstatt 2014, 30), we adopted an "inclusive" definition of innovation that accounts for the possibility of introducing changes without investing financial resources.

As shown in Table 16.2, the majority of respondents had introduced a new product or service (62 percent), improved ways to produce/offer services or products (60 percent), or invested resources to improve business tools in the last three years (55 percent). Only a minority of respondents had invested in improving business premises (41 percent). Overall, respondents had introduced at least two kinds of changes in the last three years.

To test the scalability of the items, we used the Mokken model (Mokken and Lewis 1982), which indicated that our scale was strong (Mokken H = 0.51).[2] Using the items, we created a variable (innovation), which is the sum of the value of the four items. This is the dependent variable with which we test our hypotheses.

Independent variables

Education. We measured education as the number of years of education.

Proactivity. We created a score of proactivity measured as the mean of the values of the three-item scale. The items were taken from Frese and collegues (1997). This scale has already been tested in Uganda (Rooks et al. 2016). The Cronbach's alpha test confirmed the reliability of the scale ($\alpha = 0.71$).

Self-efficacy. We created a score of general self-efficacy based on the mean of the values from the four-item scale. The scale was built from Schwarzer and Jerusalem's ten-item scale (1995). We tested the scale in a pilot study conducted in May 2015. Based on this pilot study, we selected four items. Cronbach's alpha showed that the scale is reliable ($\alpha = 0.76$).

Firm size (logarithm). Following previous research (Romero and Martínez-Román 2012; Robson et al. 2009), we measured firm size based on the number of employees. We inserted the logarithmic version in the model because the original variable had a skewed distribution.

Business age (logarithm). To measure business age we calculated the number of years since the business started. We inserted the logarithmic version in the model because the original variable had a skewed distribution.

Urbanization. We inserted the urbanization variable, indicating whether the entrepreneur was living in an urban area or in a rural one (reference category).

Control variables

Gender. Female and male entrepreneurs in the African context vary in their behaviors, their characteristics, and their contacts to a great extent (Vossenberg 2016). To account for this, we included entrepreneur gender (female being the reference category).

Sector. Innovation can vary across business sectors (Robson et al. 2009). To check for any effect of different sectors, we created three variables: (1) *industry* (whether or not a business is in the manufacturing or construction sectors); (2) *services* (whether or not a business is in the services sector), and (3) *trade* (whether or not a business is a retail or wholesale business). The reference category is *agriculture* (whether or not a business is in the agricultural sector).

Results

Table 16.3 presents the descriptive statistics. Respondents in our sample reported a medium–high score for proactivity and self-efficacy.

Although rather consolidated, because the average business age is seven years, businesses are very small (one employee, on average). Businesses are mainly in trade-related industries – retail and wholesale (50 percent) and services (31 percent). This is in line with the most recent data regarding Ugandan businesses

Table 16.3 Individual and business characteristics

Characteristics	N	M	SD	Range
Individual level				
Age	592	34.17	10.92	15–89
Male (gender)	594	.47	.49	0–1
Year of education	597	9	4.6	0–18
Proactivity	605	3.86	.70	1–5
Self-efficacy	605	3.95	.67	1–5
Firm level				
Business age (in years)	599	7.27	7.92	0–54
Number of employees	555	1.23	1.95	0–19
Trade (sector)	606	.50	.50	0–1
Industry (sector)	606	.12	.32	0–1
Service (sector)	606	.31	.46	0–1
Agricultural (sector)	606	.7	.26	0–1

(Uganda Bureau of Statistics 2011), which underlined that the majority of Ugandan businesses are rather small (two employees on average) and are in trade sectors.

To test our hypotheses, we ran a linear regression. Table 16.4 shows the correlations of the variables included in the model. The correlations between independent variables are low, except for trade and service sectors.

Table 16.5 shows the results of the linear regression for innovation. Given the high correlation between trade and service, we also ran a model only with

Table 16.4 Correlations between variables

	1	2	3	4	5	6	7	8	9	10	11
1 Innovation	–										
2 Education	.06	–									
3 Proactivity	.24***	.09*	–								
4 Self-efficacy	.23***	.15***	.34***	–							
5 Business size	.03	.08	−.08	.01	–						
6 Business age	.23***	−.32**	−.03	−.03	.14**	–					
7 Urbanization	−.15***	.18***	.06	−.01	.02	−.11**	–				
8 Gender	.11***	.12**	−.04	.07	.25***	.12**	.01	–			
9 Industry	.08*	−.03	.02	.02	.17***	.15***	.08	.24***	–		
10 Service	.02	.04	−.03	−.03	.05	−.11**	.03	−.04	−.24***	–	
11 Trade	−.01	.07	.09*	.05	−.27***	−.11**	.00	−.16***	−.36***	−.67***	–

Table 16.5 Regression analysis of innovation: whole sample

	B	SE	β
Individual level			
Education	.05***	.01	.17
Proactivity	.41***	.09	.19
Self-efficacy	.32***	.09	.15
Firm level			
Business size	.03	.99	.01
Business age	.40***	.60	.29
Context			
Urbanisation	−.54***	.12	−.18
Control variables			
Gender (male = 1)	.11	.13	.04
Sector: Industry	1.23***	.30	.27
Sector: Service	1.18***	.27	.38
Sector: Trade	1.06***	.27	.36
Constant	−2.66***	.47	
N	520		
R2	.23		
F	15.1***		
adj-R2	.21		

* $p < .05$; ** $p < .01$; *** $p < .001$. B, unstandardized coefficient, SE, unstandardized standard error, β, standardized coefficient.

service (all the other possibilities as reference category), and we obtained the same results of the model reported here.

Hypothesis 1 states that education has a positive effect on innovation. The results support our hypothesis ($\beta = 0.16; p < 0.001$).

Hypotheses 2 and *3* address the entrepreneurs' personality traits. *Hypothesis 2*, which concerns the positive effect of proactivity on innovation, is supported by our results ($\beta = 0.18; p < 0.001$). The results also show that self-efficacy has a positive effect on innovation ($\beta = 0.15; p < 0.001$). Therefore, *hypothesis 3* is confirmed as well.

Hypotheses 4 and *5* concern the firm level. Our results do not support *hypothesis 4*, which states that larger businesses are more innovative. The effect of firm size on innovation is not significant. Prior studies reported that firm size can have a nonlinear effect on innovation. In analyses not reported here, we tested the nonlinearity of firm size (Martínez-Román et al. 2011; Romero and Martínez-Román 2012). We found no effect of the quadratic versions of business size. *Hypothesis 5a* is supported and, consequently *hypothesis 5b* is not. The results show that the older a business is, the more innovative it is ($\beta = 0.28; p < 0.001$).

Finally, the results contradict *hypothesis 6*, which states that urbanization positively influences innovation. On the contrary, the results show that entrepreneurs in the urban area are less innovative than entrepreneurs in the rural environment ($\beta = -0.19; p < 0.001$).

As for control variables, our results confirm that innovation differs depending on business sectors in Uganda. In particular, businesses in the agricultural sector are less innovative than businesses in other sectors. Analyses not reported here showed that sectors (industrial, trade, and services) do not differ in innovativeness. Finally, we did not find any significant difference between male and female entrepreneurs. This is consistent with prior research, which found no gender-based differences in the level of innovation (DeTienne and Chandler 2007; Romero and Martínez-Román 2012; Sackey 2005).

Table 16.6 Hypotheses (dependent variable: innovation)

	Variable	Hypothesized effect	Findings
Hp1.	Education	+	Supported
Hp2.	Proactivity	+	Supported
Hp3.	Self-efficacy	+	Supported
Hp4.	Business size	+	Not sig.
Hp5a.	Business age	+	Supported
Hp5b.	Business age	−	Contradicted (opposite result)
Hp6	Urbanization	+	Contradicted (opposite result)

Conclusions

In this chapter, we addressed the determinants of innovation in micro and small businesses in a developing country, Uganda. Overall, our results suggest that the entrepreneur as an individual is an important driver of micro and small business innovation. Entrepreneurs who are better educated or more proactive and who have a higher degree of self-efficacy are more innovative. At the firm level, business age predicts innovation. Older businesses are more innovative than more recent ones. This can be linked with the fact that micro and small businesses in developing countries face a number of constraints and challenges (Bradley et al. 2012; DeBerry-Spence and Elliot 2012). This affects businesses especially at the nascent stage of entrepreneurship and may be linked to the fact that entrepreneurs often face financial constraints. This is particularly true in Uganda (Sserwanga 2010). Many Ugandan businesses fail within the first year (Uganda Bureau of Statistics 2012), and have difficulties in accessing finances (Rooks et al. 2016; Solano and Rooks 2018). These challenges may hinder their efforts in innovating. Another explanation is a selection effect. New companies that are more innovative are more likely to survive. Although business age is associated with innovation, business size does not appear to matter in Uganda.

Our research confirms the importance of context in which where an entrepreneur runs his or her business (Barasa et al. 2017; Robson et al. 2009; Rooks et al. 2012). However, in contrast with what we expected, entrepreneurs in a rural area are more innovative, and urbanization seems to hinder business innovation. This is a surprising finding (compared, for example, with Robson and colleagues 2009), given that more dynamic environments are normally associated with higher levels of innovation (Alvarez and Barney 2007).

Why are urban entrepreneurs less innovative, as emerged from our research? First, the literature links urban areas – which are more dynamic – to high-quality and innovative entrepreneurship (Santos-Cumplido and Linan 2006). However, less dynamic environments are also more stable (no rapid changes). Therefore, the lower dynamicity of rural areas could lead entrepreneurs to have a more long-term perspective. Previous studies on small businesses in Uganda and other developing countries (Berner, Gomez, and Knorringa 2012; Rosa Kodithuwakku and Balunywa 2006; Sserwanga 2010) confirm this by underlining that entrepreneurs tend to run urban businesses that produce quick cash and require small investments, but they invest profits in the development of rural businesses, where the context is less turbulent. Second, opportunities to find a job are higher in Kampala than in rural areas. This implies that in Kampala, talented people are likely to have better options than that of starting a business. Entrepreneurship is often a choice for the most marginal urban population. Third, a relevant number of migrants from rural areas compose the population of Kampala (Mukwaya et al. 2011; Bell et al. 2015). As also underlined by literature on the topic (Baggiani, Longoni, and Solano 2011; Longoni, Solano and Baggiani 2011; Rath et al. 2019), many of them migrated to the city and then started a business. This is also confirmed in our sample, where 65 percent of the Kampala respondents were not born in the city. These migrant entrepreneurs have few resources, often engaging in small trade. Taken together, these explanations suggest that less resourceful entrepreneurs make up the urban entrepreneurial population of Kampala, and this may be another reason for their lower level of innovation.

This chapter contributes to the field of business and development studies. In particular, the study contributes to the ongoing debate on inclusive and frugal innovation (Chataway et al. 2014; Knorringa et al. 2016; van Beers et al. 2014; Zanello et al. 2016), meaning innovation linked to small business innovation in a resource-constrained environment (Ray and Ray 2010). By analyzing the determinants of innovation, we showed what factors can foster (frugal) innovation when the innovation comes from micro and small businesses in constrained environments.

As explained in the methods section, we defined innovation in an inclusive way and we employed tailor-made questions for innovation in developing countries. By doing this, a need clearly emerged to redefine our analytical and empirical tools to study entrepreneurial activities in developing countries. These tools were often designed in developed countries and therefore might not be applicable in developing countries.

This chapter has important policy implications. It stresses the importance of the individual level and, in particular, of behaviors linked to personality (i.e., personality traits). As illustrated by the work of Frese and colleagues (Frese, Hass et al. 2016; Frese, Gielnik et al.2016), it is possible to train behaviors linked to personality. Motivating entrepreneurs to acquire a proactive, self-confident, and effective approach to entrepreneurship – and teaching them how to do this – seems to be the right way to boost innovative and successful entrepreneurship. The chapter also points to the prominent role of education. A clear indication for policymakers is to invest in education (schooling, ad-hoc trainings, etc.) with the aim of encouraging innovative entrepreneurship.

The chapter has a number of limitations, which can be addressed in subsequent studies. The study focuses on a single country in sub-Saharan Africa (Uganda). Future research on developing countries might replicate this study so as to account for developing countries in other areas of Africa (e.g., North Africa) or other continents (e.g., Asia). Furthermore, we did not collect information regarding the actual formality of the business. As informality is a relevant phenomenon in Uganda and in Africa, subsequent studies might analyze how businesses in an informal economy differ from businesses in a formal economy when it comes to innovation. Another limitation is that we measured whether or not a certain level of innovation, or better yet, four domains of innovation, was implemented. However, we did not check the "quality" of this innovation, namely how innovative the implementation was. As for domains of innovation, further research might analyze variations based on different types of innovation (e.g., comparing business model innovation and changes in technology). Finally, the set of variables included in the model is not exhaustive. Other variables could be included as possible determinants of innovation, such as employee characteristics or management characteristics (Barasa 2017; Collins and Reutzel 2017; Radas and Bozic 2009).

Notes

1 Acknowledgements: The paper is an output from the project 'Changing the Mindset of Ugandan Entrepreneurs', which is part of the research agenda of the Knowledge Platform on Inclusive Development Policies and funded by the Netherlands Ministry of Foreign Affairs through NWO-WOTRO. We are grateful to them for the financial support provided.
2 A value of H above 0.5 on the Mokken is considered to be strong (Mokken and Lewis, 1982; Meijer and Baneke, 2004).

References

Ahlin, Branka, Mateja Drnovšek, and Robert D. Hisrich (2014), "Entrepreneurs' creativity and firm innovation: the moderating role of entrepreneurial self-efficacy," *Small Business Economics*, 43 (1), 101–17.

Ahlstrom, D. (2010), "Innovation and growth: how business contributes to society." *The Academy of Management Perspectives*, 24(3), 11–24.

Altenburg, Tilman (2009), "Building inclusive innovation systems in developing countries: challenges for IS research," in *Handbook of Innovation Systems and Developing Countries*, B.-Å. Lundvall, K. Joseph, C. Chaminade, and J. Vang, eds., Cheltenham, UK and Northampton, MA: Edward Elgar Publishing, 33–56.

Alvarez, Sharon A. and Jay B. Barney (2007), "Discovery and creation: alternative theories of entrepreneurial action," *Strategic Entrepreneurship Journal*, 1 (1–2), 11–26.

Baggiani, B., L. Longoni, and G. Solano (Eds.). (2011), *Noi e l'altro? Materiali per l'analisi e la comprensione dei fenomeni migratori contemporanei*. Ravenna: Discanti.

Balasubramanian, Natarajan and Jeongsik Lee (2008), "Firm age and innovation," *Industrial and Corporate Change*, 17 (5), 1019–47.

Balunywa, Waswa, Peter Rosa, S. Dawa, R. Namatovu, Sarah Kyejjusa, and Diana Ntamu (2012), "Global Entrepreneurship Monitor Executive report – Uganda," Kampala.

Bandura, Albert (1978), "Self-efficacy: toward a unifying theory of behavioral change," *Advances in Behaviour Research and Therapy*, 1 (4), 139–61.

Barasa, Laura, Joris Knoben, Patrick Vermeulen, Peter Kimuyu, and Bethuel Kinyanjui (2017), "Institutions, resources and innovation in East Africa: a firm level approach," *Research Policy*, 46 (1), 280–91.

Baum, J. Robert, Edwin A. Locke, and Ken G. Smith (2001), "A multidimensional model of venture growth," *The Academy of Management Journal*, 44 (2), 292–303.

Beck, Thorsten and Asli Demirguc-Kunt (2006), "Small and medium-size enterprises: access to finance as a growth constraint," *Journal of Banking & Finance*, 30 (11), 2931–43.

Bell, Martin and Michael Albu (1999), "Knowledge systems and technological dynamism in industrial clusters in developing countries," *World Development*, 27 (9), 1715–34.

Bell, Martin, Elin Charles-Edwards, Philipp Ueffing, John Stillwell, Marek Kupiszewski, and Dorota Kupiszewska (2015), "Internal migration and development: comparing migration intensities around the world," *Population and Development Review*, 41 (1), 33–58.

Berner, Erhard, Georgina Gomez, and Peter Knorringa (2012), "'Helping a large number of people become a little less poor': the logic of survival entrepreneurs," *The European Journal of Development Research*, 24 (3), 382–96.

Bhattacharya, Mita and Harry Bloch (2004), "Determinants of innovation," *Small Business Economics*, 22 (2), 155–62.

Blattman, Christopher, Nathan Fiala, and Sebastian Martinez (2014), "Generating skilled self-employment in developing countries: experimental evidence from Uganda," *The Quarterly Journal of Economics*, 129 (2), 697–752.

Bogliacino, Francesco, Giulio Perani, Mario Pianta, and Stefano Supino (2012), "Innovation and Development: The Evidence From Innovation Surveys," *Latin American Business Review*, 13 (3), 219–61.

Boso, Nathaniel, John W. Cadogan, and Vicky M. Story (2013), "Entrepreneurial orientation and market orientation as drivers of product innovation success: A study of exporters from a developing economy," *International Small Business Journal*, 31 (1), 57–81.

Bradley, Steven W., Jeffery S. McMullen, Kendall Artz, and Edward M. Simiyu (2012), "Capital is not enough: innovation in developing economies: innovation in developing economies," *Journal of Management Studies*, 49 (4), 684–717.

Casson, Mark and Nigel Wadeson (2007), "The discovery of opportunities: extending the economic theory of the entrepreneur," *Small Business Economics*, 28 (4), 285–300.

Chataway, Joanna, Rebecca Hanlin, and Raphael Kaplinsky (2014), "Inclusive innovation: an architecture for policy development," *Innovation and Development*, 4 (1), 33–54.

Chen, Chao C., Patricia Gene Greene, and Ann Crick (1998), "Does entrepreneurial self-efficacy distinguish entrepreneurs from managers?" *Journal of Business Venturing*, 13 (4), 295–316.

Chudnovsky, Daniel, Andrés López, and Germán Pupato (2006), "Innovation and productivity in developing countries: a study of Argentine manufacturing firms' behavior (1992–2001)," *Research Policy*, 35 (2), 266–88.

Collins, Jamie D. and Christopher R. Reutzel (2017), "The role of top managers in determining investment in innovation: the case of small and medium-sized enterprises in India," *International Small Business Journal*, 35 (5), 618–638.

Cook, Paul (2001), "Finance and small and medium-sized enterprise in developing countries," *Journal of Developmental Entrepreneurship; Norfolk*, 6 (1), 17–40.

Crespi, Gustavo and Pluvia Zuniga (2012), "Innovation and productivity: Evidence from Six Latin American countries," *World Development*, 40 (2), 273–90.

DeBerry-Spence, Benet and Esi Abbam Elliot (2012), "African microentrepreneurship: the reality of everyday challenges," *Journal of Business Research*, 65 (12), 1665–73.

de Jong, J. P.J. and P. A.M. Vermeulen (2006), "Determinants of product innovation in small firms: a comparison across industries," *International Small Business Journal*, 24 (6), 587–609.

Deraniyagala, S. and H.H.H. Semboja (1999), "Trade liberalization, firm performance and technology upgrading in Tanzania." in *The Technological Response to Import Liberalization in Sub-Saharan Africa*, S. Lall, ed., London: Palgrave Macmillan, pp. 112–147.

DeTienne, Dawn R. and Gaylen N. Chandler (2007), "The role of gender in opportunity identification," *Entrepreneurship Theory and Practice*, 31 (3), 365–86.

Dohnert, Sylvia, Gustavo Crespi, and Alessandro Maffioli (Eds.) (2017), *Exploring Firm-Level Innovation and Productivity in Developing Countries: The Perspective of Caribbean Small States*, Inter-American Development Bank.

Fagerberg, Jan, Martin Srholec, and Bart Verspagen (2010), "Innovation and economic development," in *Handbook of the Economics of Innovation*, N. Rosenberg and B. Hall, eds., Elsevier, 833–72.

Fagerberg, Jan and Bart Verspagen (2009), "Innovation studies – the emerging structure of a new scientific field," *Research Policy*, 38 (2), 218–33.

Fay, Doris and Michael Frese (2001), "The concept of personal initiative: an overview of validity studies," *Human Performance*, 14 (1), 97–124.

Frese, Michael, Doris Fay, Tanja Hilburger, Karena Leng, and Almut Tag (1997), "The concept of personal initiative: operationalization, reliability and validity in two German samples," *Journal of Occupational and Organizational Psychology*, 70 (2), 139–61.

Frese, Michael and Michael M. Gielnik (2014), "The psychology of entrepreneurship," *Annual Review of Organizational Psychology and Organizational Behavior*, 1 (1), 413–38.

Frese, Michael, Michael M. Gielnik, and Mona Mensmann (2016), "Psychological training for entrepreneurs to take action: contributing to poverty reduction in developing countries," *Current Directions in Psychological Science*, 25 (3), 196–202.

Frese, Michael, Lydia Hass, and Christian Friedrich (2016), "Personal initiative training for small business owners," *Journal of Business Venturing Insights*, 5, 27–36.

Fu, Xiaolan and Yundan Gong (2011), "Indigenous and Foreign innovation efforts and drivers of technological upgrading: evidence from China," *World Development*, 39 (7), 1213–25.

Gebreeyesus, Mulu and Pierre Mohnen (2013), "Innovation performance and embeddedness in networks: evidence from the Ethiopian footwear cluster," *World Development*, 41, 302–16.

George, G., C. Corbishley, J. N. O. Khayesi, M. R. Haas, and L. Tihanyi (2016), "Bringing Africa in: promising directions for management research," *Academy of Management Journal*, 59 (2), 377–93.

Grant, Adam M. and Susan J. Ashford (2008), "The dynamics of proactivity at work," *Research in Organizational Behavior*, 28, 3–34.

Gries, Thomas and Wim Naudé (2010), "Entrepreneurship and structural economic transformation," *Small Business Economics*, 34 (1), 13–29.

Hadjimanolis, A. and K. Dickson (2000), "Innovation strategies of SMEs in Cyprus, a small developing country," *International Small Business Journal*, 18 (4), 62–79.

Hannan, Michael T. and John Freeman (1984), "Structural inertia and organizational change," *American Sociological Review*, 49 (2), 149–64.

Keller, Wolfgang (2004), "International technology diffusion," *Journal of Economic Literature*, 42 (3), 752–82.

Kiconco, Rebecca I., Gerrit Rooks, Giacomo Solano, and Uwe Matzat (2018), "A skills perspective on the adoption and use of mobile money services in Uganda," *Information Development*, online version.

Knorringa, P., I. Peša, A. Leliveld, and C. van Beers (2016), "Frugal innovation and development: aides or adversaries?" *European Journal of Development Research*, 28(2), 143–153.

Kumar, R. and C. Uzkurt (2011), "Investigating the effects of self-efficacy on innovativeness and the moderating impact of cultural dimensions," *Journal of International Business and Cultural Studies*, 4, 1–15.

Longoni, L., G. Solano, and B. Baggiani (Eds.). (2012), *La città nell'epoca della globalizzazione*. Roma: Aracne.

Love, James and Stephen Roper (2015), "SME innovation, exporting and growth: a review of existing evidence," *International Small Business Journal*, 33 (1), 28–48.

Lumpkin, G. T. and Gregory G. Dess (1996), "Clarifying the entrepreneurial orientation construct and linking it to performance," *Academy of Management Review*, 21 (1), 135–72.

Mahemba, Christopher M. and Erik J. De Bruijn (2003), "Innovation activities by small and medium-sized manufacturing enterprises in Tanzania," *Creativity and Innovation Management*, 12 (3), 162–73.

Martínez-Román, J. A., J. Gamero, and J. A. Tamayo (2011), "Analysis of innovation in SMEs using an innovative capability-based non-linear model: a study in the province of Seville (Spain)," *Technovation*, 31(9), 459–475.

Meijer, Rob R. and Joost J. Baneke (2004), "Analyzing psychopathology items: a case for nonparametric item response theory modeling," *Psychological Methods*, 9 (3), 354–68.

Mokken, R. J. and C. Lewis (1982), "A Nonparametric approach to the analysis of dichotomous item responses," *Applied Psychological Measurement*, 6 (4), 417–30.

Mukwaya, Paul, Yazidhi Bamutaze, Samuel Mugarura, Todd Benson, and others (2011), "Rural-urban transformation in Uganda," in *Conference on Understanding Economic Transformation in Sub-Saharan Africa*, Accra.

OECD (2012), *Innovation for Development*, Paris: OECD Publishing.

OECD (2018), *Measuring Business Innovation Activities*, Paris: OECD Publishing.

Oly Ndubisi, Nelson and Khurram Iftikhar (2012), "Relationship between entrepreneurship, innovation and performance: comparing small and medium-size enterprises," *Journal of Research in Marketing and Entrepreneurship*, 14 (2), 214–36.

Oyelaran-Oyeyinka, Banji and Kaushalesh Lal (2006), "Learning new technologies by small and medium enterprises in developing countries," *Technovation*, 26 (2), 220–31.

Prahalad, C. K. (2012), "Bottom of the pyramid as a source of breakthrough innovations: BOP as source of innovations," *Journal of Product Innovation Management*, 29 (1), 6–12.

Radas, Sonja and Ljiljana Božić (2009), "The antecedents of SME innovativeness in an emerging transition economy," *Technovation*, 29 (6–7), 438–50.

Rath, Jan, Giacomo Solano, and Veronique Schutjens (2019), "Migrant entrepreneurship and transnational links," in *The Sage Handbook of International Migration*, C. Inglis, B. Khadria, W. Li (Eds.), London: Sage.

Rauch, Andreas, Johan Wiklund, G. T. Lumpkin, and Michael Frese (2009), "Entrepreneurial orientation and business performance: an assessment of past research and suggestions for the future," *Entrepreneurship Theory and Practice*, 33 (3), 761–87.

Ray, P.K. and S. Ray (2010), "Resource-constrained innovation for emerging economies: the case of the Indian telecommunications industry." *IEEE Transactions on Engineering Management*, 57, 144–156.

Robson, Paul J. A., Helen M. Haugh, and Bernard Acquah Obeng (2009), "Entrepreneurship and innovation in Ghana: enterprising Africa," *Small Business Economics*, 32 (3), 331–50.

Rogers, Mark (2004), "Networks, firm size and innovation," *Small Business Economics*, 22 (2), 141–53.

Romero, Isidoro and Juan A. Martínez-Román (2012), "Self-employment and innovation: Exploring the determinants of innovative behavior in small businesses," *Research Policy*, 41 (1), 178–89.

Rooks, Gerrit, Leon Oerlemans, Andre Buys, and Tinus Pretorius (2005), "Industrial innovation in South Africa: a comparative study: science policy," *South African Journal of Science*, 101 (3–4), 149–50.

Rooks, Gerrit, Arthur Sserwanga, and Michael Frese (2016), "Unpacking the personal initiative-performance relationship: a multi-group analysis of innovation by Ugandan rural and urban entrepreneurs: the personal initiative-performance relationship," *Applied Psychology*, 65 (1), 99–131.

Rooks, Gerrit, Adam Szirmai, and Arthur Sserwanga (2010), "The interplay of human and social capital in entrepreneurship in developing countries: the case of Uganda," in *Entrepreneurship and Economic Development*, W. A. Naudé, ed., Houndmills, Basingstoke and New York, NY: Palgrave Macmillan.

Rooks, Gerrit, Adam Szirmai, and Arthur Sserwanga (2012), "Network structure and innovative performance of african entrepreneurs: the case of Uganda," *Journal of African Economies*, 21 (4), 609–36.

Rosa, Peter, Sarath Kodithuwakku, and Waswa Balunywa (2006), "Reassessing necessity entrepreneurship in developing countries," in *29th Institute for Small Business & Entrepreneurship*

Conference: *International Entrepreneurship – from Local to Global Enterprise Creation and Development*, Cardiff, 1–13.

Rosenbusch, N., J. Brinckmann, and A. Bausch (2011), "Is innovation always beneficial? A meta-analysis of the relationship between innovation and performance in SMEs." *Journal of Business Venturing*, 26(4), 441–457.

Sackey, Harry A. (2005), "Poverty in Ghana from an assets-based perspective: an application of probit technique," *African Development Review*, 17 (1), 41–69.

Santos-Cumplido, Francisco Javier, and Francisco Liñán (2006), "Measuring entrepreneurial quality in Southern Europe," *International Entrepreneurship and Management Journal*, 3 (1), 87–107.

Schumpeter, Joseph A. (1942), *Capitalism, Socialism, and Democracy*, New York: Harper Perennial Modern Thought.

Schwarzer, R. and M. Jerusalem (1995), "Generalized self-efficacy scale," in *Measures in Health Psychology: A User's Portfolio*, M. Johnston, J. Weinman, and S. C. Wright, eds., Windsor: NFER-NELSON, 35–37.

Siba, Eyerusalem (2016), "Enabling female entrepreneurs and beyond," *Africa in Focus, Brookings*.

Solano, Giacomo and Gerrit Rooks (2018), "Social capital of entrepreneurs in a developing country: the effect of gender on access to and requests for resources," *Social Networks*, 54, 279–90.

Sserwanga, Arthur (2010), *Entreneurial Quality in Uganda*, Kampala: Makarere University Business School.

Szirmai, Adam (2008), "Explaining success and failure in development," MERIT Working Papers, United Nations University – Maastricht Economic and Social Research Institute on Innovation and Technology (MERIT).

Szirmai, Adam, Wim A. Naudé, and Micheline Goedhuys (Eds.) (2011), *Entrepreneurship, Innovation, and Economic Development*, Oxford and New York: Oxford University Press.

Tiwari, Rajnish and Cornelius Herstatt (2014), *Aiming Big with Small Cars: Emergence of a Lead Market in India*, India Studies in Business and Economics, Cham, Heidelberg, New York, Dordrecht, and London: Springer International Publishing.

Tushabomwe-Kazooba, Charles (2006), "Causes of small business failure in Uganda: a case study from Bushenyi and Mbarara towns," *African Studies Quarterly*, 8 (4), 27–35.

Ugandan Bureau of Statistics (2011), "Report on the Census of Business Establishments 2010/2011," Kampala.

Ugandan Bureau of Statistics (2012), "Statistical Abstract," Kampala.

Ugandan Bureau of Statistics (2017), "Statistical Abstract," Kampala.

van Beers, C., P. Knorringa, and A. Leliveld (2014), Frugal Innovation in Africa Towards a Research Agenda. Position paper for 14th EADI General Conference Responsible Development in a Polycentric World: Inequality, Citizenship and the Middle Classes, Bonn, 23–26 June 2014.

Vossenberg, Saskia (2016), *Gender-Aware Women's Entrepreneurship Development for Inclusive Development in Sub-Saharan Africa*, Leiden: Include.

Wang, Edward Shih-Tse and Pei-Yi Juan (2016), "Entrepreneurial orientation and service innovation on consumer response," *Journal of Small Business Management*, 54 (2), 532–45.

Wignaraja, Ganeshan (2002), "Firm size, technological capabilities and market-oriented policies in Mauritius," *Oxford Development Studies*, 30 (1), 87–104.

Zanello, Giacomo, Xiaolan Fu, Pierre Mohnen, and Marc Ventresca (2016), "The creation and diffusion of innovation in developing countries: a systematic review" *Journal of Economic Surveys*, 30 (5), 884–912.

Zeschky, M, S. Winterhalter, and O. Gassmann (2014), "From cost to frugal and reverse innovation: mapping the field and implications for global competitiveness." *Research-Technology Management*, 57(4), 20–27.

Zhao, Hao, Scott E. Seibert, and G.T. Lumpkin (2010), "The relationship of personality to entrepreneurial intentions and performance: a meta-analytic review," *Journal of Management*, 36 (2), 381–404.

17 Microfinance programs and women's empowerment[1]

New evidence from the rural middle hills of Nepal

Mahinha Wijiesiri and Franque Grimard

Introduction

Microfinance institutions (MFIs) are hybrid type of financial institutions that pursue "double" bottom lines of social outreach and financial sustainability.[2] They are thought to play a vital role in inclusive economic growth while reducing poverty and inequality in developing economies where access to formal financial services is typically very limited. They serve the low-income households and rural microenterprises, providing a wide range of financial services and products ranging from simple credit facilities to savings, remittance, insurance, and many others (the "minimalist" lending model). Some of them extend their operations by providing clients with skill-based business training as well as consciousness-raising programs (the "plus" lending model) (Khandker 2005). Thus, microfinance programs have become an integral part of development policies by enabling institution building at the grassroots level as well as an effective poverty alleviation tool (Goetz and Gupta 1996; Mazumder, Ullah, and Lu 2015).

Although some microfinance programs serve both males and females, most target only female clients, with an explicit aim of empowering them (Pitt, Khandker, and Cartwright 2006; Pitt and Khandker 1998; Rankin 2001, 2002; Kabeer 2001; Khandker 2005; Setboonsarng and Parpiev 2008; Garikipati 2012; Ganle, Afriyie, and Segbefia 2015). Targeting only female clients is not surprising, as they are the most vulnerable and poorest segments of the society. This is particularly true in many low- and middle-income countries where social norms and religious beliefs have created a large gender gap. Women in these countries are more likely than men to be constrained in their access to credit, as well as restricted in their access to assets, education, and basic health and sanitation facilities. Even within the same market, women entrepreneurs are considerably disadvantaged in terms of less access to credit, equipment, raw materials, and information (King and Mason 2001), and consequently earn less relative to their male counterparts (Torri and Martinez 2011). In addition, women often have limited decision-making and bargaining power within the household and have limited access to assets and land ownership, indicating a significant gender gap between men and women in developing economies.

In such circumstances, providing low-income women with access to affordable microfinance services is often considered to be an effective means of women's socioeconomic empowerment (Khandker 2005). Because women are less likely to misuse loans and are therefore good credit risks, their access to microfinance services could lead to an increase in their business productivity, household income, and, ultimately, improved self-esteem and household welfare (Goetz and Gupta 1996; Garikipati 2008).

Women's empowerment is one of the main issues in the process of development in the world (Sen 1999). This is especially true for developing countries where gender inequality and women's disempowerment are very common and become a key factor operating against sustainable economic development. Access to education, credit, health, and sanitation facilities and participation in household decisions and asset ownership are among the main causes of gender inequality. Moreover, women's disproportionate burden of unpaid work which, together with paid work, contributes to overall economic growth, has serious implications for prevailing gender inequalities (Hirway 2018).

Women's equality and empowerment has, thus, become a core theme of Sustainable Development Goals (SDGs) to be implemented by 2030. Goal 5 of the SDG agenda focuses explicitly on women's issues and suggests a multi-dimensional approach to gender equality with a range of targets that include ending discrimination, exploitation, and child, early, and forced marriage; recognizing unpaid care and domestic work; promoting women's participation and opportunities for leadership; enabling ownership of land and other property; and providing access to intermediate technology (Stuart and Woodroffe 2016).

There is no universally accepted definition of "empowerment," with the term being used to represent a wide range of concepts across a range of disciplines and to describe a proliferation of outcomes (Torri and Martinez 2011). In the context of microfinance and its impact on women, Mahmud, Shah, and Becker 2012 referred to the term "women's empowerment" as a dynamic process of internal dynamism, which is difficult to examine, despite the visibility of its aggregate effects. Kabeer (1999, 2001) describes empowerment as a process by which those who have been denied the ability to exercise strategic forms of choice, voice, and influence, both within their personal lives and in the wider community, have been able to gain this ability. She further argues that this process is a rudimentary three-dimensional theory of change incorporating three indivisible dimensions of "choices": (1) women's access to *material and human and social resources:* these are the media through which "agency" is exercised. Therefore, women need resources to improve their livelihood, and those resources are acquired from the multitude of relationships in the various domains of the family, market, and community; (2) *agency:* the ability to define a woman's goals and act upon them or the ability to gain control over various aspects of a woman's life. Agency has both positive and negative connotations; and (3) *achievements:* these are the outcomes of choices (see the schematic diagram in Figure 17.1 that shows an overview of the three-dimensional theory of change, which links women's access to resources

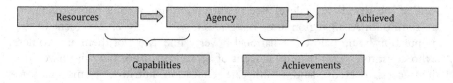

Figure 17.1 Three-dimensional theory of change
Source: Kabeer 1999

to their capacity to exercise strategic forms of agency in order to achieve valued outcomes).

Swain and Wallentin 2009 also provide a similar definition. In their case study of a self-help bank linkage microfinance program in India, they refer to it as a process in which women challenge the prevailing social and religious norms of their society in which they live to improve their well-being effectively. However, as Kabeer 1999 points out, caution is warranted when understanding the differentials of outcomes of choices. As she explained, women's household responsibilities for caring for their children do not necessarily empower women, as women's involvement in such household activities is similar to their male counterpart's responsibilities towards the family, which are recognized by societies as traditional gender roles, something which is especially true for South Asian countries. Women's commitment to such traditional roles within the family can increase their self-esteem, but it does not mean that those women are empowered.

Microfinance, in particular, has often been argued, not without controversy, to be a tool for empowering women (Ashraf, Karlan, and Yin 2010). There is a growing body of literature in economics that investigates the effectiveness of microfinance programs on women's empowerment and household welfare. The evidence, however, is far from conclusive and is heavily polarized. Whereas some studies provide evidence supporting the view that access to microfinance contributes considerably to women's empowerment (Hashemi, Schuler, and Riley 1996; Swain and Wallentin 2009), smooth consumption, and poverty reduction (Khandker, 2005; Berhane and Gardebroek, 2011; Imai et al. 2012; Dupas and Robinson, 2013), others found only modest (Karlan and Zinman, 2011; Agbola, Acupan, and Mahmood 2017) or zero empowering impacts on women's lives (Montgomery, Bhattacharya, and Hulme 1996; Coleman 1999; Kabeer 2001; Setboonsarng and Parpiev 2008). Inconclusive and ambiguous findings may reflect a relationship between microfinance programs and women's empowerment that is complex and always not linear.

The objective of this study was to investigate the link between microfinance lending and socioeconomic empowerment of female entrepreneurs in rural, hill villages in Nepal. The Nepalese case provides a significant exploration of this issue, as there is little evidence concerning the impacts of microfinance programs on women's socioeconomic empowerment and improved gender equality. According to the Asian Development Bank (ADB) 2016, Nepal is one of the world's least developed countries and the second poorest country in the South Asian region after Bangladesh, with nearly 25.2 percent of the population living below the national poverty line. Most of them are women who constitute more than 60 percent of agricultural labor but who have limited access to credit, land, health care, education, nutrition, formal markets, and participation in household decision making (IFAD 2013). This gender discrimination is considerably higher in rural areas that were home to more than 80 percent of the total population in 2015 (World Bank 2017). Moreover, Nepal is heavily vulnerable to climate change and natural disasters. Because there is a general consensus that women tend to suffer disproportionately from adverse shocks linked with various socioeconomic and environment factors (Grimard and Laszlo 2014), such disasters could impose a significant impact on the livelihood of rural women, especially given the prevailing gender inequality. For example, Pradhan et al. 2007 show that the flood-related fatality rate was higher for women and was closely associated with low socioeconomic status. Because of the high rate of poverty, lack of physical collateral, and vulnerability to various socioeconomic and environmental shocks, commercial banks often considered rural female entrepreneurs a financially unviable proposition and as a risk, and they were reluctant to take a chance on them. Thus, many poor Nepalese households remain unbanked (Ferrari, Shrestha, and Jaffrin 2007), with most of them living in rural and hill areas in Nepal. It is in this context that microfinance services are thought to fill this gap by playing a catalytic role in empowering poor and low-income rural Nepali women at the community level. But empirical evidence on the impacts of these programs on women's socioeconomic empowerment has been sparse. This study, therefore, considered the Nepali case to offer more evidence on this issue.

Our empirical analysis is based on data collected from a sample survey carried out in rural, hill villages in the Tanahun district located in the mid-hill region of Nepal. The district has reported a higher incidence of poverty (Pandey 2012). Thus, the selected villages in the Tanahun district provide an ideal focus for our study's research. For the household survey, we used the quasi-experimental pipeline design approach proposed by Coleman 1999 to select treatment and control groups. The principle of this sampling approach is based on identifying member women in the control group who have similar baseline unobservable characteristics as the member women in the treatment group who have already benefitted from microfinance services. Because the control group captures what would have been the outcomes if the microfinance program had not been implemented, the program can be said to have caused any difference in outcomes between the treatment and control groups (White and Sabarwal 2014).

Our results show that women's participation in Nirdhan Bank's microfinance program has had had a significant positive effect on their empowerment with respect to indicators such as control of income, independent savings, decisions over food purchase, asset purchases, and applying for loans. All these indicators are a proxy for women's financial empowerment. On the other hand, concerning the impact of microfinance on women's social empowerment, our results reveal that access to microfinance resulted in significant impact on all indicators for women's social development outcomes except women's household decision making regarding groceries, their children's marriage, and women's role as the household head.

Our study provides some evidence on the empowerment effects of the microfinance operations of a regulated MFI (development bank). In most countries, with the exception of Bangladesh, regulated MFIs exist as member-based cooperatives, nongovernmental organizations (NGOs), or shareholding entities such as banks and nonbank financial institutions (NBFIs), that are subject to prudential regulation and licensed by the Central Bank (D'espallier et al. 2017), thus benefiting from superior governance (Wijesiri 2016). NGO MFIs, on the other hand, are unregulated and they largely depend on donor support and various kinds of subsidized funding, but they are dedicated to service, not profit, and to the good of society (Dichter 1996; D'espallier et al. 2017). Although all MFIs have social and financial goals at their core, irrespective of the type of ownership, there is speculation that shareholding MFIs are more profit oriented, whereas NGOs put much more weight on the social impact (Wijesiri 2016). Many of the earlier empirical studies focus on women entrepreneurs in NGO MFIs, but there has been little research based on shareholding MFIs' involvement in women's empowerment that is known to the author and, thus, little evidence exists of the impacts of such initiatives in promoting women's empowerment. Using a sample from women living in rural, hill villages with low population density and poor infrastructure, where financial inclusion is a great challenge for MFIs, our study provides policymakers and practitioners with a better understanding of how microfinance programs run by a regulated microfinance bank contribute to socioeconomic empowerment of women entrepreneurs, especially those who live in rural, hill villages. Moreover, the microfinance sector in Nepal is largely under-researched despite its importance to the country's economic growth and improved gender equality. Therefore, the findings of this study will help researchers compare findings from other countries with relevant empirical evidence from Nepal.

A brief overview of the Nepalese financial market

Recent developments in the Nepalese financial sector

The Nepalese financial system compromises the banking and nonbanking institutions. Whereas the latter consists of development banks ("B" Class), financial companies ("C" Class), microfinance institutions ("D" Class), NGOs, and cooperatives, the former includes the Nepal Rastra Bank (NRB) and commercial banks ("A" Class). Figure 17.2 presents the growth of the Nepalese financial institutions over the period. From the graph, we can see that there is a downward trend in the growth of "A," "B," "C," and "D" class financial institutions

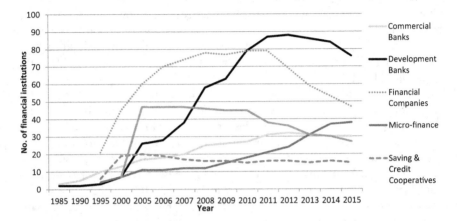

Figure 17.2 Growth of Nepalese financial institutions (1985–2015)

Source: Author's own compilation from various sources

in the past few years. For example, although the total number of "A," "B," "C," and "D" class financial institutions stood at 204 by 2014, the number slightly decreased to 191 by 2015. This could be because of the consolidation process of the Nepalese financial industry through merger and acquisition during this period. Moreover, by 2015, the number of branches of the commercial bank networks has grown to 1,672, followed by 808 development banks, 242 financial companies, and 1,116 MFIs, with 10,160 customers per branch. Credit flows from banks and financial institutions have also grown significantly by 20.5 percent by 2015, which was 18.2 percent in the previous fiscal year (see NRB 2016a, 2016b). Although this indicates a considerable growth in the Nepalese financial market that had been characterized by only two commercial and two development banks before introducing the financial sector reforms in the 1980s (NRB 2008), access to finance has still remained limited, with 18 percent of the adult population completely financially excluded, and 21 percent depended only on informal financial services by 2016 (MAP 2016).

Evolution of the Nepalese microfinance market

The history of the Nepalese microfinance industry can be traced back to the early 1950s when the first small agricultural cooperatives emerged (NRB 2008). Since then the industry has continued to grow with a view to making financial services accessible to the poor, particularly women entrepreneurs, who have often been excluded by the formal credit market. The availability of wholesale funds from microfinance wholesale banks and different programs of international agencies has given momentum to the extension of microfinance services (CMF 2016).

Despite the considerable growth of the microfinance market during the last few decades, with increased financial and nonfinancial resources devoted to financial inclusion and deepening, some geographical regions still have minimal access to financial services (NRB 2016a). Most of these villages are located in remote and hill areas (Pant, Sharma, and Dahal 2008). Moreover, poor infrastructure, limited market access, sparse population, small areas of arable land, and few economic activities have hindered the outreach of microfinance programs in Nepal (Taylor, Hailey, and Parajuli 2015). Thus, a significant portion of the rural people still depend on informal financial markets, which are normally based on small-size, short-term transactions and, particularly, on loan sharks who, quite often, exploited them with exorbitant interest rates over the years. Lack of adequate regulatory, supervisory, and client protection mechanisms has fostered these informal financial activities in Nepal (MAP 2016).

With view to eliminating these financial disparities, NRB currently implements several important policy measures aiming at increasing access to financial services for the poor, such as provision of a special refinance facility at 1 percent interest for microfinance programs to extend loans to agriculture and small business–based income-generating activities in poverty-stricken areas; encouraging the establishment of the MFIs and expanding branches, branchless banking, and mobile banking services in geographical regions with low financial access; increasing the limit of collateral-based micro enterprise credit; encouraging MFIs to go for merger and acquisition; measures to improve financial literacy among the poor; and measures to protect customers' rights. All of these services can be viewed as important policy initiatives.

Microfinance and women's empowerment: a brief review

Most studies to measure the extent to which microfinance services provided by MFIs translate into empowering impacts for rural women entrepreneurs are nonacademic projects that have relied largely on more qualitative case studies (Coleman 1999). Only a few are based on empirical studies with rigorous statistical applications (Kabeer 2001). Moreover, the findings of previous studies have been inconclusive and ambiguous due to differences in sampling locations, time periods, analytical techniques employed, and differences in operating models adopted by different microfinance ownership types, as well as different empowerment domains used in different studies (Kabeer 2001). Lack of a clear definition of "empowerment" and that which is not directly observable can only be approximated using appropriate indicators that can either be context specific or universal (Mahmud, Shah, and Becker 2012). Thus, the way to measure it and the best way to achieve it have created a major debate (Goldman and Little 2015). Moreover, MFIs' capacity to adapt to the varying environments with different cultural practices and women's social positions may also have an impact on these inconclusive outcomes (Singh 2015). Based on a study of Grameen Bank and Bangladesh Rural Advancement Committee (BRAC), and applying an ethnographic study and quantitative survey method, Hashemi, Schuler, and Riley 1996 found that participation in both programs has significantly improved women's mobility, purchasing ability, legal and political awareness, asset ownership, and involvement in household decision making and public campaigns. Although most of these domains are generic to both MFIs, some are positive only with Grameen bank, suggesting that business strategies adopted by different MFIs' can influence on their social impacts. The findings of this study also indicate that the use of a ritualistic and disciplined model in lending mechanisms by both MFIs has stimulated participants' ability to control assets and income while strengthening the level of confidence and self-esteem in the society. Using a quasi-experimental, household data sample collected from five states in India from 2000–2003, Swain and Wallentin 2009 found that women who participated in microfinance programs experienced significant and higher empowerment compared with the control group that consisted of nonparticipating households with similar characteristics. More recently, Weber and Ahmad 2014 investigated the impact of microfinance on empowerment of women in Pakistan. They focused particularly on analyzing the relationship between loan cycle and level of empowerment. Their findings show that women in higher loan cycles experienced a significant increase in empowerment compared to their counterparts in the first loan cycle.

However, other studies provide empirical evidence that microfinance has negative or a mixed impact on women's empowerment. Goetz and Gupta 1996 studied the ability of women to control loans they received from Bangladesh MFIs. Using a 5-point index of managerial control over loans as an empowerment indicator, they found that a preoccupation with credit performance affects the incentives of fieldworkers to dispense and recover credit, in ways which may outweigh concerns to ensure that women develop meaningful control over their investment activities. Using detailed datasets from two Indian villages participating in the Shelf Help Group (SHG) microfinance program in India, Garikipati 2008 investigated the impact of the credit program on core dimensions of household vulnerability and female empowerment. Her findings revealed that loans procured by women are often used to improve assets that are controlled preliminary by their husbands. Women's lack of authority over their families' productive assets adversely affected repayments and, consequently, their degree of empowerment. Her findings also suggested the importance of ownership of productive assets by women for achieving one of the key objectives of microfinance programs vis-à-vis women's empowerment. Ganle, Afriyie, and Segbefia 2015 examined the empowerment effects of the microfinance operation of an NGO-managed microfinance program to the poor women in a rural district of Ghana. They found that some women were empowered along several dimensions as a result of their access to credit, other women had little control over the use of loans and were therefore no better off, and others had been subjected to harassment and were worse off due to their indebtedness and inability to repay the loans on time. They argued that women who became more empowered could be the women who either obtained loans to expand their existing business or those who fully exercised a significant control over proceeds from the loans. On the other hand, the women who became vulnerable and even disempowered could be those who wanted to start up a new business with no proper business plan and those who used loans for direct consumption.

In reviewing the earlier studies, it is evident that different studies used different empowerment indicators in different contextual settings. Moreover, all of the earlier research studies that empirically investigated the microfinance interventions on women's empowerment are single-country studies, with most based on the case studies of larger Bangladeshi MFIs. The findings of the studies that focus on one specific program in a particular location lack internal validity, irrespective of the methodology applied. Furthermore, the microfinance sector in Nepal is largely under-researched relative to microfinance markets in other emerging economies. Our aim, as articulated in this chapter, is to address this void using a quasi-experimental survey design approach to provide policymakers and practitioners with a better understanding of how microfinance contributes to the socioeconomic empowerment of women entrepreneurs in Nepal.

Microfinance program studied, survey design, and description of the variables

Microfinance program studied

We implemented this research in close collaboration with the microfinance programs conducted by Nirdhan Utthan Bank Limited (NUBL). It is one of the largest and best-known microfinance banks providing a range of microfinance services (loans, savings, micro-insurance, and remittance services) to the low-income households and neglected sectors in rural Nepal. As a public limited company, 30 percent of NUBL's equity is held by the general public, with the remainder being held by promoters including Nirdhan NGO, Himalayan Bank, Nabil Bank, Everest Bank, Grameen Trust Bangladesh, and private individuals. Though it has operated as a microfinance development bank since 1999, its roots can be traced back six years earlier to the establishment of its predecessor, Nirdhan, an NGO. The transformation of Nirdhan into a regulated development bank enables it to access a wide range of funding sources, including public deposits, while expanding financial outreach and deepening in different geographical areas in a sustainable way. This is evident by its current operation in all 75 districts in Nepal, though 178 branch offices, that serve more than 295,000 poor entrepreneurs with 12 billion Nepal rupees (Rs.) in outstanding loans by 2017 (NLUBL 2017).

In addition to collateral-based lending to micro-entrepreneurs, NUBL provides loans on a solidarity-group lending model as well as the Self-Reliant Group (SRG) model. The latter has been developed by NUBL with the aim of providing microfinance support for the poor in hill and remote villages. The office bearers of the group (chairperson, treasurer, controllers, and secretary) manage group meetings, collections, and keep financial records. The bank has also developed a day-long module for office bearers of SRGs with the aim of upgrading their leadership capacity and financial literacy (DHC 2017). The bank has also extended its services to provide credit "plus" activities, such as entrepreneurship training and awareness programs, while allocating a share of its profits for the implementation of client protection mechanisms.

The bank uses its own targeting criteria to provide its group-based financial services. Initially it provides loans to groups for a period of 12 months, and the duration is gradually increased in subsequent cycles up to 36 months. The average loan size for a woman in a group is about Rs. 75,000, which is gradually increased in following cycles based on the woman's repayment discipline in previous cycles. Typically, a group consists of 10 women, but this can be as large as 40 in some rural villages. The bank lends to the group without collateral. The members of a group and the group itself are jointly liable for each other's repayments. Members of the group meet once a month for repayment and mandatory savings. Figure 17.3 shows the meeting of a women's reliant group in Bhimad village, Dulegauda.

The bank is also committed to providing training to its staff members. It is compulsory for newly recruited employees to go through training and development interventions for a six-month period to obtain theoretical and practical knowledge of the bank's operations. In addition, the bank organizes training

Figure 17.3 Women attending a group meeting in Bhimad village, Dulegauda, Tanahun District, Nepal

programs, both in-house and outsourced, to promote the continuous learning process of employees. All training programs are designed to enhance professional growth of staff members so as to serve the clients more effectively (Activity Report 2017).

Survey design and description of variables

Survey design

In this research, we followed the quasi-experimental sampling design approach proposed by Coleman 1999 and selected our treatment and control villages accordingly. We carried out our sample survey in the Tanahun district, located in the mid-hill region of Nepal. Our sample strategy consisted of two main steps. First, we spoke with the NUBL officials at its central office in Kathmandu, as well as mangers at its regional office in Tanahun district and its branch office in Dulegauda town, to obtain detailed information regarding microfinance lending models and group formation mechanisms used by them. We obtained a list of treatment and control villages in Tanahun district from the bank. The control group consisted of randomly selected villages, pre-identified by the microfinance bank, which would soon receive microfinance support. Women in these villages had been allowed to self-select into the microfinance programs. These women had been organized into groups but no loans had yet been disbursed to them. The treatment group, on the other hand, consisted of randomly selected villages where the bank has been in operation for at least a five-year period. Based on the eligibility criteria defined by the microfinance bank, both members and nonmembers in both treatment and control villages were surveyed.

In the second step, we randomly drew ten treatment and eight control villages from the list of villages provided by the bank. Care was also taken that the control villages in our sample reflected comparable physical and socioeconomic characteristics (availability of infrastructure facilities, level of economic developments, and social and cultural similarities) as the treatment villages. All study villages were approximately one to two hours' walking distance from the closest paved road. The randomly selected treatment and control villages for our study are indicated in Figure 17.4.

Any impact evaluation method may encounter problems related to internal and external validity. Indeed, our use of this quasi-experimental design to measure the impact of microfinance on women's empowerment is not without problems. First, the relatively small number of villages may not generate enough variation to yield tests with statistical differences, which would lead us to falsely accept the null hypothesis of no impact. Second, because one uses the villages where NUBL has already chosen (i.e., either it is in operation in the treatment villages, having established a relationship with customers, or it plans to be in operation in the control villages but has yet to start a lending relationship with the customers), it might be that these villages are different from other villages

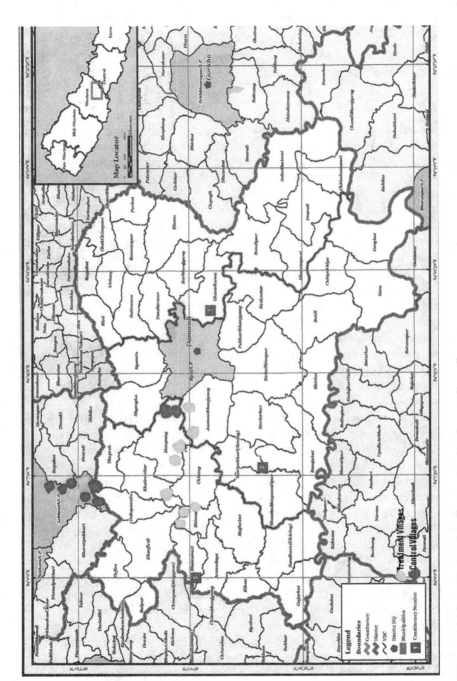

Figure 17.4 Map of the Tanahun District showing the sampling villages

Source: United Nations Office for the Coordination of Humanitarian Affairs (OCHA), Nepal.

in Nepal. For instance, NUBL might have chosen these villages to set up their operations because households in these villages have characteristics that are more suitable to banking. One might argue that microcredit, for instance, would already choose villages that have more empowered women because this would help NUBL's repayment rates and bottom line. This is a possibility. But note that if giving the loan was just a signal to identify the already empowered woman, one should not see a difference between women from the treatment and control villages. If such a difference existed, it would imply that the loan is doing something different to the treated women compared to the already empowered control women: perhaps it might empower them more or signal some other unobserved characteristic. The interpretation would then change: microfinance may then enhance empowerment, but not necessarily of average women. Third, the issue of heterogeneous treatment may arise: the design compares individuals whose treatment (i.e., loan) might have been at different time in the past, with individuals who have yet to have obtain the loan. If time is a factor in determining empowerment and yields as a result women with different levels of empowerment, the comparison with control women may not reveal enough signal to estimate the impact of microfinance.

Our use of a quasi-experimental survey design method suggested by Coleman 1999 has some advantages, as it helps us to correct the bias from unobserved household and village level heterogeneity. Although quasi-experiments generally have lower internal validity than randomized control trials (RCTs), they may tend to yield findings with a higher external validity because the interventions being evaluated in quasi-experiments have been implemented using real-life systems rather than systems designed or modified for the purpose of research. Hence quasi-experiments can be used to obtain cost-efficient consistent and unbiased estimates, though one should beware that the estimation is dependent on some assumptions that may not always hold.

We used a questionnaire survey approach to collect data. Due to budget and time constraints, we limited our sample size to 360 respondents. We conducted our household survey from March–April 2017. From both treatment and control villages, we randomly interviewed ten member women and ten nonmember women. Inclusion of the nonmember women in both village groups (treatment and control) allows for the use of village fixed effects estimation to control for the possibility that the order in which these villages received program support was endogenous (Coleman 1999). The questionnaire used to collect data consisted of four sections. In the first section, we gathered information about village characteristics (distance to nearest city center from the village, road conditions, availability of electricity and public transport). The second section of the questionnaire incorporated questions to capture eligibility and microfinance participation, and the third section included questions regarding basic household characteristics (woman's age, level of education, marital status, occupation, caste, religion, family structure). The last section included the items relevant to empowerment outcomes. After the survey, we had 356 usable questionnaires, of which 196 were from treatment villages and 160 were from control villages.

Description of variables

Women's personal and household characteristic variables

A great number of women in the survey villages were involved in the agricultural sector and small business. Most of the women are married. The summary of the personal and household characteristics of the women in treatment and control villages is presented in Table 17.1. The sample means reveal that between treatment and control groups women's personal and household characteristics are almost the same. For example, the mean age of the women was 37 years and most women believe in Hindu Dharma (mean value = 0.89). Moreover, there was no significant variation in school attendance, family size, and number of children of women belonging to either category.

Women's empowerment indicators

Following Pitt, Khandker, and Cartwright 2006, we treated the empowerment variable as being measured by a set of observed indicators. Pitt, Khandker, and Cartwright 2006 mentioned a number of proxy indicators using a large set of qualitative responses to questions that characterize women's autonomy and gender relations within the household. Selection of appropriate empowerment indicators, however, depends on the study contexts. Thus, following earlier studies (Montgomery, Bhattacharya, and Hulme 1996; Kabeer 2001; Khandker 2005; Swain and Wallentin 2009), we designed our empowerment indicators considering the Nepali social and cultural norms. These included decision-making autonomy, participation in the household, societal and financial decision making, ability to spend money independently, and awareness of their

Table 17.1 Summary statistics of the women's personal and household characteristics

Women's personal and household characteristic variables	Unit	Mean (Std. Dev.) Overall Sample	Mean (Std. Dev.) Treatment Group	Mean (Std. Dev.) Control Group
Age	Years	37.48 (9.84)	37.56 (9.77)	37.38 (9.94)
Religion	Hinduism = 1; Others = 0	0.89 (0.31)	0.89 (0.32)	0.89 (0.31)
Ever attended school	Yes = 1; No = 0	1.46 (0.50)	1.38 (0.49)	1.54 (0.5)
Household size	Persons	4.31 (1.11)	4.34 (1.11)	4.27 (1.1)
Number of children	Persons	1.11 (0.95)	1.21 (1.01)	0.97 (0.86)
Proportion of children	Percent	26.77 (21.82)	28.51 (22.06)	24.63 (21.4)

basic rights and law. Note that when it comes to some key household decisions (repairing/construction of houses, children's schooling and marriage, major asset purchases), we considered the women's empowerment in terms of both the husband's and wife's mutual agreement on those decisions. Most of those decisions seem directly linked to major household responsibilities rather than merely women's rights. Although women's increased role in key decision making in the family can lead to hindering the men's participation in household decisions (Mahmud, Shah, and Becker 2012), the ability of a household to make joint decisions could reduce household violence while increasing harmony in the family.

Table 17.2 presents the descriptive statistics of the empowerment variables used in this study. The questionnaire yielded information on potential measures of empowerment in the dimensions of financial and social empowerment. As can be seen in Table 17.2, approximately 40 percent of women reported they had independent income and savings. As for key financial decisions regarding the family's daily consumable food items, asset purchases and asset types, and taking loans, more than 65 percent of respondents tended to discuss these matters with their husbands when making these decisions. It is also clear from

Table 17.2 Descriptive statistics of the empowerment variables

Empowerment Indicator	Mean (Overall sample)	Mean (Treatment group)	Mean (Control group)	t-Statistics
Control own income	.4073	.5102	.2812	−4.53
(Yes = 1)	(.4921)	(.5011)	(.4510)	
Independent Savings	.3904	.5204	.2312	−5.90
(Yes = 1)	(.4885)	(.5008)	(.4229)	
Food purchase	.8202	.9387	.6750	−6.44
(Jointly = 2)	(.3845)	(.2403)	(.4698)	
Assets purchase	.66321	.7448	.4937	−4.97
(Jointly = 2)	(.4831)	(.4370)	(.5015)	
Assets type	.6769	.8520	.4625	−8.28
(Jointly = 2)	(.4682)	(.3559)	(.5001)	
Loan decision	.6797	.7295	.6187	−2.21
(Jointly = 2)	(.4672)	(.4453)	(.4872)	
Head of household	.1432	.1632	.1187	−1.2
(Wife = 1)	(.3508)	(.3705)	(.3245)	
Children's marriage decisions	.8848	.8775	08937	.47
(Jointly = 2)	(.3196)	(.3286)	(.3091)	
Groceries decisions	.8258	.8571	.7875	−1.68
(Jointly = 2)	(.3797)	(.3508)	(.4103)	
House repairing decision	.6038	.7295	.45	−5.51
(Jointly = 2)	(.4897)	(.4453)	(.499)	
Awareness of legal rights	.5252	.6938	.3187	−7.57
(Yes = 1)	(.5001)	(.462)	(.4674)	

Table 17.2 that there were significant differences between the treatment and control villages in terms of these key financial empowerment decisions.

As for the social empowerment indicators, most of the households surveyed were headed by men, and more than 75 percent of women reported they made joint household decisions regarding their children's marriages and groceries. Nevertheless, regarding both social empowerment indicators, there were no significant differences between the women in the treatment and control villages. Approximately 70 percent of the women in treatment villages reported they made joint decisions regarding house repairs compared to 45 percent of households in control villages. Furthermore, approximately 70 percent of women in treatment villages reported they had an awareness of women's legal rights as compared to 31 percent of households in control villages. The t-test results confirmed the difference between the women in treatment and control villages in terms of house repair decisions and awareness of women's legal rights.

Even though economic and social empowerment are separately considered by indicators, it is worthwhile to note that the process of empowerment in the "real world" cannot be confined to a particular empowerment dimension because efforts of building women's opportunities and their capacity to take advantage of these opportunities in economic sphere only become empowering when they strengthen their control over their own lives within the family and exercise more influence within their society (see Kabeer 1999, 2001, for more details).

The overall results in Table 17.2 indicate that women in treatment villages were more empowered in all of the financial empowerment indicators. Of the five social empowerment indicators, women in treatment villages seemed to be empowered on only two indicators. Thus, a more robust regression analysis is required to ascertain if the difference between treatment and control households is still significant when considering observable characteristics.

Empirical analysis

We followed Coleman 1999 and estimated the impact using following equation:

$$Y_{ij} = X_{ij} + T_{ij}\gamma + \varepsilon_{ij} \tag{1}$$

Where Y_{ij} is the empowerment outcome for women i in village j on which we want measure microfinance program outcome; X_{ij} is a vector of women and household characteristics; T_{ij} is a dummy variable (equal to 1 if women ij are in a treatment village where the microfinance program is present, and 0 otherwise). This dummy variable is a proxy for the unobservable characteristics that lead a household to self-select into a microfinance program and that might affect outcomes. This dummy variable equals 1 for both treatment members (who have already received microfinance services) and control members (who have not yet received program support); α, β, and γ are the parameters to be estimated, and ε is the error term.

Results

Table 17.3 provides the summary of results obtained from nine ordinary least squares (OLS) models to ascertain the impact of microfinance on women's empowerment outcomes, accounting for differences in observable characteristics. Each column of the table represents a separate model and t-statistics are given in parentheses. The results confirm that the women who were located in the treatment villages appeared to be more empowered, particularly on the financial dimension. Indeed, it can be seen from Table 17.3 that coefficients for treated villages in all empowerment indicators (except head of household, women's autonomy in grocery, and decisions about children's marriages) are positive and statistically significant. For example, women in the treatment villages were 18.67 percent more likely than those in the control villages to respond "yes"' to the question of whether they have their own income and that they can spend it without their husband's permission. The coefficient for treated villages for "head of household" is not significant, although the coefficient has a positive sign. Similarly, women's autonomy in decision making in groceries and children's marriage is also not significant. These results are not surprising because, in traditional Hindu society, the male partner of a couple is considered the "household head" and is involved in a number of major household decisions. All these indicators are proxies for social empowerment (that financial empowerment constructs) that is more heterogeneous and often linked with a number of exogenous factors, such as male partner's age, level of education and his adherence to traditional beliefs towards his wife, level of family income, the worth of dowry brought into the marriage by his wife, and the gender of their children (Ngo and Wahhaj 2012; Weber and Ahmad 2014). In other words, a number of other factors, such as household and village characteristics, cultural and religious norms within the society, and behavioral differences between the respondents and their family members, are critical factors for empowerment, particularly empowerment regarding women's social autonomy and, consequently, measuring it based on the observable indicators may be quite difficult (Swain and Wallentin 2009).

As for the women's personal and household characteristics (control variables), we found positive and statistically significant coefficients for the variables of age and proportion of children in all empowerment indicators except decisions regarding loans, house repairs, and awareness of legal rights. Furthermore, coefficients for school attendance are positive and significant in all empowerment indicators we used except for the head of household. Finally, household size has a negative effect on all empowerment indicators. However, coefficients for household size are significant only in asset purchases, assets types, head of household, house repairs, and awareness of legal rights. Overall, the results of this study suggest that women's participation in the Nirdhan Bank microfinance program had a considerable positive effect on their financial empowerment along the selected empowerment indicators. However, access to microfinance had not resulted in a significant impact on women's social

Table 17.3 The impact of microfinance on the women's empowerment: estimated parameters

Variables	Empowerment Indicators										
	Own Income	Own Savings	Food Purchase	Assets Purchase	Assets Type	Loan Decision	Head of Household	Children marriage	Grocery	House Repairing	Awareness of legal rights
Program-related variable Treated women	.1867★ (3.81)	.2461★ (4.24)	.2263★ (2.76)	.2068★ (2.82)	.3486★ (5.98)	.1032★ (1.93)	.0501 (1.21)	-.0113 (-.28)	.05287 (.84)	.2636★ (3.18)	.3337★ (6.49)
Woman's personal and household characteristics	.0057 (1.63)	.0053★ (1.83)	.0075★ (2.65)	.0145★ (3.57)	.0104★ (2.66)	-.0028 (-.79)	.0183★ (4.99)	-.0009 (-.54)	.0061★ (3.15)	.0068 (1.54)	-.0016 (-.44)
Age School attendance	.2109★ (4.41)	.2114★ (4.28)	.1978★ (2.96)	.1782★ (2.6)	.1634★ (2.66)	.1015★ (2.33)	-.0785 (-1.61)	-.0202 (-.48)	.08429 (1.41)	.1230★ (2.13)	.2929★ (6.47)
Household size	-.0301 (-.86)	-.0458 (-1.39)	-.0145 (-1.38)	-.0821★ (-4.55)	-.0705★ (-3.01)	-.0068 (-.25)	-.1163★ (-8.66)	-.0482★ (-2.16)	-.0176 (-.94)	-.0808★ (-4.26)	-.0587★ (-2.6)
Proportion of children	.1761★ (1.69)	.2383★ (1.88)	.1668★ (2.05)	.3846★ (2.42)	.3674★ (3.08)	-.1468 (-1.42)	.2825★ (2.90)	.0756 (.92)	.1075 (1.10)	.0895 (.75)	.0558 (.55)

★ Significant at 5% level. t-statistics are in parentheses. Standard errors are clustered at the village level. Analysis is based on 356 respondents.

development outcomes in women's household decision making regarding groceries and their children's marriage and women's role as the household head.

Discussion

The objective of this study was to investigate the link between microfinance lending and socioeconomic empowerment of female entrepreneurs in rural, hill villages in Nepal. The Nepalese case is a significant study exploring this issue, as there is little evidence concerning the impacts of microfinance programs on women's socioeconomic empowerment and improved gender equality. We used a quasi-experimental survey approach involving a survey of 356 women entrepreneurs in member and nonmember villages. The overall results of this study suggest that women's participation in the Nirdhan Bank microfinance program has had a significant positive effect on their empowerment along all selected financial empowerment indicators. However, access to microfinance has not resulted in any significant impact on women's social development outcomes in terms of women's household decision making regarding groceries and their children's marriages. Given the women's role in rural economic growth, women's simultaneous empowerment along both social and economic dimensions is crucial to achieve Nepal's sustainable development goals. Therefore, special attention needs to be paid to women's social empowerment, though such an initiative could be costly for microfinance, as it helps them to promote child education (particularly girls' school attendance), improve health and sanitation, and reduce child mortality.

The research findings are potentially of considerable interest to an audience comprising governments, policymakers, aid agencies and NGOs, and academics. The lending model adopted by the bank seems to have the potential to empower women in the given economic empowerment indicators to a certain extent. However, our findings lead us to suggest that bank managers need to further strength the delivery mechanism so as to improve women's empowerment particularly in social sphere. Use of cheaper computers, increased clients/credit officer ratio, and decreased loan losses help the bank to reduce operating costs and subsidy dependency and make a greater social impact. Reduced subsidy dependency by using innovative approaches such as "learning by doing" and relying on saving rather than credit and risk-based allocation of resources could also be useful strategic options for the bank to ensure its sustainability without compromising its social mandate.

Our findings in this research are subject to at least three limitations. First, given the available budget and resources, we limited our sample to only to 356 respondents. Thus, with a small sample size, caution must be applied, as the findings cannot be generalized to a large population in the sampled district. Second, there is no single definition of women's empowerment, and it is often considered as a multidimensional socioeconomic process that helps women to enhance their autonomy and self-reliance. The current investigation, however, was limited by several empowerment dimensions in a cross-sectional design.

Finally, there are several methodological issues. A major factor is that the setting did not allow a regular randomized control trial, with baseline and follow-up datasets on treatment and control households. Rather, we used a similar design to Coleman (1999), and we relied on the strategy that the treatment and control villages were correctly chosen, in conjunction with the NUBL organization. In addition, because of the placement of the NUBL institution in the village, our results are more suggestive of the "intent to treat" (ITT) of the NUBL program, rather than the "average treatment effect" (ATE) that the program might have. Future work will include further consideration of village characteristics and the eligibility criteria that NUBL used to allocate its loans to women, as well as considering the possible heterogeneity of treatment by further analyzing the length and number of loans women in the treatment group may have received. Clearly, more research on this topic needs to be undertaken before the association between microfinance lending and empowerment of rural female entrepreneurs is more clearly understood, though our preliminary results suggest a positive link between microcredit and some measures of women's empowerment.

Notes

1 Acknowledgements: We thank participants in the Canadian Economic Association Annual Conference (2018) at McGill University, Montréal, and staff of Nirdhan Utthan Bank Limited, especially Janardan Dev Pant and Iswar Atreya, for their guidance throughout the field surveys. Special thanks are due to Rabindra Ghimire and faculty members of School of Business Pokhara University for their support. Sadish Tiwari, Bimal Shrestha, Sagun Pokhrel, and Sujana Sapkota provided dedicated research assistance. We gratefully acknowledge financial support from the International Development Research Center, Canada (IDRC) and Fonds de recherche du Québec – Nature et technologies (FRQNT). A part of the research for this study was completed while Mahinda Wijesiri was a Postdoctoral Fellow at the IGIDR, India.
2 Whereas social outreach refers to the MFIs' ability to alleviate poverty and gender inequality, financial sustainability is defined as MFIs' ability to survive without subsidy. The potential trade-off between the two notions may be a strategic choice for the MFIs.

References

Activity Report (2017), "Developing Human Capital," A periodic publication of Nirdhan Utthan Bank Ltd. On Capacity Development Intervention. Kathmandu, Nepal.

ADB (2016), "Basic Statistics Report 2016," Economic Research and Regional Cooperation Department Development, Economics and Indicators Division, Asian Development Bank, Philipines.

Agbola, Frank W., Angelito Acupan, and Amir Mahmood (2017), "Does microfinance reduce poverty? New evidence from Northeastern Mindanao, the Philippines," *Journal of Rural Studies*, 50, 159–171.

Ashraf, Nava, Dean Karlan, and Wesley Yin (2010), "Female empowerment: Impact of a commitment savings product in the Philippines," *World Development*, 38(3), 333–344.

Berhane, Guush, and Cornelis Gardebroek (2011), "Does microfinance reduce rural poverty? Evidence based on household panel data from Northern Ethiopia," *American Journal of Agricultural Economics*, 93 (1), 43–55.

CMF (2016), "Center for Microfinance Nepal," Social performance country report.

Coleman, Brett (1999), "The impact of group lending in Northeast Thailand," *Journal of Development Economics*, 60 (1), 105–141.

D'Espallier, Bert, Jann Goedecke, Marek Hudon, and Roy Mersland (2017), "From NGOs to banks: Does institutional transformation alter the business model of microfinance institutions?" *World Development*, 89, 19–33.

DHC (2017), "Developing Human Capital," Activity Report of 2016/2017. Nirdhan Utthan Bank Ltd. Nepal.

Dichter, Thomas (1996), "Questioning the future of NGOs in microfinance," *Journal of International Development*, 8(2), 259–269.

Dupas, Pascaline, and Jonathan Robinson (2013), "Savings constraints and microenterprise development: Evidence from a field experiment in Kenya," *American Economic Journal: Applied Economics*, 5(1), 163–192.

Ferrari, Aurora, Sabin Raj Shrestha, and Guillemette Jaffrin (2007), *Access to Financial Services in Nepal*, The World Bank, Washington, DC.

Ganle, John Kuumuori, Kwadwo Afriyie, and Alexander Yao Segbefia (2015), "Microcredit: Empowerment and disempowerment of rural women in Ghana," *World Development*, 66, 335–345.

Garikipati, Supriya (2008), "The impact of lending to women on household vulnerability and women's empowerment: Evidence from India," *World Development*, 36(12), 2620–2642.

Garikipati, Supriya (2012), "Microcredit and women's empowerment: Through the lens of time-use data from rural India," *Development and Change*, 43(3), 719–750.

Goetz, Anne Marie, and Rina Sen Gupta (1996), "Who takes the credit? Gender, power, and control over loan use in rural credit programs in Bangladesh," *World Development*, 24(1), 45–63.

Goldman, Mara J., and Jani S. Little (2015), "Innovative grassroots NGOS and the complex processes of women's empowerment: An empirical investigation from Northern Tanzania," *World Development*, 66, 762–777.

Grimard, Franque, and Sonia Laszlo (2014), "Long-term effects of civil conflict on women's health outcomes in Peru," *World Development*, 54, 139–155.

Hashemi, Syed M., Sidney Ruth Schuler, and Ann P. Riley (1996), "Rural credit programs and women's empowerment in Bangladesh," *World Development*, 24(4), 635–653.

Hirway, Indira (2018), "Translating the SDG commitments into reality: Time use data for gender equality and women's empowerment in the global South," *Indian Journal of Human Development*, 12(1), 93–108.

IFAD (2013), *Enabling Poor Rural People to Overcome Poverty in Nepal*. International Fund for Agricultural Development, Italy.

Imai, Katsushi S., Raghav Gaiha, Ganesh Thapa, and Samuel Kobina Annim (2012), "Microfinance and poverty – a macro perspective," *World Development*, 40(8), 1675–1689.

Kabeer, Naila (1999), "Resources, agency, achievements: Reflections on the measurement of women's empowerment," *Development and Change*, 30(3), 435–464.

Kabeer, Naila (2001), "Conflicts over credit: Re-evaluating the empowerment potential of loans to women in rural Bangladesh," *World Development*, 29(1), 63–84.

Karlan, Dean, and Jonathan Zinman (2011), "Microcredit in theory and practice: Using randomized credit scoring for impact evaluation." *Science*, 332(6035), 1278–1284.

Khandker, Shahidur (2005), "Microfinance and poverty: Evidence using panel data from Bangladesh," *The World Bank Economic Review*, 19(2), 263–286.

King, Elizabeth, and Andrew Mason (2001), *Engendering Development: Through Gender Equality in Rights, Resources, and Voice*. The World Bank, Washington, DC.

Mahmud, Simeen, Nirali M. Shah, and Stan Becker (2012), "Measurement of women's empowerment in rural Bangladesh." *World Development*, 40(3), 610–619.

MAP (2016), "Making access possible: Nepal- detailed country report 2016," [available at www.beed.com.np/uploads/publication/file/Nepal%20Report_final%20web_2017 0205121727.pdf. Accessed on 15/04/2017]

Mazumder, Mohummed Shofi Ullah, and Wencong Lu (2015), "What impact does microfinance have on rural livelihood? A comparison of governmental and non-governmental microfinance programs in Bangladesh," *World Development*, 68, 336–354.

Montgomery, Richard, Debapriya Bhattacharya, and David Hulme (1996), "Credit for the poor in Bangladesh," in *Finance Against Poverty*, D. Hulme and P. Mosley, eds., Routledge, London.

Ngo, Thi Minh-Phuong, and Zaki Wahhaj (2012), "Microfinance and gender empowerment." *Journal of Development Economics*, 99(1), 1–12.

NLUBL (2017), "Newsletter of Nirdhan Uttan Bank Limited, May 2017," (accessed June 21, 2017), [available at www.nirdhan.com.np/wp-content/uploads/2016/08/NUBL-News-May-2017.pdf]

NRB (2008), "Micro-Financing Towards Empowerment of Disadvantaged Groups in Nepal: Innovations and Practices," Sahakarya Project Centre for International Studies and Cooperation (CECI), Nepal Rastra Bank, Kathmandu, Nepal.

NRB (2016a), "Monetary Policy for 2016/ 2017," Nepal Rastra Bank, Kathmandu, Nepal.

NRB (2016b), "Financial Stability Report. Issue No 7," Nepal Rastra Bank, Kathmandu, Nepal.

Pandey, Sushil (2012), *Patterns of Adoption of Improved Rice Varieties and Farm-Level Impacts in Stress-Prone Rainfed Areas in South Asia*, International Rice Research Institute, Los Baños, Philippines.

Pant, Harihar Dev, Prakash Raj Sharma, and Prabin Kumar Dahal (2008), "Reaching Groups of Remote Areas with Microfinance Services-A case study of the Self-Reliant Group (SRG) Model," (accessed May 10, 2017), [available at www.microfinancegateway.org/library/reaching-groups-remote-areas-microfinance-services-case-study-self-reliant-group-srg-model]

Pitt, Mark M., and Shahidur R. Khandker (1998), "The impact of group-based credit programs on poor households in Bangladesh: Does the gender of participants matter?" *Journal of Political Economy*, 106(5), 958–996.

Pitt, Mark M., Shahidur R. Khandker, and Jennifer Cartwright (2006), "Empowering women with micro finance: Evidence from Bangladesh," *Economic Development and Cultural Change*, 54(4), 791–831.

Pradhan, Elizabeth Kimbrough, Keith P. West Jr, Joanne Katz, Steven C. LeClerq, Subarna K. Khatry, and Sharada Ram Shrestha (2007), "Risk of flood-related mortality in Nepal," *Disasters*, 31(1), 57–70.

Rankin, Katharine (2001), "Governing development: Neoliberalism, microcredit, and rational economic woman," *Economy and Society*, 30(1), 18–37.

Rankin, Katherine (2002), "Social capital, microfinance, and the politics of development," *Feminist Economics*, 8(1), 1–24.

Sen, Amartya (1999), *Development as Freedom*, Oxford University Press, Oxford.

Setboonsarng, Sununtar, and Ziyodullo Parpiev (2008), "Microfinance and the Millennium Development Goals in Pakistan: Impact Assessment Using Propensity Score Matching," No. 104. ADB Institute Discussion Papers. (accessed March 10, 2017), [available at www.adbi.org/discussionpaper/2008/04/18/2526.microfinance.millennium.dev.goals. pakistan].

Singh, Swati (2015), "The effects of microfinance programs on women members in traditional societies," *Gender, Place and Culture*, 22(2), 222–238.

Stuart, Elizabeth, and Jessica Woodroffe (2016), "Leaving no-one behind: Can the sustainable development goals succeed where the millennium development goals lacked?" *Gender & Development*, 24(1), 69–81.

Swain, Ranjula Bali, and Fan Yang Wallentin (2009), "Does microfinance empower women? Evidence from self-help groups in India," *International Review of Applied Economics*, 23(5), 541–556.

Taylor, Lloyd J., Krista W. Hailey, and Bina Sharma B. Parajuli (2015), "Goldratt's theory applied to the problems associated with the distribution of microfinance services to the poor of rural Nepal," *Global Education Journal*, (4), 153–174.

Torri, Maria Costanza, and Andrea Martinez (2011), "Gender empowerment and equality in rural India: Are women's community-based enterprises the way forward?" *Journal of International Women's Studies*, 12(1), 157–176.

Weber, Olaf, and Adnan Ahmad (2014), "Empowerment through microfinance: The relation between loan cycle and level of empowerment," *World Development*, 62, 75–87.

White, Howard, and Shagun Sabarwal (2014), "Quasi-Experimental Design and Methods: Methodological Briefs-Impact Evaluation No. 8," UNICEF Office of Research, Florence.

Wijesiri, Mahinda (2016), "Weathering the storm: Ownership structure and performance of microfinance institutions in the wake of the global financial crisis." *Economic Modelling*, 57, 238–247.

World Bank (2017), "Rural Population (% of total population) Data." The World Bank. (accessed March 16, 2017), [available at http://data.worldbank.org/indicator/SP.RUR.TOTL.ZS]

18 Social entrepreneurship as a vehicle for inclusive development

The case of Siya Sebenza in South Africa

Frederik Claeyé, Michael Brookes, and Sandra Ramos

Introduction

Over the last two decades or so, the global governance system of international aid has undergone some deep changes. It has moved away from the dominance of the Bretton Woods institutions to a more polycentric architecture that includes a number of nontraditional development actors (Gore 2013; Mawdsley, Savage, and Kim 2014). The classic donor–recipient relationship is thus being replaced by a multistakeholder global partnership (Eyben and Savage 2013). One of the partners that has increasingly gained attention as an important actor in development is the private sector.

Although the private sector has been involved in some of the discussions on sustainable development since at least the 1987 Brundtland Report, it was the creation of the United Nations (UN) Global Compact in 2000 that formed a major milestone in the evolving engagement of business in development (Frey and Sabbatino 2018). With the endorsement of the Sustainable Development Goals (SDGs)—in which the business sector was strongly involved in its formulation—in September 2015, the role of the private sector has been foregrounded. This central role of the private sector in the SDGs has been hailed by some as a new paradigm in development thinking (United Nations Global Compact 2014). As Scheyvens, Banks, and Hughes (2016) point out, many assert that the private sector has particular strengths in terms of innovation capacity, responsiveness, efficiency, and provision of specific skills and resources that can be put to productive use in achieving the SDGs (see also Porter and Kramer 2011). Therefore, it seems the expectations of business as active actors in bringing about inclusive development are high (Frey and Sabbatino 2018).

It is interesting to note that this emergence of the private sector as a key player in the development process coincides with an increased interest in entrepreneurship as a way to alleviate poverty. For instance, the key claim of the bottom/base of the pyramid (BoP) concept is that poverty can be alleviated through financially profitable activity (Kolk, Rivera-Santos, and Rufin 2014). Although the original attention of the BoP literature has been on the poorest of the poor as potential consumers (Prahalad 2004), others have emphasized the entrepreneurial potential of the poor (de Soto 2000).

In parallel to this interest in BoP strategies, social enterprises have also received increasing attention as vehicles for development (Fowler 2000; Mair and Schoen 2007; Seelos and Mair 2005). The present chapter is concerned with how social enterprises may support businesses and thus promote development. Through an in-depth case study of a South African social enterprise, Siya Sebenza, we aim to show how this type of innovative organization can make a difference to the lives of disadvantaged populations by forming a link between them and the world of business, and as such promote inclusive development.

Our argument unfolds as follows: first, we sketch a picture of the South African context. Then we review the literature on social entrepreneurship and development and social enterprises in South Africa. Next, we present the case and subsequently turn to the findings of our case study. We end this chapter with some conclusions that can be drawn from the case and how this may be useful at a larger level.

The South African job market: a mismatch between supply and demand

In the 1990s the South African political, social, economic, and cultural context went through deep changes with the end of the apartheid regime and the changeover to a more democratic society. This political transition would also mark South Africa's re-entry into the global economy after years of international sanctions imposed in the late 1980s. During the process of transition to a democratic framework, several measures and policies were established in order to increase the level of development and equality of the country. However, as mentioned by Franchi, Bellucci, and Testi (2014), these programs did not succeed in solving the structural economic problems of the country. Hence, the economic transformation since 1994 has not achieved its objectives as the structure of the economy has not changed dramatically. This has led Sharma to describe the South African economy as a "cappuccino economy . . . white cream over a large black mass, with some chocolate sprinkled on top" (as cited in Bhorat et al. 2014, p. 15).

Although overall reasonable economic growth has been achieved since 1994, inequality has increased, and poverty reduction efforts have not yielded much progress. At the same time, job creation has always lagged behind the growth of the working population, leading to accusations of largely jobless growth simply fueling rising inequality (Bhorat et al. 2014). Overall, the unemployment rate since 1994 has remained above 20 percent (Mlatsheni and Leibbrandt 2014). The latest data published by the South African Office of Statistics, Stats SA, indicate an unemployment rate of 27.7 percent in the third quarter of 2017 (Stats SA 2017). Depending on how one measures unemployment, this means South Africa counts between 6.2 and 14.9 million unemployed, against an estimated working age population (aged between 15 and 64 years old) of about

37.4 million (Stats SA 2017). As Bhorat et al. (2014) indicate, it is mainly the low and unskilled segments of the working age population that are hardest hit by unemployment, reflecting racial imbalances with the African individuals (as opposed to the other racial groups) showing the highest rate of unemployment (Stats SA 2017). Whereas the unemployment rate of Africans has remained north of 25 percent, the unemployment rate of whites has consistently remained under 10 percent (Mlatsheni and Leibbrandt 2014). In addition, much of this unemployment is of long duration, which has important spillover effects in terms of social attitudes and criminality, as well as higher levels of anxiety, apathy, and helplessness and lower levels of subjective well-being (Mlatsheni and Leibbrandt 2014). Hence, Mlatsheni and Leibbrandt (2011) argue that the psychological and social costs of prolonged unemployment exceeds by far the loss of income associated with unemployment.

Part of the unemployment problem can be explained by the poor performance of the educational system. As a result, the system is not able to produce a sufficient number of graduates in key skill areas. This, in turn, has a negative effect on youth unemployment, which has been a key driver of the high unemployment rates in South Africa (Mlatsheni and Leibbrandt 2014). Recent data show staggering high unemployment rates of 52.2 percent of the working-age population between 15 and 24 years old, and 33.5 percent for the population between 25 and 34 (Stats SA 2017). This suggests a serious supply-side issue in that there seems to be a mismatch between the skills demanded by employers and those students acquire in the educational system (Bhorat et al. 2014).

As Mlatsheni and Leibbrandt (2014) indicate, it is clear that the reasons for high unemployment are too complicated for there to be a single, simple policy solution to this problem. In relation to the issue of misalignment between the educational system and the requirements of the job market, government has focused on the provision of technical and vocational skills through the Further Education and Training (FET) colleges. However, FET colleges seem to be performing poorly and do not deliver the expected employment outcomes (Bhorat and Kimani 2017; Mlatsheni and Leibbrandt 2014).

Since 1994, the South African government has implemented a number of policies and initiatives to promote entrepreneurship and boost the creation and development of small enterprises (Cassim, Soni, and Karodia 2014; Mlatsheni and Leibbrandt 2014; Rogerson 2004, 2008). Within the macro-economic context provided by the Growth, Employment and Redistribution (GEAR) strategy, a framework focusing on small, medium, and micro-enterprises (SMMEs) was set forth as from 1995 (Rogerson 2004). Despite this, South Africa shows the one of the lowest rates of early-stage entrepreneurial activity in Africa relative to other countries participating in the Global Entrepreneurship Monitor (GEM) studies (Herrington, Kew, and Mwanga 2017). The GEM study further suggests that South Africa's persistently low established business prevalence rate paints a bleak picture of the SMME sector's potential to contribute meaningfully to job creation, economic growth, and more equal income distribution. This is further exacerbated by the poor sustainability of start-ups in South Africa (Herrington, Kew, and Mwanga 2017; Mlatsheni and Leibbrandt 2011). Again, South Africa's educational system and the market structure leave participants short of skills. This has a negative effect on the success of SMMEs and thus hampers its job creation potential (Mlatsheni and Leibbrandt 2011). Hence, although there have been continuing efforts on the supply side to increase both the skills said to be required for greater employability and increased entrepreneurial activity (inter alia through the Black Economic Empowerment [BEE] strategy that seeks to empower black entrepreneurs), these have been largely ineffective (Ashman et al. 2014).

If government strategies are seen as inadequate in addressing unemployment, inequality and poverty in South Africa, this opens up space for nonstate actors to step in and try to address these scourging problems. One such actor may be social enterprises. In the following section, we turn to discussing social enterprises and how they can play a role in bringing about desired change.

Social entrepreneurship and development: moving beyond a global soup kitchen?

The rise of neo-liberalism in the 1980s together with the retraction of the state in an attempt to conform to the conditionalities imposed by Structural Adjustment Programs, meant that third-sector organizations have gained in importance as vehicles of development by trying to fill the vacuum left by the retracting state apparatus (Clark 1991; Henderson 2002; Lewis 2010; Lindenberg and Bryant 2001; Marcussen 1996). This was amplified by a growing disillusionment of many donor organizations with the poor track record of many developing nations in alleviating poverty and boosting development. This meant that they turned their eye to third-sector organizations as an alternative route to address the failings of both the state and the market in bringing about development, thus bringing nongovernmental organizations (NGOs) into the aid mainstream (Fowler 2000; Lewis 2008, 2014; Vakil 1997). This rise to prominence of the third sector was also rooted in the assumption that NGOs are more efficient and effective providers of social services than governments (Anheier 2005). However, Fowler and Biekart (2013) assert NGOs have not lived up to the (high) expectations. Around the new millennium, the label "NGO" began to lose a little of its earlier shine (Lewis 2014), and some observers argue they are the product of a rapidly fading era (Fowler 2000).

Fowler (2000) sees the rise of social entrepreneurship in the development arena as linked to a loss of legitimacy of development NGOs. It also flows from organizations' response to decreasing funding opportunities for traditional NGOs as a result of declining aid, and the homogenizing effects of global capitalism. Fueled by the dominance of a market discourse, it favors a market-inspired model of NGO identity and behavior. In addition to this, it has become clear that channeling aid through NGOs creates a dependency on donor funding that undermines the sustainability of NGOs' activities. Furthermore, it has created what may be called a "beggar mentality" (Peredo and Chrisman 2006) in many communities where there have been massive aid interventions. As such, NGOs may have become part of the problem rather than a solution to the problem.

In the last decades, the nonprofit sector has reinvented strategies to better address the social needs and to become more efficient and sustainable in their activities. One of the strategies opted by the nonprofit sector is based in an innovative and entrepreneurial approach, designated as social entrepreneurship. Despite the noticeable rise of the social enterprises and the increase of the academic research and discussions, the concept is still very blurred, with unclear frontiers and with little knowledge about their social and economic impact (Mair 2010; Mair and Schoen 2007). Banks (1972) first coined the term "social entrepreneur" in the context of the sociology of social movements, and Drucker (1979) first introduced the concept of "social enterprise" while advocating for the ethical responsibilities of corporations; however, the literature on social entrepreneurship remains fragmented and disjointed (Trivedi 2010) when it comes to a generally accepted and clear-cut definition of what is and what is not a social enterprise. Cutting a long and still ongoing debate short (Bacq and Janssen 2011; Dwivedi and Weerawardena 2018; Ferreira et al. 2017; Hossain, Saleh, and Drennan 2017; Peredo and McLean 2006; Roundy and Bonnal 2017; Sengupta, Sahay, and Croce in press), we agree with Fowler (2000, p. 645), when he describes social enterprises as organizations that link the morality and public benefit objective to characteristics commonly ascribed to commercial entrepreneurs. In other words, we adopt the view that social enterprises are hybrid organizations that combine social welfare and commercial logics to pursue social outcomes (Battilana and Lee 2014; Doherty, Haugh, and Lyon 2014; Santos, Pache, and Birkholz 2015).

Although the literature has recognized that reconciling competing social and financial objectives within hybrid organizations can be fraught with problems (Pache and Santos 2010; Santos, Pache, and Birkholz 2015), research suggests that such organizations in Africa can be both financially and socially successful (Gupta, Beninger, and Ganesh 2015; Nega and Schneider 2014). Social enterprises may be able to offer more effective and sustainable solutions because the delivery of development-focused interventions by any social enterprise is ultimately reliant upon the commercial viability of that enterprise and its activities (Brindle and Layton 2017; Dees 2008). Any surplus generated by their activities is used to sustain the social mission of the organization and, as such, any surplus generated can be used as a *means* to the end of creating social value (Santos 2012).

Several authors pointed out the role social enterprises may play in poverty alleviation and in increasing well-being by promoting the opportunity to access services and goods that otherwise people would not have the opportunity to access (Brindle and Layton 2017; Katzenstein and Chrispin 2011; Mair and Schoen 2007; McWade 2012; Seelos and Mair 2005, 2009). The argument in favor of social enterprises tends to focus on cost-effectiveness and financial sustainability of those enterprises (Katzenstein and Chrispin 2011). Gomez and Helmsing (2010) identify five main areas where social enterprises may intervene in development. The first is resolving systemic market failure. They define market failure as "the incapacity of market relations to establish themselves due to the lack of capacities of the agents and/or lack of necessary institutions to regulate the exchange relationship" (p. 396). In this area, they continue, the action of social enterprises is focused on capacity building, facilitating information flows, channeling donor money, and linking up potential partners. A second area of action they identify is direct participation in imperfect markets in delivering services free of charge or for a small fee (which may go toward recovering costs or making a profit, which, in turn, can be reinvested in the organization). The third area of action of social enterprises in the development arena is reducing government failure. Here, Gomez and Helmsing (2010) argue, social enterprises aim to secure access to basic services such as health provision, education, housing, etc. A fourth area of action they distinguish is the regulation of market institutions through advocacy. Finally, they identify channeling private philanthropy as a fifth area of action. The idea is to create value for money by channeling funds to organizations that adopt a clearer business language and approach to solving social problems and bringing about sustainable and inclusive development.

Throughout both the developing and developed world, social entrepreneurs have introduced and applied innovative business models to address social problems that businesses, governments, and NGOs could not or did not want to address. These entrepreneurs play an important role in ameliorating adverse social conditions, especially in developing and emerging economies, where resource scarcity and corruption among governments, and even NGOs, severely limit the attention given to social needs (Zahra et al. 2009). Social entrepreneurs develop new models for the provision of products and services that cater directly to basic human needs that remain unsatisfied by current economic or social institutions and thus contribute to the inclusive development of communities, regions, and countries.

Social enterprises in South Africa

Although research on social entrepreneurship in South Africa is slowly seeping into international scholarly publications, the field is still relatively under-researched and undertheorized. The terms "social enterprise" and "social entrepreneurship" are starting to gain currency; however, many social enterprises remain under the academic radar as they don't define themselves as such. Furthermore, the term "social enterprise" is used in South Africa as a general term to describe a variety of organizational forms and practices. This broad use of the term presents challenges in delimiting what it really means in South Africa and who is to be considered a social entrepreneur (Littlewood and Holt 2015; Steinman and van Rooij 2012). The absence of a legal framework on social entrepreneurship in South Africa further complicates coming to grips with the phenomenon (Claeyé 2016, 2017)

In comparison to similar countries, the rate of social entrepreneurship is low in South Africa (Herrington, Kew, and Kew 2010). Much of what is currently known as social enterprises in South Africa emerged from various NGOs that were established during the 15-year period leading up to the end of the apartheid era in 1994 (Visser, 2011). The emergence of social enterprises in South Africa is broadly similar to what we discussed earlier with regard to the emergence of social entrepreneurship in international development. As Claeyé and his colleagues observed in the organizations participating in their studies, there seems to be a shift from "do-good organizations" to becoming more business-like in the way they are running their activities (Claeyé 2011, 2014; Claeyé and Jackson 2012; Claeyé and van Meurs 2013). This shift can be explained by a number of converging factors. First, as we hinted at earlier, there was a change in the global discourse surrounding international development, which increasingly emphasized performativity in development interventions (Gulrajani 2011; McCourt and Gulrajani 2010; Murphy 2008). This changing discourse also affected organizations implementing development interventions on the ground through changes in donor requirements, which forced organizations to professionalize (Claeyé 2014). Second, the funding environment has become increasingly difficult, meaning that NGOs need to find other ways to ensure the survival and sustainability of their operations. This has led to organizations seeking to pursue income-generation activities in order to replace the funds that were no longer available through traditional channels (ILO 2013; Trialogue 2016). At the same time, companies reduced the funds they could make available through corporate social investment activities because of the global financial meltdown and the consequence this had on corporate profits. In addition to "donor fatigue" some respondents highlighted a phenomenon of "NGO fatigue," related to the fact that NGOs were perceived as not being able to deliver on the promises made to communities and thus lost legitimacy (see also Fowler 2000; Taylor 2013). This, again, diverted funds from the third sector. In response to this, some NGOs turned to income-generating activities to sustain their activities. Finally, one may also point at a fashionable phenomenon that emerged in the last decade, whereby social entrepreneurial activities seem to have gained increasing credit, as this type of development activities seemed to respond better to some donors' requirements in terms of performativity and sustainability. In this sense, it seems fashionable to set up a social enterprise rather than a traditional NGO. These converging developments have created a fertile ground for more business-like NGOs and social enterprises to emerge.

Research on social entrepreneurship in South Africa is picking up, with the last five years seeing more research being done (including PhD theses) than the preceding ten years. In addition to a number of conceptual papers (Brundin et al. 2013; Claeyé 2016, 2017; Karanda and Toledano 2012; Urban 2008; Visser 2011), others have taken a more empirical approach investigating, for example, the craft industry (Daya 2014); the role and importance of the institutional environment for social entrepreneurship in South Africa (Littlewood and Holt 2018; Urban 2013; Urban and Kujinga 2017b); or social entrepreneurial intentions, motivations, and beliefs (Boluk and Mottiar 2014; Urban 2013, 2015; Urban and Kujinga 2017a; 2017b; Urban and Teise 2015).

The general gist among both these conceptual and empirical papers is the view that social entrepreneurship may offer a promising alternative approach to combating poverty, unemployment, disease, and other issues plaguing South African society. Due to its focus on combining business logics with a social welfare agenda, it is seen as a more sustainable and cost-efficient approach to tackling South Africa's social problems.

Surprisingly few researchers have looked at the role of social entrepreneurship in development in South Africa. Visser (2011) assesses the relevance, role, and extent of social entrepreneurship in South Africa and illustrates that social entrepreneurs provide social and economic stability in communities where they provide service. Steinman and van Rooij (2012), looking at the broader context of the social and solidarity economy, note that these organizations have a significant potential for job creation, but the policy environment is not adequately conducive for them to flourish. They note, inter alia, that in terms of tax legislation, there is lack of coordination between the levels of government in the implementation of policies and unwillingness on the part of government to assist social enterprises with business development services.

This chapter helps to fill this gap by investigating how social enterprises may support businesses and thus promote development in South Africa by looking at the case of Siya Sebenza. In the following section we describe the methodology we used together with the organization under study.

Methods and data

We conducted a singled case study selecting a paradigmatic case (Flyvbjerg 2006; Yin 2009). We consider Siya Sebenza to be a pivotal case, as it reveals some key elements of a what social entrepreneurship might do in the context of developing countries for the following reasons: first, as we explain later, it has been very successful in developing its business model while at the same time creating a significant impact (it trains about 30,000 job seekers per year). Second, Siya Sebenza is unique in its approach to skills development though its focus on changing people's mind-sets in addition to providing them with skills that correspond to demands from the business sector. Third, it has been successful in developing links with the business world, thus bridging the gap between the demand and supply sides of the job market. Fourth, in relation to its labor market operations, it is the only enterprise that simultaneously supports job seekers and employers as well as operating as an employment agency.

Data were gathered through semi-structured interviews with members at the head office and facilitators in various branches and companies they work with. In total 11 semi-structured interviews were conducted. These data were complemented with information from the organization's website, Facebook posts, and YouTube videos. Both the interviews and the YouTube videos were transcribed. These transcripts and the Facebook posts were analyzed with QSR Nvivo 11 using an inductive approach. Table 18.1 summarizes the data and indicates the codes we used when presenting and discussing the data.

Table 18.1 Data sources

Respondent 1 (R1)	Founder and CEO
R2	Facilitator
R3	Facilitator
R4	Program coordinator
R5	Facilitator
R6	Facilitator
R7	Facilitator
R8	Company founder
R9	Branch manager
R10	Administrative coordinator
R11	Facilitator
FB	Facebook posts
YT 1–4	YouTube videos

Siya Sebenza is a not-for-profit social enterprise, based in Port Elizabeth (Eastern Cape province) that seeks to address the fundamental development challenge of alleviating poverty among the most disadvantaged urban communities. In order to address this, they have developed their Work 4 A Living program, which recognizes that in poorer urban communities the most effective path out of poverty is through paid employment.

The Work 4 A Living model is based on three distinct approaches. First, using an integrated approach combining labor market research, training workshops, and consultancy services, as well as acting as an employment agency. The combination of the four activities within one institution is unique and a major contributory factor to the success of the program. Second, there are innovative workshops focused upon improving the mind-set of job seekers, broadening their worldview as a catalyst to better employment outcomes, with the focus on the mind-set as a precursor, before focusing on job and entrepreneurial skills, also being a major contributor to the success of the project. Third, the project has been able to expand from a single center with a capacity 600 job seekers per year, to having 45 centers across the whole of South Africa with a capacity of 30,000 per year. This has been undertaken using a social franchise-based model recruiting social entrepreneurs, then developing and supporting them in delivering the Work 4 A Living program in their community. Again, this franchise-based approach is unique to this project and is another major contributor to its success.

The training program consists of a foundational course, the Work 4 A Living program, that is compulsory for all students. A small fee is charged to participants (100 ZAR) for this foundational program. From here, they can move into the phase 2 programs. These are more specialized paying courses (400 ZAR on average), such as computer literacy, waiting tables, office management, merchandising, business development, etc. Besides these phase 2 skills programs, Siya Sebenza has a School of Excellence, which is by invitation only and open to the very best students: The Grain (specialized artisanal bakery skills), Serv (geared at the hospitality industry), and Red Brand Barista Academy. These are typically longer programs running over several weeks.

All of these innovative activities are brought together through the operation of Work 4 A Living's recruitment agency that is offered to candidates at no cost. Employers register for free and can do a skills search, which will link them to candidates with requisite skills. Work 4 A Living then tracks their progress, and this enables them to track how many job seekers from the training program have been employed. The operation is effectively centralized, and the recruitment agency markets the database to key national employers. In addition, each center uses it locally to ensure that there is a local take-up as well with small to medium enterprises.

Findings

In the following paragraphs we will present our findings with regard to the ways in which Siya Sebenza offers support to local employers through its innovative skills development program and how this may promote development.

Empowering job seekers through changing mind-sets

Siya Sebenza, through its Work 4 A Living program, aims to provide people with the skills and attitudes necessary to be successful in the job market. The focus on both skills development and people's attitudes and behaviors in the workplace stems from the founder's observation that although unemployment in South Africa is high, many employers have enormous difficulties in attracting the right personnel. R4 describes it this way:

> So, the problem that we are trying to address it's real, we are really addressing a real problem. What creates need, creates demand. You get an employer calling you "I am struggling with my staff here, they don't treat my customers right, can you come and help, you see". So, I think we picked a good problem to address. [. . .] [T]he thing is, it's not quite easy. Jobs are very hard for young people to get and so obviously they come, and they want to be taught how to do it right. But they just want to come and get a job, they don't know that you actually get taught to do a proper job, how to become effective.

As this quote indicates, the problem identified relates to people being able to do "a proper job." This "doing a proper job" goes beyond mere skills and competencies. A lack of skills and competencies is only one part of the unemployment problem. A more important problem, according to Siya Sebenza, is situated at the behavioral level. Although skills development, financial literacy, and computer literacy are important components of the Work 4 A Living program, the core of its intervention is at the level of changing mind-sets. As one respondent put it:

> I think it's not about necessarily doing a service, so our skills development, which is your computers, merchandising, cashier and barista, I think there are many organisations that do that very well. What distinguishes us, makes us different, is that we spend a lot of time focusing on the mind-sets and it's a mind-set change.
>
> (R9)

As indicated by R4 earlier, the attitudes and behaviors job seekers bring to the job seem to be out of phase with what is expected by employers; therefore, employability interventions also need to work on the level of attitudes and behaviors. Hence, the program offers its students skills they will need to function in a business environment by providing them work ethics training and working on excellence and professionalism. The root problem, however, that the Work 4 A Living program aims to address lies deeper at the level of the "poverty mind-set," which says, "I'm poor, I'll always be poor and nothing is going to change" (YT2). Through a focus on transforming this fatalist mind-set, the Work 4 A Living program works on character development with a view of breaking both the poverty mind-set and the spirit of entitlement in which some students are trapped as a backlash of decennia of apartheid rule. This spirit of entitlement says, "I'm owed something. Somebody needs to fix my problems. Somebody needs to fix my life" (YT2). It is this culture of entitlement, together with a poverty mind-set that is intertwined with it, that the program wishes to address. Hence, in addition to building students' confidence, the program focuses on work ethics, professionalism, and standards of excellence in order to bring students in line with the expectations of the corporate world. As such, the program aims to empower people to be more confident and develop greater self-esteem. The many quotes from both the posts and review section of Siya Sebenza's Facebook page attest to this change in worldview. One commentator wrote:

> Siya sebenza [sic] offers more than what we pay to be trained. The staff at Siya Sebenza is superb, they don't only train us to be applicable for a job, but to develop our self-esteem and improve our mind-set because most of us think we ain't good enough for a specific job or whatsoever.
>
> (FB, January 21, 2017)

As the founder indicated, the program is aimed at empowering students by unleashing their potential and taking ownership of their personal and professional development. Therefore, any impact that the organization makes is measured in terms of what action students undertake as a result of their training. As the founder indicated:

> There needs to be an action. So, for us, we are not achieving what we want to achieve if there isn't a tangible result at the end of the day. So, it is just

"Oh, good, we've had an intervention with some poor people and we've done a good job." How do we know we've done a good job until there is something tangible? So, there must be a result. [...] First prize for us is they find themselves a job. Second prize is we find them a job. [Third prize,] They must have started their own business, [fourth prize] they must have decided to go back to school, so there must be an action. And we measure that action. So, for us that is critical.

(R1)

As indicated earlier, this taking action is critical in how Siya Sebenza evaluates its success. However, as a social enterprise that aims to make a difference and bring change that will affect development, its ultimate focus goes beyond the individual. The long-term goal of Siya Sebenza and its Work 4 A Living program is to affect societal change. This societal change is to be brought about by first affecting the individual, and through the individual its family, its community, and finally society at large. Again, this change is mediated through the change in behavior of the individual, which trickles down and affects others in the community through word of mouth about how the program channels many into employment and the mechanism of social comparison. Answering the question on what changes can be observed, R7 answered:

The mission is to bring about a change to the community. [...] So, it is very effective because when they [the students] come here they change, first of all, the way they think and after they change they manage to pick their lives up, they manage to get jobs and it changes the community. [...] Yes, one young person is influenced by the other to take drugs. So, when they come to the center, one of the questions asked on the form [is] how did you hear about Siya Sibenza? It is "I heard through a friend". And when another friend starts to change their behavior, start to be more focused with their studies or future, they tend to change as well, because they influence each other. So that's how it starts to affect them, the society in a good way.

(R7)

These illustrations suggest an innovative approach to thinking about empowerment, employability, and inclusive development through working on people's worldviews. As such, it goes beyond many traditional approaches that tend to focus on material aspects of underdevelopment, or capabilities that are open to individuals. Siya Sebenza's approach is to go beyond mere a skills development program. Although it certainly acknowledges that there is a skills deficit and that skills are an important factor in increasing the employability of people from disadvantaged backgrounds and communities, the most important aspect of their program is changing people's mind-sets from passive recipients to active entrepreneurial agents that take matters in their own hands.

As discussed earlier, unemployment, and especially the long-term unemployment to which many South Africans are exposed, leaves its marks. At the individual level, it reduces levels of confidence and self-esteem. At the level of the community, it may result in antisocial behavior, criminality, and other behaviors (Mlatsheni and Leibbrandt 2011, 2014) that may undermine social capital in a community. Through its program, Siya Sebenza not only works on the level of "technical" skills and competencies that make people more employable, it also works at the level of self-esteem and confidence. As such, it focuses on students' sense of self-efficacy (Ajzen 1991, 2002) and as such empowers them to take action and make a change by either finding themselves a job, creating a business, or going back to school. Through giving students back confidence and self-esteem and a sense that "I can do anything, as long as I put my mind to it" (R6), it aims to make a difference and bring about change.

In addition to professional and personal development, the program has a wider impact that goes beyond the individual that went through the training. Through its success in channeling people into (self-)employment, it succeeds in building a strong reputation. This results in word of mouth as a strong factor of attraction that helps keep a steady stream of applicants coming to the program. In addition to the economic value created through employment and income for the students and the (extended) family dependent on this income, it creates social value through its work on changing people's world view. This shift from a spirit of entitlement to a more active and entrepreneurial stance not only benefits the student directly but also seems to have wider effects on the behaviors of people surrounding the student, and in this way may have an effect on the community and society at large.

This section discussed the demand side of the job market; the next will focus on the demand side (i.e., the employers).

Supporting business through collaborating

As stated earlier, one of the drivers that led to the establishment of Siya Sebenza and its Work 4 A Living program was the disconnect its founder observed between the demands of the job market and the skills and attitudes job seekers had to offer. As such, a first role Siya Sebenza plays in supporting business is the role of intermediary, where job seekers and employers can meet each other. This is echoed by R4, when he states that

> Employers and students with skills, they are missing each other every time. But the moment we set up a centre, you find that all those people they get a meeting point. I think that is one of the most important things that we created.

In order to address the perceived disconnect between the supply and demand side of the job market, the Siya Sebenza has built strong links with employers to find out what skills they expect from prospective job seekers so as to be able to equip them with what employers are looking for. In this regard, the home page of their website states "that empowerment starts with listening" (Siya Sebenza a). This was echoed across the interviews. R2 summarizes it in this way:

> And another thing the information given to people, it's very relevant. It's very relevant in a sense that we do, our research is, we speak to the employers and the employers say, "This is what we want". And then we try and give people that, so then when they go out there, they have what the employers want.
>
> (R2)

Through this listening to employers and tailoring its skills development to the needs of employers Siya Sebenza is able to start bridging the gap between employers demands and job seekers skills and "turning the unemployed into confident and attractive employees" (YT2). As such, part of Siya Sebenza's success as a training organization can be explained by its innovative approach of actively seeking out feedback from both employers (and students) in a continuous attempt to make its skills development courses relevant for both parties. This interaction with employers not only helps the further development and fine-tuning of existing programs; employer feedback also leads to the development of new training programs, such as the Red Band Barista Academy, which trains baristas, or the Grain Baking Academy, which equips students to work as specialist bakers.

As discussed earlier, the training students receive goes beyond the mere skills and competencies people need to be effective employees. An important aspect of the training, therefore, relates to how individuals conduct themselves in the workplace. This means people are equipped with behavioral and relational skills in terms of work ethics, time management, professionalism, etc. One of the effects of this emphasis on attitudes and behaviors is that employers actively seek out Siya Sebenza's services when they need personnel because it has built a reputation of delivering high-quality, dedicated staff. One of the partner companies now uses Siya Sebenza's Work 4 A Living program as part of their induction process, putting all their new recruits through the program, because it teaches job seekers work ethic, self-governance, and financial literacy to job seekers before they get hired (Siya Sebenza b.). As one employer commented:

> I think for me the proof was in the last, like our December holidays, like our summer holidays, when the schools close and stuff like that. [. . .] [C]ompanies have problems with their staff over this period, especially where there is a lot of holidays. I have got 48 baristas now and during the month of summer holidays not one dropped me ever. They worked day shift and night shift sometimes. So, I think that stands for something. They never had, even if they have difficult times, they were all at work when they were supposed to be there.
>
> (R8)

Employers not only seek out Siya Sebenza for the perceived quality of the people they are able to supply. Another element that makes Siya Sebenza attractive is that it does not charge employers for its services. Even though some employers indicated that they would be willing to pay a fee, Siya Sebenza sees providing them for free to potential employers as part of its mission, as it wants to channel as many job seekers as possible into employment. This means relationships are not only built directly with employers, but that synergies are also created with recruitment agencies that may need qualified personnel for their own clients. In this respect, the founder argued:

> We have employment agencies contacting us all the time to get staff. I don't mind that they make money from us. At the end of the day, what do we want? Bring about change, which means somebody must be employed. If they have got the opportunity to place this person, make money, it's fine as long as the person gets placed. You know what I mean? It [. . .] must impact the individual. That was an interesting thing to work through that someone else is making money off the fruit of our labour, but it doesn't matter. If we look at what we're trying to achieve, it doesn't matter. And they do have the contacts sometimes that we don't. They do have the opportunities sometimes that we don't. I mean that's fine. We want to work with as many organisations that have opportunities as possible.
>
> (R1)

This focus on providing job opportunities by increasing people's employability is corroborated across the interviews we conducted and is summarized by R2 as follows:

> The mission and purpose of Siya Sebenza is to take unemployed young people, teach them to work to a standard of excellence and make sure that they get employment. And the long term, obviously, we want to change the work force in South Africa, but mostly the key area of focus would be "Let's change the social lives of people, let's restore hope in people who sit at home." So, it is quite an interesting mix in terms of what we want to do.

As discussed earlier, South African economy is plagued by a mismatch between the demands of the market and what the educational system is able to supply (Bhorat et al. 2014; Bhorat and Kimani 2017; Mlatsheni and Leibbrandt 2014). As the quotes earlier aim to illustrate, Siya Sebenza's success as a social enterprise rests in part on the dialogue it is able to develop and maintain with employers. By listening to what employers need, it is able to adapt its training courses to what the job market is expecting of its workforce. In this way it aims to address the mismatch between the supply and demand sides of the job market that seems to exist in South Africa (Mlatsheni and Leibbrandt 2014).

Siya Sebenza is able to intervene at two levels with regard to this mismatch. The first, and most basic, level at which it intervenes is skills development.

Through its basic Work 4 A Living and the phase 2 programs it provides participants with the skills they need to function on the work floor. In addition to basic numeracy or computer literacy skills, the management of personal finances, etc., Siya Sebenza provides job seekers with concrete skills for particular job niches. As such its vocational training program is able to channel many young unemployed persons with high potential into jobs such as, inter alia, becoming a barista or specialist baker. As indicated by a number of interviewees, this skills development aspect of Siya Sebenza's program is not necessarily different from what other players in the field might be doing, and as such it is quite similar to what others are offering.

Thus, where Siya Sebenza is able to distinguish itself from the "competition" is its work on behavioral aspects. This forms the second level where it intervenes, and it is here that it is able to make a difference in comparison to other skills development organizations, as the expectations of the employers go beyond mere "technical" skills and competencies to include the behaviors and attitudes potential employees bring with them. The data suggest that although the "technical" skills are important to employers, it is the attitudinal and behavioral ("soft") skills that make Siya Sebenza's graduates attractive to employers. By working on issues related to work ethics, time management, professionalism, commitment, etc., it produces graduates that are highly valued and sought after in the job market.

It is this combination of listening to employers with the provision of a skills development program that is tailored to both the technical and soft skills demanded by the market that makes that Siya Sebenza is able to build a bridge between the demand and supply sides of the job market. By doing so, it is able to increase the employability of its graduates. This increased employability is translated, through word of mouth, into a steady stream of both incoming students and potential employers seeking high-quality personnel. As such, it is able to create a multiplier effect that affects the lives of both individuals and the communities from which these individuals are drawn by generating income and setting an example for others in those communities.

Conclusions

We started this chapter with the observation of high unemployment and a mismatch between the demand and supply side of the job market (Bhorat et al. 2014). Despite government initiatives to tackle the problem, these seem to be inadequate in addressing unemployment, inequality, and poverty in South Africa. This opens up space for nonstate actors—such as social enterprises—to step in and try to address these scourging problems. Our findings suggest that Siya Sebenza is able to effectively address this gap by empowering job seekers and supporting business through a dialogue that aims to match the supply side to the demand side.

Conventional wisdom about case study research cautions researchers not to generalize beyond the case at hand. This is certainly the case when research draws on a single case study. However, drawing on Flyvbjerg's (2006) arguments, in this section we will venture beyond the single case study under review and suggest some ways in which the insights from the present case study may be valuable at a larger level and for other geographic settings based on the practical, context-dependent knowledge this case provides us (Flyvbjerg 2006).

So, what can we learn from this case? A first lesson that can be drawn from this case study is one of cooperation across sectors to promote inclusive development. This notion of partnerships was already part of the Millennium Development Goals and has been reiterated with the launch of the SDGs. Siya Sebenza shows that through a dialogue with the employers it can better tailor its skills development program to the needs of the employers and thus increase the employability of its graduates. These types of collaborations across sectors are important in matching supply with demand, which seems to be deficient at the moment (Bhorat and Kimani 2017; Mlatsheni and Leibbrandt 2011). It creates a win–win situation for all parties involved, as employers get employees with the skills and attitudes they need to remain competitive, and the graduates enter into gainful employment that generates income that can support the extended family, if customary and necessary.

Second, in contrast to interventions that aim to empower individuals and communities through focusing only on skills development training, Siya Sebenza takes a more radical (in all senses of the word) approach. The root problem that it identifies that holds people and communities back lies in a lack of self-esteem, self-confidence, and a drive to excellence. Both a poverty mind-set and a spirit of entitlement are put forward as underlying reasons for this observation.

Research on the effects of poverty on people's psyche have shown that it has detrimental effects on individuals and, by extension, whole communities (Carr 2013; Carr and Sloan 2003; Haushofer 2013). Recent research by Haushofer and Fehr (2014) posits feedback loops in which "poverty reinforces itself through exerting an influence on psychological outcomes" (p. 866). This, they continue, "may lead to economic behaviours that are potentially disadvantageous and may prolong the climb out of poverty for poor individuals, or even make the escape from poverty impossible" (p. 866). This undermines individuals' and communities' resilience in the face adversity. This is mirrored by research on the detrimental effects of long-term unemployment that is reported by Mlatsheni and Leibbrandt (2011, 2014). It also links back to the literature on entrepreneurial intentions that puts self-efficacy (Ajzen 1991, 2002) forward as an important factor in moving from the intention to create a business to actually creating one. Therefore, we would argue that empowerment strategies need to include a focus on addressing the mental effects of poverty in addition to skills development and other interventions (such as micro-credit schemes, etc.) by trying to break this negative downward spiral. In this sense Siya Sebenza's work on changing poor people's world view and giving them back a sense of self-worth and self-confidence is important in helping people break out of this cycle of poverty. Combined with the provision of a strong set of skills that matches the demands and expectations of employers and increases their employability, we argue this approach has a lot of merit.

We can draw a parallel here with the work of Gawad Kalinga and the School for Experiential and Entrepreneurial Development (SEED) in the Philippines. Again, the main premise is that poverty creates a "slum mentality" and that this holds people back. Hence, Gawad Kalinga favours an approach to helping people out of poverty that is based on working on values transformation and strong mentoring that gives students from the BoP a sense of self-esteem and increases their confidence that they can achieve excellence and a way out of poverty for themselves and their community (Gawad Kalinga 2014). Both approaches rest on the assumption that employability and employment is a way out of poverty. At the same time, we should also recognize that institutional barriers to entrepreneurship and business development have an impact on the demand side of the coin and need to be addressed. This is further exacerbated by material deprivation, discrimination, and the lack of access to opportunities, which further undercuts the resilience of the poor.

A third element that Siya Sebenza's example illustrates is related to the issue of the poverty mind-set – what Siya Sebenza calls a "spirit of entitlement." In South Africa this is strongly related to the legacy of apartheid and the feeling that people are owed something as a result of past wrongdoings (Hammett 2008). As many interviewees suggested, the result is an undermining of resilience such that people do not take action to deal with their circumstances. Again, Siya Sebenza aims to bring about change in individuals and communities by changing people's worldview by working on this spirit of entitlement. This links to what Peredo and Chrisman (2006) have termed a "beggar mentality" that is created in many communities as a result of massive aid interventions. Through working on people's worldviews and by building their confidence that they can achieve something in life, this approach builds their resilience in the face of adversity and provides a way forward for people to see the opportunities that are around and act on them. The underlying argument goes that through working on people's worldview and their self-perception, they are transformed from being passive recipients of charity to active agents of their own change by instilling them with a more entrepreneurial mind-set.

A link can be drawn here with the focus on entrepreneurship as a way out of poverty (Gries and Naudé 2011). As indicated earlier, this has gained some attention in recent years and is at the forefront of the pleads repeatedly made by Muhammad Yunus (2017), if we restrict our focus to social entrepreneurship and social business. This emphasis on entrepreneurship as a way forward out of poverty ties also in with the examples of Gawad Kalinga, BoP strategies and the entrepreneurial potential of the poor (de Soto 2000). Furthermore, the wider literature on economic development also underlines the importance of entrepreneurship and enterprise development as an important constituent of economic growth (Gries and Naudé 2011; Naudé 2011). As such, it seems to be in the spirit of the times.

Finally, the example of Siya Sebenza also highlights how a viable business model that generates income may be able to create social value. The literature on social entrepreneurship emphasizes the combination of entrepreneurial acumen with social objectives, where profits generated by its activities are used to sustain the social mission of the organization (Seelos and Mair 2005). By charging its students a small fee, Siya Sebenza generates income that can be used to further develop its activities with a view to increasing its social impact and channeling more job seekers into gainful employment.

To conclude this chapter, we argue that although cross-sector partnerships and skills development programs are conducive to inclusive development, real empowerment of individuals and communities depends on building resilience by changing the poverty mind-set and spirit of entitlement in which they might be trapped. Although we do not want to minimize the role of effective institutional environments, material deprivation, discrimination, or the lack of access to opportunities, we suggest that lifting mental barriers and in this way strengthening the resilience of the poor might be a way forward that merits more consideration. Social enterprises might take the lead on this by building resilience through instilling an entrepreneurial mind-set that is conducive to change and would lead to more inclusive development.

References

Ajzen, Icek (1991), "The theory of planned behavior," *Organizational Behavior and Human Decision Processes, Theories of Cognitive Self-Regulation*, 50 (2), 179–211.

Ajzen, Icek (2002), "Perceived behavioral control, self-efficacy, locus of control, and the theory of planned behavior," *Journal of Applied Social Psychology*, 32 (4), 665–83.

Anheier, Helmut K. (2005), *Nonprofit organizations: Theory, management, policy*, Abingdon, UK: Routledge.

Ashman, Sam, Ben Fine, Vishnu Padayachee, and John Sender (2014), "The political economy of restructuring in South Africa," in *The Oxford companion to the economics of South Africa*, H. Bhorat, A. Hirsch, R. Kanbur, and M. Ncube, eds., Oxford, UK: Oxford University Press, 67–74.

Bacq, Sophie and Frank Janssen (2011), "The multiple faces of social entrepreneurship: A review of definitional issues based on geographical and thematic criteria," *Entrepreneurship & Regional Development*, 23 (5–6), 373–403.

Banks, Joseph Ambrose (1972), *The sociology of social movements*, London, UK: Macmillan.

Battilana, Julie and Matthew Lee (2014), "Advancing research on hybrid organizing – Insights from the study of social enterprises," *The Academy of Management Annals*, 8 (1), 397–441.

Bhorat, Haroon, Alan Hirsch, Ravi Kanbur, and Mthuli Ncube (2014), "Economic policy in South Africa-past, present and future," in *The Oxford companion to the economics of South Africa*, H. Bhorat, A. Hirsch, R. Kanbur, and M. Ncube, eds., Oxford, UK: Oxford University Press, 1–25.

Bhorat, Haroon and Mumbi E. Kimani (2017), *The role of post-school education and training institutions in predicting labour market outcomes*, Pretoria, South Africa: Labour Market Intelligence Partnership.

Boluk, Karla Aileen and Ziene Mottiar (2014), "Motivations of social entrepreneurs: Blurring the social contribution and profits dichotomy," *Social Enterprise Journal*, 10 (1), 53–68.

Brindle, Margaret and Ron Layton (2017), *Social entrepreneurship for development: A business model*, New York, NY: Routledge.

Brundin, Ethel, Eslyn Isaacs, Kobus Visser, and Caroline Wigren (2013), "The role of social entrepreneurship in South Africa," in *Social entrepreneurship and microfinance*, J. H. Westover, ed., Champaign, IL: Common Ground Publishing LLC, 149–71.

Carr, Stuart C. (2013), *Anti-poverty psychology*, New York, NY: Springer.

Carr, Stuart C. and Tod S. Sloan (2003), *Poverty and psychology: From global perspective to local practice*, New York, NY: Springer Science & Business Media.

Cassim, Shahida, Paresh Soni, and Anis Mahomed Karodia (2014), "Entrepreneurship policy in South Africa," *Arabian Journal of Business and Management Review (Oman Chapter)*, 3 (10), 29.

Claeyé, Frederik (2011), "Hybridisation in non-profit organisations in Southern Africa: A critical cross-cultural reading," in *The third sector, dialogues in critical management studies*, R. Hull, J. Gibbon, O. Branzei, and H. Haugh, eds., Bingley, UK: Emerald, 235–58.

Claeyé, Frederik (2014), *Managing nongovernmental organizations: Culture, power, and resistance*, New York, NY: Routledge.

Claeyé, Frederik (2016), "Social entrepreneurship in South Africa: A tentative typology," ICSEM working papers series, Liège, Belgium.

Claeyé, Frederik (2017), "A typology of social entrepreneuring models in South Africa," *Social Enterprise Journal*, 13 (4), 427–42.

Claeyé, Frederik and Terence Jackson (2012), "The iron cage re-visited: Institutional isomorphism in non-profit organisations in South Africa," *Journal of International Development*, 24 (5), 602–622.

Claeyé, Frederik and Nathalie van Meurs (2013), "Power, resistance and culture in the construction of NPO identity in South Africa," in *Academy of Management Proceedings*, Lake Buena Vista, FL: Academy of Management, 16402.

Clark, John (1991), *Democratizing development: The role of voluntary organizations*, London, UK: Earthscan.

Daya, Shari (2014), "Saving the other: Exploring the social in social enterprise," *Geoforum*, 57, 120–8.

Dees, J. Gregory (2008), "Philanthropy and enterprise: Harnessing the power of business and social entrepreneurship for development," *Innovations: Technology, Governance, Globalization*, 3 (3), 119–32.

de Soto, Hernando (2000), *The mystery of capital: Why capitalism triumphs in the West and fails everywhere else*, London, UK: Bantam Press.

Doherty, Bob, Helen Haugh, and Fergus Lyon (2014), "Social enterprises as hybrid organizations: A review and research agenda," *International Journal of Management Reviews*, 16 (4), 417–36.

Drucker, Peter (1979), *The practice of management*, London, UK: Pan Books.

Dwivedi, Abhishek and Jay Weerawardena (2018), "Conceptualizing and operationalizing the social entrepreneurship construct," *Journal of Business Research*, 86, 32–40.

Eyben, Rosalind and Laura Savage (2013), "Emerging and submerging powers: Imagined geographies in the new development partnership at the Busan fourth high level forum," *Journal of Development Studies*, 49 (4), 457–69.

Ferreira, João J., Cristina I. Fernandes, Marta Peres-Ortiz, and Helena Alves (2017), "Conceptualizing social entrepreneurship: Perspectives from the literature," *International Review on Public and Nonprofit Marketing*, 14 (1), 73–93.

Flyvbjerg, Bent (2006), "Five misunderstandings about case-study research," *Qualitative Inquiry*, 12 (2), 219–45.

Fowler, Alan (2000), "NGDOs as a moment in history: Beyond aid to social entrepreneurship or civic innovation?" *Third World Quarterly*, 21 (4), 637–54.

Fowler, Alan and Kees Biekart (2013), "Relocating civil society in a politics of civic-driven change," *Development Policy Review*, 31 (4), 463–483.

Franchi, Serena, Marco Bellucci, and Enrico Testi (2014), "Social enterprise, social innovation and social entrepreneurship in South Africa: A national report," Florence, Italy: University of Florence.

Frey, Marco and Alessia Sabbatino (2018), "The role of the private sector in global sustainable development: The UN 2030 agenda," in *Corporate responsibility and digital communities: An international perspective towards sustainability*, Palgrave Studies in Governance, Leadership and Responsibility, G. Grigore, A. Stancu, and D. McQueen, eds., Cham, Switzerland: Palgrave Macmillan, 187–204.

Gawad Kalinga (2014), "How we end poverty-our model," (accessed February 14, 2018), [available at www.gk1world.com/our-model].

Gomez, Georgina M. and A.H.J. Helmsing (2010), "Social entrepreneurship: A convergence of NGOs and the market?" in *NGO management: The Earthscan companion*, A. Fowler and C. Malunga, eds., London, UK: Earthscan, 391–402.

Gore, Charles (2013), "The new development cooperation landscape: Actors, approaches, architecture," *Journal of International Development*, 25 (6), 769–786.

Gries, Thomas and Wim Naudé (2011), "Entrepreneurship and human development: A capability approach," *Journal of Public Economics, New Directions in the Economics of Welfare: Special Issue Celebrating Nobel Laureate Amartya Sen's 75th Birthday*, 95 (3), 216–24.

Gulrajani, Nilima (2011), "Transcending the great foreign aid debate: Managerialism, radicalism and the search for aid effectiveness," *Third World Quarterly*, 32 (2), 199–216.

Gupta, Sudheer, Stefanie Beninger, and Jai Ganesh (2015), "A hybrid approach to innovation by social enterprises: Lessons from Africa," *Social Enterprise Journal*, 11 (1), 89–112.

Hammett, Daniel (2008), "The challenge of a perception of 'un-entitlement' to citizenship in post-Apartheid South Africa," *Political Geography*, 27 (6), 652–68.

Haushofer, Johannes (2013), "The psychology of poverty: Evidence from 43 countries," Working paper, Princeton, NJ: Abdul Latif Jameel Poverty Action Lab, Massachusetts Institute of Technology.

Haushofer, Johannes and Ernst Fehr (2014), "On the psychology of poverty," *Science*, 344 (6186), 862–867.

Henderson, Keith (2002), "Alternative service delivery in developing countries: NGOs and other non-profits in urban areas," *Public Organization Review*, 2 (2), 99–116.

Herrington, Mike, Jacqui Kew, and Penny Kew (2010), *Tracking entrepreneurship in South Africa: A GEM perspective*, Cape Town, South Africa: Graduate School of Business, University of Cape Town.

Herrington, Mike, Penny Kew, and Alesimo Mwanga (2017), "GEM South Africa report 2016/2017: Can small businesses survive in South Africa?," National Reports, Global Entrepreneurship Monitor.

Hossain, Sayem, M. Abu Saleh, and Judy Drennan (2017), "A critical appraisal of the social entrepreneurship paradigm in an international setting: a proposed conceptual framework," *International Entrepreneurship and Management Journal*, 13 (2), 347–368.

ILO (2013), "South Africa SME Observatory: The potential of non-profit organizations in the Free State Province to adopt a social enterprise approach," Pretoria, South Africa: ILO.

Karanda, Crispen and Nuria Toledano (2012), "Social entrepreneurship in South Africa: A different narrative for a different context," *Social Enterprise Journal*, 8 (3), 201–15.

Katzenstein, James and Barbara R. Chrispin (2011), "Social entrepreneurship and a new model for international development in the 21st century," *Journal of Developmental Entrepreneurship*, 16 (1), 87–102.

Kolk, Ans, Miguel Rivera-Santos, and Carlos Rufin (2014), "Reviewing a decade of research on the 'base/bottom of the pyramid' (BOP) concept," *Business & Society*, 53 (3), 338–77.

Lewis, David (2008), "Nongovernmentalism and the reorganization of public action," in *The new development management: Critiquing the dual modernization*, S. Dar and B. Cooke, eds., London, UK: Zed Books, 41–55.

Lewis, David (2010), "Nongovernmental organizations, definition and history," in *International encyclopedia of civil society*, H. K. Anheier, S. Toepler, and R. List, eds., New York, NY: Springer, 1056–62.

Lewis, David (2014), *Non-governmental organizations, management and development*, Milton Park, UK: Routledge.

Lindenberg, Marc and Coralie Bryant (2001), *Going global: Transforming relief and development NGOs*, Bloomfield, CT.: Kumarian Press.

Littlewood, David and Diane Holt (2015), "Social enterprise in South Africa," ICSEM Working Papers.

Littlewood, David and Diane Holt (2018), "Social entrepreneurship in South Africa: Exploring the influence of environment," *Business & Society*, 57 (3), 525–61.

Mair, Johanna (2010), "Social entrepreneurship: Taking stock and looking ahead," in *Handbook of research on social entrepreneurship*, A. Fayolle and H. Matlay, eds., Cheltenham, UK: Edward Elgar, 15–28.

Mair, Johanna and Oliver Schoen (2007), "Successful social entrepreneurial business models in the context of developing economies: An explorative study," *International Journal of Emerging Markets*, 2 (1), 54–68.

Marcussen, Henrik Secher (1996), "NGOs, the state and civil society," *Review of African Political Economy*, 23 (69), 405–23.

Mawdsley, Emma, Laura Savage, and Sung-Mi Kim (2014), "A 'post-aid world'? Paradigm shift in foreign aid and development cooperation at the 2011 Busan high level forum,'" *The Geographical Journal*, 180 (1), 27–38.

McCourt, Willy and Nilima Gulrajani (2010), "The future of development management: Introduction to the special issue," *Public Administration and Development*, 30 (2), 81–90.

McWade, Whitney (2012), "The role for social enterprises and social investors in the development struggle," *Journal of Social Entrepreneurship*, 3 (1), 96–112.

Mlatsheni, Cecil and Murray Leibbrandt (2011), "Youth unemployment in South Africa: Challenges, concepts and opportunities," *Journal of International Relations and Development*, 14 (1), 118–26.

Mlatsheni, Cecil and Murray Leibbrandt (2014), "Unemployment in South Africa," in *The Oxford companion to the economics of South Africa*, H. Bhorat, A. Hirsch, R. Kanbur, and M. Ncube, eds., Oxford, UK: Oxford University Press, 236–43.

Murphy, Jonathan (2008), *The world bank and global managerialism*, Abingdon, UK: Routledge.

Naudé, Wim (Ed.) (2011), *Entrepreneurship and economic development*, Basingstoke, UK: Palgrave Macmillan.

Nega, Berhanu and Geoffrey Schneider (2014), "Social entrepreneurship, microfinance, and economic development in Africa," *Journal of Economic Issues*, 48 (2), 367–76.

Pache, Anne-Claire and Filipe Santos (2010), "When worlds collide: The internal dynamics of organizational responses to conflicting institutional demands," *The Academy of Management Review*, 35 (3), 455–476.

Peredo, Ana María and James J. Chrisman (2006), "Toward a theory of community-based enterprise," *Academy of Management Review*, 31 (2), 309–28.

Peredo, Ana María and Murdith McLean (2006), "Social entrepreneurship: A critical review of the concept," *Journal of World Business*, 41 (1), 56–65.

Porter, Michael E. and Mark R. Kramer (2011), "Creating shared value: How to reinvent capitalism – and unleash a wave of innovation and growth," *Harvard Business Review*, 89 (1–2), 62–77.

Prahalad, C. K. (2004), *The fortune at the bottom of the pyramid: Eradicating poverty through profits. Enabling dignity and choice through markets.*, Upper Saddle River, NJ: Wharton School Publishing.

Rogerson, Christian M. (2004), "The impact of the South African government's SMME programmes: a ten-year review (1994–2003)," *Development Southern Africa*, 21 (5), 765–84.

Rogerson, Christian M. (2008), "Tracking SMME Development in South Africa: Issues of Finance, Training and the Regulatory Environment," *Urban Forum*, 19 (1), 61–81.

Roundy, Philip T. and Michaël Bonnal (2017), "The singularity of social entrepreneurship: Untangling its uniqueness and market function," *The Journal of Entrepreneurship*, 26 (2), 137–62.

Santos, Filipe M. (2012), "A positive theory of social entrepreneurship," *Journal of Business Ethics*, 111 (3), 335–51.

Santos, Filipe M., Anne-Claire Pache, and Christoph Birkholz (2015), "Making hybrids work: Aligning business models and organizational design for social enterprises," *California Management Review*, 57 (3), 36–58.

Scheyvens, Regina, Glenn Banks, and Emma Hughes (2016), "The private sector and the SDGs: The need to move beyond 'business as usual,'" *Sustainable Development*, 24 (6), 371–82.

Seelos, Christian and Johanna Mair (2005), "Social entrepreneurship: Creating new business models to serve the poor," *Business Horizons*, 48 (3), 241–46.

Seelos, Christian and Johanna Mair (2009), "Hope for sustainable development: How social entrepreneurs make It happen," in *An introduction to social entrepreneurship: Voices, preconditions, contexts*, R. Ziegler, ed., Cheltenham, UK: E, 228–46.

Sengupta, Subhanjan, Arunaditya Sahay, and Francesca Croce (in press), "Conceptualizing social entrepreneurship in the context of emerging economies: An integrative review of past research from BRIICS," *International Entrepreneurship and Management Journal.*

Siya Sebenza (n.d. a), "Siya Sebenza | skills development/entrepreneurial training – port Elizabeth," (accessed February 14, 2018a), [available at https://siya-sebenza.co.za/].

Siya Sebenza (n.d. b), "Impact and media."

Stats SA (2017), "Quarterly labour force survey: Quarter 3: 2017," Pretoria, South Africa: Statistics South Africa.

Steinman, Susan and Jerome van Rooij (2012), "Developing public policies for the social and solidarity economy in South Africa," *Universitas Forum*, 3 (2).

Taylor, James (2013), "Struggles against systems that impoverish: South African civil society at the crossroads," *Development in Practice*, 23 (5–6), 617–30.

Trialogue (2016), *The Trialogue CSI handbook, 19th edition*, Cape Town, South Africa: Trialogue.

Trivedi, Chitvan (2010), "A social entrepreneurship bibliography," *Journal of Entrepreneurship*, 19 (1), 81–85.

United Nations Global Compact (2014), "The role of business and finance in supporting the post-2015 agenda," White paper, United Nations Global Compact.

Urban, Boris (2008), "Social entrepreneurship in South Africa: Delineating the construct with associated skills," *International Journal of Entrepreneurial Behaviour & Research*, 14 (5), 346–64.

Urban, Boris (2013), "Social entrepreneurship in an emerging economy: A focus on the institutional environment and social entrepreneurial self-efficacy," *Managing Global Transitions*, 11 (1), 3–25.

Urban, Boris (2015), "Evaluation of social enterprise outcomes and self-efficacy," *International Journal of Social Economics*, 42 (2), 163–78.

Urban, Boris and Leanne Kujinga (2017a), "Towards social change: South African university students as social entrepreneurs," *South African Journal of Higher Education*, 31 (1), 243–59.

Urban, Boris and Leanne Kujinga (2017b), "The institutional environment and social entrepreneurship intentions," *International Journal of Entrepreneurial Behavior & Research*, 23 (4), 638–55.

Urban, Boris and Heinrich Teise (2015), "Antecedents to social entrepreneurship intentions: An empirical study in South Africa," *Management Dynamics*, 24 (2), 36–52.

Vakil, Anna C. (1997), "Confronting the classification problem: Toward a taxonomy of NGOs," *World Development*, 25 (12), 2057–71.

Visser, Kobus (2011), "Social entrepreneurship in South Africa: Context, relevance and extent," *Industry and Higher Education*, 25 (4), 233–47.

Yin, Robert K. (2009), *Case study research: Design and methods*, London, UK: Sage.

Yunus, Muhammad (2017), *A world of three zeroes: The new economics of zero poverty, zero unemployment, and zero carbon emissions*, London, UK: Scribe Publications.

Zahra, Shaker A., Eric Gedajlovic, Donald O. Neubaum, and Joel M. Shulman (2009), "A typology of social entrepreneurs: Motives, search processes and ethical challenges," *Journal of Business Venturing*, 24 (5), 519–32.

19 Micro and small business clusters and local development policies[1]

Insights from India–Italy cooperation projects

Silvia Grandi

Introduction

As of the late 1990s, the world of international cooperation for development has been influenced by the successful Italian scientific publications on industrial districts and local development, starting with the seminal works of Bagnasco (1977) and Becattini (1987), inspired by Alfred Marshall's work on positive externalities of agglomeration. Soon, this approach was followed by Porter's cluster one (Porter 1990, 1998), and both entered into policymaking. The international diffusion of this territorial approach can be brought back, especially to the United Nations Industrial Development Organization (UNIDO), United Nations Conference for Trade and Development (UNCTAD 1998), Inter-American Development Bank (IADB), and in the World Bank. Lund-Thomsen et al. (2016) noticed that in that period, many articles and policy papers promoted local economic growth through cluster development, often by highlighting the benefits for small and medium-sized enterprises (SMEs) located in industrial districts in developing countries. However, only relatively few papers focus on real cases of industrial districts or clusters in the Global South (Nadvi and Schmitz 1993; Schmitz and Nadvi 1999; Nadvi 1999; Kennedy 1999; Pietrobelli and Olarte 2002; Pietrobelli and Rabellotti 2004; Schmitz 2004; Giuliani et al. 2005), and even fewer ones on organic handicraft clusters composed of cottage industries, tiny industries, and micro enterprises in India.

Therefore, this chapter seeks to illustrate the dynamics of this latter case by analyzing whether and how the industrial district and cluster models can be transposed from one region to another, to reveal the mixed fortunes of international development projects and national policies in India. In particular, this is done by reviewing the theoretical literature and the national and international organization policy documents, as well as using a case study regarding the cluster development program of the Indian government and the technical assistance project, funded by the World Bank, on the conservation and revitalization of leather and textile craft clusters in the Indian state of Rajasthan. In fact, this latter project has been carried out based on a comparative approach and the attempt to create interlinks with the Italian industrial district model and policies.

The content of this chapter draws on qualitative and quantitative primary and secondary data gathered mainly thanks to participation of international cooperation projects between Italy and India. Information has been collected with structured interviews as well as with ethnographic and visual geography approaches (i.e., collecting information with observations, visual analysis, and people's interaction dynamics). The most significant fieldwork has been in Italy and India in the years 2002–2006 after conducting visits and meetings in Roma, Milano, Firenze, Prato, Carpi, New Delhi, and in Rajasthan, including interviews of 12 Italian and 18 Indian public institutions, private–public intermediary bodies, and business organizations relevant for the ecosystem of the development of conservation and revitalization of leather and textile craft clusters in Italy and the Indian state of Rajasthan. Moreover, the study has been carried out with field visits of the two most significant industrial clusters on textile and clothing traditional industries in Italy (Prato and Carpi) and five significant craft clusters of Rajasthan, located in the districts of Dausa, Baran, Tonk, Churu, and Kota, with direct contacts and interviews with the local master craftsmen, local nongovernmental organizations (NGOs) and World Bank's District Poverty Initiatives Project (DPIP) officers. Further ethnographic insights have been collected through a two-day workshop organized to understand the perceived needs of knowledge transfer, to collect inputs with a participatory approach, and to test training dynamics among Italian experts and Indian ones. Moreover, four technical trainings for 125 people (master craftsmen/master craftswomen, designers, craftsman/craftswomen) and a workshop held in Italy's most important fair on ethnic and craft business have provided information about the strengths and weaknesses of the Rajasthan craft clusters and the actual feasibility of creating direct and sustainable export opportunities. Ten years later, a study to monitor and verify the signs of the evolution of Rajasthan's craft cluster policy has been carried out using statistical data, websites, reports, and publications on policy documents.

This chapter is structured as follows. The next section focuses on the review of the literature on industrial districts and clusters, starting from a theoretical point of view and attempting a contextualization with respect to the main geopolitical scenario and in the international organizations' discourses from the 1990s to the 2030 Agenda. The section describes the main features of the Italian archetypes and the role of small businesses in creating local development. Then, the following section relates the industrial districts and clusters to poverty reduction instead of, as is generally done, to innovation and economic competitiveness. In the next section, the chapter provides a brief overview of the Indian micro and small businesses and Rajasthan's traditional craft clusters. This is followed by a framework conceptualizing UNIDO's and the Indian government's approach to cluster development programs. Furthermore, the section also describes in detail the specific case study relating to Rajasthan's traditional craft clusters and the attempt to create linkages with the Italian ones. The concluding section summarizes the outcomes of the study, highlighting that in India, as in Italy, clusters can be significant in promoting jobs, foster local development, and preparing the ground for entrepreneurship empowering practices for participation in global production networks (GPNs), but it is evident that these are long-term perspective policies that need stable and interdisciplinary teams, both locally and in the partner countries, and, last but not least, appropriate funds. Moreover, if international cooperation projects are used to improve the clusters' growth, special attention has to be paid to the weaker and marginalized areas, as their rural traditional clusters might face severe social, economic, and environmental drawbacks if opened too quickly to external exposure; conversely, the action is ineffective and in fact ignored. Finally, there are substantial differences among typologies of industrial clusters and those highly rural ones that are based on micro and small businesses. The comparative analysis between Italy and India confirmed that, despite some similarities and that potential connections can be developed, there is no best model for organizing industrial districts or rural craftsmen clusters. Models cannot be transferred from one country to another without significant adaptation work; that is, models can be just inspirational according to a place-based approach and, thus, political and cultural circumstances.

Literature review: industrial clusters and poverty reduction

Industrial district and cluster models for local development

As of the 1990s, the role of businesses and of the private sector began to be more and more recognized as a determinant in inducing economic prosperity, therefore influencing development and industrial policies in the Global North and, then, in the Global South. It must be recalled that, in those years, the world was facing a significant shift in the international geopolitics scenario and in the international cooperation approaches (Bonaglia and De Luca 2006; Grandi 2013; Bianchi 2014). The consequence of the fall of the Berlin Wall affected economic as well as development studies. It cannot be forgotten, too, that in those years John Williamson proposed the ten recommendations called the Washington Consensus – an influential landmark in global economic policies, including those for the Global South. It was evident in the shift in the mainstream thoughts of the international organizations towards a neoliberal wave with a central role of the trade liberalization, foreign direct investments, and privatization of the state-owned enterprises (Williamson 2004).

In parallel, as mentioned in the introduction, the world of international cooperation for development has been influenced by the successful Italian scientific publications on industrial districts and local development followed by Porter's cluster one. Both entered the policymaking discourses and programs, as the industrial district and/or cluster represented a relatively easy model to understand for decision makers, program managers, and policymakers. In the wake of the neo-liberal wave, a neo-institutional one was rising in response (Amin 1999, 2014), and industrial districts and clusters were able to explain growth, competitiveness, agglomeration patterns, and thus job dynamics in certain areas where no large firms or cities were located. This was done thanks to linkages, efficient local institutions, collective efficiencies, and externalities (Nadvi 1999).

Regarding the Global North countries, the most common case studies referred to are the Silicon Valley and Orange County, and in France some of the most popular archetypes are Grenoble, Montpellier, and Sophia-Antipolis. In Italy, the textile industrial district of Prato has been known worldwide thanks to the seminal work of Becattini and its associated scholars. In particular, the Italian industrial district case studies refer to the local systems located in relatively small towns or cities where a large number of SMEs is concentrated. These SMEs are characterized by their specialization in a precise phase of the production chain and value chain in a specific industrial or craft sector. What makes them different is their capacity to integrate and link together, thanks to Marshallian localization externalities; to agents; to institutions; and to the effect of the local entrepreneurship skills, the relational attitude, and the educational culture (Sforzi and Lorenzini 2002).

This has been a phenomenon that has strongly characterized the Italian economic system and attracted the interest of policymakers around the world, and it still does. The fascination of the Italian case can be summarized into a classical question of how Italy can be so strong economically and in international trade without having significantly large firms. Between the 1990s and the economic crisis of the 2010s, Italy could count more than 200 industrial districts, mainly in traditional sectors such as textile, fashion, leather, small parts, and in furniture industries (IPI 2002). Both at the beginning and in the more mature phases of internationalization, the key points of success have been rooted in the SMEs' capacity to create and work in cluster ecosystems, a model that represents an example of economic growth without large firms.

Joining a cluster can help SMEs reduce the transaction costs; it creates positive externalities (Krugman 1991) and provides easier to access specialized suppliers, skilled workforces, logistics firms (Marshall 1947), local support agencies, training institutes, relevant consultants, associations, and public–private partnership processes (Becattini 1987; Becattini 1991; Becattini 1998; Lund-Thomsen et al. 2016), as well as financial support by local banks and attention by policymakers (Guigou 2001; Grandi 2007). Their proximity with other SMEs, operating in the same or related industries, would also facilitate knowledge exchange and learning (Boekema et al. 2000). All this can create the competitive advantage of a place (Porter 1990). Thus, cluster-based SMEs might address local competitions and globalization challenges and opportunities more effectively than individual SMEs, both in the Global North and Global South regions (Schmitz and Nadvi 1999).

Moreover, geography scholars highlight that successful industrial districts and clusters are rooted in pre-conditions (i.e., social, cultural, infrastructural, institutional ones, etc.) that could have been found in the region; specialized agglomerations of firms are getting different shapes and peculiarities, according to factors explained by the local development and territorial systems approach (Vallega 1995; Dematteis and Governa 2005; Bignante et al. 2008; Dansero et al. 2008; Bini 2016; Grandi 2017).

Small businesses, clusters, and poverty reduction in global policies

During the same period that industrial districts and clusters gained popularity in development discourse, the term *pro-poor* growth became popular as economists in the main international financial institutions, such as the World Bank, acknowledged that accelerating poverty reduction required both more rapid growth and lower inequality. This consequently led to policy recommendations and actions that sought to accelerate growth in the incomes of poor people and thus reduce overall poverty levels. In this perspective, a successful pro-poor growth strategy would thus need to have, at its core, measures for sustained and rapid economic growth; that is, macroeconomic stability, well-defined property rights, trade openness, a good investment climate, an attractive incentive framework, well-functioning factor markets, and broad access to infrastructure and education (Besley and Cord 2007).

Poverty reduction has been a very central discourse in international development cooperation policies as of the 1990s.[2] Moreover, as of the 2000s, poverty reduction has been moved to poverty eradication and has been the central theme in the Millennium Development Goals (MDGs)[3]. In 1990, nearly half of the population in the developing world lived on less than $1.25 a day; however, according to the UN (2015), that proportion dropped to 14 percent in 2015. Notwithstanding the fact that this is a global number, but going deeper in the analysis, one can find inequalities and significant differences among regions. Therefore, the UN general Assembly Resolution: "Transforming our World: the 2030 Agenda for sustainable development"[4] and the following Sustainable Development Goals (SDGs) recognize as first point that "eradicating poverty in all its forms and dimensions, including extreme poverty, is the greatest global challenge and an indispensable requirement for sustainable development."

Although one cannot find substantial changes in the significance of poverty in global development policies, two things seem to be significantly evolved and questioned in the late years: the meaning of development, and the role of for-profit business in international cooperation. Without going into details on the complex and elusive definition of development or into the discussion on development versus growth that can be read – among others – in Hettne (2009), Hirst (2014), Grandi (2013), and Ianni (2017), it has to be recalled that development has different meanings according to historical situation and it varies according to regions, political ideologies, and societal values (Hettne 2009: Grandi 2013). In the institutional framework, referring to the 2030 Agenda, development is the result of the challenging convergence of human rights principles, sustainable development, human development, and economic growth based on neo-liberalism and technological paradigms. In this global compromise, the private sector is recognized as more and more important in tackling poverty reduction. After both the 2030 Agenda and the Addis Ababa Action Agenda were signed in 2015, the OECD 2016 annual report for international cooperation highlighted that the significant results in poverty reduction and in strong economic growth at the macroeconomic level observed in some Asian countries are related to policies based on the belief in the market and in the private sector. The increase in cooperation between the public and the private business sector has been recognized as vital to contribute to the solution of the pressing economic, social, and environmental challenges in the Global South. The Organisation for Economic Co-operation and Development (OECD) (2016) states that, in developing countries, SMEs are considered the engine of growth, as in Asia, they represent up to 98 percent of all enterprises and employ 66 percent of the workforce.

In summary, the global policy framework identifies business as a major player in global development, and this is influencing influences policy making worldwide. For instance, the reform of the Italian international cooperation for sustainable development, human rights, and peace is significantly open to private for-profit sector, stating that "profit organizations, when acting in compliance with the principles laid down in this Law,[5] meeting the standards commonly applied to social responsibility and environmental safeguard clauses, and comply with human rights legislation in making international investments" can be counted among the actors of the development cooperation system.

Clusters and poverty reduction in the Global South

According to Nadvi and Barrientos (2004), there is an implicit assumption that clusters are beneficial for poverty reduction, as economic growth translates into rising levels of employment and incomes, with improving conditions and standards for workers. This assumption generally follows the fact that SMEs account for a significant proportion of formal and informal employment in developing countries. Therefore, if an explicit consideration of poverty is related to cluster development strategies, Nadvi and Barrientos argue that clusters can contribute to poverty reduction, as they can generate jobs and promote incomes for the poor, as well as create dynamics useful to help entrepreneurs mobilize limited resources, reaching wider markets by providing venues for collective actions. Moreover, clusters can enhance the well-being of poor communities, training, and a wider social identity that might result in broader developmental goals.

In the Global South, the most common case studies referred to are in Asia and Latin America. For instance, the Sialkot surgical instrument cluster in Pakistan, where the workers, although skilled, are largely illiterate and poor (Nadvi 1999); the Jalandhar sport goods manufacturing cluster in the Indian Punjab, where child labor is a significant phenomenon (Lund-Thomsen and Nadvi 2010) and those in India in other traditional sectors that will be further described in the following section and where UNIDO focused significant international cooperation technical assistance; the Sinos Valley in Brazil (Schmitz 1999); the Guadalajara and Leon footwear clusters in Mexico (Rabellotti 1997); and others in the traditional sector, such as garments in South America (Pietrobelli and Olarte 2002; Pietrobelli and Rabellotti 2004; Schmitz 2004; Giuliani et al. 2005).

With a focus on policies and knowledge transfer between Global North and Global South, it is relevant to highlight that a comparison of industrial district and cluster dynamics in developing countries can be grouped into at least two different main typologies:

1   Those that tend to be more formal and with structured SMEs along an industrial value chain (generally located close to urban areas).
2   Those that tend to involve micro enterprises, small-scale industries, tiny, and cottage industries that are grounded on traditional craft knowledge and often with informal and homeworking.

Both collective efficiencies and externalities of agglomeration are grounded on sectoral and localized specialization; however, the nature of workers involved, the external linkages that can help the access to distant markets or acquire new forms of knowledge, and upgradation can be significantly different. In particular, in the case (2) traditional knowledge, despite appearing linked to poverty, it is also a value in itself, as it is the expression of a local heritage that provides a distinctiveness and uniqueness of products and market patterns. Policies and projects have to carefully take this in consideration when technologies, training, and new working procedures are proposed.

The following case study, described in the third and fourth, on Indian clusters and the potential cross-fertilization and collaboration with the Italian ones, is particularly significant in this perspective. The main research questions that have been tackled are: How did Indian cluster policies evolve over time? Was international influence important? When do international cooperation projects create cluster-to-cluster self-sustainability? What are the weaknesses and the strengths of international cooperation activities in this field?

The evolution of small business clusters in practice: the case of India

A brief overview of Rajasthan and its handicraft clusters

With a population mostly located in rural areas of about 54 million in the year 2000 and 69 million in 2011, Rajasthan's economy is mainly agriculture based, despite parts of the state being extremely dry and covered by the Thar Desert. Rajasthan's territory forms a corridor between the northern and the western states in India and traditionally implies a favorable localization to access a larger market. In particular, Jaipur, the state capital, is located in the Delhi–Mumbai industrial corridor, one of the main industrialized and connected areas in India.

In the last 20 years, Rajasthan has made significant progress in the infrastructure sector on all fronts – power, roads, telecommunication, information technology, and water supply, among others – despite still being in the 2000s. The distribution of Internet connectionc, paved roads, water supply, wastewater system, and electrical power was concentrated in larger urban areas, whereas in rural ones these facilities were still scattered and unstable. Tourism is also an important part of the economy, as Rajasthan is traditionally known for its rich cultural heritage and a fine handicraft tradition.

The main industries are based on textiles and leather, as well as the manufacture of rugs and woolen goods, vegetable oils, and dyes. Other relevant industries are the heavy industry and the chemical industry, mainly concentrated in the urban areas. The main industrial complexes are at Jaipur, Kota, Udaipur, and Bhilwara. However, Rajasthan's official statistical data highlight that only a minor percentage of people are dedicated to industrial activities or small and medium-sized structured companies (less than 5 percent in 2011). The vast majority are working in rural-related activities, either farming or nonfarming ones, or in other informal sectors. Among these, handicraft small-scale industry, tiny, and cottage industries are particularly significant, as they provide the main sources of occupation in Indian villages. These activities are based on a historical, long tradition; they present significant characters of local identity, clustering, and sectoral specialization. These types of small businesses are usually carried out at home or in small craft workshops led by the master craftsmen and involving a limited number of workers that are members of the family who have inherited their work as an art form from their ancestors living in Indian villages. The goods produced include dress fabric–based products such as khadi, wool, leather, silk, cotton-woven and decorated items (embroideries, laces, tie and dye, block printing, etc.), carpets, jewelry, ornaments, and stone decorations that have both a domestic and an international market.

In terms of policy, these types of small-scale industries have been neglected in favor of an industrial policy related to attracting larger and more industrial-based firms. However, the handicraft sector is crucial for Rajasthan's economy and social structure, as it can provide a significant contribution in improving livelihoods by providing employment to at least 600,000 to 700,000 people according to World Bank estimates. Thanks to a significant uniqueness in traditional design, Rajasthan's craftworks have potential, coupled with tourism, and in export flows when quality thresholds are reached.

Fieldwork confirmed that these types of small-scale industries are generally unorganized and based on traditional and self-employed arrangements; therefore, they can present significant weaknesses in term of marketing and trade opportunities other than local markets. In fact, when analyzing the value chain structures of Rajasthan clusters in the field, the Nadvi observation related to the Knitwear Cluster of Tiruppur (Nadvi 1995) has been found in Rajasthan too: next to manufacturers, merchants follow. They are generally focused on exports and can dominate either informally or formally by controlling enterprises and product prices, leaving the master craftsmen limited to undertaking subcontracting tasks or selling to the domestic market (Nadvi 1995). Therefore, in the last 20 years, some private–public initiatives and organizations, also thanks to governmental support programs and policies (discussed next), have significantly focused on cluster and master craftsmen creating trading opportunities and creating collective stores, fairs, training programs, and export support services.

Although the exports data related to Rajasthan's artisanal clusters are not easy to catch, as the definition of cluster is not fully structured to this purpose, the overall India data showed (see Figure 19.1) that the exports of handicrafts (other than hand-knotted carpets) rose from 8,490 crores in 2000–2001 to the level of 14,527 crores in 2005–2006, then reducing the effect and restarting to grow and reaching a peak of 24395 crores in 2016–2017 (Export Promotion Council for Handicrafts 2018). Moreover, it is estimated that in terms of value, the micro and SMEs sector accounts for about 45 percent of the manufacturing output and around 40 percent of the total exports of the Indian country and thus they play an important role in export promotion of the country (MSME 2018).

The Indian cluster and international cooperation influences

Becattini's industrial cluster and the later local development approach found a place in the policy programs in India, and it was very influential in Indian national and regional institutions between 1995 and 2010 (Becattini et al. 2009; UNIDO 2010). In 1996, an initiative called the "Cluster Development Program" (CDP) was launched per a request by the Indian government to UNIDO. The guiding principle of UNIDO's approach towards SMEs is that these enterprises can play a key role in triggering and sustaining economic growth and equitable development in developing countries (Ceglie and Dini 1999), and the term "cluster" is used to indicate a sectoral and geographical concentration of enterprises that produce and sell a range of related or complementary products and are thus faced with common challenges and opportunities. According to the theory mentioned in an earlier section, the UNIDO model (see Figure 19.2) highlights that performing clusters are concentrations giving rise to external

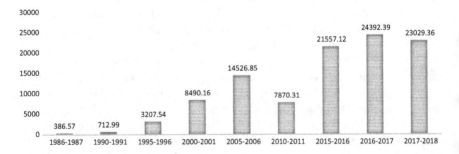

Figure 19.1 Export of handicrafts in India (in crores)

Source: Export Promotion Council for Handicrafts 2018

economies, such as the emergence of specialized suppliers of raw materials and components or the growth of a pool of sector-specific skills, and favor the emergence of specialized services in technical, administrative, and financial matters. Moreover, clusters are also a conducive ground for the development of a network of public and private local institutions which support local economic development by promoting collective learning and innovation through implicit and explicit coordination. The concept of "networking" refers to the overall action of establishing the relationships characterizing both networks and clusters. Thus, in UNIDO's approach, networking development services indicate the services aimed at promoting the development of clusters and networks (*ibid.*) within a specific region and across regions nationally or internationally along value chains.

Indian government and UNIDO studies have identified the existence of about 350 small business clusters and about 2,000 rural and craftsmen clusters, places with a marked specialization often deriving from a strong historical tradition sedimented over centuries, recalling the path dependency theories. In particular, the most frequent were the artisan/crafts types: weaving, fabric processing (tie-dye, block printing), leather, shoe manufacturing, woodworking, etc. (Russo 1999).

Compared to the other regions of the world, the Indian local economic systems showed significant similarities with the Italian case: tendency of specialization, local economy based on small businesses, significant historical tradition rooted in the "cluster"-like place, high value added, and knowledge embedded in the community transferred by a learning-by-doing approach, service-like organizations/small businesses that integrate the value chain and connect to the markets, family-based culture, etc. (IPI 2005).

However, the UNIDO analysis tends to use the cluster and industrial district approach with a normative and a managerial point of view. From this perspective, in the UNIDO technical paper by Wiesert et al. (2013), potential clusters are categorized in underperforming and performing ones according to an organizational model described in Figure 19.1 and identify a methodology to intervene in order to create an improved performance, thus a pro–poor growth (Figure 19.2). The actions proposed by UNIDO are quite standard worldwide: act to foster linkages, facilitate the consensus building in the region, build trust and social capital, and strengthen governance mechanisms. This would reduce isolation of SMEs that are identified as the main barrier for growth (*ibid.*). Such a standardized approach can be misleading, however – it builds up significantly from the Italian and Indian experiences as well as the Latin American ones, each showing specificities to be considered.

The CDP program, initially supported with funds for international cooperation from the Italian Ministry of Foreign Affairs and the Swiss Agency for Development and Cooperation, focused in the early years on some pilot projects located in Tirupur (cotton weaving), Pune (food processing), Jaipur (textile molding), and Ludhiana (knitwear), and in the following years, attention to small businesses led to the establishment of a dedicated ministry that has continued to

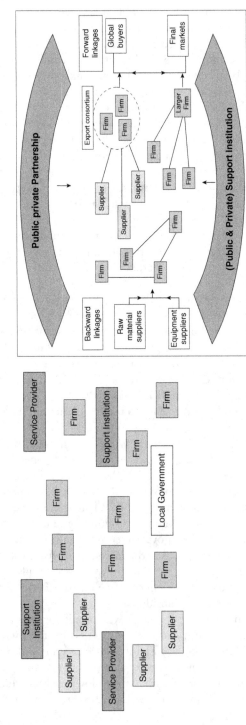

Figure 19.2 UNIDO model of an underperforming and a performing cluster

Source: Weisert et al. 2013

follow the extended program on other production districts, both of a craft and of a more industrial type, such as, Ambur (leather), Bangalore (machinery), and Ahmedabad (pharmaceuticals). The UNIDO program focused essentially on technical assistance aimed at promoting "trust and governance as well as institutional capacity building activities" on the assumption that an external agent (see Figure 19.3) could be a catalytic factor to facilitate the strengthening of these clusters regarding their ability to network with companies and institutions and to develop policies in this regard (Russo 1999; UNIDO 2010).

Applying at first the UNIDO perspective to the Indian case and then using follow-up assessments held in the late 2000s and 2010s, the government of India based the CDP on the combination of the following main elements:

- The driving role of small businesses.
- The valorization of local tradition and social capital in creating external economies.
- The positive role of exports for economic growth.
- The power of networks and value chain for their ability to reduce transaction costs
- The desired and expected result for a possible change in a more globalized district model.

As often happens in practice in international cooperation for development, experts and program managers have tried to use models already created and adopted in some regions and reapply them in other parts of the world. In this case, the inspiration was provided by the experience in Brazil, Mexico, and Chile. Moreover, the approach was affected by the discourse of the cited Becattini and Porter works. In the implementation in India, the Italian history of the Prato industrial district archetype has been evident, as well as inspiring for some further projects. For example, the focus on strengthening or creating common technical assistance and training centers, the development of export consortia, and collective participation in fairs appears in UNIDO's technical papers (Weisert et al. 2013) and implementation project activities of the World Bank (see the following section). A good deal of attention has been paid to the local dimension of firms in trying not to force them towards trajectories of exogenous technological acquisition, premature exposure to international markets, or construction of structures detached from the culture of the Indian entrepreneurial and institutional class. In fact, compared to other areas of the world, in India, there are many preconditions suitable for productive development by district/cluster models, however imperfect they may be.

These elements also emerged through another pro-poor project included in the Poverty Reduction program: the "District Poverty Initiatives Project" of the World Bank and the Department of Rural Development of the government of Rajasthan. The general objective of this program was to improve the living conditions of the craftsmen in a sustainable manner by acting on the creation of about 700 *Common Interest Groups* (CIGs) identified, theoretically, in the rural micro clusters of the traditional craftsmanship of this Indian state. The methodology was focused on strengthening the creation of CIGs through empowerment actions by networking women and people below the poverty line and encouraging them through a set of actions: meetings led by external agents (representatives of the World Bank or local development agencies) to develop a participatory decision system within the CIGs, activate basic training schemes, promote networking among CIGs and external organizations, and provide financial resources for small investments related to demand and appropriate technology.

A very interesting evolution in the following years is the decision to include the "Integrated Infrastructural Development (IID)" scheme of the Indian government has in the CDP. This aimed at providing developed sites for new enterprises and upgrading existing industrial infrastructure. Moreover, guidelines for CDP were issued after identifying the following interventions (MSME 2010):

1   Diagnostic study reports (DSR): to map the business processes in the cluster and propose remedial measures with a validated action plan.
2   Soft interventions (SI): technical assistance, capacity building, exposure visits, market development, trust building, etc., for the cluster units.
3   Detailed project report: to prepare a technically feasible and financially viable project report for setting up a common facility center for clustering small business units and/or an infrastructure development project for a new industrial estate area or for upgrading infrastructure in existing industrial ones.
4   Hard intervention and Common Facility Centers (CFC): to create tangible "assets" like a testing facility, design center, production center, effluent treatment plant, training center, research and development center, raw material bank/sales depot, product display center, information center, and any other need-based facility.
5   Infrastructure development (ID): for land development, the provision of water supply, drainage, power distribution, nonconventional sources of energy for common captive use, construction of roads, common facilities such as a first aid center, canteen, and other need-based infrastructural facilities in new industrial (multiproduct) areas/estates or existing industrial areas/estates/clusters.

The Indian Ministry for Small and Medium Enterprises stated in 2016 (MSME) that the micro, small and medium enterprise sector "remains a key driving force for India's complete transition from an agrarian economy to an industrialized one [...] A number of clusters are so large, that they account for nearly 80 per cent of production of a selected product within the country", started a financing scheme too that in the four years 2012–2015 led to supporting more than a thousand interventions and a spending of about 24 million euro (Figure 19.4). According to the MSME (*Ibid*) in those clusters where the interventions were completed, an increase in business turnover and job creation has been observed.

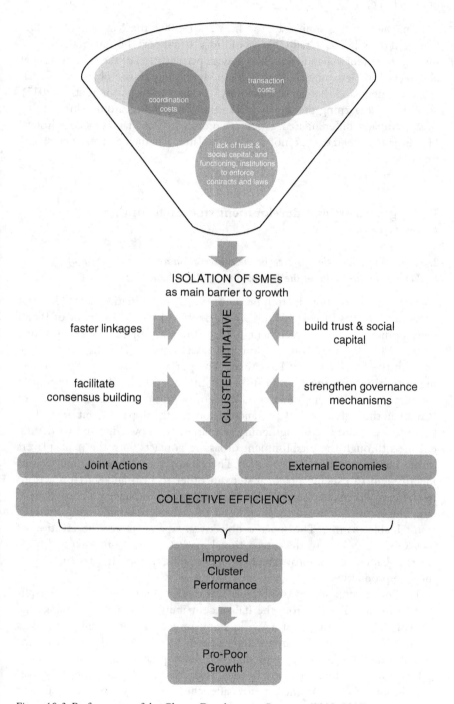

Figure 19.3 Performance of the Cluster Development Program (2012–2015)

Source; **MSME 2016**

In parallel, with a similar approach in 2001–2002, the Ministry of Textiles launched the scheme "Craft Clusters of India" to support the "integrated development of potential handicraft clusters with participation of the craft persons at all stages of implementation of the scheme with the ultimate objective of their empowerment and, hence, sustainability" (Indian Ministry of Textiles 2017). This shows a learning process in Indian policymaking regarding clusters; that is, substantially differentiated action according to the main type of clusters: However, published data do not reveal if the latter scheme has been successfully implemented.

Linking business and development studies: from theory to practice

International cooperation project for the conservation and revitalization of leather and textile crafts in the Indian state of Rajasthan

As part of the poverty reduction program, within the initiative called "District Poverty Initiatives Project" of the World Bank and the Department of Rural Development of the Government of Rajasthan, a project was also planned in the 2000s for the "conservation and revitalization of leather and textile crafts in the Indian state of Rajasthan." The purpose, chosen by the promoting institutions, was the identification and implementation of concrete actions aimed at improving the living conditions of groups of artisans in the state of Rajasthan through technical assistance actions for the improvement of production processes and the strengthening of marketing knowledge and marketing channels through the establishment of lasting contacts with the main players in the Italian craft and SMEs system. The objective of this assignment was to identify and to execute practical steps in order to plan and start-up actions to preserve, "revitalize," and "valorize" handicraft products and thus achieve tangible improvements in the livelihood of craftsmen, empowering them in a sustainable manner. The specific objectives expected were the creation of new CIGs; exposure to the international market; reducing the steps of trade intermediation; and improvement of design skills, quality, and technology to increase productivity.

The implementation of this project was carried out thanks to aid for technical assistance deriving from the Italian contribution to the World Bank. The working group consisted of a World Bank project manager and a group of Italian experts coordinated by the Italian agency for SMEs – IPI – in cooperation and the local micro-entrepreneurship development agency of rural areas (RUDA) that should have been the local agent that would implement the project locally and carry on the activities after the external intervention was over. This technical assistance project was based on an adapted local development approach linking the Italian model to the Rajasthan one. The implicit and explicit assumptions of the World Bank were based on the belief that Rajasthan had a high potential in handicraft development thanks to existing preconditions:

1   Existence of specialized micro and small businesses and localized in traditional villages that showed at least some industrial district/cluster dynamics.
2   Large variety of craft products with unique and highly worldwide potentially appreciated design, good manufacturing quality, etc.

Moreover, acting on these local systems, empowering intermediary institutions (i.e., local development agency, training, and master craftsmen) the assumption was that this would enhance knowledge, production capacity, product quality, and thus, thanks to better networking and trade, would raise the CIGs' income and thereby reduce poverty.

The attention has been on textiles and leather and traditional footwear (*mojaries*) sectors in pre-identified clusters in the state of Rajasthan, especially those close to tourist sites, namely, Dausa, Baran, Tonk, Churu, and Kota. The activities were grouped into three main parts (Figures 19.5 and 19.6):

1   First, an inceptive one aimed at territorial analysis of CIGs that were assimilated to potential industrial district-like systems as the first hypothesis. This assumption had to be verified and analyzed to understand specificities, with the aim of ensuring sustainability of the external action; that is, minimizing adverse social and environmental effects of potential externally induced fast economic growth.
2   Second, a detailed value chain analysis of the handicraft productions in the textile and leather sectors was carried out to understand institutions, as well as existing internal and external linkages and capacities. Meetings, interviews, and interactions with stakeholders and facilitators (vocational schools, RUDA, local trade and business services, etc.) and with local policymakers completed this part. This first phase paved the way to understand the potential for stronger and longer-term actions and partnerships; that is, sustainability of the project when experts and aids would not be there anymore.
3   Third, the attention moved to more business-centered activities and approaches focusing on product development and production processes, concerning aspects such as capacity building and training in design, new product ideas, product packaging (especially for handicraft products sold in the tourist markets), product quality (improving characteristics such as durability, comfort, care for details that the foreign or Indian consumer appreciates most), and, when necessary, technological upgradation of machineries and materials (by adopting "appropriate technologies" in a technological framework of sustainable development).
4   The final part of the project has been on business and marketing variables, with the aim of developing better market channels with the selection or the reduction of intermediaries' chains through the identification of more

Physical progress (cumulative up to January 31, 2016)		
	Completed	Ongoing
Diagnostic study (DSR)	408	156
Soft interventions (SI)	235	106
Common Facility Centers (CFC)	34	70
Infrastructure Projects (ID)	126	52

Financial progress (sanctioned amounts up to January 31, 2016)		
	Amount	
2012–2013	2343.92	in Lakh Rs.
2013–2014	4140.82	in Lakh Rs.
2014–2015	6317.82	in Lakh Rs.
2015–-2016 (up to Jan. 2016)	5927.28	in Lakh Rs.

Distribution and status of the physical progress in Indian states (cumulative up to January 31, 2016)

	Ongoing					Completed					Grand total
	DSR	SI	CFC	ID	total	DSR	SI	CFC	ID	total	
Andhra Pradesh	9	2	1	1	13	3	8	1	4	16	29
Arunachal Pradesh	2	1	0	1	4	2	1	0	0	3	7
Assam	7	3	0	6	16	15	10	1	9	35	51
Bihar	2	11	0	0	13	25	8	1	0	34	47
Chattisgarh	0	0	0	1	1	1	2	0	4	7	8
Delhi/UT	0	1	0	0	1	3	2	0	0	5	6
Gujarat	1	0	2	0	3	4	3	1	2	10	13
Goa	1	0	0	0	1	2	2	1	0	5	6
Haryana	9	0	6	8	23	19	4	0	21	44	67
Himachal Pradesh	3	1	0	0	4	2	2	0	1	5	9
Jharkhand	10	0	0	0	10	5	3	0	0	8	18
Jammu & Kashmir	3	3	0	3	9	4	0	1	3	8	17
Karnataka	42	9	4	0	55	24	7	3	4	38	93
Kerala	0	1	7	0	8	7	27	8	8	50	58
Maharashatra	0	15	13	1	29	29	19	2	4	54	83
Madhya Pradesh	6	1	0	4	11	7	4	0	7	18	29
Manipur	4	6	0	6	16	4	3	0	0	7	23
Meghalaya	3	1	0	0	4	4	2	0	0	6	10
Mizoram	2	0	0	0	2	5	3	0	2	10	12
Nagaland	3	5	0	0	8	9	2	0	1	12	20
Odisha	8	4	2	0	14	26	6	1	3	36	50
Punjab	14	3	1	1	19	14	14	0	2	30	49
Rajasthan	8	6	1	6	21	11	11	0	9	31	52
Sikkim	0	0	0	0	0	1	1	0	0	2	2
Tamilnadu	0	5	22	4	31	28	5	10	27	70	101
Telangana	5	1	0	3	9	8	7	0	0	15	24
Tripura	2	1	0	3	6	4	1	0	0	5	11
Uttar Pradesh	18	7	2	3	30	104	40	2	8	154	184
Uttarakhand	0	0	0	0	0	2	2	0	3	7	7
West Bengal	3	19	9	1	32	36	36	2	4	78	110
	165	106	70	52	393	408	235	34	126	803	1196

Figure 19.4 Performance of the Cluster Development Program (2012–2015) and operational activities of the conservation and revitalization of leather and textile crafts in the Indian state of Rajasthan project

Source: **MSME 2016**

effective distribution organization and strategies, as well as to explore new markets locally, regionally, and internationally. The actions were aimed at understanding the possible promotion strategies and acquiring new customers, both in India and/or in foreign markets, through implementing promotional campaigns, based, for example, on the cultural value included in artisan manufactures.

The background thought was that industrial development at the local level should ensure that the cultural dimension becomes a high-priority component to concretely improve the livelihood of the craftsmen and their communities. In particular, the valorization of cultural characteristics is essential because a marketing strategy "embedded" into the final products' unique and unrivalled characteristics make a single good recognizable within a number of international markets (increasing the "added value") and the factor of social cohesion within the cluster and the territorial context realize the production (promoting community cooperation and engagement for better living conditions and spreading achievement in welfare improvements). As reported in the second section, the social and economic promotion of local communities, cultural homogeneity, and historical traditions have to be considered as key factors in cluster dynamics because they can guide the local production towards a strong and sustainable development. For example, many Italian districts can rely on a strong cultural tradition in specific sectors such as textile, ceramics, wood, etc.

The Italian industrial district reconceptualization for the Rajasthan craft clusters

According to IPI (2005) and UNIDO (Russo 1999), the Rajasthan productive system showed several similarities with reference to the Italian economic system based on a high percentage of micro and SMEs in the productive environment, with the existence of the so-called "informal sector" (especially for handicrafts). These behaviors have been conceptualized in industrial districts and local economic systems. Traditionally, most of the Italian SMEs have been specialized in the traditional sectors of the worldwide promoted "Made in Italy" brand (textile and fashion, furniture, leather and shoes, food, ceramics, stoneware, etc.) with technological assets of medium–low complexity, but often with high creativity, traditional culture, and handicraft content. The large number of SMEs and craftsmen has triggered the spontaneous establishment of several enterprise associations locally founded and nationally confederated.[6] A large number of SMEs operating in the field of machinery production play a strong role in Italian exports, especially those used in the traditional sectors, such as Italian machinery for the textile and leather industries, food production and packaging, and ceramic plants which are renowned worldwide for their technology, reliability, and capacity for customization. Furthermore, the small dimensions of the Italian enterprises, and their consequently limited capacity to invest in research and development, has forced both the private and public institutions to provide access to a rich and extended network of technical centers focused on innovation and technology transfer to SMEs.

In the framework of the Italian industrial districts the specialized international fairs are relevant and, when relating more to the crafts than industry, are important to avoid overlooking the role of cultural institutions promoting applied arts and crafts, such as specialized museums and performing arts, that is, the creative cluster approach (Callegati and Grandi 2005). In fact, the handicraft sector in Italy has a long historical tradition, and it is effectively developed in all regions of the country with specialization at local levels (clusters). In this perspective, advances in marketing strategies consist in revitalizing the central role of the cultural and traditional content of the production, creating a mutually beneficial relationship between the territory and their craft production. Thus, after a period of crisis, Italian handicraft is again assuming a relevant role, especially coupled with increasing tourism.

The local development approach taken as a hypothesis and invariant between Italian and Indian clusters is depicted in Figure 19.6: product development and production processes (including design, product quality control practices, packaging, etc.) and promotion and distribution functions are facilitated and carried out by the firms themselves but with the support of local system institutional capacities and capabilities. These can be reinforced with empowerment

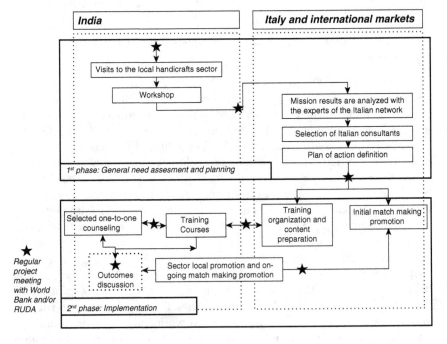

Figure 19.5 Operational activities of the project

Source: IPI 2005

activities providing new knowledge and ideas, but sustainability is thought of as a process coming from the inside, thus triggering durable initiatives that are locally promoted, as the train-the-trainer approach was considered appropriate to the case. Associations of machinery producers, cultural institutions, associations of craftsmen and SMEs, fair and exhibition organizations, and training and technical centers completed the common determinants to apply these cluster-to-cluster policy interventions between Italy and India. This territorial preliminary model was used as a reference to create the project team and the organizational chart (Figure 19.7).

The Italian organizations involved from the start in the supply of expertise and networking opportunities in the creation of the Italian–Indian relationship system in the craft sectors were Acimit – Italian Manufacturers' Association of Machinery for Textile Industry; Assomac – Italian Association of Leather Machine Builders' Association; APIs – Small and Medium-sized Industries

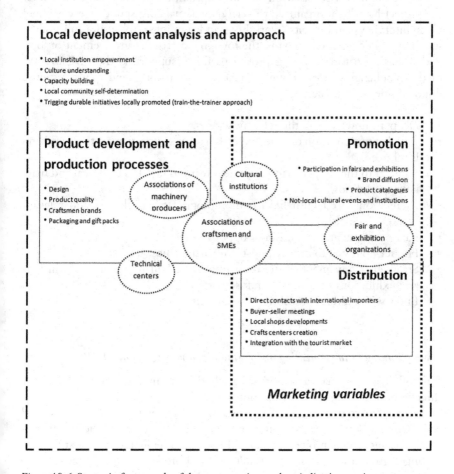

Figure 19.6 Strategic framework of the conservation and revitalization project

Association of the Province of Varese, Varese; CNA – National Confederation of Crafts and Small and Medium Enterprises, Treviso, Treviso; Confartigianato – Prato Office; Tecnotessile Srl – National Society of Technological Research of Prato; Pisie – International Polytechnic for Industrial and Economic Development of Florence; Citer – Textile Information Center Emilia-Romagna of Carpi; Polimoda, Polytechnic International for fashion of Florence; MACEF – International Home Show of Milan; Firenze Fiera; and the Museum of Textile of Prato. The Indian interface has been those of the Rajasthan RUDA and the World Bank officers that mediated the identification of Rajasthan's institutions, associations, training and technical centers, and selections of local experts and master craftsmen.

One of the first points is to find Indian–Italian correspondences and to acknowledge that these types of organizations might act in Italy in different ways when carrying out tasks, and they might have different powers compared to the Rajasthan case. Based on this assumption, the operational activities of the project have been organized to verify the actual correspondence with field visits, interviews, and events (workshops and trainings). To ensure full understanding and deployment, next to the foreign experts, the involvement of local people has been foreseen. This proved useful in supporting the revitalization of the handicraft sector's thought, creating peer-to-peer and quick-response opportunities to provide:

- Deeper knowledge in the relevant sectors.
- Quicker mobilization of other experts in these sectors to react to Rajasthan's local needs.
- Support to the Italy–Rajasthan project team to develop technical and marketing solutions.
- Facilitation to establish links to homologue Italian clusters and relevant market channels.
- Large dissemination of business opportunities.
- Higher potential to create long-term partnerships.
- Stronger involvement of the most important Italian organizations in fairs and exhibitions of the handicraft sector.
- Links with cultural promotion institutions.

From planning to implementing and evaluating: a managing model

First of all, a dilemma was posed as to whether to intervene in these realities directly, both for linguistic reasons but, above all, to avoid an excess of exposure to an exogenous model instead of focusing on generating endogenous local diffusion mechanisms. These considerations were reinforced by the fact that in some villages visited, projects had already been implemented, and next to generating a growth in commercial results of local production, problems of alcoholism and new social hardships had arisen. Moreover, after the first inceptive fieldwork, it was clear that the reference framework of the rural areas was not similar to the current Italian one, but rather to the pre-industrial Italian cluster one where the activity was organized around the skills of master craftsmen, with an excellent ability based on traditional knowledge handed down over generations, supported by both family members and sometimes by other workers. Given this context, contrary to the expectations of the donor of a strong collaboration among firms to strengthen trade, as a first step it was hypothesized to create a twinning process for the conservation of Italian craftsmanship that is dispersing due to the lack of generational turnover and labor cost dynamics.

In addition, a soft action was then chosen in line with the local development approach focusing on a train-the-trainer approach. The main output of the project was to train trainers, called for the occasion a "mobile master trainer." The people identified were both (1) Rajasthan's young people with an interest in working in the development of rural areas in the area and graduates of schools of specialization in the fields of textiles, leather processing, and design and (2) some master craftsmen, selected by the local development agency. This resulted in a relatively easy task, as vocational education institutions are quite present and due to that fact that the importance of schooling is particularly felt in India. The number of participants to the four technical trainings was 125 people (master craftsmen/master craftswomen, designers, craftsmen/craftswomen), distributed mainly in the textile and technology industries, as shown in Figure 19.8a, and the level of satisfaction that resulted was very high according to the feedback forms collected (Figure 19.8b).

The "mobile master trainers" would then report to the villages, appropriately adapted to the context, the information drawn from the seminars carried out by Italian experts, "epidemically" spreading new indications and acting as catalysts for CIGs. In particular, there were three training modules: one centered on technological improvement in weaving methods that saw the participation of 80 mobile master trainers; another one was centered on the creation and improvement of shoe models; and the third one was on international design elements. By forming groups of approximately 20 people for each course, each of these groups potentially generated an epidemic effect of knowledge estimated to be around 1,000 units. However, it turned out that mixing young and master craftsmen created inhomogeneity that was difficult to tackle in the beginning by the Italian trainers. In addition, the actual follow-up of the epidemic knowledge transfer activities has not been performed successfully to confirm the initial estimation, as the project duration was too short.

Another important activity performed to satisfy the request and the ambition to strengthen the export of the products of these clusters was the test of the potential of product marketability and product features according to international market demand. Therefore, a large sample of artefacts was collected and was evaluated by Italian importers in the context of some ethnic craft fairs (mainly the Macef one in Milan). A suitable place to focus the ambitions of exports of the project, as well as a twinning, was created with the Museum of Prato fabric. Technological purchases were not suggested, as they were not strictly necessary and not mature in

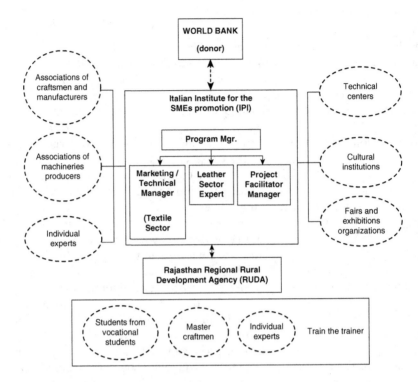

Figure 19.7 Project team organisation

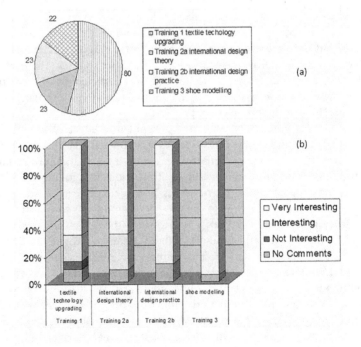

Figure 19.8 Participation in the technical trainings (a) and satisfaction feedbacks (b)

this phase of the project. Creating a sample desk, presenting questionnaires to buyers, and offering a presentation workshop made it easier to understand opinions, and it was a more affordable activity in the project's context. A stepped approach was preferred in order to avoid the cases of failure observed in other cooperation projects when phases were too quickly implemented. The results of this phase showed the limits of Rajasthan's current cluster products. The overall evaluation collected from the Italian buyers in terms of product and marketability showed that the current craft products was resulting in an average of 50 percent of overall satisfaction. In particular, style and design scored 50 percent, and appeal 75 percent, but the wearability only 30 percent. The buyers' opinions were associated with other weakness factors, such as the difficulty of access to production sites, product quality too low compared to the demands of the foreign market and the lack of international standards, the absence of trade relations skills to tackle more distant markets and international product networks directly or in forms of cooperation that could ensure local craftsmen firms a proper earning, suggesting the need to keep on working on training on quality, design, and marketing strategies and keeping a longer-term perspective for international markets.

Regarding the upgrade in technology, the project did not push for an immediate machinery upgrade. A classical mistake in international technical cooperation is to provide technologies bought with international cooperation funds that might be of the highest quality, but in the context of a rural cluster in India, they showed to quickly turn to unused and abandoned machines. After the field visit, it was clear that the level of accessibility of the road and to technology networks, even a basic one (continuous electrical power supply, drinkable and industrial water supply, wastewater system, etc.), was still weak in most of the study areas to invalidate substantially many of the top-down interventions conceived of by the international donors and requested by experts. It is then significant that in the CDP, in the 2010s, the government of India acknowledges the need to include this new component (i.e., infrastructure) in its CDP.

Conclusions

This chapter aimed at investigating the relationships between micro and small businesses, local development for poverty reduction, and the programs and policies that attempt to create a positive causation cycle based on industrial district and cluster models. The discourses on the importance of micro and small businesses and local economic growth highlight the power of entrepreneurship in generating benefits, as well as the comparative advantages of regions, the opportunities of international free trade, the advantages of externalities of localization, and the role of the place's social capital and of the networking capacity of cluster-level institutions in connection with internal and external agents. These themes have been significantly considered by economists, sociologists, economic geographers, and development studies scholars, yet only a few studies have been dedicated to clusters and industrial districts in the Global South.

This last insight has probably been more stimulated by international multilateral organizations and governments that have tended to turn descriptive models into normative ones when it is known that from theory to practice, things seems less promising and more complex and long-term based than hoped. In particular, comparing Italian and Indian cluster case studies from the 1990s to 2010s and the effects of international cooperation projects in these regions, it can be seen that interventions should be tailored to the specific place, as no one-size-fits-all programs and actions can be carried out. Elaborating Pietro-belli's (2004) work, it can be argued that there is no one best single, transposable model for organizing an industrial district or a rural craftsmen cluster, because a diversity of institutional arrangement becomes successful according to place-based and cultural circumstances: sound micro and small business organizations in industrial districts and clusters evolve over time in a unique way, balancing historical persistence with external pushes.

Regarding international cluster-to-cluster relationships, these can be sustainable when cluster typologies are significantly comparable; conversely, they can just be inspirational occasions artificially created by international cooperation for development projects. In the case analyzed, it has been observed that the survival of a co-evolution perspective to develop interactive modes of knowledge creation for common participation to GPNs could not be left to the market forces alone, as the maturity of firms in quality, design, and marketing, as well as supporting institutions, funds, and policies are strongly relevant.

Moreover, another interesting finding to highlight is that weak and marginalized areas and their rural traditional clusters might face severe social, economic, and environmental drawbacks if opened too quickly to external exposure; social, cultural, and environmental aspects should always be taken into consideration to ensure a sustainable development and poverty reduction initiatives, as these are few of the most significant capitals in crafts production when connected to GPNs. In fact, it is not just a question of concentration of specialized small businesses and Marshallian external economies that creates effective organizational structures, accelerates local economy growth, and leads to craft and industrial development. The fieldwork and activities carried out showed that the social capital of the place (traditions, shared values of people, habits, etc.) embedded in the local systems is of paramount importance. This is another reason why it is significantly difficult to turn effectively the industrial district and cluster theory from a descriptive model to a normative one and, therefore, to transpose models from one region to another. This perspective was well perceived by the Italian and Indian experts in creating cluster-to-cluster relationships: when local productions face the global markets, the cultural factor has to be sustained by a strong layer of entrepreneurship in order to get concrete reach as well as preferential networks with homologous organizations around the world. Thus, preserving traditions and heritages, fostering human resources with entrepreneurial skills, and providing connection to accessible and profitable marketing channels can become elements of the same strategy, linking business and development processes working both on preconditions and uniqueness rather than actual immediate (and likely not permanent) results from a classical industrial production standpoint.

Another factor that might affect the success of initiatives based on small businesses in the international development cooperation is the influence of official development aid dynamics. Global South governments and NGOs have been influenced by experts, programs, and project managers of international multilateral organizations as well as bilateral cooperation ones. These played a significant role in terms of dissemination of these development policies and instrument fashions. For instance, the soft action on training of the "mobile master trainer" held in 2005 within the "conservation and revitalization of leather and textile crafts in the Indian state of Rajasthan" project, although rather reduced in time and activity, was much appreciated locally by the artisans, the young designers, the institutions, and the World Bank itself, which considered it exemplary and among the most effective ones implemented in India. However, the dependency on experts and program managers that are subject to significant turnover and the lack of further grants diverted the attention from continuing an initiative that was not yet self-sustainable.

It can be concluded that the effect of international projects probably did not have immediate benefits on creating new small business, reducing poverty, or on the creation of the CIGs. However, they acted on intermediate agents to create knowledge and ownership and to develop their own cluster vision. The statement of the MSME of the government of India is significant:

> The intervention criteria/ proposal formats for cluster development through international agencies like UNIDO, GTZ, DFID, etc. do not match with that of the Ministry of Small and Medium Enterprise – Cluster Development Programme. However, sometimes it is required to join hands with such agencies with necessary international expertise for development of clusters on national/ regional level. Contribution for such programmes may be considered by the Steering Committee in relaxation of the prescribed norms.
>
> (MSME 2010)

Notes

1 Acknowledgements: This research was carried out thanks to the participation of international cooperation initiatives and projects supported by (1) the INSME (International Network of Small and Medium Enterprises) following the first OECD Ministerial Conference on SMEs and Globalization held in Bologna, Italy, in June 2000 co-organized by the Italian Government and (2) the World Bank's technical assistance project "Revitalizing Rajasthan Leather and Textile Handicrafts." The authors wish to thank all experts, officers, and other people involved in the projects that made this research possible. The views expressed in this chapter are those of the author and should not be attributed to INSME, the Italian Ministry of Economic Development, or World Bank, nor do the conclusions represent official statements.
2 https://sustainabledevelopment.un.org/topics/povertyeradication
3 MDGs Goal 1 in year 2000: "Eradicate extreme poverty and hunger (Target 1.A: Halve, between 1990 and 2015, the proportion of people whose income is less than one dollar a day; Target 1.B: Achieve full and productive employment and decent work for all, including women and young people; Target 1.C: Halve, between 1990 and 2015, the proportion of people who suffer from hunger)."

4 UN General Assembly Resolution (A/RES/70/2015)
5 Italian Law n. 125/2014.
6 The three main Italian SMEs and craftsmen's confederation were Confartigianato, CNA (National Confederation for the Craft Sector and Small and Medium Enterprise) and CONFAPI (Italian Confederation of Small and Medium-Sized Industry), lately incorporated in the main Italian business association (Confidustria).

References

Amin Ash (1999). An Institutionalist Perspective on Regional Economic Development, International, *Journal of Urban and Regional Research*, 23(2), 365–378.
Amin Ash (2014). Regions Unbound: Towards a New Politics of Place, *Geografiska Annaler: Series B, Human Geography*, 86(1), 33–44.
Bagnasco Arnaldo (1977). *Tre Italie: la problematica territoriale dello sviluppo economico italiano.* Il Mulino, Bologna.
Becattini Giacomo (1987). *Mercato e forze locali: il distretto industriale.* Il Mulino, Bologna.
Becattini Giacomo (1991). Il distretto industriale Marshalliano come concetto socio-economico. In Pyke Frank, Becattini Giacomo, Sengenberger Werner (eds), *Distretti industriali e cooperazione fra imprese in Italia.* Quad. Banca Toscana, Nardini, Firenze, 51–65.
Becattini Giacomo (1998). *Distretti industriali e Made in Italy.* Bollati Boringhieri, Torino.
Becattini Giacomo, Sforzi Fabio (eds) (2002). *Lezioni sullo sviluppo locale.* Rosenberg & Sellier, Torino.
Becattini Giacomo, Bellandi Marco, De Propis Lisa (2009). *A Handbook of Industrial Districts.* Edward Elgar, Cheltenham, UK.
Besley Timothy and Cord Louise J. (eds) (2007). *Delivering on the Promise of Pro-Poor Growth: Insights and Lessons from Country Experiences.* The International Bank for Reconstruction and Development, The World Bank and Palgrave Macmillan, Washington and New York.
Bianchi Patrizio (2014), *Globalizzazione, crisi e riorganizzazione industriale.* McGraw-Hill Education, Milan.
Bignante Elisa., Dansero Egidio, Scarpocchi Cristina (2008), Sviluppo Locale e cooperazione internazionale. Una proposta teorico-metodologica. In Bignante Elisa, Dansero Egidio, Scarpocchi Cristina (eds), *Geografia e cooperazione allo sviluppo.* Franco Angeli, Milano, 48–68.
Bini Valerio (2016). *La cooperazione allo sviluppo in Africa. Teorie, politiche, pratiche.* Memesis Kosmos, Milan.
Boekema Frans, Morgan Kevin, Bakkers Silvia, Rutten Roel (2000). Introduction to Learning Regions: A New Issue for Analysis? In Boekema Frans, Morgan Kevin, Bakkers Silvia, Rutten Roel (eds), *Knowledge, Innovation and Economic Growth.* Edward Elgar, Cheltenham, UK, 3–16.
Bonaglia Federico, De Luca Vincenzo, (2006), *La cooperazione internazionale allo sviluppo.* Il Mulino, Bologna.
Callegati Enrico, Grandi Silvia (2005). Cluster Dynamics and Innovation in SMEs: The Role of Culture. *Working Papers Ebla Center*, vol. 3, Dipartimento di economia "S. Cognetti de Martiis", Turin, 1–11.
Ceglie Giovanna, Dini Marco, (1999). SME Cluster and Network Development in Developing Countries: The Experience of UNIDO. *PSD Technical Working Papers Series*, UNIDO, Vienna.
Dansero Egidio, Giaccaria Paolo, Governa Francesca (eds) (2008). *Lo sviluppo locale al Nord e Sud. Un confronto internazionale.* Franco Angeli, Milan.
Dematteis Giuseppe, Governa Francesca (eds) (2005). *Territorialità, sviluppo locale, sostenibilità: il modello SLoT.* Franco Angeli, Milan.

Export Promotion Council for Handicrafts (2018). Exports of Handicraft, On-line statistics http://epch.in/index.php?option=com_content&view=article&id=76&Itemid=181

Giuliani Elisa, Pietrobelli Carlo, Rabellotti Roberta (2005). Upgrading in Global Value Chains: Lessons from Latin American Clusters. *World Development,* 33(4), 549–573.

Grandi Silvia (2007). Multi-Level Policies: A Geographical Approach to the Analysis of Innovation Systems /Politiche multi-livello: un approccio geografico all'analisi dei sistemi di innovazione. *AMS ACTA*, Diapason – Biblioteca Polo di Rimini, Rimini, 1–25.

Grandi Silvia (2013). *Sviluppo, geografia e cooperazione internazionale. Teorie, politiche e mappamondi*, Editrice La Mandragola, Imola.

Grandi Silvia (2017). Cooperazione decentrata tra la Regione Emilia-Romagna e Stato Del Paranà per lo sviluppo del cooperativismo e delle filiere agroalimentari di qualità: Il caso del Programma Brasil Próximo. *Revista Movimentos Sociais e Dinâmicas Espaciais (Social Movements and Spatial Dynamics Journal*, 6(2), 73–91.

Guigou Jean-Louis (2001). Les territoires-entreprises. In Pommier Paulette (ed), *Resaux d'entreprises et territoires. Regards sur les systèmes productifs locaux*. DATAR, Paris.

Hettne Bjorn (2009). *Thinking About Development*. Zed Books, London.

Hirst Gilbert (2014). *The History of Development: From Western Origins to Global Faith*. Fourth Edition. Zed Books, London and New York.

Ianni Vanna (ed) (2017). *Lo sviluppo nel XXI secolo. Concezioni, processi, sfide*. Carrocci Editore, Milan.

Indian Ministry of Textile (2017), AHVY Scheme, http://craftclustersofindia.com/ahvy-scheme/.

IPI (2002). *L'esperienza italiana dei distretti industriali*. IPI, Rome.

IPI (2005). Preservation and revitalization of leather, textiles and furniture making crafts in Rajasthan, Madhya Pradesh and Chhattisgarh states of India – Phase I Report, IPI, Rome.

Kennedy Loraine (1999), Cooperating for Survival: Tannery Pollution and Joint Action in the Palar Valley (India). *World Development*, 27(9), 1673–1691.

Krugman Paul (1991). *Geography and Trade*. MIT Press, Cambridge, MA.

Lund-Thomsen Peter, Lindgreen Adam, Vanhamme Joelle (2016). Industrial Clusters and Corporate Social Responsibility in Developing Countries: What We Know, What We Do Not Know, and What We Need to Know. *Journal of Business Ethics*, 133(1), 9–24.

Lund-Thomsen Peter, Nadvi Khalid (2010). Clusters, Chains and Compliance: Corporate Social Responsibility and Governance in Football Manufacturing in South Asia. *Journal of Business Ethics*, 93, 201–222.

Marshall Alfred (1947). Industrial Organization, Continued. The Concentration of Specialized Industries in Particular Localities. In *Principles of Economics: An introductory Volume. Eighth Edition*, Chapter X. Macmillan and Co. Ltd., London, 267–77.

MSME (2010). Modified Guidelines of MSE-CDP Background, Document of the Ministry of Micro, Small and Medium Enterprises (MSME), Government of India (GoI), New Delhi, India.

MSME (2016). Prospects & Activities Reflecting Cluster's Highlights and Achievements of MSE-Cluster Development Programme, The Development Commissioner, Micro, Small & Medium Enterprises, Nirman Bhavan, New Delhi, India.

MSME (2018). Annual Report 2017–2018. Document of the Ministry of Micro, Small and Medium Enterprises (MSME), Government of India (GoI), New Delhi, India.

Nadvi Khalid (1995). *Industrial Clusters and Networks: Case Studies of SME Growth and Innovation*. UNIDO Small and Medium Enterprise Programme, UNIDO, Vienna.

Nadvi Khalid (1999). Collective Efficiency and Collective Failure: The Response of the Sialkot Surgical Instrument Cluster to Global Quality Pressures. *World Development*, 27(9), 1605–1626.

Nadvi Khalid, Schmitz Hubert (1993). *Industrial Clusters in Less Developed Countries: Review of Experiences and Research Agenda*. Discussion Paper n. 339, Institute of Development Studies University of Sussex, IDS, Brighton.

Nadvi Khalid, Barrientos Stephanie (2004) *Industrial Clusters and poverty Reduction: Towards a Methodology for Poverty and Social Impact Assessment of Cluster Development Initiatives*. UNIDO, Vienna.

OECD (2016). *Development Co-Operation Report 2016. The Sustainable Development Goals as Business Opportunities*, OECD Publishing, Paris.

Pietrobelli Carlo (2004). Upgrading and Technological Regimes in Industrial Clusters in Italy and Taiwan. In Pietrobelli Carlo, Sverrisson Arni (eds) *Linking Local and Global Economies: The Ties That Bind*. Routledge, London, 133–159.

Pietrobelli Carlo, Olarte Barrera Tatiana (2002). Enterprise Clusters and Industrial Districts in Colombia's Fashion Sector. *European Planning Studies*, 10(5), 541–562.

Pietrobelli Carlo, Rabellotti Roberta (2004). Upgrading in Clusters and Value Chains in Latin America: The Role of Policies. In *Sustainable Development*. Department Best Practices Series. Inter-American Development Bank. Washington, DC.

Porter Michael (1998). Clusters and the new economics of competition. *Harvard Business Review*, November-December, 77–90.

Porter Michael (1990). *The Competitive Advantage of Nations*. Macmillan, London.

Rabellotti Roberta (1997). The Mexican Clusters of Guadalajara and Leon. In: *External Economies and Cooperation in Industrial Districts*. Palgrave Macmillan, London, pp 96–130.

Russo Fabio (1999). *Strengthening Indian SME Clusters: UNIDO's Experiences*. Case study Project US/GLO/95/144, UNIDO, Vienna.

Schmitz, Hubert (1999). Global Competition and Local Cooperation: Success and Failure in the Sinos Valley, Brazil. *World Development*, 27(9), 1627–1650.

Schmitz Hubert (2004). *Local Enterprises in the Global Economy – Issues of Governance and Upgrading*. Edward Elgar, Cheltenham, UK.

Schmitz Hubert, Nadvi Khalid (1999). Clustering and Industrialization: Introduction. *World Development*, 27(9), 1503–14.

Sforzi Fabio, Lorenzini Franco (2002). I distretti industriali. In IPI, *L'esperienza italiana dei distretti industriali*. IPI, Roma.

UN (2015). The Millennium Development Goals Report, United Nation, New York.

UNCTAD (1998). *Promoting and Sustaining SME Clusters and Networks for Development. Commission on Clustering and Industrialization: Introduction*. Enterprise, Business Facilitation and Development, TD/B/Com.3/EM.5/2, UNCTAD, Geneva.

UNIDO (1997). *UNIDO's Programme to Promote and Support SMI Clusters*. Paper presented at the Seminar on New Trends and Challenges in Industrial Policy, October, Vienna.

UNIDO, (2010). Cluster Development for Pro-Poor Growth: The UNIDO Approach. *Business, Investment and Technology Services Branch Technical Paper Series*, UNIDO, Vienna.

Vallega Adalberto (1995). *La regione, sistema territoriale sostenibile*. Mursia, Milano.

Weisert Natascha, Maier Kaibitsch Clara, Patacconi Gerardo (2013). *The UNIDO Approach to Cluster Development Key Principles and Project Experiences for Inclusive Growth*, Technical Paper, UNIDO, Vienna.

Williamson John (2004). A Short History of the Washington Consensus, In Fundación CIDOB – Conference "From the Washington Consensus towards a new Global Governance" – Barcelona, September, 24–25.

Index

Note: Page numbers in *italic* indicate a figure and page numbers in **bold** indicate a table on the corresponding page.